The Bluejacket's Manual

The Bluejacket's Manual

CENTENNIAL EDITION

Thomas J. Cutler

Naval Institute Press
Annapolis, Maryland

Naval Institute Press
291 Wood Road
Annapolis, MD 21402

First edition published in 1902.

ISBN 1-55750-221-8 hardcover
ISBN 1-55750-208-0 paperback

Printed in the United States of America on acid-free paper ∞
09 08 07 06 05 04 03   9 8 7 6 5 4 3

Unless specified otherwise, all illustrations are from official U.S. Navy sources.

Contents

Foreword

This is a special edition of a special book. Originally written and issued as a basic seamanship and shipboard life training manual for recruits, it was immediately valued for its clarity and pragmatism. While it has remained true to that purpose, this centennial edition gives us pause to reflect on how much more it has become. As the Navy became more complex and technical, so too *The Bluejacket's Manual* evolved to address the mission, values, traditions, and heritage of Naval service. Long before honor, courage, and commitment were chosen to represent the core values of a Sailor, character-building commentary was regularly included in *The Bluejacket's Manual*.

When wartime requirements severely shortened recruit training to as little as three weeks, Sailors were admonished to study their *BJM* en route to their fleet assignments and told that everything they really needed to know to succeed could be found there. Incredibly, that is still a fundamentally true statement.

As it taught, inspired, and motivated millions of Sailors over one full century, *The Bluejacket's Manual* gained icon status and became the most cherished and treasured of Sailor keepsakes. It is safe to say that every Sailor—active, retired, and veteran—either has their originally issued *BJM* or deeply regrets the loss of it.

Over the years you will look to your *BJM* to refresh your memory, settle arguments, plan a ceremony, write a note for the Plan of the Day, execute an order, and for many other reasons. And as you use it, it will become more than the ready reference manual it was on the day of issue. On some not-so-distant future day, you will pull it out of the drawer or off the shelf and sense something new about the old book. It will be weightier, somehow more substantial. There will be something of a sacred feel to it. Intermingled with chapters on all things Navy will be vivid, detailed memories. Shipmates and events from your Navy experience will have taken residence in the pages in ghostly but undeniably real ways. I'm not sure when it will happen for you, only that it will. So I advise you to keep your *BJM* handy, make frequent use of it, but safeguard and care for it. One day you'll be glad you did.

John Hagan
Master Chief Petty Officer
of the Navy (Retired)

Preface

In 1902, Lt. Ridley McLean, recognizing that young men entering the Navy had no source of information to introduce them to their new profession, wrote what has become an American institution: *The Bluejacket's Manual.* Lieutenant McLean probably had no idea that his creation would endure for an entire century, evolving through more than twenty revisions to keep up with the sweeping changes that have transformed the U.S. Navy from a fledgling seapower to master of the world's oceans. Although the technology has changed, new terms have been added to that strange lexicon of the sea, and the American Bluejacket is a very different sort from those who joined the Navy in Ridley McLean's day, the need for an introductory text and lasting reference has not diminished.

This centennial edition, like its predecessors, makes no attempt to be a comprehensive textbook on all things naval—to do so today would require a multivolume set that would defy practicality—but it *is* a Navy primer that will help the new recruit make the transition from civilian to Sailor and serve as a handy reference for years to come. Those who have not joined the Navy but who wish to better understand it would do well to read this explanatory book.

Among the changes to the 23rd edition is an added chapter on "Naval Missions and Heritage," expansion of the chapter on "Navy Education and Training" to include the Navy College Program and other improvements, enhanced treatment of physical fitness, the latest changes to the Navy's ratings system, and added information on threat conditions, fraternization, hazing, standards of conduct for government employees, and knowledge factors as mandated by the Navy's "NAVSTDS" system. Of course, a great deal of information was updated to keep up with the ever-evolving nature of the U.S. Navy.

Because it is designed for the neophyte, every attempt has been made to explain all new terms as they are used. The seasoned Sailor may cringe a bit when he or she encounters civilian terms used to explain the nautical ones—a *deck* described as similar to a *floor,* for example—but it should be apparent that a familiar analogy is an expeditious means of teaching new terms and concepts. For the reader who is not reading this book from cover to cover, the glossary will serve as a quick reference for finding the meanings of words that were defined earlier in the book.

In this rapidly changing world, it is vital that information be kept as accurate as possible. This latest edition represents a significant rewrite of those parts requiring it, but those areas deemed still valid have been preserved or only slightly modified. Because *The Bluejacket's Manual* is updated with each printing, and because it is in the best interests of all concerned that this manual be kept up to date, readers are invited to submit recommended changes by writing to the author, care of the Naval Institute (291 Wood Road, Annapolis, Maryland 21402), or by e-mail (tcutler@navalinstitute.org).

Older readers may note that the title of the book has been slightly modified by moving the apostrophe in *Bluejackets'* from the plural possessive to the singular possessive—*i.e. Bluejacket's*—position. This change was made because the original 1902 edition was entitled *The Bluejacket's Manual.* For reasons unknown today, the title was changed sometime after the First World War and remained that way for many decades. A return to the original makes sense not only for traditional reasons but because the singular possessive is more appropriate to the personal nature of this book. Throughout the book, the current author (a former Sailor himself) has chosen to speak directly to the Sailor who will be reading it instead of using the less personal third person.

Ridley McLean is no longer the author of this book, and much of what is presented in this hundredth-anniversary edition would be wholly unfamiliar to him, but it is a testimony to the Navy's heritage and its traditions that he would be fully comfortable with many of the terms, customs, and ceremonies that have endured for a century. *The Bluejacket's Manual* has played an important role in the preservation of our naval heritage and will continue to do so into the next millennium.

Acknowledgments

Few books are ever the work of a single author. This one is certainly no exception. Not only has *The Bluejacket's Manual* had the advantage of numerous authors and editors over its one hundred years of existence, but it has enjoyed the input of literally hundreds of others who have selflessly contributed their time and expertise toward making this a better book. This edition is the product of many who have gone "above and beyond" in helping to make this unusual book live up to its long-standing reputation.

One of the daunting challenges of updating a book such as this is obtaining access to the latest official (Navy, Department of Defense, and so on) sources of information. My early efforts in this area were aided by Debbie Bullan, who has the enormous challenge of keeping all official directives and publications for the United States Naval Academy up to date, and who gave me access to her office and shared her vast knowledge with me.

Eileen Parmeter and Carolyn Johnson of the Bureau of Naval Personnel and Pat Townsend of the Office of the Chief of Naval Operations were also very helpful in my journeys through the uncharted seas of official paper.

A special thanks is due Master Chief Petty Officer Mike McCalip, Command Master Chief at the Recruit Training Command, Great Lakes, who called me one day and said—in the age old tradition of this great Navy of ours—"reporting for duty, sir." He invited me to come to Great Lakes for a working visit that was immensely useful in helping me to understand the changes that had taken place since the days when I had marched on those same "grinders." He offered the assistance of his talented staff of Recruit Division Commanders, instructors, and administrators—an offer I did not refuse. He also insisted that he needed no recognition—the one thing he said that I have chosen to ignore.

Master Chief Gunner's Mate Joel Nissen took good care of me during my Great Lakes visit and for many months afterward he reviewed a number of sections for me and coordinated the efforts of the many people at RTC who helped immeasurably. The latter are unsung but their contributions are not.

Many people contributed to this revision and the last, and I am indebted to them. Among them were Charles Heberer and Petty Officer First Class John Whelan at Great Lakes who were helpful with RTC matters and damage control. Master Chief Petty Officers of the Navy John Hagan and Jim Herdt were most helpful in a variety of ways. I am particularly grateful to VADM Daniel T. Oliver, who as Chief of Naval Personnel mobilized the people at BUPERS to assist with many aspects of the book. Among them were CAPT W. S. Wolff, CDR B. L. Brehm of PERS 2WW; Mrs. Kathleen M. Whitsel and CAPT J. B. Frank, Jr. of PERS 3; LCDR S. Rauch of PERS 42A; Mr. Bob Sunday of PERS 46; CDR K. Maloney and HTCM (SW) Sawyer of PERS 221F; LT D. Howell of PERS 221G; CDR J. Brown and DSCS (SW) Jim Norman of PERS 221H; CDR J. Taplett, RMC (SW) T. Martin of PERS 221I; CDR T. Barge of PERS 221K; CDR B. Marsh, CTACM B. Farrell, CTICM F. Griffits, and CTMCM J. Pardun of PERS 221N; LCDR M. Crum and EACS (SCW) M.S. Kauffman of PERS 221R; CDR L. Gruendl, CDR B. Welch, LT N. Jurkovic, LT D. Kaspar, PNCS D. Cevault, and Ms. J. Douglas of PERS 222; LT Greene of PERS 251; PNC S. R. Collier of PERS 262B; Ms. B. G. Allen and GMCM P. Montgomery of PERS 333C; and LCDR Hawley of PERS 6. LT Ingrid Mueller at the Naval Personnel Command was particularly helpful on a number of personnel matters.

Senior Chief John Cole of Naval Station Annapolis deserves a special thanks for answering the phone the many times I called for help, for reviewing many parts of this new edition, and for providing many helpful materials. Also at NAVSTA Annapolis, Lorraine Seidel and John Dunning helped me with matters pertaining to the Navy's Morale, Welfare, and Recreation programs and Marilyn Lewis clarified a number of matters pertaining to Family Support Services.

Captain J. D. Scranton very kindly helped me through some of the confusing legal aspects and Chief Quartermaster Evan Soskin reviewed the chapter on navigation and made a number of useful suggestions.

The chapter on boats is almost entirely the work of Jason T. Marshall and Malcolm Whitford, naval architects at the Naval Surface Warfare Center Detachment, Norfolk, Carderock Division. These gentlemen are to be commended not only for willingly doing the work, but for *volunteering* their services. My thanks also to their boss, CAPT John S. Miano Jr., for his support of the project.

The chapter on health, hygiene, and first aid is primarily the work of the medical staff at the Naval Hospital in Great Lakes, Illinois, including CAPT Jon D. Bayer, CDR Margaret Ryan, LCDR Steven Winter, LCDR Brian Davis, Leslie Stewart, and Florence Cook. A special thanks is due to ENS Thomas Prieskorn who served as chairman of the medical chapter revision committee and was my point of contact throughout.

Andrew Bahjat made many helpful suggestions that got me started on this project, and Donald Hegelson, Arthur Doherty, Tom Sheehy, George Starkey, Dale Diefenbach, and Albert Romero pointed out some of my errors in the twenty-second edition.

This book would be a pile of meaningless paper without the combined efforts of Jim Bricker, Rebecca Hinds, Brian Barth, and Kristin Wye-Rodney of the Naval Institute Press.

I am indebted to CAPT Jim Barber, then CEO of the U.S. Naval Institute, and Ron Chambers, Naval Institute Press Director, who believed that I was up to the challenge of revising this important book the first time. I thank ADM Tom Marfiak, current Naval Institute CEO, and Ron Chambers once again for their continued confidence in allowing me the honor of authoring this centennial edition.

Fourteen years ago, in dedicating my first book, I described Deborah Welch Cutler as "typist, editor, critic, and loving wife." None of that has changed. Just as she made the many sacrifices that come with life in the Navy, she saw me through this demanding project, putting up with my preoccupation, idiosyncrasies, and absence (both real and virtual) that come with an undertaking of this magnitude. Her word-processing and editing expertise, knowledge of the Navy, and, most of all, her love and support make this work at least as much hers as mine.

The Bluejacket's Manual

Introduction to the Navy

Welcome aboard! These words carry a world of significance. They mean that you have made one of the biggest decisions a young person can—you have volunteered to enlist in the United States Navy. By raising your right hand and taking the oath of enlistment, you have become a member of one of the most important military services in the world and joined one of the biggest businesses in the United States. Not only have you proved your understanding of citizenship by offering your services to your country, but you have also taken the first step toward an exciting and rewarding career.

If you are not already familiar with names like John Paul Jones, Stephen Decatur, Doris Miller, William F. Halsey, and Marvin Shields, you soon will be. And you will feel honored to be serving, as they once did, in the United States Navy.

Today's Navy is a massive and complex organization, a far cry from the makeshift fleet that opposed the British in the Revolutionary War. Hundreds of ships, thousands of aircraft, hundreds of thousands of people, and an annual budget in the billions of dollars go together to make the U.S. Navy a powerful and important component of the American defense establishment, playing a vital role in maintaining our national security, protecting us against our enemies in time of war, and supporting our foreign policy in peacetime. Through its exercise of seapower, the Navy ensures freedom of the seas so that merchant ships can bring us the vital raw material we import from abroad, like petroleum, rubber, sugar, and aluminum. Seapower makes it possible for us to use the oceans when and where our national interests require it, and denies our enemies that same freedom.

You are now a part of all that—a *vital* part, for the ships and aircraft of the Navy are only as good as the people who operate them.

First Enlistment

Your introduction to the Navy probably started at your hometown recruiting station, with interviews and processing conducted by a Navy recruiter. He or she was specially trained to compare your desires and your qualifications with the needs of the Navy to establish the terms of your service. Your "contract" with the Navy is officially called an enlistment, but you will sometimes hear it described as a *hitch*. It began when you took the oath of enlistment, and it will last from two to six years, depending upon the terms agreed upon by you and your recruiter.

Naval Training Center, Great Lakes

All recruits begin their naval careers in what is officially called Recruit Training Command (RTC), but is more traditionally referred to as "boot camp." Although you may have relatives who once trained at boot camps in other parts of the country, currently the Navy is operating only one RTC, located at the Naval Training Center (NTC) in Great Lakes, Illinois. This 1628-acre training facility, on the shore of Lake Michigan about 40 miles north of Chicago, has been training Sailors since July 1911. During World War II, nearly a million Sailors were trained there.

You and the other recruits will make the transition from civilian to military life in the time you will spend at RTC. Nearly every minute of every day will be filled with military drills, physical training, hands-on experiences, and a busy schedule of drills and classes on naval history, traditions, customs, operations, and regulations. At first you will probably find the transition challenging—you will have completely changed your environment, diet, sleep patterns, climate, clothes, and companions—but within a relatively short period, you will make the necessary adjustments and find a great deal of pride to replace your initial anxiety.

First Weeks in the Navy

P-Days

The day of arrival at RTC is called receipt day, when your initial processing begins. The next three to five days will be your processing days (P-Days). The procedures may vary from time to time, but in general go like this: Report in, turn in orders, and draw your bedding and bunk assignment for your first night aboard. You will also fill out a bedding custody card, a stencil form, a receipt for a "chit book" (to be used instead of money for purchases at the Navy Exchange), a safe-arrival card for your parents, and other forms.

Haircuts

Every recruit will get a haircut and, chances are, it will be different from what you are used to. While male recruits won't get their heads shaved, the barber won't leave enough hair to comb either. Female recruits have two options: they must wear their hair up or get special haircuts to conform to Navy standards. Later, at your first duty station, you will have more choice in hairstyle, but you will still have to conform to Navy regulations.

Medical Examinations

As a Sailor, you will have to be in excellent health and good physical condition to perform your duties properly. Navy medical personnel will examine you from head to toe, run blood tests and urinalysis, take X-rays, and give you a series of inoculations—the works. If you need dental work, it will be scheduled.

Clothing Issue

At first you will receive an initial clothing issue that includes enough uniform clothing to make you look like a Sailor and to allow you to perform your duties while in boot camp. Eventually you will receive a complete outfit, called a seabag, worth hundreds of dollars.

Chit Book

You will not need money while in boot camp. You will be issued a chit book of coupons to be used in the Navy Exchange for toilet articles, sewing kits, shoeshine gear, notebooks, stationery, postage stamps, and pens and pencils. The total cost will be deducted from your pay.

ID Card

You will be issued an Armed Forces of the United States Identification Card—"ID card"—which identifies you as a member of the armed forces. While it is unique to you and in your possession, it remains government property and must be returned when you are discharged. Altering it, damaging it, counterfeiting it, or using it in an unauthorized manner (such as lending your card to someone or borrowing another person's card) can result in serious disciplinary action.

Your card shows your name, Social Security number, and the date your enlistment expires. Carry it at all times. Besides granting you access to ships, Navy Exchanges, and other government installations, it will identify you as one protected by the provisions of the Geneva Convention should you become a prisoner of war.

If you lose your card, you will have to sign a statement detailing the circumstances of the loss.

Boot Camp Routine

Soon after reporting in, you will be placed in a division and will meet the people you'll be with for the next several weeks. Then, during a formal commissioning ceremony, an officer will welcome you, give a brief talk on the history and mission of the Navy, assign your unit a division number and name (after a Navy ship), present a division flag (called a guidon) bearing that number, and introduce your recruit division commanders (RDCs).

Recruit Division Commander

Each division, usually about eighty-four recruits, is taken through training by its RDCs—outstanding petty officers who are intimately familiar with instructional techniques, principles of leadership, and administrative procedures. The RDCs will instruct you in military and physical drills and show you how to keep yourself, your clothing, equipment, and barracks in smart, ship-shape condition. While at boot camp, your RDCs are the most important people in the Navy. Keep in mind that your RDCs once went through recruit training just like you; by now, they have many years of naval experience. Follow your RDCs' example and you'll make a good start toward a successful Navy career.

4

Chain of Command

The Navy is organized like a pyramid, with the President of the United States at the top as commander-in-chief of the armed forces. There are many levels below the President leading eventually to you. This is known as the chain of command. Just as you must follow the orders and guidance of your RDCs, they must, likewise, follow the orders and guidance of the ship's leading chief petty officer, and he or she must follow those of the assistant squadron commander, and so on. Your chain of command will change somewhat each time you report to a new duty station, but while you are at RTC, your chain of command is as follows:

President (Commander-in-Chief)
Secretary of Defense
Secretary of the Navy
Chief of Naval Operations
Chief of Naval Education and Training
Commander NTC
Commanding Officer RTC

Executive Officer RTC
Director of Training
Department Head (Squadron Commander)
Assistant Squadron Commander
Ship's Officer
Ship's Leading Chief Petty Officer
Recruit Division Commanders (RDC)
Recruits (You)

Intro-
duction
to the
Navy

Because you are new to the Navy, you will start out at the bottom of the pyramid, but time, training, experience, hard work, and the right attitude will change that. Keep in mind that everyone in the Navy began at the bottom, and your seniors were once recruits like you.

Daily Routine

Nearly everything you do at boot camp is designed to prepare you for service in the Navy. On ships, submarines, and naval stations throughout the world, the daily routine is prescribed by a bulletin called the "Plan of the Day" or, more commonly, the POD. At RTC, the daily routine appears as a schedule on the compartment chalkboard. It issues the special orders for the day, gives the hours of meals, inspections, parades, and other events. Using the master training schedule as their guide, your RDCs will post the information you need to get through each day. Once you leave boot camp, it will be *your* responsibility to read the POD each day to find out what uniform to wear, what special events are taking place, and so on. A typical day at RTC is outlined in Table 1.1.

Back to School

You have a lot to learn in order to make the transition from civilian to Sailor. Much of your time will be spent in classrooms. A typical day of instruction includes a dozen 40-minute periods with 10-minute breaks between periods. Many topics will be covered, including:

Advancement program
Aircraft familiarization
Career incentives/medical
  benefits
Chain of command
Chemical, biological, and
  radiological defense

Code of conduct/Geneva
  Convention
Damage control
Deck equipment (basic)
Discharges
Drug/alcohol abuse
Education benefits

Equal opportunity awareness
Financial responsibility
Firefighting
First aid
General orders
Grievance procedures
Grooming standards
Hand salute and greetings
Hazing prevention
Honors and ceremonies
Inspections
Marlinespike seamanship
Military discipline
Military drill
Naval history and traditions
Navy mission and
organization
Officer rank recognition

Ordnance and weapons
Pay and allowances
Personal hygiene
Physical conditioning
Rape awareness
Rates and ratings
recognition
Sexual harassment
awareness
Ship familiarization
Small boats
Sound-powered phones
Survival at sea
Uniform Code of Military
Justice
Watch, quarter, and station
bill
Watch standing

Some of your classroom training will be augmented by hands-on training, which will give you the opportunity to work with actual equipment and simulate real conditions. Examples of this kind of training are firefighting, seamanship, chemical, biological and radiological (CBR) defense, and survival at sea techniques where you will actually fight a fire, work with lines and deck equipment, put on a gas mask in a gas chamber, and learn to stay afloat using your clothing as a life preserver.

Few jobs in the Navy are completely independent, so a great deal of emphasis is placed upon teamwork during your training at RTC. Military drill (such as marching) is one way that you and your fellow recruits will learn the importance of instant response to orders and the value of group precision. Later on—when you are helping to launch and recover aircraft on the flight deck of an aircraft carrier, or rescuing a shipmate from the sea, or taking a nuclear submarine into the depths of the ocean—you will fully understand and appreciate the importance of such training.

Training at RTC—which includes such things as the meticulous folding and precise stowage of clothing—may sometimes be seen as nitpicky or unnecessary, but in the highly technical, sometimes dangerous, and often unique surroundings you will find in the Navy, attention to detail can make the difference between success and failure, survival and disaster, victory and defeat. Everything you do in

Table 1.1. A Typical Day at RTC

0500 (5:00 A.M.)	Reveille (wake up). Begin morning routine (brush teeth, dress, etc.).
0545 (5:45 A.M.)	Breakfast
0600 (6:00 A.M.)	Sick call. Report to sick bay (the medical clinic) if you are ill.
0700 (7:00 A.M.)	Physical training (stretching, calisthenics, etc.)
0755 (7:55 A.M.)	First call to colors (warning that the color ceremony is five minutes away).
0800 (8:00 A.M.)	Colors (American flag is ceremoniously hoisted).
0820 (8:20 A.M.)	Commence instruction periods.
1100 (11:00 A.M.)	Break for noon meal (lunch).
1200 (12:00 Noon)	Resume instruction periods.
1230 (12:30 P.M.)	Sick call. Report to sick bay if you are ill.
1630 (4:30 P.M.)	Evening meal
5 minutes before sunset	First call to colors (warning that the evening colors ceremony is five minutes away).
Sunset	Evening colors (American flag is ceremoniously lowered).
1800 (6:00 P.M.)	Commence night routine (shower, study, work on uniforms, etc.).
2200 (10:00 P.M.)	Taps (end of day). Turn in for the night.

boot camp has a purpose, and the overall mission of RTC is to make you ready for the challenges and opportunities that await you in the U.S. Navy.

Boot Camp Life

Not all of your time at RTC will be spent in training. There will be administrative periods during which you will make pay arrangements, be fitted for uniforms, complete your medical and dental work, and make known your desires for future assignment. Based upon your Armed Services Vocational Aptitude Battery (ASVAB) test scores and your classification interviews, the initial path of your Navy career will be determined.

While at boot camp you will be given the opportunity to attend the church of your choice. Chapels are available in which Catholic, Jewish, Protestant, and several other religious services are conducted by chaplains, who are also available for pastoral counseling and religious education. Recruit choirs are organized and often sing at the services.

Because of the tight schedule and the great number of recruits in training, you cannot receive telephone calls while at RTC, but on

PHI Todd Cichonwicz

Figure 1.1. Military drill is one way you and your fellow recruits will learn the importance of teamwork and group discipline. Here the RTC Drill Team performs alongside a Navy ship on a pier in Chicago.

occasion, with permission from your RDC, you may make outgoing calls.

Visitors are not permitted during training, but you will be permitted to have guests attend your graduation review. Information about this will be provided for you to send home.

You will be paid twice while at RTC, but once you graduate you (and every other member of the Navy) will be paid twice a month. You will be paid by electronic transfer of funds through the direct deposit system to the banking institution of your choice.

Competition

The Navy relies upon competition as a means of enhancing readiness and promoting pride. Individual Sailors compete with other Sailors for promotions, and ships and aircraft squadrons compete with each other using appropriate exercises to measure readiness in gunnery, engineering, safety, communications, and other important areas. While at boot camp, your division will compete for awards in athletic skill, scholastic achievement, military drill, inspections, and overall excellence.

Special flags are awarded to divisions in recognition of their achievements, and at the graduation ceremony a number of individuals are selected to receive outstanding recruit awards. Honor graduates will be designated and other recruits will receive special recognition.

Battle Stations

Near the end of your training at boot camp, you and your fellow recruits will participate in a large-scale exercise called "Battle Stations," which will place you in a realistic scenario designed to test what you have learned at RTC. You will simulate handling emergencies such as the kind you might encounter while serving in the Navy, and learn how to function as part of a team while demonstrating your endurance. This physically, mentally, and emotionally demanding exercise will test your abilities in meeting the challenges of fighting a fire, preparing for an approaching hurricane, conducting a search-and-rescue operation, transporting an injured shipmate, defending a position using small arms, abandoning ship, and so on. After successfully completing this "final exam," your achievement will be recognized by replacing your recruit cap with the Navy ballcap you will wear in the fleet.

Core Values

Underlying all the training you will receive at RTC is a focus on self-respect, respect for others, and the core values of *honor, courage,* and *commitment.* These are not just words but inter-related concepts that you must take to heart to guide you in virtually everything you do as a Sailor. Before you make a decision or do something, you must consider whether your action will reflect a loss of honor, a failure of courage, or a lack of commitment. If it does, then you should not do it. You should keep in mind that honor includes the honor of your nation and your Navy as well as your own, and that maintaining honor will often require courage and commitment. You should remember that courage can be physical or moral—sometimes you have to make a decision that is not easy and may not result in you getting what you want, but because it is the right thing to do, you must find the courage to do it. And you must be committed to doing what you know is right, what is honorable, what is courageous.

These core values are embodied in the "Sailor's Creed," which you and all recruits will be expected to memorize and to live by for as long as you are in the U.S. Navy.

Sailor's Creed

I am a United States Sailor.

I will support and defend the Constitution of the United States
of America and I will obey the orders of those appointed
over me.

I represent the fighting spirit of the Navy and those who have
gone before me to defend freedom and democracy around
the world.

I proudly serve my country's Navy combat team with Honor,
Courage, and Commitment.

I am committed to excellence and fair treatment of all.

From Civilian to Sailor

The ways of the Navy are very different from what you were used to in civilian life. In boot camp you will take the first steps toward becoming a Sailor. You will be introduced to the many differences of Navy life, and for the rest of your time in the Navy, whether you stay for only one enlistment or have a 30-year career, those differences will become second nature to you.

Navy Terminology

Just as doctors, lawyers, baseball players, engineers, artists, and police officers have their own language when communicating within their professions, the Navy too has its own special terminology. Doctors speak of contusions and hemostats, baseball players have their own meanings for "in the alley" or "ahead in the count," and police officers use special words like "perp" and "SWAT." In the

Navy, special terms include *helm, anchor, leeward, port, starboard, aft, bitts, chocks,* and *bollards* for nautical equipment and concepts. Everyday items also take on new names in the Navy, where bathrooms are *heads,* floors are *decks,* walls are *bulkheads,* stairways are ladders, and drinking fountains are *scuttlebutts.* You go *topside* instead of upstairs and *below* instead of downstairs. (See Appendix K, "Glossary of Navy Terms," for more.) Many of these terms will seem strange to you at first, but you will get used to them and will soon be using them naturally. Remember that many of these terms come from a long history of seafaring and nautical traditions. By using them, you are identifying yourself as a member of a unique and very special group.

The Navy also uses short abbreviations (also known as acronyms) in place of long titles, such as OOD for officer of the deck, QMOW for quartermaster of the watch, and USW for undersea warfare. While at boot camp, you will become familiar with a number of such abbreviations, some of which are listed in Table 1.2.

Ceremonies

There are many special ceremonies in the Navy that are different from civilian life. You encountered your first one when you took your oath of enlistment. Morning and evening colors are ceremonies you will quickly become familiar with while at RTC. Just before leaving boot camp you will participate in a special pass-in-review ceremony which includes a full parade and the presentation of special awards to outstanding recruits and divisions. Later in your Navy

Table 1.2. Common RTC (Boot Camp) Abbreviations

BMO	Basic Military Orientation
DOT	Day of Training
EPO	Educational Petty Officer
FFTD	Firefighting Training Division
MD	Military Drill
MED	Military Evaluation Division
PI	Personnel Inspection
RAB	Recruit Aptitude Board
RCPO	Recruit Chief Petty Officer
RDC	Recruit Division Commander
ROD	Rate of the Day
TG	Training Group
TOD	Term of the Day
TTO	Training Time Out

PHCS Terry Cosgrove

Figure 1.2. Special ceremonies are an important part of Navy life. Here the Navy's eighth *Nimitz*-class aircraft carrier is commissioned in Norfolk, Virginia.

experience you may participate in other special ceremonies, such as ship commissionings, change-of-command ceremonies, and special awards presentations.

Dates and Time

You will find that in the Navy even dates and times are stated differently. Dates are expressed in a day-month-year format (e.g., 11 October 2001 or 30AUG99) instead of the civilian month-day-year format you are probably used to.

Time is referred to by the 24-hour clock. Hours of the day are numbered from 1 to 24 and spoken as indicated below. Never say "thirteen hundred hours." While this is acceptable practice in the Army and Air Force, the word "hours" is not used in the Navy. Just say "thirteen hundred."

Table 1.3. Navy Time

Civilian time	Navy time (24-hour clock)	Spoken as
Midnight	0000 or 2400	
1 A.M.	0100	"Zero-one-hundred" *or* "Oh-one-hundred"
2 A.M.	0200	"Zero-two-hundred" *or* "Oh-two-hundred"
3 A.M.	0300	
3:30 A.M.	0330	"Zero-three-thirty" *or* "Oh-three-thirty"
4:00 A.M.	0400	
5:00 A.M.	0500	
6:00 A.M.	0600	
6:15 A.M.	0615	"Zero-six-fifteen" *or* "Oh-six-fifteen"
7:00 A.M.	0700	
8:00 A.M.	0800	
9:00 A.M.	0900	
10:00 A.M.	1000	"Ten-hundred"
11:00 A.M.	1100	"Eleven-hundred"
11:47 A.M.	1147	"Eleven-forty-seven"
12 Noon	1200	
1:00 P.M.	1300	"Thirteen-hundred"
2:00 P.M.	1400	
3:00 P.M.	1500	
3:59 P.M.	1559	"Fifteen-fifty-nine"
4:00 P.M.	1600	
5:00 P.M.	1700	
6:00 P.M.	1800	
7:00 P.M.	1900	
8:00 P.M.	2000	"Twenty-hundred"
8:01 P.M.	2001	"Twenty-oh-one"
9:00 P.M.	2100	
10:00 P.M.	2200	
11:00 P.M.	2300	"Twenty-three-hundred"
12 Midnight	2400 or 0000	"Twenty-four-hundred" *or* "Zero-zero-zero-zero"
12:01 A.M.	0001	"Zero-zero-zero-one"

13

Liberty and Leave

Even time off from your job is referred to differently in the Navy. At the end of a normal work day when your ship is in port or if you are stationed ashore, you may be allowed to leave the ship or station to spend some time doing what you enjoy (such as going to a movie, visiting local friends, eating at a restaurant, going home to your family if they live nearby). This time off is called *liberty,* and may last until the next morning, or for an entire weekend, or it may end at midnight or some other designated time, depending upon the circumstances. Liberty overseas when your ship is visiting a foreign port is one of the great advantages of being in the Navy. Most people would have to spend thousands of dollars to take a trip to Italy or Japan, but as a Sailor you may find yourself visiting such places as part of your job.

What would be called a vacation in the civilian world is called *leave* in the Navy. If you want some time off to go back to your hometown to visit friends and relatives, you must submit a request, using the chain of command, specifying the exact days you want to be away. Of course, you cannot take leave whenever you feel like it. You will be an important member of the crew of your ship or station, so your absence will have to be carefully planned in order to keep things running smoothly while you are gone. Do not make airline reservations or other firm plans until your leave request has been approved.

Everyone in the Navy earns leave at the rate of $2^1/_2$ days per month (or 30 days per year). If you do not use all of your leave in a year, you may carry what is left over to the next year. There is a limit, however. The maximum you may carry over from one year to the next is 60 days (unless you have been unable to use your leave because of extended operations; in that case, you may be authorized to carry up to 90 days into the new year).

Occasionally, a death in the family or some other serious consideration will require you to need leave in a hurry. This is called *emergency leave* and the procedures are, of course, different from those of routine leave requests. Tell your family that the best way to get you home in an emergency is to notify the American Red Cross, who after verifying the situation will immediately notify the Navy.

While in boot camp, you will not be granted any routine leave or liberty until you have completed your training.

Orders

Before you know it, recruit training will be over. And it won't be long before you are an apprentice instead of a recruit, with two stripes on your sleeve and higher pay. Some of your shipmates, those who went through training with you, may go with you to your next assignment; some you will never see again; others you may meet years later at some far off duty station or aboard one of the Navy's many ships.

Schools

Because the Navy is a very complex organization that is frequently leading the way in adopting new technologies, and because advancement is one of the goals the Navy has in mind for you, training is an almost constant part of Navy life. Recruit training is just the first step. After boot camp you will go to apprenticeship training or to a Class A school. After that, you may receive still more schooling. Later in your career you will probably go to other schools for advanced training. Even when you are doing your job aboard your ship or station, on-the-job training will frequently be a part of your routine.

All formal training in the Navy comes under the control of the Chief of Naval Education and Training (CNET), whose headquarters are in Pensacola, Florida. CNET plans and directs training programs for several hundred activities, everything from basic recruit training to postgraduate instruction for officers. CNET also handles family educational programs.

Apprenticeship Training

If you have not been slated for a Class A school, you will attend a three-week course, called apprenticeship training, which will prepare you to be a seaman, fireman, or airman. Upon completion of the course, you will be ordered to your first ship or duty station.

Class A School

If you were selected for a Class A school, you will be going there after graduation from RTC. In Class A school you will receive specialized training that will prepare you for a specific rating (occupation). Successful completion of this training will give you the knowledge and skills necessary to do your special job and will enhance your chances for promotion.

Underway

Once you have completed your initial schooling, your orders will take you to your first duty station. Whether you are going to a destroyer, an aircraft carrier, a submarine, a naval air station, a supply depot, or a Navy medical facility, you will be a vital part of the world's greatest navy. Whether you plan on making the Navy your career or are just trying it out for one enlistment, your performance of duty at this first duty station will have an important effect on the rest of your life. And keep in mind that it will also have an important effect on the effectiveness of this greatest of all navies and on the defense of your nation.

Naval Missions and Heritage

In the brief discussion below (and in Appendix B), you will get a small taste of the Navy's heritage while learning about the Navy's missions. From the examples cited, it should be quite apparent that the Navy you are now a part of has a long history of successfully carrying out the missions assigned. Keep in mind that these examples are just a few of the many instances when Sailors like you have been called upon to contribute to the defense and well-being of our nation. The time will come when you will be called upon to do the same.

Missions

Even though the United States is the fourth largest nation in the world in terms of land area, it has always been a maritime nation, focusing on the sea as one of its most important assets. During the colonial period and in the early days of the Republic, it was much easier to travel from colony to colony or state to state by ship than by horse or on foot, and fishing, whaling, and overseas trade were among the fledgling nation's earliest businesses. One of its earliest challenges was the War of 1812, which was partially decided by a series of stellar naval victories against the world's foremost sea power at the time. A naval blockade and riverine warfare were essential elements in the Civil War, and the war against Spain at the end of nineteenth century was begun by a naval tragedy and decided largely by naval victories. American commerce would never have thrived without open sea lanes, two world wars could not have been won without the lifelines maintained across the world's oceans, and United States control of the sea was an essential element in the victory over Communism in the Cold War. Throughout the nation's history, the sea has played an important role in America's economy, defense, and foreign policy. Today, the modern United States of America continues to look to the sea for these same things and relies upon its Navy to preserve and further the nation's maritime interests.

Being a maritime nation means having a comfortable relationship with the sea, using it to national advantage and seeing it as a highway rather than as an obstacle. An illustration of this point can be seen in World War II. By 1941, Hitler had conquered much of the land of Europe, but because Germany was not a maritime power, he saw the English Channel (a mere twenty miles across at one point) as a barrier, and England remained outside his grasp. Yet the Americans and British were later able to strike across this same channel into Europe to eventually bring Nazi Germany to its knees. And in that same war, the United States attacked Hitler's forces in North Africa from clear across the Atlantic Ocean—a distance of more than 3,000 nautical miles.

The navy of a maritime nation must be able to carry out a variety of strategic missions. In general terms, the most significant ones can be described as:

- Freedom of the seas (sometimes called "sea control")
- Deterrence
- Forward presence
- Power projection

Freedom of the Seas

Because navies are expensive, the newly created United States tried to do without one in the years immediately following the American Revolution. Within a year after the termination of hostilities with England, Congress ordered all naval vessels sold or destroyed. The men who had fought for independence as Sailors in the Continental Navy during the Revolution were left high and dry by the new government's decision. John Paul Jones, the most famous American naval hero during the Revolution and later recognized as the "father of the U.S. Navy," left America and served as an admiral in the Russian Navy. No money was allocated to the building of naval vessels in the first ten years, and George Washington, the general who had shown a keen understanding of the importance of naval power during the war, as president relied upon his Secretary of War to oversee both the Army and Navy, such as they were. Thomas Jefferson viewed a navy as not only expensive but provocative and, when he became the nation's third President, oversaw the creation of an inexpensive fleet of defensive gunboats to guard the nation's shores.

But these frugal measures did not last long. World events and human nature conspired to prove that a maritime nation cannot long endure without a navy. Almost immediately, the so-called Barbary pirates—the North African states of Morocco, Algiers, Tunis, and Tripoli, ruled by petty despots whose main source of income was derived from the seizure of ships or extorting protection money— began preying on defenseless American merchant shipping in the Mediterranean Sea. Additionally, the ongoing struggle between France and England made American ships and their crews tempting targets, and both nations began taking advantage of the helplessness of the Americans by seizing merchant ships and sailors on flimsy pretexts. Under these provocations, the cost of not having a navy soon outweighed the cost of having one. Spurred to reluctant but unavoidable action by these costly and insulting blows to U.S. sovereignty, Congress approved the re-establishment of a navy and the building of several ships.

In a series of engagements on the high seas in the next two decades, the fledgling U.S. Navy successfully defended the nation's right to use the world's oceans. During the Quasi-War with France (1798–1800), the frigate *Constellation* defeated two French frigates in separate engagements, and other American ships, including the feisty little schooner *Enterprise,* managed to capture more than 80 French vessels of various sizes and descriptions. In the War with Tripoli (1801–5), a band of American Sailors and Marines led a dar-

U.S. Naval Institute Print Collection (Phillips Melville, artist)

Figure 2.1. Ships like the frigate *Constellation* have long maintained American "freedom of the seas."

ing raid into the enemy's home harbor that earned them respect throughout much of the world. At the beginning of the War of 1812, the U.S. Navy had only 17 ships while the British had over 600, yet the Americans won a number of ship-to-ship battles that contributed to the favorable outcome of the war. Considering the relative inexperience and small size of this new navy, American Sailors performed well, and the new nation secured its rights and proved its ability to use the oceans of the world. Never again would the United States be powerless to defend itself at sea.

Ever since those early days, the U.S. Navy has been on station, ensuring America's right to use the sea for trade, for security, and for its growing role as a world power. As the nation grew stronger, the Navy also grew in size and capability. The early frigates that performed so well in battle with the French and British Navies during the Quasi War and the War of 1812 gave way to the ironclad monitors of the Civil War, and these were superseded by the big-gun, armored battleships and high-speed cruisers that won the Spanish American War in 1898.

In time, the United States emerged as a world power and the Navy's mission of preserving freedom of the seas became more vital than ever. New technology led to the development of new kinds of ships, such as destroyers and submarines, and the invention of the airplane brought about naval aviation as a whole new component of the Navy. In the latter half of the twentieth century, the U.S. Navy was called upon to fight the greatest sea war in history when Germany and Japan challenged America's freedom of the seas, and maintaining that freedom was a major factor in the victory over Communism in the Cold War. Today the Navy continues its role of preserving our free use of the sea, and that is where you come in.

Deterrence

Perhaps the most obvious reason for a maritime nation to have a navy is to ensure that no other nation attacks it by sea. Even when President Jefferson was trying to avoid having a navy in order to save money, he recognized this elemental need and tried to use his gunboat fleet as a deterrent to attack. One of the reasons for the United States digging the Panama Canal in the early part of the 20th century was to permit U.S. warships to move rapidly from coast to coast and thereby deter a potential enemy from attacking our shores.

Improvements in technology—such as the development of high speed aircraft, powerful missiles, and long-range submarines—gradually increased our vulnerability to attack, and the Navy continued to play a vital role in protecting the nation by deterring our enemies, both real and potential. In 1962, the Soviet Union placed offensive nuclear missiles in Cuba. President Kennedy, a former Navy man himself, imposed a naval quarantine around the island and threatened nuclear retaliation as deterrent measures to keep the Soviets from using these missiles against the United States and other nations in the Western hemisphere and to ultimately force the Soviets to take the missiles out of Cuba.

All through the Cold War, the U.S. Navy's fleet of ballistic missile submarines patrolled the oceans of the world, armed with nuclear weapons ready to be launched on very short notice against an aggressor nation. This massive firepower, coupled with the striking power of U.S. aircraft carriers, land-based missiles, and the Air Force's long-range aircraft, served as an effective deterrent to the Soviet Union. Without this deterrence, the U.S. would have been very vulnerable to attack and would not have been able to stand up to the extremely powerful Soviet Union in moments of crisis.

An example of America's ability to stand up to Soviet intimidation occurred during the Middle East War of 1973. Although neither the Soviet Union nor the United States was directly involved in that war between Israel and most of the Arab nations, the U.S. supported Israel while the USSR backed the Arabs. When the Soviets began resupplying their clients by sending in massive quantities of weapons by airlift, the U.S. did the same for Israel. The U.S. Sixth Fleet took up station in the Mediterranean to provide protection for its aircraft flying into the war zone. When the war began going badly for the Arabs, the Soviets threatened to intervene. The United States responded by putting its forces on increased alert worldwide and by moving naval units into striking position. Faced with this deterrent, the Soviets thought better of their intervention and the war was ultimately ended and settled on equitable terms.

Several times—once as recently as the late 1990s—Communist China has threatened to attack the Nationalist Chinese on the island of Taiwan, and each time the U.S. Navy has moved into position to successfully deter the Communists from attacking.

There are many such examples when the Navy has been called upon to deter others from taking actions that were seen as dangerous to the U.S. or were not in the nation's best interests. Just as an effective police patrol can deter criminals from committing crimes in a peaceful neighborhood, so the Navy preserves the peace and keeps our nation safe and prosperous by its mere existence and by its ability to patrol the waters of the world.

Forward Presence

Another of the important missions of the Navy is based upon its ability to go virtually anywhere in the world. This capability allows the United States to be in a position to reassure our allies in a time of crisis, to intimidate potential enemies (a form of deterrence), to deliver humanitarian aid when disaster strikes, to rescue Americans or our allies from dangerous situations, or to be able to carry out offensive military action in a timely manner. This is called "forward presence" and explains why you may well find yourself serving on a deployment to a far corner of the world.

Sometimes the presence of a single destroyer visiting a foreign port is all that is needed to carry out this vital mission. On other occasions, a carrier battle group or an entire fleet moving into a region is needed to send a strong message of warning or support. If hostilities become necessary, having units already at or near enemy territory can be a major advantage.

In 1854, Commodore Matthew Perry used forward presence as a means to open diplomatic relations and, ultimately, trade with Japan, a nation that, until Perry's visit, had shunned contact with the outside world. During the latter part of the nineteenth century, American naval ships patrolled the waters of the Far East to provide protection for our economic interests and the many American missionaries in that part of the world. When war broke out with Spain in 1898, the

U.S. Naval Institute Print Collection (Tom Freeman, artist)

Figure 2.2. Sometimes "forward presence" takes Navy Sailors to far off places. Here, the gunboat *Tutuilla* stands watch at Chungking, China in 1939.

U.S. fleet already present in the Far East was able to strike a quick and decisive blow against the Spanish fleet in the Philippines. Throughout the Cold War, the U.S. Navy kept the Sixth Fleet in the Mediterranean Sea and the Seventh Fleet in the Far East to reassure our allies in those regions that we were nearby and ready to respond in the event of a crisis. Today the Fifth Fleet has been added to make our presence known in the Middle East and nearby regions. Aircraft from U.S. carriers patrol the skies near Iraq to prevent the unpredictable dictator Saddam Hussein from taking actions that will threaten U.S. interests in the region.

Today's modern American military forces have great striking power through powerful armies and long-range aircraft, and some of those forces are maintained for quick response in Europe, the Middle East, and Asia. But that kind of forward presence can only exist at the invitation of other nations who are willing to give us bases on their territory. The Navy allows us to have a presence wherever there is water. In times of increased tension, naval units can be moved to positions where American presence is needed, without having to negotiate any complicated diplomatic arrangements, without requiring much time. Today the United States is a world power, and an extremely important component of that power is the U.S. Navy with its ability to extend American influence to nearly all parts of the globe.

Power Projection

Forward presence allows the U.S. Navy to be on station the world over, but just being there is not always enough. Sometimes, despite a nation's efforts to remain at peace, the use of force becomes necessary. When that occurs, the Navy has always been particularly effective in projecting American power where it is needed.

As early as the American Revolution, an American naval squadron sailed to the British-owned Bahamas to capture needed weapons, and John Paul Jones furthered the American cause by conducting a series of daring raids against the British Isles themselves.

In 1847, during the war with Mexico, the Navy transported a force of twelve thousand Army troops to Vera Cruz, and played a crucial role in the successful capture of that port city, ultimately leading to an American victory in that war.

Union ships not only carried out an effective blockade of Confederate ports during the Civil War, they also attacked key southern ports and opened up the Mississippi river to Union use, effectively driving a wedge right into the heart of the Confederacy.

By escorting convoys, U.S. destroyers projected American power across the Atlantic to aid in an Allied victory during World War I. In the Second World War, American aircraft carriers, battleships, cruisers, destroyers, submarines, amphibious vessels, troop transports, oilers, ammunition ships, minesweepers, PT-boats, and a wide variety of other ships carried the fight to the far corners of the world, slugging it out with powerful Japanese fleets in the Pacific, dueling with German submarines in the Atlantic, safely transporting incredible amounts of supplies to the many theaters of war, and landing troops on distant islands and on the African, Asian, and European coasts.

During the Korean, Vietnam, and Gulf Wars, naval power guaranteed our ability to project our power ashore, and naval aircraft, guns, and missiles inflicted significant harm on our enemies.

When American embassies in Africa were bombed by terrorists in 1998, American cruisers, destroyers, and submarines took retaliatory action by launching a Tomahawk-missile barrage at terrorist targets in Afghanistan and Sudan. In the following year, Naval electronic warfare and strike aircraft were vital components of the air war in Kosovo, and periodic attacks on Iraq have become an almost routine form of power projection to minimize the threats of Saddam Hussein's regime.

When power needs to be projected, American naval forces have always been ready, willing, and able to accomplish the mission. As

Figure 2.3. "Power projection." Naval aircraft strike enemy targets in North Vietnam during Operation Pierce Arrow in 1964.

U.S. Naval Institute Print Collection (R.G. Smith, artist)

an American Sailor, you will sometimes hear yourself being described as the "tip of the sword" with good reason.

Other Missions and Feats

The missions described above are the more traditional ones, but the U.S. Navy has also played an important role in other realms, such as exploration and scientific discovery as well. For example, a Navy exploration team led by Commander Charles Wilkes took a squadron of ships around the world, exploring Antarctica and vast areas of the Pacific Ocean in the years 1838–42. His charts of the Pacific not only served mariners for many decades to come but were used in the invasion of Tarawa in the early part of World War II. Navy men Robert E. Peary and Richard E. Byrd were pioneers in polar exploration: Peary was the first man to reach the North Pole in 1909, and Byrd flew over the South Pole in 1929. When Captain Ned Beach and his crew took their nuclear submarine USS *Triton* around the world in 1960, it was not the first time anyone had circumnavigated the earth, but it was the first time anyone had done it *submerged* for the entire voyage of 41,500 miles in 83 days. In that same year, Lieutenant Don Walsh went deeper than any human being has ever been when he and Jacques Picard took the bathyscaphe *Trieste* to the bottom of the Marianas Trench, 35,800 feet down (more than six and a half miles beneath the sea). Alan Shepard was in the Navy when he became the first American in space, and Neil Armstrong had been in the Navy before he became the first man to walk on the moon.

The Navy has often led the way or played a crucial role in many realms of scientific and technological development, such as electricity, radio communications, radar technology, computer science, and nuclear engineering. Among her many achievements in computer science, Grace Hopper invented COBOL, one of the important computer languages that led the way in computer development. Today, a ship bears her name. The world of nuclear engineering has been forever affected by the work of Hyman Rickover, and a Navy man known to his shipmates as "Swede" Momsen changed the deep sea diving world by his inventions and his pioneering work.

Another Navy diver, Carl Brashear, worked his way up from cook to master diver, salvaging a nuclear weapon from the depths of the Atlantic and losing a leg in the process. His inspiring story was the basis for a major motion picture.

Another modern, multi-million-dollar movie included a reenactment of the feats of another Sailor who won the Navy Cross at Pearl Harbor. Dorie Miller was different from you only in circumstance, but how he responded to a crisis situation later earned him the right to have a ship named after him.

Boatswain's Mate James Elliott Williams left his southern rural home to join the Navy. Some years later he was a first-class petty officer in command of a pair of patrol boats on narrow jungle waterways in Vietnam, when he found himself facing an entire enemy regiment trying to cross a canal. Without hesitation, Williams pressed the attack. Three hours later, over a thousand enemy soldiers had been killed or captured and sixty-five enemy vessels had been destroyed. Williams was awarded the Medal of Honor and later retired from the Navy as its most decorated enlisted member, having earned the Navy Cross, two Silver Stars, the Navy and Marine Corps Medal, three Bronze Stars, the Navy and Marine Corps Commendation Medal, the Vietnamese Cross of Gallantry, and three Purple Hearts. In a second career, he won the continued respect of his fellow South Carolinians by serving as a federal marshal.

For more than two centuries, Sailors of the United States Navy have been recording an impressive history of courage, resourcefulness, sacrifice, innovation, humanitarianism, combat skill, and dedication to duty. Now it is your turn to follow in their wakes and, circumstances permitting, you may well leave *your* mark on the pages of this impressive record.

Heritage

As one who has chosen to take part in this ongoing story and to do your part in carrying out the important missions described above, you would do well to read and think about the history of the United States Navy. Even in the best fiction, you will not likely find a better story than the one that makes up the true story of the U.S. Navy in action. It is full of excitement, adventure, and heroism. It is also a story of harrowing moments and great challenges, and there are times when those who served before you made mistakes or were not up to the challenges placed before them. By learning about yesterday's Navy, you will be better prepared to serve today's Navy. You will better understand why the Navy is so important to national security, you will be inspired by the heroic actions of other Sailors who served before you, you will learn from the mistakes of the past, and you will share the pride of a heritage that became yours when you took the oath of enlistment. All of this will help you to do a better job and to feel good about why you are doing it.

While there are many good books, some magazines, and a few movies that will help you better understand the legacy you have been entrusted with, there are other ways that you can learn about and grow to appreciate the proud heritage you are now a part of. When you report to a ship, find out why she has the name she does. You may learn that the name once belonged to someone much like you, a Sailor carrying out the missions of the Navy to the best of their ability. You may also be surprised to learn that there may well have been other ships that have had the same name and have passed it on to this latest bearer of the name. When ships are lost in battle or die of old age, their name is often given to a newly built ship to carry on the legacy of the name. This is similar to the ongoing process you are now participating in. As older Sailors move on to retirement, they pass the legacy on to younger Sailors who then are entrusted to carry out the Navy's vital missions. This is obviously no small responsibility, but it is also a privilege that only a select group of Americans have had.

When you go ashore and notice a monument on the base, take a moment to read the accompanying plaque. It was placed there to honor some aspect of the Navy's (and your) heritage. You may find yourself walking just a little taller as you move on.

History can be the most boring thing in the world, but heritage is written in a special ink that is a blend of the blood of sacrifice, the sweat of hard work, and the tears of pride that you are bound to feel when you realize the importance of what you are doing. Learn your heritage, be proud of it, and work hard to carry it on.

3 Ranks, Rates, Ratings, and Paygrades

One of the best things about military service is the opportunity to advance. With advancement comes increased pay, privileges, authority, and responsibility. How far you advance depends upon your abilities and how willing you are to work and learn. The Navy advancement system is explained in detail in a later chapter, but before you can think about advancing you must first understand the Navy structure of paygrades, ranks, rates, and ratings. These terms may seem confusing at first, but you will quickly adapt to their usage. Keep in mind that "paygrades," "ranks," and "rates" all refer to a person's relative position within the Navy, while the term "rating" refers only to an occupational specialty.

Everyone in the Navy is either nonrated, rated, or a commissioned officer. Men and women who enlist in the Navy begin as nonrated personnel. A combination of experience and specialized training will allow them to move up into a rated category and to advance through a number of levels. Rated personnel are called "petty officers." Nonrated and rated personnel together are referred to as "enlisted personnel." Commissioned officers are appointed using special criteria that usually include a college education and a special selection process.

Paygrades

Everyone wearing a Navy uniform has a paygrade. For that matter, everyone in the armed forces (Army, Navy, Air Force, Marines, and Coast Guard) has a paygrade. A paygrade defines a person's relative standing in the Navy and, of course, determines how much money he or she will be paid. (See chapter 11, "Navy Pay and Benefits," for more information.) There are officer paygrades and enlisted (rated and nonrated) paygrades. Rated personnel whose technical skills and performance are outstanding may earn a commission as a warrant officer, a special category that falls in between the other officer and enlisted paygrades.

A new recruit enters the Navy as an E-1, which is the first enlisted paygrade. Paygrades E-1 through E-3 are the nonrated paygrades, meaning that they are not tied to a specific occupation. However, based upon screening and testing, they are placed within a broad occupational category—known as a general apprenticeship (such as seaman or airman)—for advancement through the nonrated paygrades. Specific advanced occupational training leads to advancement into the rated paygrades (E-4 through E-9). Officer paygrades are designated O-1 through O-10. The various Navy paygrades and their titles are listed in Table 3.1.

Ratings

A rating is an occupational specialty in the Navy. You might call it a "job" in the civilian world. Before you can qualify for a rating, you must first work your way through the general apprenticeship levels (E-1 to E-3), which will help prepare you for your rating. Once you are promoted to E-4, you will have a rating and, except in special circumstances, you will keep that rating for the rest of your career.

Strikers

If you are seeking to be promoted into a specific rating, you are said to be "striking" for that promotion. Personnel who are E-1s, E-2s, or E-3s and have achieved a significant level of experience and/or training toward a particular rating may be formally designated as a "striker." This is an official recognition of your progress and is an important step toward achieving that all-important promotion to petty officer. If you become a designated striker, it means that you have achieved the minimum skills required (through on-the-job experience and/or formal training) for a particular rating. A rating abbreviation will be formally added to your general rate abbreviation to indicate your achievement. For example, a seaman (SN) who demonstrates significant skills in the electronics technician (ET) rating would be designated as a striker by the new rating abbreviation ETSN.

Ratings Categories

In order to advance beyond the E-3 paygrade, you must have a rating. This, of course, requires a significant amount of training. Each of the Navy's ratings is identified by a two- or three-letter abbreviation such as ET (for electronics technician) or GSM (for gas turbine system technician—mechanical). Each rating is further identified by a unique symbol, called a specialty mark, that becomes a part of your

Table 3.1. Navy Paygrades for Officers and Enlisted

Paygrade	Rank	Abbreviation
Officers		
O-10	Admiral	ADM
O-9	Vice Admiral	VADM
O-8	Rear Admiral (Upper Half)	RDML
O-7	Rear Admiral (Lower Half)	RADM
O-6	Captain	CAPT
O-5	Commander	CDR
O-4	Lieutenant Commander	LCDR
O-3	Lieutenant	LT
O-2	Lieutenant (junior grade)	LTJG
O-1	Ensign	ENS
W-4	Chief Warrant Officer	CWO4
W-3	Chief Warrant Officer	CWO3
W-2	Chief Warrant Officer	CWO2
W-1	Not currently in use	WO1
Enlisted		
E-9	Master Chief Petty Officer	MCPO
E-8	Senior Chief Petty Officer	SCPO
E-7	Chief Petty Officer	CPO
E-6	Petty Officer First Class	PO1
E-5	Petty Officer Second Class	PO2
E-4	Petty Officer Third Class	PO3
E-3	Seaman	SN
	Fireman	FN
	Airman	AN
	Constructionman	CN
	Hospitalman	HN
	Dentalman	DN
E-2	Seaman Apprentice	SA
	Fireman Apprentice	FA
	Airman Apprentice	AA
	Constructionman Apprentice	CA
	Hospitalman Apprentice	HA
	Dentalman Apprentice	DA
E-1	Recruit	

rating badge worn on the left sleeve of your uniform. There are three categories of ratings: general, service, and emergency.

General Ratings

Occupations for paygrades E-4 through E-9 are called general ratings. Each general rating has a distinctive badge. Examples of general ratings are operations specialist, gunner's mate, and storekeeper. General ratings are sometimes combined at the E-8 or E-9 level, when the work is similar. For example, the work done by a senior chief utilitiesman and by a senior chief construction electrician is very similar, so when these individuals are promoted to master chief, both would become master chief utilitiesmen.

Service Ratings

Some general ratings are further subdivided into service ratings. For example, the general rating of gas-turbine system technician (GS) is subdivided into two service ratings: GSE (electrical) and GSM (mechanical). There are service ratings at any petty officer (PO) level; however, they are most common with E-4s through E-6s. In the higher paygrades (E-8 and E-9), service ratings often merge into a general

U.S. Naval Institute

Figure 3.1. Operations specialists (OS) man the combat information center (CIC) in a Navy combatant.

rating. For example, those gas-turbine system technicians who specialized in electrical and mechanical systems (GSE and GSM) would become simply GSs once they are promoted to senior chief petty officer (E-8), because a senior chief gas-turbine system technician needs to know about both the electrical and mechanical systems.

Emergency Ratings

In wartime or other national emergency, it may be necessary to create special ratings not normally needed in the Navy. These are called, appropriately enough, emergency ratings. For example, during World War II the special needs of the war caused the Navy to create the emergency ratings of stevedore, transportationman, and welfare and recreation leader. The Navy has not created any emergency ratings since the late 1950s and there are no emergency ratings in use today.

Current Ratings

In the days before the Civil War, the Navy had an urgent need for sailmakers but did not have any call for missile technicians. The number and types of ratings change as the needs of the Navy change. Each of the current ratings in the Navy is briefly described in the following pages. The service ratings within each general rating are also included. You will find a wide variety of occupational specialties in the Navy and that the skills required vary a great deal. Whether you enjoy working indoors or out, using tools or computers, are better in technical subjects or clerical, there are ratings that will suit your desires and abilities. The specialty mark of each rating is included with the rating description. Specialty marks, added to enlisted uniforms in 1866, were created to represent the instrument originally used to perform a particular task. For example, the quartermaster (QM) mark is a ship's helm, while the signalman (SM) mark is two crossed signal flags. The custom of representing the type of work with a specialty mark for each rating continues, but many of the designs have been stylized. For instance, the journalist (JO) is represented by a crossed quill and scroll, neither of which is still in use, but they serve as a traditional representation of the skills needed and the tasks performed in that rating.

AB

Cross anchors,
winged

Aviation Boatswain's Mate: ABs operate, maintain, and repair aircraft catapults, arresting gear, and barricades. They operate and maintain fuel- and lube-oil transfer systems. ABs direct aircraft on the flight deck and in hangar bays before launch and after recovery. They use tow tractors to position planes and operate support equipment used to start aircraft. (Service ratings: ABE [launching and recovery equipment]; ABF [fuels]; ABH [aircraft handling].)

AC

Microphone, winged

Air Traffic Controller: ACs assist in the essential safe, orderly, and speedy flow of air traffic by directing and controlling aircraft under visual (VFR) and instrument (IFR) flight rules. They operate field lighting systems, communicate with aircraft, and furnish pilots with information regarding traffic, navigation, and weather conditions. They operate and adjust GCA (ground-controlled approach) systems. They interpret targets on radar screens and plot aircraft positions.

AD

Two-bladed propeller, winged

Aviation Machinist's Mate: ADs maintain jet aircraft engines and associated equipment, or engage in any one of several types of aircraft maintenance activities. ADs maintain, service, adjust, and replace aircraft engines and accessories, as well as perform the duties of flight engineers.

33

AE

Globe, winged

Aviation Electrician's Mate: AEs maintain, adjust, and repair electrical-power generating, converting, and distributing systems, as well as lighting, control, and indicating systems in aircraft. They also install and maintain wiring and flight and engine instrument systems, which include automatic flight control, stabilization, aircraft compass, attitude reference, and inertial navigation systems.

AG

Circle on vertical arrow, winged

Aerographer's Mate: The Navy has its own weather forecasters, AGs, who are trained in meteorology and the use of aerological instruments that monitor such weather characteristics as air pressure, temperature, humidity, wind speed, and wind direction. They prepare weather maps and forecasts, analyze atmospheric conditions to determine the best flight levels for aircraft, and measure wind and air density to increase the accuracy of antiaircraft firing, shore bombardment, and delivery of weapons by aircraft.

AK

Crossed keys,
winged

Aviation Storekeeper: AKs ensure that the materials and equipment needed for naval aviation activities are available and in good order. They take inventory, estimate future needs, and make purchases. AKs store and issue flight clothing, aeronautical materials and spare parts, ordnance, and electronic, structural, and engineering equipment. (This rating is expected to merge with *Storekeeper* by 2003).

AM

Crossed mauls,
winged

Aviation Structural Mechanic: The maintenance and repair of aircraft parts (wings, fuselage, tail, control surfaces, landing gear, and attending mechanisms) are performed by AMs working with metals, alloys, and plastics. AMs maintain and repair safety equipment and hydraulic systems. (Service rating: AME [safety equipment].)

AO

Flaming spherical
shell, winged

Aviation Ordnanceman: Navy planes carry guns, bombs, torpedoes, rockets, and missiles to attack the enemy on the sea, under the sea, in the air, and on land. AOs are responsible for maintaining, repairing, installing, operating, and handling aviation ordnance equipment; their duties also include the handling, stowing, issuing, and loading of munitions and small arms.

AS

Crossed maul and
spark, winged

Aviation Support Equipment Technician: ASs perform intermediate maintenance on "yellow" (aviation accessory) equipment at naval air stations and aboard carriers. They maintain gasoline and diesel engines, hydraulic and pneumatic systems, liquid and gaseous oxygen and nitrogen systems, gas-turbine compressor units, and electrical systems.

AT

Helium atom, winged

Aviation Electronics Technician: ATs perform preventive and corrective maintenance on aviation electronic components supported by conventional and automatic test equipment. They repair the electronic components of weapons, communications, radar, navigation, antisubmarine warfare sensors, electronic warfare, data link, fire control, and tactical displays.

AW

Spark-pierced electron orbits over wave, winged

Aviation Warfare Systems Operator: AWs operate airborne radar and electronic equipment used in detecting, locating, and tracking submarines. They also operate equipment used in antisurface, mine, and electronic warfare, and play key roles in search-and-rescue and counternarcotics operations.

AZ

Two-bladed propeller on open book, winged

Aviation Maintenance Administrationman: AZs perform clerical, administrative, and managerial duties necessary to keep aircraft-maintenance activities running smoothly. They plan, schedule, and coordinate maintenance, including inspections and modifications to aircraft and equipment.

BM

Crossed anchors

Boatswain's Mate: BMs train, direct, and supervise others in marlinespike, deck, and boat seamanship; ensure proper upkeep of the ship's external structure, rigging, deck equipment, and boats; lead working parties; perform seamanship tasks; are in charge of picketboats, self-propelled barges, tugs, and other yard and district craft; serve in or in charge of gun crews and damage-control parties; use and maintain equipment for loading and unloading cargo, ammunition, fuel, and general stores.

BU

Carpenter's square on plumb bob

Builder: Navy BUs are like civilian construction workers. They may be skilled carpenters, plasterers, roofers, cement finishers, asphalt workers, masons, painters, bricklayers, sawmill operators, or cabinetmakers. BUs build and repair all types of structures, including piers, bridges, towers, underwater installations, schools, offices, houses, and other buildings.

CE

Spark on telephone
pole

Construction Electrician: CEs are responsible for the power production and electrical work required to build and operate airfields, roads, barracks, hospitals, shops, and warehouses. The work of Navy CEs is like that of civilian construction electricians, powerhouse electricians, telephone and electrical repairmen, substation operators, linemen, and others.

CM

Double-headed
wrench on nut

Construction Mechanic: CMs maintain heavy construction and automotive equipment (buses, dump trucks, bulldozers, rollers, cranes, backhoes, and pile drivers) as well as other construction equipment. They service vehicles and work on gasoline and diesel engines, ignition and fuel systems, transmissions, electrical systems, and hydraulic, pneumatic, and steering systems.

CT

Crossed quill and
spark

Cryptologic Technician: Depending on their special career area, CTs control access to classified material, translate foreign-language transmissions, operate radio direction-finding equipment, employ electronic countermeasures, and install, service, and repair special electronic and electromechanical equipment. CTs require special security clearances. (Service ratings: CTA [administrative]; CTI [interpretive]; CTM [maintenance]; CTO [communications]; CTR [collection]; CTT [technical].)

DC

Crossed fire axe
and maul

Damage Controlman: DCs perform the work necessary for damage control, ship stability, firefighting, and chemical, biological, and radiological (CBR) warfare defense. They instruct personnel in damage control and CBR defense, and repair damage-control equipment and systems.

DK

Key on data card

Disbursing Clerk: DKs maintain the financial records of Navy personnel. They prepare payrolls, determine transportation entitlements, compute travel allowances, and process claims for reimbursement of travel expenses. DKs also process vouchers for receiving and spending public money and make sure accounting data are accurate. They maintain fiscal records and prepare financial reports and returns.

DM

Draftsman's
compass on triangle

Illustrator-Draftsman: DMs prepare mechanical drawings, blueprints, charts, and illustrations needed for construction projects and other naval activities. They may specialize in structural drafting, electrical drafting, graphic arts mechanics, and/or illustrating.

DT

"D" on caduceus

Dental Technician: Navy dentists, like many civilian ones, are assisted by dental technicians. DTs have a variety of "chairside," laboratory, and administrative duties. Some are qualified in dental prosthetics (making and fitting artificial teeth), dental X-ray techniques, clinical laboratory procedures, pharmacy and chemistry, or maintenance and repair of dental equipment.

37

EA

Measuring scale
fronting level rod

Engineering Aide: EAs provide construction engineers with the information needed to develop final construction plans. EAs conduct surveys for roads, airfields, buildings, waterfront structures, pipelines, ditches, and drainage systems. They perform soil tests, prepare topographic and hydrographic maps, and survey for sewers, water lines, drainage systems, and underwater excavations.

EM

Globe with
longitude, latitude
lines

Electrician's Mate: The operation and repair of a ship's or station's electrical powerplant and electrical equipment are the responsibilities of EMs. They also maintain and repair power and lighting circuits, distribution switchboards, generators, motors, and other electrical equipment.

EN

Gear

Engineman: Internal-combustion engines, either diesel or gasoline, must be kept in good order; this is the responsibility of ENs. They are also responsible for the maintenance of refrigeration, air-conditioning, and distilling-plant motors and compressors.

EO

Bulldozer

Equipment Operator: EOs work with heavy machinery such as bulldozers, power shovels, pile drivers, rollers, and graders. EOs use this machinery to dig ditches and excavate for building foundations, to break up old concrete or asphalt paving and pour new paving, to loosen soil and grade it, to dig out tree trunks and rocks, to remove debris from construction sites, to raise girders, and to move and set in place other pieces of equipment or materials needed for a job.

ET

Helium atom

Electronics Technician: ETs are responsible for electronic equipment used to send and receive messages, detect enemy planes and ships, and determine target distance. They must maintain, repair, calibrate, tune, and adjust electronic equipment used for communications, detection and tracking, recognition and identification, navigation, and electronic countermeasures.

EW

Spark through
helium atom

Electronics Warfare Technician: EWs operate and maintain electronic equipment used in navigation, target detection and location, and the prevention of electronic spying by enemies. They interpret incoming electronic signals to determine their source. EWs are advanced electronic technicians who do wiring and circuit testing and repair. They determine performance levels of electronic equipment, install new components, modify existing equipment, and test, adjust, and repair cooling systems. (Rating is expected to merge with *Cryptologic Technician [Technical]* by 2003.)

FC

Range finder
with inward spark
on each side

Fire Controlman: FCs maintain the control mechanism used in weapons systems on combat ships. Complex electronic, electrical, and hydraulic equipment is required to ensure the accuracy of guided-missile and surface gunfire-control systems. FCs are responsible for the operation, routine care, and repair of this equipment, which includes radars, computers, weapons-direction equipment, target-designation systems, gyroscopes, and rangefinders.

FT

Range finder

Fire-Control Technician: FTs maintain advanced electronic equipment used in submarine weapons systems. Complex electronic, electrical, and mechanical equipment is required to ensure the accuracy of guided-missile systems and underwater weapons. FTs are responsible for the operation, routine care, and repair of this equipment.

GM

Crossed cannons

Gunner's Mate: Navy GMs operate, maintain, and repair all gunnery equipment, guided-missile launching systems, rocket launchers, guns, gun mounts, turrets, projectors, and associated equipment. They also make detailed casualty analyses and repairs of electrical, electronic, hydraulic, and mechanical systems. They test and inspect ammunition and missiles and their ordnance components, and train and supervise personnel in the handling and stowage of ammunition, missiles, and assigned ordnance equipment.

39

GS

Turbine with
ducting

Gas-Turbine System Technician: GSs operate, repair, and maintain gas-turbine engines, main propulsion machinery (including gears, shafting, and controllable-pitch propellers), assigned auxiliary equipment, propulsion-control systems, electrical and electronic circuitry up to printed circuit modules, and alarm and warning circuitry. They perform administrative tasks related to gas-turbine propulsion-system operation and maintenance. (Service ratings: GSE [electrical]; GSM [mechanical].)

HM

Caduceus

Hospital Corpsman: HMs assist medical professionals in providing health care to service people and their families. They act as pharmacists, medical technicians, food-service personnel, nurses' aides, physicians' or dentists' assistants, battlefield medics, X-ray technicians, and more. Their work falls into several categories: first aid and minor surgery, patient transportation, patient care, prescriptions and laboratory work, food-service inspections, and clerical duties.

HT

Crossed fire axe and maul with carpenter's square

Hull Maintenance Technician: HTs are responsible for maintaining ships' hulls, fittings, piping systems, and machinery. They install and maintain shipboard and shore-based plumbing and piping systems. They also look after a vessel's safety and survival equipment and perform many tasks related to damage control.

IT

Four sparks

Information Systems Technician: ITs are responsible for the Navy's vital command, control, communications, computer and intelligence systems and equipment. They use state-of-the-art multimedia technology such as fiber optics, digital microwave, and satellites on a global basis and work with telecommunications equipment, computers, and associated peripheral devices.

IC

Telephone receiver over globe

Interior Communications Electrician: ICs operate and repair electronic devices used in a ship's interior communications systems—SITE TV systems, public-address systems, electronic megaphones, and other announcing equipment—as well as gyrocompass systems.

IS

Magnifying glass
and quill

Intelligence Specialist: Military information, especially secret information about enemies or potential enemies, is called intelligence. The IS is involved in collecting and interpreting intelligence data. An IS analyzes photographs and prepares charts, maps, and reports that describe in detail the strategic situation all over the world.

JO

Crossed quill
and scroll

Journalist: JOs are the Navy's information specialists. They write press releases, news stories, features, and articles for Navy newspapers, bulletins, and magazines. They perform a variety of public-relations jobs. Some write scripts and announcements for radio and TV; others are photographers or radio and television broadcasters and producers. The photo work of JOs ranges from administrative and clerical tasks to film processing.

LI

Crossed lith crayon
holder and scraper

Lithographer: LIs run Navy print shops and are responsible for producing printed material used in naval activities. LIs print service magazines, newspapers and bulletins, training materials, and official policy manuals. They operate printing presses, do layout and design, and collate and bind printed pages. The usual specialties are cameraman, pressman, and binderyman.

41

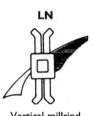

LN

Vertical millrind
crossing quill

Legalman: Navy LNs are aides trained in the field of law. They work in Navy legal offices performing administrative and clerical tasks necessary to process claims, to conduct court and administrative hearings, and to maintain records, documents, and legal-reference libraries. They give advice on tax returns, voter-registration regulations, procedures, and immigration and customs regulations governing Social Security and veterans' benefits, and perform many duties related to courts-martial and nonjudicial hearings.

MA

Star embossed in
circle within shield

Master-at-Arms: MAs help keep law and order aboard ship and at shore stations. They report to the executive officer, help maintain discipline, and assist in security matters. They enforce regulations, conduct investigations, take part in correctional and rehabilitative programs, and organize and train Sailors assigned to police duty. In civilian life, they would be detectives and policemen.

MM

Three-bladed
propeller

Machinist's Mate: Continuous operation of the many engines, compressors and gears, refrigeration, air-conditioning, gas-operated equipment, and other types of machinery afloat and ashore is the job of the MM. In particular, MMs are responsible for a ship's steam propulsion and auxiliary equipment and the outside (deck) machinery. MMs may also perform duties in the manufacture, storage, and transfer of some industrial gases.

MN

Floating mine

Mineman: MNs test, maintain, repair, and overhaul mines and their components. They are responsible for assembling, handling, issuing, and delivering mines to the planting agent and for maintaining mine-handling and minelaying equipment.

MR

Micrometer and
gear

Machinery Repairman: MRs are skilled machine-tool operators. They make replacement parts and repair or overhaul a ship engine's auxiliary equipment, such as evaporators, air compressors, and pumps. They repair deck equipment, including winches and hoists, condensers, and heat-exchange devices. Shipboard MRs frequently operate main propulsion machinery in addition to performing machineshop and repair duties.

MS

Crossed keys with
quill on open ledger

Mess Management Specialist: MSs operate and manage Navy dining facilities and bachelor enlisted quarters. They are cooks and bakers in Navy dining facilities ashore and afloat, ordering, inspecting, and stowing food. They maintain food service and preparation spaces and equipment, and keep records of transactions and budgets for the food service in living quarters ashore.

MT

Guided missile and
electronic wave

Missile Technician: MTs perform organizational and intermediate-level maintenance on ballistic missile weapon systems; operate and maintain their fire-control systems, guidance subsystems, and associated test equipment, as well as missile and launcher/tuber groups and all ancillary equipment. They operate and maintain strategic weapons systems, associated ship/weapon subsystems, and test and handling equipment.

MU

Lyre

Musician: MUs play in official Navy bands and in special groups such as jazz bands, dance bands, and small ensembles. They give concerts and provide music for military ceremonies, religious services, parades, receptions, and dances. Official unit bands usually do not include stringed instruments, but each MU must be able to play at least one brass, woodwind, or percussion instrument. Persons are selected for this rating through auditions.

43

NC

Anchor crossed
with quill

Navy Counselor: NCs offer vocational guidance on an individual and group basis to Navy personnel aboard ships and at shore facilities, and to civilian personnel considering enlistment in the Navy. They assess the interests, aptitudes, abilities, and personalities of individuals.

OS

Arrow through
oscilloscope

Operations Specialist: OSs operate radar, navigation, and communications equipment in a ship's combat information center (CIC) or on the bridge. They detect and track ships, planes, and missiles. They operate and maintain IFF (identification friend or foe) systems, ECM (electronic countermeasures) equipment, and radiotelephones. OSs also work with search-and-rescue teams.

PC

Postal cancellation
mark

PH

Lens pierced by
light lines, winged

PN

Crossed manual
and quill

PR

Parachute, winged

QM

Ship's helm

Postal Clerk: The Navy operates a large postal system manned by Navy PCs, who have much the same duties as their civilian counterparts. PCs collect postage-due mail, prepare customs declarations, collect outgoing mail, cancel stamps, and send the mail on its way. They also perform a variety of recordkeeping and reporting duties, including maintenance of an up-to-date directory service and locator file.

Photographer's Mate: PHs photograph actual and simulated battle operations as well as documentary and newsworthy events. They expose and process light-sensitive negatives and positives; maintain cameras, related equipment, photo files, and records; and perform other photographic services for the Navy.

Personnelman: PNs provide enlisted personnel with information and counseling about Navy jobs, opportunities for general education and training, promotion requirements, and rights and benefits. In hardship situations, they also assist enlisted persons' families with legal aid or reassignments. PNs keep records up to date, prepare reports, type letters, and maintain files.

Aircrew Survival Equipmentman: Parachutes are the lifesaving equipment of air-crewmen when they have to bail out. In time of disaster, a parachute may also be the only means of delivering badly needed medicines, goods, and other supplies to isolated victims. PRs pack and care for parachutes as well as service, maintain, and repair flight clothing, rubber life-rafts, life-jackets, oxygen-breathing equipment, protective clothing, and air-sea rescue equipment.

Quartermaster: QMs are responsible for ship safety, skillful navigation, and reliable communications with other vessels and shore stations. In addition, they maintain charts, navigational aids, and records for the ship's log. They steer the ship, take radar bearings and ranges, make depth soundings and celestial observations, plot courses, and command small craft. QMs stand watches and assist the navigator and officer of the deck (OOD).

RP

Globe on anchor within compass

Religious Program Specialist: RPs assist Navy chaplains with administrative and budgetary tasks. They serve as custodians of chapel funds, keep religious documents, and maintain contact with religious and community agencies. They also prepare devotional and religious educational materials, set up volunteer programs, operate shipboard libraries, supervise chaplains' offices, and perform administrative, clerical, and secretarial duties. They train personnel in religious programs and publicize religious activities.

SH

Crossed key and quill

Ship's Serviceman: Both ashore and afloat, SHs manage barbershops, tailor shops, ships' uniform stores, laundries, drycleaning plants, and cobbler shops. They serve as clerks in exchanges, soda fountains, gas stations, warehouses, and commissary stores. Some SHs function as Navy club managers.

45

SK

Crossed keys

Storekeeper: SKs are the Navy's supply clerks. They see that needed supplies are available, everything from clothing and machine parts to forms and food. SKs have duties as civilian warehousemen, purchasing agents, stock clerks and supervisors, retail sales clerks, store managers, inventory clerks, buyers, parts clerks, bookkeepers, and even forklift operators.

SM

Crossed semaphore flags

Signalman: SMs serve as lookouts and, using visual signals and voice radios, alert their ship of possible dangers. They send and receive messages by flag signals or flashing lights. They stand watches on the signal bridge, encode and decode messages, honor passing vessels, and maintain signaling equipment. SMs must have good vision and hearing.

ST

Earphones pierced
by arrow

SW

I-beam suspended
from hook

TM

Torpedo

UT

Valve

YN

Crossed quills

Sonar Technician: STs operate sonar and other oceanographic systems. They manipulate, control, evaluate, and interpret data for surface and submarine operations. STs coordinate submarine and auxiliary sonar and underwater fire-control interface, operate surface-ship underwater fire-control systems and associated equipment for the solution of antisubmarine warfare problems, and perform organizational and intermediate maintenance on their respective sonar and allied equipment. (Service ratings: STG [surface]; STS [submarine].)

Steelworker: SWs rig and operate all special equipment used to move or hoist structural steel, structural shapes, and similar material. They erect or dismantle steel bridges, piers, buildings, tanks, towers, and other structures. They place, fit, weld, cut, bolt, and rivet steel shapes, plates, and built-up sections used in the construction of overseas facilities.

Torpedoman's Mate: TMs maintain underwater explosive missiles, such as torpedoes and rockets, that are launched from surface ships, submarines, and aircraft. TMs also maintain launching systems for underwater explosives. They are responsible for the shipping and storage of all torpedoes and rockets.

Utilitiesman: UTs plan, supervise, and perform tasks involved in the installation, operation, maintenance, and repair of plumbing, heating, steam, compressed-air systems, fuel-storage and -distribution systems, water-treatment and -distribution systems, air-conditioning and refrigeration equipment, and sewage-collecting and disposal facilities.

Yeoman: YNs perform secretarial and clerical work. They greet visitors, answer telephone calls, and receive incoming mail. YNs organize files and operate duplicating equipment, and they order and distribute supplies. They write and type business and social letters, notices, directives, forms, and reports. They maintain files and service records.

Occupational Fields

Ratings are organized into twenty-four occupational fields reflecting the similarities in their functions and the training required to qualify. Table 3.2 shows these occupational fields, which ratings belong to each, and which apprenticeships will prepare you for them.

Table 3.2. Occupational Fields

Field No. and Title	Ratings	Apprenticeship
1. General Seamanship	BM, SM	Seaman
2. Ship Operations	OS, QM	Seaman
3. Marine Engineering	EM, EN, GS, IC, MM	Fireman
4. Ship Maintenance	DC, HT, MR	Fireman/Seaman
5. Aviation Maintenance/ Weapons	PR, AE, AT, AD, AZ, AO, AM	Airman
6. Aviation Ground Support	AB, AS	Airman
7. Air Traffic Control	AC	Airman
8. Weapons Control	ET, FT, FC	Seaman
9. Ordnance Systems	GM, MN, MT, TM	Seaman
10. Sensor Systems	EW, ST	Seaman
11. Weapons System Support	[None currently]	
12. Construction	BU, CE, CM, EA, EO, SW, UT	Constructionman
13. Health Care	DT, HM	Hospitalman/ Dentalman
14. Administration	LN, NC, PC, PN, RP, YN	Seaman
15. Logistics	AK, DK, MS, SH, SK	Seaman/Airman
16. Media	DM, JO, LI, PH	Seaman/Airman
17. Music	MU	Seaman
18. Master-at-Arms	MA	Any
19. Cryptology	CT	Seaman
20. Communications Information Systems	IT	Seaman
21. Intelligence	IS	Seaman
22. Meteorology and Oceanography	AG	Airman
23. Aviation Sensor Operations	AW	Airman

47

Ranks and Rates

Traditionally, the term "rank" was applied only to the officer paygrades, and the term "rate" was used to describe the enlisted paygrades. In more recent times, this distinction has become less clearcut, and enlisted paygrades are sometimes referred to as ranks as well. The term "rate" really has two meanings. Like "rank," it is roughly equivalent to paygrade, and is often used that way. For example, "Seaman Apprentice" or "Petty Officer Third Class" are rates. But rate is also often considered a combination of paygrade and rating. Remember that rating refers to an occupation and only applies to petty officers (E-4s and above). If someone referred to you as a "radioman," they would be identifying you by your rating. But if they called you a "radioman second class," they would be referring to your rate (your occupation and your paygrade combined). This is somewhat confusing, but you can stay out of trouble if you remember that rating *always* refers to occupation and rate involves paygrade.

General Apprenticeships

There are six general apprenticeship fields: seaman, fireman, airman, constructionman, hospitalman, and dentalman. All naval personnel who are in paygrades E-1, E-2, or E-3 belong to one of these groups, and their particular status, reflecting both apprenticeship field and paygrade, is called their "general rate." Assignments to these general apprenticeships are based upon the individual's desires and aptitudes and the needs of the Navy. Each general apprenticeship field leads to one or more ratings. (See "Occupational Fields.") For example, a person hoping to be a signalman would first be a seaman; one wanting to be an engineman would first be a fireman; and a would-be aviation ordnanceman would first be an airman.

Some of the duties and skills of each general apprenticeship are described below.

Seaman (SN): Keeps ships' compartments, lines, rigging, decks, and deck machinery shipshape. Acts as a lookout, member of a gun crew, helmsman, and security and fire sentry.

Fireman (FN): Cares for and operates ships' engineering equipment (such as turbines, boilers, pumps, motors). Records readings of gauges, and maintains and cleans engineering machinery and compartments. Stands security and fireroom watches.

Airman (AN): Performs various duties for naval air activities ashore and afloat. Assists in moving aircraft. Loads and stows equipment and supplies. Maintains compartments and buildings. Acts as member of plane-handling crews.

Constructionman (CN): Operates, services, and checks construction equipment (such as bulldozers and cranes) Performs semiskilled duties in construction battalions. Stands guard watches.

Hospitalman (HN): Assists doctors, nurses, and hospital corpsmen with care of patients. Renders first aid. Prepares dressing carriages with sterile instruments, dressings, bandages, and medicines. Applies dressings. Keeps medical records.

Dentalman (DN): Assists dental officers in the treatment of patients. Renders first aid. Cleans and services dental equipment. Keeps dental records.

E-1s, E-2s, and E-3s are considered "general rates" and are identified by a two-letter combination that identifies their general apprenticeship and their paygrade. For example, someone who has gone into the construction general apprenticeship would start at the E-1 level as a CR (constructionman recruit); a promotion to E-2 would make that individual a CA (constructionman apprentice); and an E-3 would be a CN (constructionman). Table 3.3 lists all of the general rates.

Rated Personnel

Petty officers (E-4 through E-9) are identified by a combination of letters and/or numbers that represent the individual's paygrade and rating. The first two or three letters represent the general or service rating; the number or letter(s) following indicate the paygrade. Table 3.4 shows the progression of a Sailor who has had a successful career as a boatswain's mate.

If your rate is BM2, it will be apparent that you are a petty officer second class (E-5) and your rating is boatswain's mate. A PNC is a personnelman who has achieved the paygrade of a chief petty officer (E-7). An AOCM is a master chief aviation ordnanceman, an STS3 is a third-class sonarman whose service rating specialty is submarine sonar systems, and an ABFCS is a senior chief aviation boatswain's mate whose service rating specialty is fuels. As you can see, those few letters and/or numbers reveal a lot about the individual who has earned them.

Naval Enlisted Classification (NEC) Codes

NEC is a special code used to identify a skill, knowledge, aptitude, or qualification not included in your general or service rating training.

Table 3.3. General Rates

General Apprenticeship	E-1	E-2	E-3
Seamanship, Operations, Administration, etc.	SR (Seaman Recruit)	SA (Seaman Apprentice)	SN (Seaman)
Engineering and Maintenance	FR (Fireman Recruit)	FA (Fireman Apprentice)	FN (Fireman)
Construction	CR (Constructionman Recruit)	CA (Constructionman Apprentice)	CN (Constructionman Apprentice)
Aviation	AR (Airman Recruit)	AA (Airman)	AN (Airman)
Health Care (Medical)	HR (Hospitalman Recruit)	HA (Hospitalman Apprentice)	HN (Hospitalman)
Health Care (Dental)	DR (Dentalman Recruit)	DA (Dentalman Apprentice)	DN (Dentalman)

Table 3.4. Boatswain's Career

Paygrade	Rate	Title
E-9	BMCM	Master Chief Boatswain's Mate
E-8	BMCS	Senior Chief Boatswain's Mate
E-7	BMC	Chief Boatswain's Mate
E-6	BM1	Boatswain's Mate First Class
E-5	BM2	Boatswain's Mate Second Class
E-4	BM3	Boatswain's Mate Third Class
E-3	SN	Seaman
E-2	SA	Seaman Apprentice
E-1	SR	Seaman Recruit

For example, if you are a boatswain's mate (BM), you would have many of the same skills and qualifications that other boatswain's mates have. But not all BMs are qualified tugmasters. If you became qualified as a tugmaster, the Navy would assign you an NEC code of BM-0161. That would tell the detailers—the administrative people at the Navy Personnel Command (NAVPERSCOM) in Millington, Tennessee, who match individuals to specific assignments in the Navy—that you have the knowledge and skills necessary to be a tugmaster. With that NEC code in your record, a detailer could then consider you for a billet (assignment) in a shipyard where a tugmaster is needed.

With a few exceptions, NECs are assigned to personnel by the Enlisted Personnel Management Center (EPMAC) in New Orleans. Changes in your NECs are made only when a training command reports that you have completed a course (earning you a specialty code), when a command shows that your specialty code should be canceled, or when a command reports that you have earned a code through on-the-job training (OJT).

Because NECs identify billets and the personnel qualified to fill them, make sure your NECs actually reflect your qualifications. Not keeping your codes up to date may keep you from getting the duty you want. There is no limit on the number of NECs you may have, but the two most important ones will appear as your primary and secondary codes. All of them are kept in your permanent record at NAVPERSCOM and are available to the detailers there when you become eligible for reassignment.

There are six types of NEC codes: entry series, rating series, special series, alphanumeric, numerical, and planning.

Entry Series

These NECs are assigned to personnel who are not yet designated as strikers but who have received training, are in training, or have the aptitude to be trained for the appropriate rating. There are two types of entry-series NEC codes: defense grouping (DG) codes and rating conversion codes. Entry NECs are always primary codes.

Defense Grouping Codes

All DG codes end in 0 (zero) and are assigned to personnel in paygrades E-1 through E-3, except for designated strikers and men and women in the ratings of hospital corpsman (HM) and dental technician (DT). The code DG-9700, for example, is assigned to Sailors who will become either boatswain's mates (BMs) or quartermasters (QMs).

Rating Conversion Codes

Those personnel who are converting from one rating to another are assigned rating conversion codes. These codes end either in 99 or a letter plus 9. For example: a PN-2699 is a person converting to the personnelman (PN) rating; a YN-2599 is converting to the yeoman (YN) rating.

Rating Series

These NECs supplement the general and service ratings. Most rating-series NECs are prefixed by two-letter abbreviations (but there are exceptions). Rating-series NECs may appear as either primary or secondary codes. For example, an HM1 (hospital corpsman first class) who has experience in the preparation and maintenance of eyeglasses would have an NEC of HM-8463, which identifies that person as an optician.

Special Series

Secondary skills are identified by these NECs. They are not usually directly related to a particular rating. An example of a special-series NEC is locksmith, 9583.

Alphanumeric NECs

These NECs identify equipment-specific skills and training levels when management requirements and the complexity of training call for such identification.

Numerical NECs

This is a special category of codes that applies to personnel working in the nuclear, aircraft systems maintenance, fleet ballistic missile, and aircrew fields.

Planning NECs

These NECs identify skill requirements for planning purposes only. Planners and personnel managers use the classifications in developing training courses, projecting manpower needs for upcoming projects, and other similar purposes. Planning NECs are not assigned to personnel.

Enlisted Service Record

All of this information about you—paygrade, rating, rate, NECs—has to be recorded somewhere so that you and the Navy can keep track of it. This is accomplished by your enlisted service record. It is the Navy's official file on you. Actually, you have *two* service records. One is called the field service record and is kept in the personnel office of your ship or station. This record goes with you when you are transferred to another duty station. The other record is referred to as your permanent service record and is kept at the Navy Personnel Command (NAVPERSCOM). At the end of your naval service, the two records are combined and sent to a records-storage center. Check your record at least once a year to make sure that it is correct and up to date. When looking it over, remember that it is government property. Do not take anything out, put anything in, or make any changes. If you have comments or questions, the YN or PN on duty will help you. A look at your service record can be arranged through your division officer or division chief. Some ships and stations have regular hours for Sailors to check their service records.

Your record is important during your Navy career and after. While you are in the Navy, your service record will be used to help decide what assignments you will get and whether or not you will be promoted. When you leave the Navy, you may need information from your record for collecting veterans' benefits, for federal or civilian employment, or for school credits.

Your service record contains copies of such vital documents as school certificates and letters of commendation. Like most things in the military, there is a standardized way of keeping service records. You will not have to know the details of this standardization unless your chosen rating is in the administrative occupational field (personnelman or yeoman), but an understanding of the basic arrangement will help you find your way around your record when you review it for accuracy.

Service records are kept in standard folders throughout the Navy. On the left side of the folder, you will find applicable documents relating to your security clearance (see chapter 8), permanent change of station orders, documents pertaining to your eligibility for certain educational benefits, and certain forms you signed upon enlistment. Beneath a special cardboard separator on the left side of your folder you will find copies of all your letters of commendation, citations for awards, evaluations of your performance, and any records pertaining to a prior enlistment. The right side of your record contains a number of important documents, some of which will immediately appear in your record, others that will come as your career progresses. The pages are numbered and arranged in reverse order with the first page on the bottom. Keep in mind that because there have been changes in the format of the service record over the years, some numbered pages are no longer used. Also be aware that more than one piece of paper can make up a numbered page; for example, page 1 of your record actually consists of several pieces of paper.

Enlistment/Reenlistment Document
Page 1 of your service record is the document you signed when you joined the Navy. It is a contract and formally establishes the relationship between you and the United States government.

Agreement to Extend Enlistment
Should you decide to extend your period of service, this form will be added to your service record as page 1A.

Dependency Application/Record of Emergency Data
In a personal sense, page 2 is the most important part of your record and should be constantly updated. It contains the names and addresses of persons to be notified in case of emergency or death, persons to receive the death gratuity, persons to receive earned pay and allowances, family member to receive allotment of pay if you're missing or unable to transmit funds, commercial insurance companies to be notified in case of death, and information about government life insurance.

You should make out a new form in the event of any of the following: change of permanent address of those to be notified in case of emergency, change in the names of those to be notified, and any major change in status, such as marriage, an additional child, or divorce.

Enlisted Qualifications History
Page 4 provides a complete chronological record of your occupa-

tional and training-related qualifications. It also contains a record of your awards and commendations.

History of Assignments
This is a record of your duty assignments, ashore and at sea, and is designated page 5.

Record of Unauthorized Absence
Hopefully, you will not have need of a page 6 in your record. This page is used to record unauthorized absences of more than 24 hours but not more than 3 days of lost time due to confinement by civil authorities or sickness or injury resulting from misconduct on your part. More than 3 days will require a Page 7 for unauthorized absence.

Court Memorandum
This is a record of court-martial action when a guilty finding is made by the court and approved by the convening authority. Page 7 is also used to report nonjudicial punishment (NJP) that affects pay.

Administrative Remarks
Designated page 13, this is a place for significant entries not provided for elsewhere; it is also used when more detailed information may be required to clarify entries on other pages.

4 Uniforms

Your Navy uniform marks you as a professional, a member of a military service over 200 years old, and a person currently in the service of your country. While one of the main reasons that you wear a uniform is to look the same or similar to other members of the service, you will soon discover that there are a great many differences in the uniforms that naval personnel wear. As you become familiar with those differences, you will be able to "read" a person's uniform in such a way as to be able to tell a great deal about him or her. An obvious difference will be whether a person is an officer or enlisted. A closer look may tell you such things as what the person's rank or rate is, how many years he or she has served in the Navy, what her or his occupational specialty is, and whether or not he or she has had any special assignments in the Navy or has achieved any special qualifications. If you are really good at reading uniforms, you will be able to tell some of the places in which a person has served and whether or not he or she has received special recognition while serving in one or more billets. After you have absorbed the material in this chapter, you will be able to meet a woman in uniform and tell that she is a second-class petty officer with at least four years of service whose occupational specialty is photography, that she has served on sea duty, and that she has been to the Middle East at least once. Even the great detective Sherlock Holmes might be impressed by that kind of deduction.

Uniform Variations

Many different kinds of uniforms are worn in the Navy. There are versions for the different seasons of the year. There are uniforms designed for work and those meant for show. Some are only worn for special occasions. In the accompanying photographs you can see some of the different types of uniforms worn by naval personnel. "Service-dress blue" and "service-dress white" uniforms are appropriate for most occasions when good appearance is the intended purpose. Blue uniforms are worn during cool or cold months and white uniforms are normally worn during warmer months. Officers and chiefs also wear khaki (tan-colored) uniforms at various times. Camouflage uniforms are sometimes worn by naval personnel in special occupations or in certain areas of the world. There are full-dress uniforms for more formal occasions in both the blue and white versions. Variations on the basic uniforms, such as wearing skirts or trousers with service-dress uniforms, are permitted in some cases. For the official word on what makes up the various uniforms, you should consult *U.S. Navy Uniform Regulations* (NAVPERS 15665). Bear in mind that changes to the various uniforms do occur, so be sure to consult the most recent version of *Uniform Regulations* for the most up-to-date information on uniforms and how to wear them. (See Appendix J for more information on official publications and directives.)

Sometimes the uniform you wear will be your choice, but more often you will be told which uniform is appropriate. Within a command or geographical area, the commanding officer or regional coordinator will designate the "uniform of the day" and will announce it in the Plan of the Day (POD). There will often be more than one uniform designated; different ones may be prescribed for officers and for enlisted and there may be different ones for work and for after-hours purposes.

All uniforms have a basic configuration, which will be discussed below, but keep in mind that certain changes (such as substituting slacks for skirts or replacing dress shoes with safety shoes) may be prescribed by your command. You will also be given certain options (such as sweaters, earmuffs, overshoes, and scarves) as conditions warrant. When consulting *Uniform Regulations,* keep in mind that those items that are listed as "prescribed" are up to your command (and will probably appear in the POD); those items listed as "optional" are up to *you* to decide whether to wear or not.

You will always want to make certain that you are wearing the appropriate uniform. Few things are more embarrassing than to show up at morning quarters or at your workstation in the wrong uniform. Equally important, you should always strive to ensure that your uniform reflects pride in your appearance. Bear in mind that your uniform is more than a set of clothing. Whether it is a full-dress uniform or a set of working utilities, your uniform tells the world that you are a part of the United States Navy, and it represents hundreds of years of proud history and tradition. You have earned the right to wear the uniform of your nation's Navy, and there are many who will envy you when they see you in it. Always wear your uniform with pride.

Uniforms for Enlisted Men (E-1 through E-6)

Service-Dress Blue

This is sometimes referred to as the "when in doubt" uniform, because if you are ever not sure what uniform to wear, such as when reporting to a new duty station, you will always do right to wear service-dress blue. Normally, it is worn during the colder months of the year. As you can tell from the name, it is a *dress* uniform, worn on occasions when your appearance is particularly important. Sometimes referred to informally as the "cracker-jack" uniform, it consists of wool blue bell-bottomed trousers, and a blue wool top piece that is something between a shirt and jacket, called a "jumper." A special necktie called a "neckerchief," a white hat (see section on "Covers," below), white undershirt, black shoes, and black socks are also worn. If you have earned any ribbons, you must wear them on this uniform.

Service-Dress White

The same as service-dress blue except that the trousers and jumper are white instead of blue. This uniform is prescribed under the same circumstances as service-dress blue and you will be told to wear it during the warmer months of the year.

Figure 4.1. Enlisted men wearing service dress blue and service dress white uniforms.

Full Dress (Blue or White)

On very special occasions when the most formality is required, full-sized medals are substituted for ribbons on the left side of the service-dress blue (or white) jumper to create the full-dress uniform. Ribbons that do not have corresponding large medals are worn on the right side of the jumper.

Dinner Dress (Blue or White)

For very formal occasions when evening wear is required, miniature versions of your medals are worn instead of ribbons on your service-dress blue or white uniforms. Unlike with full dress, no ribbons are worn on the right side of the jumper with this uniform. An optional version that you may choose to wear on these occasions (at your expense) consists of a dinner jacket (both blue and white versions are available), evening trousers, a formal dress shirt, silver cufflinks, bow tie, a cummerbund (black with the blue version and silver with the white), and miniature medals. An optional tropical version sub-stitutes a short-sleeve uniform shirt for the dinner jacket. Covers (caps) are not normally worn with this uniform except when wearing the all-weather coat (raincoat) as outer wear.

59

Summer White

An alternative to service-dress white used when less formality is required, such as for office work, watch-standing, or business ashore during hot weather conditions, summer white consists of a short-sleeved white shirt with flap pockets, white trousers, white belt with a pewter buckle and tip, white hat, and black shoes and socks. Ribbons are also worn on this uniform.

Tropical White

When in extremely warm climates, white shorts and knee socks may be substituted for those worn with the summer white uniform to create this specialized uniform.

Winter Blue

Standard-cut trousers (not bell-bottomed and worn with a black belt with pewter tip and buckle), a blue, flap-pocketed shirt with black necktie, black shoes, and black socks make up this uniform. The same white hat worn with the service-dress uniforms can be worn; an alternative is the blue garrison cap (see "Covers"). Ribbons are also worn with this uniform.

Winter Working Blue

Remove the necktie and the ribbons from the winter blue uniform and you have winter working blue.

Utilities

For those times when you are performing work that is likely to soil your clothing or when safety considerations require it, utilities are the uniform of choice. Utility trousers are worn with a light blue, long-sleeved utility shirt, black web belt with pewter buckle, a blue baseball cap, and black steel-toed safety shoes and socks.

Tropical Utilities

Changing the utility trousers to shorts, the shirt to short sleeves, and adding black knee socks converts utilities to a uniform more appropriate to tropical working conditions.

Coveralls

The coverall uniform is designed to be the principal underway uniform of the day. When worn aboard ship in port, it may be worn on the pier in the immediate vicinity of the ship. In some working environments ashore (such as industrial areas or on airfields), coveralls may be worn but in the immediate workspaces only. You may also be authorized to wear them while traveling to and from eating facilities. Coveralls are not authorized for wear outside the confines of a military installation.

Uniforms for Enlisted Women (E-1 through E-6)

Service-Dress Blue

Just as with the male version of service-dress blue, this uniform is the appropriate one to wear whenever in doubt (such as when reporting to a new duty station and you are not sure what is the uniform of the day). It consists of a blue coat and unbelted skirt, white short-sleeve shirt, neck tab, combination cap or black beret (see section on "Covers"), black dress shoes, and fleshtone hose. Blue, unbelted slacks may be prescribed for wear with this uniform instead of the skirt. Any ribbons you have earned should be worn with this uniform.

Service-Dress White

The warm-weather equivalent of service-dress blue consists of a white skirt topped by a white jumper (virtually identical to the one worn by males), white undershirt, combination cap (beret optional), Navy neck-

Figure 4.2. Enlisted women wearing different variations of the service dress blue uniform. The Sailor on the left is wearing the optional beret and slacks, while the Sailor on the right is wearing the more common combination cover and a skirt.

Figure 4.3. Enlisted women wearing different versions of the service dress white uniform.

erchief, fleshtone hose, and black shoes. White slacks may be prescribed instead of the skirt. Ribbons are worn with this uniform as well.

Full Dress (Blue or White)

On very special occasions when the most formality is required, full-sized medals are substituted for ribbons on the left side of the service-dress blue (or white) jumper to create the full-dress uniform. Ribbons that do not have corresponding large medals are worn on the right side of the jumper.

Dinner Dress (Blue or White)

For very formal occasions when evening wear is required, miniature versions of your medals are worn instead of ribbons on your service-dress blue or white uniforms. Unlike with full dress, no ribbons are worn on the right side of the jumper with this uniform. An optional version that you may choose to wear on these occasions (at your expense) consists of a dinner jacket (both blue and white versions are available), floor-length formal skirt, a formal dress shirt, dress neck tab, a black cummerbund, black dress handbag, black formal shoes, and miniature medals. An optional tropical version substitutes a short-sleeve uniform shirt for the dinner jacket and formal dress shirt and is worn with a blue knee-length skirt. Covers (caps) are not normally worn with this uniform except when wearing the all-weather coat (raincoat) as outer wear.

Summer White

An alternative to service-dress white, used when less formality is required, such as for office work, watch-standing, or business ashore during hot weather conditions, summer white consists of a short-sleeved white shirt with flap pockets, white skirt (although white slacks may be prescribed), white belt with pewter buckle and tip, combination white hat (black beret optional), fleshtone hose, and black shoes. Ribbons are also worn on this uniform.

Tropical White

When in extremely warm climates, white shorts and knee socks may be substituted for those worn with the summer white uniform to create this specialized uniform.

Winter Blue

A blue, flap-pocketed shirt with black necktie, blue skirt (slacks may be prescribed instead), black belt with pewter tip and buckle, fleshtone hose, black shoes, and either the white combination cover, the black beret, or the blue garrison cap make up this uniform. Ribbons are also worn.

Winter Working Blue
Remove the necktie and the ribbons from the winter blue uniform and you have winter working blue.

Utilities
For those times when you are performing work that is likely to soil your clothing or when safety considerations require it, utilities are the uniform of choice. Utility trousers are worn with a light blue, long-sleeved utility shirt, black web belt with pewter buckle, a blue baseball cap, and black steel-toed safety shoes and socks.

Tropical Utilities
Changing the utility trousers to shorts, the shirt to short sleeves, and adding black knee socks converts utilities to a uniform more appropriate to tropical working conditions.

Coveralls
The coverall uniform is designed to be the principal underway uniform of the day. When worn aboard ship in port, it may be worn on the pier in the immediate vicinity of the ship. In some working environments ashore (such as industrial areas or on airfields), coveralls may be worn but in the immediate workspaces only. You may also be authorized to wear them while traveling to and from eating facilities. Coveralls are not authorized for wear outside the confines of a military installation.

63

Uniforms for Chief Petty Officers and Officers
Male chiefs and officers wear uniforms that are very different from those worn by men in paygrades E-1 through E-6, but the differences for women are less pronounced. Most of the uniforms worn by female CPOs and officers are modified versions of the uniforms worn by women in paygrades E-1 through E-6. Male chief petty officers and officers do not wear the so-called cracker-jack uniforms, relying on straight-legged trousers and jackets (called "blouses") that are more like conventional suit jackets. Female chief petty officers also do not wear the white "Cracker Jack" uniform, but instead wear a white version of the service dress blue jacket and skirt (or slacks). All officers and chiefs (both women and men) have khaki (tan)-colored

Navy Exchange Service Command

Figure 4.4. An officer (*left*) and a chief petty officer (*right*) wearing service dress blue uniforms.

Navy Exchange Service Command

Figure 4.5. Chief petty officers in summer khaki (*left*) and summer white (*right*) uniforms.

uniforms that they wear for working or for less-formal working conditions. CPOs and officers who work in aviation also wear an additional uniform called "aviation working green." For more information about the uniforms worn by CPOs and officers, see a current edition of *Uniform Regulations*.

Covers

In the Navy, what you wear on your head is sometimes called a "cap" or a "hat" but usually is referred to as your "cover." Rarely worn indoors and nearly always worn outside, the cover is an important component of your uniform. Remembering to wear your cover at the appropriate times will soon become second nature to you. Once you have adjusted to Navy life, you will become immediately aware that something is wrong if you step outside without your cover on your head.

What your cover looks like will depend on your rank or rate, whether you are in a working or dress uniform, and whether you are a man or woman. As with all components of your uniform, you will want to ensure that your cover is shipshape at all times.

Enlisted (E-1 through E-6)

The standard cover worn with the jumper-style uniform, the summer white, winter blue, and winter working blue uniforms by all enlisted men other than chief petty officers is the "white hat," sometimes informally referred to as a "dixie cup" (see fig. 4.1). Enlisted women wear a different style cap called a "combination cover" (or cap), with the sides turned up and a pewter eagle with wings spread upward and the letters "USN" placed horizontally between the wing tips and centered above the eagle's head (see fig. 4.2).

For women, a black beret with the same crest that is worn on the combination cover is an optional replacement for the combination cover with the service-dress blue and white, summer white, tropical white, winter blue, and winter working blue uniforms. A blue garrison cap (sometimes called a "fore-and-aft cap") with a metal eagle (and chevrons as appropriate) on the left side may be worn with the winter blue and winter working blue uniforms by both men and women. (E-1 through E-3 do not wear an eagle or any other device on their garrison caps.)

With utilities and coveralls, both men and women wear a baseball-type cap. The standard ballcap issued at boot camp is dark blue with the word "NAVY" on the front in gold letters. When you serve in other commands, such as ships or air stations, you may be authorized to wear a "command cap" instead, which is a ballcap with the name of the ship (or other command) on it instead of the word "NAVY." Ball caps may be worn with working uniforms on or in the immediate vicinity of ships or shore-based work centers.

Chief Petty Officers

Female CPOs wear a dress cover similar to that worn by E-1 through E-6 personnel, but male CPOs do not wear the white hat worn by other enlisted men. Their dress covers are also called combination covers and have a shiny visor (or bill) and a glossy black chin strap just above the visor (see fig. 4.5). Even though it is called a chin strap, it is rarely pulled down and used for that purpose, serving instead more as ornamental.

The crest worn by all CPOs (male and female) is a vertical gold anchor with the letters "USN" in polished silver centered in front. Senior chief petty officers (E-8) also have a silver star mounted above the anchor, and master chief petty officers (E-9) have *two* silver stars above the anchor. One person in the Navy serves in the important role of master chief petty officer of the Navy (MCPON) and he or she wears *three* stars above the anchor.

Chief petty officers also wear garrison caps (with a metal rank device worn on the right side) and baseball-type working caps. Female CPOs may also wear the optional black beret.

Officers

For dress purposes male officers wear combination covers with visors similar to those worn by chief petty officers, and female officers wear a modified version of the combination cover worn by enlisted women. Male officers wear a gold chin strap just above the visor of their caps and women wear the chin strap in the same relative position on their combination cover. Above the chin strap is an officer's crest, consisting of a silver federal shield with crossed gold anchors behind it and a silver eagle perched above. Male commanders and captains replace their shiny visors with ones adorned with a row of gold oak leaves and acorns (frequently referred to as "scrambled eggs"). Female commanders and captains wear the row of oak leaves and acorns on their hat band since their covers do not have the large visor. Flag officers (admirals) wear *two* rows of leaves and acorns on their visors (for males) or hat bands (for females).

Garrison caps are sometimes worn with khaki and some blue uniforms. On the left side of these caps, officers wear a smaller (half-size) version of the same crest (shield, eagle, and anchors) that is worn on the combination cover. On the right side, officers wear a metal device indicating their rank.

Women officers may also wear a black beret with some uniforms. The same smaller version of the officer's crest worn on the garrison cap is attached to the beret when it is worn.

In a working environment, officers sometimes also wear baseball-type caps. The exact design and the appropriate times for wearing these caps is specified by each command.

Ranks and Ratings

An individual's uniform is appropriately modified to display his or her rank or rating. Different identifying marks are worn on the upper arm, the collar, the shoulders, or the lower sleeve (near the cuff), depending upon the uniform and whether the individual is enlisted or an officer.

Nonrated Enlisted Personnel

You will remember from the last chapter that Sailors in paygrades E-1 through E-3 are nonrated personnel. Those in paygrade E-1 do not wear any indication on their uniforms, but two diagonal stripes worn on the upper left sleeve identify the wearer as an apprentice (E-2); three of these diagonal stripes are worn by an E-3. These stripes are three inches long and are worn at a 30-degree angle with the lower end of the stripe to the front of the arm. They are worn on the left sleeve of all of your dress and service uniforms and on your winter working blue uniform, but not on your peacoat, utility shirt, working jacket, all-weather coat (raincoat), or blue windbreaker.

You will also recall from your reading of chapter 3 that nonrated personnel belong to one of six general apprenticeship fields. Which field you belong to will determine what your diagonal stripes look like. Seamen (SN) and seaman apprentices (SA) wear white stripes on their blue uniforms and dark blue stripes on their white uniforms. Firemen (FN) and fireman apprentices (FA) wear red stripes on all their uniforms. Airmen (AN) and airman apprentices (AA) wear green stripes on all their uniforms. Constructionmen (CN) and constructionman apprentices (CA) wear light blue stripes on all their uniforms. Hospitalmen (HN) and hospitalman apprentices (HA) wear a specialty mark (a medical caduceus) above their stripes. Both the specialty mark and the stripes are white on blue uniforms and dark blue on white uniforms. Dentalmen (DN) and dentalman apprentices (DA)

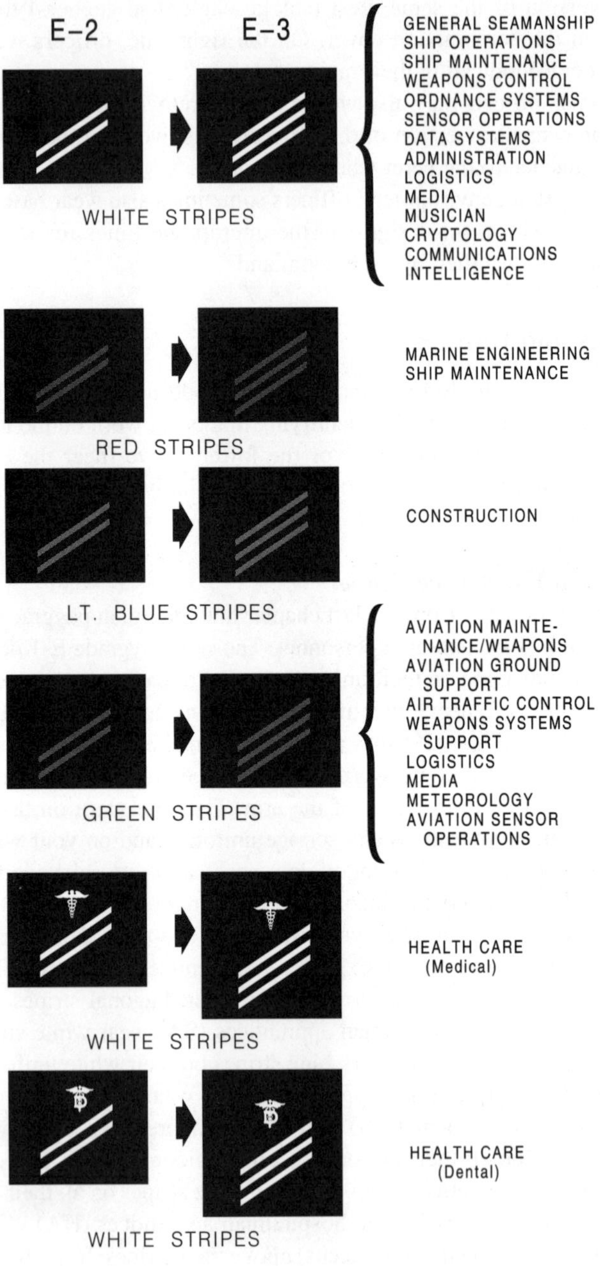

Figure 4.6. Nonrated personnel rate insignia. (E-1 personnel do not wear rate insignia.)

wear a specialty mark (a medical caduceus with a superimposed *D*) above their stripes. Both the specialty mark and the stripes are white on blue uniforms and dark blue on white uniforms.

Apprentice Training Graduates

Above their stripes, graduates of apprentice training schools wear one of the symbols shown in fig. 4.7 until they either are designated a striker or until they are promoted to petty officer.

Striker Marks

Once they have been designated, strikers wear the specialty of the rating they are striking for above their diagonal stripes. This mark replaces the one worn as a graduate of an apprentice training school. For example, if you were designated a boatswain's mate striker, you would wear crossed anchors above your diagonal stripes.

Petty Officers

As discussed earlier, enlisted men and women who have achieved paygrades E-4 and above are considered "rated personnel" and are known as "petty officers." On their left upper sleeve (taking the place of the diagonal stripes worn by nonrated personnel), petty officers wear a rating badge with three parts: an eagle with up-raised wings and its head facing right (popularly known as a "crow"); one or more V-shaped stripes called "chevrons," which tell the individual's paygrade; and, between the eagle and the chevrons, a specialty mark representing the individual's rate (crossed anchors for boatswain's mate, a quill and scroll for a journalist, and so on). All three parts of the rating badge are dark blue when worn on white uniforms, but on blue uniforms the eagle and specialty mark are white and the chevrons are red. An exception is that an individual who serves for 12 consecutive years or more under conditions of good conduct (that is, he or she has

SEAMAN   FIREMAN   AIRMAN

Figure 4.7. Graduates of apprentice schools wear one of these symbols above their stripes until they are rated.

been eligible for a Good Conduct Medal for all those 12 years), wears gold chevrons instead of red, and the eagle and specialty mark are silver instead of white on his or her blue uniforms.

Rating badges are worn on all uniforms, including utilities (although the specialty mark is not included when the rating badge is worn on the utility shirt or the working jacket). Unlike nonrated personnel, petty officers *do* wear rating badges on their peacoats (*with* specialty mark) and working jackets (*without* specialty mark).

The chevrons on rating badges are 3¹/₄ inches wide for men and 2¹/₂ inches wide for men. The length of the rating badge will vary depending upon the number of chevrons.

An E-4 (petty officer third class) wears one chevron on her or his rating badge, an E-5 (petty officer second class) has two, and an E-6 (petty officer first class) has earned three.

Chief Petty Officers

When an individual has been promoted to chief petty officer (E-7), he or she adds an arc (popularly known as a "rocker") that connects the ends of the top chevron and passes over the specialty mark on the rating badge. An E-8 (senior chief petty officer) adds a star centered above the eagle, and a master chief petty officer (E-9) has *two* stars symmetrically arranged above the eagle.

CPOs wear rating badges on some of their uniforms (service-dress blue, for example), but on others (such as winter blue and working khaki) they wear metal collar devices instead. The CPO collar device is a miniaturized version of the device chiefs wear on their covers, a gold anchor with silver block letters "USN" centered on the shank of the anchor. To distinguish E-8s and E-9s, one or two silver stars are added above the anchor. A soft shoulder board is also worn on white dress shirts and black sweaters.

PETTY OFFICER
THIRD CLASS

PETTY OFFICER
SECOND CLASS

PETTY OFFICER
FIRST CLASS

Figure 4.8. Rating badges for petty officers. Note the crossed anchors, which symbolize the boatswain's mate rating. This symbol changes with different ratings.

CHIEF
PETTY OFFICER

SENIOR CHIEF
PETTY OFFICER

MASTER CHIEF
PETTY OFFICER

Figure 4.9. Rating badges for paygrades E-7, E-8, and E-9.

MCPON, FLTMC, FORMC, CMDMC, and COB

Outstanding master chief petty officers who are appointed as Master Chief Petty Officer of the Navy (MCPON), Fleet Master Chief (FLTMC), Force Master Chief Petty Officers (FORMC), Command Master Chief Petty Officer (CMDMC), and (on submarines) Chief of the Boat (COB) wear special rating badges that identify them as holding these important offices.

On his or her rating badge, the MCPON replaces the specialty mark with a gold star and wears three gold stars above the eagle. A third star is added to his or her collar device as well.

FLTMCs and FORMCs replace their specialty marks with a gold star and wear *two* gold stars above the eagle on their rating badges. There are no changes to their collar devices.

CMDMCs and COBs replace the specialty mark with a *silver* star and wear two *silver* stars above the eagle on their rating badges. When an E-7 or E-8 is appointed to a command chief billet, her or his rating badge does not change. Collar devices remain the same for CNOMCs, CMDMCs, and COBs.

71

Officers

Naval officers wear their rank in a number of ways. On full, dinner, and service-dress blue uniforms they wear gold stripes on both lower sleeves (near the cuffs). On their overcoats (called "bridge coats"), reefers (similar to the enlisted peacoat), and on white uniforms, officers wear shoulder boards (sometimes called epaulets) with the same gold stripes that they wear on their blue uniforms. (An exception is that female officers wear gold stripes on the sleeves of their white full, dinner, and service-dress uniforms.) On khaki and winter blue shirts, officers wear metal collar devices that indicate their rank. An enlarged version of the collar device is worn on the shoulder straps of jackets and raincoats. A soft version of the shoulder board is also worn on white dress shirts and on sweaters. On their green jackets, aviation officers wear the same kind of stripes on the lower sleeves as they wear on their service-dress blues, except they are dark blue instead of gold.

Refer to Appendix C and you will see that the Navy and Coast Guard wear similar shoulder boards and sleeve markings, but Army, Air Force, and Marine officers do not wear anything comparable. The collar devices shown for the other services are virtually the same ones worn by naval officers, but the rank names are different.

The stars worn above the stripes on shoulder boards and sleeve markings indicate that the officer is what is known as a "line officer," which means that she or he is eligible for command of line units (such as ships or aircraft squadrons). Some officers are in special staff corps—such as doctors, lawyers, and chaplains—and they wear different symbols above their stripes. (See fig. 4.10.) Metal versions of these symbols are also worn on their left collar point (with the rank device on the right). Line officers wear rank devices on both collar points.

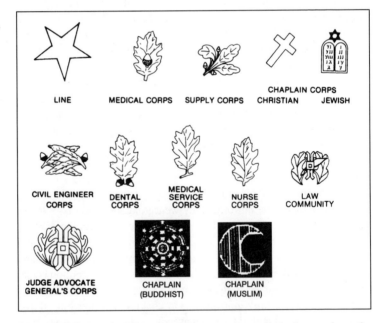

Figure 4.10. Line and staff corps insignia are worn on both sleeves, above the stripes, and on shoulder boards. Officers other than line officers also wear them on the collar tips of khaki and blue shirts.

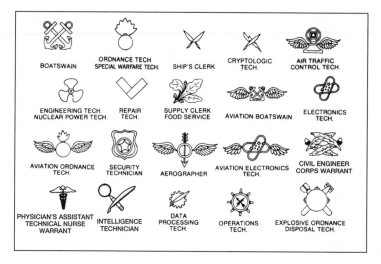

Figure 4.11. Some of the warrant officer insignia worn on sleeves, above the stripes on sleeves, on shoulderboards, and as pin-on collar devices.

Warrant officers also wear special symbols above their stripes, in a manner similar to staff corps officers. (See fig. 4.11.)

73

Unit Identification Marks (UIMs)

Once you are assigned to a ship or some other duty station, you will be issued a number of unit identification marks to wear on your uniforms. UIMs are arch-shaped dark blue patches approximately five inches long and half an inch high with ¼-inch white letters spelling the name of your command (unit). They are worn on the right sleeve of your shirts, jumpers, and jackets (both blues and whites, but not on utilities). They are sewed on ⅜ of an inch below the stitching at the shoulder that joins the sleeve to the rest of the garment. Only personnel in paygrades E-1 through E-6 wear UIMs.

Service Stripes

Service stripes, informally known as "hashmarks," indicate how long you have been in the service. Each stripe signifies the completion of four full years of active or reserve duty (or any combination thereof) in any of the armed forces. They are long diagonal stripes worn on the left sleeve below the rating badge (on the forearm) by all enlisted personnel who have earned them. Service stripes are red when worn on your blue uniforms and Navy blue when worn on your white uniforms. Aviation personnel wearing the green uniforms (E-7s and above) also have dark-blue service stripes.

Enlisted personnel with a total of 12 years of active duty or drilling reserve service in the Navy and/or the Marine Corps who have fulfilled the requirements for successive awards of the Navy Good Conduct Medal, Reserve Meritorious Service Award, or Marine Corps Good Conduct Medal (see section on "Awards and Decorations," below) change the color of their rating badge and service stripes to gold on their service-dress blue, service-dress white, dinner-dress blue, and dinner-dress white jackets. Since each stripe represents four years of service, and it takes 12 years to qualify for the gold stripes and rating badge, you will have to have a minimum of three hashmarks before you can switch from red to gold.

Awards and Decorations

In the armed services, special awards are given to personnel who have done something beyond the normal expectations of duty. These awards are either medals or ribbons. Medals are metal pendants hung from pieces of colored cloth. Ribbons are rectangular pieces of colored cloth $1\frac{1}{2}$ inches long and $\frac{3}{8}$ inch high. Medals always come with a ribbon, but some awards consist of only a ribbon and do not have a corresponding medal.

The term "award" is used to describe any medal, ribbon, or attachment. "Decoration" is usually used to describe an award given to an individual for a specific act of personal gallantry or meritorious service.

Extraordinary bravery is what most people think of when they see these awards and that *is* the reason behind many of the awards, but many others are given for other reasons. We have already mentioned the Good Conduct Medal (and ribbon), which is given to individuals in recognition of consistent achievement and conduct over a period of four years. The Purple Heart (medal and ribbon) is awarded to individuals who have been wounded in combat. The Meritorious Unit Commendation (ribbon only) is given to all members of a unit (an entire ship's crew, for example) when that unit has been singled out for some notable achievement. Some awards are issued for a particular war or campaign (such as the Vietnam Service Medal and the Southwest Asian Service Medal), and all who actively participated in those campaigns were given those awards. There are awards recog-

nizing proficiency with rifles and pistols, a Humanitarian Service Medal (awarded to those involved in a rescue mission or similar operation), and a ribbon that represents deployments overseas. Some awards (such as the Bronze Star and the Joint Service Commendation Medal) are the same for all the armed services and others are unique to one service (such as the Naval Reserve Meritorious Service Medal
and the Air Force Cross).

Proper Wearing of Awards

You will only wear your medals on very formal occasions when the prescribed uniform is full dress. Miniature versions of the medals are worn with dinner-dress uniforms. Ribbons are worn on summer and tropical white, winter blue, and service-dress blue and white uni- forms. Ribbons are not worn on working uniforms.

Arrangement

When you earn your first ribbon, you will wear it centered $1/4''$ above your left breast pocket. As you add ribbons, you will build them in rows of three. You may see members of other services wearing large numbers of ribbons in rows of four, but in the Navy the most you can wear in a row is three. If you have a number not divisible by three, the uppermost row contains the lesser number, with the extra one or two ribbons centered over the row beneath. On full-dress occasions, when you are wearing your medals, you should line them up in rows of three, side by side, or you may put five in a row if you overlap them. Any awards that only have a ribbon (no corresponding medal) should be worn on the *right* breast when full-size medals are worn. Do not wear any ribbons, however, when you are wearing miniature medals (dinner-dress occasions).

Attachments

If you earn the same award more than once, you will not receive the medal or ribbon again, but will receive a special metal attachment that goes on the original medal or ribbon. Attachments are also some- times added to awards to represent something other than repeated awards (such as the number of missions flown or an "S" on a pistol or rifle ribbon to indicate qualification as a sharpshooter).

Precedence

It is important that you wear your awards in the proper order. Whenever you earn a new award, you must determine where it goes in relation to the other awards you have already earned. Below is a list of all the medals and ribbons you might earn while in the Navy. They are listed in the correct order of precedence, with the highest precedence (the Medal of Honor) at the top of the list.

The awards with the higher precedence are worn closer to your heart (called "farthest inboard"). For example, if you have earned an Armed Forces Expeditionary Medal, a Navy Unit Citation, a Combat Action Ribbon, a Navy and Marine Corps Achievement Medal, and a National Defense Service Medal, you would arrange them in two rows, with three ribbons on the lower row and two on the upper row. Since the Navy and Marine Corps Achievement Medal has the highest precedence (nearest the top of the list), it would go on the top row, closest to your heart (farthest inboard). Next to it would be the Combat Action Ribbon. The bottom row would have the Navy Unit Citation farthest inboard, with the National Defense Service Medal next in line (in the middle), and the Armed Forces Expeditionary Medal last, on the bottom row, farthest from the heart (farthest outboard).

Precedence of Awards

1. Medal of Honor
2. Navy Cross
3. Defense Distinguished Service Medal
4. Distinguished Service Medal
5. Silver Star
6. Defense Superior Service Medal
7. Legion of Merit
8. Distinguished Flying Cross
9. Navy and Marine Corps Medal
10. Bronze Star
11. Purple Heart
12. Defense Meritorious Service Medal
13. Meritorious Service Medal
14. Air Medal
15. Joint Service Commendation Medal
16. Navy and Marine Corps Commendation Medal
17. Joint Service Achievement Medal
18. Navy and Marine Corps Achievement Medal
19. Combat Action Ribbon
20. Presidential Unit Citation
21. Joint Meritorious Unit Award
22. Navy Unit Commendation

23. Meritorious Unit Commendation
24. Battle "E" Ribbon
25. Prisoner of War Medal
26. Navy Good Conduct Medal
27. Naval Reserve Meritorious Service Medal
28. Fleet Marine Force Ribbon
29. Navy Expeditionary Medal
30. China Service Medal
31. Navy Occupation Service Medal
32. National Defense Service Medal
33. Korean Service Medal
34. Antarctic Service Medal
35. Armed Forces Expeditionary Medal
36. Vietnam Service Medal
37. Southwest Asia Service Medal
38. Kosovo Campaign Medal
39. Armed Forces Service Medal
40. Humanitarian Service Medal
41. Military Outstanding Volunteer Service Medal
42. Sea Service Deployment Ribbon
43. Navy Arctic Service Ribbon
44. Naval Reserve Sea Service Ribbon
45. Navy and Marine Corps Overseas Service Ribbon
46. Navy and Marine Corps Recruiting Service Ribbon
47. Armed Forces Reserve Medal
48. Naval Reserve Medal
49. Philippine Presidential Unit Citation
50. Republic of Korea Presidential Unit Citation
51. Republic of Vietnam Presidential Unit Citation
52. Republic of Vietnam Gallantry Cross Unit Citation
53. Republic of Vietnam Civil Actions Unit Citation
54. United Nations Service Medal
55. United Nations Medal
56. NATO Medal
57. Multinational Force and Observers Medal
58. Inter-American Defense Board Medal
59. Republic of Vietnam Campaign Medal
60. Kuwait Liberation Medal (Kingdom of Saudi Arabia)
61. Kuwait Liberation Medal (Kuwait)
62. Rifle Marksmanship Medal
63. Pistol Marksmanship Medal

Warfare and Other Qualification Insignia

Navy men and women may earn additional qualifications as their careers progress, and some of these are reflected in special insignia for their uniforms. For example, pilots wear gold wings, scuba divers wear a silver pin showing a diver's face-mask and regulator, and enlisted women or men who have qualified in surface warfare wear a pewter pin consisting of a ship, crossed sabers, and ocean waves. These qualifications may be in warfare areas such as aviation or submarine warfare, or they may signify special occupations such as explosive ordnance disposal or parachuting. These insignia are usually metal pins attached to the uniform but may be embroidered or stenciled in some cases. Those who earn these special insignia wear them on the left breast above the ribbons and/or medals (except for command insignia, which are worn on the right breast when the individual is actually in command and are moved to the left breast, below the ribbons/medals, once the individual is no longer in command). If you earn more than one of these special insignia, you may wear a maximum of *two,* one above your ribbons and one below. (See *Uniform Regulations* for more information.)

Identification Badges

Personnel in certain unique assignments (such as working in the White House or on the Joint Chiefs of Staff) are authorized to wear distinctive identification badges on their uniforms. The rules for proper wear of these badges vary from badge to badge, so you should refer to the latest version of *Uniform Regulations* if you are authorized to wear one of them.

Miscellaneous Uniform Items

Aiguillettes

These colored cords are worn by naval personnel who are serving as naval attachés, aides to high-ranking officials (such as admirals or the president of the United States), recruit division commanders, members of the U.S. Navy Ceremonial Guard, and various other specialized duties. There are service and dress versions and they vary in color and the number of loops depending upon the duty assigned. Aides to the president, vice-president, and foreign heads of state, as well as various other White House aides, all wear their aiguillettes on the right shoulder. All others are worn on the *left* shoulder.

Figure 4.12. Some of the warfare and other qualification insignia worn by officers and enlisted personnel.

Brassards

Brassards are bands of cloth, suitably marked with symbols, letters, or words, indicating a temporary duty to which the wearer is assigned, such as officer of the day (OOD), junior officer of the day (JOOD), master-at-arms (MAA), or shore patrol (SP). They are worn on the right arm, midway between shoulder and elbow, on outer garments.

Another variation is the mourning badge, made of black crepe, which officers wear on the left sleeve of the outer garment, halfway between shoulder and elbow. Enlisted personnel wear it in the same position, but on the right sleeve.

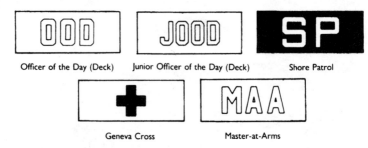

Officer of the Day (Deck)   Junior Officer of the Day (Deck)   Shore Patrol

Geneva Cross   Master-at-Arms

Figure 4.13. Brassards are worn on the right arm midway between the shoulder and elbow. The officer of the day (or deck) wears the OOD brassard, the junior officer of the day (or deck) wears JOOD, shore patrol wear the SP, corpsmen the Geneva Cross, and masters-at-arms the MAA.

Flight Deck Colored Jerseys

Sailors working on flight decks and airfields wear color-coded jerseys to identify their jobs as follows:

Purple — Aviation fuel handlers.

Blue — Plane handlers, aircraft elevator operators, tractor drivers, messengers, and phone talkers.

Green — Catapult operators, arresting gear crewmen, maintenance personnel, cargo handlers, hook runners, photographers, quality control personnel, and helicopter landing signal enlisted personnel (LSEs).

Yellow — Plane directors, aircraft handling officers, catapult officers, and arresting gear officers.

Red — Ordnancemen (weapons handlers), crash and salvage crews, and explosive ordnance disposal (EOD) personnel.

Brown — Plane captains and air wing line leading petty officers.
White — Squadron plane inspectors, landing signals officers, liquid oxygen (LOX) crews, safety observers, and medical personnel.

Name Tags

You may be required to wear a name tag for easy identification during conferences, VIP cruises, open houses, or similar occasions, or in the performance of duties where some easy method of identification by name is desirable or beneficial. Name tags are rectangular, not exceeding dimensions of 1 inch by $3^1/_2$ inches, and may be any color as long as the same color is used throughout the command. Name tags are worn on the right breast, but are not worn when medals are prescribed.

Jewelry and Accessories

Tie clasps, cufflinks, and shirt studs are prescribed for certain uniforms, and you may choose to wear one ring per hand (in addition to a wedding ring), a wristwatch, and a bracelet. Thumb rings are not authorized in uniform. You may wear one necklace with your uniform, but it must not be visible. Enlisted women may wear small silver ball ($^1/_4$-inch post or screw) earrings with a brushed matte or shiny finish while in uniform. Officers and CPOs wear gold with a brushed matte or shiny finish. Small, single-pearl earrings are authorized for wear with dinner- and formal-dress uniforms. Men may not wear earrings while in uniform.

81

Ownership Markings

Uniform components of all E-1 through E-6 personnel must be marked with the owner's name and the last four digits of his or her service (Social Security) number. Use white markings on all dark-blue uniform items and black markings on white uniform articles and utility shirts. Some uniform components have label areas for you to use, but on many items you will have to use a stencil cut with half-inch-high letters and numbers.

In the instructions provided below, the word "right" or "left" means the owner's right or left when the article is worn. Markings on all articles, properly rolled or laid out for sea bag inspection, will appear right-side up to the inspecting officer and upside down to the person standing behind them. Optional articles of clothing are marked similarly to comparable items of required clothing.

Enlisted Men E-1 through E-6

All-weather coat (Raincoat): Inside on lining, 3 inches below collar seam and inside of outer shell on manufacturer's tag.

Belts: Inside, near clip.

Covers:

Garrison: On designated nameplate.

Navy/Command (ball cap): Initials and last four digits of social security number on sweatband.

Watch cap (knit): Initial and last four digits of social security number on inside label.

White hat: In back of brim. When brim is turned down, next to seam between brim and crown, so that marking will not show when brim is turned up.

Coveralls: On waistband inside front at the right centerline.

Gloves: Initials on inside only, near the cuff.

Jackets:

Black Jacket: Inside hem at right of centerline on the back.

Blue windbreaker: On inside of hem at right of center line on back.

Blue working: On inside of hem at right of center line on back. Also your last name must be embroidered in white directly on the fabric of the jacket or on a sewed-on name tape on the right breast three inches above a straight horizontal (imaginary) line connecting the armpits of the jacket.

Jumpers (blue or white): Turn jumper inside out, front down, collar away from you, stencil your three initials, $1/4$ inch below collar seam to left of center, and last four digits of your social security number $1/4$ inch below collar seam to right of center; fill in manufacturer's tag, using indelible ink pen.

Neckerchief: Diagonally across center, initials only.

Necktie (black, four-in-hand): Center back, inside, initials only.

Peacoat: Last name, initials, and last four digits of social security number on left side of tail lining, three inches from and parallel to bottom edge.

Sea (duffel) bag: Along short strap on outer side, and on opposite side from carrying strap, centered, one foot from top.

Shirts: Vertically, beginning 1 inch from bottom on inner side of right front fold on which buttons are sewn. Blue utility shirts must also be embroidered with your last name (only) on right front, $1/4$ inch above the pocket.

Shoes: Initials only, inside, near top.

Socks: Initials only on foot.

Sweater: On designated nameplate.

Towel: As the towel is laid out for inspection, the marking should appear on the corner to your right, on the hem, parallel to end.

Trousers:

Blue (bell-bottomed; worn with jumper): Turn trousers inside out, fly down, waistband away from you. Stencil three initials and last four digits of social security number on rear pocket, $1/4$ inch below horizontal seam using white ink; fill in manufacturer's label using indelible ink.

Blue (straight-legged): On designated nameplate.

Utility: On front inside waistband, at right of center line; last name only, embroidered on outside, $1/4$ inch above right hip pocket.

White: Turn trousers inside out, fly down, waistband away from you, and stencil three initials and last four digits of social security number on left rear pocket in between the two horizontal seams; also fill in manufacturer's label using indelible ink.

Trunks (swimming): Inside on hem on right center of back.

Undershirt: On outside of front, 1 inch from the bottom of the shirt and at right of center.

Undershorts: On outside of right half of waistband, or immediately underneath waistband on undershorts with elastic waistbands.

Enlisted Women E-1 through E-6

Anklets: On foot, initials only.

All-weather coat (Raincoat): Inside on lining, 3 inches below collar seam and inside of outer shell on manufacturer's tag.

Belts: Inside, near clip.

Brassiere: Initials only on the inside back strap.

Coat, service-dress blue: On designated nameplate.

Covers:

Beret: On designated nameplate.

Combination: On designated nameplate. Cap cover should be stenciled on center back, inside band.

Garrison: On designated nameplate.

Navy/Command (ball cap): Initials and last four digits of social security number on sweatband.

Watch cap (knit): Initial and last four digits of social security number on inside label.

Gloves: Initials only, near the cuff.

Handbag: On designated nameplate.

Hosiery: Initials only, near the top.

Jacket:

Black Jacket: Inside hem at right of centerline on the back.

Blue windbreaker: On inside of hem at right of center line on back.

Blue working: On inside of hem at right of center line on back. Also your last name must be embroidered in white directly on the fabric of the jacket or on a sewed-on name tape on the right breast three inches above a straight horizontal (imaginary) line connecting the armpits of the jacket.

Jumpers: Turn jumper inside out, front down, collar away from you, and stencil three initials, $1/4$ inch below collar seam to left of center, and last four digits of your social security number $1/4$ inch below collar seam to right of center; also fill in manufacturer's tag, using indelible ink pen.

Neckerchief: Diagonally across center, initials only.

Neck tab: Center back; inside.

Peacoat: Last name, initials, and last four digits of social security number on left side of tail lining, three inches from and parallel to bottom edge.

Sea (duffel) bag: Along short strap on outer side, and on opposite side from carrying strap, centered, one foot from top.

Shirts: Vertically, beginning 1 inch from bottom on inner side of right front fold on which buttons are sewn. Blue utility shirts must also be embroidered with your last name (only) on right front, $1/4$ inch above the pocket.

Shoes: Initials only, inside, near top.

Skirts:

Blue (belted and unbelted): Initials and last four digits of social security number inside right pocket.

Blue formal: Center front, inside, on waistband.

White belted: On name tag sewn on right pocket.

Slacks:

Blue (belted and unbelted): Initials and last four digits of social security number inside right pocket.

Utility: On inside waistband in front, at right of center line; last name only, embroidered on the outside, $1/4$ inch above right hip pocket.

White: Initials and last four digits of social security number on inside right front pocket.

Slips: Center in back below the elastic band; last name and initials only.

Socks: Initials only on foot.

Sweater: On designated nameplate.

Towel: As the towel is laid out for inspection, the marking should appear on the corner to your right, on the hem, parallel to end.

Undershirts: On outside of front, 1 inch from bottom of shirt and at right of center.

Underpants: Center in back below the elastic band; last name and initials only.

New Ownership

Normally, you may not give, sell, or trade articles of uniform clothing to someone else. However, the commanding officer may authorize the transfer of clothing under special circumstances. When that occurs, the name of the former owner is stamped over with the red letters "D.C." (discarded clothing) and the new owner's name is placed above, below, or next to it, wherever it best fits.

Grooming Standards

Wearing a sharp-looking uniform will not mean much if not accompanied by comparable grooming standards. Neatness and cleanliness are essential components of your military image.

The grooming standards established for naval personnel are intended to promote a favorable image for the Navy, not to isolate you from the rest of society. While a certain degree of uniformity is, of course, intended, the standards *do* permit a degree of individuality.

Men

You should be neat, clean, and presentable at all times. Your hair may not exceed four inches in length, never touch your ears or your collar, and must be tapered around the sides and neck. The hair on the top of your head, after you have combed or brushed it, may not extend more than two inches above the scalp. If your hair interferes with the wearing of any headgear (covers, helmets, etc.), or if it can be seen protruding from beneath the front edge of your cover, it is too long. You are permitted to have only one part, and plaited or braided hair may not be worn while in uniform. Sideburns, if you choose to wear them, must be neat and trimmed, and must end at the middle of the ear in a clean-shaven horizontal line with no flare. Using hair color to give your hair more than one color is not authorized.

Beards are not permitted except when medically authorized, and then only until the problem clears up. If you wear a mustache, keep it trimmed and neat. Don't grow your mustache below the top line of your upper lip, and do not allow it to extend more than $1/4$ inch beyond the corners of your mouth.

Fingernails must be kept clean and must not extend beyond the tips of your fingers.

Women

Keep your hair clean, neatly arranged, professional in appearance, and no longer than the lower edge of your collar. In the case of the white jumper, which has no collar, your hair should not extend more than $1^1/_2$ inches below the top of the jumper flap. Your hair must not interfere with the wearing of any headgear (covers, helmets, etc.) and must not show under the front brim of any covers except the beret. Pigtails and ponytails are not authorized. You may wear french braids or have a multiple braided hairstyle, but you should read the details provided in *Uniform Regulations* before doing so. You may not braid any foreign material (beads or other decorative items) into your hair, but you may use rubber bands or bobbypins and one or two small barrettes, combs, or clips, provided they are similar in color to your hair. Hairnets may be worn only if authorized for specific duties, such as in hospitals or galleys. Using hair color to give your hair more than one color is not authorized.

When wearing cosmetics, keep in mind that a natural appearance is the goal. Artificial, exaggerated, or faddish cosmetics are not authorized. For example, lipstick and fingernail-polish colors must be conservative and long false eyelashes cannot be worn while in uniform. Fingernails must not extend more than $^1/_4$ inch beyond the fingertips.

You may have your ears pierced for your earrings (one per ear), but no other body piercing jewelry is permitted while in uniform.

Leadership, Discipline, and Personal Relations

5

In the plotting room far below, Ensign Merdinger got a call to send up some men to fill in for the killed and wounded. Many of the men obviously wanted to go—it looked like a safer bet than suffocating in the plotting room. Others wanted to stay—they preferred to keep a few decks between themselves and the bombs. Merdinger picked them at random, and he could see in some faces an almost pleading look to be included in the other group, whichever it happened to be. But no one murmured a word, and his orders were instantly obeyed. Now he understood more clearly the reasons for the system of discipline, the drills, the little rituals . . . all the things that made the Navy essentially autocratic but at the same time made it work.

Walter Lord, *Day of Infamy*

The scene described above actually took place aboard the battleship *Nevada* during the Japanese attack on Pearl Harbor at the beginning of World War II. Besides its dramatic appeal, this glimpse of history demonstrates an important fact of military life. The Sailors in *Nevada*'s plotting room did not carry out their orders because they wanted to or because they were seeking a bonus in their paycheck. They did what Ensign Merdinger directed because their fears and sense of self-preservation were overcome by a combination of his leadership and their self-discipline. This is not easily achieved, yet in order for a military organization to function properly, particularly in life-threatening situations, leadership and discipline are absolutely vital.

Leadership

Leadership can be simply defined as the art of causing people to do what is required to accomplish a task or mission. But *good* leadership is not so easily defined. Good leaders are concerned with more than simply getting a job done. *How* the job gets done is also important. What good is a leader who gets a job done but loses the respect of his or her crew in the process? What good is a leader whose methods result in dissension, disorganization, ineffectiveness, or poor morale?

Leadership is characterized by responsibility and authority. As a leader, you are responsible for the tasks or missions assigned, and you are responsible for leading your subordinates in a manner that will not only get the job done but will preserve their dignity and minimize any negative effects that may be part of a difficult task. A leader's authority in the armed forces comes from the Uniform Code of Military Justice (UCMJ) which spells out the laws and the punishments that give the leader official power over her or his subordinates. Technically speaking, this authority is all a leader needs to make people do what he or she wants. But good leaders rely on much more than their authority to lead people. They recognize that subordinates are human beings just like themselves, not mere tools that can be used for a job and put back in a box. Good leaders find ways to cause individuals to carry out an assignment *willingly* rather than out of fear of reprisal.

Even though you start your Navy career as a follower, it will not be long before you will be called upon to exercise leadership. You might be selected as a recruit chief petty officer (RCPO) in boot camp, or become leading seaman in your division aboard ship, or be promoted to petty officer. So it is never too soon to begin thinking about how to be a good leader.

Principles

Because leadership is an art and not an exact science, there is no exact formula for success and it cannot be broken down into absolute rules. However, certain principles, if practiced on a consistent basis, will go a long way toward making you a good leader.

Reverse roles. This is a form of the so-called Golden Rule that appears in the culture of all civilized societies. Whenever you are dealing with subordinates, always treat them the way you would want to be treated if your roles were reversed. If you keep this principle in mind at all times, you will be well on your way to being a good leader.

Take responsibility. One of the fastest ways to lose the respect of your subordinates and undermine your leadership ability is to shirk responsibility. If you make an error, *admit it.* Do not try to hide your mistakes from your superiors or your subordinates. It will be very tempting to try to cover up your mistakes for fear that others will think less of you if they are revealed. This is magnified when you are in a leadership position. But very rarely does hiding a mistake work, and the damage done when you are discovered is always far greater than any damage that might occur from whatever mistake it was that you made in the first place.

Set the example. Always conduct yourself in a manner that will bring credit to yourself and will provide a model of behavior for your subordinates. *Never* say or imply that your subordinates should "do as I say, not as I do."

Praise in public; correct in private. When you have something good to say about your subordinates, do it so that all or many will hear. This will give added recognition to the individual(s) being praised and it will inspire others to do well in hopes of being similarly recognized. When you have to correct a subordinate, do it in privacy. Embarrassing an individual adds nothing to the learning experience, and learning is the intended purpose of correcting someone who has done something wrong.

Be consistent but not inflexible. This is a difficult principle to uphold, because there are no clear guidelines. For the most part, consistency is extremely important and should be your goal. You should try to do things in a manner that your subordinates will come to know and expect so that they do not have to second-guess you. You should most especially be consistent in your praising and correcting and in your rewards and punishments. But you must also recognize that conditions and even people change. Because everything around you is not always consistent, you must be flexible when that is what is needed. For example, you should be very consistent in expecting your subordinates to be on time for quarters every morning, but if an unexpected overnight snowfall has traffic slowed down one morning, you should not hesitate to excuse the latecomers.

Know your job. Few things are more uninspiring for subordinates than to recognize that their leader does not know her or his job. As a leader, you will earn the confidence and respect of those who work for you if you know everything you possibly can about your job. You should also strive to learn as much as you reasonably can about the jobs of your subordinates, but use this knowledge to improve your communications with subordinates, to instruct when necessary, and to monitor what they are doing. Do not use this knowledge to *intrude* on their work.

Do not micromanage. This ties in with the "know your job" principle. While it is important for you to assign, instruct, direct, and monitor, you should not overdo these things. Consistent with safety and efficiency, allow your subordinates to carry out their tasks in a manner that suits their abilities and preferences. People appreciate clear instructions, concerns for their safety, and suggestions for efficiency, but they rarely like having someone looking over their shoulder during the entire job, telling them each and every step to take and exactly how to do it. When giving instructions and directions, try to sort out what is important for safety and efficiency from what is merely your personal preference. This will go a long way in promoting a positive attitude when a subordinate is doing a job. He or she will feel "ownership" and a greater sense of accomplishment if allowed to put some of themselves into a project.

Practice good followership. There are several advantages to being a good follower even when you have been made a leader. First, you will never become a leader if you have not been a good follower. No one is going to recommend you for a leadership position if you have been poor at responding to the leadership of others. Second, no leader is *only* a leader. Every leader is also a subordinate. The chain of command discussed in chapter 1 should make that clear. And even the president, who is commander-in-chief of the armed forces and appears to be at the top of the chain of command with no superior, must answer to the American people or he or she will not long remain their leader. So it is obvious that to *remain* a leader, you must also be a good follower. The third and most important reason goes back to the second principle in this discussion. As a leader you must always *set the example.* If you are a poor follower, it will not take long for your subordinates to begin following your example and it does not take a rocket scientist to figure out where that will leave you.

Don't be one of the gang. Nearly everyone wants to be liked, and being a good leader does not mean that you cannot also be liked. There is absolutely nothing wrong with a leader having a sense of humor and showing concern for each subordinate as an individual. But it is important to avoid the temptation of being too friendly, of putting your desire to be liked above your need to accomplish the mission. Whether it's as simple as an unpleasant clean-up job or as dramatic as having to tell someone to place themselves in danger as Ensign Merdinger did at the beginning of this chapter, as a leader you are going to have to tell people to do things they do not want to do. You will not be able to do this if you have allowed yourself to be too friendly with your subordinates, to become "one of the gang."

Keep your subordinates informed. No one likes to be kept in the dark. And a person is usually better able to do a job if he or she understands why that job needs to be done and how it fits into the "big picture." For these reasons, you should keep your subordinates informed as much as possible. Sometimes, for security or other reasons, there will be things you cannot share with your subordinates. But unless these conditions exist, you should make it a common practice to give your subordinates as much information as you can about what they are doing and why they are doing it. This will improve morale and will often help them do a better job.

Leadership Styles

Leaders, like their followers, are individuals, and because of this you will quickly learn that different leaders have different leadership styles. Just because two different leaders seem very different in the way in which they lead does not necessarily mean that one is doing it wrong. Two athletes may have very different styles of playing, yet both can be quite good at what they do. Leaders, as well as athletes and anyone else who is striving to be successful, will do well to take advantage of their natural strengths and to compensate for their natural weaknesses. Some people are gifted with a natural sense of humor while others are inspirational speakers. Some people are naturally talkative while others are more sparing with their words. These characteristics are going to show themselves in each individual's leadership style, yet all can be effective leaders as long as they adhere to the basic principles discussed above.

Chief petty officers (CPOs), by definition and in practice, are leaders. They are at the top of the enlisted chain of command and got there by a combination of thorough knowledge of their ratings and of proven leadership. When asked what leadership meant to them, a group of randomly selected CPOs gave what at first appears to be different answers. But if you think about what they are saying, you will hear many of the principles discussed above echoed in their words.

CPO 1: In the past, leaders were more educated than their followers. Since they knew more, they took charge. But today, those expected to follow are educated and, in many cases, may be smarter than the people who outrank them. Today's educated followers need motivation. They want to know the reason for their work. If their boss can't give a reason and fails to motivate them, the job will suffer.

CPO 2: Honesty is a key to leadership, honesty with yourself and those you work with. By listening to others' ideas before forming opinions and deciding what to do, a leader earns respect, more respect than one who decides immediately to do everything "my way." A leader should be flexible and willing to compromise when necessary. Leaders should be friendly, willing to help, and knowledgeable about the Navy and its professional fields.

CPO 3: I like the personal touch. By personal example, close direction, and a soft approach, I can get people to do their jobs well. And this makes my job easier. We don't have to yell and scream at our people. We treat them as intelligent people, which they are.

CPO 4: A leader doesn't have to be exceptionally smart as long as she knows the capabilities of her people.

CPO 5: I always try to act the way I want my subordinates to act. I don't go for this "do as I say, not as I do" garbage.

CPO 6: Always stand up for your people. Back them up and they'll back you up. The chain of command involves respect down as well as up.

CPO 7: I don't ask anyone to do anything that I can't do myself.

CPO 8: Sometimes you've got to be paternalistic—kind of a father-to-kid relationship. When you have to lay down the law, be firm, but be sure of what you're doing.

CPO 9: Sarcasm and ridicule have no place in leadership.

CPO 10: Treat young Sailors under your command as you'd want to be treated. Respect their problems. They may seem trivial, but they're important to them. Offer them the guidance they need. But avoid the trap of becoming one of the gang. There is a fine line between being one of the gang and being their leader. Stay on the right side of that line.

Responsibility Before Authority

It has probably occurred to you by now that much of leadership is merely common sense. Just by remembering and practicing the "reverse roles" principle, you will make few mistakes as a leader. But human nature is complex, and leadership is never easy. Whenever you are entrusted with a leadership role, whether you are leading one person or thousands, you must take it very seriously. Remember that with every leadership position comes added responsibility as well as added authority. Always keep the responsibility foremost in your mind and the authority secondary, and you will be well on your way to being a good leader.

Discipline

The word *discipline* comes from a Latin word that means "to teach." What is being taught in a system of discipline is the controlling of an individual's actions, impulses, or emotions. Undisciplined children are those who have not been properly taught how and when to control their actions. Many times in our everyday lives we deliberately do things that are counter to our first impulse or what we may want to do, and this is a result of the discipline that was taught us by those who raised us. Discipline is what prevents us from getting into line ahead of others and what causes us to study for a test when our favorite television show is on.

Methods

Discipline is often confused with punishment, but the two words do not mean the same thing. Rewards and punishments are tools that are used to create and maintain discipline. As a child, you may have received an ice cream cone or a raise in your allowance for good behavior, and you more than likely were restricted from watching television or saw your allowance reduced because you did something you should not have. If these things worked as they were meant to, someone probably referred to you at one time or another as a "well-disciplined child." This same system works when we are adults. Pay raises and parking tickets replace ice cream cones and allowance reductions, but the principles are the same.

Rewards and punishments are not the only means to achieve discipline. Love, religious beliefs, and other values contribute to discipline in individuals as well.

In the Navy, such things as promotions and medals serve as rewards, while demotions and restricted liberty are sometimes imposed as punishments. Unit pride and patriotic devotion are some of the values relied upon to create a system of discipline that will ensure that Sailors will do what is expected of them even when it is different from what they may want to do. When discipline is working best within a unit, the individuals who make up the unit have the right attitude, do their work efficiently, and exhibit high morale. In a well-disciplined unit, the members do the right thing because they *want* to, not because they *have* to. Such men and women perform with enthusiasm, individually or in groups, to carry out the mission of their organization, often with little guidance.

Standards

The Navy has several written standards, or codes, which help in the establishment and maintenance of discipline. One of these, "The Sailor's Creed" (see chapter 1), with its core values of honor, courage, and commitment, is unique to the Navy, but the Uniform

Code of Military Justice and the Code of Conduct apply to all the armed forces of the United States.

Uniform Code of Military Justice (UCMJ)

As a civilian, you were subject to the criminal laws of local, state, and federal governments. To a large extent you still are. But by enlisting you have submitted yourself to the jurisdiction of the Uniform Code of Military Justice as well. The basic criminal laws of the Navy are stated in the UCMJ. It is a "uniform" code of law because Congress made it apply equally to the Army, Navy, Air Force, Marine Corps, and Coast Guard, and it is under this code that the various services bring criminal charges against personnel who violate military law. You have the right to see a copy of the UCMJ at any time and it is always posted in an accessible place on every ship and station in the armed forces.

The UCMJ consists of 146 articles. Those dealing with the punishment of various crimes (numbers 77 through 134) are called the "punitive articles" and are explained to all Navy personnel when they enter active duty, six months thereafter, and on reenlistment. Articles 77 through 133 deal with specific crimes, such as desertion, failure to obey an order, or robbery. Article 134 is called the "general article" and gives the government authority to prosecute for crimes not specifically covered in the other punitive articles.

Unauthorized Absence (UA). Many of the offenses that are covered in the UCMJ require no special explanation. Theft is theft and arson is arson no matter what system of justice you answer to. But one article requires some additional explanation and emphasis. Article 86 of the UCMJ deals with unauthorized absence, sometimes referred to as "AWOL" (absence without leave).

In civilian life, your presence at your job is very important and, in the case of some occupations such as doctor or fireman, it can mean the difference between life or death for someone. In the military, since defending the nation is your foremost reason for being, the potential for a life-or-death situation is always there. Whether you are the loader on a gun, the person who inspects parachutes, or the cook who prepares meals for the crew, you are an important part of a team that depends upon every member to function properly. Any mission, whether it is one involving combat, rescue, or routine operations, will be adversely affected if one or more of the team is not there to do his or her job. Because of this, UA is considered a very serious breach of discipline and is subject to severe penalties.

Because of the punishment you may receive and because of your responsibility to the Navy and to your shipmates who are counting on you, you must make every effort to avoid being absent without proper authorization. This requires sensible planning on your part. Always leave extra time in your travel plans, whether you are facing a 20-minute drive or a 14-hour flight. If, for reasons beyond your control, you are going to be late, notify your duty station immediately. If you cannot get in touch with your duty station (for example, if you are attached to a ship and she got underway without you), contact the nearest naval activity or the American Red Cross. Don't use the mail, use the telephone. Furnish enough information so that your commanding officer can understand the situation and provide appropriate instructions. You can always reach the duty officer of any station or a shore patrol headquarters on any Navy base. In most cities, naval activities are listed in the telephone directory under "U.S. Government"; otherwise the information operator can give you the number. Also, even if you are in a region where there are no naval bases or installations, keep in mind that the Navy has recruiting offices in nearly every major U.S. city; the officer or petty officer on duty there can advise you of the best course to follow. If you are sick or in jail, a family member, a friend, the hospital, or the shore patrol can send a message for you. The bottom line is that there may be a valid excuse for your being late—such as sickness, accident, or other emergency—but there is never an excuse for not notifying your commanding officer, the nearest naval activity, or the American Red Cross.

Shore Patrol and Other Armed Forces Police. The shore patrol (SP) is the military police force of the Navy. Personnel assigned shore-patrol duties can be officers and/or petty officers, and it is their duty to function much as any police force in civilian life does, providing assistance and maintaining order among naval personnel off ship or station. They are identified by brassards (armbands) with the letters *SP*.

The other services have police as well, called military police (MPs) in the Army and air police (APs) in the Air Force. In some areas, a combined or unified armed-forces police detachment (AFPD) is organized, with military police from all the services under one command. You must obey all of these police, no matter what service they represent and no matter what their rank.

Military police from the various services assist military personnel and investigate accidents and offenses involving military personnel.

They have the authority to stop, question, apprehend, or take into custody any member of the armed forces. You are required show them your ID card, leave papers or other orders, and obey any directions they give you.

MAAs and Police Petty Officers. While SPs, MPs, and APs function as police off base, onboard your ship or duty station personnel are assigned similar duties as masters-at-arms (MAA). They are appointed by the executive officer (second in command) and function as her or his assistants. Large ships or stations will have a chief master-at-arms (CMAA) with several assistants. Personnel are usually assigned to the MAA force for several months or longer. While acting as MAAs, they are relieved of most of their normal watches and duties.

Police petty officers usually remain with their divisions for work and watches, but they have been assigned additional duties that contribute to good order and discipline, such as making reveille (morning wakeup) and taps (shutting things down for the night), directing traffic during times of heavy personnel movement, and turning lights on and off at the appropriate times.

Nonjudicial Punishment (NJP). You have probably heard of the military term "court-martial" and you would be correct if you understood it to be roughly equivalent to a trial in civilian life. However, some of the terminology and many of the procedures are different.

An even greater difference between military and civil justice exists in a procedure called "nonjudicial punishment" which is a hearing in which the commanding officer (CO) would handle a relatively minor offense rather than send it to a court. Because these proceedings are nonjudicial, the offender may be punished but will not have a criminal record. In the Navy, NJP is usually referred to as "captain's mast."

On hearing the evidence, both for and against, the commanding officer determines whether the accused is guilty or not and then, if necessary, assigns an appropriate punishment. Some of the punishments that a CO may award are:

Restriction of not more than 60 days;
Extra duties for not more than 45 days;
Reduction in grade (for E-6 and below);
Correctional custody for not more than 30 days (for E-3 and
below); or
Forfeiture of not more than half a month's pay per month for
two months.

The accused has certain rights during a captain's mast:

To be present before the officer conducting the mast;
To be advised of the charges;
Not to be compelled to make any statement;
To be present during testimony of witnesses or the receipt of
  written statements;
To question witnesses or to have questions posed to witnesses;
To have available for inspection all physical and documentary
  evidence;
To present evidence in the accused's own behalf;
To be accompanied by a personal representative who may or
  may not be a lawyer and whose presence is arranged for by
  the accused;
To appeal the imposition of punishment to higher authority; and
If assigned to a shore activity, to refuse captain's mast and
  demand trial by court-martial instead.

Other "Masts." To avoid confusion, you should also be aware
that there are other forms of "mast" in the Navy that have nothing to
do with the UCMJ. Besides the captain's mast, you might find yourself involved in a "meritorious mast," which is used to present awards
or commendations for achievement, or, if you asked to see the commanding officer for an important reason, this would be called a
"request mast."

Courts-Martial. If an alleged offense is too severe to dispose of
by captain's mast, or if the accused exercises his or her right to refuse
NJP, the case will go to court-martial. As already mentioned, there
are three types of court-martial: summary, special, and general.

Summary Court-Martial. If the offense is minor, and if nonjudicial action has been ruled out, the CO may refer the charges to trial
by summary court-martial. This involves a summary or shortened
procedure where actions are judicial in nature. One officer serves as
the judge, jury, prosecution, and defense counsel. The officer takes
evidence on the charges and makes judgment according to judicial
standards. The accused may be represented by an attorney if he or she
desires, but this is not mandatory. The accused may also refuse trial
by summary court-martial and receive a special court-martial instead.

If an accused is convicted by summary court-martial, the court
may impose the following punishments:

Confinement at hard labor of up to one month (E-4 and below);
Hard labor *without* confinement for 45 days (E-4 and below);

Restriction to specified limits for a total of 60 days;
Loss of two-thirds of one month's pay; or
Reduction in grade (E-5 and above may be reduced only one
grade, while E-4 and below may be reduced to the lowest
enlisted paygrade).

Special Court-Martial. If a commanding officer feels that an alleged offense against a service person is moderate to severe, or if the accused has refused trial by summary court-martial, the CO may refer the charges to trial by special court-martial. A legally trained military judge is assigned by the convening authority and a three-member jury is appointed. If you are brought before a special court-martial, you may waive the right to trial before the court-martial jury and face the military judge alone. If you decide to go with the jury, you may also request that an enlisted person serve as at least one of the jurors. You may have a military attorney assigned to you, you may request a specific military counsel, or you may hire your own civilian attorney at your own expense. Some of the punishments that may be awarded at a special court-martial are:

A bad-conduct discharge;
Six-month imprisonment;
Forfeiture of two-thirds pay per month for six months; or
Reduction to the lowest enlisted paygrade.

General Court Martial. The general court-martial is reserved for more serious charges, such as common-law felonies (murder, rape, robbery, and arson) and more serious military charges (lengthy unauthorized absence and desertion). The court is composed of a military judge, five or more members who serve as the jury, and military defense and prosecution attorneys. The accused in a general court-martial may request trial before a military judge alone, but if he or she is enlisted and elects to be tried by the full court-martial, at least one-third of the court members *must* be enlisted persons.

This is by far the most serious of all military courts. Its sentencing power extends to the death penalty and life imprisonment. The *Manual for Courts-Martial* lists the maximum sentence that may be imposed for each offense by a court-martial under the UCMJ.

Although there are certain reservations, service personnel are also subject to civilian trial and punishment. Service personnel are not answerable to civil authorities for violations of a strictly military nature, such as unauthorized absence, desertion, or misbehavior before the enemy. These offenses are subject to trial by military authorities only. Service personnel, however, may be subjected to joint jurisdiction (both civil and military) for offenses such as murder, robbery, rape, or driving under the influence of drugs or alcohol. Under these circumstances, you could be tried twice for the same offense.

Military law is a complex subject covered by thousands of books. The finer points of military law are not understood by most nonlegal personnel. But Navy lawyers are at your disposal, should the need arise, and will advise you at no cost on all matters of military justice matters.

Code of Conduct

United States Navy Regulations require you to be thoroughly familiar with the Code of Conduct for Members of the Armed Forces of the United States, more commonly referred to as simply the "Code of Conduct." Like the UCMJ, the Code of Conduct will always be posted in an accessible place in every command so you should have no problem reviewing it from time to time. The six articles of this code make it clear what is expected of you if you are in a combat situation and if you are unfortunate enough to become a prisoner of war (POW).

Each article of the Code of Conduct is presented here and followed by a brief discussion of its meaning. Read the Code carefully and think about what it says. Its potential importance cannot be overestimated.

ARTICLE I

I am an American, fighting in the forces which guard my country and our way of life. I am prepared to give my life in their defense.

As a member of the armed forces it is always your duty to oppose the enemies of the United States. This applies whether you are in active combat or confined as a prisoner of war.

Your responsibility is to guard "our way of life" and to be prepared to sacrifice your life if that is what it takes to accomplish this mission. You need only watch the evening news to know that there are problems in America, that this is not a perfect nation. But anyone who has traveled the world (as you may well do before your time in the Navy is over) will tell you that the United States of America is the greatest of all nations. And anyone who pays close attention to the evening news will also note that, despite the many problems, there is a never-ending struggle to find solutions. This nation was born and continues to survive because Americans have always jealously guarded their freedom and have been willing to sacrifice themselves rather than yield their hard-won rights. You must do no less.

ARTICLE II

I will never surrender of my own free will. If in command, I will never surrender the members of my command while they still have the means to resist.

You must not surrender unless you have no other choice except senseless death. As long as you have the ability to resist being captured, either by engaging the enemy in combat or by evading, you must do so. If your continued resistance would result in your death and it would serve some useful purpose to the mission (such as delaying the enemy from taking an important position or providing additional time for others to escape), then you should *not* surrender. But if your continued resistance would result in your death and have no effect on the outcome of the mission, then surrender is acceptable.

This responsibility extends to anyone in command as well. The commander must not surrender the people in her or his command unless they can no longer fight or avoid capture and the only other choice is for them to die for no useful purpose.

ARTICLE III

If I am captured I will continue to resist, by all means available. I will make every effort to escape and aid others to escape. I will accept neither parole nor special favors from the enemy.

The duty of a member of the armed forces to continue resistance by all means available is not lessened by the misfortune of capture. You should escape by any means possible and help others to escape. Parole agreements are promises given the captor by a POW to fulfill stated conditions (such as not to bear arms or not to escape) in consideration of special privileges (such as release from captivity or better living conditions). You must never sign or enter into any parole agreement.

ARTICLE IV

If I become a prisoner of war, I will keep faith with my fellow prisoners. I will give no information or take part in any

*actions which might be harmful to my comrades. If I am
senior, I will take command. If not, I will obey the lawful
orders of those appointed over me and will back them up in
every way.*

Informing, or any other action that harms a fellow prisoner, is shameful. Prisoners of war must not help the enemy identify fellow prisoners who may have knowledge of value to the enemy, and who may therefore be tortured.

Strong leadership is essential to discipline, and being in a POW situation does not lessen this. Without discipline, camp organization, resistance, and even survival may be impossible. Personal hygiene, camp sanitation, and care of the sick and wounded are imperative, and it is up to the leaders to ensure these things are accomplished to the best of everyone's ability.

Officers and petty officers (known as noncommissioned officers in the Army, Air Force, and Marines) will continue to carry out their responsibilities and exercise their authority after capture. The senior line officer, petty officer, or noncommissioned officer within the POW camp or group will assume command according to rank (or precedence), without regard to branch of service. Responsibility and accountability may not be evaded. If the senior officer or noncommissioned officer is incapacitated or unable to act for any reason, the next senior takes over.

ARTICLE V

*When questioned, should I become a prisoner of war, I am
required to give name, rank, service number, and date of birth.
I will evade answering further questions to the utmost of my
ability. I will make no oral or written statements disloyal to my
country and its allies or harmful to their cause.*

Navy Regulations explains that the United States has agreed to abide by an international agreement entitled the Geneva Convention Relative to the Treatment of Prisoners of War (known more commonly as simply the "Geneva Convention"), and as a member of the U.S. armed forces, you are subject to the requirements and protections of this agreement.

In accordance with the Geneva Convention, a POW is required to reveal her or his name, rank, service (Social Security) number, and date of birth. A POW may tell the enemy about his or her individual health or welfare and, when appropriate, about routine matters of camp administration, but the following are forbidden:

Oral or written confessions (whether true or false);
Filling out questionnaires;
Providing personal-history statements;
Making propaganda recordings and broadcasts; or
Signing peace or surrender appeals, criticisms, or any other oral
or written communication on behalf of the enemy or that is
critical or harmful to the United States, its allies, its armed
forces, or other prisoners.

It is a violation of the Geneva Convention for captors to subject a POW to physical or mental torture or any other form of coercion to secure information of any kind. If, however, a prisoner is subjected to such treatment, he or she must strive to avoid by every means the disclosure of any information, or the making of any statement or the performance of any action, harmful to the interests of the United States or its allies, or that will provide aid or comfort to the enemy.

ARTICLE VI

I will never forget that I am an American, fighting for freedom, responsible for my actions, and dedicated to the principles which made my country free. I will trust in my God and in the United States of America.

The provisions of the UCMJ continue to apply to members of the armed forces while POWs, and they have a continuing obligation to remain loyal to country, service, and unit. Should you become a prisoner, never give up hope and always resist enemy indoctrination. This will, of course, serve the best interests of the nation, but it will serve *your* best interests as well. The life of a POW is hard. If all nations lived up to the terms of the Geneva Convention as it is intended, a POW experience would be difficult enough, but Americans who have been captured by the enemy have, more often than not, been subjected to terrible living conditions and have often been tortured. Experience has proven that POWs who stand firm and united against the enemy help one another survive this ordeal.

After POWs are released, their conduct will be examined and evaluated. For this reason alone, you should strive to uphold the Code of Conduct while a POW. But, just as important, you will have to live with yourself after your release, and experience has proven that those POWs who upheld the Code of Conduct to the best of their ability are much better prepared to lead a normal life after their POW ordeal is over. Those who failed to uphold the Code must live with the shame and dishonor of knowing that they failed their nation and their fellow POWs.

Hope that you never become a prisoner of war. Do everything in your power, consistent with honor, to avoid becoming a POW. But if you are captured, remember the Code of Conduct and uphold it. Your chances of survival will be enhanced and your personal sense of honor will be undamaged.

Personal Relations

Getting along in the Navy means more than just learning new duties, obeying regulations, standing watches, and showing up for drills. It also means working and living with all kinds of people. While this is part of the American ethic, it takes on particular significance when you find yourself in the crowded and challenging working conditions that are often a part of Navy life. Going to sea means a lot of people living and working in a relatively small area. It means not only putting up with crowded living conditions but also with extreme operating conditions and long working hours, in intense heat or bitter cold, for perhaps weeks at a time. The combination of these challenges coupled with the high standards of conduct demanded by the Navy means that you will have to place a great deal of emphasis on your personal behavior and on your relations with others.

Getting along with others is always in your own best interests. But even if it were not, you need to be aware that one of the quickest ways to end a successful career, and to face other harsh penalties as well, is to take part in such ugly practices as ethnic discrimination and sexual harassment. The Navy is committed to fair and equitable treatment of all hands, by all hands, at all times and simply *will not tolerate* anything less.

Ethnic Discrimination

Because Americans join the Navy from all walks of life and come from all parts of the country, you will be living and working with people of different races, people with different social and educational backgrounds, people whose religious faith might be very different from what you are used to, people whose family background and customs are different from yours. All of these variations are defined as "ethnic" differences, and while they are very real and cannot be ignored, they must also be *irrelevant* in your relations with one another. Despite all these potential differences, the people you share the Navy with are guaranteed to have two things in common with

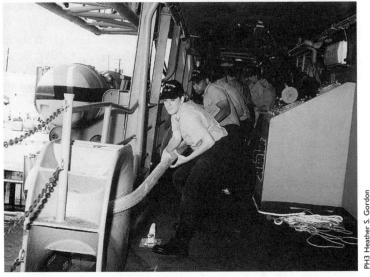

Figure 5.1. Different races and genders must pull together to make the Navy run well.

you. They are *people* and they are *in the Navy*. These are strong bonds when you think about it.

This is not to say that you must *like* everyone in the Navy. Human nature being what it is, it is almost guaranteed that you will meet, and even work closely with, some people you will not like. But your evaluation of an individual should be based upon their words and actions, not on their ethnic differences.

Men and women who have been in combat will tell you that they never gave a thought to the religion of the medic who stopped the bleeding of their wounds. They never once wondered if the pilot who was providing covering fire for them was black or white. They never asked about a fellow Sailor's family background before letting him help put out a fire on an aircraft loaded with live bombs.

The Navy has taken a great many steps to eliminate ethnic prejudice and discrimination. There have been programs, educational campaigns, and regulations enacted to this end. All of these are important steps that need to be taken, but what is going to be the most effective means is how *you* deal with these matters. The following principles should guide you in your everyday activities:

Treat every person as an individual and evaluate them on their words and actions, not on their ethnic makeup.

Never tolerate ethnic discrimination in others. If a subordinate is practicing discrimination or exhibiting ethnic prejudice, correct it. If a superior is doing so, *report* it. If you are the *victim* of such activities, report it.

If you need some help in deciding whether you are involved in ethnic discrimination—either as a victim or as the one doing the discriminating—the Navy has provided a telephone counseling service that you may call. This is *not* for reporting ethnic discrimination. It is there for you to call to get advice on your rights and responsibilities should you be discriminated against or if someone is accusing you of doing so. This is a confidential service—you need not give your name when calling. The number to call is 1-800-253-0931 if you are in the continental United States. If you are outside the continental United States, call *collect* at 1-703-614-2735. If you are working in the Department of Defense, call 224-2735.

If you follow these guidelines at all times, you will be taking a large step toward the prevention of ethnic discrimination in the Navy, and you will be protecting yourself from the very serious consequences that are the result of such practices.

Sexual Harassment

It should come as no surprise to you that sexual harassment is prohibited in the Navy. Sexual harassment is defined, in simple terms, as making unwelcome advances toward another person. But human interaction is rarely simple. There can be a fine line between acceptable and unacceptable behavior when it comes to interactions between men and women. Sexual harassment can be sexually oriented communications, comments, gestures, or physical contact. It can also be offers or threats to influence or alter, directly or indirectly, an individual's career or other conditions of service in order to secure sexual favors.

Despite the terminology used, sexual harassment is really about *power,* not about sex. Both men and women are capable of harassment and either men or women can be victims of it.

Men and women in the Navy have an obligation to each other and to their service to respect each other's dignity. That is the basis of civil rights and is required conduct for all service people.

Guidelines

The Secretary of the Navy has issued specific guidance concerning sexual harassment in SECNAVINST 5300.26. The instruction states that sexual harassment occurs when a person in a supervisory or command position uses or condones sexual behavior to control, influence, or affect the career, pay, or the actual job of a military member or civilian employee. Unwelcomed verbal comments, gestures, or physical contact of a sexual nature are also considered sexual harassment. If an individual feels that his or her job performance is affected by such behaviors or feels that such activities are creating an intimidating, hostile, or offensive environment in the workplace, this is a clear sign that sexual harassment is taking place. It is also a violation for a supervisor or commanding officer to condone or ignore acts of sexual harassment or to ignore reports of such behavior. Violations also include making false accusations or retaliating against a person who reports sexual harassment.

The SECNAV instruction uses the three colors of a traffic light to explain the wide range of behaviors of sexual harassment. Green-light behavior is acceptable under any circumstances; yellow-light actions cover areas that are possibly offensive; red-light conduct constitutes blatant sexual harassment.

Green Light. These behaviors, which are not sexual harassment, include:

Performance counseling;
Touching that could not reasonably be perceived in a sexual way
    (such as touching someone on the elbow);
Counseling on military appearance; and
Social interaction, such as showing concern, encouragement, a
    polite compliment, or a friendly conversation.

Yellow Light. Many people find the following behaviors unacceptable and consider them sexual harassment:

Violating "personal space" (lingering close enough to make that
    person uncomfortable);
Repeated requests for dates;
Unwanted letters or poems;
Questions about personal life;
Foul language;
Touching, comments, jokes, posters, calendars, whistling, leer-
    ing, or staring that is sexually suggestive; and
Sitting or gesturing sexually.

Red Light. The following behaviors are always considered sexual harassment:

Sexual favors in return for employment rewards;
Threats if sexual favors are not provided;
Sexually explicit remarks or pictures (including calendars or
posters);
The use of status to request dates; and
Obscene letters or comments.

The most severe forms of sexual harassment, such as sexual assault (ranging from forcefully grabbing to fondling, forced kissing, or rape), constitute criminal behavior and will result in prosecution.

Keep in mind that the examples used here are for guidance only, that individuals believe they are being sexually harassed based on their perception of the situation, that each incident is judged on the totality of facts in that particular case, and that each individual's judgment may vary on the same facts. Therefore, caution in this area is advised. Some basic principles that will help guide you in your day-to-day activities:

Any time sexually oriented behavior *of any kind* is introduced into the work environment or among coworkers, the behavior may constitute sexual harassment. *If in doubt, don't do it.*

Never tolerate sexual harassment in others. If a subordinate is sexually harrassing someone, correct it. If a superior is doing so, *report* it.

If you are the *victim* of such activities, report it.

Action

The Secretary of the Navy's guidance prescribes specific actions that should be taken in the event that sexual harassment is committed or suspected.

Assistance. If you need some help in deciding whether you are involved in sexual harassment—either as a victim or as the one doing the harassing—the Navy has provided a telephone counseling service that you may call. It is the same line used for assistance in matters of ethnic discrimination described above and is staffed by trained counselors who can provide the assistance you need. This line is *not* for reporting sexual harassment. It is there for you to call to get advice on your rights and responsibilities should you be sexually harassed or if someone is accusing you of sexual harassment. This is a confidential service—you need not give your name when calling. The number to call is 1-800-253-0931 if you are in the continental United States. If you are outside the continental United States, call *collect* at 1-703-

614-2735. If you are working in the Department of Defense, call 224-2735. You may also obtain more information at the BUPERS website http://www.bupers.navy.mil/pers61.

Responsibilities. If you believe that you are being sexually harassed, you must take appropriate action to get it stopped. You should do the following:

Tell the harasser to stop. Because people's perceptions are often different in such matters, you must make the harasser aware that her or his behavior is unwanted. Politeness is always appropriate, but be clear and firm about what it is that is bothering you.

Talk with coworkers. See if any of them have witnessed what is happening to you and find out if they, too, are feeling harassed.

Keep a written record of what has been occurring. The record of each incident should include:

When it occurred (date and time);
Where it occurred;
A description of *what happened;*
What was said (by the harasser and by you);
How you felt when the incident was occurring and afterwards; and
The *names* of any witnesses, anyone you told about the incident, and anyone else who is also a victim of the same harassment.

Report the harassment up the chain of command. If telling the harasser to stop has not had the desired effect, tell your supervisor what is occurring and ask that it be stopped. If it is your supervisor who is doing the harassing, report it to his or her supervisor or commanding officer.

File a formal grievance. If the chain of command does not respond adequately, file a grievance.

Fraternization

Hundreds of years of Navy experience have demonstrated that seniors must maintain thoroughly professional relationships with juniors at all times. "Fraternization" is the term traditionally used to identify personal relationships that violate the customary bounds of acceptable senior-subordinate relationships.

While it is impossible to define every situation which might be considered fraternization, common sense dictates that activities which can affect a senior's ability to be objective are not appropriate.

For example, dating, sharing living accommodations, intimate or sexual relations, commercial solicitations, private business partnerships, gambling, and lending or borrowing money are all activities that can damage senior-subordinate relationships.

Personal relationships that include any of these characteristics are forbidden under the following circumstances:

—between officers and enlisted personnel
—between chief petty officers (E-7 through E-9) and juniors (E-1 through E-6) who are assigned to the same command
—between instructors and students within Navy training commands
—between recruiters and recruits (or potential recruits).

Violations of these rules may result in disciplinary action under the Uniform Code of Military Justice (UCMJ).

One last caution. Fraternization rules are "service specific," which means they are not identical in each of the armed services. What is allowed or forbidden in another service, such as the Army, may or may not be allowed in the Navy, so do not make assumptions. If in doubt, ask for assistance from a senior in your chain of command to determine what is appropriate behavior and what might be considered fraternization.

Homosexuality

The Department of Defense (DOD) has long held that, as a general rule, open homosexuality is incompatible with military service because it interferes with some of the factors critical to combat effectiveness, including unit morale, unit cohesion, and individual privacy. But DOD also recognizes that individuals with a homosexual orientation have served effectively and sometimes with distinction in the armed services of the United States.

With those facts in mind, the policy of DOD regarding homosexuality can be summed up as "Don't Ask—Don't Tell—Don't Harass." What this means is that (1) no individual in the Navy will be *asked* (either in writing or verbally) about their sexual orientation, (2) no servicemember is expected to, nor should they, *tell* anyone what their sexual orientation is, and (3) hostile treatment or violence against a servicemember based on a perception of his or her sexual orientation will not be tolerated. This latter warning means that you must not tell any jokes, say anything derogatory, threaten, or harm anyone because you suspect or think they are, or are not, homosexual. In other words, to protect yourself and others from any misunderstandings and/or punitive action, you should avoid the subject and any related actions altogether.

Hazing

Good-natured fun, such as mild teasing, can enhance relationships among shipmates, but when it goes too far, it is no longer fun and is illegal. Your Navy has no tolerance for behaviors that are demeaning, humiliating, abusive, oppressive, or cruel to others. Neither must you.

Games or playing tricks on others that include such things as shaving, taping, greasing, painting, tattooing, striking, threatening, forcing the consumption of food, alcohol, drugs, or any other substance are forbidden. Such practices as "tacking on," "pinning," and "blood wings" are a quick way to find yourself the subject of a court martial. Following two simple rules will keep you from making a mistake that may do significant physical or psychological harm to others and bring serious consequences to you. (1) Do not do anything to someone else that you would not want done to you. (2) If you have any doubt, don't do it.

Public Relations

Because you represent the U.S. Navy whenever you put on your uniform, you are in effect performing public relations duty every time you come into contact with someone outside the Navy. What people think about the Navy is influenced by what they see its members doing. This is true whether you are a seaman recruit or an admiral. When you put on the Navy uniform, you represent the U.S. Navy. It should be apparent that it is in your best interests as well as the Navy's that you never forget your importance as a representative of the service and always conduct yourself in a manner that will bring credit to you, your Navy, and the nation you serve.

Overseas Diplomacy

When you are visiting or working in other countries—and, as a Sailor in the U.S. Navy, the odds are that you *will* find yourself in one or more foreign nations at some point in your career—you not only represent the Navy, but the United States of America as well. You will still be on public relations duty, but you will, in effect, be an American ambassador as well. Fair or not, people in the other nations you visit will often judge all Americans by what you do.

Standards of Conduct

Whether you are overseas, in your homeport, or visiting your hometown, as a representative of the Navy you must always practice standards of conduct that will reflect favorably upon you and your Navy. These standards are explained in detail in the Secretary of the Navy's instruction number 5370.2, but the list of "nevers" below will guide you in maintaining the expected standards of conduct:

Never use your position as a member of the Navy for private gain.

Never give preferential treatment to any person or organization.

Never do things that will reduce government efficiency or economy.

Never give up your independence or lose your impartiality.

Never make decisions or take actions that will bypass the chain of command or go outside official channels.

Never do anything that will adversely affect the public's confidence in the Navy or in the U.S. government.

Never take part in any business or financial dealings that result in a conflict between your private interest and the public interest of the United States.

Never engage in any activity that might result in or reasonably be expected to create the appearance of a conflict of interest.

Never accept gifts from defense contractors or others who are trying to do business with the government.

Never use your official position to influence any person to provide any private benefit.

Never use your rank, title, position, or uniform for commercial purposes.

Never accept outside employment or take part in any activity that is incompatible with your duties or may bring discredit to the Navy.

Never take or use government property or services for other than officially approved purposes.

Never give gifts to your superiors or accept them from your subordinates.

Never conduct official business with persons whose participation in the transaction would be in violation of law.

Examples of violations of these standards would be wearing your uniform while filming a television commercial or taking part in a political rally. Or accepting money or a gift in exchange for a tour of your ship. Or taking a piece of Navy electronic test equipment home to work on your stereo. Or posing for pictures for a magazine that some may find offensive. The list of examples could go on for pages and pages. For the most part, simple common sense will serve you well. But if you are not sure about something, before you do it, ask someone who can help: a more senior petty officer in your division, your division chief, a chaplain, or your division officer.

24/7

From the time you join the service until you are discharged or retire, your duty and commitment to the Navy is a 24-hour-a-day, seven-days-a-week obligation. This means that you must comply with the codes, standards, regulations, and policies described in this chapter and elsewhere in this book at all times, in all places. Unacceptable conduct is not excused because you are "not at work."

Finally, three simple rules will guide you well in your conduct as a Sailor in the United States Navy:

Always be aware that you are a representative of the Navy and your nation.

Always assume that someone is watching.

Never do anything you would not want to read about in the newspaper or that you would not want to have to explain to your commanding officer or the people who raised you.

Courtesies, Customs, and Ceremonies

6

Fleet Admiral Chester Nimitz, one of the key figures in the U.S. Navy's victory at sea in the Pacific during World War II, once said that "a naval ceremony should follow the long established rules for its execution carefully and exactly. Such attention to detail honors those who, long before us, established the ritual, and all those who, past, present, and future, take part in that ceremony."

There is no question that life in the Navy is a unique experience. Once you have been to sea, or flown on naval air missions, or taken part in the many different things that Sailors the world over are doing every hour of every day, you will know from first-hand experience how different a job in the Navy can be from what your counterparts in civilian life are doing. It is only fitting, therefore, that we celebrate our uniqueness through special ceremonies and demonstrate our differences through special customs that remind us of our very different heritage. Not only will these practices make you feel special, they will remind the rest of the world of the unique contributions made by the men and women who serve in the U.S. Navy.

Because some of the things we do in the Navy are very different from what you were used to in civilian life, it is only natural to feel somewhat embarrassed the first few times you practice these new courtesies and customs or take part in these unusual ceremonies. But remember that everyone around you in the Navy is also doing these things, and that most everyone outside the Navy may not understand what they are seeing but are favorably impressed whenever they witness these unique practices. Think about what you felt if you ever saw a military drill team perform before you entered the Navy. More than likely, you did not laugh but instead felt a kind of awe as you watched the precision and skill displayed by this military unit. What you felt is much like what most civilians feel when they see Sailors dressed in their best uniforms, smartly lined along the rails of a ship returning from a long deployment overseas, or when they hear the roar of a gun salute. Practice these new customs and soon pride will overtake any embarrassment you might feel.

The Salute

After learning how to stand at attention, the next military custom you will most likely learn how to use is the hand salute. It is a centuries-old custom, and it probably originated when men in armor raised their helmet visors so they could be identified. The tradition continues today as a means of showing respect among naval warriors.

Salutes are customarily given with the right hand, but there are exceptions. If your right arm is injured in such a way as to prevent you from saluting, or if you are using your right hand for some military purpose, such as holding a boatswain's pipe while blowing it, then it is considered appropriate for you to salute with your left hand. Interestingly, people in the Army and Air Force never salute left-

Figure 6.1. Saluting is a centuries-old military tradition that is impressive when done correctly, embarrassing when done poorly. Here, a Chief instructs a Sailor on the proper method of saluting.

handed. On the other hand, a soldier or airman may salute uncovered (without cap on), while Sailors must be covered if they are going to salute. Be aware that these differences in custom among the services should be modified if the circumstances warrant. Consider, for example, if you are in an office with several soldiers and none of you are covered. An Army officer enters, and the soldiers jump to their feet, come to attention, and salute. Your naval custom would not include the salute, since you are uncovered, but not to salute would seem disrespectful under the circumstances, so you should do as the soldiers do and salute. The old (and *customary*) saying, "When in Rome, do as the Romans do," is good advice.

How to Salute

Salute from a position of attention if you are standing still. If you're walking, salute from an erect position. Your upper arm should be parallel to the deck or ground, forearm inclined at a 45-degree angle, hand and wrist straight, palm slightly inward, thumb and fingers extended and joined, with the tip of the forefinger touching the lower edge of your cap, slightly to the right of the right eye. Face the person saluted or, if you're walking, turn your head and eyes toward the person. Allow time for the person being saluted to see and return the salute; if both of you are walking, a distance of about six steps is

AT ATTENTION

FOREARM INCLINED AT 45°

TIP OF FOREFINGER TOUCHING SLIGHTLY TO RIGHT OF RIGHT EYE

UPPER ARM PARALLEL TO DECK, ELBOW SLIGHTLY FORWARD

HAND AND WRIST IN A STRAIGHT LINE, PALM SLIGHTLY INWARD

Figure 6.2. How to salute properly.

about right. Hold the salute until the officer has returned or acknowledged it, then bring your hand smartly to your side.

In most cases, a salute is accompanied by a verbal greeting. For example, when you meet an officer you know, you should accompany your salute with "Good Morning, Lieutenant Jones." If you do not know the officer's name, "Good morning, Ma'am" or "Good morning, Sir" is appropriate. For more guidance on how to address people in the Navy, see "The Address" section below.

Whom to Salute

Salute all officers of all U.S. services and all allied foreign services. Officers in the U.S. Merchant Marine and Public Health Service wear uniforms that closely resemble Navy uniforms, and they too rate a salute.

Salute the person standing an OOD watch no matter what their rank or rate (see "Boarding and Departing the Ship"). The same applies to anyone taking a division muster.

A good rule to remember about saluting is: When in doubt, salute. If you salute someone who does not rate a salute, you may cause yourself some slight embarrassment by appearing less informed than you should be. But if you fail to salute someone who does rate one, you appear to be unmilitary, discourteous, and a shirker. No one ever got into trouble for saluting when it was not expected, but the opposite cannot be said.

Because you are in uniform, young children will often salute you; they rightfully associate saluting with military behavior. Return the salute. The smile you will get in return will make your whole day.

When Not to Salute

There are times when other considerations override the desirability of a military salute. Do *not* salute in the following circumstances:

When engaged in work and saluting would interfere with what you are doing. If you are part of a work detail, the person in charge of the detail will salute for the entire group.

When engaged in athletics or some other recreational activity.

When carrying something with both hands and saluting would require you put all or part of your load down. A verbal greeting is still appropriate in this case.

In public places where saluting is obviously inappropriate (such as on a bus or while standing in line at a theater). A verbal greeting is still appropriate, however.

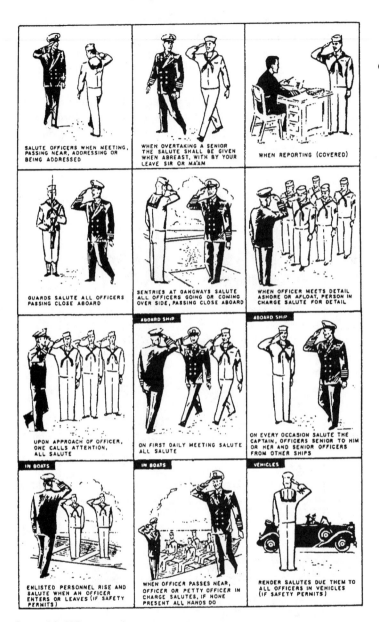

Figure 6.3. Whom to salute.

In combat or simulated combat conditions.

At mess. If you are addressed by an officer while eating, you should stop eating and sit at attention until the officer has departed. Courtesy dictates that the officer will keep the interruption brief.

When guarding prisoners.

In formation. The person in charge will salute for you or, in some cases, will give the order for you and the others in the formation to salute, but you are relieved of any responsibility to salute on your own when in formation.

Figure 6.4. When not to salute.

Saluting While Armed

If you have a sidearm (pistol) in a holster, you would salute the same as if you were unarmed. The same is true if you are carrying a rifle at "sling arms," except that it is appropriate to reach across the front of your body with your left hand to prevent the butt of the rifle from swinging forward.

When carrying a rifle (other than at "sling arms"), there are three different ways in which to salute.

Present Arms

"Present arms" is a salute in itself and is the one most often used. (The word "present" is pronounced with the emphasis on the second syllable, not the first.) Hold the rifle vertically in front of you, parallel to your body, with the muzzle about three inches higher than your eyes.

Rifle Salute at Order Arms

If you are already at order arms or if present arms is not practical because of confined space, saluting at order arms is appropriate. When you have your rifle at order arms, it is resting on the deck next to your right foot and held in place by the V formed between the thumb and index finger of your right hand. To salute from this posi-

119

Figure 6.5. Saluting while at sling arms.

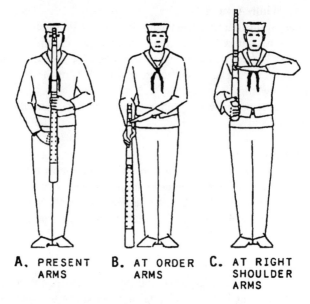

A. PRESENT ARMS   **B.** AT ORDER ARMS   **C.** AT RIGHT SHOULDER ARMS

Figure 6.6a–c. Rifle salutes.

tion, you should smartly move your left hand across your body and, holding it flat in a position similar to that used when saluting normally, touch it to the rifle just below the muzzle.

Rifle Salute at Shoulder Arms

Rifles are often carried—particularly when marching—at shoulder arms (resting smartly on the shoulder at about a 45-degree angle with your arm parallel to the deck). Rather than stop marching, come to attention, and then present arms, it is appropriate to salute from right shoulder arms by bringing your left arm smartly across your body, keeping your hand flat in appropriate salute fashion, and touching your fingertips to the rifle while keeping your arm parallel to the deck.

The Address

There are really two different situations you must consider when it comes to addressing people in the Navy: introductions and conversation. Introducing people requires a degree of extra formality over merely addressing them in other conversation.

When you are introducing someone, you should use their entire title, but some—such as vice admiral or lieutenant commander—are too long and cumbersome to use in normal conversation, so you would shorten them by dropping the first part of their titles. You would *introduce* "Lieutenant Commander Jones" but you would then refer to her or him in conversation as "Commander Jones," or simply "Commander." However, if several people of the same rank are together, it is proper to use both title and name, such as "Admiral Taylor" or "Chief Smith," to avoid confusion.

In the military, rank establishes the order of introduction: introduce the junior to the senior, regardless of either one's age or sex.

Officers

Officers are always addressed and referred to by their title or rank, such as admiral, captain, or commander. By tradition, the commanding officer of any ship or station, no matter what his or her rank, is addressed and referred to as "Captain." An officer in the medical corps or dental corps is addressed and referred to by rank, or as "Doctor." A chaplain may be called "Chaplain" no matter what the rank.

Army, Air Force, and Marine Corps officers are addressed and referred to by their ranks.

Enlisted Personnel

A chief petty officer is addressed as "Chief Petty Officer Smith," or more informally as "Chief Smith" or "Chief" if you do not know his or her name. Master and senior chief petty officers are customarily addressed and referred to as "Master Chief Smith," "Senior Chief Smith," "Master Chief," or "Senior Chief" if you do not know their names.

Other petty officers are addressed and referred to by their specific rates. For example, you would introduce GMG2 Johnson as "Gunner's Mate Second Class Johnson" or "Petty Officer Second Class Johnson," and refer to her as "Petty Officer Johnson."

Nonrated personnel—those in paygrades E-1 through E-3—are introduced as "Seaman Wells" or "Fireman Apprentice Clifton" and referred to in the same manner or by their last names only in informal situations.

The Reply

When an officer asks you a question that can be answered either "yes" or "no," you should answer "Yes, sir" or "Yes, ma'am" or "No, sir" or "No, ma'am," whichever is appropriate. If your answer requires more than a simple yes or no, you should still add "sir" or "ma'am" to your answer, such as "The boat is ready for launching, sir." But if an officer gives you an order, the proper answer is "Aye, aye, sir" or "Aye, aye, ma'am." This means that you have heard the order, you understand it, and you will carry it out.

When a senior wants to indicate that she or he has heard and understood a report from a junior, she or he will answer, "Very well." A junior never says "Very well" to a senior. Observe the following conversation:

> Lieutenant Washington: "Seaman Nelson, is the boat ready for launching?"
> Seaman Nelson: "Yes, sir."
> Lieutenant Washington: "Excellent. Make certain there are enough life-jackets on board."
> Seaman Nelson: "Aye, aye, sir."
> [Nelson checks]
> Seaman Nelson: "There are seven life-jackets on board, sir."
> Lieutenant Washington: "Very well."

This way of speaking is different from what you are probably used to, but it is one of the differences that makes life in the Navy special and interesting. The terms "Aye, aye" and "Very well" come from centuries of tradition going way back to the days when ships were powered by sails and Sailors fought with cannons and cutlasses. Just as you would never say "Aye, aye" back in the neighborhood where you grew up, so you should not say "Yeah," "Yup," or "Okay" when speaking to an officer in the Navy. Once you have used terms like this a few times, you will get past the strangeness and feel pride because it is one of the things that marks you as a Navy professional.

Flags and Flag Etiquette

Showing respect to the American flag is probably not new to you. In school, or perhaps in a scout troop, you may have recited the pledge of allegiance before starting the day's activities. You have probably been to a sporting event where the national anthem is played while everyone in the stadium stood as a mark of respect.

The American flag is, in truth, a piece of colored cloth. But what it *represents* causes us to want to show respect for it. The American flag is a symbol of the democracy we hold so dear, that men and

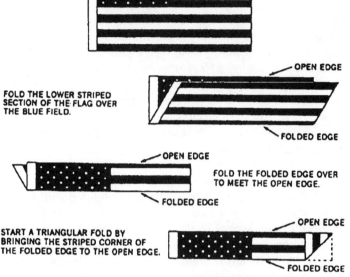

OPEN EDGE

FOLD THE LOWER STRIPED
SECTION OF THE FLAG OVER
THE BLUE FIELD.

FOLDED EDGE

OPEN EDGE

FOLD THE FOLDED EDGE OVER
TO MEET THE OPEN EDGE.

FOLDED EDGE

START A TRIANGULAR FOLD BY
BRINGING THE STRIPED CORNER OF
THE FOLDED EDGE TO THE OPEN EDGE.

OPEN EDGE

FOLDED EDGE

FOLD THE OUTER POINT INWARD
PARALLEL WITH THE OPEN EDGE
TO FORM A SECOND TRIANGLE.

CONTINUE FOLDING UNTIL THE ENTIRE
LENGTH OF THE FLAG IS FOLDED INTO
A TRIANGLE WITH ONLY THE BLUE
FIELD AND MARGIN SHOWING.

TUCK THE REMAINING MARGIN INTO
THE POCKET FORMED BY THE FOLDS AT
THE BLUE FIELD EDGE OF THE FLAG.

THE PROPERLY FOLDED FLAG SHOULD
RESEMBLE A COCKED HAT.

Figure 6.7. Correct method of folding the national ensign. It takes a minimum of
two people to keep the flag taut while folding..

women have died protecting, that is the essence of what the United States of America is truly about.

In the Navy, as in all the armed forces, the American flag is no less a symbol of democracy, and it takes on extra significance because it is in the military services that many Americans have sacrificed their lives defending "the republic for which it stands." The first official salute of the American flag by a foreign government took place on 14 February 1778 when a Navy ship, the sloop-of-war *Ranger* under the command of Captain John Paul Jones, exchanged salutes with the French ship *Robuste,* in Quiberon Bay on the Atlantic coast of France. As an American bluejacket, you will see the American flag often, and you will participate in many ceremonies in which the flag plays a part and is honored.

You may be called upon to fold an American flag and you should know the proper way of doing it. It takes a minimum of two to do it properly, so practice with a friend using a bath towel until you are comfortable with the procedure.

As with many aspects of the Navy, you must learn some new terms and new customs when it comes to the American flag. To begin with, we don't normally refer to it as the American flag. In the Navy, it is called the "national ensign" and is sometimes referred to as "the colors." You will also see a flag used in the Navy that is just the blue rectangular part of the national ensign with the white stars. It is called the "union jack" and its use will be explained below.

There are other special flags used in the Navy besides the union jack and many special customs go along with these special flags as well.

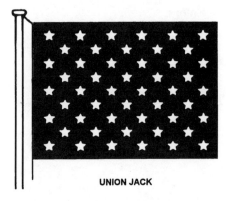

UNION JACK

Figure 6.8. The union jack is a special flag used by the U.S. Navy.

The National Anthem

Many customs and ceremonies are associated with the national ensign. One that you will have some familiarity with is showing respect during the playing of the national anthem. Just as you would stand during the playing of "The Star Spangled Banner" before a ballgame, all naval personnel show similar respect whenever the national anthem is played. This is accomplished by standing at attention and facing the national ensign if it can be seen, or facing in the direction of the music if the ensign is not in sight. If in uniform and covered, salute from the sounding of the first note to the last. If you are uncovered, in uniform, it is customary to stand at attention during the playing of the anthem. If you are wearing civilian clothes or athletic gear, stop and face the colors at attention. If you are a man wearing a hat with your civilian clothes, remove it with your right hand and hold it over your heart throughout the ceremony. If you are not wearing a hat, salute by holding your right hand over your heart. If you are a woman in civilian clothes, with or without a hat, stand at attention and place your right hand over your heart.

If you are a passenger in a boat, stand at attention if that is practical. Obviously, safety takes precedence over ceremony, so if you are seated and it would be unsafe for you to stand, remain seated at attention throughout the ceremony. The boat officer or coxswain will salute for all aboard.

Drivers of motor vehicles pull over and stop if traffic safety permits. Sit at attention but do not salute.

The same marks of respect prescribed during the playing of the national anthem are shown during the playing of a foreign national anthem.

Passing of the Colors

Whenever the national ensign is being carried by a color guard and passes by you, as in a parade, for example, you should stand (if you were sitting) and render a salute until the ensign has passed by. If you are in civilian clothes, the same rules apply as during the national anthem: hat or hand over your heart.

Morning and Evening Colors

The ceremonies of hoisting the national ensign (raising the flag) at 0800 in the morning and lowering it at sunset are called morning colors and evening colors, respectively. These ceremonies take place every day on every Navy shore station in the world. Ships at sea do not observe either of these formal ceremonies, but ships in port—

whether moored to a pier or anchored offshore—*do* observe both morning and evening colors. Aboard ships, the ceremonies have an added factor in that the union jack is also hoisted and taken down at the same time as the national ensign. The union jack is always hoisted on a pole called a "jackstaff" at the bow (front end) of the ship, while the national ensign is always hoisted onto a pole called a "flagstaff" at the stern (back end) of the ship.

If there is more than one Navy ship in port at the same time, the one having the most senior officer (called SOPA, or "senior officer present afloat") holds colors normally, that is, raising or lowering the national ensign and union jack using a clock (or chronometer) to determine when it is time to do so. But all the other ships (those with officers junior to SOPA) ignore the time and simply follow the lead of SOPA. This ensures that all ships hold colors simultaneously, which makes for a much more impressive ceremony than if each ship acted independently.

Morning Colors

"First call to colors" is sounded on the ship's announcing (1MC) system precisely at 0755. Most often this is a special bugle call that you will come to recognize. Few Navy ships today have a bugler aboard as part of the ship's company (crew), as was common in earlier days, so the tradition is often kept alive by using a recorded bugle call. An alternative is for the officer of the deck to pass the word "first call to colors" over the 1MC. This serves to alert everyone that the morning colors ceremony will take place in five minutes. A special yellow and green pennant called the PREP (for "preparative") pennant will be hoisted to the yardarm on ships. You will be able to tell youth from experience at this point because the veterans of battle with enemies or the elements will often come out to take part in the ceremony, while the young and inexperienced will hurry inside to avoid participating because they have not yet come to appreciate what it symbolizes.

At 0800, the bugle sounds "Attention" (or a whistle is blown) and the national ensign and union jack are hoisted. At that moment, the PREP pennant will be hauled to the dip (lowered to the halfway point) and remain there until the ceremony is completed. While the colors are being briskly hoisted, one of several things will happen:

> The band plays the national anthem (if the ship or shore station has a band).
> The bugler plays "To the colors" (if the ship or station has a bugler assigned).

A *recording* of the national anthem is played over the 1MC.
A *recording* of "To the colors" is played over the 1MC.
Silence is observed while the colors are being hoisted (if none of the choices above are available).

During colors everyone within sight or hearing renders honors. If you are outside, stop working (or whatever else you were doing when attention was sounded), face the colors, and salute until you hear, "Carry on" (either by bugle, whistle, or voice). If you are aboard ship and cannot see the national ensign, face aft (toward the stern) because you know the colors are being hoisted there. If you are on a shore station and cannot see the national ensign, face in the direction you hear the music or whistles coming from. If you are in ranks, follow the orders of the person in charge of the formation.

During the colors ceremony, you may of course think about whatever you like, but those who have grown to love the Navy and appreciate this nation through their years of experience will tell you that it is an excellent time to reflect upon what this Navy and this nation are all about, to think about what it is that makes the United States the greatest nation on Earth. If you are unmoved by the sight of your nation's flag bursting forth on a morning breeze in all its colorful glory, it is because you have not yet traveled the world and witnessed how other people live, and it is because you have not yet experienced the pride of being a part of a crew that works hard and gives what it takes to make the U.S. Navy the best the world has ever seen.

Once the colors have been hoisted and the music has ended, "Carry on" will be signaled either by bugle, by whistle, or verbally over the announcing system. That is the signal for you to resume what you were doing before the color ceremony.

Evening Colors

Sunset is the time for evening colors in the Navy. The exact time of sunset changes (ranging anywhere from 1700 to 2100) depending upon your latitude and the time of year but will be published each day in the POD of your ship or station. Five minutes before sunset, "First call to colors" is sounded just as in the morning and, if you are aboard a ship, the PREP pennant will again be raised to the yardarm. At sunset, the colors ceremony begins when "Attention" is sounded on a bugle (in most cases a recording) or when a whistle is blown. PREP is hauled to the dip just as in the morning and the procedures for standing at attention and saluting are the same as in the morning. While the national ensign is being lowered, the bugler (or recording) will play "Retreat" (instead of "To the Colors," as is played in the morning). Another difference in the two ceremonies is that at morning colors the national ensign is hauled up smartly (quickly), while at evening colors it is hauled down slowly and ceremoniously.

Just as morning colors will often cause a great surge of pride as the national ensign makes its dramatic appearance, so evening colors is a time for quiet reflection. As you stand saluting in the evening twilight, watching your nation's colors slowly descend the mast to the haunting notes of the bugle playing "Retreat," do not be surprised if you feel a special bond with your nation and an appreciation for the sacrifices that have been made by people just like you in its defense. It is one of those moments that civilians never exactly share and which you will remember for the rest of your life whether you leave the Navy after one enlistment or remain in service for 30 years.

"Carry on" will signal the end of the ceremony just as in the morning.

Half-Masting the National Ensign

When an important official dies, it is often the practice to lower the ensign halfway down the mast or flagstaff as a means of honoring the deceased official. A list of officials so honored is contained in *U.S. Navy Regulations.*

If the ensign is flying when word is received that the ensign is to be half-masted, it should be immediately lowered. If the ensign is not already flying (for example, word is received during the night), morning colors will be held as normal except that after the ensign is hoisted all the way to the peak (top of the mast or jackstaff), it is then lowered to the half-mast position. In other words, it is not appropriate to merely hoist the colors directly to half mast; the ensign must first be two-blocked (hoisted as far as it will go), then lowered to half mast. The reverse is true in the evening. Before the national ensign can be brought down for the evening, it must first be ceremoniously two-blocked and then lowered all the way down.

On Memorial Day, the national ensign is always half-masted when first hoisted at morning colors. At 1200 (noon), a special twenty-one-gun salute is sounded: one every minute until twenty-one shots have been fired to honor those who have given their lives in the defense of our nation. At the conclusion of the firing, the national ensign is hoisted to the peak and flown that way for the remainder of the day. If a twenty-one-gun salute cannot be fired, the ensign is raised to the peak at precisely 1220.

During burial at sea, the ensign is at half mast from the beginning of the funeral service until the body is committed to the deep.

Aboard ship in port, anytime the national ensign is lowered to half mast, so is the union jack.

Shifting Colors

Another custom, far less formal than morning or evening colors, yet unique to the sea services, is what we call shifting colors. As already discussed, the national ensign is flown from the flagstaff at the stern (and the union jack is flown from the jackstaff at the bow) when a Navy ship is in port. But when a ship gets underway (no longer moored to a pier or anchored) the national ensign is flown from the gaff (a short angled pole that is higher up and toward the middle of the ship). When the last line is brought on board, or the anchor is lifted clear of the bottom of the harbor (aweigh), a long whistle blast is blown over the ship's general announcing system (1MC) by the BMOW and the national ensign is hoisted to the gaff while, simultaneously, the national ensign and union jack are taken down from the flagstaff and jackstaff respectively. This is all done smartly (quickly); the union jack and ensign should virtually disappear from the bow and stern while a different ensign leaps to the gaff. A ship that does not shift colors smartly will soon have a reputation she does not want. (*Note:* It is an old tradition of the sea that ships are referred to as "she.")

When a ship returns from sea, the exact opposite procedure takes place. The ensign is taken down from the gaff and raised along with the union jack at the stern and bow when the first mooring line is passed to the pier or the anchor touches bottom. All of this is done smartly, of course, to preserve the ship's reputation as "a taut ship" (efficient and proud).

Underway

Ships at sea do not make morning or evening colors, but they do fly an ensign at the gaff from sunrise to sunset. The union jack is not flown at sea.

When far out at sea and very few other vessels are around, the ensign is often taken down. This is done because a flag flying in the wind suffers a great deal of wear and tear, making it necessary to replace them frequently, and flying the national ensign at times when there is no one around to see it is wasteful. The ensign is flown at sea at the following times:

Getting underway and returning to port.
When joining up with other ships.

When cruising near land or in areas of high traffic.
During battle.

Dipping

A very old custom of the sea is that merchant ships "salute" naval vessels by dipping their ensigns as they pass by. When a merchant ship of any nation that is formally recognized by the United States salutes a ship of the U.S. Navy, she lowers her national colors to half mast. The Navy ship returns the salute by lowering her ensign to half mast for a few seconds, then closing it back up. The merchant vessel then raises her ensign back up.

If a naval ship is at anchor or moored to a pier and a passing merchant ship dips her ensign, the salute should be returned by lowering the national ensign halfway down the flagstaff, pausing for a moment, then returning it to the peak. The union jack is *not* dipped as well but remains two-blocked on the jackstaff.

If a naval vessel is underway and not flying the ensign (as discussed above) and a passing merchant ship dips her ensign in salute, the Navy ship will hoist her colors, dip for the salute, close them up again, and then haul them down again after a suitable interval.

Naval vessels dip the ensign only to answer a salute; they never salute first.

Other Flags

Many other flags besides the national ensign are used in the Navy. There are flags that represent numbers and the letters of the alphabet that are used by ships to communicate (see chapter 22) and there are special flags used for a variety of purposes as discussed below.

Union Jack

This replica of the blue, star-studded field of the national ensign has already been discussed in some detail because it is closely associated with the national ensign in its normal use. It is half-masted if the ensign is half-masted, but it is not dipped when the ensign is dipped. Besides being flown from the jackstaff in port from 0800 to sunset, the union jack is also hoisted at a yardarm (crossbar on a mast) when a general court-martial or a court of inquiry is in session.

Commission Pennant

The commission pennant is long and narrow, with seven white stars on a blue field and the rest of the pennant divided lengthwise, red on top and white below.

The commission pennant flies, day and night, from the time a ship is commissioned until she is decommissioned (in other words, while she is in service as a U.S. Navy ship), except when a personal flag or command pennant is flying instead (as explained below). One other exception is that a Navy hospital ship flies a Red Cross flag instead of a commission pennant.

The commission pennant is hoisted at the after truck (top of the mast closest to the rear of the vessel) or, on board a mastless ship, at the highest and most conspicuous point available.

A commission pennant is also flown from the bow of a boat if the commanding officer is embarked (riding in the boat) to make an official visit.

The commission pennant is not a personal flag, but sometimes it is regarded as the personal symbol of the commanding officer. Along with the national ensign and the union jack, it is half-masted on the death of the ship's commanding officer. When a ship is decommissioned, it is the custom for the commanding officer to keep the commission pennant.

Personal Flags

You will frequently hear the terms "flag officer" or "flag rank." These refer to admirals (or generals in other services) and have come about because officers in paygrades O-7 through O-10 in the Navy have special flags that accompany them wherever they go in an official capacity. For Navy admirals the flags are blue and have the same number of stars that these officers wear on their collars and on their shoulder boards: one star for a rear admiral (lower half), two stars for a rear admiral (upper half), three stars for a vice admiral, and four stars for an admiral.[1] These flags are flown on the fenders of their official cars, in front of their headquarters ashore, and from the main truck (top of the tallest mast) on board ships in which they are embarked.

The commission pennant and the personal flag of an admiral are never flown at the same time, so if a vice admiral boards your ship, the commission pennant is hauled down from the after truck and the admiral's three-star flag is hoisted instead at the main truck. The admiral's personal flag remains flying for as long as the admiral is officially embarked, even if he or she leaves the ship for a period of less than 72 hours.

---

1. You may also have heard of a "five-star admiral." This is a rank, called "Admiral of the Fleet" (or "Fleet Admiral"). The rank is not used anymore but was awarded to four outstanding admirals of World War II: Nimitz, King, Leahy, and Halsey.

Some very high-ranking officials, such as the Secretary of the Navy and the Chief of Naval Operations, have their own specially designed personal flags which are flown in the same manner as the starred flags of admirals.

Command Pennants

Officers who are not admirals but have command of more than one ship or a number of aircraft rate a command pennant. These pennants are flown in the same manner as an admiral's personal flags. When commanding a force, flotilla, squadron, cruiser-destroyer group, or aircraft wing, the officer rates a "broad command pennant," which is white with blue stripes along the top and bottom. An officer in command of any other unit, such as an aircraft squadron, flies a burgee command pennant, which is white with *red* stripes top and bottom.

Absence Indicators

When a commanding officer or any flag officer is temporarily absent from a ship, an absentee pennant is flown. When the admiral or unit commander whose personal flag or command pennant is flying departs the ship for a period less than 72 hours, his or her absence is indicated by hoisting the "first substitute" pennant to the starboard yardarm. The second substitute, flown from the port yardarm, indicates that the admiral's chief of staff is absent. The third substitute, also flown from the port yardarm, indicates the absence of the ship's commanding officer. (If the commanding officer is to be gone more than 72 hours, the pennant indicates the temporary absence of the executive officer.) The fourth substitute flying from the starboard yardarm means that the civil or military official whose flag is flying (such as the Secretary of Defense) is absent. It is flown from the starboard yardarm.

Church Pennant

While church services are conducted by a chaplain, the church pennant is placed on the hoist above the ensign. It is the only flag or pennant ever flown above the national ensign in this manner.

Other Flags and Pennants

Both in port and at sea, it is the custom for ships to fly other flags or pennants with special meanings. Some of these will be discussed in the chapter on communications (see chapter 22). The senior officer present afloat (SOPA) will fly a special green and white flag (which is also the "starboard" pennant used in flag communications) so that all ships in sight will know where SOPA is embarked. Ships who have earned them fly special flags representing awards for battle efficiency, the Presidential Unit Citation (PUC), Navy Unit Commendation (NUC), or Meritorious Unit Commendation (MUC) from sunrise to sunset.

Honors

Some of the special customs and ceremonies that are unique to Navy life are carried out as a way of honoring individuals or celebrating special events. Nautical and military tradition have brought about a number of ways in which we honor deceased presidents, senior officers, national holidays, foreign ambassadors, and others.

Gun Salutes

In the old days it took as long as 20 minutes to load and fire a gun, so that when a ship fired her guns in salute, thereby rendering herself temporarily powerless, it was a friendly gesture. That practice has come down through the years to be a form of honoring an individual or a nation.

The gun salutes prescribed by Navy regulations are fired only by ships and stations designated by the Secretary of the Navy. Salutes are fired at intervals of five seconds, and always in odd numbers. A salute of twenty-one guns is fired on Washington's Birthday, Memorial Day, and Independence Day, and to honor the president of the United States and heads of foreign states. Other high-ranking government officials are honored by a lesser number of guns; for example, the vice-president of the United States is honored by nineteen guns and the Under Secretary of the Navy receives a seventeen-gun salute. (See *U.S. Navy Regulations* for details.) Senior naval officers are also honored by gun salutes, and the number of shots fired depends upon their rank. Salutes for naval officers are as follows:

Admiral	17 guns
Vice admiral	15 guns
Rear admiral (upper half)	13 guns
Rear admiral (lower half)	11 guns

Officers below the rank of rear admiral (lower half) do not rate a gun salute.

Manning the Rail

In the days of sail, a custom evolved in which the crew would "man the yards" by standing evenly spaced on all the ship's yards (cross-bars on masts from which sails were suspended) and giving three cheers to honor a distinguished person. Today, the crew is stationed along the rails and superstructure of a ship when honors are rendered to the president, the head of a foreign state, or the member of a reigning royal family. Men and women so stationed do not salute.

Ships will sometimes man the rail when entering port after a long deployment to honor those who were left behind to await the ship's return.

Dressing and Full-Dressing the Ship

Commissioned ships are "dressed" on national holidays and "full-dressed" on Washington's Birthday and Independence Day. When a ship is dressed, the national ensign is flown from the flagstaff and usually from each masthead. When a ship is full-dressed, in addition to the ensigns a "rainbow" of signal flags is displayed from bow to stern over the mastheads, or as nearly so as the construction of the ship permits. Ships are only dressed and full-dressed in port, never underway and only from 0800 to sunset.

Passing Honors

When naval vessels pass close aboard (600 yards for ships, 400 yards for boats) other naval vessels with officers more senior to them in command or embarked, it is the custom to initiate passing honors. Such honors are exchanged between ships of the U.S. Navy, between ships of the Navy and the Coast Guard, and between U.S. and most foreign navy ships.

The junior vessel initiates the passing honors by passing the word "Attention to port" or "Attention to starboard" depending upon which side of the vessel the senior ship is on. All members of the crew who are outside on the weather decks and not in ranks will stop what they are doing (unless their work is safety-related and it would be dangerous for them to stop) and face the direction indicated at attention. The vessel being honored will likewise call its crew to attention. Next, the word "Hand salute" is passed on the junior vessel and the hand salute is rendered by all persons on deck. This also is returned by the senior vessel. "Two" (the command for ending the salute) is then passed by the *senior* vessel, followed by the junior. Once the vessels are clear, "Carry on" is sounded and everything returns to normal routine.

Frequently, you will find that the entire process is accomplished using whistle signals blown with a police-type whistle. It is important that you know what the procedure is and what the whistles mean so that you are not embarrassed when the occasion arises to participate in a passing honors situation. One blast indicates attention to starboard; two blasts indicate attention to port. Subsequent commands are one blast for hand salute, two blasts for ending the salute, and three blasts for carrying on.

Side Boys

Side boys are a customary part of the quarterdeck ceremonies when a person comes aboard or leaves a ship that rates special attention, such as a senior officer or a high-ranking civilian official. To carry out this honorary ceremony, the BMOW blows a special call on her or his boatswain's pipe while anywhere from two to eight side boys, depending on the rank of the officer, line up at attention on either side of the gangway (entrance/exit of the ship) forming a human corridor for the dignitary to pass through. The side boys salute on the first note of the pipe, holding their salute as the person being honored walks through the human passageway, and finishing the salute together on the last note of the boatswain's pipe.

Side boys must be particularly smart in appearance and well groomed, with brightly polished shoes and immaculate uniforms. If women are detailed as side boys they are still referred to by the traditional term "side *boys.*"

135

Figure 6.9. Side boys render honors to an admiral.

PHI Denis C. Dube

Other Shipboard Customs

Ships have been plying the waters of the world for many centuries and this long history has resulted in many unique customs. By observing these special customs, you will be forming a special link with Sailors from the past and keeping alive traditions that, in some cases, are thousands of years old.

The Bridge

When a ship is underway, the area known as the bridge serves as the control point for the vessel. A team of people will always be on watch serving the ship's special needs. The OOD heads that team and, serving as the captain's direct representative, is responsible for the safe navigation of the vessel and for carrying out the ship's routine. He or she is assisted by a team of watchstanders, who carry out a number of functions such as steering the ship and making announcements on the general announcing (1MC) system.

There is a formality associated with the bridge, and many ships require all nonwatch personnel to request permission from the OOD to come on the bridge, accompanying their request with a salute. This

is more than a mere tradition since it allows the OOD to control access to the bridge, ensuring that the watch team is not inhibited in carrying out its important duties by having too many people in the way. Another custom that serves a useful purpose is the calling out "Captain is on the bridge" by the first person to see the commanding officer enter the bridge area. This alerts the OOD and the other watchstanders to the captain's presence, which is important since it is the OOD's responsibility to report significant happenings to the captain and since the captain's authority supersedes that of the OOD when she or he is on the bridge.

The Quarterdeck

The quarterdeck in many ways replaces the bridge as the control point of the ship when the ship is not underway. It has both functional and ceremonial purposes and, just like the bridge, is manned by a watch team. The OOD shifts his or her watch from the bridge to the quarterdeck once the ship enters port and, until the ship gets underway again, the ship's routine is run from there. The location of the quarterdeck will vary according to the type of ship and, because the quarterdeck also normally serves as the point of entry and exiting for the ship, it may actually move to different locations on board the same ship, depending upon which side is facing the pier or whether or not the ship is anchored and using boats.

Frequently the quarterdeck is marked off by appropriate lines, deck markings, decorative cartridge cases, or fancy work (nautical decorations made from pieces of line). The quarterdeck is always kept particularly clean and shipshape.

Watchstanders on the quarterdeck must be in the uniform of the day and present a smart and military appearance at all times. Personnel not on watch should avoid the quarterdeck unless their work requires them to be in that area.

Larger vessels, such as aircraft carriers, may have two or more entry and exit points for the ship. Only *one* is designated as the quarterdeck, however.

Boarding and Departing the Ship

The officer of the deck in port, or the OOD's assistant—known as the junior officer of the deck (JOOD)—will meet all persons leaving or boarding the ship. There are specific procedures to be followed by Navy personnel when boarding or departing and, to avoid serious embarrassment, you must learn them.

Because of security considerations, you will nearly always be expected to show your ID card to the OOD (or her or his representative) whenever you board a naval vessel, whether you are a member of the crew or not.

Boarding

If the ship is alongside a pier, you will use a "brow" (a walkway that bridges the gap between the pier and the ship) to come aboard. If the ship is anchored out in the water, you will, of course, ride in a boat to get to the ship, and to get from the water up to the ship's main deck you will use an "accommodation ladder" (a kind of stairwell that has been rigged over the side of the ship). The opening in the ship's rail, where you actually board the ship (whether you are using a brow or an accommodation ladder), is called the "gangway." At the gangway, you should turn and face aft (where the national ensign is flying from the jackstaff), come to attention, and smartly salute if the ensign is flying. The OOD will return your salute to the national ensign. On some larger ships, you will not be able to actually *see* the national ensign but you should salute anyway. You will know whether it is flying or not by the time of day. If it is after 0800 and before sunset, you will know that the ensign is flying. After you have smartly saluted the national ensign, turn and face the OOD (or her or his representative), salute, and say, "I request permission to come aboard, ma'am" (or "sir"). The OOD will return your salute and say, "Very well," or "Permission granted," and you should proceed. (*Note:* These salutes take place no matter what the ranks or rates of the individuals involved. If the OOD is a chief petty officer and the boarding individual is a commander, the latter will still salute the CPO, who, as OOD, represents the captain.)

If you are not in uniform, you should not salute but still face aft at attention to honor the national ensign and then, still at attention, face the OOD and request permission to come aboard.

If you are not a member of the crew of the ship you are boarding, you should state the reason for your visit when requesting permission to come aboard.

Departing

The procedure for leaving a ship is much the same as boarding, except that the steps are reversed. Step up to the vicinity of the gangway, salute the OOD, and say, "I request permission to leave the ship, sir" (or "ma'am"). When the OOD says, "Very well," or "Permission granted," and returns your salute, drop your salute and step to the gangway. If the ensign is flying, face aft, salute smartly, and leave.

Crossing Nests

Destroyers and smaller ships sometimes tie up in nests (clusters) alongside a tender or pier, and you may have to cross one or more ships to get to your own. The usual quarterdeck procedure described for boarding and leaving is modified somewhat in this case. When you board the inboard ship, salute the colors and the quarterdeck, and, addressing the OOD, say, "I request permission to cross, ma'am" (or "sir"). When the OOD says, "Very well," or "Permission granted," and returns your salute, drop your salute and head across the ship to the brow that leads to the next ship in the nest. It is not necessary to salute the colors on leaving, but be sure to do so when boarding the next ship in the nest. Repeat this procedure on each ship until you reach your own.

Officers' and CPO Country

The area on board ship where officers eat (the wardroom) and sleep (staterooms), as well as the halls (passageways) surrounding these areas, is known as "officers' country." Correspondingly, the area where chief petty officers eat and sleep is known as "CPO country."

You should avoid these areas unless you are on official business. If your duties require you to enter any of these spaces, you should knock before entering and remove your hat. Watchstanders wearing a duty belt or sidearm remain covered, unless a meal is in progress.

Enlisted Mess Deck
The eating area for enlisted personnel is called the mess deck and is treated with the same courtesy as the wardroom. Always uncover when on or crossing mess decks, even if you are on watch and wearing the duty belt.

Sick Bay
In a ship, that area that functions as a hospital or medical clinic is known as the sick bay. In the days of sailing ships, it was customary to uncover when entering sick bay, out of respect to the dying and dead. Though modern medicine has transformed the sick bay into a place where people are usually healed and cured, the custom remains. In areas where patients are resting, you should avoid making noise, just as you would in any hospital ward.

Divine Services
When divine services are held on board, the church pennant is flown, and word is passed that services are being held in a certain space of the ship and to maintain quiet about the decks. A person entering the area where services are held uncovers unless the services are for a religion that requires the head to be covered during worship.

Boat Etiquette

A ship is judged, among other things, by her boats and their crews. Whether in utilities or dress blues, crews should observe the courtesies and procedures that build and maintain their ship's reputation. Boats play an important part in naval ceremonies, and each crewmember ought to know what is expected of the boat and of him or her.

Some boats will have only an enlisted man called a "coxswain" (pronounced "cock-sun") in charge, while others will have a "boat officer" specifically assigned to be responsible for boat and passenger safety.

Boarding and Departing
The basic rule in Navy manners, as in civilian life, is to make way for a senior quickly, quietly, and without confusion. The procedure for

entering boats and vehicles is *seniors in last and out first*. The idea is that the captain should not have to wait in a boat for anyone. Seniors get out first because normally their business is more important and pressing than that of the men and women of lesser rank.

If the boat is clearly divided into two sections (forward and aft), enlisted Sailors should sit in the forward section and officers in the after section. In any case, the rule is that *seniors take the seats farthest aft*.

The boat coxswain salutes all officers boarding and leaving the boat. Enlisted personnel seated well forward in a large boat do not rise and salute when officers enter or leave. Enlisted personnel in the after section of a boat always rise and salute when a commissioned officer enters or leaves.

Saluting

Boats exchange salutes when passing, as enlisted personnel and officers do when passing on shore. It is not the size or type of boat that determines seniority, but who is embarked; a small whaleboat carrying a commander is senior to a large boat with only an ensign aboard.

When one boat passes another, the coxswain and the boat officer (if there is one embarked) render the hand salute. Others in the boat stand or sit at attention. If standing, they face the boat being saluted; if seated, they sit at attention but do not turn toward the passing boat. The senior officer in the boat also salutes, while remaining seated, if he or she is visible outboard.

It is usually possible to tell by the uniform of the passenger officer or the flag flown which boat is senior, but if in doubt, *salute*.

If a boat is carrying an officer or official for whom a salute is being fired, the engine is slowed and the clutch disengaged after the first gun is fired, and the person honored rises, if safety permits. If personnel are working in a boat, they should not stop to salute.

Other Courtesies

Attention on Deck

Whenever important visitors, the captain, or other senior officers approach an area or enter a compartment (room) where there is a gathering of personnel, the first person to see them coming should call out "Attention on deck." All present should immediately come to attention and remain that way until the senior person present gives the command "Carry on." This courtesy applies (even the use of the word "deck") both on and off ships.

Gangway

The command "Gangway!" should be given by anyone who observes an officer approaching where passage is blocked. Do not wait for someone else to call it out, even if you are not the most senior person present. The first person to see the approaching officer should call out "Gangway," and everyone present should move out of the officer's way.

Enlisted personnel do not clear a passage for themselves or other enlisted crewmembers in this way, but should say "Coming through" instead. "Make a hole" is *not* the correct term to use, although you will sometimes hear it being used (incorrectly).

By Your Leave

Do not overtake and pass an officer without permission except in an emergency. When it is necessary to walk past an officer, overtake him or her on his or her left side, salute when you are abreast, and ask, "By your leave, sir [or "ma'am"]?" When the officer returns the salute and replies, "Very well," drop your salute and continue past.

141

Accompanying a Senior

When walking with a senior, always walk on that person's left, that is, with the senior on your right.

7 Military Fundamentals

As an American Bluejacket, you are, of course, a Sailor, and that requires you to know and do many things differently from civilian life. But you are also a member of the armed forces and this requires a certain amount of *military* knowledge as well.

Even though you may never see a parade field again after you leave boot camp, it is important to know the fundamentals of military drill. Long-distance marching in the Navy may be rare, but it is not uncommon to see a division formed up in ranks for morning quarters aboard a destroyer or to see thousands of Sailors in military formation covering the flight deck of an aircraft carrier during a personnel inspection. Military drill is an efficient way to keep groups of people together in an orderly fashion, it is an effective method of promoting discipline, and it provides experience in giving and following commands.

We often associate guard duty with soldiers, yet people and equipment must be safeguarded in the Navy as well. You may find yourself standing sentry duty on a pier in a foreign country or walking the rounds on your ship as part of a security patrol.

As part of your military duties, you may be required to carry and perhaps even use a firearm. You will, of course, receive practical training in the use of weapons before you will be expected to carry one, but certain universal fundamentals will help to prepare you.

Military Drill

Besides the benefits already mentioned, military drill encourages teamwork, instills habits of precision and instantaneous response, and improves bearing and demeanor.

Formations
Various kinds of formations are used in different parts of the Navy. Depending upon whether you are assigned to a ship, a training facility, a Navy construction battalion, or some other naval activity, you

PHC Terry C. Mitchell

Figure 7.1. Sailors standing in a military formation at parade rest.

will encounter terms like "squad," "detail," "platoon," "section,"
"company," and "division," all referring to military formations. You
will see military formations used for morning quarters, for personnel
inspections, to welcome dignitaries, or for many other reasons. But
no matter what the occasion and no matter what the units are called,
some things are common to all military formations.

The two basic structures of all military formations are "ranks"
(also called "lines"), where people are lined up side by side—in other
words, everyone is standing uniformly next to one another—and
"files" (also called "columns"), where people are uniformly lined up
one behind the other. There can be a single rank (or line) or a single
file (or column), or the two can be combined. Anytime you have
more than one rank, you automatically have formed columns (and
vice versa).

FRONT

_ _ _ _ _ _ _ _ _ _ _ _

Rank

I I I I I I I I I I I FRONT

File

FRONT

_ _ _ _ _ _ _ _ _ _ _ RANK
_ _ _ _ _ _ _ _ _ _ _ RANK
_ _ _ _ _ _ _ _ _ _ _ RANK

F F F F F F F F F F F
I I I I I I I I I I I
L L L L L L L L L L L
E E E E E E E E E E E

In a formation with several ranks and files, the front rank is referred to as simply the front or first rank. Subsequent ranks are called the second rank, third rank, and so on.

There are a number of other terms associated with formations that you should learn.

Interval

The space between individuals, from shoulder to shoulder, who are standing in a rank is called the interval. "Normal interval" is one arm's length.

Close Interval

This is used when space is limited and is determined by the individuals in the rank placing their left hand on their hip, fingertips down.

Distance

The space between individuals in a file (or column), measuring approximately 40 inches between the chest of one person and the back of the one directly in front.

Guide

In a formation, someone must serve as the reference point on which the others align themselves. This person is called "the guide." In a single file, the guide must be the person in the very front because it would be impossible for you to guide on an individual behind you (unless you have the proverbial "eyes in back of your head "). In a single rank, the guide is *usually* (though not always) on the extreme right of the line. In a formation with several ranks and files, the guide is usually the person on the extreme right of the front rank.

Commands

The difference between a command and an order is in timing. Both must be carried out if given by a superior in a military organization, but a command is to be carried out at a precise moment, whereas an order need not be instantaneously executed. For example, if your recruit division commander in boot camp calls "Attention on deck" because the base commander has just entered the auditorium to deliver an address, this is a *command* and you must jump to your feet and assume the position of attention the instant you hear the words. If you are standing watch as a messenger aboard ship and the OOD tells you to sweep down the quarterdeck, this is an *order* and, while you certainly would not dawdle in carrying out the OOD's instructions, you would not be expected to begin sweeping instantaneously.

In military drill, commands are usually given in two parts. The first part is the "preparatory command," which serves to warn you what is coming so that when you hear the second part, known as the "command of execution," you will be able to carry it out instantaneously. No two military drill commands begin with the same preparatory command, so once you have learned the various commands you will know what is coming every time you hear a preparatory command. For example, the command to get the members of a squad moving along together is "Forward, march." The word "forward" is the preparatory command and, because this command is the only one that begins with the word "forward," all members of the squad know that the next word they hear will be the command of execution "march," and they will all begin marching the instant they hear it. This method ensures the precision that is essential in military drill.

Some commands have a "secondary command" that follows on to complete a move. For example, when you are told to salute while in formation, you will execute the hand salute and hold it until the secondary command "two" is given. On the command "two," everyone in the formation will end the salute together.

When *giving* military drill commands, you should always speak in a firm tone loud enough to be heard by everyone under your command. You should also develop the habit of giving the preparatory command, pausing briefly to allow everyone time to anticipate what is coming, and then giving the command of execution with emphasis. You will quickly pick up this technique once you hear an experienced drill instructor giving commands.

Sometimes the preparatory command will be preceded by the name or title of the group concerned, for example, "First Division" or "Squad" or "Platoon." This is especially important for avoiding confusion if there are a number of groups in the vicinity.

Some military drill commands, such as "Fall in" and "At ease," cannot be carried out with the same precision that is normally expected. These commands do not have separate preparatory and execution commands and are simply given as one command.

If the person calling the commands gives a preparatory command and then decides to call back or revoke that command, he or she may cancel it by saying "As you were." For example, "Second Squad, FORWARD . . . As you were." The members of second squad would do nothing in this case, remaining as they were before the command began.

Most of the military drill commands you will encounter in the Navy are listed and explained below. In the section below, military drill commands will be indicated by **bold** letters. Preparatory commands will be indicated by *italics* and commands of execution by UPPERCASE LETTERS. For example, "*Forward* . . . MARCH."

Forming Up

A number of commands are associated with creating a formation.

"Fall in." (Given simply as one command: "FALL IN.") All personnel will immediately line up in the appropriate ranks and files using the standards of distance and interval discussed above.

"Dress right/left." (Given as "*Dress right* . . . DRESS" or "*Dress left* . . . DRESS".) If dressing to the right, the person on the right of each rank is the guide. The guide will extend his or her left arm straight out, parallel to the deck (floor), and the person to his or her left will move until the guide's fingertips are barely touching his or her shoulder. That second person will also extend his or her left arm to establish the interval for the next person in the rank, and so on. The last person in the rank will not extend her or his arm since there will be no one there to line up on it. The guide will look straight ahead, but everyone else in the rank will turn her or his head smartly to the right. If dressing to the left, the guide will be on the left, and everyone but the guide will look to the left, but it is still the left arm that is extended.

If there is not enough room for everyone to stand at a normal (arm's length) interval, a close interval may be ordered. (Given as "*At close interval, dress right* . . . DRESS.") In this case, your left hand is placed on your left hip, fingers pointed down, and the person next to you will use your elbow instead of your fingertips as the measure of interval.

At the command "*Ready* . . . FRONT," everyone smartly drops their arms to their sides and snaps their heads to the front, leaving them in the position of attention (see below).

Disbanding the Formation

Of the two methods of breaking up a formation, one is temporary and the other permanent.

"Fall out." (Given simply as "FALL OUT.") When this command is given, the formation is temporarily disbanded and everyone breaks ranks but remains nearby. When the command "FALL IN" is given, everyone should return to their original positions in the formation and stand at attention.

"Dismissed." (Given as "DISMISSED.") This signals the end of the formation. Everyone will break ranks and go about their business.

Basic Commands

Once the formation is set up, you will need to know a number of basic commands.

"Attention." (Given as "*A-ten* . . . SHUN" or "*A-ten* . . . HUT.") Your heels are brought together (smartly and audibly), and your feet are turned out to form an angle of 45 degrees, with hips level and body erect. Your weight rests equally on the heels and balls of your feet. Your shoulders are squared, chest arched, arms hanging down without stiffness so that the thumbs are along the seams of the trousers or skirt, palms and fingers relaxed. Draw your chin in and keep your head straight. Do not look around; keep your head still and your eyes looking straight ahead.

"Parade rest." (Given as "*Parade* . . . REST.") Move the left foot smartly 12 inches to the left of the right foot. At the same time, clasp the hands behind the back, palms to the rear, the right hand inside the left with thumbs interlocking. Despite the word "rest," you should be very still and silent with your eyes looking straight ahead. The only command that may be given after "Parade rest" is "Attention."

"At ease." (Given as "AT EASE.") You may move any part of your body (such as stretching or looking about) except your right foot (this marks your place in the formation) and your mouth (meaning that you are not permitted to talk).

"Rest." (Given as "REST.") The same as "At ease" except that you may also talk.

"Hand salute." (Given as "*Hand* . . . SALUTE.") At the command "SALUTE," raise the right hand smartly in the hand salute. Hold the salute until you hear the follow-on command "TWO," then drop your arm to its normal attention position by your side in one brisk movement.

Facing Movements

Facing movements are used to turn everyone in the formation to face in a different direction.

"Right/left face." (Given as "*Right* . . . FACE" or "*Left* . . . FACE.") For a right facing movement, on the command "face," slightly raise the left heel and right toe. Face right (90 degrees), turning on the right heel, putting pressure on the ball of the left foot and holding the right leg straight. Then place the left foot smartly beside the right one so that you are standing at attention again. The exact opposite will cause you to execute a left face.

"About face." (Given as "*About* . . . FACE.") This command is used when the person in charge of the formation wants everyone to turn and face in the exact opposite direction. At the command "face," place the toe of the right foot about half a foot to the rear and slightly to the left of the left heel without moving the left foot. Put the weight of the body mainly on the heel of the left foot, left leg straight. Then pivot to the rear, moving to the right on the left heel and on the ball of the right foot. Place the right heel beside the left to complete the movement, ending up at attention. Remember, you always turn to the right when executing an about face, never to the left.

Marching Commands

Military formations are sometimes moved, either to get from one place to another or to put on a parade or what is called a "pass in review."

It will help to remember that all movements except "Right step" begin with the left foot.

"Forward, march." (Given as "*Forward* . . . MARCH.") At the preparatory command "Forward," shift the weight of your body to the right leg. At the command of execution "march," step off smartly with the left foot and continue marching with 30-inch steps taken straight forward without stiffness or exaggeration. Swing the arms

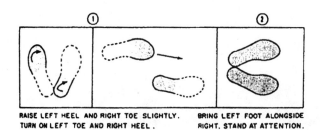

RAISE LEFT HEEL AND RIGHT TOE SLIGHTLY.
TURN ON LEFT TOE AND RIGHT HEEL.

BRING LEFT FOOT ALONGSIDE
RIGHT. STAND AT ATTENTION.

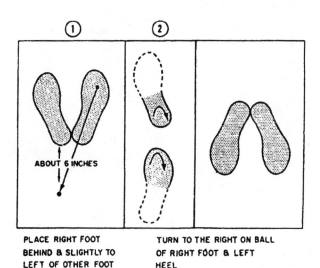

PLACE RIGHT FOOT
BEHIND & SLIGHTLY TO
LEFT OF OTHER FOOT

TURN TO THE RIGHT ON BALL
OF RIGHT FOOT & LEFT
HEEL

Figure 7.2a–b. a. Right face. b. About face.

easily in their natural arcs about six inches straight to the front and three inches to the rear of the body. Continue marching straight ahead until another command is given.

"Halt." When the person in charge wants to stop the formation from marching ahead, she or he will use the "Halt" command. The preparatory command used with "Halt" is the name of the formation, for example, squad, platoon, detail, company, or battalion. If you were in charge of a squad and you wanted them to stop marching, you would give the command "*Squad . . .* HALT." You could give the command of execution ("halt") as either foot struck the ground. If you gave it on the left foot, each squad member would take one more step with the right foot and then bring up the left foot to stop alongside the

PHI Alexander Hicks

right foot so that all motion would stop and everyone would be standing at attention.

"**Half step.**" (Given as "*Half-step* . . . MARCH.") Begin taking steps of 15 inches instead of the normal 30 inches. To resume the full step from half step, the command is "*Forward* . . . MARCH."

"**Right step.**" (Given as "*Right-step* . . . MARCH.") At the command "march," move your right foot 12 inches to the right. Then place the left foot beside the right, keeping your left knee straight. "Right step" is ordered from a halt and for short distances only.

"**Left step.**" (Given as "*Left-step* . . . MARCH.") At the command "march," move your left foot 12 inches to the left. Then place your right foot beside the left, keeping your right knee straight. "Left step" is ordered from a halt and for short distances only.

"**Back step.**" (Given as "*Back-step* . . . MARCH.") At the command "march," take steps of 15 inches straight to the rear. The back step is used for short distances only.

Flanking movements. (Given as "*By the right/left flank* . . . MARCH.") When it is desired for the whole formation to change direction by everyone simultaneously facing in a different direction while marching, the flanking commands are used. For a right flanking movement, the command "march" will be given when your right foot hits the ground. You should then take another step with your left foot. With your left foot extended out in front of your right, you should pivot on both feet, causing your whole body to turn 90 degrees to the right. Step off with your left foot as soon as you are turned, and continue marching normally in the new direction. Everyone who was in the right file before the command was given will end up in the front rank after the command is executed, and everyone who was in the rear rank before the command will end up in the right file afterwards.

A left flanking movement is executed in the same but opposite manner.

Reversing direction. (Given as "*To the rear* . . . MARCH.") The command "march" will be given as the right foot strikes the ground. You should take another step with your left foot, then turn to the right all the way about on the balls of both feet and then step off with the left foot.

Figure 7.3. Navy and Marine honor guard members at the commissioning ceremony of USS *Abraham Lincoln* (CVN 72).

"Route step." (Given as *"Route-step . . .* MARCH.*"*) At the command "march," adopt an easy natural stride; there is no requirement to keep step or to maintain silence. In other words, walk normally while staying with your unit.

Sentry Duty

One of the first military duties you will perform as a new recruit is a sentry or security watch. As such, you will be charged with the responsibility for guarding against sabotage, theft, or damage by storm or fire. Such duties will not end with boot camp. Unless your time in the Navy is very unusual, you will be called upon for guard duty, fire watches, barracks watches, pier sentry, and other similar military duties. You may be assigned to patrol an area on foot or in a vehicle, to guard a specific area for a specified period, or merely be available to answer a phone, check people in and out, turn lights off and on, and preserve order and cleanliness.

Requirements for standing sentry duty are the same as those for all watches: keep alert, attend to duty, report all violations, preserve order, and remain on watch until properly relieved. Your immediate superior may be called the "petty officer of the guard," the "petty officer of the watch," the "officer of the deck," the "command duty officer," or some other title. (For the purposes of this discussion, we will refer to your immediate superior as the petty officer of the watch.) Whatever your superior is called, you must take your orders from that person. When you are detailed to a sentry watch, you will conduct yourself according to both special and general orders.

Special orders apply to a particular watch and will be rather specific. These orders will be passed on and explained to you before you assume the watch. You may receive these orders directly from the petty officer of the guard, or you may receive them from the sentry you are relieving.

The eleven general orders are the same throughout the Navy (and the other armed forces for that matter) and never change. You will—on any watch or duty, now and in the future—be responsible for carrying them out, even if no one has explained them to you or reminded you of them. For that reason, you must memorize these eleven general orders and be prepared to recite all or any of them whenever called upon to do so. Because these general orders were written for all the armed forces, you will see some terminology in them that may be unfamiliar. Each of the general orders is listed and briefly explained below.

The General Orders of a Sentry

1. To take charge of this post and all government property in view.

When you are a sentry, you are "in charge." This means that no one—no matter what their rank or position—may overrule your authority in carrying out your orders. The only way that you may be exempted from carrying out your orders is if your orders are changed by your superior. For example, if your orders are to allow no one to enter a fenced-in compound, you must prevent everyone from entering, even if an admiral tells you it is all right for him or her to enter. The petty officer of the watch (or whomever is your immediate superior) may modify your orders to allow the admiral to enter, but without that authorization you must keep the admiral out. Situations such as this will not often—if ever—occur, but it is important that you understand the principles involved.

It is also your responsibility to know the limits of your post. This information will be conveyed to you among your special orders. You must also treat all government property that you can see as though it were your own, even if it is not technically part of your assigned post.

2. To walk my post in a military manner, keeping always on the alert and observing everything that takes place within sight or hearing.

"Keep your eyes peeled," as the expression goes. Be vigilant by looking around at all times. Do not be tempted to hide from the rain or cold in poor weather. If you see or hear anything unusual, investigate it.

3. To report all violations of orders I am instructed to enforce.

If, for example, someone is climbing a fence near your post, you must report it, even if the offender stops climbing and runs away after your challenge. In this case, even though it appears that the threat to security is over, there is no way for you to know whether this violator is the only one involved. And even though the climber may have just been seeking a shortcut back to her or his ship, you cannot be certain that there is not something more sinister involved. Let your superiors make the judgment calls; your job is to report what happens on or near your post.

4. To repeat all calls from posts more distant from the guardhouse than my own.

In these days of modern communications, sentries will probably have telephones or radios at their disposal with which to make their reports. But if they do not, or if there is a power failure or some other reason that the modern equipment fails, the age-old practice of relaying the word is very important.

The term "guardhouse" in this general order refers to the command post or point of control for the watches. It might be the quarterdeck on board ship or a tent in the field.

5. To quit my post only when properly relieved.

It should be fairly obvious that you should not leave your post until someone has come to take your place or until the petty officer of the guard has told you that the watch is no longer necessary. If the person relieving you is late, report it to the petty officer of the watch but do *not* quit your post. If you become ill and can no longer stand your watch, notify the petty officer of the watch and he or she will provide you a proper relief.

6. To receive, obey, and pass on to the sentry who relieves me all orders from the commanding officer, command duty officer, officer of the deck, and officers and petty officers of the watch.

It is essential that you receive and obey all of the special orders that apply to your watch. It is also essential that you pass these orders on to your relief.

7. To talk to no one except in the line of duty.

Having conversations about matters not pertaining to your duty is distracting and must be avoided. If someone tries to engage you in casual conversation while you are standing your watch, it is your responsibility to inform them courteously that you are on duty and cannot talk with them.

8. To give the alarm in case of fire or disorder.

While this is rather straightforward and obvious, keep in mind that a fire or disorder of some kind might be a deliberate distraction to keep you from observing some other disorderly or subversive activity. If you are certain that a fire is not meant to be a distraction, you should fight the fire if you have the means to do so. Remember, however, that your first responsibility is to *report* whatever is amiss.

9. To call the petty officer of the watch in any case not covered by instructions.

The rule here is "When in doubt, ask." If you are not sure what you are supposed to do in a particular situation, it is better to ask for clarification than to make an assumption or to guess.

10. To salute all officers, and all colors and standards not cased.

Even though you are in charge of your post and everyone, including officers, must obey your instructions insofar as they pertain to your duties, you must still extend the appropriate military courtesies. (Refer to chapter 6 for instructions on saluting if armed.)

Both terms, "colors" and "standards," refer to the national ensign. The national ensign may be referred to as "the colors" when it is fixed to a staff, mast, or pike (e.g., when flown from a flagstaff or carried in a parade). When it is fixed to a vehicle it is often called "the national standard."

A flag is considered "cased" when it is furled and placed in a protective covering.

If your duties allow, you should take part in morning or evening colors ceremonies, but do not sacrifice your vigilance by doing so. For example, if your assignment requires that you watch a certain area and the national ensign is being hoisted in a different direction, you should stand at attention and salute but do not face the colors; keep looking in the direction you are supposed to be watching.

11. To be especially watchful at night, and during the time for challenging, to challenge all persons on or near my post, and to allow no one to pass without proper authority.

Challenging persons while you are on sentry duty is accomplished by a mix of custom and common sense. When a person or party approaches your post, you should challenge them at a distance that is sufficient for you to react if they turn out to have hostile intentions. You should say in a firm voice, loud enough to be easily heard, "Halt! Who goes there?" (or "Who is there?"). Once the person answers, you should then say "Advance to be recognized." If you are challenging a group of people, you should say, "Advance *one* to be recognized." If you have identified the person or persons approaching, permit them to pass. If you are not satisfied with that person's identification, you must detain the person and call the petty officer of the watch.

When two or more individuals approach from different directions at the same time, challenge each in turn and require each to halt until told to proceed.

Use of Weapons

Standing sentry duty will usually mean that you are armed. In addition to sentry watches, other duties may require you to be armed, such as when carrying official mail, guarding prisoners, and, sometimes, when part of a shore patrol party. Armed personnel are authorized to fire their weapons only under the following conditions:

> To protect their own lives or the life of another person where no other means of defense will work.
> To prevent the escape of a dangerous prisoner.
> To prevent sabotage, arson, or other crimes against the government after all other means have failed.

No one is to be assigned to any duty requiring the use of a weapon until he or she has been properly trained in its use, including all safety precautions.

Whenever you are armed, always treat your weapon with the utmost respect. (See chapter 15 for guidance in the proper handling of weapons.)

Make certain that you know the special orders of your watch pertaining to weapons. In some situations, your orders will be to carry your weapon with a clip or magazine of ammunition inserted but no round (bullet) in the chamber; in others you will be expected to carry your clips or magazines in a pouch on your belt and only insert them when imminent danger threatens.

When being relieved of the watch and your orders are to carry a loaded weapon, you should remove the clip or magazine from the weapon, point it in a safe direction, and check the chamber, making sure there are no rounds present. Release the slide, and with the weapon still pointed in a safe direction, let the hammer go home (return it to the uncocked position). Your relief should repeat this procedure after you have turned the weapon over to her or him.

Physical Fitness

The need for a Sailor to be physically fit goes well beyond health and appearance. While both of these things are important, a Sailor's strength and endurance can be the deciding factors in saving a ship from sinking or an aircraft from going down. Even if your main duties do not routinely entail much physical exertion, the time may come when your ability to shore up a collapsing bulkhead may make the difference in keeping your ship afloat, or a shipmate may live or die depending on your ability to continue holding a line.

For these reasons the Navy places great emphasis on physical fitness, and because an emergency is not the time to find out if you are up to challenge, the Navy requires all Sailors to periodically test their

fitness. Twice a year, you will be given a physical fitness assessment
(PFA) that consists of several parts. To begin with, you will be given
a Physical Activity Risk Factor Screening Questionnaire, and it is
very important that you answer all the questions truthfully. The next
part of the assessment consists of a Body Composition Assessment
which will determine, through measurements, whether your weight
is acceptable or needs adjustment. The last part of the assessment is
the Physical Readiness Test (PRT). This consists of a flexibility component (sit-reach), a muscular strength and endurance component
(pushups and curl-ups), and an aerobic capacity component (either a
mile-and-a-half run, a 500-yard swim, or a 450-meter swim). The
PFA is organized and conducted by the Command Fitness Leader
(CFL) who may or may not have a number of assistants, depending
upon the size of your command.

The standards you will be expected to meet will depend upon your
age and gender, and your assessment for each segment will be evaluated as low, medium, or high within the performance categories
of satisfactory, good, excellent, and outstanding. If you do not meet
the minimum standards, you will be required to participate in a com-
mand-directed Fitness Enhancement Program, which will include
monitored training, monthly fitness assessments, and, if warranted,
nutrition and weight-management counseling. Should you fail the
PRT three times in four years, you will be ineligible for advancement
in rate until you are able to pass it.

While your command is required to aggressively integrate physical readiness activities into the workweek while meeting mission and
operational requirements, it is also your responsibility to maintain
a lifestyle that promotes optimal health and physical readiness. At a
minimum, you should exercise at least three times a week and ensure
that these exercise periods include at least 20-30 minutes of brisk aerobic activity, a strength and flexibility component, and warm-up and
cool-down periods. At shore stations, there often are many fitness
resources available. Take advantage of them when you can. Staying
fit at sea is more challenging, depending on the size of ship you are
serving in, but it is imperative that you do what you can, when you
can, to stay fit. The stakes are too high to do otherwise.

For more information about the Navy's physical requirements, see
the latest version of OPNAVINST 6110.1 or talk to your CFL.

8 Security

The word *security,* as it is used in the Navy, can mean many things. Its most common usage refers to the safeguarding of classified information, but it can also mean the protection of ships and stations and all the people and equipment associated with them.

Security of Information

Because the safety of the United States and the success of naval operations depend greatly on the protection of classified information, it is important that you understand what classified information is, who may have access to it, and some rules and guidance for safeguarding it.

Security Classification
Information is classified when national security is at stake. It is assigned a classification designation, which tells you how much protection it requires. There are three classification designations, each of which indicates the anticipated degree of damage to national security that could result from unauthorized disclosure:

Top secret	Exceptionally grave damage
Secret	Serious damage
Confidential	Damage

All classified material—such as publications, software, equipment, or films—must be plainly marked or stamped with the appropriate classification designation. Following the classification, some material may have additional markings that signal extra precautions in handling. For example, "restricted data" means that the material pertains to nuclear weapons or power and cannot be released to anyone who is not a U.S. citizen.

Unauthorized disclosure, or "compromise," means that classified information has been exposed to a person not authorized to see it.

There is another category of government information, "for official use only" (FOUO). This is not classified information because it does not involve national security, but it is information that could be damaging in other ways and cannot, therefore, be divulged to everyone. Results of investigations, examination questions, bids on contracts, and so on, are "privileged information" and are kept from general knowledge under the designation FOUO.

Security Clearance

Before a person is allowed to have access to classified information, he or she must have a security clearance. You will be assigned a security clearance based upon how much classified material you will need to work with in order to do your job. If you have a need to work with top-secret material, you must first obtain a top-secret clearance. If all you will need to see is confidential information, you will be assigned a confidential clearance.

The standards for clearance are listed in the *Information and Personnel Security Program Regulation* (OPNAVINST 5510.1) or *Security Manual,* as it is commonly called. In general you must be trustworthy, of reliable character, and able to show discretion and good judgment. A person may be loyal to his or her country but unable to meet the standards for a position of trust and confidence. Conduct such as drug abuse, excessive drinking, and financial irresponsibility can lead to denial of clearance. This could cost a promotion, cause a rate conversion, or lead to separation from military service. A clearance may be denied or revoked because of mental or emotional condition, general disciplinary causes, AWOL (absent without leave), falsification of official documents, or disregard for public laws or Navy regulations.

Investigations

Before you can be granted a security clearance, an investigation is conducted into your background to make certain that you can be trusted with classified information. Government agents will look into your past records and question people who have known you. This process takes a while, so you may be given an "interim" clearance based upon some preliminary investigating before your "final" clearance comes through. The word "final" in this case means that the routine investigating is over and that you have been granted the clearance you need. It is not "final" in the sense that it cannot be taken away. Should you involve yourself in any of the disqualifying activities mentioned above (such as drug use or financial irresponsibility) your clearance may be revoked.

Access and Need to Know

Security clearances are granted only when access to classified material is necessary to perform official duties and only at the appropriate level. If your job requires you to see confidential material but not secret or top secret, you will only receive a confidential clearance. This is no reflection on you or the level of trust the government places in you. If you are ever denied the access you *need,* that is a cause for concern, but as long you receive the level of clearance required for the performance of your assigned duties, you should be satisfied.

It is important to understand the concept of "need to know." Just because you may have a secret clearance, that does *not* give you access to *all* secret material. Your secret clearance allows you to see all the secret material you need to know in order to do your job, but it does not entitle you to see information classified at that level in other locations or departments not related to your job. If circumstances change and your duties no longer require access, or require a lower level of access, your security clearance will be administratively withdrawn or lowered without prejudicing your future eligibility. Commanding officers may reinstate or adjust your security clearance as the need arises.

Safeguarding Classified Information

Classified information or material is discussed, used, or stored only where adequate security measures are in effect. When removed from storage for use, it must be kept under the continuous observation of a cleared person. It is never left unattended.

You are responsible for protecting any classified information you know or control. Before giving another person access to that information, it is your responsibility to determine that the person has the proper clearance and a need to know. If you are uncertain whether someone has the proper clearance and a need to know, find out before you allow them access. Never tell someone something classified just because they are curious, even if they have the proper clearance. Remember, there are *two* requirements for someone to have access to classified material: they must have the proper clearance and they must have an official need to know the information.

Voice Communications
Some radio circuits and telephones in the Navy are what we call "secure." This means they are protected by special equipment that encrypts (scrambles) your voice so that an enemy cannot listen in and understand what you are saying. Never discuss classified information over a telephone or a radio circuit unless you know it is secure.

Figure 8.1. Never discuss classified information on an unsecured telephone line or radio circuit.

Stowage and Transport

Classified material may not be removed from the command without permission. Authorized protective measures must be used when classified material is sent or carried from one place to another and it must be stowed (stored) properly. Do not, for example, take a classified manual home to study at night. It is admirable that you want to improve your knowledge so that you can do your job better, but you probably do not have the means to transport the material safely, you almost definitely do not have the means to stow it safely in your home, and since you will not have the permission of your commanding officer, you will be in very serious trouble should anything happen to the material.

Discovery of Classified Information

If you accidently come across some classified material that has been left unguarded, misplaced, or not secured, do not read or examine it or try to decide what to do with it. Report the discovery immediately and stand by to keep unauthorized personnel away until an officer or senior petty officer arrives to take charge.

Security Areas

Spaces where classified materials are used or stowed or that serve as buffers are known as security areas. Some areas are more sensitive or are more likely to risk compromise than others, so to meet these varying needs, a system has been developed to identify security areas properly. The government has established three types of security areas and identified them by levels. All three of these areas are clearly marked by signs with the words "Restricted Area." The level of the area is *not* identified on the signs, however.

Level I No classified material is actually used or kept in a level I space; it is used as a buffer or control point to prevent access to a higher-level security area. A security clearance is not required for access to a level I area, but an identification system is usually in place to control access to the area.

Level II Classified material *is* stowed or used in these areas. Uncontrolled access to a level II area could potentially result in the compromise of classified information. Therefore, it is mandatory that anyone not holding the proper clearance must be escorted while visiting a level II area.

Level III Classified material is used in a level III area in such a manner as mere entry into the area risks compromise. An example would be a command and control center where large decision-making displays have classified information posted on them. Only people with the proper clearance and the need to know are permitted access to a level III area. All entrances must be guarded or properly secured.

Censorship

In war or during certain peacetime emergency conditions, censorship of personal mail may be imposed. The intent of censorship is to avoid security violations that might occur through carelessness or lack of judgment in writing letters. Under such emergency conditions, all letters written aboard a ship, or in a forward area, must be passed by a censor. When censorship is imposed, instructions will be issued explaining what can and cannot be discussed in letters. You should avoid subjects such as ships' movements, combat actions, or details of weapons in your letters under these circumstances.

Photographs may be censored as well. Cameras may be barred and all pictures taken aboard ship may require clearance for release.

Limitations may also be imposed upon other forms of communication, such as telephone calls and ham radio operations.

Threats to Security

Foreign nations may be interested in classified information on new developments, weapons, techniques, and materials, as well as movements and the operating capabilities of ships and aircraft.

The people who collect such information cannot be stereotyped or categorized, which is why they succeed in their work. A person who has access to classified material should never talk to any stranger about any classified subjects. A foreign intelligence agent collects many odd little bits of information, some of which might not even make sense to the agent, but when they are all put together in the agent's own country they may tell experts much more than the Navy wants them to know.

Espionage agents prey upon the vulnerabilities of their intended targets. For example, service people with relatives in foreign countries can sometimes be intimidated into cooperation by threats to their relatives. Members of minorities sometimes can be tempted to divulge information if they feel the system within which they live isn't fair to them. People with financial problems or drug habits can be coerced into doing favors for the enemy. Some people may feel a need for attention. If a stranger offers to solve your problem, you could be placed in the awkward position of accepting, without even knowing that your new friend is indeed from an unfriendly foreign nation. All this may sound like a scene from a spy movie but, unfortunately, it happens in real life. Enemy agents also like to infiltrate social gatherings where U.S. service personnel dance, drink, and talk. These agents may gather important pieces of information merely by listening to the conversation around them or by actively engaging in talk with service personnel. Then they pass on whatever is heard. Some agents even move into communities with service people so they can collect information from their neighbors.

Listed below are some ways to prevent being exploited by a foreign agent:

Don't talk about a sensitive job to people who don't need to know—not even to your family or friends.

Be careful what you say in social situations. Even seemingly trivial information can be valuable in the wrong hands.

Know how to handle classified material properly.

Don't be careless with carbons and typewriter ribbons used in connection with classified material. They are as classified as the original material.

If you have personal problems you feel might be exploited, use the chain of command to solve them. No one in the Navy is going to hit you over the head because you have a problem that might be solved by a senior petty officer or officer. If one of them can't help, go to the chaplain. Chaplains are in the service for more than promoting religion; they are there to help, whatever your problem is.

Reporting Threats

Report any suspicious contact. If someone seems more curious about your job than seems normal and presses you for information in any way, report it to your superiors. If the person is innocent, no harm will come of it. If the person is guilty, you will have done a great service to your country by calling attention to the incident.

If you are contacted by someone whom you are certain is attempting espionage, do not try to be a hero by taking action yourself. *Report it!*

Report any contact with someone you know who is from a nation that is hostile or potentially hostile to the United States, even if the contact seems innocent. Remember that spies rarely start out trying to get classified information from their targets. If you are unsure whether the nation is considered a potential threat, *report it*. In matters of security, it is always better to be overly cautious than not cautious enough.

If you feel that your superior in the chain of command cannot be trusted with the information you have to report, request permission to see the next higher-up. And the next, if necessary. If you feel you can't approach the people in your chain of command, go to the Naval Criminal Investigative Service (NCIS) office. If you can't find one, look in the white pages of the phone book under U.S. Government, Naval Activities.

If you are going to make a report, make a note of the date, time, place, and nature of the encounter. Describe how you were approached and mention who else in the Navy was also approached. Provide names if you know them. State your own name, grade, Social Security number, and anything else you feel is pertinent.

Operational Security

Operations are military actions, missions, and maneuvers. They involve the movement of ships and planes and their cargoes, personnel assignments, information gathering, communications, and the deployment and usage of weapon systems.

Much information can be gathered by an enemy or potential enemy without resorting to espionage. With enough information, an enemy can determine what an operation is for and sabotage it. Cargo loaded aboard a ship or plane may seem unimportant, but it can be vital information for an enemy wondering whether it is destined for the tropics or the arctic regions. The kind of ship carrying the cargo does not escape the enemy's attention. Is it a troop carrier or an icebreaker? Are the planes involved bombers or supply transports? Does an increase in radio traffic signal the beginning of a big operation? The slightest change in daily routine can be noted and reported to an expert who knows that any change, no matter how innocent or trivial it may seem, could be a piece in the puzzle of U.S. operations. For example, if medical supplies are being loaded aboard a supply ship at the same time that Marines are boarding an amphibious assault ship and an air squadron makes an urgent request for maps of a certain area that would be ideal for an amphibious assault, an enemy gathering these three facts can deduce that an amphibious assault is likely in that area and will know something about its timing and components. This information will allow the enemy to take the necessary steps to oppose or confuse the landing, causing a failure of the operation or the loss of American lives that might otherwise not have occurred.

"Operational security" (OPSEC) is the term used in the military to define those measures used to prevent an enemy or potential enemy from gathering too much information about our military operations. There are four main components to OPSEC.

Communications security. Measures taken—such as encryption and coding or methods of controlling the flow of message traffic—to prevent the disclosure of information by telephone, telegraph, radio, teletype, Internet, FAX transmissions, mail, and any other means of communicating.

Electronic security. This includes the prevention of giving away valuable information by means of radar, sonar, or any other noncommunicating electronic emission. For example, if you use your radar to search for aircraft, your radar signal can be detected by the enemy to let them know you are in the area.

Operational information security. This refers to the protection of plans, maps, photographs, documents pertaining to attack and defense tactics, and information regarding unit movements and locations.

Physical security. Guarding classified areas, equipment, buildings, and people from unauthorized access, sabotage, and other dangers.

Physical Security

Protecting classified material is essential to a military organization, but there are other considerations in the security of a ship or other naval unit. Naval personnel assigned to ships—whether on watch or not—must always be security-minded and on the alert for any sign of danger to the ship. A ship can be threatened by any number of dangers, including hurricanes, tidal waves, flooding, fire, explosions, sabotage from within the ship, foreign saboteurs, sneak attacks, civil disorders, and riots.

External Security

Threats to security may originate outside the ship. Strangers approaching the ship should be regarded with suspicion, even though they appear to be ordinary visitors, salespersons, newspaper carriers, or delivery people. All individuals coming aboard must be identified by the OOD or his or her representative, and all items such as packages, parcels, briefcases, and toolboxes should be inspected. Persons standing gangway or quarterdeck watches assist the OOD in identifying approaching boats, screening visitors, and checking packages.

Sentries and guards posted for security purposes are guided by written instructions and must know how to challenge approaching boats in order to identify occupants before they come alongside. All sentries may be armed when the situation demands. Armed guards should be well trained in the use of their weapons.

Moored or anchored ships are vulnerable to sneak attacks and sabotage, particularly at night. Ships can be approached by swimmers, small boats, or submarines. Saboteurs may mingle with a returning liberty party, pose as visitors, or sneak aboard when ships are moored to a pier. During times of heightened danger, extra watches will be assigned for added protection to the ship.

If an attack is expected, U.S. military authorities will change the "Threat Condition" or "ThreatCon" as appropriate, which will in turn require heightened security measures. If there is no perceived threat, *ThreatCon Normal* will be set and only routine precautions will be required. Other conditions are described as follows:

ThreatCon Alfa. General threat, the nature and extent of which are unpredictable.

ThreatCon Bravo. Increased and more predictable threat; no target identified.

ThreatCon Charlie. An incident has occurred or intelligence indicates some form of terrorist action is imminent.

ThreatCon Delta. A terrorist attack has occurred, or intelligence indicates terrorist action against a specific target is likely.

As the ThreatCon increases, your command will have certain specific actions to take that will heighten security, ranging from required ID checks to posted sentries and armed patrols. These will vary, depending on the nature of your command, and you should learn what they are.

Internal Security

The safety of a ship may also be threatened from within by accidental or deliberate causes. Fire and flooding—whether caused by equipment failures or deliberate sabotage—are always a serious threat to the internal security of a ship. Someone intent upon doing harm to a ship, for whatever reasons, can do grave damage from within if adequate security measures are not in place.

In addition to the quarterdeck watches already discussed, there are a number of routine watches set up to enhance the internal security of most naval vessels.

The sounding and security watch. Manned both underway and in port, personnel assigned to this watch patrol the ship, making routine checks for watertight closures and security. If you are assigned to this watch, you will watch for fire hazards, take soundings (checks for flooding), and make draft readings (watch special markings on the ship for signs of gradual sinking).

The cold-iron watch. When a ship is in port and all or part of her engineering plant is shut down, a "cold-iron watch" is set. This watch checks all machinery spaces for violations of watertight integrity and any other problems that might occur.

Security alert teams. Shipboard personnel may be assigned to a security alert team to respond when some sort of emergency situation arises. These Sailors do not man any particular posts but are ready to respond on a moment's notice (much like firefighters in your community) if called away to provide additional security to the ship.

Bomb Threats

A bomb threat may happen anytime or anywhere. Many bomb threats are not real, but you should not assume that this is the case. If you receive a bomb threat by telephone, keep your head and take the following actions if at all possible:

- Try to keep the caller on the line and obtain as much information as you can.
- Write down the exact words of the caller (or as close to the exact words as possible) as quickly as you can.
- Try to determine the sex, approximate age, and attitude of the caller.
- Ask the caller when and where the bomb is to go off, what kind of bomb it is, what it looks like, and where the caller is calling from.
- Listen for background sounds that might give an indication of the caller's location.
- Note any accent or peculiarity of speech that may help identify the caller.

Each telephone at your command should have a copy of the "Telephonic Threat Complaint" form readily available to guide you if you receive a bomb threat.

There are certain defensive actions you can take to reduce the chance of a real bomb attack:

- Strictly comply with and enforce procedures for personnel identification and access control by always carrying your own identification card and, if you are on watch, carefully examine the ID cards of personnel boarding your ship or visiting your command, particularly if you do not recognize them.

- Be suspicious of packages if you do not know where they came from.
- Be suspicious of articles that are obviously out of place.
- Maintain tight control of locks and keys.
- Lock spaces that are not in use.
- Report suspicious personnel and their actions.

Wartime Security

In times of war or when the potential for hostile action is very high, extra precautions must be taken to provide additional security to the ship. These precautions may be very elaborate and involve highly trained personnel, or they may be relatively simple and affect everyone on board.

EMCON. Because modern technology enables an enemy to detect almost any electronic emission, a condition known as EMCON (emission control) may be set. When EMCON is imposed aboard ship, powerful equipment such as radio transmitters and radars will be shut down or tightly controlled. Even your personal radio may be prohibited if it has signal-emitting characteristics (which many do).

Darken ship. If a vessel does not want to be detected at night, "darken ship" will be set and must be observed by everyone on board. The glow of a cigarette can be seen for miles on a dark night. The light from an improperly shielded doorway will let a submarine make a successful periscope attack.

Quiet ship. Sound travels better in water than in air. Unnecessary noises can aid an enemy in detecting a ship or submarine. When "quiet ship" is set, all banging and hammering will be prohibited and everyone on board will be expected to avoid making any loud noises.

Shipyard Security

Ships sent into shipyards for major repairs will have many civilians coming aboard to do their work. This increased traffic can make a ship more vulnerable to problems of theft, damage, and even sabotage, because it becomes more difficult to keep track of so many people on board. All workers coming aboard a ship must be identified. The shipyard itself will assist in this process by providing proper identification cards to its workers. Compartments containing classified matter must be secured, either by locks or with sentries.

U.S. Naval Institute

Figure 8.2. A Marine on sentry duty.

Shipboard personnel may be assigned as "fire watches" to each welder and burner who comes on board because of the increased potential for fire. Also, special precautions must be taken after each shift to inspect spaces for fire hazards.

Duty Assignments and Advancements

During your time in the Navy, two things will occur on a periodic basis: you will change duty stations and you will advance in paygrade. In order for you to vary and broaden your experience and for you to contribute to the needs of the Navy, you will periodically change duty stations. The longer you stay in the Navy, the more transfers from one duty station to another you will experience. If you are doing your job well and striving to learn and improve yourself, you will also be advanced in rate.

U.S. Naval Institute

Figure 9.1. A Sailor at work in the combat information center.

Duty Assignments

Whenever you are assigned to a duty station, you will have what is called a "planned rotation date" or, as you will more commonly hear it called, a PRD. This is the day that the Navy is planning to transfer you to a different duty station. It is important to note the word "planned" in this term. This date is for *planning* purposes. You may or may not be transferred on that date. You may in fact be transferred on or close to your PRD, you may be transferred earlier or later than your PRD if circumstances arise that make it necessary, or your PRD may be changed at some point during your stay at a particular duty station. The thing to remember is that most transfers do take place on or about the date set in your PRD, but you must be prepared for other eventualities. Do not embarrass yourself by trying to tell a Navy official that you *have* to be transferred on a certain date because it is your PRD.

It should be obvious that transferring Navy people from one duty station to another is a fairly complicated process. A number of factors (or details) have to be considered before a successful transfer can be accomplished. In the Navy, the people who make these changes are called "detailers" and they must consider the needs of the Navy (including who is needed where and what it will cost to get them there), the needs and desires of the individuals involved, and the qualifications of the individuals who are going to fill specific billets.

Duty Preferences

Your desires are among the factors that detailers will consider in making duty assignments. It is important to let the detailers know what your desires are for your next duty assignment. This is accomplished by the use of a special form called a "Duty Preferences Form" (NAVPERS 1306/63). This form allows you to tell the detailer what kind of ships or squadrons you would like to serve in, what home ports you prefer, where you would like to serve on shore duty, and what overseas duty you would most like to have.

Submission of the duty preferences form is an individual responsibility. If you have no duty preference on file, your detailer will not know what you want and will have no choice but to assign you to fill any valid requirement without considering what your needs and wants are. You should fill out a 1306/63 when you arrive at your duty station and submit a new one every time your duty preferences change.

The 1306/63 has a "remarks" section that allows you to provide additional information that might help your detailer make an appropriate assignment. Use this section to tell the detailer about such things as the expected delivery date if you have a child on the way, any special needs that members of your family may have, or special skills that you or your spouse may have (such as foreign language proficiency).

Detailing

At any one time, about two-thirds of the enlisted personnel in the Navy are in seagoing billets and the other third are in shore billets. To make certain that everyone gets a fair share of each kind of duty assignment, a system of centralized detailing has been set up by the Bureau of Naval Personnel (BUPERS). Full details of how this system works are contained in the Enlisted Transfer Manual (TRANSMAN, NAVPERS 15909), but because this system is somewhat complicated, you should make it a habit to consult a career counselor before making any requests under this system.

Duty Types

It would not be fair if some people always had sea duty and others only shore duty. And it should come as no surprise that not all sea assignments are alike—some are more challenging than others—and not all shore assignments are equal in their challenges and benefits. Therefore, different kinds of duty have been classified by a system that assists detailers in making equitable assignments. These types of duty are assigned (and, when necessary, changed) exclusively by BUPERS. With these type designations, detailers are able to make fair assignments. For example, if you and a shipmate both requested a shore assignment to Hawaii, you would have a better chance of getting it than your shipmate if your record showed that you had more time at sea.

The various types of duty are described below.

Shore Duty (Type 1)

Duty performed in the United States, Hawaii, or Anchorage, Alaska, at land-based activities where you are not required to be away from the station more than 150 days a year. Also, if you are assigned as a student to a school that lasts more than 18 months, it is considered Type 1 (shore) duty.

Sea Duty (Type 2)
Duty performed in ships and deployable aircraft squadrons that are home-ported in the United States (including Hawaii and Anchorage, Alaska). Also applies to embarked staffs (senior officers and their staffs who ride on a ship but are not permanently assigned to it) and land-based activities that are home-ported in the United States (including Hawaii and Anchorage, Alaska) but deploy (go away from their home port or base) for more than 150 days per year.

Overseas Remote Land-based Sea Duty (Type 3)
Duty performed in a land-based activity that does not require you to be away from your base more than 150 days each year but, because of its undesirable location, is counted as sea duty.

Nonrotated Sea Duty (Type 4)
Duty in ships and aircraft squadrons that are permanently located overseas and whose duties require them to be away from their home base for more than 150 days each year. Also applies to embarked staffs or land-based activities who are required to be away from their home base for more than 150 days each year.

Neutral Duty (Type 5)
This type of duty is no longer recognized.

Overseas Shore Duty (Type 6)
Duty performed at overseas locations that does not meet the special criteria of Type 3 duty counts the same as shore duty in the United States for rotational purposes. In other words, you can expect to go to sea following a Type 6 assignment.

Special Assignments
In addition to the various kinds of duty described above, there are a number of special assignments that require additional attention by detailers and may require additional qualifications or special screening procedures. Some of these are instructor duty, recruiting duty, career counseling, Food Management Teams, Fleet Technical Support Centers, brigs and correctional custody units, Military Assistance Advisory Groups in foreign countries, State Department Support Units, Blue Angels flight demonstration team, Underwater Demolition Teams (UDT), Sea-Air-Land (SEAL) teams, Special Warfare Combat Crewman (SWCC) teams, explosive ordnance disposal (EOD) units, deep sea and salvage diving, and personnel exchange programs (PEP)

Figure 9.2. Because food is vital to the readiness of the Navy, special Food Management Teams travel to ships and shore stations to provide on-the-job training in food preparation, mess management, and sanitation.

with foreign navies. If you are interested in any of these special assignments, see your command career counselor for more information.

Humanitarian Assignments

Detailers are aware of the hardships confronting Navy families and of the additional aggravation imposed by long absences of service members from their families. Emergency leave sometimes provides sufficient time to alleviate hardship; however, when an individual requires more time than leave can provide and has a reasonable chance of resolving the hardship within a specified time frame, reassignment for humanitarian reasons (HUMS) may be required.

Figure 9.3. Sailors must complete an arduous training program to become Navy
SEALS.

Specific requirements are contained in the TRANSMAN, and
your personnel office can give you additional information regarding
HUMS assignments and help you determine your eligibility for one,
but bear in mind that these assignments are made under rather narrow guidelines. The situation has to be *very* serious and there has to
be reason to believe that the problem can be solved within a reasonable amount of time (six months is the norm).

Exchange of Duty
There are occasions when the assignment of an individual to a specific area would be highly beneficial to the individual's morale, but
not justifiable in view of the expenditure of government funds
required. The Navy may effect such transfers, provided the individuals involved agree to bear all expenses involved. There are two
types of duty exchange, usually called "swaps." One is negotiated by
NAVPERSCOM and is based on a letter of request from you. The
other is self-negotiated and should be requested on a NAVPERS
1306/7 (enlisted transfer and special-duty request) form. The specific
requirements are contained in the TRANSMAN.

Transfers

Once your new duty assignment has been made and you have received your official orders, it will be time for you to check out of your old duty station, move yourself and your belongings to the new location, and report in to the new duty station. Sometimes a transfer can be as simple as walking across a street or a pier. Other transfers can involve moving you and your family halfway around the world. The Navy will provide you a great deal of assistance in making the transfer as smooth as possible, but you must also do your part to ensure a smooth transition.

Departing

Make certain when you are checking out from your old duty station that you understand your orders. If they authorize DELREP (delay in reporting) to count as leave, make certain you know the date on which you must report to the new station. If commercial transportation is authorized at government expense, pick up the tickets or travel vouchers. If you have any questions at all, ask the transfer yeoman or personnelman before you leave; this may save you a lot of trouble later.

If you have a spouse and/or children who will be going with you to your new duty assignment, it is a good idea to write to the local housing office at your new duty station to get housing information.

Make certain that you file a change of address form at your old duty station so that your mail can catch up to you.

En Route

While you are en route to your new duty station, you may encounter some problems. For example, if you are assigned to a ship, you may get to the port where she is supposed to be only to find that she got underway the day before because an airliner went down off the coast and the ship is needed for rescue operations. There may be no way to join the ship until she returns from the rescue operation. What do you do?

Remember, it's all one Navy, and no matter where you are you can find someone to help. Always keep your orders, records, and pay accounts with you, not in your baggage, which may be lost. With them, you can obtain further transportation if needed and draw some of your pay if you are running out of money. If you are in an area where there are no Navy facilities, Army and Air Force activities can help you with these matters as well.

If you are in doubt as to the location of your new duty station when you arrive in the area, check in with the Navy Shore Patrol or look in the local telephone directory under "U.S. Government" to find some naval activity where you can obtain help. Most areas have a local Navy or other armed forces recruiting station, and they can help you find your new station.

If you have dependents (spouse and/or children) with you, get them settled into a temporary lodging facility (a hotel, motel, or Navy Lodge if one is available) before reporting to your new duty assignment.

Reporting

When reporting to your new duty station, be in complete and proper uniform. Because you are going to be making a first impression and you want it to be a good one, look your sharpest, and present yourself well when you report in.

Be sure you have all your necessary gear with you; the ship may sail the same day you report, and what you check in with could very well be all you will have for a while. But also keep in mind that you will have only a limited amount of space to store your personal belongings, so bringing large items like "Boom-boxes," computers, and even oversized luggage can cause you problems.

Hand your orders to the watch, either at the main gate or the quarterdeck, so that they can be endorsed and stamped with the time and date of reporting, and you can be logged in.

As soon as is practical, deliver your original orders and your records to the personnel office. You certainly want to be paid on time, so turn in a copy of your orders to the disbursing office.

Enlisted Advancement System

Advancement in the Navy means better pay, more privileges, greater responsibility, and increased pride. Advancement to petty officer rates in the Navy are made through centralized competition. Because the requirements sometimes change, it is always best to consult with your personnel office or educational-services office for the latest information. While the Navy will assist you in various ways, meeting the requirements for advancement in rate is ultimately up to you. Think ahead and prepare, so that you are ready for advancement once you have met the time-in-rate (TIR) requirements.

General Requirements

While there are a number of requirements for advancement (length of service, awards earned, test scores, etc.), the most heavily weighted aspect is your performance. Throughout your Navy career, you will receive performance evaluations describing how well you perform your duties. What those evaluations in your record say about you is the most important factor in determining whether you will be advanced. Advancement to E-3 depends entirely upon your performance and your having spent the required amount of time as an E-2. If you have a favorable recommendation for advancement on your most recent evaluation, you will be automatically advanced to E-3 when you have served the required time in rate [see below]. But to advance to E-4 through E-7, you must also compete in the semiannual or annual Navy-wide examinations for advancement in rate. Before you can take these exams you must meet certain eligibility requirements. You must meet physical readiness and body fat standards, must complete any required courses for the rate you are seeking, and must complete all required Personnel Qualification Standards (PQS) [see Chapter 10]. If you are seeking advancement to E-6, E-7, or E-8, you must also attend the Leadership Training course for your rate to be eligible.

Time in Rate (TIR)

You must spend a minimum length of time in any given rate before you can even try to advance to the next higher one. This period is called "time in rate" and is designed to ensure that a Sailor spends some time at each level gaining experience before she or he is eligible for advancement to the next higher rate. The specific TIR requirements do change from time to time, but currently they are as follows:

E-1 to E-2	9 months as an E-1
E-2 to E-3	9 months as an E-2
E-3 to E-4	6 months as an E-3
E-4 to E-5	12 months as an E-4
E-5 to E-6	36 months as an E-5
E-6 to E-7	36 months as an E-6
E-7 to E-8	36 months as an E-7
E-8 to E-9	36 months as an E-8

Keep in mind that these are *minimum* times. Except for advancement to E-3, you should not expect to necessarily get advanced within these periods of time. Few people do. Advancement tests are only given at certain times of the year, and it takes time to process and grade them. That factor alone will make it very difficult for you to be advanced within the minimum times shown above.

Naval Standards (NAVSTDS) and Occupational Standards (OCCSTDS)

Volume one of the *Manual of Navy Enlisted Manpower and Personnel Classifications and Occupations Standards* (NAVPERS 18068) lists the minimum things you should know or be able to do in order to be eligible for your next advancement. NAVSTDS are general military requirements that do not apply to a specific rating and that all Sailors at each paygrade should know. OCCSTDS are the things you should know for the specific rating (such as quartermaster or storekeeper) you are trying to achieve. Keep in mind that there will be questions related to both on your exam. Also keep in mind that you are responsible for knowing not only those NAVSTDS and OCCSTDS for the rate you are trying to achieve but also all those of the lower rates. In other words, if you are preparing to be advanced to Quartermaster Second Class, you should be studying and reviewing the NAVSTDS for E-2 through E-5 and the OCCSTDS for QM3 as well as QM2.

Preparation Aids

For most advancements you must take a written advancement examination. The people who write these exams have also prepared guides to help you study. For each rate there is a Bibliography for Advancement-in-Rate Exam Study (known more commonly as a BIBS) and an Advancement Handbook (AH). Together, these two publications make up a comprehensive study package that will help you prepare for advancement.

The BIBS for your rate gives you a list of all the publications that will help you prepare for advancement such as training courses, instructions, and technical manuals. BIBSs can be obtained from your educational services officer (ESO) or from the Internet at *www. cnet.navy.mil/netpdtc/nac/bibs/bibs.htm*.

Advancement Handbooks tell you what you need to know and must be able to do in order to pass the advancement exam for your particular rate by breaking the requirements down into logical packages of general skill areas, specific skills, knowledge required to perform the skill, references you should study, and suggestions as to what to expect on the exam. AHs can be obtained from your ESO or from the Internet at *www.cnet.navy.mil/netpdtc/nac/download/ ah.intro.htm*.

Training Manuals (TRAMANs) and Non-Resident Training Courses (NRTCs)

To help you prepare for advancement, the Navy supplies TRAMANs, which serve as textbooks, and NRTCs (often called "correspondence courses"), which are courses based on the TRAMANs, that you can take without having to go to a school. Many of these courses are required for advancement. See your Educational Services Officer or Command Career Counselor for assistance in determining which courses to take and how to obtain them. Most are available on the Internet at *http://www.advancement.cnet.navy.mil* and *http://courses.cnet.navy.mil.*

Personal Preparations

Next to good performance, perhaps the most important requirement for your advancement is a good study plan. There is a lot to learn no matter what rate you are trying to achieve so you must make time on a regular basis to prepare yourself for advancement. Try studying three days a week right after breakfast or every night before taps—whatever works best for you. Try to allot at least an hour, but settle for less on occasion rather than not study at all. Every little bit helps.

Find a study partner or start a study group. Two (or more) heads are usually better than one as long as all participants are sincere about learning. Study partners can help each other understand difficult concepts by pooling their knowledge, and quizzing one another is an excellent way of preparing for exams.

When it comes time to take the exam you have been preparing for, it is a good idea not to attempt any last-minute studying the night before. Relax. Go out for dinner if possible. Take a walk, spend some time with friends, or have a moderate workout at the gym. Most important of all, get a good night's sleep.

While taking the exam, pace yourself. Begin by reading all the questions and the answer choices. Then go through the exam again, this time answering all those questions you are certain you know. Go through again with the time remaining and work on those questions you are not certain about. Take an educated guess rather than leave a question blank. You will not be graded by the number of wrong answers, but on the number of correct responses.

Professional Development Board (PDB)

To ensure that your professional development is adequately cared for, your command will have a PDB consisting of the Command Master Chief, Command Career Counselor, Personnel Officer,

Educational Services Officer, and other assistants as deemed necessary who meet periodically to review the career development issues of the crew as they see them or as individuals bring to their attention. For example, should you be having difficulty reaching career goals in a timely manner, the PBD will find ways to help you. Or if you wanted to apply for an officer program, the PBD would assist you in determining your eligibility and in fulfilling the application requirements.

Advancements

Obviously the Navy cannot advance everyone who wants to be advanced. Because the Navy needs only a certain number of petty officers, it is not even always possible to advance everyone who passes the examination and meets the other qualification requirements. The Navy has therefore devised an equitable system to select the most qualified people for advancement.

Final Multiple Score (FMS)

Once you have met all the requirements and have taken the competitive examination, your results will be computed as a "final multiple score." This is determined by combining a number of factors to determine who, of all those competing, will be advanced. The factors considered include how you did on the written examination, your performance marks, how long you have served in your current paygrade, how long you have been in the Navy, how many awards you have received, and whether or not you have taken the exam before and how well you did. You will receive a certain amount of credit for each of these factors, depending upon what paygrade you are seeking, and the end computed result will be your FMS. Your FMS is then compared to the FMSs of everyone else who took the exam, the Navy determines how many people it needs to advance, and those with the highest FMSs are advanced. For example, if you are seeking advancement from seaman to QM3, and the Navy needs 100 new QM3s, you will be advanced if your FMS was among the top 100 of those who are competing. If 100 or more people did better than you once the FMSs are calculated, you will not be advanced. But if only 99 or fewer did better, you will be a new QM3.

Passed But Not Advanced (PNA)

For every written examination, there is a minimum passing grade established. If you pass the exam but do not end up with a high enough FMS to be advanced, you are designated as PNA, which means "passed, but not advanced." This is certainly frustrating, but it's not all bad news. The next time you compete for advancement, you will receive some additional credit toward your FMS by having a PNA in your record. And if you do not get advanced the second time you try, but you once again pass the exam, you will receive even more credit the next time around. You can see that it is a good idea to take the exam each time it is offered even if you feel that you have little chance of being one of those who will get advanced. It also is a good idea because, even though it is a different exam each time, chances are you will do better each time you take it.

Senior Enlisted Rates

The higher you go in the rate structure, the more emphasis you will see placed upon leadership and performance. Advancements to the top two enlisted grades, E-8 and E-9, are not determined by a written examination at all. Those chiefs who have three years in rate, have satisfactorily completed military course requirements for senior and master chief petty officer, and are recommended by their commanding officers will automatically be eligible for selection-board consideration. This is where a good record becomes extremely important—those with the best records are selected over those with records that may be good, but not good enough.

There are a number of special positions held by senior enlisted people in the Navy. Only the best of the best of the best will find their way to these positions.

Division Chief/Leading Petty Officer

Every command, whether afloat or ashore, is divided into departments and divisions, and in every division the senior enlisted person is the division chief or the leading petty officer (LPO). The division chief or LPO is responsible for the morale and welfare of his or her subordinates, but also functions as the technical expert for the division. In a larger division, there may be several work centers to which supervisors are assigned. The primary duty of the division chief/LPO is then in the area of personnel management, with the work-center supervisors responsible for the more technical aspects of the division's assignments. The division chief/LPO is responsible for all work performed by his or her division, and he or she reports directly to the division officer. The division chief/LPO also maintains liaison with the Command Master Chief (see below) on all matters that concern the morale, welfare, and proper employment of enlisted members of the division.

Command Master Chief (CMDMC)

By having direct communication with the commanding officer, command master chiefs (CMDMCs) serve as the commanding officer's principal enlisted advisor, fostering sensitivity to the needs and viewpoints of enlisted men and women and their families.

CMDMCs have the responsibility of keeping their commanding officers up to date on situations, procedures, and practices that affect the welfare, morale, and well-being of the enlisted crew.

Navy commands with 250 or more personnel are eligible to have a CMDMC billet. Personnel assigned to these billets actually change their rate to CMDMC. Commands that do not meet this criterion may designate a master chief petty officer from within the command to serve as a collateral-duty command master chief. In commands with no master chief petty officers assigned, a collateral duty command senior chief may be designated from within the existing crew, and where there are no master chiefs or senior chiefs, a collateral duty command chief may be designated. Collateral duty command chiefs (no matter what their rate) do not change their rating.

Chief of the Boat (COB)

The Navy's submarine service has assignments similar to those of CMDMCs, but call these individuals the chief of the boat instead of the command master chief. There are other differences as well. The COB assigns bunks and lockers; details personnel to compartment cleaning, mess cooking, and special details; and assists the executive officer in maintaining the watch, quarter, and station bill. The COB is responsible for ship cleanliness and proper stowage of all special clothing and safety equipment (life-jackets, escape hoods, breathing equipment, lines, and cables). In addition, the COB is responsible, under direction of the commanding officer, for ensuring strict compliance with all safety regulations.

One of the most important functions of the COB is serving as qualification officer for the on-board enlisted submarine-qualification program. The COB coordinates and supervises—through division LPOs—the conduct, performance, and administration of all enlisted personnel. Another responsibility is monitoring leave and special liberty.

The COB, considered an executive petty officer in all matters affecting enlisted personnel, is charged with departmental coordination at the level of LPO. As such, this person reports directly to the commanding officer and is the senior petty officer on board. By virtue of the position, the COB works closely with the executive officer and all officers on board.

CNO-Directed Command Master Chief Petty Officers (CNOMCs)

A number of special Navy commands, such as the Naval Academy, the Navy Recruiting Command, and the Naval Training Center at Great Lakes, have command master chiefs assigned who are specially designated as CNOMCs. These individuals, like primary duty CMDMCs, change their rating (to CNOMC).

Fleet and Force Master Chiefs (FLTMCs and FORMCs)

These command master chiefs serve as principal enlisted advisors to the commanders of larger commands, such as the Commander in Chief of the Atlantic Fleet or the Commander of the Naval Reserve Force. They also change their ratings (to either FLTMC or FORMC, as appropriate).

Master Chief Petty Officer of the Navy

Assigned to the Office of the Chief of Naval Operations, there is only one master chief petty officer of the Navy (MCPON) and he or she serves as senior enlisted leader of the Navy and as senior enlisted advisor to the Chief of Naval Operations and the Chief of Naval Personnel in all matters pertaining to enlisted personnel and their families.

The MCPON also serves as an advisor to many boards dealing with enlisted personnel, accompanies the Chief of Naval Operations on some trips, serves as the enlisted representative of the Department of the Navy at special events, and testifies before Congressional committees on enlisted issues.

10 Navy Education and Training

Education in the Navy begins with recruit training and continues throughout your naval career, whether it lasts for four years or thirty. You will probably attend one or more Navy vocational/technical schools, you may be able to receive college credit for your military training and experience, you may qualify for specialized training (such as nuclear engineering or diving school), and you might even be eligible to enter a commissioning program that will lead to becoming an officer. General Military Training (GMT) applies to everyone in the Navy and is an ongoing process throughout your career no matter what your rank or rate. There are self-study courses available for those who wish to improve and advance themselves. And every Sailor is frequently involved in formal or informal on-the-job training.

Young men and women who have the desire and the ability to expand their personal educational horizons will find a number of programs offering correspondence courses, tuition assistance, college opportunities, high school equivalency, and other ways to improve themselves. You will never find a shortage of educational opportunities and requirements while you are in the Navy.

Professional Development

One of the easiest and yet most effective forms of professional training is what is called on-the-job training (OJT). It can be as simple as a coworker showing you how to turn on the office copier, or it can be more involved, such as your chief letting you shift electrical distribution under supervision. Other forms of training are more structured and require either formal schooling or a system of written standards and requirements. However it is accomplished, professional training that contributes directly to your effectiveness as a Sailor—improving your vocational and/or your military capabilities—is essential to both you and the Navy as long as you are wearing a uniform.

PH3 Heather S. Gordon

Figure 10.1. One of the most effective forms of professional training is OJT (on-the-job training).

Navy Military Training (NMT) and General Military Training (GMT)

NMT is required training for all enlisted personnel during their first year of service that is designed to round out the training you received at Boot Camp. GMT is non-occupational training required periodically for all Navy personnel (officer and enlisted) throughout their time in the Navy.

NMT is designed to help you make the transition from the highly structured environment of recruit training to one of personal accountability and responsibility. You will probably complete your NMT requirements while in apprentice training or at "A" school.

GMT falls within four curriculum areas (Navy Heritage, Personal Growth and Professional Relationships, Managing Risk, and Wellness) and covers a wide variety of subjects, including such things as naval history, fraternization, the Navy College Program, suicide awareness, etc.

Personnel Qualification Standards (PQS)

Before you can operate or maintain a specific piece of equipment, you must learn certain skills and acquire a certain amount of knowledge. The same is true of standing a watch or doing a job. The PQS program provides a written list of the skills and specific knowledge that you must have in order to qualify for a specific watch station, to be able to do a certain job, or to operate or maintain a specific piece of equipment. That list tells you exactly what you need to know and serves as a guide through your qualification process.

As part of the PQS process, you will be given a PQS book that allows you to record your progress by obtaining the signatures of already qualified people who are convinced that you have met the standards for qualification. For example, you may be working toward qualification as a small boat operator. Your card might say, among other things, that you must demonstrate the ability to tie certain knots. The person helping you to qualify would have you tie a square knot several times until she or he was convinced that you could do it sufficiently well. Then he or she would sign your book on the appropriate signature line. This process would continue until you had obtained all of the required signatures and met any additional requirements leading to your qualification.

Service Schools

Navy service schools are located at NTC Great Lakes and at Pensacola, Florida; Gulfport and Meridian, Mississippi; Norfolk, Virginia; and Port Hueneme (pronounced "why-nee-mee"), California, among other places. For some ratings, graduation from a particular service school is necessary for advancement. Selection for a service school depends on your rate, time in service, current duty assignment, school quotas, and the operational schedule of your unit. Although you can be sent to a service school from your current duty station on what the Navy calls a TAD (temporary additional duty) basis, most school assignments are made as part of your formal transfer process when changing duty stations and will be assigned on your PCS (permanent change of station) orders.

Since the eligibility requirements for schools vary, and change frequently, you should check the *Catalog of Navy Training Courses* (CANTRAC), NAVEDTRA 10500. CANTRAC has information on schools and courses under the direction of the Chief of Naval Education and Training (CNET). Besides CANTRAC, you have three other sources of information on schools—your educational services office, your career counselor, and your personnel office.

The different types of service schools are listed and explained below.

Class A. These schools provide basic technical knowledge required for job performance in a given rating. A Navy enlisted classification (NEC) code may be awarded once the school has been completed.

Class C. Advanced skills and techniques needed to perform tasks beyond those of the normal rating are taught in these schools. This category includes schools and courses previously identified as Class B. An NEC code may also be awarded to identify the level of skill.

Class E. This identifies schools designed for professional education leading to an academic degree.

Class F. Schools that train fleet personnel who are en route to or are members of ships' companies. These schools also provide individual training such as refresher, operator, maintenance, or technical training of less than 13 calendar days. An NEC code is not awarded.

Class P. These are officer-acquisition schools, designed to provide undergraduate education and training for midshipmen, officer candidates, and all other newly commissioned officers (except aviators).

Class R. This is the basic school that provides initial training after enlistment, also known as "boot camp" or "recruit training." It prepares the recruit for early adjustment to military life by inculcating basic skills and knowledge about military subjects. Currently, everyone attends Class R school in Great Lakes. Class R schooling does not include apprenticeship training, but follow-on apprenticeship training is conducted at the Naval Training Center in Great Lakes for seaman and fireman apprentice and in Pensacola for airman apprentice.

Class V. Training that leads to designation as a naval aviator or naval flight officer is conducted at schools designated as Class V.

Specialized Training

If you choose and are qualified to go into a specialized part of the Navy—such as submarines, underwater demolition, deep-sea diving, or a foreign language specialty—you will be specially trained. Some programs, such as the nuclear-power program, require a substantial amount of additional schooling, and, if you are accepted, will require an added service obligation. The nuclear field, for example, requires the Navy to provide more than a year's additional training to participants—training worth thousands of dollars which will make the individual receiving it more qualified for good civilian engineering jobs—so it is a fair trade that the Navy expects those selected for such training to serve some additional time in the Navy to make the investment worthwhile.

Most specialized training programs are voluntary in nature and all require personnel to meet extra qualifications beyond those of the average enlistee. For example, nuclear-field personnel must be able to handle a great deal of mathematics and physics training, while those who would be deep-sea divers must pass a very rigorous physical before entering that program.

Leadership Training

Although leadership comes more easily to some than to others and there is no complete substitute for experience, acquiring leadership skills can be enhanced by schooling. To assist you in understanding and accepting your responsibilities as a leader, the Navy provides extensive leadership training at various times throughout your career. These courses, called the "Leadership Continuum," vary in length and are taught at major training centers throughout the fleet. Leadership-oriented training is available for petty officers, for chiefs, and for officers, both senior and junior. If you are selected to be a command master chief, you will be eligible to attend the Senior Enlisted Academy at the Navy Education and Training Center at Newport, Rhode Island. This course provides in-depth study in communications skills, leadership and management technique, national security affairs, management of Navy resources, and other selected topics.

Along with the promotions you receive in your Navy career come increased responsibilities as a leader and manager. These courses are designed to help you attain the level of skill required to accept such responsibilities and perform effectively.

Personal Development

The Navy provides a wide variety of training experiences that help Sailors do their jobs better. But because the Navy also recognizes the value of education outside that required for a Sailor to do his or her job, a number of programs and methods have been created and/or endorsed which are designed to enhance the personal development of individual Sailors. The Navy's voluntary education program is called Navy College and encompasses many avenues to help active-duty personnel complete high school diplomas, work on technical/occupational certifications, improve academic skills, or pursue college degrees.

PH3 L. B. Weaver

Figure 10.2. To advance your Navy career, you must study and stay abreast of the latest developments in your field.

Navy College Program (NCP)

NCP brings together a number of different programs designed to help you obtain a college degree while in the Navy, at a pace that you are comfortable with. Some of these programs have existed for quite some time and have been proven effective, while others are newer initiatives.

One of the newest advancements is the cooperation of a number of colleges and universities that recognize your Navy training and experience as partial fulfillment of requirements for a degree. These colleges have partnered with the Navy to work with you to maximize the amount of credits you can earn through successful completion of training within your rating.

The Navy College Center (NCC) coordinates and provides information for the NCP. You can ask questions of special education advisors via the NCC website at *www.navycollege.navy.mil* or by calling 1-877-253-7122 seven days a week, 15 hours a day (0700-2200 EST). You can also reach the NCC advisors by e-mailing them at *ncc@smtp.cnet.navy.mil*.

There are also local offices, called Navy College Offices (NCOs), at many locations around the world that can help you get the education you seek. The NCO can answer your educational questions, provide advice, get you the courses and testing you need to earn a high-school diploma or high-school equivalency certificate, and tell you what college courses are being offered at times that fit your schedule. To find the nearest NCO to you, go to the website *www. navycollege.navy.mil.*

Servicemembers Opportunity Colleges, Navy (SOCNAV)

A worldwide network of more than eighty colleges provides college education opportunities that cross traditional academic boundaries and allow Sailors to work toward and ultimately earn degrees while serving in various duty stations around the world. First, credit is awarded for past experience, nationally recognized standard tests, and military training. You will then determine what additional schooling is necessary to earn a degree, and then take those courses from SOCNAV sites near your duty stations until you have fulfilled the requirements for the degree you are seeking. If you are transferred before earning a degree, credits are readily transferable within the network and arrangements can also be made to take required courses from colleges outside the network. Participating colleges have agreed to limit their residency requirements to make your participation more feasible.

Navy College Program for Afloat College Education (NCPACE)

Tuition-free college preparatory and college credit courses are available at some remote shore sites and on ships and submarines on extended deployment. These courses are taught by on-site instructors in some cases and electronically (using computer-based and modern communications technology) in others. You pay for the textbooks while the Navy pays all other costs. Courses are offered by colleges in the SOCNAV network [see above] so NCPACE credits earned can be combined with those earned in the SOCNAV program in your quest for a degree.

Tuition Assistance (TA)

The Navy pays a substantial percentage of tuition costs at accredited educational institutions for courses leading to a vocational-technical certification or a college degree (associate, bachelor's, or graduate). For high school diploma or equivalency courses, the Navy pays the full cost. Check with your local NCO or the NCC for more information.

Navy College Learning Center (NCLC)

Fully funded courses designed to provide improvement in basic reading, mathematics, and grammar skills are offered at many locations worldwide. These courses are designed to improve your ability to succeed in college-level studies and may be conducted by on-site instructors or through computer interaction, depending upon the circumstances.

Sailor/Marine American Council on Education Registry Transcript (SMART)

SMART is a formal record of your educational achievements that is similar to a college transcript. It tracks your educational progress by validating military occupational experience and training, listing college-level exams completed as well as credits earned, and incorporating other learning experiences. Under this system, for example, you earn college credit by successfully completing recruit training. Recognized by the American Council on Education (ACE), these recommended credits can be applied toward a college degree at many colleges and universities. To review your SMART or have it sent to an academic institution, visit your local NCO, or call 1-877-253-7122, or send an e-mail to *ncc@smtp.cnet.navy.mil,* or go to the website *www.navycollege.navy.mil.*

Rating Roadmap

Some of your on-the-job experience and training is worth college credits as recommended by the American Council on Education. Rating roadmaps tell you how many credits may be earned in a career for a particular rating. You can obtain them at your local NCO or from the NCC website.

Navy National Apprenticeship Program (NNAP)

Under an agreement between the Navy and the U.S. Department of Labor, some Navy skills can lead to apprenticeship certification in jobs comparable to civilian career fields. See your Educational Services Officer for more information about application procedures.

Job-Oriented Basic Skills Program (JOBS)

This program provides preparatory training for enlisted personnel with insufficient ASVAB scores to qualify for "A" School.

Defense Activity for Nontraditional Education Support (DANTES)

DANTES is a Department of Defense activity that supports voluntary education programs of all active and reserve military services. The organization provides tests to service members (the majority are offered free), which are administered at NCOs and on large ships. Navy students can take the GED high-school equivalency test, earn college credit upon successful completion of tests such as the College Level Proficiency Examination (CLEP), take college admission tests such as the SAT, ACT, and GRE, and also take certification examinations and guidance tests. DANTES also publishes and provides education centers with catalogs listing independent study/distance learning courses and degree programs offered by accredited colleges and universities and private educational institutions.

Information Technology (IT) Courses
The Department of Defense has made many IT courses available to you free of charge through the Internet. These computer courses range in scope from beginning applications such as MSWord, Powerpoint, Access, and Excel to more advanced technology such as C, C++, Java, and Visual Basic. Successful completion of these courses can lead to professional certifications, such as Microsoft Certified System Engineer (MCSE), Database Administrator, A+ certification and many others. You can access these courses at *http://USN.netg.com* or *http://dl.damneck,navy.mil* or *http://192.215.136.73*.

Montgomery GI Bill (MGIB)
The MGIB provides educational assistance in the form of money paid directly to the member for tuition and registration fees. To qualify for these benefits, you must agree to participate when you enter active duty, have a minimum two years of obligated service, agree to have money deducted from your pay to go toward the program as your share, and complete a high school diploma or equivalent before the end of your first enlistment. You may use these benefits while on active duty (after a specified qualifying period) or you may use them after you leave the Navy (provided you receive an honorable discharge), but you must use these benefits within 10 years of your discharge.

Once you elect coverage in the MGIB, you cannot change your mind and the money reduced from your pay is not refundable if you decide later not to participate.

Navy College Fund (NCF)
The Navy College Fund provides an additional educational benefit (or "kicker"), added to the MGIB, for those qualified Sailors who agree to strike for certain critical or hard-to-fill ratings.

Commissioning Opportunities

There are a number of ways to become an officer in the U.S. Navy. Minimum requirements are that you must be a U.S. citizen, and must meet certain age, physical, and additional service requirements. In general, a college degree is also a minimum requirement, although there are exceptions. If you are interested in any of the programs briefly described below, you should contact your educational services officer or command career counselor for additional information and assistance.

The United States Naval Academy

Most midshipmen are appointed from among high school or prep school graduates, but about ten percent of every entering class consists of prior enlisted Sailors and Marines. To be a candidate for appointment, you must be a U.S. citizen, at least 17 but not more than 23 years of age in the entering year, unmarried with no children, and have a combined math and verbal Scholastic Aptitude Test (SAT) score of at least 1050 or an American College Test (ACT) combined score of 46. You must also meet certain physical requirements and be recommended by your commanding officer.

Midshipmen pay no tuition, room, and board and are paid while attending the Academy in Annapolis, Maryland, for four years. Upon graduation, they receive a bachelor of science degree and a commission in the Navy or Marine Corps.

For further information, consult your educational services officer or contact the Candidate Guidance Office, 117 Decatur Road, U.S. Naval Academy, Annapolis, MD 21402-5018. Or call the fleet coordinator toll-free at 1-800-638-9156. The Naval Academy website is also available at *www.nadn.navy.mil.*

Naval Reserve Officers Training Corps (NROTC)

Enlisted persons may also compete for NROTC scholarships. To be eligible, you must be a U.S. citizen, a high school graduate or equivalent, physically qualified, have a good performance record, and be under $27^{1}/_{2}$ years of age on 30 June of the year you become eligible for commissioned status. Tuition, fees, books, uniforms, and a monthly subsistence allowance are paid for by the scholarship program. The program is available at more than fifty civilian colleges and universities. A NROTC student may earn a bachelor's degree in various academic fields, although at least 80 percent of the program's participants must be majoring in engineering, mathematics, physics, or chemistry.

Officer Candidate School (OCS)

If you have a baccalaureate degree (BA, BS) from an accredited academic institution, you may be eligible to attend OCS at Pensacola, Florida. The program is about 13 weeks long and provides basic knowledge of the naval profession. You will also receive specialized follow-on training after OCS to further prepare you for your initial fleet assignment as an officer. If you are an E-4 or below, you will be designated as an officer candidate and advanced to E-5 for pay purposes upon reporting to OCS. If you are an E-6 or above, you will continue to be paid in your current grade. Besides having the required degree, you must meet age and physical requirements, and you must be a U.S. citizen. Upon completion of the program you will incur a minimum active duty obligation of four years.

Broadened Opportunity for Officer Selection and Training (BOOST)

This is an excellent educational opportunity for men and women who have demonstrated leadership potential but have not had enough education to compete successfully for commissioning programs. If selected, you will attend a rigorous college preparatory course in Newport, Rhode Island studying mathematics, science, communications skills, computer science, and campus skills to acquire the knowledge and academic discipline you will need to compete for admission to a commissioning program.

There are a number of admission requirements, but probably the most important one is that you must be serious about a career in the Navy. You will probably incur an additional service obligation, must meet certain age and physical requirements, and must be recommended by your commanding officer.

Seaman to Admiral Program (STA)

The seaman to admiral program provides a commissioning path for outstanding career-motivated enlisted personnel. It is open to E-5 and above (or E-4s who have passed the E-5 exam) active-duty personnel who have at least four years active duty. The Seaman to Admiral Board meets annually to select the fifty most-qualified applicants and sends them to selected schools to earn a bachelor's degree within 36 months on a full-time, year-round basis. After successful completion of that phase, candidates will go to Officer Candidate School to earn their commissions.

To be eligible to apply for this program, applicants must meet all eligibility requirements, including being a U.S. citizen, having a high school diploma or service-accepted equivalent, meeting age and physical requirements, and having a superb performance record as well as strong academic potential.

Seaman to Admiral-21 (STA-21)

A relatively new program has been created to make applying for a commissioning program easier and more beneficial. The STA-21 program consolidates four of the programs listed above into one. Included are the Enlisted Commissioning Program (ECP), Naval Reserve Officer Training Corps (NROTC), Broadened Opportunity for Officer Selection and Training (BOOST), and the Seaman to Admiral program (STA). With STA-21 you need only make one application and you will automatically be considered for all four programs. Additionally, under this new program the Navy provides full pay and benefits and up to $10,000 per year to cover college costs (tuition, books, etc). STA-21 will ultimately replace the ECP, NROTC, BOOST, and STA programs but the older versions will not be phased out until fiscal year 2006. The Naval Academy and OCS programs are unaffected by the STA-21 program, and you must apply to them separately.

Warrant Officer Program

Chief petty officers (paygrades E-7 to E-9) may apply for the warrant officer program. There is no age requirement but applicants must have completed at least 12 but not more than 24 years of naval service. Appointments are made to the grade of chief warrant officer (W-2). E-9s with two years in grade may apply for appointment to chief warrant officer (W-3).

Other specific requirements are that a candidate must be a U.S. citizen, have a high school diploma or equivalent, have a good performance record, be physically qualified, and be recommended by the commanding officer. Applications are considered by a board convened by the Secretary of the Navy annually. Names of selectees are released by a BUPERS notice or an ALNAV (all-Navy commands) message. Those not selected are not notified.

Applicants accepted into the warrant officer program must agree to remain on active duty for three years from the date they are promoted to chief warrant officer.

Limited Duty Officer (LDO) Program

The LDO program is open to warrant officers with one year time in grade as of 1 September in the year application is made. The program is also open to enlisted applicants in paygrades E-6 through E-8. Enlisted applicants must have completed at least eight but not more than sixteen years of active naval service. E-6 personnel must compete in the E-7 examination and be designated LDO selection-board-eligible. The LDO program has some of the same basic requirements as the warrant officer program. Warrant officers who are accepted into the LDO program are appointed to the grade of lieutenant (junior grade); enlisted applicants who are accepted are appointed as ensigns.

Because those appointed through this program are specialists in a particular field (having come from an enlisted rating), officers who receive their commissions as LDOs continue to receive assignments related to their specialties. For example, a gunner's mate who is commissioned through the LDO program is likely to be assigned to a ship as the weapons officer. Because these officers are "limited" to assignments related to their specialties, they are called "limited duty officers." Applicants accepting commissions through the LDO program must agree to remain on active duty for three years from the time they are commissioned.

Enlisted Commissioning Program (ECP)

The ECP is an undergraduate education program for enlisted personnel on active duty who have previously earned college credits. Selectees are ordered to the ECP on a permanent change of station (PCS) basis and enrolled as full-time students in a participating NROTC (Naval Reserve Officers Training Corps) host college or university to complete their degrees. If you are selected and are in a technical degree program, you will have up to 36 months to complete your degree. If you are in a nontechnical program, you may have up to 30 months to complete your degree. You will maintain your enlisted status during training, receiving all pay and allowances, but you must pay any expenses incurred in the education program (such as tuition, fees, and books). Upon graduation you will be commissioned. There are medical, aviation, and nuclear options available for this program.

Other Commissioning Opportunities

Besides the programs listed above, there are a number of other ways for you to earn a commission. All commissioning programs are covered in a consolidated manual called the Enlisted to Officer Commissioning Programs Application Manual (OPNAVINST 1420.1). See your educational services officer for assistance.

Navy Pay and Benefits

While no one gets rich serving in the U.S. Navy, there are many benefits—some financial, some in other forms—that are part of the Navy career. One benefit that cannot be spent in any consumer outlet, but is of inestimable value, is the satisfaction of knowing that you are serving your nation. By being a part of the finest Navy the world has ever seen, whether in the throes of combat or carrying out the daily routine, you are helping to preserve freedom in the United States of America, and that is a special satisfaction you will not find in many walks of life.

No one expects you to survive or thrive on pride alone, however. Just as in any profession, you will be paid for your work. And, because there are special demands and sacrifices that go with life in the Navy, there are also other benefits that come with the job.

Pay and Allowances

You will receive two kinds of financial remuneration while you are in the Navy, pay and allowances. There are certain legal and economic distinctions between the two, but the most practical way to distinguish them is that pay is much like the salary a civilian would receive in her or his job and is, therefore, subject to federal income tax. Allowances are extra payments designed to help you meet certain expenses of Navy life, and these are *not* subject to federal income tax.

Because there are these two types of remuneration in the Navy, when you are comparing how much money you make with how much a civilian counterpart makes you should not merely compare dollar for dollar because some of your dollars are tax free.

Defense Joint Military Pay System (DJMS)

Your Navy pay is handled by a sophisticated pay system known as DJMS, but you are responsible for knowing what you should be getting paid and ensuring that what you actually receive is correct.

PHI Alexander C. Hicks, Jr.

Figure 11.1. Because there are special demands—such as periods of family separation—that come with a career in the Navy, there are also many benefits for both the Sailor and his family.

Every month you will receive a DFAS Form 702, known as a leave and earnings statement (LES), showing you your entitlements, deductions, and allotments. Read and keep these forms each month. If your pay varies significantly and you don't know why, or if you have any questions after reading your LES, contact your disbursing office.

DEFENSE FINANCE AND ACCOUNTING SERVICE MILITARY LEAVE AND EARNINGS STATEMENT

ID	NAME (LAST, FIRST, MI)			SOC. SEC. NO.		GRADE	PAY DATE	YRS SVC	ETS	BRANCH	ADSN/DSSN	PERIOD COVERED

	ENTITLEMENTS		DEDUCTIONS		ALLOTMENTS		SUMMARY	
	TYPE	AMOUNT	TYPE	AMOUNT	TYPE	AMOUNT	+AMT FWD	
A							+TOT ENT	
B								
C							-TOT DED	
D								
E							-TOT ALMT	
F								
G							=NET AMT	
H								
I							-CR FWD	
J								
K							=EOM PAY	
L								
M								
N								
O								
	TOTAL							

LEAVE	BF BAL	ERND	USED	CR BAL	ETS BAL	LV LOST	LV PAID	USE/LOSE	FED TAXES	WAGE PERIOD	WAGE YTD	M/S	EX	ADD'L TAX	TAX YTD

FICA TAXES	WAGE PERIOD	SOC WAGE YTD	SOC TAX YTD	MED WAGE YTD	MED TAX YTD	STATE TAXES	ST	WAGE PERIOD	WAGE YTD	M/S	EX	TAX YTD

PAY DATA	BAQ TYPE	BAQ DEPN	VHA ZIP	RANT AMT	SHARE	STAT	JFTR	DEPNS	2D JFTR	BAS TYPE	CHARITY YTD	TPC	PACIDN

REMARKS   YTD ENTITLE_____   YTD DEDUCT_____

DFAS Form 702, May 92

Figure 11.2. Leave and earnings statement (DFAS Form 702).

Navy Pay
and
Benefits

201

Below is a list of the names of the various blocks as they appear on the LES with a brief explanation of each. Because DJMS is run by the Defense Department instead of the Navy Department, some of the terms are different from the old Navy terminology.

BLOCK NAME   EXPLANATION

The first nine blocks are listed on a line marked by the letters "ID" (for "identification").

NAME   Your name in last, first, and middle initial format.

SOC. SEC. NO.   Your Social Security number.

GRADE   Your current paygrade.

PAY DATE   The date you entered active duty for pay purposes in YYMMDD (year, month, day) format. The old Navy term for this was "pay entry base date (PEBD)."

YRS SVC   In two digits, the actual years of creditable service you have.

ETS	Expiration term of service in YYMMDD format. This is the date when your obligated service ends. This is the equivalent of the term EOAS (end of active obligated service) used more commonly in the Navy.
BRANCH	The branch of service you belong to (i.e., Navy).
ADSN/DSSN	The unique identifying number assigned to your disbursing office (Disbursing Station Symbol Number).
PERIOD COVERED	The period covered by this individual LES. Normally this would be a calendar month.
ENTITLEMENTS	This large block lists the pay and allowances you are receiving. There is room for fifteen separate entitlements and they are listed by type and amount. If you should rate more than fifteen, the others would be continued in the remarks block.
DEDUCTIONS	Such things as taxes and deductions for the dependent dental plan are listed in this large block by type and amount. Like the entitlements block, there is room for fifteen entries in this block.
ALLOTMENTS	Allotments (explained below) that you have set up are listed in this large block by type and amount. There is room for fifteen entries.

The next seven blocks are listed under the heading "SUMMARY."

+AMT FWD	The amount of all unpaid pay and allowances due from a previous LES.
+TOT ENT	The total of all your pay and allowances.
–TOT DED	The total of all your deductions.
–TOT ALMT	The total of all your allotments.
=NET AMT	The dollar amount of all unpaid pay and allowances, minus all deductions and allotments.
–CR FWD	The dollar amount of all unpaid pay and allowances due to be reflected on the next LES as the +AMT FWD.

=EOM PAY   The actual amount of the payment to be
                  paid to you on payday.

The next eight blocks are listed as items pertaining to your LEAVE
(earned vacation days).

BF BAL   The "brought forward" leave balance. This
                  is the number of days of leave you had
                  earned as of the last LES.

ERND   The amount of leave earned during the
                  period covered by this LES.

USED   The amount of leave used during the period
                  covered by this LES.

CR BAL   Your current leave balance.

ETS BAL   The leave balance you would have if you
                  took no more leave during the remainder
                  of your obligated service (until the expi-
                  ration of your term of service).

LV LOST   The number of days of leave you have lost
                  (remember, there is a limit to the number
                  of days of leave you can carry "on the
                  books").

LV PAID   The number of days you have paid for
                  instead of taken (normally only occurs at
                  the end of your service).

USE/LOSE   The number of days of leave you will lose
                  if not taken by the end of the fiscal
                  year. This is figured on a monthly
                  basis.

The next six blocks are listed "FED [federal] TAXES" items.

WAGE PERIOD   The amount of money you earned this LES
                  period that is subject to federal income
                  tax withholding (FITW).

WAGE YTD   The total amount of money you have earned
                  this calendar year ("year to date") that is
                  subject to federal income tax. Note that
                  this is figured on "calendar year" and not
                  on the "fiscal year" (explained below);
                  this is because your taxes are figured on
                  the calendar year.

M/S	Your marital status (used to compute the FITW).
EX	The number of exemptions used to compute the FITW.
ADD'L TAX	The dollar amount you have specified to be withheld in addition to the amount computed using the M/S and EX figures.
TAX YTD	The total amount of FITW withheld so far this calendar year.

The next five blocks are listed at "FICA [Federal Insurance Contributions Act] TAXES" and pertain to Social Security and Medicare.

WAGE PERIOD	The amount of money you have earned this period that is subject to FICA.
SOC WAGE YTD	The total amount of money you have earned this calendar year that is subject to FICA.
SOC TAX YTD	The total amount of FICA that has been withheld so far this calendar year.
MED WAGE YTD	The wages earned so far this year that are subject to Medicare.
MED TAX YTD	Cumulative total of Medicare taxes paid so far this year.

The next six blocks are listed as "STATE TAXES" items.

ST	The two-digit postal abbreviation for your official home state.
WAGE PERIOD	The amount of money you earned this LES period that is subject to state income tax withholding (SITW).
WAGE YTD	The total amount of money you have earned this calendar year that is subject to SITW.
M/S	Your marital status (used to compute the SITW).
EX	The number of exemptions used to compute the SITW.
TAX YTD	The total amount of SITW withheld so far this calendar year.

The next thirteen blocks contain additional "PAY DATA."

BAQ TYPE — Basic Allowance for Housing (BAH) was once called Basic Allowance for Quarters (BAQ). Although it may eventually be changed, the LES still uses the old term.

BAQ DEPN — Again using the old term (BAQ instead of BAH), this block contains a code that indicates the type of dependent(s) you have for pay purposes. The codes are as follows:

I = Member married to member (your spouse is also in the service)

R = You

A = Spouse

C = Child

W = Member married to member, child under 21

G = Grandfathered (special case where an old policy is continued)

D = Parent

K = Ward of the court

L = Parents-in-law

S = Student (age 21–22)

T = Handicapped child over 21

Note: Keep in mind that these categories must be officially established in order for you to draw the associated BAH. Just because you have parents-in-law, for example, does not mean that code L would show up on your LES—they must be your legal dependents for that to happen.

VHA ZIP — VHA (Variable Housing Allowance) is an old term that no longer is used (what used to be VHA is now incorporated into BAH).

RENT AMT — The amount of rent you are currently paying for housing (if applicable).

SHARE	The number of people that are sharing your housing costs (if applicable).	
STAT	Indicates whether you are authorized to be "accompanied" (i.e., spouse is with you at your duty station) or "unaccompanied."	
JFTR	The joint federal travel regulations code based on your location—used for cost-of-living adjustments (COLA).	
DEPNS	The number of dependents you have.	
2D JFTR	The JFTR code based on the location of your dependents—used for COLA purposes.	
BAS TYPE	A code indicating the type of basic allowance for subsistence you are receiving, if applicable. Codes are as follows:	

B = Separate rations
C = Temporary duty (TDY) or permanent change of station (PCS)
H = Rations in kind not available
K = Rations under emergency conditions

CHARITY YTD	The total amount of charitable contributions you have made out of your pay so far this year.
TPC	This block is not used by the Navy.
PACIDN	The activity unit identification code. (*Note:* Every naval activity has a unique number assigned that identifies it. The number of the activity that is processing your pay appears in this block.)
REMARKS	Amplifying information that may be necessary appears in this block.
YTD ENTITLE	The total of all entitlements (pay and allowances) that you have received so far this year.
YTD DEDUCT	The total amount of money that has been deducted from your entitlements so far this year.

Basic Pay

Basic pay depends on your paygrade and years of service. It is the largest single item in your pay. You will be paid twice a month, usually on the first and the fifteenth. Through the direct-deposit system (DDS), your pay and entitlements will be electronically transferred to the banking institution of your choice. With DDS, no matter where you are—aboard ship, on shore, at an overseas station, in a travel status, or on leave—when payday rolls around you will have immediate access to your money because your pay will be in your account, on time.

Basic Allowance for Housing (BAH)

There are two kinds of BAH. If you have family members—spouse, children, or stepchildren (under 21 years old), parent or step-parent—who rely on you for more than half of their support, you can draw "with-dependents BAH." This allowance is not paid to you, however, when you are occupying public (government) quarters. "Without dependents BAH" is a lesser amount and is available to you if you do not have any of the family members described above. Because the cost of housing varies from place to place, the amount of BAH you receive will depend upon the geographic location of your duty station (your home port if you are assigned to a ship or squadron).

Family Separation Allowance (FSA)

Persons entitled to BAH (at the with-dependents rate) may also draw a family separation allowance (FSA) if (1) their ship or squadron is deployed for more than 30 days; (2) transportation of family members at government expense to a new duty station is not authorized; or (3) they are on temporary additional duty (TAD) for a period of 30 days or more.

Basic Allowance for Subsistence (BAS)

If you are serving aboard ship or on a base, your meals will be provided on the mess decks or in a mess hall. Sometimes, however, you will not be able to eat in these facilities on a regular basis. In those cases, you will receive BAS to cover your increased food costs.

The rates vary depending on whether (1) "rations in kind" (a government or government-provided mess) are available; (2) permission has been granted to mess separately (commuted rations or leave rations); or (3) you are assigned to duty under emergency conditions where no government messing facilities are available. Separate rations (SEPRATS) are usually limited to people living off base who have permission to eat away from their duty station. If you are receiving SEPRATS and choose to eat a meal at a government-run mess hall, you must pay for the meal.

Sea and Foreign Duty Pay

In general, sea pay begins the day you report aboard ship for duty if you have more than three years' prior sea duty and are in paygrade E-4 or above. Foreign-duty pay begins the day you report aboard a designated foreign-duty station. The rates vary for each paygrade.

Selective Reenlistment Bonus (SRB)

As the name implies, this retention incentive is paid to members serving in certain selected ratings or with certain NECs that are critically undermanned who have agreed to stay in the Navy for a specified amount of time. The actual amount received depends on a number of factors and can be rather complicated. You will do well to check with your career counselor or personnel office for additional facts.

Incentive Pay for Hazardous Duty

There are a number of different types of incentive payments. The most common types are aviation pay and submarine-duty pay. Rates for those two types are based on your paygrade and years in service.

Additional monthly incentive payments are made for flight-deck hazardous duty (FDHD), parachute duty, demolition duty, and experimental stress duty. Handlers of toxic pesticides, fuels, and propellants also receive incentive payments.

Diving pay, for members serving in an authorized diving billet, varies according to the skills involved. A scuba diver gets less per month than a master saturation diver, for example.

Imminent danger/hostile-fire pay may be given to members under certain circumstances.

Clothing Allowances

The first clothing allowance you received while at boot camp is the initial clothing monetary allowance (ICMA). Because men's and women's uniform items are not identical and different costs are associated with the various items, the ICMA for men and women is different.

If you must wear a uniform not worn by the majority of Navy personnel (if you serve in a Navy band that wears a special uniform for performances, for example), you will receive a special initial clothing monetary allowance (SICMA). This allowance is also paid to you upon promotion to chief petty officer, since chief uniforms are very different from other enlisted uniforms.

You also will receive a yearly clothing maintenance allowance (CMA). This allowance varies depending upon a number of circumstances. See your disbursing office to determine how much you are eligible for.

Travel and Transportation Allowances (T&T)

The T&T allowances are paid to you when you receive orders to travel. You might be authorized to travel by privately owned vehicle (POV) or by government or commercial transportation. In addition, you may be paid a per diem (daily) allowance to cover the cost of lodging, meals, and other incidentals not included in the cost of transportation. How much you receive for per diem expenses will depend upon the area you are traveling through. An allowance for transportation of family members at government expense is also provided for a permanent change of station (PCS). You may also receive an allowance for transportation of household goods (HHGs) or personal effects when you make a PCS move. A reduced weight allowance is sometimes allowed for temporary additional duty (TAD) orders. Partial reimbursement for incidental expenses incurred in a PCS move of HHGs is also paid as a dislocation allowance (DLA). Single and married personnel may qualify for this entitlement.

Several other allowances are specifically designed to help you with excessive costs while you are on permanent duty outside the continental United States (CONUS). Some overseas stations will give you an overseas housing allowance (OHA) or cost-of-living allowance (COLA) and a temporary lodging allowance (TLA). The OHA is based on the average cost of local housing in the overseas area, compared with your BAH. Items considered include rent, utilities, minor maintenance expenses, and initial occupancy expenses. COLA is derived by comparing the cost of living in your overseas area with the average cost of living in CONUS for a similar area. TLA provides partial reimbursement for the expenses incurred when you are moving to or from overseas areas. The amount is a graduated percentage, depending on the number of family members and the per diem allowances for travel to that specific area. Be sure you see your disbursing office for all the details before making the move.

Family Subsistence Supplemental Allowance (FSSA)

This supplemental pay program is designed to ensure that all military members' household income is at least 130% of the federal poverty line and to ensure that no military members must use food stamps in order to subsist. The amount received is based upon monthly income and family size. If you have a spouse and/or dependent children and are having serious financial difficulty, see your division chief or division officer to find out whether you may be eligible for FSSA.

Allotments

Through allotments you may assign part of your pay regularly to a spouse, parents, bank, or insurance company so that they will receive payments without you having to take any further action. You may also take part in the Navy's savings bond program or make a donation to certain charity organizations through the allotment system. Once the appropriate forms have been filled out, the specified amount of money is automatically deducted from your pay each month and payments will automatically be made by the Navy.

Benefits

There's no doubt that the pay in today's Navy is one of the real benefits. There are others, such as commissary and exchange privileges, medical and dental care for you and your family, and an extensive educational program. Other somewhat less tangible benefits also go to you (and in some cases to your family) because you are in the Navy.

Legal Assistance

A legal-assistance officer can help you draw up wills, powers of attorney, deeds, affidavits, contracts, and many other documents. She or he also can advise you on transfer of property, marriage and divorce, adoption of children, taxation, personal injury, and other legal problems. The advice is free, and may help you avoid a lot of trouble. The Navy's legal-assistance program is specifically designed to advise and assist Sailors and their dependents who have legal problems. All matters are treated confidentially.

Family Housing

The family housing program includes public quarters (government rental units), mobile-home parks, government-insured privately owned projects, and leasing of privately owned units. The Navy tries to make sure adequate housing facilities are available for Sailors and their family members at a reasonable cost and within reasonable commuting distance.

Because on-base housing is a popular benefit (more convenient and less expensive than renting or buying a place to live off base) there is usually a waiting list for those who want it. When you are preparing to transfer to a new duty station, contact the housing office at your new location as soon as possible to see what the housing situation is and to get yourself on the list as soon as you are eligible. Where Navy housing is not available, housing referral offices will assist you in locating private housing in the community.

Health Benefits
Under the Uniformed Services Health Benefit Program (USHBP), care is provided in Uniformed Services Medical Treatment Facilities (USMTFs) when possible. Other care is provided in civilian facilities at full or partial expense to the government when necessary.

Active-duty members must be provided all *necessary* medical care. The primary source of care for all eligible beneficiaries is the USMTF. When care is not available from the USMTF for an active-duty member, it may be provided at government expense under the Non-Naval Medical Care Program and must be preauthorized. Each USMTF can provide acute medical and surgical care to varying degrees. Since not all USMTFs have the same medical capabilities, the health benefits advisor (HBA) should be contacted to determine what services are available.

Dependents and retired personnel are provided care at a USMTF if space, facilities, and proper medical staff are available. Dental care may also be provided on a space-available basis.

Defense Enrollment Eligibility Reporting System (DEERS)
The DEERS system verifies who is entitled to health care at military medical treatment facilities and who is eligible for TRICARE benefits [see below]. Active duty and retired personnel are automatically enrolled in the system, but family members must be enrolled (including newborns) to be eligible. Be sure to report all changes (such as marriages, divorces, adoptions, changes of address, etc.). To enroll family members or make changes, see your personnel office.

TRICARE
TRICARE is a regionally managed health care program for active duty and retired personnel and their dependents that brings together the health care resources of the Army, Navy, and Air Force. There are three components of this program: TRICARE Prime (where military medical facilities are the primary source of care), TRICARE

Standard (a fee-for-service option), and TRICARE Extra (a preferred provider option that saves money).

Active duty personnel are automatically enrolled in TRICARE Prime and pay no fees. Family members must choose a TRICARE option and apply for enrollment but they pay no enrollment fees. Retired personnel must choose an option and in some cases pay enrollment fees.

The best option for you and your family depends upon a number of factors, and making the right choice can be challenging. A lot of information is available in the form of pamphlets and booklets but do not hesitate to seek advice from your command health benefits advisor.

Family Dental Plan

The Navy's family dental plan is a contracted insurance program that allows spouses and children of active-duty members to obtain basic dental care from the civilian sector. Family members must reside in the United States, Puerto Rico, or the U.S. Virgin Islands to be eligible. Participants pay a monthly payroll deduction, plus there may be copayments for certain kinds of care. First-term enlisted personnel must have at least 24 months until expiration of active obligated service (EAOS) to enroll their family.

Counseling Assistance

The Navy has human relations experts ready to advise and help Sailors with difficult personal and family affairs. A Navy chaplain, like a minister or priest at home, can offer counseling as well as perform religious ceremonies like baptisms, marriages, and funerals.

Professionally trained specialists are also available through Fleet and Family Support Centers (FFSC) for counseling of problems relating to alcoholism, drug abuse, family and personal affairs, and the effects of discriminatory practices in and out of the Navy.

Death Benefits

If you should die while on active duty, your family members would be eligible for certain benefits to help them financially.

Death Gratuity

If you die while serving on active duty in the Navy (or within 120 days after leaving the Navy, and if your death is determined to be service-related), your spouse or another designated surviving family member will receive a death gratuity of $6000. Also, your family will be eligible to receive 90 days worth of BAH or will be permitted to remain in government housing for 90 days rent-free.

Social Security
Your family will also be eligible for certain Social Security benefits if you die while in the Navy. Your uniformed service may qualify you for extra consideration above the amount you would receive as a civilian. You may obtain additional information about your Social Security benefits by calling 1-800-772-1213.

Dependency and Indemnity Compensation (DIC)
Regardless of your paygrade, your surviving spouse will also be eligible for a monthly payment from the Department of Veterans Affairs should you die while serving on active duty. These payments will continue as long as your spouse does not remarry.

If your spouse has one or more children under the age of 18, he or she will receive an additional payment per child. If only your children survive you and they are under the age of 18, they will receive additional payments depending upon the number of children.

Servicemen's Group Life Insurance (SGLI)
You may also have a $200,000 life-insurance policy while on active duty, through servicemen's group life insurance. The cost is $18.00 per month. If you do nothing, you will automatically be covered for $200,000 at a cost of $18.00 per month. You must request to be covered for less than $200,000. You may request that the amount be reduced in increments of $10,000 or you may choose not to be covered at all. On separation, SGLI can be converted to a five-year nonrenewable term policy, veterans' group life insurance (VGLI). The moderate cost of VGLI is based on age at the time of separation.

Survivor Benefit Program
This program is for retired personnel only and provides a guaranteed lifetime income to your surviving spouse (providing he or she does not remarry before age 55). While this is an optional program, most responsible sources recommend that you take advantage of this benefit.

Navy Mutual Aid Association
While this is not a government benefit, the Navy Mutual Aid Association was organized for the purpose of aiding its members and

their families by providing assistance and a low-cost life insurance program. If you are interested in learning more about this popular program, call 1-800-628-6011 or write to: Navy Mutual Aid Association, Henderson Hall, 29 Carpenter Road, Arlington, Virginia, 22212.

Leave

As already discussed in chapter 1, all personnel on active duty, from seaman to admiral, earn leave at the rate of 2.5 days each month, for a total of 30 days a year. The only exceptions are time spent in the brig or if you are absent without authorization for 24 hours or more. "Earned leave" is the amount credited to you on the books at any given date. Under certain circumstances, you will be permitted to take more leave than you are entitled to. This is called "advance leave" and will give you a negative balance, which will show up on your LES. Advance leave is paid back as you earn it.

As leave accumulates, it is carried over from one fiscal year to the next. Except for special circumstances involving extended deployments and/or hostile conditions, no more than 60 days can be carried over on the books. This means that if you have 67 days of leave on the books on 30 September (the end of the fiscal year), you will lose seven days of leave. For this reason, you should watch your leave balance on your LES and plan accordingly.

Persons discharged with leave still on the books are paid a lump sum equal to their daily pay for each day. The most leave you can "sell back" in a military career is 60 days. Those discharged with minus leave will pay back approximately a day's pay for each day's leave owed.

Your commanding officer has the authority to grant all earned leave on a yearly basis, plus up to 45 days' advance leave. Personnel lacking enough earned leave during an emergency can be granted advance leave up to 60 days.

"Convalescent leave" is an authorized absence while you are under medical care and treatment. It must be authorized by your commanding officer on orders of a medical officer, or by the commanding officer of a military hospital. It is usually granted following a period of hospitalization and is not charged as leave.

In a personal emergency, such as a death in the family or a serious illness, you will normally be granted emergency leave to take care of personal matters that no one else can handle. Such emergencies must be verified by the Red Cross.

Overseas Schools for Family Members

The Department of Defense (DOD) operates many educational facilities for minor family members of all U.S. active-duty military and DOD civilian personnel stationed overseas. There are approximately 190 DOD schools overseas and 90,000 students; about 20 of these schools are Navy-sponsored. There are Navy schools from Spain to Japan, from Iceland to the West Indies. Army and Air Force schools in many countries are open to Navy family members. From first grade through high school, family members can receive an education overseas at the government's expense.

Credit Unions

Although not a government-supplied benefit, your special status as a member of the armed services has caused the development of specially oriented credit unions. Most major Navy installations provide credit-union facilities for Navy personnel and the Navy Federal Credit Union (NFCU) in Washington, D.C., serves Navy men and women the world over. NFCU has worldwide wire facilities, an 800 number that allows members to call toll free anywhere in the continental United States, and a website (*www.navyfcu.org*). NFCU offers credit cards, signature loans, loans based on equal collateral, automobile loans, and personal loans for mobile homes and furniture as well as mortgage loans in some areas. NFCU also has a policy of free life insurance that ensures loan protection for members. Recruits at Great Lakes are eligible for membership and can sign up immediately.

215

Morale, Welfare, and Recreation

Morale, welfare, and recreation (MWR) programs provide many different recreational, social, and community support activities for all Navy personnel. Some of these activities are described below.

Sports and fitness program. The sports and fitness program is designed to provide the Navy community with sports and fitness opportunities that enhance the overall quality of life and contribute to physical and mental readiness. The base-level sports and fitness program consists of informal or recreational sports (where individuals participate for fun and fitness) and organized (intramural) sports (i.e., individual, dual, team, and meet events) where the element of competition is included for events within and between individual commands. Some MWR programs also offer "Captain's Cup Field Day" competitions that are designed to build morale and teamwork while providing a means to have a great deal of fun.

Navy higher level sports program. The higher level sports program (armed forces sports program) is for active-duty members who demonstrate exceptional athletic abilities. Competitive forums for the higher level sports program include Navy trial camps, which are used to evaluate and select athletes for Navy teams and the armed forces championships. These two competitive forums provide a pathway for athletes to represent the armed forces in competition at the international level.

Youth recreation program. This program provides comprehensive, year-round recreation activities and services for youth of all ages ranging from kindergarten to twelfth grade. The program contains six core elements: school-age care, day camps, teen programming, social/recreational activities, sports/physical fitness, and personal development.

Outdoor recreation program. Facilities may include outdoor equipment rental centers, parks, picnic areas, archery ranges, recreational vehicle (RV) parks, skeet and trap ranges, campgrounds, stables, marinas, beaches, swimming pools, cabins, cottages, off-base recreational areas, outdoor obstacle/challenge courses, paint-ball competition courses, and climbing walls. Instructional classes, outdoor equipment rentals, specialty equipment sales, organized group activities, special events, self-directed activities, and seasonal/geographic activities are also provided in various areas.

Information, tickets, and tours (ITT) program. An information, tickets, and tours program is located on virtually every shore installation in the Navy. ITT serves the military community with local recreation information (on and off base), entertainment tickets, and local tour services. Additionally, a hotel reservation system is available to assist travelers in finding quality, low-cost accommodations while on vacation.

Auto craft skills center program. Provides automotive enthusiasts with a quality, value-based program for the repair and maintenance of their vehicles. Auto-craft skills centers are not service stations, but are facilities where patrons can work on their vehicles and learn automotive skills.

Afloat recreation program. Sea duty is a difficult and demanding part of Navy life and it is important that Sailors are provided quality leisure time activities that can be accommodated within the limited space aboard ship. Whether in port or at sea, a wide variety of individual and group recreational activities are available, including sports, fitness center facilities, tours ashore, leisure reading, ticket rebates, board games, and underway athletics.

Golf program. The Navy golf program is offered at over forty bases, providing course play, snack bars, pro shops, driving ranges, cart rentals, as well as classes and personalized lessons.

Bowling program. The Navy bowling program offers open and league bowling, and special youth programs at many shore facilities.

Navy Clubs. The Navy Club System provides food, beverage, entertainment, and recreation programs at most bases.

Child care. The Navy operates child-development centers at almost all naval installations. This program provides high-quality child care in conveniently located child-development centers at moderate cost to the Sailor (fees are based on pay grade). Additionally, at naval installations having government housing, family child care is provided in government housing and is run by government-certified child-care providers. Commanding officers of installations that have child-care centers may establish priority of access in child-development centers (for example, single parents, dual military couples).

Fleet and Family Support Centers (FFSC)

Fleet and Family Support Centers are located at most Navy installations and are staffed by program specialists and clinical counselors to assist with adaptation to Navy life, to facilitate personal and family readiness, and to provide services and skills for self-sufficiency and personal success. They offer a wide variety of programs and services, some of which are discussed below.

Information and referral programs. Provide a convenient way to find out what family support services are available in both the military and civilian community.

Counseling services. Helps Sailors and their families deal with personal issues and stresses. FFSCs provide short-term, individual, marital, family, and group counseling to address situational problems in day-to-day living such as depression/grief after a loss, troubled relationships, occupational concerns, and family and parenting issues.

Crisis response. Provides help in a time of crisis that affects many people or a group of people at an installation. Such incidents can include natural disasters, aircraft accidents, major fires, terrorist activity, a collision at sea, or mission-related casualties. The help provided is designed to minimize the negative effects and long-term human-resource losses associated with traumatic incidents.

Deployment support. Helps Sailors and their families successfully manage the challenges of deployment.

Personal financial management assistance. Sailors in need of financial guidance can find it at their local FFSC.

Spouse employment assistance. Assists civilian spouses in locating and obtaining local employment by providing workshops on how to search for a job, plan a career, write a resume, have a successful job interview, and network.

Family advocacy program. Provides help with the problems of child and spouse abuse. Services include prevention classes and individual help for victims and offenders. FSC staff members work closely with military and civilian agencies in dealing with these issues.

Exceptional family member support. Ensures that the special needs of family members will be met by ensuring the service member's assignments are compatible with those needs. Because special needs cannot be met at every duty station throughout the world, EFM enrollment is mandatory for active-duty sponsors who have family members with chronic illness or incapacity, mental illness, or learning disabilities.

Transition assistance. Assists service members who are transitioning from military to civilian life. These services include seminars designed to address social, financial, job-search, and professional issues.

Relocation assistance. Helps Sailors and families adjust to new duty stations. Typical services include destination area information, intercultural relations training, settling-in services, and help in finding a home.

Sexual assault victim intervention services. Victims are helped directly and educational services are provided to individuals, commands, and community groups to improve awareness of these problems.

New parent support. A voluntary program of identification, screening, home visitation, information, and referral for new and expectant parents. Prevention education programs and referrals to community support services are also offered.

Service Organizations

Many organizations provide assistance and services to Sailors and their families. Three of the most important are listed below.

Navy–Marine Corps Relief Society. Supported entirely by private funds, the Navy–Marine Corps Relief Society assists Sailors/Marines and their families in time of need. Though not an official part of the Navy, this society is the Navy's own organization for taking care of its people. It is staffed and supported largely by naval personnel and provides financial aid to those in need in the form of an interest-free loan, a grant, or a combination of both.

American Red Cross. The Red Cross supplies financial aid to naval personnel, does medical and psychiatric casework, and provides recreational services for the hospitalized. It also performs services in connection with dependency discharge, humanitarian transfer, emergency leave, leave extensions, and family welfare reports.

Navy Wives Club of America. This group is composed chiefly of wives of enlisted men serving at sea in the Navy, Coast Guard, and Marine Corps. Besides its many social activities, NWCA sponsors a special scholarship fund for the children of Sailors. The club assists chaplains and participates in the blood-donor and NRS projects. Local chapters participate in community projects and hold dances, picnics, and similar affairs.

Reenlistment

A Sailor who completes an enlistment in the Navy and then reenlists is said to "ship over." If you reenlist on the expiration date of your current term of service, or within three calendar months after discharge, it is called a continuous-service reenlistment. Those who reenlist after more than three calendar months of being released from active duty make a "broken service reenlistment." The first type is better; on the broken service reenlistment, you may have to come back in a lower rate. Also, if your rate is SRB eligible, you may lose a substantial portion of your reenlistment bonus.

Reenlistment is not a right, it's a privilege. To earn that privilege, you must be recommended by your commanding officer, be physically qualified, and meet certain standards of performance.

You may choose to reenlist for anywhere from two to six years. In cases where a reenlistment bonus is available, the more years you ship over for, the more money you will receive.

In some cases, you may choose to *extend* your current enlistment rather than reenlist. There are two types of enlistment extension. "Conditional extensions" may be made at any time during an enlistment if you wish to qualify for advancement, for a cruise or a deployment, for entrance into a service school, for a special program, for any other duty requiring additional obligated service, or to obtain maternity benefits for your wife. Extensions are executed in increments of one or more months, not to exceed a total of 48 months on any single enlistment. "Unconditional extensions" may also be made at any time for a period of not less than 24 or more than 48 months.

Incentive Programs

A number of programs in the Navy offer various incentives to help a Sailor decide in favor of staying in the Navy.

Selective Training and Reenlistment (STAR) Program

A number of incentives are available under this program, including early reenlistment, a variety of school programs, automatic advancement, and payment of a selective reenlistment bonus (SRB). In order to apply for STAR, you must be an E-5, E-4, or qualified E-3, and you must have at least 21 months, but not more than six years, of continuous naval service. You must also be recommended by your commanding officer, be serving in your first enlistment, meet the minimum test-score requirements for entrance into the appropriate Class A school, and agree to reenlist for or extend your enlistment to a period of four, five, or six years. Although all ratings are eligible, your chances of getting into the STAR program are enhanced if you are serving in a critical rating or if you have a critical NEC. (*Note:* "Critical" means that there is a shortage of that rating or NEC in the Navy at the time that you apply.)

Selective Conversion and Reenlistment (SCORE) Program

This program allows you to change your rating as an incentive for reenlistment. SCORE works best for people in ratings that are overmanned or have limited advancement opportunities and are willing to shift into a critical rating. The program offers a variety of incentives, depending upon the individual's particular situation, and may include schooling guarantees, automatic advancement, early reenlistment, and, in some cases, payment of a selective reenlistment bonus. To be eligible, you must be in paygrade E-6, E-5, E-4, or be an identified E-3 striker who has more than 21 months of continuous active naval service (but not more than 12 years of total active military service). You must be recommended by your commanding officer, be within one year of end of active obligated service (EAOS), meet the obligatory service and test-score requirements to enter the appropriate Class A school for your new rating, and be willing to extend your service obligation. Candidates frequently are given the opportunity to work in the rating to which they are converting before being assigned to school. See your command career counselor for more information.

Guaranteed Assignment Retention Detailing (GUARD) Program
Although there are no schools guaranteed under this program, GUARD is a reenlistment incentive program that guarantees assignment to all petty officers and eligible E-3s with less than 25 years of service. If you are within six months of your EAOS you should first talk to your career counselor, then contact your detailer (by personal letter, telephone, or e-mail) to discuss your options. GUARD guarantees two assignments in exchange for your reenlistment. One assignment must be used at first reenlistment, while the second may be used at the end of any other enlistment, up to your seventeenth year of service.

To be eligible for GUARD, you must not be more than six months away from your EAOS and cannot already have a set of PCS (permanent change of station) orders in hand. You must also be recommended by your commanding officer, be eligible for the duty requested in accordance with the sea/shore rotation pattern, be willing to reenlist for four or more years, and have a consistent record of above-average or steadily improving performance.

Assignment to School as a Reenlistment Incentive
The Navy also has provisions to guarantee reenlistees a specific school. Generally, a Sailor must meet the service and entrance requirements for the appropriate school. Consideration of requests is based on composite training, sea/shore rotation, paygrade-versus-skill requirement, and fleet-reserve eligibility. Assignments to schools normally occur at the member's projected rotation date (PRD).

Changes in Rate or Rating
Since the Navy wants each Sailor to serve in the rate or rating for which he or she has the greatest aptitude and interest, regulations provide for lateral changes in rate and rating. "Lateral change" means that you can change your apprenticeship field or occupational specialty without changing your paygrade. Changes in rate or rating may be accomplished via formal school training or "in-service training," through direct conversion, through successful competition in a Navy rating exam, and, in rare cases, through forced conversion. The program is rather complex, so if you are contemplating a change in rate or rating, you would do well to check current directives or consult with your career counselor, personnel office, or educational services office.

If you are not yet rated and want only to change your apprentice-ship field, this is less complicated and your commanding officer can authorize it. Normally it will be approved if a greater need exists in the apprenticeship you want to switch to.

Discharges

If you choose not to reenlist, or if the Navy does not invite you to reenlist, or if other circumstances dictate that you must leave the service, you will receive a discharge.

Types of Discharge

There are different types of discharges and the type you receive is very significant because it can affect your life in important ways after you leave the Navy. Certain discharges eliminate some veterans' rights and benefits, and many employers will reject a former military person who cannot produce an honorable-discharge certificate. The various types of discharge are discussed below.

Honorable discharge. An honorable discharge means separation from the service with honor. It is given for one of the following reasons: expiration of enlistment, convenience of the government, dependency, or disability. To receive an honorable discharge, the final average of your performance marks must meet minimum specifications. You can't have been convicted by a general court-martial, or convicted more than once by a special court-martial.

General discharge. A general discharge is given under honorable conditions for such reasons as minority enlistment (meaning that you lied about your age to get into the Navy and were later discovered), ineptitude, and unsuitability. In most cases, it goes to those whose conduct and performance, though technically satisfactory, has not been good enough to deserve an honorable discharge.

Other discharges. These are the ones you especially do not want. They are, in order of increasing severity, the undesirable discharge (UD), bad conduct discharge (BCD), and dishonorable discharge (DD). The UD is given by administrative action for misconduct or breach of security, the BCD only by approved sentence of a general or special court-martial, and the DD only by approved sentence of a general court-martial.

Formal Reasons for Discharge

There are twelve formal reasons for discharge that the government uses to officially determine the nature of your discharge. They are listed and briefly explained below.

Expiration of enlistment. An enlistment normally ends the day before the anniversary date of the enlistment. Depending on circumstances, it may be later. If you have lost days because of injury, sickness, or disease caused by misconduct, you can be kept on active duty until the lost days are made up. Your expiration date may also be postponed if you are undergoing medical care or awaiting trial or official papers. All enlistments can be extended by the government during war or national emergency.

Fulfillment of service obligation. This discharge is given to regular Navy enlisted men and women on completion of their service obligation (if different from your original enlistment period), or to reservists released to inactive duty after completing their active obligated service.

Disability. Given to Sailors unable to carry out their duties because of a mental or physical disability.

Convenience of the government. This term includes general demobilization after a war, acceptance of a permanent commission, and for certain parenthood issues.

Dependency. Discharges for reasons of dependency or hardship are authorized when it is shown that undue and general hardship exists at home. The hardship must be permanent and must have arisen or worsened since the person joined the Navy. Dependency discharges, commonly called hardship discharges, are not authorized for financial or business reasons, or for personal convenience.

Misconduct. A misconduct discharge is given to deserters who have not returned to military jurisdiction, persons convicted by civil authorities, and those who have made fraudulent enlistments.

In absentia. Deserters absent longer than 18 months can be discharged *in absentia.* These discharges cover those who flee to foreign countries, where the United States has no jurisdiction, or for those who have not been found and the statute of limitations has run out.

Security. Given to personnel considered security risks.

Sentence of court-martial. Self-explanatory.

Unsuitability. Given for such reasons as ineptitude, apathy, alcoholism, and financial irresponsibility, as well as character and behavior disorders.

Personal abuse of drugs. Given to a drug abuser identified either by urinalysis or by the abuser's own admission.

Good of the service. This type of discharge can be issued instead of taking action under the UCMJ. Although a Sailor may request an administrative discharge under other-than-honorable (OTH) conditions, he or she is still subject to the results of any disciplinary proceedings in the case.

Retirement

When enlisted men and women complete more than 20 years of active service, they are eligible for release to inactive duty and for transfer to the fleet reserve. After 30 years of combined active service and inactive duty in the fleet reserve, they are transferred to the Navy's retired list. Those with 30 or more years of active service may be transferred directly to the retired list. Technically, the pay received by a fleet reserve member is a retainer, while that received by those on the retired list is retired pay, though both are popularly called retired pay. For the rest of this discussion, we will simply refer to both retirement pay and retainer pay as "retirement pay."

Currently, if you joined the Navy after July 1986, you have to make a choice of what kind of retirement benefit you will receive once you reach the 15-year point of your career. One choice is to accept a $30,000 bonus at the 15-year point and receive less retirement money once you actually retire. The other choice is to not take the $30,000 bonus at the 15-year point but receive more retirement money once you actually retire. The difference between the two is based on more complicated formulas but can be summed up as follows.

High-3. Whether you take the $30,000 bonus option or not, you will first need to figure your "high-3" pay. This is obtained by averaging your annual basic pay for the 3 years of service in which you received the most pay (usually the last 3 years of service). For example, if your basic pay was $32,000 in your last year of service and $30,000 in the two years preceding that, you would average them (32,000 + 30,000 + 30,000 divided by 3) to get your "high-3" of $30,666. (These figures are for illustration only; real Navy pay would not normally work out to such even figures.)

Without 15-Year Bonus. If you chose not to take the bonus at the 15-year point, you will receive 50% of your High-3 pay if you retire at the 20-year point. For every year beyond 20 that you serve, you will receive an additional 2.5%, up to 75%. So, using the high-3 example above ($30,666), if you retired at the 20-year point, you would receive 50% of that—$15,333—every year for the rest of your life [see the discussion of inflation below]. If you waited another year to retire, your retired pay would be increased by another 2.5% (to $16,099). [Be aware that dollar figures are always rounded down when figuring retirement.] If you stayed on active duty for 25 years, your retired pay would be 62.5% of your high-3 ($19,166). Once you reached 30 years, you would receive the maximum 75% ($22,999) and could not go any higher.

Taking the 15-Year Bonus. This option puts cash in your pocket before you retire, which can be a big help, but you should weigh the advantages against the disadvantages before making a decision either way. To begin with, you should know that income taxes will be withheld from the bonus money, so you will not receive a full $30,000. You should also know that if you decided to leave the Navy before reaching retirement (or Fleet Reserve) eligibility, you would be required to pay back $6,000 for each year less than twenty you did not serve. When you reach the twenty-year point, you will be eligible to receive 40% of your high-3 money ($12,266 per year in our example). Each year served beyond that would earn you another 3.5%, so at the 21-year point you would be eligible for $13,339, and at the 25-year point it would be $17,632 per year. By the time you reached 30 years, you would have reached the 75% maximum just as you did with the other option [see the discussion of inflation below].

Inflation. One other thing to consider is that the rate of inflation adjustment is different for the two options described above. The no-bonus option includes full inflation adjustment each year, but the bonus option is capped each year at 1 percentage point below the inflation rate, with a one-time adjustment at age 62 to raise your pay to what it would have been without the cap.

Obviously, there is a lot to consider before making your choice. Be sure to weigh all the variables (how long you plan/hope to stay on active duty, what are/will be your financial needs, etc.) before making that important decision at the 15-year point in your career. No matter what decision you make, military retirement is an important benefit that you should think about before deciding when to leave the Navy.

Another thing to consider is the Thrift Savings Plan offered by the Navy. This is not a substitute for the retirement plans described above but is an added benefit you can choose to supplement your retirement. The plan allows you to have some of your pay automatically deducted and invested. There are several options available, and you should see your career counselor for more information.

Second Career

For most people, retirement from the military is not retirement in the traditional sense. Either because you want to make more money or because you are still young enough to do more with your life, you will probably want to start a second career after you leave the Navy. Planning for a second career is an important step that should be care-

Figure 11.3. A chief petty officer retires from the Navy after 30 years of service.

fully considered. Your new life can offer fun, zest, or relaxation—or it can be one big headache.

The first step is getting to know yourself, especially if you want to find a new job. Often a Sailor undersells his or her talents or, worse yet, his or her potential. If you have climbed the promotion ladder to senior petty officer or officer, you've shown not only talent but potential and leadership. In examining your career, look for areas that will support your job aims in civilian life. Don't think that because you've spent 20 years as a signalman, the only job you're qualified for on the outside is that of a construction flagman. In general, don't limit yourself to work directly related to your Navy occupation. Your experience as a supervisor or manager is probably even more important in the eyes of an employer.

You should also brace yourself for the social and psychological shock that comes from leaving military society, where rules and paths are well defined. Even though you were a civilian before you joined the Navy, going back to the civilian world will take some adjustment. Even though you always looked sharp in your uniform and passed every inspection with flying colors, you may find that dressing yourself for your new job is a real challenge. You will probably be surprised at how missing a little sleep is a much bigger deal to a civilian than it is to you. You may find that what is early morning to your civilian coworkers is midday to you. You will probably get some quizzical looks the first time you ask a coworker where the head is or explain that you are "going topside for a minute."

Don't expect this transition to happen overnight. It may take weeks, months, or even longer. The important thing to remember is that it is perfectly normal and you're not the first who has had to make this adjustment.

As you venture out on this second career, whatever it is, bear in mind that your years of service in the Navy have strengthened you as a person, taught you a great many things, and prepared you to handle many of the challenges of life. Don't be cocky, but be confident. As a former Sailor, there isn't much you can't handle.

12 Ship Construction

Ships are the basic element of the Navy. There are other important components—aircraft, submarines (a kind of specialized ship actually), construction battalions (known as Seabees), commando teams (known as SEALS), shore installations, and so on—but ships have been the centerpiece of navies since ancient times. Because of their long existence, ships are steeped in tradition and talking about them requires a specialized vocabulary. Among the traditions that you will learn to observe is that ships are always referred to in the feminine gender. Sailors use the words "she" and "her" when talking about ships, never "it."

Navy ships are highly complicated machines with their own propulsion plants, weapons, repair shops, supply spaces, and facilities for living, sleeping, and eating. Although there are great differences in the types and missions of ships, all ships have certain essential characteristics.

Figure 12.1. Ships are the basic element of the Navy.

Armament is the combat "punch" of a ship. In some ships, that punch is primarily offensive, such as heavy-caliber guns or long-range missiles. Other ships, whose mission may be supportive, such as oilers or ammunition replenishment ships, carry armament that is primarily defensive in nature. A ship's armament may consist of guns, missiles, torpedoes, depth charges, rockets, mines, or aircraft. Most ships are armed with more than one type of weapon. An aircraft carrier, for example, uses her airplanes as the primary means of attack and defense, but she also may carry a close-in missile defense system to handle any attackers that may have penetrated her outer defenses.

Survivability refers to those features that help a ship survive the effects of combat. Aside from weapons, a ship's sturdy construction is her best protection. Compartmentation, double bottoms, and other structural components all make a ship less vulnerable to attack or damage by other means. A ship's fire-fighting and flooding-control systems are also important components of her survivability.

Seaworthiness means those features that enable a ship to operate in high winds and heavy seas. A ship's stability, or the way she recovers from a roll, is an essential part of her seaworthiness. You will sometimes hear a ship referred to by her "sea-keeping abilities," which refers to how well she is able to perform her mission when the sea and weather conditions are bad.

Maneuverability is the way a ship handles in turning, backing down (going in reverse), moving alongside another ship, or evading enemy weapons. Many factors contribute to a ship's maneuverability, such as the size of her rudder, the power of her engines and how quickly they respond to changes, her draft (how much of the ship is under the water), or her sail area (how much of the ship is above the water where the wind can affect her).

Speed determines how quickly a ship can get to a scene of action, helps her overtake an enemy or avoid being overtaken, and plays a role in a ship's maneuverability and vulnerability. Key factors are the power of her engines in relation to her size, and the shape of her underwater hull.

Endurance is the maximum time a ship can steam at a given speed. Most oil-powered ships can steam for days or even weeks without refueling. The Navy's nuclear-powered ships can cruise for years, limited only by their need to replenish food and other consumables.

No matter how specialized your professional training, you must still be thoroughly familiar with basic nautical terminology referring to ship construction. You will find that this terminology is used throughout the Navy whether you are on a naval air station, in a Navy school, or actually aboard ship. So you will need to learn this new vocabulary in order to communicate in your new profession. After a time, such language will become second nature to you and you will find yourself using these terms more naturally than the ones you used to use.

In some respects a ship is like a building. She has outer walls (forming the *hull*), floors (*decks*), inner walls (*partitions* and *bulkheads*), corridors (*passageways*), ceilings (*overheads*), and stairs (*ladders*). But, unlike a building, a ship moves, so you will also have to learn new terms for directions and getting around. For example, when you cross from a pier to a ship you are using the *brow* to go *aboard,* and what might be an entrance hall or foyer in a building is the *quarterdeck* on a ship. The front (*forward*) part of a ship is the *bow;* to go toward the bow is to *go forward.* The back (*after*) part of the ship is the *stern;* to go toward the stern is to go *aft.* Something located further aft than another object is said to be *abaft* the other. The uppermost deck that runs the entire length of the ship from bow to stern is the *main deck.* [An exception to this rule is the aircraft carrier, whose main deck is the hangar deck, not the flight deck, which would seem to fit the normal definition of main deck.] Above the main deck

is the *superstructure.* "Floors" below the main deck are called *lower decks,* but those above the main deck are called *levels.* In a building you would go upstairs or downstairs, in a ship you go *topside* and *below.* The forward part of the main deck is the *forecastle* (pronounced "fohk-sul"), and the after part is the *fantail.* As you face forward on a ship, the right side is *starboard,* and the left side is *port.* An imaginary line running full-length down the middle of the ship is the *centerline.* The direction from the centerline toward either side is *outboard,* and from either side toward the centerline is *inboard.* A line from one side of the ship to the other runs *athwartship.*

Although an explanation of the term *displacement* is more complicated, for most practical purposes this term refers to the weight of a vessel.

Basic Ship Structure

While you are not expected to be a naval architect, you will need to know some of the basics of how ships are constructed in order to understand how they work and where things are in relation to each other. This knowledge will not only keep you from getting lost on a ship, it may help you some day to save your ship or yourself should a disaster strike.

The Hull

The hull is the main body of the ship. *Shell plating* forms the sides and bottom, and the *weather deck* or *main deck* forms the top. Where the sides join the main deck is called the *gunwale* (pronounced as though rhyming with "funnel"). The outermost layer of plating and decking is called the *skin of the ship.*

The shape and construction of the hull depend on the type of ship. Ships designed for high-speed operations—destroyers and cruisers, for example—have long, narrow hulls with fine lines. Aircraft carriers and auxiliary ships have hulls with square center sections, vertical sides, and flat bottoms for greater carrying capacity. Submarines, designed to operate under water, have hulls that are rounded, like an egg, because that shape withstands great pressure.

The keel is the backbone of the ship. The keel usually looks like an I-beam running the full length of the ship along the bottom. The forward end of the keel, extended upward, is the *stem;* the after end, extended upward, is the *sternpost. Frames* are beamlike structures fastened to the keel. They run athwartship, like ribs, and support the watertight skin or shell plating. Most ships built for the Navy also have *longitudinal frames* running fore and aft. The longitudinal and athwartships frames form an egg-crate structure in the bottom of the ship which, when inner-bottom plating is welded to it, creates what is called a *double bottom.* What would be walls in a building are called *bulkheads* if they are weight-supporting and watertight, and *partitions* if they are not. Solid (except for the openings for doors, ventilation ducts, and so on) "walls" inside the hull, extending from one side of the ship to the other, are called *transverse bulkheads.* Deck beams, transverse bulkheads, and *stanchions* (posts) support the decks and help strengthen the sides against water pressure.

When weight is added to a ship's inner bottom to balance her topside weight, making her more stable, it is called *ballast.* Some ships carry permanent concrete ballast; others pump saltwater into tanks to serve as temporary ballast, pumping it out when it is no longer needed.

Where the hull meets the surface of the water on a ship is called the *waterline.* Any part of the ship that is under water is below the waterline; any part of the ship that is in air instead of water is above the waterline.

Vertical extensions of the shell plating above the deck edge, which serve as a kind of solid fence, are called *bulwarks.* They shield deck areas from the direct effect of waves and keep personnel and equipment from going overboard. The latter purpose is also served by *lifelines,* which are wire ropes mounted on short stanchions and stretched tight by turnbuckles to form a kind of safety fence around the edges of the ship's weather decks (where there are no bulwarks).

The vertical distance from the waterline to the keel determines a ship's *draft*. Measured in feet and inches, draft markings are six-inch-high numbers marked on the hull near the stem and stern post. Because these numbers are six inches high and are six inches apart, the bottom of each number indicates foot marks and the top indicates half-foot marks.

That part of the ship's hull that extends from the waterline to the first weather deck is called *freeboard*.

To protect the ship's propellers (also called *screws*) from damage when coming alongside a pier or mooring next to another ship, steel braces are mounted at the stern, directly above the propellers. These are appropriately called *propeller guards*.

When a ship is properly balanced fore and aft (that is, the bow and stern are at the levels they were designed to be), the ship is said to be in *trim*. If the bow is lower than the stern, the ship is said to be *down by the head* or *down by the bow*. When her stern is lower, she is said to be *down by the stern*.

A ship with one side higher out of the water than the other has a starboard or port list. *List* is a temporary condition caused by uneven loading of the ship. If fuel is added to the port-side tanks more rapidly than to the starboard-side tanks, the ship will list to port until the weight is balanced. List is measured in degrees by a device called an *inclinometer,* which is either a liquid-level or pendulum-like device mounted exactly at the ship's centerline. When the ship is perfectly level, the inclinometer reads "zero"; when she has a list the inclinometer will tell you how much.

Superstructure

All structures above the main deck are collectively referred to as the *superstructure*. Different kinds of ships have different types of superstructure. Often, the superstructure is topped off by one or more *masts*. At its simplest, a mast is a single pole fitted with a crossbar, called a *yardarm,* which extends above the ship and carries flag *halyards* (lines used to hoist the flags), navigational and signal lights, and various electronic devices. If the ship has two masts, the forward one is called the *foremast,* the after one the *mainmast*. Modern ships do not normally have three masts, but in the days of sail, when masts also played a role in the propulsion of the ship by supporting her sails, some ships had a third mast, called the *mizzen,* which was mounted after the mainmast. On single-masted ships, the mast,

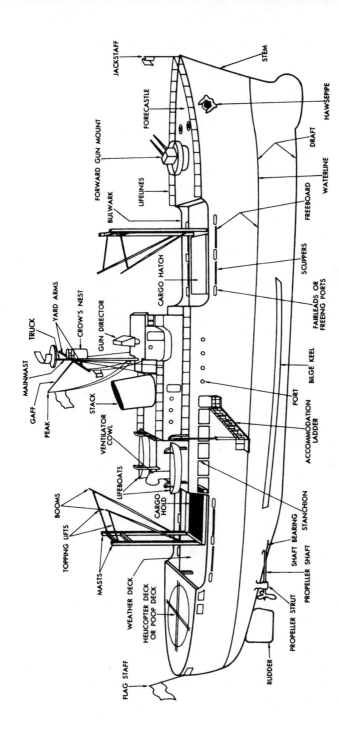

Figure 12.2. Some of the principal parts of a ship.

whether forward or amidships, is usually part of the superstructure and is simply called the mast.

The top of a mast is called the *truck.* The top of the foremast is the *foretruck,* while the top of the mainmast is the *main truck.* The *pigstick* is a slender vertical extension above the mast from which the ship's commission pennant or an admiral's personal flag flies. The *gaff* usually extends abaft the mainmast and is used to fly the national ensign when the ship is under way. The vertical *spar* (short pole) at the bow and the slightly raked one at the stern are called the *jackstaff* and *flagstaff,* respectively. As discussed in chapter 6, when a Navy ship is at anchor or moored to a pier it flies the union jack on the jackstaff and the national ensign on the flagstaff from 0800 to sunset.

The *stack* of a ship serves the same purpose as the smokestack on a powerplant ashore. It carries off smoke and hot gases from the boilers and exhaust from the diesel engines. (Nuclear-powered ships do not need stacks since their reactors produce no smoke or gas.) Some diesel-powered ships release their exhaust from the sides. On some ships, the masts and stacks have been combined to form large towers called *macks.*

234

Decks and Levels

Decks divide a ship into tiers or layers of compartments the way floors of a building divide it into stories. The deck normally consists of steel plates strengthened by transverse (athwartships) deck beams and longitudinal (fore and aft) girders. Decks above the waterline are usually *cambered* (arched) to provide greater strength and drain off water.

Decks are named according to their position and function in the ship. For purposes of compartment identification, decks are also numbered. The *main deck* is usually the uppermost of the decks that run continuously from bow to stern. The *second, third,* and *fourth decks,* continuous decks below the main deck, are numbered in sequence from topside down. A partial deck (that does not run continuously from bow to stern) is called a *platform.*

A partial deck above the main deck is numbered with a zero in front and called a *level* to distinguish it from the full decks. So the first partial deck above the main deck would be the 01 level, the next one up would be the 02 level, and so on. The term *weather deck* means just what it sounds like—a deck that is exposed to weather. *Flats* are removable platings or gratings installed as working or walking surfaces.

The *quarterdeck* is not a true deck or a structural part of the ship, but rather a location designated by the commanding officer as a place for ceremonies. Likewise, the word *mess deck* refers to a specific place (where the crew eats) and is not actually a deck in the strict sense of the word. A *flight deck* is an area used by airplanes and/or helicopters to land and take off.

Compartmentation and Watertight Integrity

Compartments are the rooms of a ship. Some compartments are called rooms, such as *wardroom, stateroom,* and *engineroom,* but generally speaking "room" is not often used. Don't refer to the area where you sleep as the "bedroom" or the place where you eat as the "dining room." They are called *berthing compartment* and *mess deck,* respectively.

You will also hear the term *space* used often to describe a compartment or any enclosed area of a ship.

If a ship were built like a rowboat, one hole below the waterline could sink her. To prevent this from happening, naval ships are built with bulkheads that divide the hull into a series of watertight compartments. The term *watertight* means that when these compartments are sealed up, water cannot enter or escape. *Watertight integrity* is the overall quality of being watertight. A ship with good watertight integrity is far more survivable than one with poor watertight integrity. If a ship experiences flooding, the affected spaces can be sealed off and the other watertight spaces will keep the ship afloat. There are limits to this concept, of course. If enough compartments on a ship become flooded, the remaining watertight compartments may not have enough *buoyancy* (floatability) to keep the ship afloat. The more compartmentation a ship has, the more chance her crew has of confining the flooding to an acceptable level that will permit the ship to stay afloat (remain buoyant). The tradeoff is, of course, that too much compartmentation would interfere with the arrangement of mechanical equipment and with her operation.

An important bonus is that just as flooding can be isolated through this compartmentation system, so can fire.

Watertight doors allow access through bulkheads when opened but can prevent flooding and the spread of fire when closed. Watertight *hatches* serve the same purpose by providing sealable access through decks. Be sure to note the difference here. People—even some Sailors—often confuse doors and hatches on a ship. Ships have doors just as buildings ashore do. The difference between shipboard doors and those ashore is that those found on ships can be watertight or nonwatertight. Watertight doors contribute to the compartmentation and overall watertight integrity of the vessel, while nonwatertight doors serve the same kinds of purposes as those ashore—privacy and noise suppression. Watertight doors pass through bulkheads and nonwatertight doors pass through partitions. *Hatches,* on the other hand, are always horizontal—never vertical like a door—and allow passage through *decks,* not bulkheads or partitions. All watertight fittings (doors and hatches) are specially marked to tell you when it is all right to open them and when it is not. These markings will be explained in the chapter covering damage control.

Obviously, holes must also be placed in watertight bulkheads and decks to allow ventilation ducts, fluid piping, and electrical and electronic cabling to pass through. These holes are specially constructed to prevent leaking and thereby preserve the watertight integrity of the ship.

Large ships have outer and inner *double bottoms.* These are divided athwartships and longitudinally into tanks, which are used to stow fuel oil or fresh water.[1] These tanks can also be used to bring in seawater for ballast.

Tanks at the extreme bow and stern, called the *forward peak* (or *forepeak*) tank and the *after peak* (or *aftpeak*) tank, are used for trimming (leveling) the ship. Sometimes these tanks are used to carry potable (drinking) water. A strong watertight bulkhead on the after side of the forepeak tank is called the *collision bulkhead.* If one ship rams another head-on, the bow structure of the latter collapses at a point somewhere forward of the collision bulkhead, thus absorbing some of the shock of the collision and, hopefully, preventing the flooding of compartments aft of it.

All tanks are connected to a pumping and drainage system so that fuel, water, and ballast can be transferred from one part of the ship to another or pumped overboard.

Deck and Compartment Identification
Trying to find your way around a multideck ship that is several hundred feet long can be a difficult process. Just as a town or city has a system using street signs and addresses to help you find your way around, so does a Navy ship. Each deck on a ship has a number, as we have already discussed, and each compartment on a ship has an

---

1. The nautical term for "store," when it is used as a verb, is *stow.* When used as a noun, the correct term remains *store.* For example: "A load of stores was delivered to the ship and stowed below." The nautical term for "storage" is *stowage.*

identifier that is roughly equivalent to a street address in a city. Once you understand this system, you will know where you are at any given time on a ship, and you will be able to find any space on ship even if you haven't been there before.

Every space aboard ship is assigned an identifying number-letter symbol, which is marked on a label plate above the entrance(s) to the space and on a sign on the bulkhead inside the space. Compartment identifiers contain the following information in the following format: Deck number–Frame number–Number representing the space's relation to the centerline of the ship–Letter(s) explaining the function of the compartment

EXAMPLE: 4–95–3–M

The *deck number* is the first part of the compartment number. Since the main deck of a ship is always numbered "1," we know that our example compartment is three decks below the main deck. If our example had been numbered "04," we would know that it was four decks *above* the main deck. If a compartment extends through more than one deck (such as an engineering space that must be large enough to hold a boiler or turbines), the deck number of that compartment refers to the bottommost deck.

The second number refers to the *frame number*. As explained earlier in this chapter, frames are beamlike structures that are fastened to the keel and run athwartships. They are numbered sequentially, fore to aft, so that the frame nearest the stem of the ship would be numbered "1" and the next one aft would be numbered "2," and so on. When you are first assigned to a ship, it is a good idea to find out and memorize the number of frames she has, because then you will have a better idea what part of the ship you are in once you know the frame number of the compartment. In our example compartment, the frame number is 95. If we know that the ship has a total of 207 frames, we would then be able to deduce that we are located about halfway between the bow and stern of the ship. The frame number always refers to the forwardmost bulkhead of a compartment.

The third part of the compartment identifier refers to the compartment's relation to the centerline. Compartments located directly on the centerline are numbered "0" (zero). Those on the starboard side of the centerline are numbered with odd numbers, and those on the port side are numbered evenly. The first compartment on the starboard side of the centerline would be numbered "1," the next one outboard would be numbered "3," the next one outboard of that one would be "5," and so on until we reach the skin of the ship. The first compartment on the port side of the centerline would be numbered "2," and the ones outboard of it would be "4," "6," and so on. Our example compartment is identified by the number "3," so we know that it is the second compartment off the centerline on the starboard side of the ship.

The fourth and last part of the compartment identifier is the letter that identifies the compartment's primary function. On cargo ships, cargo spaces (where goods are stowed for delivery to other ships or stations) are identified by a two-letter symbol, but all others are simply one letter. From the following list, it can be seen that our example compartment is used for the stowage or handling of ammunition.

Compartment Letter Identifiers

A — Stowage spaces: store and issue rooms; refrigerated compartments

AA — Cargo holds: cargo holds and refrigerated compartments

C — Control centers for ship and fire-control operations (normally manned): the combat information center (CIC); internal communications (IC) rooms; plotting rooms; pilot house; electronic equipment-operating spaces

E — Engineering control centers (normally manned): main machinery spaces; evaporator rooms; steering-gear rooms; pump rooms; auxiliary machinery spaces; emergency generator rooms

F — Oil stowage compartments (for use by the ship itself, that is, not as cargo): fuel-, diesel-, and lubricating-oil compartments

FF — Oil stowage compartments (cargo): compartments carrying various types of oil as cargo

G — Gasoline stowage compartments (for use by the ship itself): gasoline tanks, cofferdams, trunks, and pump rooms

GG — Gasoline stowage compartments (cargo): spaces for carrying gasoline as cargo

J — JP-5 (aviation) fuel (ship or embarked aircraft use): jet-fuel stowage spaces

JJ — JP-5 fuel (cargo): spaces for carrying JP-5 fuel as cargo

K — Chemicals and dangerous materials (other than oil and gasoline)

L — Living spaces: berthing and messing spaces; staterooms; washrooms; heads; brig; sick bay; and passageways

M   Ammunition spaces: magazines; handling rooms; turrets; gun mounts; shell rooms; ready service rooms
Q   Miscellaneous spaces not covered by other letters: laundry; galley; pantries; wiring trunks; unmanned engineering; electrical and electronic spaces; shops; offices
T   Vertical access trunks: escape trunks
V   Voids: spaces that are normally empty
W   Water stowage spaces: drainage tanks; freshwater tanks; peak tanks; reserve feedwater tanks

Propulsion Plant

A ship is of little use unless it has mobility, and the source of that mobility is the ship's propulsion plant. In previous centuries, the source of propulsion was oars or sails, but in modern times more sophisticated forms are used.

Oil-fired Steam Plants

For the better part of a century, steam has been the primary method of marine propulsion for sizable ships and is still used in many U.S. Navy vessels. Steam plants consist of *boilers* that transform fresh water into steam and *turbines* that convert that pressurized steam into usable power that turns the ship's propellers. *Condensers* convert the spent steam back into fresh water, which returns to the boilers to be reheated into energy-filled steam again. This "steam cycle," as it is called, is repeated over and over to propel a ship through the water. Even though this is a *closed* cycle—meaning that the water and steam are theoretically contained in the system and not allowed to escape— a certain amount of the fresh water is used up, so that a continuous supply of *feed water* is required for sustained operations. This is generated by *distilling plants,* which convert sea (salt) water into fresh. A steam plant also needs a supply of fuel to provide the heat in the boilers, and this must be carried in fuel tanks onboard—much as an automobile has a gas tank—and periodically replenished (either in port or from oilers at sea).

239

Nuclear Power

Nuclear power is a very specialized form of steam propulsion. Instead of using oil-fired boilers, nuclear-powered ships have a *reactor* that produces the heat to convert fresh water to steam. Nuclear powerplants give a ship the advantage of great endurance at high speed. Instead of refueling every few thousand miles like an oil-burning ship, a nuclear-powered ship can operate for years on one reactor core. Because there is no need to replenish oil, nuclear-powered ships can steam almost indefinitely, limited only by their need to replenish food and spare parts (and ammunition in wartime).

Another favorable feature of nuclear power is that, unlike conventional oil-fired systems, the generation of nuclear power does not require oxygen. This makes it particularly useful as a means of submarine propulsion. Submarines can operate completely submerged for extended periods of time.

Gas Turbines

Gas turbines are very similar to aircraft jet engines, but have been adapted for use on ships. The burning fuel spins turbines in the engines that convert the energy created by the burning fuel into usable power that turns the ship's propellers.

Although some of the principles are the same, some of the primary differences between these propulsion plants and those that use steam are that the gas turbines combine the functions of the boiler and the turbines into one element and gas turbines have no need of feedwater. This means that they are smaller, more efficient, and easier to maintain. They are also much more quickly "brought on the line" (turned on). A steam-powered vessel requires *hours* to prepare to get underway, while gas turbine-powered ships can be ready in *minutes*.

The obvious advantages of gas-turbine technology have caused the U.S. Navy to build more and more of these ships. Whereas steam was once the main means of naval propulsion, today there are more gas-turbine ships in the Navy than any other kind of propulsion.

Diesel Engines

For relatively small ships that need no more than 5000 to 6000 horsepower, diesel engines are frequently used. Diesels are lighter, take up less space, and are more efficient than steam turbines. The diesel can be coupled directly to the shaft through reduction gears and perhaps a clutch; or it can drive a generator that produces current for the main drive.

Diesel engines are preferred over gasoline engines because highly volatile gasoline fumes are heavier than air and tend to collect in low places a ship, making them very dangerous. Diesel fuel, which does not vaporize as readily, is much safer.

Propellers

A vital component of a ship's propulsion system is the propeller(s). Some ships have only one, others have two or more (an aircraft car-

rier has *four* giant propellers). Another term you will hear when referring to ships' propellers is *screw*.

Propeller *shafts* carry the power generated by the propulsion plant
to the propellers. Shafts run from the *reduction gears* (which change
the high-speed spin of the turbines into a more suitable speed for the
propellers) through long watertight spaces, called *shaft alleys,* in the
bottom of the ship. These shafts go out through the hull using special watertight sleeves and are often supported outside the hull by
struts.

Propellers on some ships are fixed while others are of the controllable-pitch type. Fixed propellers are solid in their construction and
change speed by speeding up or slowing down the spin of the whole
propeller. Controllable-pitch propellers, on the other hand, pivot their
blades in such a way as to change the amount of thrust they create and
thereby control the speed. For a fixed-type propeller to *back down*
(go in reverse), it must be slowed down, stopped, and then spun in the
opposite direction. A controllable-pitch propeller need only change
the pitch sufficiently to reverse the thrust. For this reason, the latter
type of propeller is much more common in modern naval ships.

The Steering System

The basic component of nearly every ship or boat steering system is
the *rudder*. The simplest rudder design is a flat board or blade that
extends into the water beneath the vessel's stern. When it is turned
one way or the other while the vessel is moving, flowing water builds
up on the front side and pushes the stern of the vessel in the opposite
direction. Because the rudder acts by the force of water pushing
against one side of it, there is no rudder action when the ship is
motionless. And the greater the speed of the vessel through the water,
the greater the effect the rudders have. For this reason, the rudder
is usually mounted just astern of the screws, where the wash created
by the moving propeller pushes directly against it and increases the
effect.

The rudder is controlled by a *tiller* in an open boat (such as a
motor whaleboat or motor launch) or by a wheel in the cockpit of
a larger boat or on the bridge of a ship. This wheel is often called a
helm on a ship. In a boat, the motion of the wheel is transmitted to the
rudder by a cable or shaft. In a ship, the rudder is turned by an electric or steam engine in the steering-engine room. This electrical or
hydraulic engine is controlled by the helm on the bridge. When the
helm is turned on the bridge, it transmits a signal to the steering
engine which then moves the rudder.

Ships can have more than one rudder, but in the case of multiple rudders the rudders do not act independently but are controlled together.

To prevent loss of control in case of damage to the bridge, there is usually a second steering wheel mounted elsewhere in the ship. This back-up control station is called *secondary conn.* If that wheel is also disabled, the ship can be hand-steered by several Sailors using special gear in the steering-engine room. There is also a duplicate set of steering engines and connecting cables on naval vessels to serve as backup in the event of damage.

Ships or boats with two screws can be steered fairly well without a rudder by using the engines. If one screw turns faster than the other, the bow will swing toward the slower screw. If one screw goes ahead while the other goes astern, the bow of the ship will swing toward the backing screw. Boats, and even very large ships, can turn within the diameter of their own lengths using this method, which is appropriately called *twisting.*

Ground Tackle

A ship is *moored* when she is held in position by an anchor on the ocean bottom made fast either to a mooring buoy or a pier. To moor to a pier, a ship uses her mooring lines. To anchor or moor to a special mooring buoy, the ship uses her *ground tackle* (such as anchors, anchor chains, or windlasses). Ground tackle is normally located on the forecastle, but some ships, particularly amphibious craft that run up onto beaches, may also carry a stern anchor used to help haul themselves off the beach when it is time to return to sea.

Ladders, Booms, and Brows

When a ship is not moored alongside a pier, her freeboard (distance from the water up to her main deck) causes a problem for boarding or leaving the ship. Boats coming alongside a ship will be too low for personnel to get out of the boat and up to the main deck. A special stairway leading from the deck down close to the water is suspended over the side to take care of this problem and is called an *accommodation ladder.* It has a platform at the bottom that serves as a landing for boats, and a suspended line, called a *sea painter,* to which boats secure themselves when coming alongside.

Some ships have *boat booms,* which are special spars swung out from the ship's side when the ship is moored or anchored. These special booms have lines suspended to the water for boats to tie up to and they also have a *Jacob's ladder* (basically a rope ladder, although it can be made of metal or have wood components) that allows boat crews to climb into their boats or to leave their boats and come aboard the mother ship.

Boat booms require some athletic ability and are provided primarily for boat-crew use. Accommodation ladders are used by other ship's personnel and visitors.

When a ship is moored to a pier (or alongside another ship), boarding and departing are less difficult and can be accomplished by placing a simple crossway, called a *brow,* to bridge the gap between the ship and pier (or between the two ships).

Specialized Spaces

Just as a building has specialized rooms or areas, such as the lobby, parking garage, heating plant, or boardroom, ships have special spaces with distinct purposes necessary to the operation or utility of the vessel. Some ships have very special areas—such as Primary Air Control on an aircraft carrier—not found on all ships, but other special areas are found on most naval ships.

The Bridge

This is the primary control position for the ship when she is under way, and the place where all orders and commands affecting the ship's movements and routine originate. The captain will be on the bridge a lot of the time underway—especially during most special sea evolutions and when the ship is entering and leaving port—but obviously cannot be there 24 hours a day. The officer of the deck (OOD)—a rotating watch position manned only by highly qualified personnel—who is the captain's primary assistant in charge of safely running the ship is always on the bridge when the ship is under way.

On the bridge are various instruments and equipment used to control the movements of the ship. The ship's helm and engine controls are located here, as well as radar repeaters, navigation light switches, wind indicators, radios, speed indicators, and compasses.

The Chart House

The chart house is normally just aft of the pilot house and on the same deck, but it can also be on another deck and some distance away. This is where the navigator and his or her team of quartermasters do much of their work. Using navigational equipment and instruments such as sextants, stadimeters, bearing circles, stopwatches, parallel rulers, dividers, protractors, position plotters, electronic devices, and navigational books and tables, the navigational team keeps a constant plot of the ship's position (location) at any given moment and a plan of where the ship is going.

Signal Bridge

This is an open platform located near (often just above) the navigational bridge and equipped with devices used to communicate visually, such as signal searchlights and signal flags. The signal lights allow ships to communicate with one another by flashing the lights on and off in Morse code (see Appendix E). The signal flags are kept in a specially designed stowage locker, known as a *flag bag,* which allows quick access to the flags. The lower ends of the halyards, on which signal flags are hoisted, are secured here so that the signalmen can quickly attach flags from the flag bag and hoist them into the air where other ships can see them.

Combat Information Center

The combat information center (CIC) is the nerve center of the ship. A wide range of electronic equipment is installed in the CIC to process information received from a wide variety of sources, including radio, radar, sonar, electronic-warfare intercept receivers, IFF (identification friend or foe) transponders, visual communications, satellites, fathometers (depth gauges), and computers. All of this information is collected, processed, displayed, evaluated, and disseminated to other parts of the ship (or to other ships) for use in decisionmaking and in properly employing the ship. CIC is the place where the ship's tactical operations are controlled. Such operations include the evaluation of targets, weapons firing, the control of friendly aircraft, surveillance operations, navigational assistance, submarine tracking, and many others.

Damage Control Central (DCC)

Damage Control Central serves as the central information site for matters affecting the safety of the ship. By monitoring conditions aboard ship and maintaining control of vital systems such as those used in firefighting and flooding control, and by maintaining careful records, damage-control charts, and liquid-loading diagrams, DCC sees that the ship is prepared for any emergency conditions that may arise.

Storerooms

A ship cannot operate at sea for extended periods of time unless it has adequate stowage for consumable supplies and spare parts. These areas are known as storerooms.

Magazines

Magazines are special storerooms used for the stowage of missiles, rockets, and gun ammunition. For obvious reasons, these important but potentially dangerous areas aboard ship are kept locked and under close control. They also are protected by various alarm and firefighting systems and are usually located in spaces well below the waterline so that, in case of fire, they can be flooded.

Crew Accommodations

The living spaces aboard ship are essential to accommodate the needs of the crew. Berthing (sleeping) compartments, heads (lavatories), wardrooms (living and dining areas for officers), officers' cabins (or staterooms), galleys (kitchens), messes (where enlisted personnel eat), laundries, barber shops, and sick bay (medical clinic) are all living areas necessary for the daily routine of the men and women who live aboard ship. Larger ships may have other spaces for the health and comfort of the crew, such as tailor shops, libraries, chapels, weight/aerobic rooms, and crew lounges. Virtually all ships have a ship's store where you can purchase toiletries, uniform items, gedunk (snacks), and—depending upon the size of the ship and its store—a variety of other items. An added benefit of using your ship's store is that the profits go to the ship's Morale Welfare and Recreation fund (see chapter 11).

Shops and Offices

Shops and offices can be found on virtually every Navy ship. The number of each depends upon the size and the purpose of the ship. An aircraft carrier will have hundreds of each. A patrol craft may have only one or two.

Most Navy ships will have at least an electrical shop and perhaps a carpentry shop as well. A tender, whose mission is maintenance and repair, will have many shops, including ones that do specialty work, such as instrument calibration, printing, photography, torpedo overhauls, and pump refurbishment. An aircraft carrier will have a large specialized repair facility called the aircraft intermediate maintenance department (AIMD), which performs a wide variety of maintenance functions to keep aircraft flying while the ship is at sea.

The captain and executive officer will probably have their own offices (or, on smaller ships, they will be combined into one, called the ship's office). On ships with adequate room, individual departments and divisions will have their own offices.

Ships' Vital Systems

A number of systems are essential to every Navy ship. Without these important systems, ships could not carry out their missions. Because they carry on vital functions for the ship similar to functions for the human body, these systems are analogous to our nervous, circulatory, respiratory, and excretion systems.

Electrical System

At one time, ships functioned without electricity, and for many years electrical power provided only a few important services, such as lights and a few motor-driven appliances. But today's modern ship uses an incredible amount of electrical power to carry out a wide array of functions. A modern vessel depends upon its electrical power system to power complex weapon and communications systems, to compute the solutions to a vast spectrum of tactical problems, to power ammunition hoists and aircraft elevators, to detect incoming enemy missiles and aircraft, and to run in-house television systems for entertainment. These and hundreds of other functions make electricity as vital to a modern vessel of war as ropes were to a sailing vessel.

Ships generate their own electricity and all have backup systems to provide power when the primary system fails. Vital electrical circuits are also frequently duplicated so that power can continue to flow after battle damage occurs.

Ventilation System

This system supplies fresh air where it is needed and carries off unwanted exhaust. This system is made up of many subsystems that operate independently of each other.

Supply ventilation brings fresh (external) air into the ship and, in the event of cold weather, heats the air by means of a preheater installed in the ducting. *Exhaust* ventilation carries away the air that has served its purpose and needs to be replaced. In those spaces containing equipment that generates heat and/or humidity (such as main engineering spaces, galley, or head facilities), the exhaust system is particularly vital. *Recirc* ventilation is provided to spaces containing electronic equipment (which requires a cool environment for proper operation), as well as to berthing, messing, and office spaces. As its name implies, this system recirculates internal air to prevent stagnation and, when necessary, draws the air through a cooling system to maintain the proper temperature.

In the event of fire, flooding, or some other danger requiring the isolation of a space or spaces, ventilation systems can be secured by de-energizing the fan motor and can be segregated by closing valve-like devices in the ducting (often found where the ducting penetrates decks, overheads, and bulkheads).

Potable Water System

Water for drinking, showers, and cooking is provided by this piping system. Potable water is made in the ship's distilling units (evaporators) from saltwater taken from the sea and stowed in tanks specifically designated for potable water only. Piping systems carry the water from the tanks to the heads, galleys, and drinking fountains (scuttlebutts) where it can be used.

Because the evaporators can only make so much water at a time, care must be exercised not to waste fresh water while a ship is underway or at anchor. You should never take what is popularly called a "Hollywood shower" while at sea. (This is the kind of shower you probably take at home, where you let the water run for as long as you are in the shower without giving any thought to water conservation.) While at sea, it is important to get in the habit of wetting down (quickly), turning the water off and leaving it off while you soap and scrub, and then turning the water on again just long enough to rinse off.

In a steam-powered ship, water conservation is complicated by the boilers' need for feedwater. Saltwater cannot be used in boilers, so you must compete with the engineering plant for whatever fresh water the evaporators can produce.

When moored to a pier where the appropriate connections are available, the ship's potable water system can be hooked up to receive fresh water. At these times, abundant fresh water is available so that the strict water conservation practices you use at sea are not necessary. The ship's potable water tanks will all be *topped off* (filled to capacity) before the ship gets underway.

Saltwater System

Saltwater is drawn out of the sea through underwater intakes and pumped throughout the ship using a different piping system from the one used for potable water. This water is available for firefighting when needed and is used on a routine basis as flushing water for the heads. It also is used as cooling water for certain items of machinery and electronic equipment and can be piped into tanks for ballast (to stabilize the ship). Special sprinkler heads mounted all over the outside of the ship can be opened to allow a washdown of the ship to rid her of contaminants in the event of a chemical, biological, or radiation (CBR) attack.

Drainage System

This system includes the piping, valves, and pumps that discharge water from the ship. Its functions include the removal of seawater that has entered the hull because of damage, collision, or heavy weather.

The main drainage system is composed of large piping located in the main engineering spaces and used for pumping their *bilges* (the lowest parts of the ship's hull where water collects). The secondary drainage system is composed of smaller piping located in other spaces, such as pump rooms and shaft alleys.

The main and secondary drainage systems are often coupled with the saltwater system to maintain the proper trim (stabilize) of the ship.

Since weather-deck drains collect natural rain and seawater, the drains connected to these areas are piped directly overboard. But internal drains (from sinks, showers, galleys, and urinals) are carefully controlled for environmental reasons. Drainage from these sources is collected in specially designed tanks for appropriate disposition.

Fuel System

This system includes fuel-stowage tanks, pumps, filling lines, transfer lines, and feed lines to the ship's boilers or engines. Like the other liquid systems aboard ship (potable water, saltwater, and drainage) the fuel system is also constantly monitored and moved about to help maintain proper trim.

Compressed Air System

Ships use compressed air for a number of reasons. Ejecting gases from guns after they have fired is one important use of this system. Compressed air is also used for charging torpedoes, operating pneumatic tools, running messages through dispatch tubes, powering automatic boiler controls, and various other uses. Compressors create the compressed air and special piping carries it where needed in the ship.

Submarines

Because they are designed to operate under water, submarines have very few topside features and practically no superstructure. About all that projects above the hull is the *sail*, a streamlined tower that houses the periscopes and certain control stations and where a few watch-standers can stand when the submarine operates on the surface.

Submarine hulls have nearly circular cross-sections and are built to withstand tremendous pressure. The hull consists of the bow compartment, containing living accommodations; the operations compartment, containing the control room, sonar and radar rooms, the torpedo room, and some state rooms; the reactor compartment; the missile rooms (on fleet ballistic missile submarines); and the engine-room. Submarines have special ballast tanks that can be quickly flooded when the boat is to submerge, or pumped out when she is to surface.

The controls by which a submarine is maneuvered are more like those of an aircraft than those of a surface ship (which merely steers left or right), because a sub also moves up and down. In fact, when operating submerged, she banks in her turns much like an aircraft. Aside from these basic differences, a submarine is still a ship (although submariners traditionally refer to their vessel as a "boat") and therefore contains many of the same systems and features found in a surface vessel.

13 Ships and Aircraft

Ships and aircraft are what the Navy is all about. While it is not difficult to tell the difference between the two, their missions and operational capabilities are tightly interwoven, and it is rare that a significant naval operation is undertaken without relying upon some combination of both for its execution. Seapower and air power go hand in hand.

There are many different kinds of ships and aircraft in the Navy, and while you cannot be expected to know every detail about each, as an effective Sailor you will need and want to have a substantial understanding of these vital components of your Navy.

Ships

The U.S. Navy operates hundreds of ships. Some of these are *active* ships, which means they have a full complement of personnel and, unless they are temporarily undergoing heavy maintenance or repair, are fully capable of carrying out an assigned mission on short notice.

The Navy also keeps a number of vessels in *reserve* status, which means that they are partially manned with active duty personnel. The rest of the crew is made up of reserve personnel, who only man the ships periodically for training and when called upon in a national emergency.

The Navy also operates a number of vessels under what is called the Military Sealift Command (MSC). These ships usually have only a very small contingent of Navy personnel on board, and the majority of the crews are civilians. MSC ships have a support role and are not used as front-line combatants. They are considered to be "in service" rather than "in commission." Some ships, such as "Roll-on, roll-off" vehicle cargo ships (AKRs) and transport oilers (AOTs) serve the Army and Air Force as well as the Navy.

Other MSC ships perform special-duty projects, such as ocean-bottom laying and repairing of cables used for detecting enemy submarines. Surveying ships (AGSs) and oceanographic research ships (AGORs) explore the oceans.

Of special interest is a group of various MSC ships of the Naval Fleet Auxiliary Force (NFAF). As with other MSC ships, they have civilian officers and crews. They operate under Navy orders and have a military department of Navy personnel aboard, performing visual and radio communications and otherwise assisting the ship's civilian master and crew in operations with other naval units. These vessels include a variety of replenishment ships, fleet ocean tugs, and several specialized mission types.

Ship Identification

Most Navy ships have both a name and what we call a *ship's designation* to identify them. While the name is a convenient and traditional means of identification, there have been Navy ships bearing the same name throughout history, so the ship's designation—which is unique to that ship—is the only way to identify a specific naval vessel. The ship's designation tells what *type* the ship is (such as destroyer, submarine, or cruiser) and assigns a specific *hull number* to the vessel.

Ships are also grouped into *classes* to identify those with identical, or nearly identical, characteristics.

Name

The name is unique to a ship in that there can only be one Navy ship in commission at a time with a given name. But, as already mentioned, there may have been other ships with the same name in the past—in fact, it is fairly common practice in the Navy for ships to carry the name of an earlier ship who served with honor. For example, there have been six U.S. Navy ships named *Enterprise*. (*Note:* This count does not include the starship *Enterprise* of Star Trek fame, but the creator of the hit television and movie series, Gene Roddenberry, recognized the long tradition of passing on ship names and carried it on in his futuristic vision.)

The name of a Navy ship in commission (active or reserve) is preceded by the letters "USS," which stands for "United States Ship," for example, USS *Enterprise*. Because they are considered to be "in service" rather than "in commission," names of MSC ships are preceded by the letters "USNS" (for United States Naval Ship) instead of "USS." In the British Navy, vessels carry the prefix "HMS" before their name, which stands for "Her Majesty's Ship" (or "*His* Majesty's Ship" if there is a reigning king instead of a queen). The navies of other nations are similarly identified.

Sailors have traditionally added nicknames to their seagoing homes. Among aircraft carriers, for instance, the USS *Enterprise* is known informally as the "Big E," the *Constellation* is the "Connie," and the *Dwight D. Eisenhower* is "Ike."

Designation

While a ship's name gives her some identity, the ship's designation—which consists of a combination of letters and numbers—tells you two additional things about a ship: her type and her place in the construction sequence. The USS *Theodore Roosevelt,* for instance, has the designation CVN 71. CVN is her type classification, *CV* standing for aircraft carrier and *N* meaning nuclear propulsion; 71 indicates that she is the seventy-first aircraft carrier authorized for construction. The term *hull number* actually refers only to the number part of the ship's designation, but you will commonly hear it used instead of "ship's designation." Ships' hull numbers are frequently painted on their bows and near the stern. Aircraft carriers have their hull numbers painted on the forward part of the flight deck and on the "island" (superstructure).

Since 1920, the Navy has used letter symbols to identify the types of ships and service craft. This is called "type classification" and is used as part of the ship's designation. Some of the more common type classifications are listed below. Keep in mind that some of these type classifications may not be currently be in use, but are listed because you may come across them historically or they may be reactivated at some later date. Those not currently in service are listed in italics.

AD	Destroyer tender
AE	Ammunition ship
AFS	Combat store ship
AGF	Miscellaneous command ship
AH	Hospital ship
AO	Oiler
AOE	Fast combat-support ship
AOR	Replenishment oiler
APL	Barracks craft (non-self-propelled)
ARS	Salvage ship
AS	Submarine tender
ASR	Submarine rescue ship
ATF	Fleet ocean tug
BB	*Battleship*
CA	*Heavy cruiser*

CG	Guided-missile cruiser
CGN	*Guided-missile cruiser (nuclear propulsion)*
CL	*Light cruiser*
CV	Multipurpose aircraft carrier
CVA	*Attack aircraft carrier*
CVN	Multipurpose aircraft carrier (nuclear propulsion)
CVS	*Antisubmarine warfare aircraft carrier*
DD	Destroyer
DDG	Guided-missile destroyer
DE	*Destroyer escort*
DL	*Destroyer leader*
DSRV	Deep-submergence rescue vehicle
FF	*Frigate*
FFG	Guided-missile frigate
IX	Unclassified miscellaneous
LCAC	Landing craft, air cushion
LCC	Amphibious command ship
LCM	Landing craft, mechanized
LCPL	Landing craft, personnel, large
LCU	Landing craft, utility
LCVP	Landing craft, vehicle, and personnel
LHA	Amphibious assault ship (general purpose)
LHD	Amphibious assault ship (multipurpose)
LPD	Amphibious transport dock
LPH	*Amphibious assault ship (helicopter)*
LSD	Dock-landing ship
LSSC	Light SEAL support craft
LST	Tank-landing ship
MCM	Mine-countermeasures ship
MCS	Mine-countermeasures support ship
MHC	Coastal minehunter
MSC	*Coastal minesweeper*
MSO	*Ocean-going minesweeper*
PBR	River patrol boat
PC	Coastal patrol craft
PCF	*Fast patrol craft ("swift boat")*
PT	*Patrol torpedo boat*
SS	*Submarine*
SSBN	Ballistic-missile submarine (nuclear propulsion)
SSN	Submarine (nuclear propulsion)
YP	Yard patrol
YTB	Large Harbor Tug

253

| YTL | Small Harbor Tug |
| YTM | Medium Harbor Tug |

Ships of the Military Sealift Command (MSC) are distinguished from other Navy ships by having a "T" before their letter designations. Below are some examples of MSC ship types.

T-AFS	Combat stores ship
T-AE	Ammunition ships
T-ATF	Fleet ocean tug
T-AH	Hospital ship
T-AGOS	Ocean surveillance ship
T-AGS	Oceanographic Survey
T-ARC	Cable repair
T-AK	Maritime pre-positioning ship
T-AOT	Tankers
T-AKR	Roll-on/Rolloff

Class

Within a type classification of vessels there are *classes*. Ships belonging to a particular class are built from the same plans and are very much alike; in many cases, they are identical except for the different hull number painted on their bows. The first ship built of a class determines the name of the class. For example, after World War II the United States redesigned its aircraft carriers to accommodate the newly invented jet aircraft then entering the fleet. The first of these new aircraft carriers to be built was commissioned as USS *Forrestal* (CV 59). She was the fifty-ninth aircraft carrier, but the first of this new class. Satisfied with these new ships, the Navy built three more—USS *Saratoga* (CV 60), USS *Ranger* (CV 61), and USS *Independence* (CV 62)—all of which are referred to as *Forrestal*-class carriers.

Later, some major improvements were deemed necessary, so the Navy redesigned its aircraft carriers significantly enough that they were considered a new class of carrier. The first of these new and different carriers was named USS *Kitty Hawk* (CV 63), so the next ship built after her, USS *Constellation* (CV 64), was considered a *Kitty Hawk*–class aircraft carrier.

Ship Types and Their Missions

The many different types of vessels have specific functions. Some exist primarily to engage in combat with enemy forces (other vessels, aircraft, or land targets) and are generally referred to as *combatants*. Others exist to deliver the supplies (fuel, ammunition, food, and repair parts) needed to keep a ship operating, and are generally referred to as *auxiliaries*. Still others, known as *amphibious* ships, are designed to take troops where they are needed and get them ashore.

Aircraft Carriers

These gigantic ships are among the world's largest. They have been described as the world's largest combatant ships and the world's smallest airfields. The various classes range in displacement between 75,000 and 96,000 tons and carry between 75 and 85 aircraft of various types. The number of personnel required to operate an aircraft carrier and its aircraft is more than 5000.

Aircraft carriers carry an assortment of aircraft capable of performing a wide variety of missions, including air support to troops ashore, bombardment missions, antisubmarine operations, rescue missions, reconnaissance, and antiair warfare. Because of their powerful engines and four screws, carriers are capable of high speed, and they are capable of staying at sea for long periods of time, making them a potent weapon in a wide variety of scenarios. Some of the

255

PH3 Greg Welch

Figure 13.1. The aircraft carrier USS *Abraham Lincoln* (CVN 72).

U.S. Navy's carriers are driven by oil-fired boilers; others, designated CVN, are nuclear-powered.

Cruisers

These medium-sized (around 10,000 tons displacement) ships are particularly potent in antiair missions, but are capable of a number of other missions as well, including antisurface and antisubmarine. They are equipped with missiles that can knock out incoming raids from enemy aircraft or missile attacks. With other specially designed missiles, they are able to hit land or sea targets at substantial distances.

Currently, the Navy's cruisers are all *Ticonderoga*-class (designated CG) ships, which are powered by gas turbines and equipped with the very sophisticated Aegis combat system. This integrated combat system is highly automated, exceptionally fast, and capable of conducting antiair, antisurface, and antisubmarine warfare simultaneously.

Destroyers

In today's Navy, destroyers perform a wide range of duties. They can serve as part of a screen unit in a carrier task group, protecting it from

Figure 13.2. The guided-missile cruiser USS *Port Royal* (CG 73).

U.S. Naval Institute

various forms of attack. They can detect and engage enemy sub-marines, aircraft, missiles, and surface ships. In an amphibious assault, a destroyer's weapons can help protect against enemy forces at sea and ashore. In short, destroyers have a well-deserved reputation of being the "workhorses" of the fleet.

Previous classes of destroyer were rather small—some displacing as little as 400 tons—but today's *Spruance*-class destroyers are 563 feet long and 55 feet in beam, displace 7800 tons, and have a crew of 250. The *Spruances* were the first major ships to be powered by gas turbines. Their 80,000-horsepower, gas-turbine-drive engineering plants can go from "cold iron" (meaning no engines on the line) to full speed in 12 minutes. Their weaponry consists of torpedoes, guns, antisubmarine rockets, and short-range antiair missiles. Some have received the vertical launching system (VLS) to handle antiair and antiaircraft missiles. Others have cruise-missile launchers.

The newer *Arleigh Burke* class, like the *Ticonderoga*-class cruisers, is equipped with the Aegis system, making it the most potent

Figure 13.3. A *Spruance*-class destroyer, USS *Fife* (DD 991) underway in the Gulf of Mexico.

Figure 13.4. A starboard-bow view of the guided-missile destroyer USS *Carney* (DDG 64).

class of destroyer ever built. At one time, the differences between cruisers and destroyers were significant. Today, the differences are not so obvious.

Frigates
The frigate first appeared in the U.S. Navy during World War II as the destroyer escort (DE). In 1975, they were re-designated as *frigates* (FF).

A number of classes have been built since then, but today the *Oliver Hazard Perry*–class frigates are the only ones in commission in the U.S. Navy. These ships carry crews of a little more than 200 and may be viewed as scaled-down destroyers. They protect amphibious forces, underway replenishment operations, and merchant-ship convoys.

Submarines
The Navy has two types of submarine: one is called *attack* and is designated SSN, while the other is called *fleet ballistic-missile* and is designated SSBN. All U.S. submarines currently are nuclear-powered.

Figure 13.5. A guided-missile frigate, USS *Taylor* (FFG 50).

The SSN's primary mission is to attack other submarines and ships, but they are also assigned secondary missions, which may include surveillance and reconnaissance, direct task-force support, landing-force support, land attack, minelaying, and rescue.

The SSN's principal weapons are high-speed, wire-guided torpedoes and cruise missiles for use against surface and land targets.

The fleet ballistic-missile submarines (SSBN) have a strategic mission, in that they are meant to deter or participate in a nuclear-

Figure 13.6. A starboard-beam view of the nuclear-powered attack submarine USS *Boise* (SSN 764) underway in the Atlantic Ocean.

missile exchange. Their highly sophisticated, very potent ballistic missiles are capable of hitting targets many thousands of miles away and causing tremendous destruction.

These vessels must remain submerged for long periods of time, virtually out of contact with the rest of the world, waiting to carry out a mission that could be devastating to the whole world. This is a stressful environment for the crews and, to alleviate some of that stress, SSBNs are operated during alternate periods by two separate crews. One is called the blue crew and the other the gold crew. On return from an extended patrol, one crew relieves the other, and the ship returns to patrol following a brief period alongside her tender or in port. The relieved crew enters a month-long period of rest, recreation, and leave, followed by two months of training. This system allows each crew time ashore, while keeping the entire force of SSBNs cruising on deep patrol except for very brief periods.

Patrol Combatants

Some smaller coastal and riverine craft are also in service. Among the more prevalent types are the coastal patrol ships of the *Cyclone* (PC 1) class. Measuring 170 feet long with a 35-knot speed and armed with two 25mm guns, Stinger missiles, and lighter weapons, the *Cyclones* are used for special warfare and coastal interdiction missions.

Figure 13.7. A fleet ballistic-missile submarine, USS *Maine* (SSBN 741).

PHI Michael J. Rinaldi

U.S. Naval Institute

Figure 13.8. Coastal patrol vessel, USS *Firebolt* (PC 10).

Mine-Warfare Ships

Three types of mine-warfare vessel are currently in use in the U.S. Navy. The *Osprey* (MHC 51)-class designation is for minehunters and the *Avenger* (MCM 1)-class ships are mine-countermeasures ships. The MHCs specialize in detecting and locating today's highly sophisticated mines and the MCMs are tasked with removing or destroying them. A former amphibious assault ship, USS *Inchon,* has been converted to a mine-countermeasures support ship (MCS) which serves as a mine-force flag ship, carrying a contingent of mine-countermeasures helicopters and specially trained explosive ordnance disposal (EOD) personnel.

Amphibious Warfare Ships

Often referred to as the "amphibs" or "gators," these ships work mainly where sea and land meet, and where assault landings are carried out by Navy–Marine Corps teams. Such operations call for a variety of types of ships. Many are transports of varied designs, used to sealift Marines and their equipment from bases to landing beaches. The differences lie in ship design and the way troops and their gear are moved from ship to shore, which can be done by means of landing craft, helicopters, or tracked amphibious vehicles.

Figure 13.9. The minehunter USS *Osprey* (MHC 51).

Tank-landing ship (LST). LSTs can run up to the beach, lower their extended bow ramp, and offload tanks, artillery, and logistic vehicles. Amphibious vehicles can also be launched from a stern gate into the water. These vessels displace 8400 tons and carry over 400 troops.

Dock-landing ship (LSD). These ships have a well deck inside the vessel that can be flooded so that waterborne landing craft and vehicles can be floated out of the ship's stern gate. They can also have a limited capacity for handling troop-carrying helicopters.

Figure 13.10. Port-bow view of mine-countermeasures ship, USS *Guardian* (MCM 5).

Figure 13.11. The dock landing ship USS *Ashland* (LSD 48).

Amphibious transport dock (LPD). These ships are similar to the LSD in that they deliver troops and equipment in landing craft or vehicles carried in a well deck and floated out through a stern gate, but their helicopter capacity is more extensive.

263

General-purpose assault ship (LHA). Of all the ship types discussed so far, only aircraft carriers are larger than these. The five ships of the *Tarawa* (LHA 1) class displace more than 39,000 tons.

Figure 13.12. The amphibious assault ship USS *Peleliu* (LHA 5).

They resemble aircraft carriers and are capable of simultaneous heli-copter and landing-craft operations, for they have both flight and well decks.

Multipurpose-assault ship (LHD). These large ships resemble the LHA but incorporate many changes as a result of experience with the *Tarawa* class. LHDs operate air-cushion landing craft (LCACs) and heavy helicopters. They function as sea-control ships, when neces-sary, by operating antisubmarine helicopters and AV-8B Harrier V/STOL (vertical/short takeoff and landing) airplanes.

Amphibious command ship (LCC). LCCs serve as floating com-mand centers, providing control and communication facilities for embarked sea, air, and land commanders and their staffs.

Underway-Replenishment Ships

If they are going to be combat-effective, warships must be able to remain at sea for weeks at a time with fuel, provisions, parts, and ammunition. The U.S. Navy is highly proficient at underway replen-ishment (UNREP) techniques that use special cargo-handling gear to make transfers from one ship to another while the two are steaming abreast or, in some cases, astern. Vertical replenishment (VERTREP) is a form of UNREP in which cargo-carrying helicopters are used to transfer goods from one ship to another. Much of the UNREP capa-

U.S. Naval Institute

Figure 13.13. The amphibious command ship USS *Mount Whitney* (LCC 20).

National Steel and Shipbuilding Company

Figure 13.14. Fast combat support ship USS *Rainier* (AOE 7).

bility of the Navy today is carried out by MSC ships (such as T-AOs
and T-AEs) but *Fast combat–support ships (AOE)* are the largest and
most powerful of the Navy's noncombatant seagoing units. Because
of their high-speed capability, these 50,000-ton sea-going warehouses
are capable of operating with fast task forces. AOEs carry fuel,
ammunition, and stores.

Fleet Support Ships
UNREP vessels are only one type of the auxiliaries that help carry out
the Navy's many missions. A number of other ships play vital roles
in keeping the fleet operating at peak efficiency.

Tenders. Submarine tenders (AS) and destroyer tenders (AD) are
full of maintenance and repair shops and are manned by technicians
with a wide variety of skills so that vessels coming alongside can
receive rather extensive repairs or have major maintenance performed on them.

Salvage vessels. Rescue, salvage, and towing ships (ARS) provide
rapid firefighting, dewatering, battle-damage repair, and towing assistance to save ships that have been in battle or victims of some other
disaster from further loss or damage. Equipped with specialized
equipment and manned by salvage divers, these ships can also perform rescue and salvage operations underwater.

Figure 13.15. F/A-18 Hornet.

Command Ships (AGF)

Two former amphibious ships have been converted into command ships to serve in a command-and-communications role in the Middle East. They are painted white to help their air conditioners cope with the intense heat of the region and are equipped with a great deal of highly sophisticated sensors and communications systems.

Service Craft

Also among the Navy's waterborne resources is a large and varied group of service craft. Some are huge vessels like the large auxiliary floating drydocks that can take very large vessels aboard and raise them out of the water for repairs. Barracks craft accommodate crews when their ships are being overhauled or repaired. Lighters are barges used to store and transport materials and to house pier-side repair shops. Some gasoline barges, fuel-oil barges, and water barges are self-propelled; those that are not depend on tugs. Floating cranes and wrecking derricks are towed from place to place as needed. Diving tenders support diving operations, and ferryboats or launches, which carry people, automobiles, and equipment, are usually located at Navy bases where facilities are spread out over large distances. Best known of the service craft are the harbor tugs, large and small, that aid ships in docking and undocking, provide firefighting services when needed, perform rescues, and haul lighters from place to place.

Aircraft

Naval aircraft are an essential component of seapower. The U.S. Navy has thousands of aircraft in its inventory, performing a wide variety of missions, many from the decks of ships and others from naval air stations. The many kinds of fixed-wing and rotary-wing (helicopter) aircraft flown by the Navy include fighters, attack, combined fighter-attack, antisubmarine, patrol, early warning, general utility, inflight refueling, transport, and trainers. Naval aircraft are organized into *squadrons* and these are further grouped into *air wings*.

Basic Aircraft Nomenclature

Because aircraft are such an important component of the Navy, you should be familiar with certain basic terms concerning the structure of airplanes and helicopters.

The *fuselage* is the main body of the aircraft. The *wings* are strong structural members attached to the fuselage. Their airfoil shape provides the lift that supports the plane in flight. Wings are fitted with flaps for increased lift and may carry fuel tanks, guns, rockets, missiles and other weapons, engines, and landing gear. Helicopters (also called "rotary-wing aircraft"), instead of having wings in the traditional sense, have rotors (which are actually wings that rotate).

The *tail assembly* of a fixed-wing aircraft consists of vertical and horizontal stabilizers, rudder(s), and elevators. These components are key elements in the flight controls of the aircraft.

The *landing gear* usually means the wheels, but in certain aircraft these may be replaced by skids, skis, or floats.

The *powerplant* develops the thrust or force that propels the aircraft forward, providing mobility and (in combination with the wings) the lift necessary to keep the aircraft aloft. In the case of helicopters, the powerplant provides the power to keep the rotors spinning, which keeps the aircraft aloft and allows it to hover as well as move through the air. The powerplant may consist of reciprocating (piston) engines that drive propellers, jet engines that develop thrust (turbojet and turbofan), or turbine engines and propellers or rotors in combination (turboprop or turbo shaft).

Another useful term is *Mach,* which is commonly used to measure the speed capability of an aircraft or missile. Formally defined as the ratio of speed of an object to the speed of sound in the surrounding atmosphere, it is used as follows. An aircraft traveling at Mach 1 would be moving at the speed of sound. One going Mach 2 would be

267

going twice the speed of sound, and Mach 1.5 would be one-and-a-half times the speed of sound. Depending upon the altitude, temperature, and some other variables, the speed of sound varies, but a rough figure to use for approximation is 650 miles per hour. So an aircraft flying at Mach 2 would be moving at a speed of *approximately* 1,300 miles per hour. An aircraft that is able to fly faster than the speed of sound (Mach 1) is said to be *supersonic* and one than cannot is called *subsonic*.

Aircraft Designations

Many types, designs, and modifications of aircraft form the naval air arm of the Navy. Like ships, aircraft have names, usually chosen by the designers or developers and approved by the Navy. For example, one type of the Navy's combat aircraft are named "Hornets," while its most prevalent patrol aircraft are known as "Orions." A more revealing system of letters and numbers (aircraft designations) is used to distinguish among the many types and variations of naval aircraft in service. Both the names and the designations are applied to all aircraft of a given type; individual aircraft are identified with a unique number.

The aircraft designation is a letter/number combination that tells you certain basic facts about the aircraft. All the various letter/number combinations can be confusing to the uninitiated, but it helps to remember that the one thing common to all aircraft designations is the hyphen. Where the various letters and numbers are placed in relation to the hyphen will help you to keep their intended meaning clear in your mind. "F-14," for example, indicates a Tomcat fighter plane. The *F* before the hyphen represents the *basic mission* (or *type*) of the aircraft and stands for "fighter." The "14" following the hyphen is the *design number*. To reduce confusion, these designations are used by all the U.S. armed forces so an F-14 in the Air Force means the same thing as an F-14 in the Navy. One other thing to keep in mind (to avoid confusion) is that this system has not always been in effect; earlier in aviation history other designation systems were used, so if you are reading about aircraft in World War II, for example, the aircraft designations will not be the same.

Basic Mission and Type Symbols

A	Attack	C	Cargo/
B	Bomber		transport

E	Special electronics	S	Antisubmarine	
	installation	T	Trainer	
F	Fighter	U	Utility	
H	Helicopter	V	V/STOL	
O	Observation		(Vertical/short	
P	Patrol		takeoff and landing)	

Future modifications to the F-14 would call for a *series symbol* indicating an improvement on or a major change to the same design. This symbol is placed after the design number. The first such change would cause the aircraft to be called an "F-14A," the next major modification would result in an "F-14B," and so on.

When the basic mission of an airplane has been considerably modified, a *modified-mission symbol* is added before the original basic mission symbol. For example, an F-14C modified to act primarily as a reconnaissance plane would become an "RF-14C."

Modified-Mission Symbols

C	Transport	O	Observation	
D	Director	Q	Drone	**269**
H	Search/rescue	R	Reconnaissance	
K	Tanker	V	Staff transport	
L	Cold weather	W	Weather	
M	Mine countermeasures		reconnaisance	

Finally, there is the *special-use symbol,* a letter prefix indicating that the aircraft is being used for special work and experimentation, or that it is in planning or is a prototype.

Consider our imaginary RF-14C. If it were to be used as an experimental aircraft to test some new design modification, it would have an *X* added to the designation and become an XRF-14C. Despite this, the basic airplane is still the F-14, and most Navy personnel would recognize it as such despite its changes. To avoid confusion, these special-use symbols are different from other letters used in aircraft designations.

Special-Use Symbols

J   Special test, temporary (after test, aircraft will be returned to its original configuration)

N Special test, permanent (aircraft has been too drastically
   altered for testing to permit returning it to its original
   configuration)
X Experimental (developmental stage in which basic mission
   has not been established)
Y Prototype (only a few procured for development of design)
Z Planning (used for identification during planning)

Types of Naval Aircraft

There are many different types of aircraft in the U.S. Navy's inventory. Some of these were designed specifically for naval use, but many are used by the other armed forces as well. Some are fixed-wing while others are helicopters.

Fighters

The primary function of fighters is to destroy other aircraft and incoming missiles. They are the aircraft you would normally see involved in a "dogfight." Fighters are very fast and highly maneuverable. They intercept and engage enemy aircraft, defend surface forces, escort other kinds of aircraft when they are carrying out their missions in hostile areas, and support ground troops.

The Navy currently operates two types of fighter aircraft. The **F-14 Tomcat** is a twin-engine, variable-sweep-wing (meaning that the wings can be swept backward or forward depending on what the pilot is trying to accomplish), all-weather fighter-interceptor. It has a powerful gun system and fires air-to-air missiles to destroy enemy aircraft. The aircraft's sophisticated radar/missile combination enables it to track twenty-four targets simultaneously and attack six with missiles while continuing to scan the airspace. It can select and destroy targets up to 100 miles away. The F-14D has improved computerization, radar, communications and electronics, and weaponry. It can fly at Mach 1.88 and has a range of nearly 2,000 miles without refueling (less when involved in high-speed maneuvering).

The **F/A-18** Hornet is designed to carry out *two* missions: the *F* stands for *fighter* and the *A* for *attack*. This is a supersonic (meaning it can fly faster than the speed of sound), twin-engine jet that can carry a variety of armament depending upon the mission, including various missiles, rockets, and bombs. It has an effective combat radius of several hundred miles and can fly in virtually all weather conditions.

A newer, more capable variation of the Hornet is the **Super Hornet,** which will eventually replace the F-14 Tomcat as the primary fighter aircraft on carriers.

JO2 Charles Neff

Figure 13.16. Marine Corps AV-8B Harrier.

Attack

The attack aircraft's main job is to destroy enemy targets, at sea and ashore, with rockets, guided missiles, torpedoes, mines, and bombs. As already mentioned, the F/A-18 Hornet performs this role for the Navy. The **AV-8B Harrier** also serves as an attack aircraft. Its vertical landing and takeoff ability means it does not need a runway (or even a full-length aircraft carrier flight deck) to function, which makes it particularly well suited for ground combat-support operations. A light-attack, single-engine aircraft, it is flown by Marine Corps pilots from shore sites or amphibious assault ships. The Harrier's armament includes cluster, general-purpose, and laser-guided bombs, as well as rockets, missiles, and guns.

Patrol

These large airplanes, with lower speeds but very long flying range, have the primary mission of antisubmarine patrol. They also can be used to drop mines or bombs and can fire missiles. They have infrared, acoustic, and magnetic-detection devices for finding and tracking submarines. The **P-3C Orion** is a propeller-driven, land-based, long-range, over-water antisubmarine patrol plane. Since the prototype first flew in 1958, the P-3 has undergone many improvements and continues to play a major antisubmarine role for the Navy. The P-3 flies with a normal crew of ten (pilots, flight engineers, sensor operators, and in-flight technicians). It has a maximum speed of 473 MPH but normally cruises at 377 MPH. Its maximum-mission radius is more than 2,000 miles.

Figure 13.17. A P-3C Orion patrol aircraft.

Antisubmarine

Searching out submarines visually, by radar and magnetic detection, or by signals sent from floating sonobuoys, these aircraft attack with rockets, depth charges, or homing torpedoes.

The P-3 Orion [see above] is a land-based antisubmarine aircraft, but the **S-3 Viking** is carrier-based. A subsonic, all-weather, long-range, high-endurance turbofan-powered aircraft, the Viking can locate and destroy enemy submarines, including newer high-speed, deep-submergence, quiet versions. With a crew of four, the Viking can operate independently or in tandem with long-range, land-based

Figure 13.18. A carrier-based S-3B Viking antisubmarine warfare aircraft.

antisubmarine units, such as the P-3. Weapons carried by the S-3 include various combinations of torpedoes, depth charges, missiles, rockets, and special weapons.

The **SH-60B Seahawk** is a helicopter designed to operate from surface ships to increase their antisubmarine capability. The SH-60F version is designed to operate from aircraft carriers for the same purpose. These sophisticated helicopters employ a long-range dipping sonar in addition to dropping sonobuoys to track submarines. They are capable of attacking as well as detecting enemy submarines. An older seagoing helicopter, the **SH-3H Sea King,** is still in service and it too can play a role in antisubmarine operations.

Mine Warfare

Helicopters are particularly well suited for both laying and sweeping mines. The **MH-53E Sea Dragon** is used on CVs, LPDs, LHDs, and LHAs for minesweeping, mine neutralization, mine spotting, floating mine destruction, and channel marking.

Command and Control

Maintaining communications is absolutely vital in modern warfare. The land-based **E-6A Mercury** is used in conjunction with ballistic-missile submarines to insure a viable strategic deterrence role. The **E-2C Hawkeye** is a carrier-based, propeller-driven aircraft that provides airborne early warning, threat analysis, and air-control functions for carrier battle groups. By flying high above the battle group, the E-2 uses its powerful radar system to watch over and control a much larger area than could be covered by shipboard radar systems.

273

Figure 13.19. A shipboard-based SH-60B Seahawk helicopter.

Figure 13.20. An E-2C Hawkeye command and control aircraft.

Its sophisticated communications systems help to control the employment of the aircraft sent aloft by the carrier.

Electronic Warfare

The **EA-6B Prowler,** the first Navy plane designed and built specifically for tactical electronic warfare, is an all-weather, four-seat, subsonic, carrier-based plane. It is the most advanced airborne electronic-warfare aircraft in existence. Its missions include the jamming of enemy electronic signals to render them incapable of performing and thereby provide a significant tactical advantage.

The **EP-3E Orion (Aries II)** is an electronic surveillance version of the P-3 Orion. Operating from land bases and using the highly

Figure 13.21. The C-9B Skytrain can carry more than 16 tons of cargo.

sophisticated Aries II surveillance system, this aircraft is capable of collecting valuable electronic data from real or potential enemies while remaining in international airspace.

Transport

Transport planes carry cargo and personnel. Some are land-based and others can be operated from aircraft carriers.

The **C-9B Skytrain II** is a Navy version of the commercial DC-9 series airliner that can carry a significant payload of cargo or passengers.

The **C-130 Hercules** was originally a transport aircraft for personnel, weapons, and supplies for all the services, but this four-engine, turboprop aircraft is also used by the Navy in a variety of roles. As an EC-130, it is an electronic surveillance aircraft. As a KC-130, it is used for aerial refueling of tactical aircraft from jets to helicopters. Probably the most versatile tactical-transport aircraft ever built, the Hercules is also used in search and rescue, space-capsule recovery, landing (with skis) on snow and ice, and special cargo delivery. It has even landed and taken off from a carrier deck without the benefit of arresting gear or catapults.

The **C-2A Greyhound,** a twin turboprop aircraft, has the primary mission of transporting people and cargo to and from aircraft carriers (called "carrier on-board delivery"—COD). The Greyhound provides critical support between shore facilities and aircraft carriers deployed throughout the world. Its cabin can be readily configured to accommodate cargo, passengers, or a combination of both. It is used for

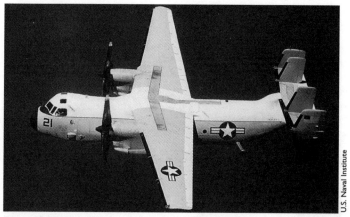

U.S. Naval Institute

Figure 13.22. The C-2 Greyhound transports people and cargo to and from aircraft carriers at sea.

transporting personnel, mail, key logistics items, mission-essential cargo such as jet engines, and litter patients for medical evacuation.

The **CH-46 Sea Knight** serves as a vertical-replenishment helicopter in the fleet, meaning that it is used to lift cargo from one ship and place it on another while the ships are underway. It has a crew of three and can carry approximately 6000 pounds of cargo in a sling beneath the fuselage.

The **CH-53 Sea Stallion** transports supplies, equipment, and personnel. It is useful for personnel evacuations or can be used to insert troops where needed. It can carry thirty-seven fully equipped troops, twenty-four litter patients plus four attendants, or 8000 pounds of cargo.

The **CH-53E Super Stallion** is the largest and most powerful helicopter in production. Despite its large size, it is shipboard-compatible and configured for the lift and movement of cargo, passengers, and heavy, oversized equipment. It can move large quantities of cargo, transfer damaged aircraft or vehicles, provide mobile-construction support, move nuclear weapons, and participate in various mine-warfare missions.

Trainer

Trainers are generally two-seat airplanes that allow instructors and students to go aloft together to learn or perfect the techniques of fly-

Figure 13.23. The CH-46D Sea Knight serves as a vertical-replenishment helicopter in the fleet.

ing. There are several types of trainers in use, but the most sophisticated type is the **T-45A Goshawk** used in the training of prospective tactical Navy and Marine Corps jet pilots.

Aircraft Squadrons

Naval aircraft are organized into squadrons for administrative and operational purposes. Some squadrons are carrier-based, spending part of their time on board aircraft carriers. Others are land-based and, if their mission requires it, periodically deploy to other locations. Some squadrons are subdivided into detachments and are scattered to ships or various bases.

Squadrons are identified by letter-number designations that, like ship hull numbers, tell something about their mission while giving them a unique identity. The first letter in a squadron designation is either a *V* or an *H*. The latter is used for squadrons made up entirely of helicopters. *V* indicates fixed-wing aircraft. If a squadron has both helicopters and fixed-wing aircraft, it is designated by a *V*. In the days when there was a third type of aircraft, the lighter-than-air (or dirigible) type, those squadrons were designated by a *Z*. The letter or letters following the *V* or *H* indicate the squadron's mission or missions. For example, a squadron whose primary purpose is training pilots to fly fixed-wing aircraft would be designated "VT." By adding a number, an individual squadron takes on a unique identity; for example, "VT-3." The numbers, in most cases, have some logic to them—such as even numbers indicating Atlantic Fleet squadrons and odd numbers designating Pacific Fleet—but movement and the periodic establishment and disestablishment of various squadrons has clouded some of the original intended logic.

Aircraft Squadron Designations

HC	Helicopter combat support
HCS	Helicopter combat-support special
HM	Helicopter mine countermeasures
HS	Helicopter antisubmarine
HSL	Light helicopter antisubmarine
HT	Helicopter training
VA	Attack
VAQ	Tactical electronic warfare
VAW	Carrier airborne early warning
VC	Fleet composite
VF	Fighter
VFA	Strike fighter

VFC	Fighter composite
VP	Patrol
VQ	Reconnaissance/strategic communications
VR	Fleet logistics support
VRC	Carrier logistics support
VS	Sea control (antisubmarine warfare, etc.)
VT	Training
VX	Test and evaluation

Air Wings

Aircraft squadrons are typically grouped into larger organizational units called *air wings*. A carrier air wing (CVW) is usually made up of about eight squadrons, each serving different but integrated purposes. With these various squadrons on board, an aircraft carrier can carry out a wide variety of missions. Table 13.1 shows a typical carrier air wing.

Table 13.1. Typical Carrier Air Wing

Squadron	Function	Type	Aircraft Number
VF	Fighter	F-14	14
VFA	Strike Fighter	F/A-18	12
VAW	Early Warning	E-2	4
VAQ	Electronic Warfare	EA-6B	4
VS	Sea Control	S-3	8
HS	Antisubmarine/Rescue	SH-60	8
VRC[a]	Carrier Logistics	C-2	2

a. Detachment

Ship and Squadron Organization

Because the missions and number of people assigned differ for each type of ship or aircraft squadron, each one is organized differently. An aircraft carrier, for example, has more departments and divisions than a destroyer, which is much smaller and has fewer people assigned. An aircraft carrier has need of an air department, but a submarine does not.

Despite these differences, all ships and squadrons have certain things in common. All commissioned ships and aircraft squadrons have a *commanding officer* who has overall responsibility and an *executive officer* who is second in command. All are divided into *departments,* and these are in turn subdivided into *divisions.*

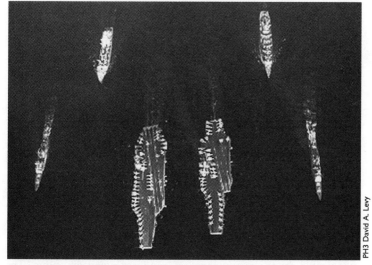

PH3 David A. Levy

Figure 14.1. Different kinds of ships will be organized differently, but all will have some things in common, such as a CO and XO and departments that are subdivided into divisions.

Ships

Every Navy ship operates under the authority of an officer assigned by BUPERS as that ship's commanding officer. The CO, as she or he is sometimes called, may be a lieutenant if the vessel is small, or a captain if the ship is very large. But no matter what the rank, the commanding officer is always called "Captain."

In case of absence or death, the CO's duties are assumed by the line officer next in command, whose official title is executive officer. The XO, as he or she is often called, is responsible for all matters relating to personnel, ship routine, and discipline. All orders issued by the XO have the same force and effect as though they were issued by the CO.

Executive Assistants

Depending on the size of the ship, certain officers and enlisted personnel are detailed as executive assistants. All answer to the XO, but some, such as the ship's secretary, will work directly for the captain in some matters. These jobs may be full-time assignments or may be assigned to individuals as collateral (secondary) duties, depending upon the size of the ship's crew. Some are always filled by officers, others are always enlisted, but many can be either. Even those with "officer" in the title are sometimes filled by qualified enlisted personnel. A lot depends upon the size of the command and the relative qualifications of the individuals concerned.

The executive assistants are listed below in alphabetical order for convenience. Those listed are the most common; there may be others on board your ship as well.

Administrative assistant. This individual can be an officer or a senior petty officer and his or her duties are to relieve the XO of as many administrative details as possible. This individual will, under the XO's guidance, manage much of the ship's incoming and outgoing correspondence, take care of routine paperwork, and assist the XO with various other administrative functions.

Chaplain. Normally assigned only to larger ships, this specially qualified staff corps officer's duties are primarily religious in nature, but she or he is also involved in matters pertaining to the mental, moral, and physical welfare of the ship's company.

Chief master-at-arms. The chief master-at-arms (CMAA) is responsible for the maintenance of good order and discipline. The CMAA enforces regulations and sees that the ship's routine is carried out. This duty is normally carried out by a chief petty officer.

Career counselor. The career counselor runs the ship's career-counseling program and makes sure that current programs and opportunities are known and available to crewmembers. His or her job is to stay informed about all of the Navy's current programs affecting the actual or potential careers of the men and women in the ship's crew.

Drug/alcohol program adviser. Every Navy command is required to have at least one drug and alcohol program adviser (DAPA) on board. In larger commands, there should be one DAPA for every 300 personnel assigned. DAPAs advise the CO and XO on the administration of the drug and alcohol abuse program aboard ship, and on the approaches necessary to cope effectively with any problems that may exist in this area. The adviser must stay informed on all Navy policies and procedures on drug and alcohol education, rehabilitation, identification, and enforcement.

Educational services officer. The educational services officer (ESO) assists the XO in administering and coordinating shipboard educational programs for crewmembers.

Lay leaders. When a chaplain is not available to meet the individual needs of crewmembers, a lay leader is appointed. For instance, if a unit has a Protestant chaplain, but no priest or rabbi, the command may appoint Roman Catholic and Jewish lay leaders. Those appointed must be volunteers, either officer or enlisted, and will receive appropriate training.

Legal officer. The legal officer is an adviser and staff assistant to the CO and XO on the interpretation and application of the Uniform Code of Military Justice (UCMJ), the Manual for Courts-Martial (MCM), and other laws and regulations concerning discipline and the administration of justice within the command.

Personnel officer. Assisting the XO in personnel matters, the personnel officer is responsible for the placement of enlisted personnel and for the administration and custody of enlisted personnel records. She or he will supervise the personnel office (if there is one) and oversee the processing of all enlisted performance evaluations, leave papers, identification cards, and transfer orders.

Postal officer. The postal officer looks after the administration of mail services to the command. He or she must learn and stay current on all applicable postal regulations and supervise those personnel who handle the ship's mail.

Public affairs officer. The public affairs officer prepares briefing material and information pamphlets, assists with press interviews, generates newsworthy material about the unit's operation, and publishes the command's newspaper.

Safety officer. On ships that do not have safety departments, the safety officer will advise the CO and XO on matters pertaining to safety aboard ship. She or he will be accorded department-head status for safety matters and will coordinate the ship's safety program.

Command Master Chief. The command master chief (CMDMC) assists the CO in matters of morale and crew welfare. [See chapter 9 for more detail.]

Senior watch officer. The senior watch officer is responsible for assigning and supervising all deck watchstanders, underway and in port. He or she coordinates the ship's watch bill, ensuring that trained personnel are equitably assigned to all necessary stations under all conditions. The senior watch officer is usually the most senior person among those who are standing watches.

Ship's secretary. Administering and accounting for correspondence and directives, and maintaining officers' personnel records, are among the responsibilities of the ship's secretary. He or she also supervises the preparation of the captain's official correspondence.

Training officer. The training officer coordinates the ship-wide training program. He or she will obtain and administer school quotas, provide indoctrination training to newly arrived personnel, coordinate with the operations officer in scheduling training exercises, and supervise the ship's personnel qualifications system (PQS).

Security manager. The security manager is responsible for information-systems and personnel security, the protection of classified material, and security education.

3-M coordinator. The various aspects of the ship's maintenance and material management (3-M) program are supervised by the 3-M coordinator.

Departments and Divisions

Different ships have different departments, depending upon their size and mission. Some examples of commonly seen departments are *engineering, operations,* and *supply.* Ships whose primary mission is combat may have a *weapons* department, or it may be called *combat systems* on more sophisticated ships. Ships whose primary mission is logistical—involving replenishment of fuel, ammunition, or other supplies at sea—will often have a *deck* department.

Departments are subdivided into divisions, and divisions are often further subdivided into work centers, watches, and/or sections with petty officers in charge of each.

Each ship's department has a department head, an officer who is responsible for its organization, training, and performance. The larger the ship, the more senior the department head will be. In a destroyer the department head is often a senior lieutenant, while in aircraft carriers department heads are usually commanders.

Divisions have a division officer responsible for them. The division is the basic working unit of the Navy. It may consist of twenty specialists on small ships or as many as several hundred persons in a division on an aircraft carrier. The division officer is the boss; he or she reports to the department head and is frequently a junior officer but can be a chief petty officer or a more senior petty officer if the situation calls for it. The division officer is the one officer with whom division personnel come into contact every day. The division chief and the leading petty officer are the division officer's principal assistants. Larger divisions may have more than one chief assigned and may even have other junior officers assigned as assistants. These larger divisions may also have one or more technical and material assistants—usually warrant officers or limited-duty officers—to supervise the maintenance and repair of material or equipment.

In the first chapter of this book, you read about the chain of command, learning that it changes from assignment to assignment. When you report to your first ship, you will have a new chain of command that might begin with your section leader or work center supervisor, who reports to the division chief, who in turn reports to your division officer, who answers to the department head, whose boss is the executive officer, who reports directly to the captain, and so on.

Departments aboard ship belong to one of three different categories: command, support, or special.

Command Departments

Depending upon the type of ship, the command departments found on board are air, aircraft intermediate maintenance, aviation, combat systems, communications, deck, engineering, executive, navigation, operations, reactor, safety, and/or weapons.

Air. The Air Department is headed by the air officer (informally referred to as the "air boss"), who supervises and directs launchings, landings, and the handling of aircraft and aviation fuels.

On a ship with only a limited number of aircraft, the department consists of a V division with the V division officer in charge. On ships with large air departments, additional divisions are assigned: V-1 (plane handling on the flight deck), V-2 (catapults and arresting gear), V-3 (plane handling on the hangar deck), V-4 (aviation fuels), and V-5 (administration). The division officers responsible for these four divisions are known as the flight deck officer for V-1, the catapult and arresting gear officer for V-2, the hangar deck officer for V-3, and the aviation fuels officer for V-4.

Aircraft intermediate maintenance. The head of this department (usually referred to simply as "AIMD") is the aircraft intermediate maintenance officer, who supervises and directs intermediate maintenance for the aircraft on board the ship. The AIMD also keeps up ground-support equipment. When there is only one division aboard ship, it is called the IM division. Ships having more than one division include the IM-1 division (responsible for administration, quality assurance, production and maintenance/material control, and aviation 3-M analysis), the IM-2 division (for general aircraft and organizational maintenance of the ship's assigned aircraft), the IM-3 division (for maintenance of armament systems, precision measuring equipment, and aviation electronic equipment, known as "avionics"), and the IM-4 division (for maintenance of other aviation support equipment).

Combat systems. Because of their complexity and sophistication, submarines and certain classes of cruisers, destroyers, and frigates have a combat systems department instead of a weapons department. Some of the functions covered by the operations department on those ships with a weapons department are included in combat systems on these vessels. Some of the divisions found in these departments are CA (antisubmarine warfare), CB (ballistic missile), CD (tactical data systems), CE (electronics repair), CF (fire control), CG (gunnery and ordnance), CI (combat information), and CM (missile systems).

Communications. In ships large enough to have a communications department, the head of the department is the communications officer, who is responsible for visual and electronic exterior communications. Her or his assistants may include a radio officer, a signal officer, a communications security material system (CMS) custodian, and a cryptosecurity officer. The department may be divided into CR (for radio) and CS (for signals) divisions. In smaller ships, the communications officer is a division officer reporting to the operations officer. In this case, the division is usually called OC division.

Deck. Some ships, such as aircraft carriers, have both a deck department and a weapons department; other ships have only one or the other, depending upon their mission. On ships with a deck department, the first lieutenant is the head of that department which consists of divisions called 1st Division, 2nd Division, and so on. On ships that do not have a deck department, there is a division in the weapons department, usually called 1st Division, and the first lieutenant in this case is a division officer rather than a department head. Aboard those ships having only a deck department (such as an AO) and not a weapons department, ordnance equipment, small arms, and other weapons are the responsibility of a division headed by a gunnery officer. Personnel assigned to the deck department (or division) carry out all seamanship operations, such as mooring, anchoring, and transferring cargo from ship to ship while underway.

Engineering. This department, headed by the engineering officer (also called the chief engineer), is responsible for the operation and maintenance of the ship's machinery, the provision of electrical power and fresh water, damage control, hull and machinery repairs, and the maintenance of underwater fittings. Ships large enough to have more than one division in the engineering department might have a B division for boilers, M for main engines, MP for main propulsion, A for auxiliaries, E for electrical, IC for interior communications, and/or R division for repair.

Executive. Some ships have an executive department made up of one or more divisions. (Aircraft carriers have an administrative department, which is similar in nature and function to the executive department in other ships.) This department is headed by the XO and may have an X division, which includes personnel assigned to work in the CO's office, XO's office, chaplain's office, print shop, security office, training office, legal office, and sick bay (when no medical officer is assigned). It may also include an I division used for the indoctrination of newly reporting personnel.

Navigation. This department, headed by the navigator, is responsible for the ship's safe navigation and piloting and for the care and maintenance of navigational equipment.

Operations. This department, often called "Ops," is headed by the operations officer, who is responsible for collecting, evaluating, and disseminating tactical and operational information. For ships with more than one division, the department could include OA, OC, OD, OE, OI, OP, OS, and OZ divisions. OA includes intelligence, photography, drafting, printing and reproduction, and meteorology. OC handles communications, but on ships having a large air contingent, such as CVs, LPHs, and LHAs, OC is the carrier air-traffic-control-center division. OD division covers the data-processing functions. OE is the operations electronics/material division. OI includes the combat information center (CIC) and sometimes the lookouts. OP is the photographic intelligence division. OS division handles communications intelligence. OZ is the intelligence and/or cryptologic operations division.

The following officers, when assigned, will usually report to the Ops officer: air intelligence, CATCC officer, CIC officer, communications (COMM) officer, electronics material officer (EMO), electronic warfare (EW) officer, intelligence officer, meteorological officer, photographic officer, strike operations officer, and computer programmer (or computer-maintenance officer).

Reactor. CVNs have this department in addition to the engineering department. The reactor officer, who heads this department, is responsible for the operation and maintenance of reactor plants and their associated auxiliaries. Divisions found in the reactor department include RA (auxiliaries), RC (reactor control), RE (electrical), RL (chemistry), RM (machinery), and RP (propulsion). Because of the special responsibilities of running a reactor plant and its obvious close ties with the engineering functions of the ship, the reactor and engineering officers must closely coordinate their activities.

Weapons. The weapons officer supervises and directs the use and maintenance of ordnance and (in ships without a deck department) seamanship equipment. On ships with antisubmarine warfare (ASW) arms and a weapons department, the ASW officer is an assistant to the weapons officer. Other assistants, depending upon the ship and its weapons capabilities, are the missile officer, gunnery officer, fire-control officer, and nuclear weapons officer. On some ships, the CO of the marine detachment may also answer to the weapons officer.

Some of the divisions that may be included in the weapons department are F division (fire control), F-1 (missile fire control), F-2 (ASW), F-3 (gun fire-control), G (ordnance handling); GM (guided missiles), V (aviation, for ships without an air department but with an aviation detachment embarked), and W (nuclear-weapons assembly and maintenance).

Support Departments

Because of its obvious importance, most Navy ships will have a supply department. Smaller ships will have one or more hospital corpsmen assigned to handle the medical and health needs of the crew, but larger ships will have a medical department and a dental department with one or more doctors, dentists, nurses, and/or medical service corps officers assigned. Ships with one or more judge advocate general (lawyer) officers on board will have a legal department.

Supply. Headed by the supply officer, this department handles the procurement, stowage, and issue of all the command's stores and equipment. The supply officer pays the bills and the crew and is responsible for supervising and operating the general and wardroom messes, the laundry, and the ship's store. Ships large enough to have multiple divisions may have an S-1 division (general supply support),

S-2 division (general mess), S-3 division (ship's stores and services), S-4 division (disbursing), S-5 division (officers' messes), S-6 division (aviation stores), and S-7 division (data processing).

Medical. The medical officer is responsible for maintaining the health of personnel, making medical inspections, and advising the CO on hygiene and sanitation conditions. Assistant medical officers may be assigned. H division is normally the only medical division.

Dental. The dental officer is responsible for preventing and controlling dental disease and supervising dental hygiene. Assistant dental officers are sometimes assigned to larger ships. D division is normally the only dental division.

Legal. The legal officer is responsible for handling all legal matters, particularly those pertaining to the UCMJ.

Special Departments

Certain ships have unusual missions and therefore require special departments. Included among these are aviation, boat group, deep submergence, marine detachment, repair, safety, transportation, and weapons repair.

Aviation. On a nonaviation ship with a helicopter detachment embarked, an aviation department is organized and headed by the aviation officer. The aviation officer is responsible for the specific missions of the embarked aircraft. His principal assistant may be a helicopter control officer, but often one officer performs both functions.

Boat group. Assault transports (LPDs and LSDs) have a boat-group department whose responsibilities include the operation and maintenance of the embarked boats.

Deep submergence. This specialized department, which is found on only a few naval vessels, launches, recovers, and services deep-submergence vehicles (DSVs) or deep-submergence rescue vehicles (DSRVs).

Marine detachment. The marine detachment assigned to some ships serves as the ship's landing party, provides ship security, operates the ship's brig, and provides orderlies for certain senior officers. The head of the marine detachment is not technically a department head, nor does he or she function as a division officer. She or he is the commanding officer of the detachment, in charge of matters pertaining strictly to the Marine Corps, but often is subordinate to the weapons officer in shipboard matters.

Repair. On ships with a large repair function, there will be a full department with a department head called the repair officer. On multiple-division ships, there may be an R-1 division (hull repair), R-2 division (machinery repair), R-3 division (electrical repair), R-4 division (electronic repair), and R-5 division (ordnance repair).

Safety. Larger ships, particularly those who conduct potentially hazardous operations on a routine basis, will have a safety department assigned.

Transportation. Only Military Sealift Command (MSC) transports have this department, headed by the transportation officer. The department is responsible for loading and unloading, berthing and messing, and general direction of passengers. On ships without a combat cargo officer, the transportation officer is also the liaison with loading activities ashore. Larger ships may have a T-1 division, which has the physical transportation responsibilities, and a T-2 division, which handles the administrative end of transportation.

Weapons repair. This department, found only on tenders, usually has a single division, designated SR. A large department may be subdivided into the SR-1 division (repair and service) and the SR-2 division (maintenance of repair machinery).

Aircraft Squadrons

Operating squadrons, like ships, have a CO, an XO, department heads, and division officers.

Commanding Officer

The CO, also known as the squadron commander, has the usual duties and responsibilities of any captain insofar as they are applicable to an aircraft squadron. These include looking after morale, discipline, readiness, and efficiency, and issuing operational orders to the entire squadron.

Executive Officer

The XO, the second senior naval aviator in the squadron, is the direct representative of the CO. The XO sees that the squadron is administered properly and that the CO's orders are carried out. The executive officer, as second in command, will take over command of the squadron whenever the CO is not present.

Squadron Departments

Operational squadrons are organized into several departments, each with its own department head who is responsible for organization, training, personnel assignments, departmental planning and operations, security, safety, cleanliness of assigned areas, and maintenance of records and reports. Just as in ships, the number and functions of departments vary somewhat according to the squadron's mission. Most squadrons have at least four departments: operations, administration, maintenance, and safety. Many have a training department as well.

Operations. This department is responsible for aircraft schedules, communications, intelligence, navigation, and (in squadrons without a separate training department) squadron training. Working for the operations officer are a number of assistants with special duties, including the communications officer, classified material security officer, intelligence officer, navigation officer, tactics officer, landing signal officer, and (in squadrons without a separate training department) several training assistants.

Administrative. The administrative department is responsible for official squadron correspondence, records maintenance, legal matters, and public affairs. An officer designated as first lieutenant ensures that squadron spaces and equipment are maintained and clean. Other assistants to the admin officer are the personnel officer, educational services officer, public affairs officer, legal officer, and command security manager. The personnel division takes care of personnel records, human-resources management, and equal-opportunity programs.

Maintenance. This department is typically the largest in the squadron and oversees the planning, coordination, and execution of all maintenance work on aircraft. It also is responsible for the inspection, adjustment, and replacement of aircraft engines and related equipment, as well as the keeping of maintenance logs, records, and reports.

Safety. The safety department head ensures squadron compliance with all safety orders and directives and is a member of the accident (investigation) board.

Training. Some squadrons have separate training departments to handle the training requirements of the squadron. Squadrons designated as *fleet replacement squadrons* (once known as readiness air groups or RAGs) exist to train new or returning squadron personnel in preparation for assignment to operational squadrons. Pilots and naval flight officers train in these squadrons after their initial basic flight training and before returning to an operational squadron after an extended assignment to other duties. Enlisted maintenance personnel are also trained in these squadrons in a special program known as FRAMP (Fleet Readiness Aviation Maintenance Personnel). Sometimes there is a separate FRAMP department.

15 Weapons

The Navy's overall mission is to maintain sufficient military capability to effectively deter a would-be enemy from using military power against the United States and its allies, to defend against any attacks that might occur, and to take offensive action against the enemy once hostilities have begun. Weapons are the mainstay of the military. Without them, the Navy could not carry out its combat missions or defend its ships, planes, bases, and personnel.

To understand the weapons used by the Navy, one should first be familiar with the following terms.

Ordnance. This term applies to the various components associated with a ship's or aircraft's firepower: guns, gun mounts, turrets, ammunition, guided missiles, rockets, and units that control and support these weapons.

U.S. Naval Institute

Figure 15.1. Without weapons, the Navy could not carry out its combat missions or defend its ships, planes, bases, and personnel.

Weapon system. When a number of ordnance components are integrated so as to find, track, and deliver fire onto a target, this is called a weapon system. For example, a gun would be called a weapon, but the gun plus the radars used to find and track the target and the ammunition-handling equipment used to load it would be called a weapon system.

Gun. In its most basic form, a gun is a tube closed at one end from which a projectile is propelled by the burning of gunpowder. A projectile (bullet) fired from a gun gets all of its traveling energy at the instant it is fired (unlike rockets and missiles whose burning fuels continue to propel them through the air).

Rocket. A weapon containing a propulsion section to propel the weapon through the air and an explosive section used to do damage to an enemy. A rocket is unable to change its direction of movement after it has been fired.

Missile. Originally called a *"guided* missile" this weapon is essentially a rocket (that is, it has a propulsion section and an explosive section), but also has a *guidance* section that allows its direction to be changed in mid-flight in order to better hit the target.

Torpedo. A self-propelled underwater weapon used against surface and underwater targets. Some torpedoes function like underwater rockets in that they cannot be controlled once they have been launched, while other, more sophisticated versions can be guided, like an airborne missile, after they have been launched.

Mine. An underwater explosive weapon put into position by surface ships, submarines, or aircraft. A mine explodes only when a target comes near or into contact with it.

Depth charge. Antisubmarine weapons fired or dropped by a ship or aircraft, and set to explode either at a certain depth or in proximity to a submarine.

Bomb. Any weapon, other than a torpedo, mine, rocket, or missile, dropped from an aircraft. Bombs are free-fall (that is, they have no propulsion power to deliver them to the target) explosive weapons and may be either "dumb" (unguided) or "smart" (with a guidance system to steer them to their target).

Missiles and Rockets

The Navy has a great many missiles and some rockets in its weapons inventory. The chief advantages of rockets and missiles over gun and bomb systems is their extended range, and missiles are, of course, more effective than rockets because of their increased accuracy. The major disadvantage of these weapons is their added cost. Both missiles and rockets can be fired from either ships (including submarines) or aircraft.

Rocket and Missile Components

Rockets have three major components—the airframe, the powerplant, and the warhead. As already explained, missiles have a fourth component—the guidance system.

The airframe is the body of the rocket or missile which determines its flight characteristics and contains the other components. It must be light, because the other parts are heavy. Airframes are made of aluminum alloys, magnesium, and high-tensile (high-stress) steel. These metals can withstand extreme heat and pressure.

The powerplant is similar to the engines of an aircraft except that the aircraft's engines are reusable while the missile's propulsion unit is expended in its one flight. The powerplant must propel the rocket or missile at very high speeds to minimize its chance of being shot down before reaching its intended target. Some must be able to operate at very high altitudes where there is little or no atmosphere, and therefore are required to carry both the fuel and an oxidizer in order to sustain combustion. Other, less expensive powerplants are air-breathing plants that carry only the fuel, but they cannot operate above about 70,000 feet.

The warhead is the part that does the damage. Its explosive may be conventional or nuclear.

Missile Guidance Systems

The guidance system in missiles constantly corrects the flight path until it intercepts the target. There are four different types of guidance systems: inertial, homing, command, or beam riding. Many missiles use a combination of two of these systems—one guiding the missile through mid-course and the other used during the terminal stage.

Inertial Guidance

This type of guidance uses a predetermined path programmed into an on-board missile computer before launch. Missile speed and direction are checked constantly, and the computer makes corrections to keep it on course.

Homing Guidance

In this type of guidance, the missile picks up and tracks a target by radar, optical devices, or heat-seeking methods.

In an *active* homing system, the missile itself emits a signal that is reflected off the target and picked up by a receiver in the missile.

In a *semiactive* homing system, the signal comes from the launching ship or plane rather than from the missile itself and is then received by the missile which uses the information received to correct its flight.

A *passive* homing system does not require either the missile or the firing ship or aircraft to emit a signal, but uses the *target's* emissions to home in on. For example, some passive homers use a target's own radar signals to home on; a heat-seeking missile can home in on the heat put out by the target's engines.

Command Guidance
After the missile is launched on an intercept course, a computer evaluates how it is doing in relation to the target and transmits orders to the missile to change its track as necessary to ensure that it hits the target.

Beam-Riding Guidance
The missile follows a radar beam to the target. A computer in the missile keeps it centered within the radar beam. Several missiles may ride the same beam simultaneously. If the missile wanders outside the beam, it will automatically destroy itself.

Missile and Rocket Designations
Navy rockets and missiles are often identified by a three-letter designation, followed by a number. For example, the Sparrow missile is known as an AIM-7. The *A* tells you that the missile is launched from an airplane. If the first letter is an *R*, it means the missile is launched from a ship; *U* means that it is submarine-launched.

The second letter tells you the mission. *I* indicates air intercept (shoots down other aircraft), *G* means surface attack (ships or land targets), and *U* means the target is a submarine.

The third letter is either *M* (for missile) or *R* (for rocket).

The number(s) used differentiate between one similar system and another and represent the sequential development of the missile; for example, the first missile of a particular type that was developed was designated number *1* and the next was number *2*, and so on.

Missile Categories
Missiles can be launched from aircraft, ships, and submarines and, depending upon their intended target, may be categorized as air-to-

air, air-to-surface, surface-to-air, and so on. Some missiles can be used against air and surface targets alike.

Air-to-Air

Carried by naval aircraft to shoot down enemy aircraft, some of the current ones in use are listed below.

Sparrow. Designated the AIM-7, this highly maneuverable radar-guided missile can attack enemy aircraft from any direction in virtually all weather conditions and has a range of more than 30 nautical miles.

Sidewinder. The AIM-9 is an all-weather heat-seeking missile with a range of five to ten nautical miles depending upon conditions.

Phoenix. The AIM-54 is a highly sophisticated, radar-guided, long-range (more than 100 miles) missile that is fired only by the F-14 Tomcat fighter aircraft.

AMRAAM. The AIM-120 is a radar-guided sophisticated missile with a range of approximately 30 miles. "AMRAAM" stands for "*a*dvanced *m*edium-*r*ange *a*ir-to-*a*ir *m*issile."

Air-to-Ground

Despite the name, these missiles can be used against ships at sea as well as inland targets.

Shrike. Designated AGM-45, this missile is delivered by fighter aircraft and is designed to home in on enemy antiaircraft radars.

HARM. The AGM-88 is named for its capabilities as a "*h*igh-speed *a*nti*r*adiation *m*issile." It homes in on enemy radar-equipped air defense systems.

Figure 15.2. An F/A-18 Hornet fires an AMRAAM missile.

Hughes Aircraft Company

Maverick. The AGM-65 is an infrared-guided missile designed for day or night sea warfare (antiship) and land interdiction missions.

Surface-to-Air

Designed to shoot down incoming enemy aircraft and missiles, these weapons can be used in concert with or instead of friendly interceptor aircraft.

Standard. The missiles currently in use by the Navy are grouped together in several variations of what are called the Standard (RIM-66) missiles. The SM-1 MR (medium range) and SM-2 MR are two common variations. There is also an extended range version that is designated "ER" instead of "MR."

Sea-Sparrow. A modified version of the Sparrow air-to-air missile, this missile is carried by ships having no Standard missile capabilities. This missile has a range of about 10 nautical miles and is designed to provide close-in protection when other means of antiair defense have been ineffective.

Cruise Missiles

These missiles can be fired from surface ships to strike other surface ships and could therefore be called surface-to-surface missiles, but because they may also be fired from submarines or from aircraft to hit surface targets, they are more generically referred to as cruise missiles.

295

Harpoon. Because Harpoons can be fired from virtually every combatant in the Navy (surface ships, submarines, and aircraft) the Harpoon is designated as the RGM-84, the UGM-84, and the AGM-84. It has a range of 75+ miles and a version called SLAM (for *s*tand-off *l*and *a*ttack *m*issile) is used to attack land targets.

Tomahawk. The BGM-109 can be used in several variations, including a TASM (*T*omahawk *a*ntiship *m*issile), a TLAM (*T*omahawk *l*and-*a*ttack *m*issile), and a TLAM(N) (nuclear) version. These missiles vary in range from 250+ nautical miles in the TASM version to 750+ nautical miles and 1200+ nautical miles in the TLAM and TLAM(N) versions, respectively.

Fleet Ballistic Missiles

With nuclear warheads capable of hitting multiple targets and doing massive damage, these missiles are designed for strategic deterrence and attack. They represent some of the greatest advances in modern weapons technology and can be launched from submerged submarines over a wide range of the earth.

U.S. Naval Institute

Figure 15.3. A surface-to-surface Harpoon (RGM 8) is fired from a canister launcher aboard a destroyer.

Trident. These subsurface-to-surface missiles, in their most advanced version, the *Trident II,* have a range of more than 6000 miles and are capable of carrying up to eight independent thermonuclear warheads.

Missile Launching Systems

Earlier missile systems had "dedicated" launchers—separate magazine-loaded launchers for each type of missile. This took up valuable space on board ship and increased topside weight. Later launchers

U.S. Naval Institute

Figure 15.4. On board SSBN submarines, Trident missiles are carried in vertical silos—here seen with their hatches open.

handled more than one type of missile, but still had to be individually loaded. The newest launcher is the Mark 41 VLS (vertical launch syctem), going into current *Ticonderoga-* and *Arleigh Burke*–class ships and being retrofitted into the *Spruance* class. Missiles are carried in below-deck ready-to-launch tubes; any needed mix of missiles can be fired right from these tubes in quick succession without the delays involved in reloading topside launchers.

Bombs

Bombs have four chief parts. The *case* is normally made of steel and contains the explosive. The *fuze* causes the bomb to explode when desired. The *fin* or *tail assembly* stabilizes the bomb during flight. The *arming-wire* assembly keeps the fuze or fuzes from being armed until after the bomb is dropped.

Bombs are classed as explosive, chemical, or practice. *General-purpose* (GP) bombs, weighing 100–2000 pounds, are explosive-type bombs and are generally used against unarmored ships or ground targets for blast or fragmentation. *Semi-armor-piercing* (SAP) bombs are used against targets that are sufficiently protected so as to require the bomb to have some penetration capability in order to be effective. *Fragmentation* bombs are usually smaller explosives dropped in clusters against troops and ground targets.

Chemical bombs contain specialized chemical agents that are used for a specific purpose. They can contain chemicals that are designed to disable or kill enemy personnel—such as mustard gas, phosgene, tear gas, or vomiting gas—or they can be smoke bombs containing white phosphorus that ignites during the explosion and spreads heavy smoke over the target area in order to conceal movements of ships or troops. *Incendiary* or *napalm* bombs, containing a mixture of gasoline or jet fuel and a thickening agent, are a form of chemical bomb that produces intense fire when ignited and are used against troops and ground targets.

Practice and drill bombs used in training may be loaded with sand or water but are inert (carry no explosive) and will cause no damage other than simple impact.

Torpedoes

The torpedo is a self-propelled, explosive-carrying, underwater weapon. Early torpedoes were basically of the "point-and-shoot" variety, but modern versions have some sort of guidance system that markedly increases the accuracy of the weapon.

A torpedo consists of a tail, afterbody, midsection, and head. The tail section includes the screws, fins, and control surfaces. The propulsion system is contained in the afterbody. The midsection houses batteries, compressed air, or liquid fuel. The head contains the explosive charge, fuze, and any acoustic or magnetic sensing devices.

Torpedo guidance systems are either preset, wire-guided, or homing. Preset torpedoes follow a set course and depth after they are launched. Wire-guided torpedoes have a thin wire connecting the torpedo and the firing vessel, through which guidance signals can be transmitted to the torpedo to direct it to intercept the target.

Homing torpedoes are either active, passive, or a combination of active/passive. The active versions depend on the sensing signals generated and returned to the torpedo through a sonar device inside the torpedo. Passive types pick up tell-tale signals (such as noise or magnetic disturbances) to home in on. In the active/passive mode, the torpedo searches passively until a target is acquired, then active terminal guiding finishes the target destruction.

Surface ships launch torpedoes from tubes mounted topside, or propel them to the target area with a rocket called an ASROC (antisubmarine rocket). Submarines launch torpedoes through specially designed tubes, and aircraft deploy their torpedoes by parachute so as to reduce the impact when the weapon strikes the water.

Mines

Mines are passive weapons that are planted under the water to await the passage of enemy vessels to explode and do damage. Their advantage is that they operate independently (that is, no personnel are required to operate them once they have been planted). Their chief disadvantage is that they are indiscriminate (they can damage friendly or neutral vessels as well as enemy ones if precautions are not taken). You might be confused a bit if you read naval history and see the word "torpedo" used. In earlier times, what we now call a mine was called a torpedo. Today they are, of course, very different weapons.

Mines can be classified according to the method of actuation (firing), the method of planting, and their position in the water.

Mines may be actuated by contact and/or influence. A contact mine fires when a ship strikes it. Influence mines may be actuated by the underwater sound generated in a passing ship's current, by the ship's magnetic field, or by the mine's sensitivity to reduced water pressure caused by a passing ship.

Mines may be planted by surface craft, submarines, and aircraft. Planting mines using surface craft is the most dangerous method because the ship doing the planting is vulnerable to attack. Submarines can plant mines more secretly and aircraft are able to plant mines quickly and with less risk.

Moored contact mines are anchored in place and float near the surface of the water where a ship might strike them. Bottom mines, which lie on the ocean floor, are used only in relatively shallow water. They are influence mines, set off by sound, magnetism, or pressure.

Naval Guns

Guns have been a major component of naval armament for centuries. Early guns were highly inaccurate, often very dangerous devices that had to be loaded from the front end and aimed simply by pointing at a visible enemy. Today's guns are much more powerful and accurate, far safer, and aimed and controlled by sophisticated electronic and hydraulic systems.

Early cannons had smooth bores (inside the barrel) and usually fired round shot. Modern guns have *rifling* in their barrels which is a network of ridges (called *lands*) and grooves shaped in a spiral that causes an elongated projectile to spin on its long axis (much as a well-thrown football). This increases the range and accuracy of the gun.

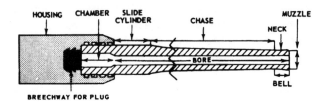

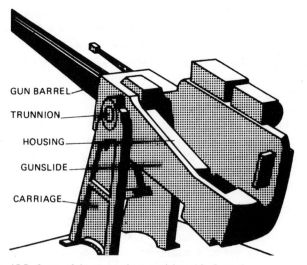

Figure 15.5. Some of the parts of a typical (simplified) naval gun.

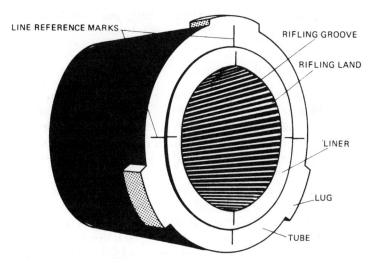

Figure 15.6. A view into the barrel of a naval gun shows the spiraling lands and grooves known as rifling.

Guns are not nearly as important to naval ships as they once were. The advent of sophisticated missile systems, with their greater range and superior accuracy, have taken the place of the gun as the main-stay of naval armament. There is, however, still a need for naval guns. Certain missions are better performed by guns, and missiles tend to be much more expensive than guns.

U.S. Navy guns are classified by their inside barrel diameter and by their barrel length. These two figures are expressed in a rather cryptic manner that may seem confusing at first, but makes sense once you understand what it is telling you. The first figure in a Navy gun classification is the inside barrel diameter, expressed in inches or millimeters (mm). The second part follows a slash and, when it is multiplied by the first number, tells you the length of the gun's bar-rel. Thus, a 5-inch/54 gun would have an inside barrel diameter of five inches and a barrel length of 270 inches (5 × 54 = 270).

In years past, guns such as the 8-inch/55 and the 16-inch/50 were the main armament of large cruisers and battleships. Today, the most prevalent guns in the U.S. Navy are the 5-inch/54 (on cruisers and destroyers), the 76mm/62 (on frigates), and a specialized close-in weapons system (CIWS) known as the 20mm/76 Phalanx system (mounted on many ships as a protection against incoming missile attacks). Many Navy ships also carry saluting guns, which are used for ceremonial purposes and have no combat capability.

Weapon Control Systems

A weapon, however powerful, is only as good as its accuracy. The process by which a projectile, missile, bomb, or torpedo is guided to its target is called weapon control. A potential target is first detected by a sensor (radar, sonar, or lookout). It is then evaluated, either by human judgment, or by computer, or by a combination of the two. If the target is evaluated to be hostile, a decision is made, according to prescribed weapons doctrine, whether or not to engage. If the target is to be engaged, the appropriate weapon is selected. All available information is assimilated to produce a weapon-control solution that will guide the weapon to contact. The weapon is then fired.

Weapon systems and their components are identified by a "Mark" and "Mod" (modification) system. A new weapon system may be designated the "Mark 22" system, for example. If it is later modified, the improved system would be called the "Mark 22 Mod 1" system.

Sensors

Before electronics arrived on the scene, enemies were detected and aimed at using the human senses, primarily the eyes. Modern weapons rely on electronic systems for detection of targets and to control weapons. Most common are *radar* and *sonar*. Both operate on the same principle but differ in the medium used.

In its most elemental form, radar (radio detection and ranging) uses a *transceiver* to send out (transmit) a radio-like electronic signal that reflects off a target and then returns the signal to a receiver where a very accurate timing system measures the amount of time that the signal took to travel to and from the target and, using the known speed of the signal, calculates the range to the target. A built-in direction-finding system also provides a bearing (direction) to the target.

Sonar works on the same principle, except that the signal used is *sound* rather than radio waves. Because radio signals work well in air and sound is more effective underwater, radar is used effectively in the detection of surface or air targets, but sonar is the sensor used in the detection of subsurface (underwater) targets.

Radar, sonar, and other Navy electronic equipments are identified by the joint electronics type designation system. This system was originally called the "Army-Navy nomenclature system" and still retains the prefix identifier "AN" (for "Army-Navy"). The rest of the designation consists of three letters plus a number. Each letter tells you something about the equipment and the number is the series number. For example, using Table 15.1, you can see that the designation AN/SPY-1 describes a multifunction (Y) radar (P) that is installed on surface ships (S). It is the first in the series of this type of radar, hence the number 1. If another radar of this type is later developed, it will be the AN/SPY-2.

Systems

Ships, aircraft, and submarines all incorporate various types of weapon-control systems. Surface- and air-search radars have been continuously improved since World War II to detect high-performance targets at long ranges in any weather. The newer surface-ship control systems work with guns and missiles, and include radars and digital computers that can quickly acquire and track targets while directing shipboard weapons.

The Mark 86 fire-control system is used in destroyers and larger ships, while the lightweight Mark 92 system is used in missile frigates. The most sophisticated weapon system currently used in U.S. Navy warships is the *Aegis* system, a rapid-reaction, long-range fleet air-defense system capable of effectively handling multiple surface and air targets simultaneously. It includes the very capable AN/SPY-1 radar, a quick-reaction tactical computer for overall command control, a digital weapon-control system, and state-of-the-art guided-missile launchers. Found in *Ticonderoga*-class cruisers and

Table 15.1. Joint Electronics Type Designation System

Installation	Type of Equipment	Purpose
A Airborne	A Invisible light, heat, radiation	D Direction finder or reconnaissance
B Underwater (submarine)	L Countermeasures	E Ejection (e.g., chaff)
S Surface ship	P Radar	G Fire control
U Multiplatform	Q Sonar	N Navigation
W Surface ship and underwater	R Radio	Q Multiple or special purpose
	S Special	R Receiving, passive detection
	W Weapon related	S Search
	Y Data processing	W Weapon control
		Y Multifunction

Arleigh Burke–class guided missile destroyers, the Aegis system gives a force commander the capability of controlling all the surface and aerial weapons of an entire battle group in a multithreat environment.

The SQQ-89 surface-ship ASW (antisubmarine warfare) combat system is an integrated system for detecting, identifying, tracking, and engaging modern submarines.

Submarines and aircraft have their own control systems, similar in general principle to those used in surface ships.

Fleet ballistic missiles fired from submarines are controlled by a missile fire-control system, which is connected to the submarine's inertial navigation system. The navigation system keeps accurate track of the ship's position. When missiles are to be fired, the fire-control system takes current position data and quickly computes firing information to put missiles on the proper ballistic course. While in flight, the missile keeps itself on course with the aid of a built-in navigational system.

Small Arms

The Navy also uses a variety of small arms (pistols, rifles, shotguns, grenade launchers, and machine guns) for various purposes, including sentry duty, riot control, and landing parties.

Just as with larger Navy guns, small arms are differentiated by the inside diameter (bore) of the barrel. Like larger naval guns, this diameter may be expressed in either inches or millimeters, but unlike larger guns, small arms do not include a follow-on figure representing the length of the barrel [see previous section]. When the figure is in inches, it is referred to as "caliber" as in ".45-caliber pistol," but when it is expressed in millimeters, the term caliber is not used, as in "9-mm pistol."

Shotguns are an exception. They are usually differentiated by "gauge," which still refers to the bore but is defined as the number of lead balls of that particular diameter required to make a pound. For example, it would take twelve lead balls of the diameter of the 12-gauge shotgun to equal one pound; sixteen balls for the 16-gauge shotgun. This means that the 12-gauge shotgun has a larger bore than the 16-gauge, which seems backwards at first but makes sense when you think about it.

Any weapon with a bore diameter of 0.6 inches (.60-caliber) or less is called a small arm. The largest Navy small arm is the .50-caliber machine gun.

Small arms are considered to be "automatic" if holding down the trigger causes the weapon to continuously fire and "semiautomatic" if the weapon reloads automatically when fired but requires another pull of the trigger to fire off another round.

Some small arms you may encounter are identified by the Army system of terminology. An "M" preceding a number identifies a particular weapon, such as the "M14 rifle." Modifications are identified by a follow-on letter and number combination. For example, the M16 rifle has been modified twice as the M16A1 and M16A2 versions. Sometimes the Navy system of "Mark" (abbreviated "Mk") and Modification (abbreviated "Mod") is used, as in the "20-mm Mk 16 Mod 5 machine gun."

Pistols

One of the oldest weapons in the Navy inventory is the M1911A1 .45-caliber semiautomatic pistol. It is commonly (though erroneously) referred to as the "45-automatic." Because you must pull the trigger each time you fire a round, this pistol is *semi-automatic*. Its magazine holds seven rounds and it has a maximum range of a little over 1,600 yards but is usually effective only at about 50 yards. One of its chief advantages is stopping power—where a .38-caliber revolver can be just as lethal as the .45, the latter is more likely to knock a man off his feet, even one who is pumped up on adrenalin. This can be a major asset when dealing with a charging fanatic, for example.

The 9-mm M9 semiautomatic pistol is a similar weapon to the .45-caliber pistol. Slightly lighter in weight, it has a maximum range of 1,800 meters (1,962.2 yards) and an effective range of 50 meters (54.7 yards). A major advantage is that its magazine has a capacity of 15 rounds, more than double that of the .45 pistol.

The .38-caliber revolver has maximum and effective ranges similar to the .45 pistol, but is lighter in weight. This makes it more suitable for flight personnel. It has a six-round capacity and its relatively simple design makes it unlikely to jam.

The 9-mm pistol is the official replacement for both the .45 and .38 pistols, but you may find the latter weapons still in service at some commands.

Rifles

As mentioned earlier, there are two versions of the M16 rifle you may encounter—the M16A1 and M16A2. Both versions are magazine-fed weapons that fire a 5.56-mm (just slightly larger than a .22-caliber) round. The caliber may seem small, but the high muzzle velocity (more than 3,000 feet per second) makes this a very powerful weapon. The M16A1 has a selector lever that allows the user to fire in automatic or semi-automatic mode, and the M16A2 has a similar selector that permits semi-automatic or burst (3 rounds) modes. The magazine capacity is either 20 or 30 rounds, depending upon the type used, and the maximum range is 460 meters (503 yards).

While the M16 is the replacement rifle for the Navy, you may still encounter some M14 rifles. Firing a 7.62-mm round in either automatic or semi-automatic mode, this was the last of the wooden-stock rifles before lighter, plastic ones appeared on the M16. Fully loaded, this rifle weighs in at 11 pounds and has a maximum range of about 4,075 yards.

Shotguns

The most common shotgun in the Navy is the Remington M870. Manually operated, this 12-gauge pump-action shotgun can fire 4 rounds without reloading. The Mossberg M500 is also a 12-gauge shotgun similar to the M870.

Machine Guns

The .50-caliber M2 Browning machine gun (abbreviated "BMG") is mounted on many surface ships and patrol craft for close-in defense. Ammunition is belt-fed at a rate of 450–500 rounds per minute. The BMG has a maximum range of 7,400 yards and an effective range of 2,000 yards. This is a highly effective weapon, but because it is air-cooled, there is the danger of a cook-off situation after a burst of 250 rounds or more; you should therefore always keep the weapon laid on target or pointed in a safe direction during breaks in firing. In an extreme case—called runaway firing—the BMG can actually continue firing after the trigger has been released. This can be remedied by twisting the ammunition belt at the feed slot to jam the weapon.

A lighter, but very effective machine gun is the 7.62-mm M60. With a maximum range of 3,725 meters (4,075 yards) and an effective range of 1,100 meters (1,200 yards), the M60 was originally designed for use by ground troops but has been adapted for naval use as well. Firing in short bursts is preferable to continuous firing to prevent overheating.

Grenade Launchers

You may encounter three different kinds of grenade launchers in the Navy. The 40-mm M79 is hand-held, like a shotgun, and fires one round (grenade) at a time. The Mk 19 Mod 3 machine gun is a

mounted weapon that fires multiple 40-mm grenades in fully automatic bursts. The M203 grenade launcher is actually an accessory
that can be attached to the M16A1 rifle.

Safety Precautions
The following general safety precautions apply whenever you are
handling any type of firearm:

1. Treat every weapon with respect. Consider it to be loaded
   even if you are certain it is not.
2. Always be aware of where the muzzle (open end of the barrel) is pointed. *Never point a weapon at a person unless you
   intend to shoot that person.*
3. Always make sure the bore (inside of barrel) is clear and that
   all oil and grease have been removed from the outside of the
   weapon before firing.
4. Use only the proper size of ammunition.
5. Unload firearms before transporting them unless they may be
   needed during the transit.
6. Keep the safety on until you are actually ready to fire the
   weapon.
7. Never shoot until you have positively identified the target.
8. Unload unattended weapons. If you have weapons at home,
   stow them with trigger locks installed and keep ammunition
   out of the reach of children.
9. Do not climb trees or fences with a loaded firearm if it can be
   avoided.
10. Do not pull a firearm toward you by the muzzle.
11. Be aware of the possibility of ricochet when firing. Keep in
    mind that a bullet may skip like a stone on water if fired at a
    shallow angle over a hard or liquid surface.
12. It should be obvious that firearms and alcohol don't mix. Be
    aware that many prescription drugs also have side effects that
    can add to the danger of handling weapons.
13. Know your weapon—its shooting characteristics, its safeties,
    and its loading and handling procedures.
14. Never play around when carrying a weapon.

Firing Techniques
When firing a small arm, whether on a target range or in an actual
real-life combat situation, remembering some basic rules will help
you to be more effective.

Figure 15.7. Effects of correct and incorrect small arms sight alignment.

Proper sight alignment is essential to accuracy. Although it may seem illogical to you, the point at which you are aiming should be resting on top of the two aligned sights. When aiming, you want the front and rear sights to be perfectly aligned and the target appearing to rest directly on top of them.

Blackening your sights will prevent glare. Use a smudge pot, carbide lamp, candle, cigarette lighter, or ordinary match to blacken your sights.

Take a normal breath before firing, exhale part of it, and hold the rest as you squeeze the trigger. Squeeze the trigger steadily—do not jerk it. If your sight alignment shifts while you are squeezing, do not release the pressure on the trigger; hold it while you realign the sights, then continue squeezing. You should be surprised when the weapon fires.

16 Shipboard Life

As a Sailor in the U.S. Navy, you will more than likely serve aboard ship. In previous chapters, you have learned some things about shipboard organization and routine. You know, for example, that each day's events are listed in the Plan of the Day (POD). You have learned that there are certain rituals regarding the national ensign and that ships have a commanding officer we traditionally call "Captain," a second in command whose title is executive officer or XO, and that each ship is organized into a variety of departments and divisions. In this chapter, you will learn more about the routine and the not-so-routine of shipboard life.

Standard Organization and Regulations of the U.S. Navy

If you had to learn a new set of regulations and an entirely different organization every time you moved from one division, department, or ship to another, you would waste a great deal of time and probably become very confused. The Navy has standardized everything—routine, regulations, and organization—as much as possible on all ships, so that transferring from one to another will require only minor adjustments on your part. The basis for this standardization is the current edition of the *Standard Organization and Regulations of the U.S. Navy* (OPNAVINST 3120.32). Your daily and weekly routine aboard ship will be governed by this book, no matter which ship you might serve in. (*Note:* You serve "in" a ship, not "on.") Your division and department will be organized in accordance with this manual, and the ship's governing regulations and instructions will have been drawn up using this book as the basis.

The various chapters of OPNAVINST 3120.32 deal with unit organization, safety, training, maintenance, and administration, and you would do well to familiarize yourself with each of these.

General Guidance and Regulations

Chapter 5 of OPNAVINST 3120.32, entitled "General Rules and Regulations," spells out those regulations that are common to all Navy ships, most of which will apply directly to you. For example, it contains rules concerning the proper operation of the ship's general announcing system (1MC), telling you that you must never use the 1MC without permission from the OOD. In chapter 5, you will also find that:

Alcohol must never be consumed aboard a Navy ship except when authorized for medicinal purposes.

Wearing shoes while in a berth (bed) is forbidden.

Gambling is illegal.

Nothing is to be sold aboard ship except in the ship's store.

Any electrical appliances brought on board must be approved by the ship's electrical officer.

Fresh water must be conserved.

Government property may not be removed from the ship without permission.

Any communicable disease you have (or *think* you have) must be reported.

Intoxication may lead to restraint.

Red lights are the only lights authorized in certain areas at night (to preserve night vision for watchstanders).

Cups, silverware, and other materials must not be removed from the mess decks.

Ship's parties and other social events or celebrations must not glorify or encourage the consumption of alcohol, include sexually suggestive activities, or show disrespect to religious beliefs.

Frayed, torn, dirty, or otherwise mutilated clothing is prohibited.

Paint and other flammable substances must be properly stowed.

Pets are not allowed without permission of the commanding officer.

Nothing should be thrown overboard without permission.

Swimming over the side of the ship is not permitted without permission from the commanding officer.

Personal mail may be subject to censorship for security reasons.

Specific routes must be followed when going to battle stations (if you must go forward or up, do it on the starboard side of the ship; use the port side to go aft or down).

These are not all of the regulations discussed in chapter 5, and because you will be held accountable for all applicable ones, you should make certain that you read and understand them.

Unit Bills

Another important feature of OPNAVINST 3120.32 is found in chapter 6, which describes the various bills used to assure that the required stations are manned for all important evolutions. Once these bills are set up on your ship, they tell you where you are supposed to be and what your duties will be for a given evolution. For example, the man overboard bill tells you where you are supposed to go and what you are supposed to do if anyone falls off the ship. If your ship is headed for some bad weather, the heavy weather bill explains who does what in order to prepare. Quite a few bills are listed and explained in chapter 6 to cover virtually every contingency, but not all of them apply to every type of ship. The unit bills covered in chapter 6 may be used as written or may be used as a guide in writing bills tailored for a specific ship.

The bills in chapter 6 are grouped according to the function they provide and are included as either administrative, operational, emergency, or special.

Administrative Bills

Included in this group are the bills that take care of routine functions in the daily administration of the ship. Some of the bills found in this section are listed below.

Berthing and locker bill. This bill ensures that you and all your fellow crew members have a place to sleep and to stow clothing and other personal effects.

Cleaning, preservation, and maintenance bill. Procedures for cleaning and preservation (such as painting and lubricating) are provided so that department heads and division officers can make the appropriate personnel assignments.

Formation and parade bill. Identifies the areas of the ship to be used for various formations, such as morning quarters, personnel inspection, quarters for entering and leaving port, and ceremonial manning of the rail. Both fair- and foul-weather plans must be drawn up for many of these evolutions.

General visiting bill. Used to specify procedures for controlling visitors to the ship, ensuring adequate security for the ship and safety of the visitors.

Orientation bill. Designed to provide an indoctrination program for newly reporting personnel, this bill calls for briefings and/or counseling on the ship's history, mission, organizations, regulations, routine, current operating schedule, and a wide variety of other topics.

Zone inspection bill. Under the guidance of this bill, the ship is divided into zones small enough to allow an experienced officer to conduct a thorough inspection in a reasonable amount of time. Zone inspections are conducted at least quarterly and each zone has a senior officer (ideally a department head) assigned on a rotational basis to ensure a fresh look at the zone each time.

Other administrative bills include the official correspondence and classified material control bill, the personnel assignment bill, the personnel recall bill, and several types of security bills.

Operational Bills

These bills cover a wide variety of operations that a ship may conduct as part of its mission, such as operating the ship's boats, launching and recovering aircraft, fueling helicopters while they are hovering above your ship, collecting intelligence, defending the ship against attack while it is in port, preparing for heavy weather, operating in extreme cold, navigating under various circumstances, replenishing supplies while underway, rescuing individuals or other vessels in distress, putting divers in the water, performing salvage operations, and towing other vessels. Some of the other bills of special interest are discussed below.

Darken ship bill. When ships steam at night all unnecessary lights must be extinguished for navigational safety (and to avoid enemy detection in war). When darken ship is set, all topside doors and hatches are closed and ports are blacked out. To perform efficiently during darken ship, you must be able to find your way around the ship's topside in complete darkness and know how to open and close doors, plug in telephones, locate switches, and handle all other equipment at the underway or general-quarters station. During darken ship, only flashlights or hand lanterns with red lens covers can be used topside, and only when absolutely necessary.

Dry-docking bill. On occasion, ships need to come out of the water in order to allow major repairs to their hull, rudder, propellers, or other underwater fixtures. This is accomplished by putting the ship into a special dock that can be pumped dry, leaving the ship perched on special blocks so that workers can get to her underside. This is obviously a delicate operation that must be accomplished without error. The ship's dry-docking bill establishes the procedures and ensures that all personnel involved know what needs to be done.

EMCON bill. Enemy forces with the right kind of equipment can locate your ship by picking up and homing in on the ship's emitters (equipment that puts electronic signals into the air, such as radar and radio). To counter this, the ship will have an emission control (EMCON) bill, which will ensure that the ship's emitters are turned off or very tightly controlled when the threat of enemy detection is a concern.

Equipment tag-out bill. Common sense dictates that you must turn off the power before you work on a piece of electrical or electronic equipment, but aboard ship the power cutoff switch may be located some distance from the equipment it serves. The same is true for steam lines, fluid lines, and other potentially dangerous systems found aboard modern ships. Sometimes, for safety reasons, it is essential to turn off equipment you are not even working on; for example, if you are going up on the mast to change the bulb of the ship's masthead light, it is vital to turn off the radars and transmitting radio antennas to keep you from being harmed by them. The last thing you want to happen is for someone to turn on a piece of equipment accidentally or open a valve that presents a hazard to you. To prevent such accidents, ships employ equipment tag-out procedures, which involve labeling all secured components, making periodic announcements over the ship's general announcing (1MC) system, and ensuring interdepartmental coordination and cooperation.

Special sea and anchor detail bill. When ships get underway or return from sea, many more people must man stations and perform tasks not necessary during routine steaming. For example, the ship's anchors must be manned (either actually to anchor the ship or to be ready in case of an emergency) whenever the ship enters shallow water. This bill provides the organization necessary to ensure that the ship is properly manned and ready for safe navigation when entering or leaving port.

Emergency Bills

The nature of life at sea and the dangers encountered in wartime create the need for advance preparation for a wide variety of emergencies. The emergencies covered in this section of chapter 6 of OPNAVINST 3120.32 include aircraft crash and rescue, man overboard, nuclear-reactor casualties, nuclear-weapon accidents, and encounters with toxic gas.

The *jettison bill* is used when the ship's stability is threatened and can only be improved by throwing overboard (called jettisoning) heavy items, particularly those located high in the ship. For example, a fire, collision, or some other disaster on an aircraft carrier may result in the ship taking on large quantities of water, which threatens stability. By throwing aircraft and flight-deck tractors off the flight deck the situation can be improved.

Because steering is so vital to a ship (besides the obvious reasons, losing the ability to steer in a heavy storm can result in a ship capsizing), the crew must be able to improvise with emergency steering measures when the time comes. The *emergency steering bill* sets up the procedures for contending with this emergency.

Special Bills

Several bills that do not fit into the other categories are listed as special bills.

Antisneak/antiswimmer attack bill. When ships are in foreign ports, particularly during times of crisis or war, it is prudent to defend against sneak attacks. Because ships are particularly vulnerable to underwater attack by swimmers, extra measures of security must be employed to prevent such attacks.

Evacuating civilians bill. Crisis situations such as foreign wars or natural disasters sometimes require civilians to be evacuated. Because U.S. Navy ships are deployed to many parts of the world, they are often the most efficient means of carrying out evacuations. This bill provides the guidance for preparing for such a contingency.

Prisoners of war bill. Should your ship be involved with the taking or transport of enemy prisoners of war, this bill establishes the procedures required in this unusual situation.

Strip ship bill. During battle, many items found aboard ship during peacetime conditions can become very hazardous. Certain flammable materials in particular may be perfectly safe for shipboard use during normal conditions, but under combat conditions greatly enhance the ship's chances of sustaining lethal damage. The strip ship bill establishes procedures for removing these items in a methodical and logical manner.

Troop lift bill. Should your ship be required to transport troops from one place to another, this bill will help your ship properly organize for the task.

Watch, Quarter, and Station Bill

Most significant of all the bills found in your ship is the watch, quarter, and station (WQ&S) bill. This bill is prepared by your division officer and summarizes the personnel assignments within the division, based upon the other unit bills and the actual people assigned to

315

the division. You should know where this bill is posted and be very familiar with those parts that apply to you. Your name will actually appear on this bill and it will list your responsibilities under various conditions.

Some ships are equipped with a computer-generated system called the shipboard nontactical ADP (automated data processing) program (SNAP), while others continue to use the old WQ&S manual system, which uses a bulletin board–size chart to list all the required stations and the people who are assigned to them.

By referring to the WQ&S bill, you will see your bunk and locker number, your cleaning station, your in-port and at-sea watch assignments, your assignments during special situations covered by other unit bills (such as fire, collision, or rescue and assistance) and what you are supposed to do during various readiness conditions (explained below).

Shipboard Duties

As you have probably gathered from the previous discussion, life aboard ship has many aspects. Some days you will primarily be doing cleaning and maintenance tasks, while others will find you taking part in evolutions such as entering and leaving port, refueling, receiving a helicopter, providing gunfire support, rescuing victims of some natural disaster, or any number of other activities that Navy ships take part in around the world. Your day may very well also include standing a routine watch or two, and training is an ever-present part of shipboard life.

Maintenance

Just as a car must receive periodic maintenance in order to keep functioning at peak efficiency, a ship and all of its many types of equipment must be maintained in order to meet all the challenges that may come along in both peace and war.

Broadly speaking, maintenance is either *preventive* or *corrective*. Preventive maintenance forestalls equipment or material failure. It includes such things as inspecting, cleaning, painting, lubricating, and testing. Corrective maintenance is another name for repair and becomes necessary when a piece of equipment fails or some part of the ship needs to be fixed. Such things as replacing worn-out parts in a piece of machinery, patching holes in the hull of one of the ship's boats, or rewiring an electronic component would be examples of corrective maintenance.

Because of the Navy's size and complexity, and the variety of equipment that must be maintained for ready use, a carefully planned program is required. The program must be the same for all equipment of the same type, regardless of the type of ship or location, so that a person transferred from one location to another can take on a new task easily. The Navy has such a program, called the 3-M (maintenance and material management) system.

Compartment Responsibility

Every compartment on a ship is assigned to a particular division for cleaning and maintenance responsibilities. While the responsible division officer will be aware which spaces have been assigned to her or him, it is important to have some means by which anyone can find out which division is responsible for a given space. On an aircraft carrier, for example, there are hundreds of compartments and the executive officer may not be able to remember who is responsible for every space, but in his or her travels about the ship he or she may be disappointed in the condition of one of the passageways. You may be going from one deck to another through a ladder well and notice that the nonskid surface is peeling up on one of the ladder rungs, creating a safety hazard. The carrier XO and you need an efficient system for finding the responsible division to report your findings.

This basic but important need is met by a system of compartment responsibility markings. Every compartment on every ship in the Navy is required to have one of these markings. It consists of a 12- by 15-inch rectangle painted with photoluminescent paint (so that it can be easily found in low-light conditions) with two-inch black letters stenciled in its center. It should, whenever possible, be located at eye level where it can easily be seen. The information placed in this rectangle is standard throughout the Navy.

4-95-3-M
FR 95-99
GM

The first line tells you the compartment number (see "Deck and Compartment Identification" in chapter 12). The second line tells you the extent of the compartment in terms of how many frames it spans, and the last line tells you which division is responsible for the space.

Damage-Control Function. The subject of damage control is treated in some detail in chapter 18, but it is important to note here that the compartment-responsibility marking system serves another important function besides telling you which division is responsible for a particular space. It also serves to identify the compartment quickly so that anyone can report it in the event of a fire or other emergency. If you discovered a fire in this space, you could report it without confusion, even if you had never been to this space before and were not familiar with it. By reading its number off the first line, you could tell the damage-control party exactly where they needed to go to fight the fire. This saves valuable time, which would be especially essential in the example used above since the space identified in this example is a magazine used for stowing ammunition!

Finding Your Way. The compartment-identification marking serves one more important purpose. It can help you find your way around the ship by serving as a kind of street-sign system. Again referring to chapter 12, you know that the first number in the first line tells you what deck you are on; the second tells you the frame number of the compartment (so if you begin walking and the next compartment you enter has a higher frame number, you know you are heading aft); and the third number in the first line tells you which side of the ship you are on (even numbers indicate the port side and odd numbers are for starboard). Using this information as you travel around the ship, you can never get too lost—even on a giant aircraft carrier.

The Maintenance and Material Management (3-M) System

As already mentioned, the Navy has standardized much of its maintenance requirements with the maintenance and material management (3-M) system. This system establishes service-wide maintenance procedures so that you can maintain a piece of equipment using the same procedures no matter what ship you may be serving in. This system also standardizes the *scheduling* of maintenance so that it is the same everywhere you go. It also allows for the standardized collection of data, which is useful in analyzing the reliability of specific equipments and thereby leads to the improvement of maintenance scheduling and procedures. The two main features of the system with which you will be concerned are the planned maintenance system (PMS) and the maintenance data system (MDS).

Planned Maintenance System (PMS). PMS is designed to standardize and simplify maintenance procedures. It defines types of maintenance, sets up maintenance schedules, prescribes the tools and methods used for a particular type of maintenance, and helps you detect and prevent impending casualties. PMS also provides a good foundation for training in equipment operation and maintenance.

This portion of 3-M also gives shipboard department heads the means to manage, schedule, and control the maintenance of their equipment. There are three major components of PMS: the PMS manual, maintenance schedules (cycle, quarterly, and weekly), and maintenance requirement cards (MRCs).

You will probably use MRCs almost daily. Your work center will have a complete set of them. When the weekly schedule names you for a job, pull the appropriate MRC from its holder and take it with you for step-by-step guidance while performing your task. The MRC has a periodicity code that tells when or how often a job is done (see Table 16.1).

If the MRC indicates a "related maintenance," it means there are two jobs and that they should be done together to save time. Safety precautions are listed for each job. Make sure you read, understand, and observe all precautions. The word "Caution" on an MRC means that a careless worker can damage the equipment; "Warning" means that the equipment could injure the worker. The section labeled "Tools, parts, materials, and test equipment" tells you exactly what to use. Don't substitute without authorization. If a particular grease is called for but not available, don't use just any grease. Check with your supervisor to see if there is an approved substitute.

Table 16.1. Periodicity Codes for Maintenance Requirement Cards

MRC	Periodicity Codes
D	Daily
2D	Each second day
3D	Each third day
W	Weekly
2W	Each second week
M	Monthly
2M	Each second month
Q	Quarterly
A	Annually
18M	Each 18 months
24M	Each 24 months
C	Cycle[a]
R	Situational[b]

[a]Cycle means that the designated maintenance is to be done once between major overhauls (approximately three years).
[b]Situational requirements would include such things as "before getting under way" or "after firing the guns."

Maintenance Data System (MDS). MDS is a management tool used by systems commands and fleet and type commanders to identify and correct maintenance and logistics support (supply) problems. This system has resulted in improvements in maintenance procedures, equipment design, the allocation of resources, and long-range cost accounting.

MDS is a means of recording planned and corrective maintenance actions. All maintenance actions, except daily and weekly preventive maintenance and routine preservation, are recorded in substantial detail using the MDS system. Recorded information concerns the number of man hours required to make a repair, materials used, delays encountered, reasons for delay, and the technical specialty or activity involved. Once this data has been submitted using MDS forms and procedures, the information gathered is used to improve PMS and supply procedures and can result in modifications to or replacement of equipment. The amount of time you spend recording information for the MDS system will be worthwhile because it is extremely valuable to those who must make important decisions on how to spend the Navy's money and how to improve equipment and procedures that will affect you and the others who must do the maintenance and operate the Navy's equipment.

Cleaning

The most basic form of preventive maintenance is cleaning. It is also the least glamorous of the many duties you will perform while living aboard ship, but this function is just as vital as anything you will do. You may have heard the term "shipshape" used to describe something that is clean and well organized; this term did not come into the English language by accident. A dirty or improperly maintained vessel will not function at peak efficiency and will create psychological as well as material problems that can mean the difference between victory and defeat when the time comes for the crew to perform under difficult circumstances.

Ships, by their very nature, cannot hire out to professional cleaning services, nor can they afford the luxury of having cleaning specialists in the crew whose only function is to do the cleaning. Therefore, the responsibility for cleanliness falls upon the crew, and these duties must be carried out in addition to other responsibilities that come with being a Sailor aboard ship.

As already discussed, the WQ&S bill will include your routine cleaning assignments so that you will know what your responsibilities are in this area. This does not mean that what is listed in the

WQ&S will be your *only* cleaning assignments. You may be given additional assignments from time to time by persons senior to you.

Sweepers

One of the routine evolutions you will encounter aboard every Navy ship is "sweepers." Shortly after reveille, at the end of the regular working day, and at other times as necessary, the word is passed on the ship's 1MC for sweepers. At these times, all men and women assigned as sweepers draw their gear, sweep and/or swab (mop) their assigned areas, and empty trash receptacles. If you are assigned as a sweeper or are placed in charge of a sweeper detail, make certain that trash and dirt are always picked up in a dustpan, never just swept over the side. Besides the potential environmental impact, sweeping dirt and trash over the side may result in the wind blowing it back on board, or it may stick to the side, giving the ship an unsightly appearance.

Compartment Cleaners

If you are assigned duty as a berthing-compartment cleaner, you will be responsible for keeping the compartment scrupulously clean. This may not be the most exciting or the most glamorous duty you will perform in the Navy, but it is extremely important. The close living conditions aboard ship make cleanliness not only desirable but absolutely essential. Few things can affect the combat effectiveness of a unit more than the spread of communicable disease, and unpleasant living conditions can have serious effects upon morale.

Topside Surfaces, Decks, and Deck Coverings

Topside surfaces, because of their constant exposure to weather and sea spray, must be kept clean in order to minimize the need to remove rust and other forms of corrosion. It is a lot easier and more economical to sweep and swab a deck than it is to remove rust and old paint and then repaint it.

There will be many inclement days at sea when weather and sea conditions prevent the crew from cleaning topside surfaces, but at the first opportunity these should be cleaned with fresh water and inspected for signs of rust and corrosion. If you see the beginnings of rust or signs of corrosion (aluminum surfaces, for example, will develop a white powdery residue in the early stages of corrosion), tend to the area immediately. A little work in the beginning will save a lot of work later.

Besides painting to prevent corrosion, decks are often covered with various other substances for a variety of reasons. For example, nonskid materials are often applied to decks or ladder steps to prevent slipping, and decks near electronic equipment are frequently covered with special rubber matting to minimize the hazard of electrical shock. Deck coverings receive more wear than any other material and must be replaced early and at great cost unless proper care is given.

You will frequently encounter tile on decks inside the skin of the ship. The tile used in the Navy is more resilient and prevents fewer hazards than many forms you may have encountered in other walks of life (pun not intended). Tile-covered decks are kept up by sweeping loose dirt daily and wiping away spills as soon as possible. Frequent clamp-downs (cleaning with a wet swab) are important to prevent the buildup of unwanted substances. After a clamp-down, allowing the deck to dry and then buffing it with an electric buffing machine will improve the deck's appearance. For a more thorough cleaning when the deck is unusually dirty, apply a solution of warm water and detergent with a stiff bristle brush or circular scrubbing machine. Use water sparingly. Wet the deck with the cleaning solution, but do not flood it. Remove the soiled solution with a swab and rinse with clean water to remove residual detergent. Stubborn dirt and black marks left by shoes can be removed by rubbing lightly with a scouring pad, or fine steel wool, or a rag moistened with mineral spirits.

Waxing will greatly improve the appearance of a tiled deck but it should not be done to excess and should never be done when the ship is going out to sea or when heavy weather is anticipated. This is an added precaution against slipping, even though approved emulsion floor waxes are designed to be slip-resistant.

When rubber matting needs cleaning, it should be washed with a detergent solution, rinsed with a minimum amount of water, and dried.

Static conductive linoleum is ordinarily used as a deck covering in the medical operating room. This material should be cleaned in the same way as resilient deck covering, except that wax, oil, and polish should be avoided. These substances act as insulators and reduce the electrical conductivity of this type of deck covering. The deck's gloss may be increased by buffing lightly with fine steel wool and a floor-polishing machine.

Nonskid paint should be cleaned with a solution of one pint detergent cleanser and five tablespoons dishwashing compound or ten tablespoons of a substance called "metasilicate." This preparation is diluted with fresh water to make 20 gallons of solution. Apply with a hand scrubber, let it soak for five minutes, then rinse with fresh water. Nonskid deck coverings should never be waxed or painted; otherwise their nonskid properties will be reduced.

Field Day
Periodically, a field day is held. Field day is cleaning day, when all hands turn to and clean the ship inside and out, usually in preparation for an inspection by the captain or his representatives. Fixtures and areas sometimes neglected during regular sweepdown (such as overhead cables, piping, corners, spaces behind and under equipment) are thoroughly cleaned. Bulkheads, decks, ladders, and all other accessible areas are scrubbed; the "knife edges" around watertight doors and their gaskets are checked, and any paint, oil, or other substances are removed; brightwork is shined; and clean linen is placed on each bunk. Field days improve the ship's appearance and sanitary condition, preserve her by extending paint life, and reduce the dirt around equipment. Besides the obvious effects that dirt can have on health, appearance, and morale, accumulated dirt can cause sensitive electronic equipment to overheat and can cause serious abrasion problems for moving parts on machinery.

Preservation

One of the most effective means of preventive maintenance is what we call "preservation." Preservation may be accomplished in a number of ways, such as applying protective grease to machinery parts that are subject to corrosion or lubricating moving parts to reduce abrasion. Simple cleaning procedures are a basic form of preservation, but the most common method of preserving the surface areas of ships is painting. Whether your stay in the Navy is one enlistment or a full 30-year career, and no matter what your rating, chances are you will be expected to paint something at some time. The old saying, "If it moves, salute it; if it doesn't, *paint* it," is more humor than fact but it contains a kernel of truth. Paint is vital because it seals the pores of wood and steel, arrests decay, and helps prevent rust. It also promotes cleanliness and sanitation because of its antiseptic properties and because it provides a smooth, washable surface. Paint is also used to reflect, absorb, or redistribute light. And, properly applied, it can improve the appearance of things markedly.

Despite all of its advantages, paint that is improperly applied can cause many problems. Proper painting is a skill that must be learned. While experience is the best teacher, there are procedures and methods that you can learn to prepare yourself for the challenges of becoming a skilled painter. Before painting, you must be able to select suitable paints for the surfaces to be covered and you must know how to effectively prepare those surfaces. Then you must learn the correct methods of actually applying the paint.

Types of Paint

Different surfaces require different kinds of paint. Different conditions (for example, whether the area will be exposed to water or air) will also dictate the kind of paint compounds that are to be used.

Primers. Primers are base coats of paint that adhere firmly to wood and metal, providing a smooth surface for finishing coats. They also seal the pores. Those applied on steel are rust inhibitors as well. At least two coats of primer should be used after the surface is cleaned to a bright shine. A third coat should be added to outside corners and edges. At least eight hours' drying time should be allowed between primer coats.

Exterior Paints. The ship's bottom (part that is underwater all of the time, except when the ship is in drydock) is painted with two special kinds of paint. *Anticorrosive* paint inhibits rusting and *antifouling* paint slows down the attachment and development of marine growth (popularly known as "barnacles"), which if allowed to grow can slow down a ship considerably. Remember that antifouling goes on *after* anticorrosive paint. The latter, if allowed to come into direct contact with the hull, will cause pitting.

The waterline area, which is sometimes under water and sometimes exposed to air, is called the "boot topping" and is painted black with a special paint compound.

Vertical surfaces above the upper limit of the boot topping are given two coats of haze gray. Horizontal surfaces are painted with exterior deck gray, which is darker than haze gray. The underside of deck overhangs are painted white.

A nonskid deck paint is used on main walkways. It contains a small amount of pumice, which helps to give a better footing.

The top of stacks and top hamper, subject to discoloration from smoke and stack gases, are painted black.

Interior Paints. Depending on the use to which individual compartments are put, several color schemes are authorized or prescribed for interior bulkheads, decks, and overheads. Some spaces may be painted at the discretion of the individual ship, but many areas must be painted as prescribed by Naval Sea Systems Command (NAVSEASYSCOM). Deck colors, for example, are dark green in the wardroom and officers' quarters, dark red in machinery spaces, and light gray in enlisted living spaces. Common bulkhead colors are green for offices, radio rooms, the pilot house, and medical spaces; gray for the flag plot, combat information center, and sonar control; and white for storerooms and sanitary and commissary spaces. Overhead colors are either the same as bulkhead colors or white.

Others. Many other types of paints are used for special purposes in the Navy. Aluminum surfaces require special primers and outer coats. Canvas preservatives, antisweat coating systems, varnishes, machinery paints, and many others are used aboard ship for different purposes. Never paint a surface without making certain that you have selected the correct paint. When in doubt, ask.

Surface Preparation

For paint to adhere to a surface, all salt, dirt, oil, grease, rust, and loose paint must be removed completely, and the surface must be thoroughly dry.

Salt and most dirt can be removed with soap or detergent and fresh water. Firmly embedded dirt may require scouring with powder or with sand and canvas. Do not use lye or other strong solutions because they might burn or soften the paint. When oil and grease fail to yield to scrubbing, they must be removed with diesel oil or paint thinner, and extreme caution is necessary. If you use diesel oil, scrub the surface afterward to remove the oil. After scrubbing or scouring, rinse the surface with fresh water.

To remove rust, scale, and loose paint, you need hand tools or power tools, paint and varnish removers, or blowtorches. Hand tools are usually used for cleaning small areas; power tools are for larger areas and for cleaning decks, bulkheads, and overheads covered with too many coats of paint.

Hand Tools. The most commonly used hand tools are sandpaper, steel wire brushes, and hand scrapers.

Sandpaper is used to clean corners and feather paint. Paint will adhere best to a clean surface that has been lightly sanded. A wire brush is useful for light work on rust or light coats of paint. It is also used for brushing weld spots and cleaning pitted surfaces.

Scrapers are made of tool steel, the most common type being L-shaped, with each end tapered to a cutting edge like a wood chisel. They are most useful for removing rust and paint from small areas and from plating less than one-quarter-inch thick, when it is impractical or impossible to use power tools.

Occasionally, it is necessary to use a chipping or scaling hammer, but care must be taken to exert only enough force to remove the paint. Too much force dents the metal, resulting in the formation of high and low areas. In subsequent painting, the paint is naturally thinner on the high areas. Consequently, thin paint wears off quickly, leaving spots where rust will form and eventually spread under the good paint.

Power Tools. The most useful power tool is the portable grinder. It is usually equipped with a grinding wheel that may be replaced by either a rotary wire brush or a rotary cup wire brush. Light-duty brushes, made of crimped wire, will remove light rust. Heavy-duty brushes, fashioned by twisting several wires into tufts, remove deeply embedded rust.

Scaling may be done with a chisel and pneumatic hammer. When using this tool, you must take care that the chisel strikes the surface at approximately a 45-degree angle.

The rotary scaling and chipping tool (commonly called a "deck crawler") is particularly helpful on large deck areas.

The electric disk sander is another handy tool for preparing surfaces. However, great care must be exercised in its use. If too much pressure is applied, or if the sander is allowed to rest in one place too long, it will quickly cut into the surface, particularly wood or aluminum.

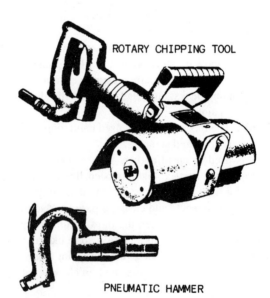

ROTARY CHIPPING TOOL

PNEUMATIC HAMMER

Figure 16.1. The rotary chipping tool (more commonly called a "deck crawler") and the pneumatic hammer are useful tools for removing paint from decks and bulkheads.

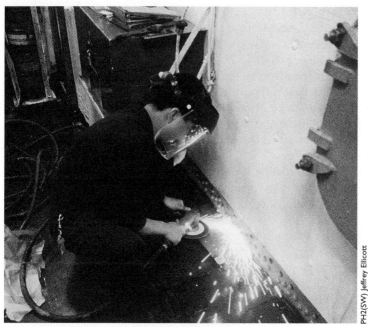

Figure 16.2. A Sailor using a disk sander aboard ship.

PH2(SW) Jeffrey Ellicott

Paint and Varnish Removers. Chemical paint and varnish removers are used mostly on wood surfaces but may be applied to metal surfaces that are too thin to be chipped or wire-brushed. Three types of removers are in general use: flammable, nonflammable, and water-base alkali. All three are hazardous, and safety precautions must be observed. These chemicals should be used only in well-ventilated spaces. Alkali remover is not to be used on aluminum or zinc because of its caustic properties.

Procedures for using these chemical removers are the same regardless of type. Wet the surface with a smooth coat of remover. Permit it to soak in until the paint or varnish is loosened, then lift the paint off with a hand scraper. After the surface is cleaned, wet it again with the remover and wipe it off with a rag. Finally, wash the surface thoroughly with paint thinner or soap and water. This final rinse gets rid of any wax left by the remover and any acids that may have worked into the grain of the wood.

Fillers. Holes, dents, and cracks in surfaces and open-grained woods should be filled before finishing.

Putty, wood fillers, and even sawdust mixed with glue can be applied to wood. Deep cracks in wooden booms, spars, and the like should first be caulked with oakum or cotton caulking and then covered with putty.

Epoxy cements are available for use on steel and aluminum surfaces. Methods of application vary with the type of cement, so carefully follow instructions.

All fillers should be allowed to dry and then sanded smooth before you apply the first finishing coat.

Using Brushes and Rollers

Smooth and even painting depends as much on good brush-work as on good paint. There is a brush for almost every purpose, so pick the proper brush and keep it in the best condition.

With a flat brush, a skillful painter can paint almost any shipboard surface. Flat brushes are wide and thick, hold a lot of paint, and give maximum brushing action. Sash brushes are handy for painting small items, for cutting in at corners, and for less accessible spots. The fitch brush also is useful for small surfaces. The painter's dusting brush cleans surfaces.

328

Handling a Brush. Grip paintbrushes firmly but lightly. Do not put your fingers on the bristles below the metal band. This grip permits easy wrist and arm motion; to hold the brush otherwise restricts your movement and causes fatigue.

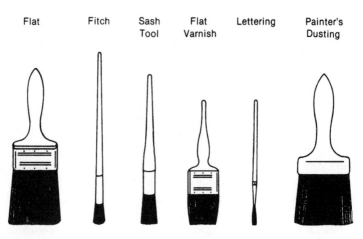

| Flat | Fitch | Sash Tool | Flat Varnish | Lettering | Painter's Dusting |

Figure 16.3. Types of paint brushes used in the Navy.

When using a flat brush, don't paint with the narrow edge. This
practice wears down the corners and spoils the shape and efficiency of the brush. When using an oval brush, don't let it turn in your hands. An oval brush, if revolved too much, soon wears to a pointed shape and becomes useless. Don't poke oversized brushes into corners and around moldings; this bends the bristles, eventually ruining a good brush. Use a smaller brush that fits into such odd spots.

Dip the brush into the paint halfway up the bristles. Remove excess paint by patting the brush on the inside of the pot. (If you oversoak the brush, paint will drip and run down the handle.) Hold the brush at right angles to the surface with the bristles just touching it. Lift the brush clear of the surface when starting the return stroke. If the brush is held obliquely and not lifted, the painted surface will have overlaps, spots, and a daubed appearance. A brush held at any angle other than a right angle will soon wear away at the sides.

For complete and even coverage, follow the Navy method and first lay on, then lay off. Laying on means applying the paint first in long strokes in one direction. Laying off means crossing your first strokes. This way the paint is distributed evenly over the surface, the surface is covered completely, and a minimum amount of paint is used.

Always paint overhead first, working from the corner that is farthest from compartment access. By painting the overhead first, you can wipe drippings off the bulkhead without smearing its paint. Coats on overhead panels should normally be applied in a fore-and-aft direction, those on the beams athwartships. But where panels contain many pipes running parallel with the beams, it is often difficult to lay off the panels fore and aft. In this case, lay off the panels parallel with the beams.

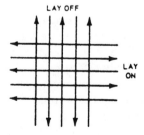

Figure 16.4. The Navy method of painting, known as "laying on and laying off."

To avoid brush marks when finishing up a square, use strokes directed toward the last square finished, gradually lifting the brush near the end of the stroke while the brush is still in motion. Every time the brush touches the painted surface at the start of a stroke, it leaves a mark. For this reason, never finish a square by brushing toward the unpainted area; instead, brush back toward the area already painted.

When painting pipes, stanchions, narrow straps, beams, and angles, lay the paint on diagonally. Lay off along the long dimension.

Always carry a rag to wipe up dripped or smeared paint. Carefully remove loose bristles sticking to the painted surface.

Paint on interior surfaces must be applied in the lightest possible coat, only enough to cover the area. Heavy layers of paint are a fire hazard—the thicker they are, the faster they will burn; they are likely to entrap solvents and thinners that burn rapidly; they have a greater tendency to crack and peel; they are uneven, and may show marks and scratches more readily than thinner coats; and they do not penetrate as well as thinner coats or dry as well. Moreover, heavy layers of paint, which add noticeably to the weight of the ship, may cut her speed.

Paint Rollers. The dip paint roller used in the Navy is equipped with a replaceable cylinder of knitted plush over a solvent-resistant paper core. It rotates on the shaft of a corrosion-resistant steel frame.

Large areas, such as decks and ship's sides (free of rivets, bolts, cables, pipes, and so on), can be covered with paint quickly by the roller method. Paint should be laid on and laid off the same way as with brushes. A moderate amount of pressure must be applied to the roller so that the paint is worked into the surface. If pressure is not exerted, the paint will not adhere and soon it will peel off. With the proper amount of pressure, a roller applies a more even coat and uses less paint than a brush.

Care of Painting Supplies and Equipment

Unfortunately, far too many good brushes and rollers are ruined simply because painters have little or no idea how to care for them. A perfectly good can of paint can be ruined after using only a little if the painter is careless. When painting, treat the paint, brushes, and rollers as though you paid for them yourself.

Do not let a brush stand on its bristles in a pot of paint for more than a few minutes. The weight of the brush bends the bristles, making it almost impossible to do a good paint job.

Never allow paint to dry on a brush. If you intend to leave a paint-filled brush for an hour or more, fold wax paper or some other heavy paper around the bristles to keep air out. Twist the paper around the handle and secure it with rope yarn or sail twine. Cover your pot of paint, and place both it and the brush in a safe place. Before resuming your job, stir the paint thoroughly with a paddle—not with the brush.

At the end of the day, before turning in your paint and brush to the paint locker, clean as much paint from the brush as possible by wiping it across the edge of the paint pot or mixing paddle. Ordinarily, those working in the paint locker will clean and stow any brushes turned in. They may require your help, and you may be detailed to the job. If so, follow instructions carefully, and thoroughly clean the brushes.

Paint lockers usually have containers with divided compartments for temporarily stowing brushes that have been used for different purposes (such as paint, varnish, or shellac). Most of these containers have tight covers and suspend brushes so that the bristles and the lower part of the ferrule are covered by thinner or linseed oil. Brushes to be used the following day should be cleaned in the proper thinner and placed in the proper compartment of the container. Those not to be used again soon should be cleaned in thinner, washed in soap or detergent and water, rinsed thoroughly in fresh water, and hung to dry. After drying, they should be wrapped in waxed paper and stowed flat. Do not leave a brush soaking in water. Water causes the bristles to separate into bunches, flare, and become bushy.

Paint rollers are cleaned differently. The fabric cylinder should be stripped from the core, cleaned in the solvent recommended for a particular type of paint, washed in soap and water, rinsed thoroughly in fresh water, and replaced on the core to dry. Combing the fabric's pile while it is damp prevents matting.

Conservation

Every job in the Navy, whether it has to do with maintenance, cleanliness, or almost anything else, requires conservation. Conservation doesn't mean that you should set aside extra stores like a packrat because you think you might need them sometime. Nor does it mean that you should try to save a bit by using one coat of paint when two are required. It *does* mean that you should make effective use of material and time to do the most work at the least possible cost. Although in many ways it is very different from your typical civilian corporation, the Navy is a business, and everything used—whether it is consumable supplies or your time—must be paid for. Just because all you do is sign a chit to draw something from supply doesn't mean it's free. Someone has to pay for it. And keep in mind that you, as an American taxpayer, help pay.

Inspections

Conducted to ensure the readiness of personnel and equipment and to maintain the high standards required of an impressive, combat-ready organization, inspections are a periodic part of shipboard life. Because inspections are similar in many ways to tests we have all encountered in school, it is only human nature to become somewhat apprehensive before an impending inspection. But, besides their obvious necessity, inspections are a time for you to show what you can do, to demonstrate what you have learned, and to prove that you are the kind of person that will meet the unique challenges that life in the U.S. Navy sometimes brings. Whether it is a personnel inspection, a zone inspection, or some other type, it is an opportunity to you to excel. If you are properly prepared, it will be an enjoyable experience and will contribute to overall unit readiness. If you are not adequately prepared, an inspection can be a very uncomfortable experience.

If you are in charge of a compartment that is being inspected, present the space to the inspecting officer by saluting and greeting her or him in the following manner: "Good afternoon [morning], ma'am [sir]; Seaman Jones, compartment [name and number], ____ Division, standing by for inspection."

Watchstanding

Unlike many civilian businesses, ships cannot shut down for the night. Someone has to keep the engineering plant running whether it is night or day. When the ship is underway, someone must be constantly navigating and someone else must steer. Even in port, many functions must be performed aboard ship around the clock. Because of this, and because the same people obviously cannot carry out these functions without rest, Sailors serving in ships must often stand watches. Watchstanding, in its simplest form, could be described as an organized means of "taking turns." Watch organization is covered in chapter 4 of OPNAVINST 3120.32.

Conditions of Readiness

The watch organization is determined by the ship's condition of readiness. These are described below, and it should be apparent that, generally speaking, the lower the number of the readiness condition, the more people will be required to be on watch. Material conditions of readiness (discussed in chapter 18) are set accordingly as well.

Condition I. Known as "general quarters." All hands are at battle stations and the ship is in its maximum state of readiness. This condition is set on board ship if the ship is expecting combat or if some other emergency situation (such as a bad fire) occurs. Everyone on board has an assigned station that he or she must go to whenever Condition I is set.

Condition II. This condition is set only on large ships and is used when the ship is expecting to be in a heightened state of readiness for an extended period of time but the operations at hand are such that some relaxation of readiness is permissible.

Condition III. Wartime cruising with approximately one-third of the crew on watch. Weapon stations are manned in accordance with the threat and other stations are manned or partially manned to fit the particular circumstances.

Condition IV. Normal peacetime cruising. Only necessary persons on watch, while the rest of the crew engages in work, training, or recreation as appropriate. This condition ensures an adequate number of qualified personnel are on watch for the safe and effective operation of the ship, yet allows for the most economical use of personnel in watch assignments.

Condition V. Peacetime watch in port. Enough of the crew is on board to get the ship under way if necessary or to handle emergencies.

Condition VI. Peacetime watch in port where only minimum personnel are required to keep an eye on the ship in order to maintain minimum security and to watch for fire or flooding. The ship will not be able to get underway without bringing more personnel on board and will require outside assistance to fight anything more than a minor fire.

There are also several variations of Condition I designed to meet special circumstances.

Condition IA. All hands on station to conduct amphibious operations and a limited defense of the ship during landing operations.

Condition IAA. All hands on station to counter an air threat.

Condition IAS. All hands on station to counter a submarine threat.

Condition IE. Temporary relaxation from full readiness of condition I for brief periods of rest and distribution of food at battle stations. This condition is set for brief periods during a lull in operations.

Condition IM. All hands on station to take mine countermeasures.

Watch Organization

Literally hundreds of different kinds of watches are stood throughout the Navy. They differ in length and the type of duties performed depending upon circumstances. But there is a model that is either used in actuality or is departed from as necessary. This model is based upon normal shipboard conditions and has been traditional for centuries. It is based upon four-hour watches that run around the clock. Four hours is the standard because that is widely accepted as the optimum time for a person to carry out the duties associated with operating a ship without suffering the dangerous effects of fatigue.

Table 16.2 shows the four-hour model, running from midnight to midnight.

Ship's Bells

For many centuries, Sailors did not have the luxury of a personal timepiece. If watches were to be relieved on time, some means of telling the time had to be devised. A system that used a half-hour sand-glass and the ship's bell was created and used for hundreds of years.

At the beginning of a watch, the sand-glass was turned over to start it running. As soon as it ran out, the watchstanders knew the first half-hour had passed, so they rang the ship's bell once and immediately turned the sand-glass over to start the second half-hour. Everyone on board the ship could hear the bell being rung so they could keep track of the time. When the sand ran out the second time, the watchstanders rang the ship's bell twice. They continued this until eight bells had been rung (representing the passage of four hours or one complete watch). The watch was then relieved, and the new

Table 16.2. Watch Organization

Period	Known as
0000–0400	Midwatch
0400–0800	Morning watch
0800–1200	Forenoon watch
1200–1600	Afternoon watch
1600–1800	First dog watch[a]
1800–2000	Second dog watch[a]
2000–2400 (0000)	Evening watch[b]

[a]The first and second dog watches straddle the time when the evening meal is traditionally served. Those with the first dog eat the evening meal after being relieved and those with the second dog eat before assuming the watch.
[b]Also called the "first watch."

watch team started the whole cycle over by ringing one bell once the first half-hour had passed, and so on. This bell-ringing tradition has been continued on board many Navy ships even though clocks and watches are now very common. Today, because bells are rung more out of tradition than for real function, they are not normally rung between taps and reveille (normal sleeping hours for Sailors not on watch), nor are they rung during divine services or in fog, when the ship's bell is used as a fog signal. Another tradition, still observed in many Navy ships, is the custom of the youngest member of the crew striking eight bells at midnight on New Year's Eve to ring in the new year.

Table 16.3 shows the cycle of daily bell-ringing and what the various bells mean in terms of time and watches.

Watch Sections

On board ship, you will more than likely be assigned to a watch section. When the word is passed that a specific section has the watch, everyone in that section immediately reports to his or her watch station. Different ships will have different numbers of watch sections, depending upon the size of the ship and upon the condition of readiness in effect.

Relieving the Watch

When relieving the watch, you should always report at least 15 minutes before your watch is scheduled to begin so you can receive information and instructions from the off-going watch. Most ships muster oncoming watch sections to make sure each watchstander is ready ahead of time, but even if there is not a formal muster, you should always arrive early (at least fifteen minutes—longer if there is a lot going on). This is to allow you enough time to be sure that you fully

Table 16.3. Cycle of Daily Bell-Ringing

Bells	Mid	Morning	Forenoon	Afternoon	Dogs	Evening
1 bell	0030	0430	0830	1230	1630	2030
2 bells	0100	0500	0900	1300	1700	2100
3 bells	0130	0530	0930	1330	1730	2130
4 bells	0200	0600	1000	1400	1800	2200
5 bells	0230	0630	1030	1430	1830	2230
6 bells	0300	0700	1100	1500	1900	2300
7 bells	0330	0730	1130	1530	1930	2330
8 bells	0400	0800	1200	1600	2000	2400 (0000)

understand all that is going on and all that is expected of you before you assume responsibility for the watch. Relieving the watch is a controlled and precise function and should always be treated as very serious business. Formality is the rule and casual behavior is clearly out of place.

The following steps are the minimum requirements for a good watch turnover:

1. State to the person you are relieving, "I am ready to relieve you." (Use these exact words so there is no possibility of confusion. "What'cha got?" or "I'm ready" is not sufficient).

2. Once the off-going watch has explained everything that is going on or is likely to happen and you have asked all the questions you need to ask, you and the person you are relieving should report your readiness to assume the watch to the next senior person in the watch organization by saying, "Request permission to relieve the watch."

3. The senior watchstander will respond by saying, "Permission granted."

4. The offgoing watch will render a salute to the senior watchstander and state, "[Watchstation] properly relieved by [your rate and name]."

5. You should then signify to all present that you have formally accepted the duties of the watch by saluting the senior watchstander and stating, "I assume the duties of [watchstation]."

This procedure unequivocally transfers the responsibility for the watch from the previous watchstander to you. Thereafter, you assume complete authority and responsibility for the watch until someone follows the same procedure to relieve you of the watch.

Watch Stations

As already stated, there are hundreds of different watches in the Navy—too many to be discussed here—but several of the key shipboard stations are worth mentioning.

Bridge Watches

While a ship is underway, the bridge watch team ensures the safe navigation of the ship, supervises the daily routine, monitors communications, conducts drills, and generally oversees the safety and smooth operation of the ship. The OOD is in charge of this team and is the captain's direct representative for these duties.

Before an individual can stand OOD watches, the nature of the responsibilities involved requires that he or she must earn the trust of the captain. This is accomplished through an intensive training program that includes adequate testing. Because no two ships are exactly alike—either in their physical layout or in their procedures—qualification as OOD on one ship does not automatically qualify the individual to stand OOD watches on other ships. OODs must requalify each time they join another ship.

Depending upon the ship, the OOD may be assisted by a junior officer of the deck (JOOD) and, on larger ships, there may be a junior officer of the watch (JOOW) as well.

Other members of a typical bridge watch team are:

Boatswain's mate of the watch (BMOW). The BMOW supervises and trains the enlisted members of the watch team, passes the word over the ship's general announcing (1MC) system, and assists the OOD and JOOD as directed. It is his or her responsibility that all deck watch stations are manned and that all hands in previous watch sections are relieved. Although it is the duty of the section leader and the division petty officer to instruct the people they send on watch, the BMOW must verify that every person on watch has been properly instructed and trained. A BMOW must also be a qualified helmsman.

Quartermaster of the watch (QMOW). Assigned from the navigation department, the QMOW maintains the ship's log and assists the OOD in navigational matters, including changes of weather and the movement of shipping. This watchstander is also a qualified helmsman.

Helmsman. Steers the ship as directed by the conning officer.

Lee-helmsman. Controls the engines as directed by the conning officer.

Lookouts. These watchstanders function as extra pairs of eyes for the OOD, scanning the sea and sky and reporting all significant objects and events. Navy regulations require that night lookouts report on the ship's navigational lights every half hour to make sure they are burning. By tradition, the starboard lookout reports, "Starboard side light, masthead light, bright lights, sir"; the port lookout reports, "Portside light, range light, bright lights, sir." (See chapter 21 for more information regarding lookout watches.)

Phone-talkers. These individuals man those sound-powered telephone circuits as necessary to maintain communication with other key watch stations (such as the lookouts and engineering watchstanders).

Messenger. This watchstander delivers messages, answers telephones, wakes up watch reliefs, and carries out other duties assigned by the OOD.

PH3 Philip J. Fraga

Figure 16.5. Standing lookout watches is one of the duties you may be required to perform aboard ship.

Quarterdeck Watches

In port the OOD shifts the watch from the bridge to the quarterdeck. Although the ship is not underway, the OOD must still be vigilant about the safety of the ship, checking mooring lines or anchor chains as appropriate, monitoring weather conditions for any significant changes, and controlling access to the ship. The OOD and her or his watch team supervise and carry out the ship's routine, conduct honors and ceremonies as appropriate, control the ship's 1MC system, conduct drills, and carry out any additional orders from the captain, the executive officer, or the command duty officer (an officer placed in charge of the ship in the captain's absence).

Just as at sea, the OOD is assisted by a watch team in port. The OOD's principal assistant is the petty officer of the watch (sometimes called the BMOW just as when underway). There will nearly always be one or more messengers of the watch assigned and, depending upon circumstances, there may be a JOOD, JOOW, and/or a QMOW assigned as well. If the ship is at anchor, lookouts may be required, and an anchor watch will normally be added to keep an eye on the anchor chain and report any strain or other problems to the OOD.

Engineering Watches

The engineering watch team is headed by the engineering officer of the watch (EOOW). He or she is responsible for the safe and proper performance of all engineering watches and ensures that all orders from the OOD are promptly and properly executed. The EOOW is assisted by a number of watchstanders that vary depending upon the type of engineering plant.

Damage-Control Watches

The damage-control watch team is responsible for maintaining the proper material condition of readiness and for checking, repairing, and keeping in full operation the various hull systems affecting watertight integrity, stability, and other conditions that affect the safety of the ship.

339

Combat Information Center (CIC) Watches

The number and types of watches in CIC will vary considerably according to the condition of readiness and the types of operations being conducted. Under routine underway operations, there will be a CIC watch officer (CICWO) who will be assisted by one or more radar and radio operators. This team detects, reports, tracks, and evaluates air, surface, and submarine contacts during the watch.

When conditions warrant (combat potential is increased) a tactical action officer (TAO) may be assigned by the commanding officer to take timely and decisive action in matters concerning the tactical employment and defense of the unit. The TAO is responsible for the safe and proper operation of combat systems.

Departmental Duty Watches

Because members of the crew go ashore in port, it is important to have qualified personnel assigned to carry out normal or emergency departmental functions. Each department will assign a duty department head and additional personnel as necessary to be responsible for departmental functions. The supply department, for example, may assign a duty supply officer, a duty storekeeper, or duty cooks as necessary.

Logs. A log is a permanent, written record that can have legal status in a court of law. For these reasons, log entries should be complete, accurate, and in standard naval language. Names should be printed, and figures must be recorded carefully. The ship's deck log, engineering log, compass record, and engineer's bell book are the official records of a ship. Because of their legal status, no erasures may be made in any of these logs. When a correction is necessary, a line can be drawn through the original entry so it remains legible and the correct entry inserted. Corrections, additions, or changes in any log are made only by the person required to sign it, and initialed by that person in the margin of the page.

Ship's deck log. This is the official chronological record of events occurring during a bridge or quarterdeck watch, which may concern the crew, operation, and safety of the ship, or may be of historical value. The OOD supervises the keeping of the log, and the QMOW (or other designated watchstander) actually writes the log. Each event is recorded in accordance with standing instructions. All log entries are made with a ballpoint pen, using black ink. Sample deck-log entries are contained in the *Watch Officer's Guide.*

The navigator examines the log daily, and the commanding officer approves it at the end of each month. The original ship's deck log goes to the chief of naval operations every month. A duplicate copy is kept on board for six months, after which it may be destroyed.

Compass record book. This is a complete record of the reading of all compasses on board. It also records gyrocompass errors. When the ship is under way, comparisons between compasses are made on every course change and entered in the book.

Engineering log. This log is the official record of important information about the operation of the propulsion plant and auxiliary equipment. It contains entries such as the total miles steamed for the day, the ship's draft and displacement, engineering casualties experienced, and other pertinent information as described in OPNAVINST 3120.32.

Engineer's bell book. This is a chronological record of all orders issued by the bridge that pertain to the propulsion plant.

Shipboard Training

One aspect of shipboard life that you can count on is *training.* Some of it will be traditional, involving lectures and books, but a lot of your shipboard education will take the form of on-the-job training. Drills, in which you will simulate an actual situation and use the equipment involved as much as possible, are another means of training frequently employed on board naval vessels.

On-the-Job Training

Frequently referred to as "OJT," this is probably the most frequently employed method of training on board a Navy ship. It is usually the least formal method of training and relies upon the experience of those who have been doing a particular task for a while to pass on their acquired expertise to those just learning the ropes. On a well-run ship, where pride in performance is evident, OJT will take place—without having been directed or scheduled—nearly every time two or more individuals stand a watch or conduct some routine maintenance together. Rather than an experienced individual merely doing a task, she or he will explain to another less-experienced individual what she or he is doing as they do it. Or he or she will let the less-experienced individual actually do the task while the experienced person supervises and assists. For example, you may be standing a bridge watch as messenger with an experienced petty officer who is the quartermaster of the watch (QMOW). Sunrise has just occurred, and it is time to turn off the ship's navigational lights. Rather than merely turn off the lights herself, the QMOW shows you where the light panel is, identifies each of the switches for you, explains what the various positions of the switches do, and then lets you actually turn off the lights—checking the secondary filaments as you do so—while she observes.

This kind of training is to everyone's advantage. The experienced person receives some assistance and has an opportunity to reinforce his or her own knowledge through teaching others, and you, as the inexperienced person, get an opportunity to improve yourself, increasing your chances for advancement, making you more useful to the organization and your shipmates, and giving you a source of pride in accomplishment. An added advantage of this type of training is that the more people there are who are capable of carrying out a task, the less chance of a problem in an emergency or when someone is ill or wants to go on leave.

Drills

This type of training is extremely important, particularly when practicing for emergencies such as fire and man overboard. It is vital that you know exactly where to go, where to find what you need, and be familiar with the equipment and procedures involved. It is also vital that you and everyone involved in complex evolutions are able to function as a team. You might think of drills as a form of advanced OJT which is more organized and usually involves more people.

Safety and Emergencies

17

U.S. Navy ships are, for the most part, very safe places to live and work. More than 200 years of experience, a high state of training and readiness, and many technological developments have minimized the dangers that must necessarily exist in a vessel that ventures onto the sometimes unpredictable waters of the world carrying ammunition, fuel, and other potentially hazardous materials. But the safety enjoyed aboard an American naval vessel is only as effective as the safety practices of its individual crew members. You must not go around in constant fear while serving in a ship, but you must always be aware that there are dangers that must be protected against. Safety precautions are an essential element of shipboard life, and you owe it to yourself and to your shipmates to make safety precautions a part of your everyday routine.

This chapter will introduce you to some of the more important safety precautions that must be continually practiced in the Navy. Because safety precautions are sometimes ignored or forgotten, and because accidents occasionally happen despite all attempts to prevent them, this chapter will also discuss some of the emergencies you may face aboard ship.

Safety

As already stated, safety is a job for all hands at all times. Every single operation aboard a naval vessel poses danger. Going to sea involves working with powerful machinery, high-speed equipment, steam of intensely high temperature and pressure, volatile and exotic fuels and propellants, heavy lifts, high explosives, stepped-up electrical voltages, and the unpredictable forces of weather. It is the responsibility of everyone aboard ship to observe all safety precautions.

Safety precautions for each piece of equipment used in the Navy are available and should be read and understood. The *Naval Ships' Technical Manual* (more often referred to as the NAVSHIPSTECH-MAN), the *Standard Organization and Regulations of the U.S. Navy,* and numerous bureau and systems manuals contain written safety regulations.

Another important part of safety is the regular maintenance of equipment and systems. Maintenance involves much more than just cleaning and painting. For safety and efficiency, every item aboard ship—from the simplest valve to the most complicated electronic gear—must be clean and operable.

The following general instructions, listed alphabetically for easier reference, serve as an introduction to the most important principles regarding shipboard safety.

Aircraft Operations

During aircraft operations, only those personnel actually involved are allowed in the flight-deck area. All other personnel must remain clear or below decks. Personnel involved in flight operations must wear appropriate safety equipment (helmet, goggles, etc.).

Before aircraft operations can actually begin, the flight deck must be checked for loose materials that might cause damage if sucked into an aircraft engine. This procedure is called a "FOD" walkdown. FOD stands for foreign object damage, and the procedure involves personnel walking slowly along the flight deck, carefully watching for any loose debris or objects that might cause damage. A single small screw or a chip of paint can spell disaster for the turbines in an engine and must therefore be removed.

Passengers must be led to and from a helicopter or aircraft by a member of the transfer crew, handling crew, or flight crew. All loose gear in the flight-deck area is stowed elsewhere or secured to the deck. Personnel are taught about the shrapnel effect of rotor blades or propellers striking a solid object. Be careful around propellers and helicopter rotors. When turning, they are nearly invisible but are extremely dangerous. Rotor tips cover a wide area and often dip close to the deck when the helo lands. An aircraft making a turn while taxiing can put you in harm's way very quickly. The engine noise of the plane you are watching will drown out the noise of planes you are not watching. Don't move without looking in all directions, and don't direct all your attention to a single aircraft.

Also beware of jet blast. Any place within 100 feet of a jet engine is dangerous. A jet blast can burn, knock down, or blow a person over the side.

Ammunition Handling

Everyone who handles ammunition must be instructed in safety regulations, methods of handling, and the stowage and uses of ammunition and explosives. Only careful, reliable, mentally sound, and physically fit Sailors are permitted to work with explosives or ammunition.

Anyone who knows of defective ammunition or other explosive ordnance, defective containers or handling devices, the rough or improper handling of ordnance, or the willful or accidental violation of safety regulations must report the facts to his or her immediate superior.

Anyone supervising the inspection, care, preparation, handling, use, or disposal of ammunition or explosives must see that all regulations and instructions are observed, remain vigilant throughout the operation, and warn subordinates of the need for care and vigilance. Supervisors must also ensure that subordinates are familiar with the characteristics of explosive materials, equipment used to handle them, safety precautions, and the catastrophes that safety regulations are designed to prevent.

Matches, lighters, and any other spark- or flame-producing devices are not permitted in the vicinity of ammunition except under specific circumstances when necessary and when approved by the commanding officer.

Crews working with explosives or ammunition are limited to the minimum number required to perform the operation properly. Unauthorized personnel are not permitted in magazines or in the immediate vicinity of loading operations. All authorized visitors must be escorted.

The productivity of persons or units handling explosive ordnance is never evaluated on a competitive basis that will lead to unsafe practices.

Live ammo, rockets, or missiles are loaded into guns or on launchers only for firing, except where approved by the Naval Sea Systems Command or as permitted below.

Nothing but inert (nonexplosive) ammo is used for drill purposes, except under certain special circumstances.

Supervisors must require good housekeeping in explosive spaces. Nothing is to be stored in magazines and other ammunition-handling spaces except explosives, their containers, and authorized handling equipment.

No warhead detonator should be assembled in or near a magazine containing explosives. Fuzing is performed only at a designated fuzing area.

Boats

In motor launches, only the coxswain and the boat officer or senior line officer may ride on the coxswain's flat. No boat may be loaded beyond the capacities established by the commanding officer (published in the boat bill) without his or her specific permission, and then only in emergencies.

To provide adequate traction, all members of a boat's crew wear rubber-soled canvas shoes in the boat. Boat crews must demonstrate a practical knowledge of seamanship, rules of the road, and safety regulations. Qualification for serving as a member of a boat crew is granted by the ship's first lieutenant. The engineering officer is responsible for all boat engines and their electrical systems, and will ensure that qualified personnel are available to operate and maintain them. Only personnel designated by the engineering officer will fuel the ship's boats, operate boat engines, or work with any component of the boat's electrical system, including the battery.

No one should ever board a boat from a boat boom unless someone is standing by on deck or in a boat at the same boom (to render assistance in case of a fall or some other difficulty).

All boats leaving the ship must have local charts with courses to and from their destinations plotted on them. They must have an adjusted and lighted compass installed and enough life preservers to accommodate each person embarked. These should be readily available when rough seas, reduced visibility, or other hazards threaten.

Chemicals

Adequate precautions should be taken when stowing, handling, and disposing of hazardous chemicals and materials. All chemicals, particularly unfamiliar ones, should be treated with respect. Unless you know otherwise for certain, always assume a chemical substance is hazardous and treat it accordingly.

A review of all potential hazards is not possible here, but substantial chemical-safety information is available in a number of references. Material Safety Data Sheets (MSDS) are provided by the manufacturers of hazardous materials (HAZMAT) stored on board ship. MSDS sheets include information on immediate actions to be taken in case of emergencies (such as when chemicals are spilled or when personnel come into unprotected contact with these dangerous materials).

The *Naval Ships' Technical Manual* (NAVSHIPSTECHMAN) has requirements and safety guidelines on a wide variety of hazardous chemicals, including cleaning agents, solvents, paints and associated chemicals, chlorinated hydrocarbons, mercury, oxidizing materials, corrosive liquids, and materials in aerosol containers.

Safety Precautions for Shore Activities (OPNAV Instruction 5100.23) includes information on the hazards of and precautions to be taken in using laboratory, photographic, and painting chemicals, as well as alkalies, acids, solvents, cleaning agents, cyanides, organic phosphates, toxic metals/dusts, and halogenated hydrocarbons.

Hazardous Material Information System (DOD Instruction 6050.5) lists hazardous items in federal stock, classifies material according to the type of hazard, and recommends proper stowage.

Afloat Supply Procedures (NAVSUP P-485) contains information on the receipt, custody, and proper stowage of hazardous materials.

Navy Hazardous Material Control Program (NAVSUP Instruction 5100.27) provides guidelines for procedures to follow when seeking information on the nature, hazards, and precautions of unknown chemicals and materials.

Electrical and Electronic Equipment

Electrical equipment includes generators, electrically powered machinery and mechanisms, power cables, controllers, transformers, and associated equipment. Electronic equipment includes radars, sonars, power amplifiers, antennas, electronic-warfare equipment, computers, and associated controls. The most important precautions with all such equipment are to treat them with respect and never work on them alone.

As a basic rule, no one is to operate, repair, or adjust any electrical or electronic equipment unless he or she has been assigned that duty, except in definite emergencies. However, common sense must prevail here: electric lights and bulkhead-mounted electric-fan switches are exempted, for example. If you have *any* doubt about whether or not you should be operating a piece of electrical or electronic equipment, *don't*. A Navy training film about electrical safety, *The Deadly Shipmate,* has been around for many years. That is an apt description of electricity. It is truly a shipmate that can be relied upon to provide comfort, convenience, and combat readiness, but it is unquestionably *deadly* when improperly used.

You should never remove, paint over, destroy, or mutilate any name plates, cable tags, or other identification marks on electrical or electronic equipment. Never hang anything on, or secure a line to, any power cable, antenna, wave guide, or other piece of electrical or electronic equipment.

Only authorized portable electric equipment that has been tested and certified by the electric shop may be used.

Electric equipment should always be de-energized and checked with a voltage tester or voltmeter before being serviced or repaired. Circuit breakers and the switches of de-energized circuits must be locked or placed in the off position while work is in progress, and a suitable warning tag should be attached to them.

Work on live circuits or equipment is carried out only when specific permission has been received from the commanding officer. The person performing the work must be insulated from the ground and must follow all safety measures. Rubber gloves are worn and another person stands by to cut the circuit and render first aid if necessary. Medical personnel are alerted before such work begins.

Personal electronic equipment (such as tape players or radios) must be inspected by the electrical or electronic workshop to ensure that it conforms to NAVSHIPSTECHMAN regulations.

Only authorized light fixtures with protective screens or shields are installed in machinery spaces.

Going aloft (onto upper areas of the superstructure or onto the ship's masts where there are radio, radar, or electronic warfare antennas mounted) can be very dangerous for a number of reasons. Electrical shock is an obvious hazard, but you can also be seriously injured by electronic emissions or struck by a rotating antenna. The emissions from such equipment can also charge the ship's rigging with enough electricity to do you serious harm. You should never go aloft unless adequate safety precautions have been employed, which will normally include securing all potentially hazardous equipment in the vicinity and making certain that equipment tag-out procedures are in effect to prevent the accidental energizing of secured equipment. These procedures are formalized and controlled by what is called a "man-aloft chit." This check list requires all pertinent departments to be notified that someone is going aloft, so that they can take the appropriate safety precautions (turn off their antennas, etc.). As a precaution, duty department heads must sign the chit, acknowledging that a person is going aloft.

Because you do not have to be in actual contact with many of these equipments for them to do you serious harm—just being in the vicinity of a transmitting radar can do serious internal organ damage, for example—it is important to remember that an adjacent ship (one moored next to you in port) can also be hazardous to you if you go aloft on your ship. In these situations, all necessary precautions must be taken on *both* ships before anyone may go aloft on either.

Electrical and electronic safety precautions must be conspicuously posted. Personnel are to be instructed and drilled in their observance and anyone who routinely works on electrical and electronic equipment must be qualified to administer first aid for shock. He or she should also be capable of performing emergency resuscitation procedures and able to use airway breathing tubes. Instructions for these procedures are posted in spaces containing electronic equipment.

Rubber matting (except where vinyl sheet is specified) is installed in areas where the potential for electrical shock exists.

Fire and Explosion Prevention

Reducing fire and explosion hazards is every Sailor's responsibility. Whenever possible, hazards should be eliminated, including nonessential combustibles (things that will burn). Replace combustible materials with less flammable ones if you can. Limit the number of combustibles whenever possible. Those combustibles that are essential should be properly stowed and protected to reduce the chances of fire.

Whenever possible, you should prevent the accumulation of oil and other flammables in bilges and inaccessible areas. Stow oily rags in airtight metal containers and paint, brushes, rags, thinners, and solvents in authorized locations only. Do not use compressed air to accelerate the flow of liquid from containers of any type.

Forklifts

Only authorized persons should operate forklifts. Before operating one, check its condition. Keep feet and hands inside the running line. No one other than the operator should ride a forklift, unless it has a second permanent seat.

On wet or slippery decks and when turning corners, always slow the forklift down. Never stand under loads being hoisted or lowered, and never permit anyone else to do so.

All cargo should be transported with the load-lifting rails tipped back. When you are moving, keep forks four to six inches above the deck, whether loaded or not. Do not exceed the specified load capacity. Lower and rest forks on deck when they are not in use.

Never bump or push stacks of cargo to straighten them. Forks should be worked all the way under their loads. Inspect each load before lifting. An unstable load should be rearranged or banded before being lifted.

Always come to a full stop before reversing the direction of travel. Put on the parking brake when you complete your work, park the forklift in a fore and aft position near the centerline of the ship, if possible, and secure it with chains or cables.

Hand Tools

You probably have worked with various tools before joining the Navy. Hammers, pliers, and screwdrivers are all common tools that most people use on occasion. If you have used these tools, you have learned that certain precautions must be taken in order to keep from injuring yourself. In most cases, injuries from these tools are usually minor—a bruised thumb or a pinched finger. But serious injury can occur when a hand tool is not used in a safe manner and when certain precautions are not taken. Striking tools—hammers and chisels, for example—are particularly dangerous because they are used with sufficient force to cause serious injury if care is not exercised. Because of the importance and vulnerability of your eyes, safety goggles should be worn anytime you use a striking tool. Also be sure that anyone else in the vicinity is wearing safety goggles as well, or have them leave the area before you begin your work. Flying chips can travel a good distance and do serious harm if everyone in the area is not protected.

Select the right hammer for the job. The head should be wedged securely and squarely on the handle, and neither the head nor handle should be chipped, cracked, or broken. Keep the hammer clean and free of oil or grease; otherwise it might slip from your hands, or the face of the hammer might glance off the object being struck. Grasp the handle firmly near the end, and keep your eye on the part to be struck. Strike so the hammer face hits the object squarely.

Cold chisels should be held between the thumb and the other four fingers. On horizontal cuts, the palm should be up. Don't use a burred chisel, one with a mushroomed head, or one that is not properly tempered or sharpened.

Wood chisels should be free of cracks. Don't use one with a mushroomed head. Cup the chisel handle in the palm of your hand and exert pressure away from the body. Be sure no one is close enough to be hurt if the chisel slips.

Hydraulic Machinery

Hydraulically operated equipment can be extremely powerful. The lift in your hometown garage, which suspends entire automobiles six or more feet off the ground, is an example of a hydraulic system. Such equipment must never be used until all personnel are clear of moving parts. Imagine what would happen to you if you were under that garage lift when the mechanic decided to bring it down. While this is not a pleasant picture, it should serve to warn and remind you of the danger associated with hydraulic machinery. Such things as periscopes, rudders, diving planes, gun mounts, and missile launchers are all moved using hydraulic machinery that makes that garage lift seem puny by comparison. Always treat hydraulic systems with respect and stand well clear when they are operating. Hydraulic machinery should always be secured and all equipment thoroughly checked when a hydraulic leak is detected or suspected.

Life-Jackets

Life-jackets can be a Sailor's best friend at certain times. Anytime you go topside in heavy weather you must wear a life-jacket. Being washed overboard is a very real danger when seas get rough, and being washed overboard without a life-jacket greatly reduces your chances of ever seeing your ship, home, or family again.

Life-jackets are also worn at times when the nature of your work increases the chances of your falling or being knocked overboard. Working on replenishment stations where booms or swinging cargo

U.S. Naval Institute

Figure 17.1. Sailors working over the side of the ship wear life jackets and safety harnesses.

may push you over the side is one example of a time you will need to put on a life-jacket. Life-jackets are also worn when working over the side in port and at sea, whether you are suspended over the side on a stage or in a "boatswain's chair," or using a small boat. You may be required to wear a life-jacket when traveling in a boat if weather or sea conditions warrant.

Lifelines and Safety Nets

The lifelines (railings) on a ship are there to prevent people from falling overboard. You should never lean, sit, stand, or climb on any lifeline whether the ship is underway or in port. People working over the side in port may climb over lifelines when necessary, but only if they are wearing life-jackets and safety lines that are tended.

No lifeline should be dismantled or removed without specific permission from the first lieutenant, and then only if temporary lifelines are promptly rigged.

No weights should be hung or secured to any lifeline unless authorized by the commanding officer.

Safety nets are also rigged around flight decks to catch anyone who may be blown over the side by an aircraft's propeller wash or jet blast. You should never enter a flight-deck safety net except as authorized.

Line Handling

Lines are used for many purposes aboard ships. True Sailors know that while lines are very useful, they can also be very dangerous. A mooring line (one that is used to secure a ship to a pier) that parts under strain is quite capable of instantaneously severing limbs. Always treat lines with respect. Do not, under any circumstances, stand in the bight (loop) of a line. If that line suddenly goes taut it can seriously injure you or drag you into danger. Never step on a line that is taut. Only a fool tries to check a line that is running out rapidly by stepping on it.

Synthetic lines (such as nylon) are widely used for mooring and rigging because of their durability and strength. These lines are characterized by high elasticity and low friction so extra turns will be required when the line is secured to bitts, cleats, capstans, and other holding devices. Nylon line stretches one and a half times its original length and then snaps back with tremendous force if the line parts. Do not stand in its direct line of pull when heavy loads are applied.

Materials Handling

You will probably—more than once—find yourself part of a working party that is bringing stores aboard or moving materials from one part of the ship to another. While you will not be able to avoid the hard work involved, you can avoid injury by taking some basic precautions. Safety shoes (with toe protection) must be worn when handling heavy stores or equipment. Always wear gloves when carrying, lifting, or moving objects that have sharp edges or projecting points. Always remove rings when wearing gloves.

Material should not be thrown from platforms or trucks to the floor or ground; use suitable lowering equipment if available.

Don't overload hand trucks. When working on a ramp or incline, keep the load below you—pull it up and push it down.

To lift a load, stand close to it with your feet solidly placed and slightly apart. Bend your knees, grasp the object firmly, and lift by straightening your legs, keeping your back as straight as possible.

Personal Protective Equipment

You only have one body. And while you may have two eyes, ten fingers, and two hands, you really cannot spare any of them. Protective clothing and equipment (such as hard hats, gloves, ear plugs and muffs, respirators, glasses and goggles, coveralls, and steel-toed shoes) were designed to help you keep your body intact and to ensure that all of your body parts continue to operate at peak efficiency. *Use them!*

353

Suitable gloves must be worn when working on steam valves or other hot units.

Keep the body well covered to reduce the danger of burns when working near steam equipment.

Welding goggles and a protective welding jacket must be worn when brazing, welding, or cutting. Personnel assigned as fire watches during welding operations must also wear protective goggles.

Protective goggles should also be worn whenever working with corrosive substances such as acid, alkali, and vinyl paint. Water in plastic squeeze bottles or other containers should be readily available.

Plastic face shields must be worn when handling primary coolant under pressure, and suitable eye protection—a shield, goggles, or safety glasses—must be used when buffing, grinding, or performing other tasks potentially hazardous to the eyes.

Do not wear clothing with loose ends or loops when working on or near rotating machinery.

Paint-Removing Tools

Paint-removing tools, whether they are simple hand tools such as a chipping hammer, or electrical and pneumatic tools, such as chippers, grinders, and scalers, are useful but potentially hazardous tools if not used with care. Because flying paint chips are an obvious hazard to your eyes, you must *always* wear protective goggles or face shields when using tools of this type. The high noise levels associated with these tools also requires hearing protection equipment as well.

Always check the rated speed of a grinding wheel before using; it should not be less than that of the machine or tool on which it is mounted. Grinders must have wheel guards to prevent injury.

To prevent a power tool from causing injury if it gets away from the user, the "deadman switch" automatically turns it off when not actually being held properly by the user. Always test this feature before operating a tool.

Radiation Hazard

As already discussed in the section about electrical and electronic safety, the high-powered radio-frequency (r-f) energy emitted by electronic transmitting equipment (such as radios or radars) can cause serious injury if you get too close to it. Areas where this hazard exists will have warning signs posted to help you remain clear.

If you must work on equipment of this type, be sure to follow all safety precautions. For example, you should never inspect a radar's wave guide (a kind of square pipe that carries the radar's r-f signal between the antenna and the other components) for damage while it is activated because a leak can mean serious exposure to damaging r-f energy.

Respect all posted r-f hazard signs. Never assume a piece of equipment is secured unless you are absolutely certain and precautions have been taken to ensure that it is not accidentally reenergized.

Be aware that r-f energy can also accidentally detonate or damage certain weapons. When these weapons are on deck or in other exposed areas for loading or maintenance, radiation hazard (RAD-HAZ) procedures will be put into effect. Follow all RADHAZ instructions and procedures, and if in doubt as to what you should or should not be doing, *ask*.

Radioactive Materials

Radioactive material is present in nuclear reactors and warheads, in the sources used for calibration of radiation-monitoring equipment, and in certain electronic tubes. Treat these objects with respect. Obey radiation warning signs and remain clear of radiation barriers unless your job requires you to do otherwise.

Radiation sources must be installed in the radiation-detection equipment or stowed in their shipping containers in a locked storage area. Spare radioactive electronic tubes and fission chambers are stored in clearly marked containers and locked stowage.

Replenishment at Sea

Ships often come alongside one another to transfer fuel, ammunition, or stores; this is called underway replenishment (UNREP). Sometimes these transfers are accomplished by helicopters; this is vertical replenishment (VERTREP).

Safety regulations should always be reviewed immediately before each replenishment operation. Only essential personnel are allowed near any transfer station.

For UNREPs, topside personnel engaged in handling stores and lines must wear safety helmets and orange-colored, buoyant life-preserver vests. If the helmets are not equipped with a quick-acting breakaway device, you should fasten the chin strap *behind* your head or wear it unbuckled.

For VERTREPs, personnel may wear flight-deck vests and cranial impact helmets instead of the types used during UNREP.

Cargo handlers must wear safety shoes. Those handling wire-bound or banded cases wear work gloves.

If involved in a replenishment operation, be sure to keep clear of bights (loops) in the lines being used and keep at least six feet between you and any block (pulley) through which the lines pass. Keep clear of suspended loads and rig attachment points until loads have been landed on deck. Do not get between a suspended load and the rail or ship's superstructure. Be alert to the possibility of shifting cargo.

When line-throwing guns or bolos are used to throw lines between ships, the word will be passed just before the line is passed. If you are on the receiving ship, take cover while the line is being fired or thrown across.

Deck space near transfer stations should be covered with something slip-resistant.

During replenishments, a Sailor will be stationed well aft on the engaged side of the ship to act as a "lifebuoy watch." He or she will toss a life ring to anyone who falls or is knocked overboard and will immediately pass the word. Normally another ship will follow behind those involved in replenishment operations to act as a lifeguard ship to retrieve anyone lost overboard. If no lifeguard ship is available, a boat or rescue helicopter should be kept ready for immediate use in rescuing anyone who falls overboard.

Measures must be taken to avoid hazards associated with r-f hazards. This is important when handling ammunition and petroleum products. Dangerous materials, such as acids, compressed gases, and hypochlorites, are transferred separately from one another and from other cargo.

When transferring personnel by highline, only double-braid polyester line (hand-tended by at least 25 people) is used. Persons being transferred wear orange-colored life-preservers (except patients in litters equipped with flotation gear). When the water temperature is 59° Fahrenheit or below, or when the combined outside air/water temperature is a total of 120° or below, immersion suits should be worn by personnel being transferred.

When fuels are received or transferred, no naked light (meaning all forms of oil lanterns, lighted candles, matches, cigars, cigarettes, cigarette lighters, and flame or arc welding and cutting apparatus) or electrical or mechanical apparatus likely to spark is permitted within 50 feet of an oil hose, an open fuel tank, the vent terminal from a fuel tank, or an area where fuel-oil vapors may be present. Portable electric lights used during fueling must have explosion-proof protected globes and must be inspected for proper insulation and tested prior to use. Portholes in the ship's structure on the engaged side are closed during fueling operations to prevent the accumulation of dangerous vapors inside the ship.

Safety Devices

Mechanical, electrical, and electronic safety devices must be inspected at intervals specified by the planned maintenance system (PMS), by type-commander instructions, or as usual circumstances or conditions warrant. When practical and safe, these inspections are conducted when the equipment or unit is in operation. Machinery or equipment should never be operated unless safety devices are working.

No one should tamper with or render ineffective any safety device, interlock, ground strap, or similar device without the commanding officer's approval.

Safety Tags

DANGER, CAUTION, OUT OF COMMISSION, and OUT OF CALIBRATION tags and labels must be posted for the safety of personnel and to prevent misuse of equipment. Safety tags must never be removed without proper authorization.

Shore Power

When ships are moored to piers they will usually hook up to shore power instead of continuing to generate their own electricity as they must do at sea. This involves running heavy electric cables from the ship to terminal boxes on shore. Like all electrical equipment, that associated with shore power must be treated with great respect.

All on-board shore-power equipment must be checked for safety. Shore power cables should be thoroughly inspected before using. Spliced portable cables are dangerous and should not be used except in an emergency. Cables should be long enough to allow for the rise and fall of the tide, but not so long as to allow the cable to dip in the water or become wedged between the ship and the pier. Cables should not rest on sharp or ragged edges such as ship gunwales. Personnel should not step or walk on shore-power cables.

Smoking

Environmental Protection Agency findings, and the surgeon general's statement that smoking is the number-one preventable cause of death, have caused smoking policy revisions everywhere. DOD bans smoking tobacco products in all DOD workplaces worldwide. The Navy prohibits smoking in its ships, vehicles, and buildings with few exceptions.

On board ship, the CO may allow smoking on weather deck spaces as safety and operations permit, and in one or more normally unmanned spaces that ventilate directly out of the vessel. Smoking is not allowed in work spaces, watch stations, berthing areas, lounges, messing areas, libraries, ready rooms, exercise areas, and medical areas.

At shore facilities, smoking areas may be designated outdoors away from common areas used by nonsmokers. Smoking is allowed in individually assigned family and bachelor living quarters and designated lodge rooms when quarters are not serviced by a common heating/air-conditioning ventilation system.

Smokeless tobacco is prohibited during briefings, meetings, classes, formations, inspections, on watch, or whenever proper decorum is required.

Tanks and Voids

No one is permitted to enter any closed compartment, tank, void, or poorly ventilated space aboard a naval or Navy-operated ship until the space has been ventilated and determined to be gas-free by a qualified gas-free engineer. In an emergency, if a space must be entered without gas freeing, a breathing apparatus such as an airline mask must be worn. In all cases, at least two persons must be present when such a space is occupied. One remains outside the space and acts as line tender and safety observer.

The space entered should be continuously ventilated, and a reliable person must be stationed at the entrance to keep count of the number of persons inside as well as to maintain communications. Suitable fire-extinguishing equipment must be on hand, nonsparking tools are to be used, and persons entering should not carry matches or lighters or wear articles of clothing that could cause a spark.

Toxic Materials

Solvents, refrigerants, paint thinner, fumigants, insecticides, paint removers, dry-cleaning fluids, antifreeze, and propellants for pressurized containers are all examples of toxic materials that may be hazardous if inhaled, absorbed through the skin, or swallowed. Even small amounts of some of these and similar substances can cause permanent blindness or death. The use of all hazardous materials is controlled by the medical officer or some other designated person. These substances should be used only in well-ventilated spaces, and contact with the skin should be avoided.

Welding

Welding is performed only with the permission of the commanding officer or officer of the deck. The area where "hot work" is done must be cleared of flammable matter beforehand. Fire watches are posted until materials cool.

Various synthetic materials yield toxic gases when burned or heated. Use caution when burning or welding resin-coated vinyl surfaces. Vinyl coating must be chipped or scraped clear in the work area whenever possible; welders, fire watchstanders, and others required to be in the immediate area are equipped with line respirators. Exhaust ventilation in the work area has a minimum capacity of 200 cubic feet per minute for each three-inch suction hose.

Although ship's personnel do not normally do welding work on the hull, if such work is required proper precautions must be taken and the hull must be x-rayed at the first opportunity to determine if any structural damage has taken place.

Personnel are always assigned to function as a "fire watch" for the purpose of detecting and immediately extinguishing fires caused by welding operations. The watch usually consists of at least two persons—one with the operator, the other in the space behind, below, or above the site of cutting, grinding, or welding. Remember, heat generated by welding or burning passes through bulkheads and decks and can ignite material on the other side. If you are assigned as a fire watch, you must remain alert at all times, even though the assignment may grow boring. Make sure that the equipment you are issued is in working condition and, if you don't know how to operate it or have even minor questions, do not hesitate to ask for assistance. Inspect the work site with the welder. Make sure you know where all firefighting equipment is in the work space and adjoining spaces and know how to use it. Also make sure you know where and how to sound the fire alarm and know the assigned escape routes from the space.

When the hot-work operation is complete, fire watchstanders should inspect both sides of the work area and remain on station for at least 30 minutes to be sure that there are no more smoldering fires or sparks and that the hot metal has cooled to the touch.

Working Over the Side

At times it is necessary for work to be done over the side of a ship (such as rust removal or painting). No work is done over the side without the permission of the OOD. Crews working over the side on stages, boatswains' chairs, and work floats or boats wear buoyant life-preservers and are equipped with safety harnesses with lines tended from the deck above. When another ship comes alongside, all personnel working over the side should be cleared.

All tools, buckets, paint pots, and brushes used over the side must be secured by lanyards (pieces of line) to prevent loss overboard and injury to personnel below.

No person may work over the side while the ship is under way without permission of the commanding officer.

Emergencies

Despite all the safety precautions that are taken in the Navy, emergency situations will occasionally take place. The consequences of an emergency situation may depend to some degree upon luck and circumstances, but a major determining factor will be the preparedness and performance of the crew.

Because of this, shipboard drills will be frequently conducted so that you and the other members of the crew may prepare for those emergencies before they happen. Take advantage of these opportuni-

ties. They just may save your life or prevent serious injury some
day.

General Quarters

During a major emergency—such as a serious fire or a gunboat
attack—you will hear the continuous sounding of the general quarters
alarm plus the words passed over the 1MC: "General quarters!
General quarters! All hands man your battle stations!" If you hear
this, don't try to find out what has happened. Just *move!* You will find
out soon enough what is happening. Proceed as quickly as you can
(being careful not to run into others or forget to duck when passing
through low doors) to your assigned general quarters station. To
ensure a smooth flow to stations, everyone adheres to the rule of
"FUSDAP"—forward, up starboard; down, aft, port. This means that
if you need to go forward or up to get to your general quarters station,
you should move to the starboard side of the ship. Conversely, if you
need to move aft or down to a lower level, you must go the port side
of the ship. This will keep people from running into each other as
they hurry to their stations. When everyone on board is at his or her
battle (general quarters) station, the ship is most prepared for any
emergency that may occur.

Man Overboard

When someone goes overboard, prompt action is essential. If you see
someone go overboard, immediately sound the alarm, "Man overboard, port [starboard] side," and throw a life ring or life-jacket. If a
smoke float and a dye marker are available, drop them in, too. If possible, keep the person in sight. Everyone who sees the individual in
the water should point at him or her. This will help the conning officer to bring the ship around to make a speedy recovery.

Every underway watch is organized to handle this situation. The
conning officer maneuvers the ship to a recovery position. At the
same time, the word is passed twice over the ship's 1MC system,
and six or more short blasts are sounded on the ship's whistle. The
lifeboat crew stands by to lower away when directed. If available,
a helicopter may be launched. If the identity of the person is not
known, a muster of the crew will be held to find out who is
missing.

If *you* are the person who falls overboard, make every effort to
keep your head. Hold your breath when you hit the water; the buoyancy of your lungs will bring you to the surface. There is an old
wives' tale that says the ship's screws will suck you under if you are

too close to the ship. Because this isn't true, you should not waste your valuable energy by swimming frantically away from the ship. Use your energy to stay afloat and try to stay in one place. The ship will maneuver right back down her track toward you. (*Note:* The exact placement of a person overboard is pinpointed in the combat information center using a dead-reckoning tracer.) Even if no one saw you go over, keep afloat and conserve your energy. Fight the impulse to panic. When a shipmate is missed, ships and aircraft begin an intensive search.

If a person goes overboard in port, the alarm is sounded as usual and the OOD follows the best available rescue procedure. Boats in the water assist in the emergency.

CBR Attack

In modern warfare, it is possible that an enemy may resort to what are commonly referred to as unconventional weapons. In the Navy, these are called CBR weapons, which stands for chemical, biological, and radiological. While these weapons are very different in some ways, many of the defensive measures employed against them are the same. In the event of a CBR attack, the crew can do a great deal to minimize casualties and damage.

For those ships located at or near "ground zero" (the point of detonation) in a nuclear attack, or in an area of high concentration of biological or chemical agents, casualties and damage will, of course, be great. However, tests have shown that ships not receiving the direct effects of such attacks have a good chance of survival with relatively few casualties, and with weapons systems intact. If a formation of ships is widely dispersed as a defensive measure, it is probable that nearly all fleet units will escape the direct effects of a CBR attack.

Protecting the Ship

When a CBR attack is expected, the ship will go to general quarters and all topside areas will be washed down using the built-in water wash-down system. The entire outer surface of the ship is kept wet so that CBR contaminants will wash overboard and not adhere to the external surfaces of the ship.

All nonvital openings of the ship are closed to maintain an envelope as gas-tight as possible. Some areas of the ship (such as engineering spaces) must continue to receive air from the outside; personnel who are manning stations in those spaces will have gas masks readily available.

Chemical-warfare directional detector sensor units are operated by signalmen on the signal bridge. The AN/KAS 1 sensor unit uses infrared sensing to indicate the presence and location of chemical clouds.

Protecting Personnel

The extreme effectiveness of some bacteriological agents, the toxicity of chemical agents, and the danger of radioactive fallout mean that protective clothing must be worn to increase the chances of survival. It is also essential that this clothing be worn properly, so it is mandatory that all personnel be periodically retrained in the use of protective clothing and masks.

The CPO Suit. The "chemical protective overgarment" (often called a "CPO suit") effectively protects against all biological and chemical agents for at least six hours of exposure. The CPO suit is *not* to be used for radiological contamination, however. It consists of a parka (smock) and trousers, with two layers of material: an inner (antigas charcoal absorbent) and an outer (modacrylic/nylon) which protects against liquid agents. The parka has a sleeve patch that

362

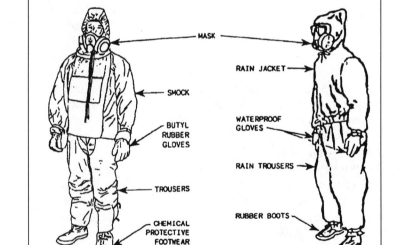

Figure 17.2. The CPO suit and foul-weather gear provide protection against some CBR contaminants.

holds detector paper which will indicate the presence of toxins. Adjustments are made by velcro fastenings at wrist, waist, and ankle. The CPO is issued in a sealed plastic envelope.

Foul-Weather Gear. Aboard ship, wet-weather clothing (often referred to as "foul-weather gear") is available for working outside in heavy rains and seas. This clothing—consisting of a parka with hood, overalls, rubber boots, and waterproof gloves—provides some extra protection during a CBR attack. When worn with normal battle-dress clothing, it will protect you from all but the most potent forms of radiological effects. When worn with the CPO suit, it provides an extra layer of protection from chemical and biological agents.

Protective Masks. Several protective masks are available for general use in the Navy, and some can be used in CBR defense. Masks are generally of two types: those that have a closed breathing system that actually supplies oxygen to the user and those that do not provide oxygen to the user but employ mechanical and chemical filters that remove solid or liquid particles and absorb or neutralize toxic and irritating vapors.

The oxygen-breathing apparatus (OBA) (see chapter 18, "Damage Control") is an example of the first type of mask. The chemicals in

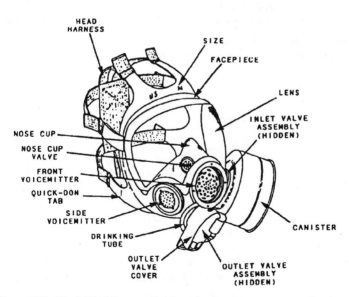

HEAD HARNESS

SIZE

FACEPIECE

LENS

INLET VALVE ASSEMBLY (HIDDEN)

NOSE CUP

NOSE CUP VALVE

FRONT VOICEMITTER

QUICK-DON TAB

SIDE VOICEMITTER

DRINKING TUBE

OUTLET VALVE COVER

OUTLET VALVE ASSEMBLY (HIDDEN)

CANISTER

Figure 17.3. The MCU-2P gas mask. Note the front voicemitter used in face-to-face communications and the side voicemitter used with communication equipment.

the OBA canister provide oxygen for about 45 minutes of light activity or 30 minutes of heavy work.

The MCU-2P gas mask is a good example of the second type. Its filters will protect against the inhalation of harmful chemical, biological, and radiological agents. The filters are issued separately and must be periodically replaced. It is important to remember that this type of mask will not protect you against carbon monoxide, carbon dioxide, ammonia, and many fuel gases or vapors. This mask is not used in connection with firefighting or smoke, or in an atmosphere containing less than 20.8 percent oxygen, the amount necessary to support life. In these cases, the OBA or some other type of oxygen-supplying mask is what you want.

Mission-Oriented Protective Posture (MOPP). Because protective clothing can be cumbersome and hot, and it interferes with basic human needs and functions, the MOPP system provides a standardized system that permits the commanding officer a means of choosing—depending upon the level of threat—the best balance between comfort and protection. The higher the risk of CBR attack, the higher the MOPP number that will be put into effect (see Table 17.1).

Detection of CBR Contaminants

The detection of CBR agents—which generally are invisible, odorless, tasteless, and give no hint to the senses of their presence—requires special equipment and training.

Table 17.1. MOPP Levels for CBR Attacks

MOPP Level	Protective Measure to be Taken
1	Protective equipment is issued to crew. Each crew member adjusts her/his mask for proper fit and stows it. Protective suits and filters for masks are located at battle stations.
2	Protective suits are put on. Hood is left down. Mask is either carried or its location is known and readily available.
3	Suit (with hood down) and boots are worn. Mask is fitted with fresh filter canisters. Mask and gloves are carried.
4	All protective equipment is worn. Hood is put up and secured around mask.

Radioactive particles betray their presence by giving off several kinds of radiation, which can be detected by instruments known as radiacs (radiation, detection, indication, and computation). These instruments can be personal dosimeters, which measure the amount of radiation a person has been exposed to, or they can be survey instruments used to detect the accumulated radiation in various parts of the ship.

In biological-warfare detection, samples must be taken, cultured, and subjected to thorough laboratory testing before the agent can be identified. This is slow, exacting work; if viruses are involved, they can greatly increase the difficulty of identification. Since identification is difficult, by the time the agent has been identified there could already be many casualties.

Chemical agents are somewhat easier to detect, but no one procedure can detect all known chemical agents. Some of these are lethal in extremely small concentrations and hence could be deployed upwind over a great area with devastating results.

The monitoring and surveying of ships and stations is a vital part of CBR defense. Locating a hazard, isolating contaminated areas, recording the results of a survey, and reporting findings up the chain of command are the functions of every military unit encountering contamination.

Decontamination

With early detection of CBR contamination, many lives can be saved by prompt and efficient decontamination. One of the most effective methods is flushing the contaminated surfaces with large amounts of water. The water wash-down system can be used for external surfaces, along with a more thorough subsequent scrubbing by personnel wearing protective clothing. For internal contamination, fire hoses and manual scrubbing are employed. Steam is also a useful agent for decontamination, especially if biological-warfare agents are suspected or if the contamination is lodged in greasy or oily films.

Emergency Destruction

In the event that your ship or station is in serious danger of being overrun or captured by enemy forces, the commanding officer may order the destruction of classified documents and equipment to prevent their falling into enemy hands. There are specific procedures for this unpleasant business and special equipment has been created for this purpose. As with all potential emergency situations, periodic drills will be conducted so that all involved personnel will be ready to carry out their duties in an expeditious manner.

Abandon Ship

Despite all precautions to prevent such a catastrophe, ships can sometimes be so badly damaged by battle or fire or some other cause that it becomes necessary for the crew to leave the ship before it sinks. During an emergency of this sort, many senior officers and petty officers may be lost as battle casualties, so you may find yourself with less supervision and assistance than usual. It is, therefore, a good idea to make sure you have a clear picture in your mind what you should do in the event the decision is made to abandon ship. Know your abandon-ship station and duties. Know all escape routes to the ship's topside from berthing spaces or working spaces below decks. Know how to inflate a life-jacket. Know how to lower a boat or let go of a life-raft. Know how to handle survival gear. And know how to do all of this *in the dark!* Disaster can strike suddenly at sea. A ship can go down within three minutes of a collision or explosion. If you don't know what to do before this happens, there won't be time to find out after it does.

Abandon-ship stations and duties are noted on the WQ&S bill. Careful planning is required to determine who goes in which boat or raft, what emergency equipment is to be supplied, and who supplies it.

Only the commanding officer can order abandon ship. She or he will do so only after all efforts to save the ship prove futile. If the commanding officer is killed or incapacitated, the executive officer or next senior surviving officer will take command and make this decision if necessary.

When the abandon-ship alarm sounds, act fast. Always wear a soft cover hat. Take note of important information, such as bearings and distance to nearest land and the water temperature. If there is time, this information will be passed to everyone by bridge personnel.

Going Over the Side

Make certain your life-jacket is secured properly and is equipped with a whistle, dye marker, and chemical lights. Go down a cargo net, boat falls, fire hose, or line if you can, but don't slide down and burn your hands. If you have to jump, look out for wreckage or swimmers in the water. Don't dive head-first into the water; jump feet-first, with legs crossed and arms crossed across your chest, firmly gripping your triceps. If you have a pneumatic life-jacket, don't inflate it until you are in the water—otherwise you will pop right out of it and possibly injure yourself because of the extreme buoyancy and force an inflated jacket exerts on your neck and body.

If possible, go over the windward side (in other words, jump into the wind) and swim upwind. If you go over the leeward side (side opposite the wind), the wind may blow the ship or burning oil down on you. Swim underwater to avoid burning oil; when you come up for air, splash the oil away as you break the surface. To protect yourself from underwater explosions, swim away for at least 150 yards, then climb aboard a raft, boat, or piece of wreckage, or float on your back. Stay calm.

In the Water

Rafts, boats, nets, and floating wreckage should be tied together; this makes it easier for searchers to find you. Wounded personnel should be put in boats or rafts first. Those strong enough to do so should hang on the sides if overcrowding is a problem.

In cold water, everyone must get into a raft or boat as soon as possible. If you must remain in the water, stay as still as possible to prevent heat loss. Heat escapes most rapidly from the head, hands, and feet; use whatever clothing is available to protect these areas. Numbness occurs in waters below 35° Fahrenheit. Breathe slowly and remain still. If overcrowding is a problem in cold waters, you may have to follow a rotation plan to get uninjured persons in and out of life-rafts. Frostbite and immersion foot can occur quickly in cold water. Don't rub, as this will damage frozen tissues. Warm affected parts against your own body or a shipmate's.

In a hot climate, keep your shirt, trousers, and shoes on—you'll need them for protection against sun and saltwater.

Boat Handling

In a power boat, the slowest possible speed will give the best mileage. If the boat is fitted for sails, use them and save the motor for an emergency. Otherwise, jury-rig a mast and sails out of oars, boat hooks, clothing, and tarpaulins. If wind and sea are driving you away from the nearest land or rescue area, rig a sea anchor (something dragged along behind the boat or raft in the water) to slow the drift.

Organization

The abandon-ship bill assigns an officer or senior enlisted person to each boat or raft, but serious casualties may make you the senior person in a boat. If so, take charge.

Make the wounded as comfortable as possible. Make a list of all survivors, and try to list all known casualties. Inventory all water and provisions and set up a ration system based on the expected number of days to land. No one should eat or drink for the first 24 hours.

Organize a watch. Lookouts must be alert and know how to use available signal gear. Get underway for the nearest known land or well-traveled shipping route. Time permitting, the nearest landfall and coordinates by compass will be passed over the 1MC. Each boat and raft will be equipped with a compass.

Secure all gear so nothing will be lost. If you have fishing gear aboard, use it; otherwise, make some. Rig a tarp for protection against the sun and to catch rainwater.

Try to keep all hands alert and cheerful. Save energy; unnecessary exertion uses up food and water.

Equipment

The vest-type life-preserver is the most important item of abandon-ship equipment. Learn how to use it. The vest preserver goes over other clothes. Adjust the chest strap and fasten the snap hook into the ring; tie collar tapes to keep them down under your chin; and pull straps between the legs from behind, as tightly as possible without becoming uncomfortable. Adjust the straps on an unconscious person before he or she is put overboard; the design of this preserver will keep the person's head upright and prevent drowning.

The inflatable life-preserver is carried in a pouch at your back and fastens around your waist on a web belt. It can be inflated with a carbon-dioxide cartridge or by blowing into the attached hose. To inflate the preserver, pull the pouch around in front, remove the preserver, slip it over your head, and jerk the lanyard down as far as possible to release the gas into the chamber. For more buoyancy, you can add air through the mouthpiece of the oral inflation tube. To reduce buoyancy, open the valve on the tube. Never attempt deflation with the tube in your mouth.

The twenty-five-man Mark 6 inflatable lifeboat, the type carried aboard most ships, is a compact, relatively light, easily stowed, and easily launched boat. It is constructed of separate tubes so that if one or more is punctured the boat will still retain some buoyancy. The upper, lower, and canopy support tubes are inflated by carbon-dioxide cylinders; the thwart tubes are inflated with hand pumps. A fabric bottom is attached to the lower tube to support manually inflatable decks, which are equipped with hand lines and are removable for emergency use.

The boat has a carrying case with a release cable extending outside; pulling the cables will open and inflate the boat in about 30 sec-

A. LIFE PRESERVER DONNED JACKET TIED AT UPPER CHEST AND WAIST; WAIST TIE PULLED SNUG, SNAP HOOK BEING FASTENED INTO RING ON CHEST STRAP.

B. LEG STRAPS BEING REMOVED FROM BACK OF PERSERVER; WILL BE LED BETWEEN LEGS.

C. BOTH STRAPS PULLED BETWEEN LEGS, ONE FASTENED TO D RING ON LEFT SIDE, OTHER BEING FASTENED.

D. TYING THE COLLAR.

Figure 17.4 a-d. Donning the vest-type life preserver.

onds. Normally the boat should be inflated in the water. As soon as the boat is inflated, use the boarding net and grab ladders to board it. The first person to enter stays at the entrance to help others; the second aboard goes forward to open the opposite entrance, check the sea anchor, and help others board at that end.

Secured inside the boat is a waterproof equipment container filled with survival gear, including the following items: food-ration packets, canned water, can openers, de-salter kits, water-storage bags, batteries, sea dye marker, mirror, sponges, pocket knife, whistle, mea-

A. WEB BELT FASTENED.

B. POUCH IN CARRY POSITION.

C. POUCH HAS BEEN PULLED AROUND TO THE FRONT. COVER OF POUCH HAS BEEN UNSNAPPED PRESERVER HAS BEEN PULLED OUT AND IS BEING PUT OVER THE HEAD.

D. PRESERVER IN POSITION, HAND JERKING DOWN ON LANYARD.

Figure 17.5 a–d. The inflatable life preserver.

suring cup, motion-sickness tablets, two-quart bailer, first-aid kit, signaling kit, fishing kit, and five flashlights.

The signaling equipment is extremely important because life-rafts are difficult to spot from the air and from the surface in heavy weather. The signal mirror you will find among the supplies provided, if used properly, can be seen at a distance of 10 miles or more. To be effective, you must hold the mirror so that it reflects sunlight onto a nearby object. Then looking through the hole in the center of the mirror, you will see a bright spot that shows the direction of the reflected beam of sunlight. Keep your eye on the dot and move the mirror slowly until the dot is on the target.

The signal kit also contains Mark 13 distress signals for day and night use, which can also be used to provide wind-drift information to helicopters that have come to rescue you. One end of the signal tube produces an orange smoke for day use; the other end produces a red flare for night use. If it is very dark, you can tell which end is the flare by feeling the series of small beadlike projections embossed around the edge. Each signal will burn for about 18 seconds.

Dye markers have a powder that produces a brilliant yellowish-green fluorescence when sprinkled on the water. In good conditions, the dye will be best seen for about an hour, but it will retain some of its color for up to four hours. From an altitude of 3000 feet, the detection range of the dye marker may be as great as 10 miles. The range decreases as the dye deteriorates. Unless the moonlight is very bright, the dye is not effective at night.

Because water is essential for life, and seawater is not fit for consumption, you should never discard any article that will hold water. When it rains, every container that can hold water will be invaluable. To assist you in filling the containers, a rain-catcher tube is attached to the lifeboat canopy. Some types of rafts, such as those carried in aircraft, have primitive but effective solar stills for converting seawater into fresh water. In polar areas, fresh water can be obtained from old sea ice, which is bluish, splinters easily, and is nearly free from salt. Fresh water may also be obtained from icebergs, but be careful. As the berg's underwater portion melts, it gets top-heavy and can capsize without warning.

Fire

When fire breaks out on board a ship, the ship's bell is rung rapidly to get everyone's attention. At the end of the ringing, the bell is struck once distinctly to indicate that the fire is in the forward third of the ship, twice if the fire is in the middle third of the ship, or three times to indicate that the fire is in the after third of the ship. The word is then passed twice over the 1MC system, giving the exact location of the fire by compartment number and name if known.

If you discover a fire, it is vital for you to get the word to the bridge (if the ship is at sea) or the quarterdeck (in port). Always report the fire first, then take action to fight it if you can. If anyone else is around, you may send them to report the fire while you fight it, but do not make the mistake of trying to put out the fire without first making sure that it is reported. Too often, a fire has gotten out of control because a person tried to put it out without calling for help.

If you have begun to fight the fire, do not leave the scene until the fire or repair party arrives, unless you are endangered and must leave the scene for your safety. (See chapter 18, "Damage Control," for more details on firefighting.)

Damage Control

18

Damage control (DC) is every Sailor's job—no matter what his or her rate or paygrade. A ship's ability to do her job, and indeed her survivability, may someday depend on her crew's damage-control response. Because basic DC qualification is a requirement for everyone on board, one of the first things a newly reporting individual receives is his or her damage-control personal qualification (PQS) package. This training package will guide you in learning about your ship, learning how to fight fires and control flooding, and reviewing basic first aid and the proper use of the ship's damage-control equipment.

The two major elements of damage control aboard ship are fighting fires and controlling flooding. The latter is often described as maintaining the ship's watertight integrity. To accomplish these vital tasks, you need to have an understanding of some basic principles of flooding, combustion, and the Navy's DC organization. You also need to know how to work with equipment that you most likely never heard of before joining the Navy. You may also have to find in your-

U.S. Naval Institute

Figure 18.1. Fighting fires is one of the two major elements of damage control aboard ship.

self an extra measure of courage and cool-headedness under pressure. Doing what is needed in a damage-control situation—with thousands of gallons of water rushing into a compartment you are trying to save, or the roar and heat of flames just a few feet away as you try to put down a fuel fire—can be a frightening experience. But if you prepare yourself by making sure that you know what is expected of you in case a DC situation arises, you will be able to keep your head in these stressful situations. Knowledge—understanding what the dangers are and how to combat them—is the most important ingredient to courage.

Damage-Control Organization

The damage-control assistant (DCA) usually answers directly to the chief engineer and is responsible for preventing and repairing damage, training the crew in damage control, and caring for equipment and piping systems assigned to the organization.

The ship's DC organization consists of two elements: the damage-control administrative organization and the battle organization. The former exists primarily to *prevent* damage on a routine basis while the latter is called into action to *control* damage once a problem has occurred.

DC Administrative Organization

To prevent or minimize damage, the ship will have an administrative organization in place to ensure that all DC-related preventive maintenance is accomplished on a routine basis. Each division in the ship will designate a damage-control petty officer (DCPO). Under the supervision of the DCA and his or her specially trained DC personnel, these DCPOs will:

Inspect division spaces daily for fire hazards and cleanliness;
Perform preventive maintenance on selected damage-control systems and equipment, portable firefighting equipment, and access closures (doors, hatches, scuttles) within their division spaces;
Maintain compartment checkoff lists and the setting of specified material conditions of readiness within their division spaces; and
Aid in teaching division Sailors damage-control, firefighting, and chemical-biological-radiological (CBR) warfare defense procedures.

DC Battle Organization

The ship's damage-control battle organization is directed from Damage Control Central (DCC) and includes a number (depending upon the size and mission of the ship) of repair parties and battle dressing stations (BDSs). DCC is the battle station for the DCA. To aid the DCA and his assistants in coordinating the damage-control activities of the ship, DCC is equipped with a variety of graphic displays that show the subdivisions of the ship and her systems. These displays include:

A casualty board to visualize damage and any corrective action in progress (based on repair-party reports);

A piping diagram and stability board showing the vessel's liquid loading status, the location of flooding boundaries, the effect of flooding and liquid transfer on the ship's list and trim, and the corrective action taken;

A corrective damage-control status board;

An electrical systems status board;

An electronic casualty status board; and

Deck plans to show areas contaminated by CBR agents, the location of battle dressing stations and decontamination stations, and safe routes to them.

375

Repair Parties

A key element in the damage-control battle organization is the repair party, the primary unit in the damage-control organization. Parties may be subdivided and spread out to cover a greater area more rapidly, and to prevent loss of the entire party from a single hit. The number and ratings of personnel assigned to a repair party, as specified in the battle bill, are determined by the location of the station, the size of the area assigned to that station, and the total number of personnel available for all stations.

Each repair party will usually have an officer or chief petty officer in charge (called the repair locker officer or repair party leader), a scene leader to supervise all on-scene activities (who also functions as the assistant repair-party leader), a phone talker, several OBA (oxygen-breathing apparatus) or Scott Air-Pak 4.5 personnel, and a number of messengers. The repair party is rounded out by additional petty officers and nonrated persons from various departments, such as electrician's mates (EMs), hull technicians (HTs), storekeepers (SKs), and hospital corpsmen (HMs).

Typical repair parties and teams are often designated as follows:

Repair 1. Main-deck repair. Includes a number of boatswain's mates who are familiar with the winches, capstans, and other equipment found on the ship's main deck.

Repair 2. Forward repair. Covers the forward third (roughly) of the ship's interior spaces.

Repair 3. After repair. Covers the after third (roughly) of the ship's interior spaces.

Repair 4. Amidship repair. Covers the middle third (roughly) of the ship (excluding engineering spaces).

Repair 5. Propulsion repair. Covers the engineering spaces of the ship. Comprised of an engineering officer or chief and a broad cross-section of engineering ratings. Personnel assigned to Repair 5 must be qualified in the various engineering watchstations, as well as highly proficient in damage-control skills.

Repair 6. Ordnance repair. Comprised primarily of gunner's mates, fire-control technicians, and electrician mates. Responsible for damage control and emergency repairs to the ship's weapons systems and magazines. This party is sometimes subdivided into forward and after groups.

Repair 7. Gallery deck and island structure repair. This unit is used primarily on aircraft carriers and other ship types where it is needed.

Repair 8. Electronics repair. Comprised primarily of personnel with ratings in the various electronic specialties (ETs, FTs, STs, and EWs).

Because of their special needs, aircraft carriers and ships equipped for helicopter operations also have aviation-fuel repair teams and crash and salvage teams.

Ships that carry large amounts of ordnance (ammunition ships and aircraft carriers, for example), have an explosive ordnance disposal (EOD) team made up of specially qualified personnel. These highly trained individuals are capable of disarming fuzed bombs and taking care of other ordnance-related emergencies. The EOD team is usually administered as a part of the ship's weapons department.

Within each repair party there are hose teams; de-watering, plugging, and patching teams; investigation teams; shoring, pipe repair, structural repair, casualty power, interior-communications (IC) repair, and electrical repair teams; chemical detection, biological sampling, radiological monitoring, and CBR decontamination teams; and stretcher bearers.

In general, repair parties must be capable of the following:

Maintaining watertight integrity (preventing leaks and flooding).
Maintaining the ship's structural integrity (shoring up weakened decks and bulkheads).
Controlling and extinguishing all types of fires.
Giving first aid and transporting the injured to BDSs.
Detecting, identifying, and measuring the amount of chemical, biological, and/or radiation contamination, as well as carrying out decontamination procedures.
Evaluating and reporting correctly on the extent of damage in an area.

The equipment needed by repair parties is stowed in repair lockers. Included are such things as patches for ruptured water and steam lines, broken seams, and the hull; plugs made of soft wood for stopping the flow of liquids in a damaged hull or in broken pipes; assorted pieces of wood used for shoring; radiological defense equipment; an electrical repair kit for isolating damaged circuits and restoring power; and tools for forcible entry, such as axes, crowbars, wrecking bars, claw tools, hacksaws, bolt cutters, oxyacetylene cutting torches, and portable exothermic cutting units. The equipment stowed in a repair locker is reserved for damage control only and should never be used for any other purpose.

Communication is vital to the damage-control organization. Systems used by repair parties and the DCA to communicate include battle telephone (sound-powered) circuits, interstation two-way (MC) systems, ship's service telephones, the internal voice communication system (IVCS), wire-free communication (WFCOM), and messengers.

Battle Dressing and Decontamination Stations (BDSs)

Most ships have at least two BDSs equipped to handle personnel casualties. They are manned by medical personnel and are located so that stretcher cases may be brought directly to them by the repair party. Emergency supplies of medical equipment are also placed in first-aid boxes throughout the ship. Signs are also posted throughout the ship directing you to the nearest BDS.

To handle CBR problems, at least two "decontamination stations" are provided in widely separated parts of the ship, preferably near BDSs. Signs pointing the way to these stations are painted with photoluminescent markings so that they can be seen in low-light conditions. To prevent recontamination after personnel have been decontaminated, each station is divided into two areas: a clean section, and a contaminated or unclean section with a washing area. Stations are manned by trained medical and repair-party personnel to ensure that proper decontamination procedures are followed.

Watertight Integrity

A ship cannot survive without maintaining its watertight integrity. Leaking or flooding in a ship obviously leads to its sinking. For this reason ships are designed so that damage resulting in leaks or flooding can be controlled and its effects minimized. Because of these design features, ships can experience an amazing amount of damage and still survive if proper precautions are taken in advance and the right corrective action is taken once damage is sustained.

Compartmentation

As explained in an earlier chapter, a network of bulkheads and decks—designed to prevent the flow of water or other fluids from one space to another when they are properly secured—ensures that a ship is protected from sinking. If one compartment experiences flooding, it can be sealed off from the others so that little of the ship's overall buoyancy is affected, thus reducing the danger of sinking. If a ship did not have this protection, one leak would cause the eventual sinking of the ship.

A ship is divided into as many watertight compartments as practical. In general, the more watertight compartments a ship has, the greater her resistance to sinking. This system, which permits the isolation of individual compartments, is useful not only to control flooding, but also to prevent the spread of fire and smoke and to reduce the effectiveness of CBR attacks.

Closures

For ideal buoyancy and protection against fire and other dangers, each compartment within a ship would be completely sealed up all of the time. This is obviously not practical since it would mean that no one could ever enter or leave a space on a ship. In order for a ship to function, it must have openings to permit passage through bulkheads and decks.

Because an opening in a deck or bulkhead obviously compromises watertight integrity, these openings must have closures (also called fittings) that can be used to restore watertight integrity when it is needed.

In ships, these closures are called *watertight doors* (WTD) when they seal openings in bulkheads, and *hatches* when they seal openings in decks.

Doors

Watertight doors are designed to resist the same amount of pressure as the bulkheads they are a part of. WTDs are sealed shut by rubber gaskets which are fixed to the door in such a way as to create a seal between the door and bulkhead where they come into contact. This point of contact is called the *knife edge.* The "latches" that press the door shut and hold it there are called *dogs.*

On a WTD, the dogs will be placed all around the door to ensure a proper seal. Some doors have dogs that must be individually closed and opened. Others, known as *quick-acting watertight doors,* have mechanisms that operate all dogs simultaneously. Some doors, because of their location, do not need to be watertight. These are, not surprisingly, called *nonwatertight doors* (NWTD).

Some doors, though not watertight, are *airtight* (ATD) to retard the spread of flames or gases. Some doors have small tubelike openings in them which allow ammunition to be passed through without having to open the whole door. These are called *passing scuttles.*

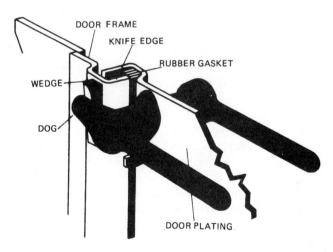

Figure 18.2. This cutaway section of a watertight door shows how the knife edge presses against the rubber gasket for a tight seal.

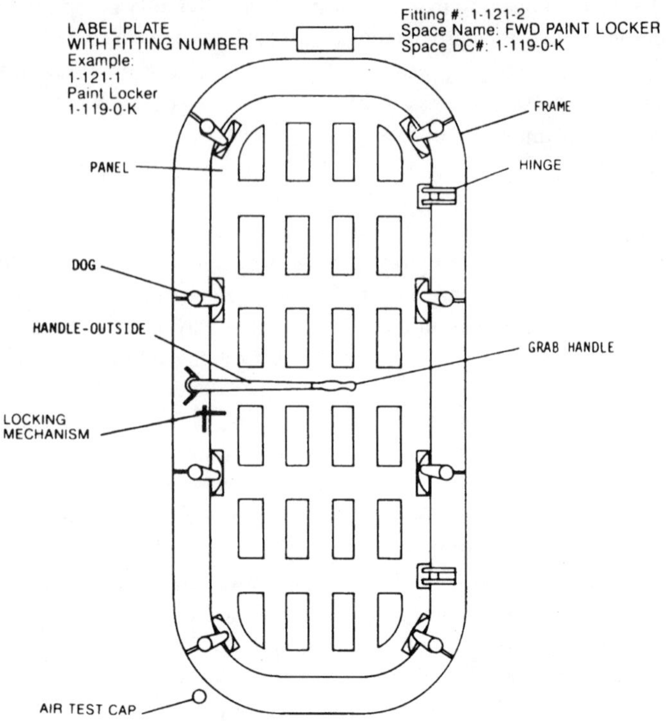

LABEL PLATE
WITH FITTING NUMBER
Example:
1-121-1
Paint Locker
1-119-0-K

Fitting #: 1-121-2
Space Name: FWD PAINT LOCKER
Space DC#: 1-119-0-K

FRAME

PANEL

HINGE

DOG

HANDLE-OUTSIDE

GRAB HANDLE

LOCKING
MECHANISM

AIR TEST CAP

Figure 18.3. An outside view of a quick-acting watertight door. Note the dogs all the way around for a tight seal.

Some openings, such as between offices, do not require watertight integrity and the doors they have look and function like normal doors you are used to seeing in buildings ashore. These are called *joiner doors*.

Hatches

Hatches can be thought of as horizontal doors that close the openings that allow access between decks. A hatch is either set with its top surface flush with the deck or on a *coaming* raised above the deck. The latter is preferable in an area (such as on a weather deck) where water might frequently wash over the deck. The coaming provides some protection that will prevent much of the water from pouring into the compartment below.

Some hatches, because they must cover relatively large openings in the deck, are heavy and difficult for one person to handle. To take

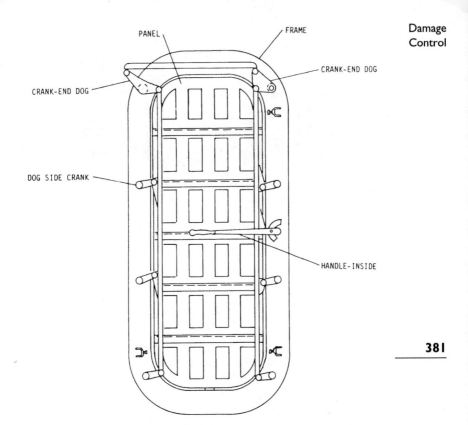

PANEL

FRAME

CRANK-END DOG

CRANK-END DOG

DOG SIDE CRANK

HANDLE-INSIDE

Figure 18.4. An inside view of a quick-acting watertight door, showing how the dogs are linked together for simultaneous opening and closing.

care of this problem, larger hatches have an *escape scuttle.* This is a round opening with quick-acting closures that can be placed in a hatch (and sometimes in a bulkhead or deck) to permit rapid escape from a compartment.

Manholes provide access to spaces that must be entered only on rare occasions, such as voids and tanks used to store water and fuel. The covers to these openings are normally bolted in place. Manholes are also occasionally placed in bulkheads.

Other Fittings
Certain other fittings must be closed at times to prevent the unwanted flow of air or fluids. These would include certain valves and vents. For example, if an enemy aircraft sprays your ship with a toxic gas,

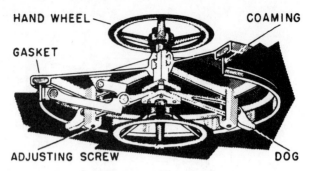

HAND WHEEL

COAMING

GASKET

ADJUSTING SCREW

DOG

Figure 18.5. A cutaway section of an escape scuttle showing the quick-acting handwheels above and below.

it would be necessary to close the vents that bring air into the ship until the danger has passed.

Compartment Checkoff Lists

In every compartment, posted where it can easily be seen, is a compartment checkoff list. This list tells you every DC fitting (hatch, door, valve, vent, and so on) in that compartment. It also tells which division is responsible for that fitting, where it is located, and what it is used for. Other useful information, such as a list of all DC equipment (for example, fire extinguishers and hoses) is also included on this list. If you are familiar with the Navy's method of numbering compartments, you will find this checkoff list very useful in locating important fittings and equipment. It is a good idea to take the time to study the compartment checkoff list in those compartments in which you spend a lot of time (such as your berthing compartment or work spaces), so that you will know what types of damage-control fittings and equipment are in those compartments and where you can find them in an emergency.

Maintenance and Usage of Closures

All doors, hatches, scuttles, and manholes giving access to compartments must be securely "dogged" (closed down). Manhole covers should always be bolted except for inspection, cleaning, or painting. They must never be left open overnight or unattended when crews are not actually working in them.

Watertight doors and hatches will work longer and require less maintenance if they are properly closed and opened. When closing a door, first set a dog opposite the hinges, with just enough pressure to keep the door shut. Then set a dog opposite the first one. Close the others, making sure you work with opposites as you go. This will maintain uniform pressure all around.

When opening a door, start with the dogs nearest the hinges. This procedure will keep the door from springing and make it easier to operate the remaining dogs. Open the rest as you would when closing, shifting to opposite sides as you go.

Never paint the gaskets—the rubber must remain pliable for a proper seal—and never strike a knife edge—dents or burrs will prevent a proper seal.

When the ship sustains damage, watertight doors, hatches, scuttles, and manholes should be opened only after making sure that the compartment is dry, or nearly so, to prevent further flooding when the closures are opened. Closures should not be opened without permission from DCC. Extra caution is always necessary in opening compartments below the waterline.

Material Conditions of Readiness

In order to determine when a ship's fittings should be opened for convenience and when they should be closed for safety, the Navy has devised a standardized system called the "material condition of readiness" system. This formal system permits the ship flexibility in adjusting to changing situations and thereby providing the right compromise between adequate safety and practical need. It should be fairly obvious, for example, that a ship at sea in a powerful storm is going to require a great deal more protection from flooding than is a ship moored to a pier in a safe harbor. To allow this flexibility, Navy ships have three material conditions of readiness that can be set to accommodate various situations, each representing a different degree of tightness and protection. These conditions are called X-RAY, YOKE, and ZEBRA. The various closures on a ship have damage-control markings on them to identify which ones should be closed depending upon the material condition of readiness in effect.

Condition X-RAY provides the least protection but the most convenience. It is set when the ship is in little or no danger of attack, such as when she is at anchor in a well-protected harbor or secured at home base during regular working hours. During this condition, all closures (such as doors and hatches) marked with a black or circled *X* are secured. They remain closed when setting the higher conditions of readiness YOKE and ZEBRA.

Condition YOKE provides somewhat more protection than condition X-RAY and is set when a ship is involved in routine underway operations. In port, YOKE is set after regular working hours and is also maintained at all times during war. YOKE closures, marked with a black or circled *Y*, are secured during conditions YOKE and ZEBRA.

Condition ZEBRA provides the maximum protection and is set before going to sea or when entering port during war. It is also set immediately, without further orders, whenever general quarters (GQ) stations are manned. Condition ZEBRA can also be set to localize and control fire and flooding when GQ stations are not manned. When condition ZEBRA is set, all closures (doors, hatches, porthole covers, and valves) marked with a red *Z,* a circled red *Z,* or a red *Z* within a black *D* are secured.

This basic system is modified to allow for special circumstances as follows:

CIRCLE X-RAY and CIRCLE YOKE fittings may be opened without special permission when going to or from GQ stations, when transferring ammunition, or when operating vital systems during GQ. These fittings must be immediately closed once the need to have them open has passed.

CIRCLE ZEBRA fittings may be opened during prolonged periods of GQ, when the condition of readiness is modified by the commanding officer to enable personnel to prepare and distribute battle rations, open limited sanitary facilities, and ventilate battle stations, and it provides access from ready rooms to the flight deck. When open, these fittings must be guarded for immediate closure if necessary.

DOG ZEBRA fittings, secured during condition ZEBRA, are also secured separately during darken ship conditions. These are doors, hatches, or porthole covers that if left open would allow light from inside the ship to be seen outside. The reason for these fittings is obvious in wartime, because allowing lights to show outside at night might help the enemy to detect your ship. DOG ZEBRA fittings are also important in peacetime conditions, because stray lights coming from inside a ship can make it confusing for mariners to see your navigational lights properly, and because stray bright lights can temporarily blind watchstanders so that they cannot see in the darkness.

WILLIAM fittings, marked with a black *W,* are kept open during all material conditions. These fittings are only closed under extraordinary conditions that you will probably never encounter. Examples of WILLIAM fittings are sea-suction valves supplying important engineering equipment and fire pumps.

CIRCLE WILLIAM, marked with a circled black *W,* are normally kept open but must be secured against CBR attack. These are primarily ventilation-system closures that must be secured to prevent the spread of CBR contaminants (radiation, chemical gases, and germs or viruses).

Remember that it is the responsibility of all hands to maintain the material condition in effect. If it is necessary to break the condition, permission must be obtained (from the OOD or DCC). A closure log is maintained in DCC at all times to show where the existing condition has been broken; the number, type, and classification of fittings involved; the name, rate, and division of the man or woman requesting permission to open or close a fitting; and the date a fitting was opened or closed.

Damage Repairs

Timely and efficient repairs of damage to your ship may someday be necessary to keep her afloat. The difference between survival and sinking for your ship may depend upon how you and your shipmates are able to effect repairs. Damage-control drills will go a long way to preparing you for this eventuality you certainly hope will never come to pass.

In an emergency repair situation, do your best with what you have. If you are calm, alert, and work quickly with the tools you have, you can do much to keep the ship afloat and make her ready for action again.

Any rupture, break, or hole in the ship's outer hull plating, particularly below the waterline, can let seawater in. If flooding is not controlled, the ship will sink. When the underwater hull is pierced, there are only two possible courses of action. The first, obviously, is to plug the holes. The second is to abandon the space or spaces where the penetration has taken place, then establish and maintain flood boundaries within the ship to prevent more extensive flooding.

There are two general methods of temporarily repairing a hole in the hull: put something *in* it or *over* it. In either case, the effect is to reduce the area through which water can enter the ship, or through which water can pass from one compartment to another. Holes may be effectively plugged by pounding in a wooden plug or stuffing it with something larger—such as a kapok life-jacket or a mattress—depending upon the size of the hole. Prefabricated box patches may be placed over a hole with jagged or uneven edges, and a flexible sheet-metal patch may be appropriate for certain types of holes.

Cracks may be sealed using gaskets or some filler material such as caulking or *oakum*.

Shoring (perhaps best described as *bracing*) is often used aboard ship to support ruptured decks, strengthen weakened bulkheads and decks, build up temporary decks and bulkheads against the sea, support hatches and doors, and provide support for equipment that has broken loose. Knowing the proper time to shore is a problem that cannot be solved by any one set of rules. Sometimes the need for shoring is obvious, as in the case of loose machinery or damaged hatches. But sometimes dangerously weakened supports under guns or machinery may not be noticeable. Although shoring is not always necessary, the best general rule is, "When in doubt, *shore!*"

The basic materials used in shoring are shores, wedges, sholes, and strong-backs. A *shore* is a portable beam. A *wedge* is a block, triangular on the sides and rectangular on the butt end. A *shole* is a flat block that may be placed under the end of a shore for the purpose of distributing pressure. A *strongback* is a bar or beam of wood or metal, often shorter than a shore, which is used to distribute pressure or to serve as an anchor for a patch. Many other pieces of equipment can also be used in connection with shoring.

Fire Prevention and Fighting

Fire is a constant threat aboard ship, and all measures must be taken to prevent it. Fires may start from spontaneous combustion, carelessness, hits by enemy shells, collision, or many other causes. If a fire is not controlled quickly, it could mean loss of the ship.

Whether you are a member of a repair party or not, it is essential that you learn all you can about fires—how they start, how to prevent them, and how to fight them.

Fire Basics

The old adage, "Know thine enemy," is appropriate, for fire is the Sailor's deadly enemy and if you understand the nature of fire, you will greatly improve your chances of keeping it from appearing and defeating it if it does.

The Fire Triangle

The three essential elements for any fire to start and continue burning are *fuel, heat,* and *oxygen.* These three things make up what is called the "fire triangle." Remove any one and you no longer have a triangle. Remove any one of these three elements and the fire will be put out. Think about your backyard barbecue. To start the fire to cook the food, you need charcoal or gas (fuel), a match or lighter (heat), and good ventilation in the barbecue stove (oxygen). If the charcoal gets used up or the gas is turned off, the fuel is removed from the triangle and your cooking is over. If it rains, your fire will cool down (the heat is removed) and go out. If you place a tight cover over your grill and shut the ventilation openings, your fire will go out as soon as all of the oxygen inside is used up.

Aboard ship, the principles are the same as with your barbecue grill, although probably not as easy to accomplish. It is not always possible, for instance, or even practical, to eliminate fuel. If, however, a flammable liquid fire is being fed by a pipeline, the flow of fuel can be stopped by closing valves in the pipe.

Removing heat is the most common method of extinguishing a fire. The usual cooling method is to use lots of water.

Oxygen can be removed from a shipboard fire by using carbon dioxide (CO_2) to dilute the oxygen content of the air or by smothering the fire with a blanket of foam or sand.

Classes of Fire

Fires can be classified into four different types, identified by the first four letters of the alphabet. Once you know the class of fire you are dealing with, you will be able to fight the fire intelligently and in the most effective manner.

Class Alfa. These fires involve solid substances—wood, cloth, paper—that usually leave an ash. Class Alfa fires are usually characterized by white smoke. Explosives are included in this category. The usual means of extinguishing Class A fires is to use water. In a large fire, the flame is usually knocked down (cooled) with fog (spray), then a solid stream of water is applied to break up the material. Fog is then used for further cooling.

Class Bravo. Class B fires involve flammable liquids, such as oil, gasoline, or paint. These fires usually are characterized by heavy black smoke. For small fires CO_2 is effective. For large fires other agents, such as water and aqueous film-forming foam (AFFF [see below]), must be used. *Never* use a solid stream of water to fight Class B fires. It will only make the fire worse because the water penetrates the fuel's surface, flashes to steam, scatters the fuel, and spreads the fire. Spaces subject to major fuel- or lube-oil spills (firerooms, enginerooms, or fuel-transfer and manifold rooms) are equipped with HALON 1301 (fluorocarbon gas) dispensing systems which, when activated, will knock down a Class B fire.

Class Charlie. Fires in electrical or electronic equipment are classified as Class C. A fire of this type is usually characterized by smoke with a bluish tint along with arcs, sparks, and a distinctive smell you are not likely to forget once you have experienced it. The primary extinguishing method is to de-energize the equipment, which reduces the fire to Class A or B. The preferred extinguishing agent is CO_2, since it does not leave any residue that may harm or interfere with the efficient operation of the equipment. PKP (a special firefighting chemical powder [see below]) may be used as a last resort, but its corrosiveness will further damage the equipment.

Class Delta. Fires involving combustible metals (for example, magnesium, sodium, or titanium) and any fires that require special handling fall into the category of Class D. Special metals are used for building certain parts of aircraft, missiles, electronic components, and other equipment. An example is the magnesium aircraft parachute flare, which can burn at a temperature above 4000° Fahrenheit. Water used on this type of fire will break down into its natural elements of hydrogen and oxygen, which by themselves are unstable and liable to cause small explosions. You should use low-velocity fog at extreme range and remain upwind of this type of fire and stay behind cover as much as possible. One important safety precaution: the intense light produced by this type of fire can easily cause permanent damage to the eyes, so never look directly at the fire, and wear protective welder's goggles with very dark lenses if they are available.

Fire Prevention

Any fire, however small, is bound to cause damage. For this reason, and because of the potential for disaster, a fire prevented is much preferred to a fire that must be fought.

The first step in fire prevention is to keep things squared away—clean, shipshape, and in their proper places. Keep flammable products (gasoline, oily rags, paint) away from fire-starting articles such as torches and sparking equipment. Don't take open flames near gasoline tanks, and don't bring flammable liquid near a welder's torch.

Make sure firefighting equipment is in the right place and in good condition. If a fire does start, you'll want to have the equipment on hand and ready to go. Even if you may not be able to prevent a fire from starting, you can prevent a little one from getting bigger.

The different classes of fire require different methods of prevention.

To prevent Class A fires, you should never throw lighted tobacco products or matches in trash cans and always be careful of where and how you stow rags and oily, paint-smeared cloth and paper. When welding or burning, maintain a proper fire watch, protect Class A

Table 18.1. Classes of Fire and Extinguishing Agent

Combustible	Class of Fire	Extinguishing Agent
Woodwork, bedding, clothes, combustible	A	1. Fixed water sprinkling 2. Slid water stream or fog 3. Foam (AFFF) 4. Dry chemical (PKP) 5. CO_2
Explosives, propellants	A	1. Magazine sprinkling 2. Solid water stream or fog 3. Foam (AFFF)
Paints, spirits, flammable liquid stores	B	1. CO_2 (fixed system) 2. Foam (AFFF) 3. Installed sprinkling system 4. High-velocity fog 5. Dry chemical (PKP) 6. CO_2
Gasoline	B	1. Foam (AFFF) 2. CO_2 (fixed) 3. Water sprinkling system 4. Dry chemical (PKP)
Fuel oil, JP-5, diesel oil, kerosene	B	1. Foam (AFFF) 2. Dry chemical (PKP) 3. Water sprinkling or fog 4. CO_2 (fixed system)
Electrical and radio apparatus	C	1. CO_2 2. High-velocity fog. 3. Fog foam or dry chemical (only if CO_2 not available)
Magnesium alloys	D	1. Jettison overboard 2. Wide-angle fog

materials from the open flame and hot droppings, and be sure to inspect the other side of a bulkhead where such "hot work" is taking place.

The danger of Class B fires requires some special methods of prevention. Be aware that in low places in the ship—such as bilges, tanks, and bottoms—there is the danger of the accumulation of flammable gasoline or oil vapors. Don't carry matches, lighters, or keys, and don't wear metal buttons or nylon clothing near gasoline or oil vapors. Use only nonsparking tools in areas where Class B substances have been or are stored. Don't turn on lamps, flashlights, or electrical equipment that are not certified as spark-proof in an area where gasoline or oil fumes can accumulate.

When working with electrical and electronic equipment, where the possibility exists of a Class C fire, do not paint or splash paint, oil, grease, or solvents on electrical insulation or wires. Report all frayed or worn wires and all sparking contacts, switches, and motors. Report any electrical equipment that is hot, smokes, or makes any unusual noise. In case of fire, secure all electrical equipment in the space. Don't use personal electrical and electronic equipment, such as hot-plates, shavers, extension cords, stereos, or radios, unless they have been inspected and authorized by qualified engineering department personnel.

Protect Class D fuels from welding and burning operations. Do not store Class D fuels in areas that are susceptible to intense heat.

Fighting Fires

Despite the most careful precautions, fires can occur. If you discover a fire, report it immediately so that firefighting operations can begin. When reporting a fire, state the type of fire and its location (compartment name and designation), then do what you can to fight it. Always report the fire before taking any action. A delay of even half a minute might result in a minor fire becoming a major one.

After you have reported the fire, do what you can to fight or contain it. The efforts of one person may be enough to contain the fire until the fire party arrives. Use discretion, however. Do what you can consistent with safety. Your becoming a casualty will not help the fire party in its efforts.

To some extent, the procedures for fighting a fire depend on the conditions under which it occurs. Fires that break out during combat, normal steaming, or when a full crew is aboard are handled as battle casualties and the ship goes to GQ. These fires, which may occur in port or at sea, are normally fought by the firefighting party from the repair station in that section of the ship. Aboard larger ships, it may not always be feasible to go to GQ for every fire that occurs, so a nucleus fire party will handle those fires that can be kept isolated and under control. If control is lost, the ship will immediately go to GQ. When a fire occurs in port and only a partial crew is on board, the duty repair party handles it.

While fighting fires, effective communications can be extremely important. A modern means of communicating, using hand-held radios specifically designed for shipboard use, is called damage-control wire-free communications (DC WFCOM). This means of communication allows personnel at various locations (especially DCC and the scene of the fire) to talk to one another so as to coordinate their efforts and keep the commanding officer informed. Fires that seem to be out may start again (reflash) from a smoldering fragment or through vapor ignition. The final step in firefighting is the establishment of a reflash watch.

Firefighting Equipment
All firefighting equipment is located in readily accessible locations and inspected frequently to ensure reliability and readiness. At any time, you may be called upon to serve on a repair/fire party, or you may be the only person present to combat a fire. If you don't know how to use the equipment, or what equipment to use, the result could be disastrous.

Firemain
The firemain system is designed to deliver seawater to fireplugs, sprinkler systems, and AFFF stations throughout the ship. The firemain (also called simply "the main") has a secondary function of supplying flushing water and of providing coolant water for auxiliary machinery.

Firemain piping is configured as either a single line, horizontal loop, vertical loop, or composite system depending on the type of ship. On small combatant ships, a single-line system runs fore and aft near the centerline. On many large combatant ships, horizontal-loop systems circle around the ship, providing versatility in case of damage. Some ships have vertical-loop systems winding through their superstructures. Composite systems (a combination of any of the other systems) are used on aircraft carriers because of their size and extensive compartmentation. There are many cross-connection points and cutout valves throughout the system to allow damaged sections of piping to be isolated or "jumped" by attaching hoses at bypass points. Risers (pipes that carry water vertically) and branch lines (horizontal pipes) lead from the main to fireplugs and AFFF systems throughout the ship.

Special attachments called "wye-gates" and "tri-gates" at the fireplugs allow two or three hoses to be attached simultaneously to one fireplug. Reducing fittings allow smaller hoses to be attached to larger fittings when necessary.

Fire Hoses
The standard Navy fire hose has an interior lining of rubber, covered with two cotton or synthetic jackets. It comes in 50-foot lengths with

a female coupling at one end and a male coupling at the other. The female coupling is connected to the fireplug. The male coupling is connected to another length of hose or to a nozzle. When rigging hoses, remember that the male end always points toward the fire and the female end of the hose is rigged in the direction of the fireplug.

Ships generally use 2½-inch hose on the weather decks and 1½-inch hose in the ship's interior. One or more racks at each fireplug are used to stow the fire hose. The hose must be faked on the rack so that it is free-running, with the ends hanging down and the couplings ready for instant use. On large ships, each weather-deck fire station has 100 feet of 2½-inch hose faked on a rack and connected to the plug. Below deck, 200 feet of 1½-inch hose are stowed by each plug, but only two lengths (100 feet) are connected to the plug. On smaller ships, 100 feet of 1½-inch hose are faked on the racks, with 50 feet connected to the plug. A spanner wrench for disassembling the connections is also stowed at each fire station. Spare lengths of hose are rolled and stowed in repair lockers.

Sprinkler Systems

Sprinkler systems are installed in magazines, turrets, ammunition-handling rooms, spaces where flammable materials are stowed, and hangar bays. Water for these systems is piped from the firemain. Some systems are automatically triggered when a compartment reaches a certain temperature, but most are opened manually by control valves.

Aqueous Film-Forming Foam (AFFF)

Aqueous film-forming foam (sometimes referred to as "light water"), a clear, slightly amber-colored liquid, is a concentrated mixture that was developed to combat Class B fires. In solution with water, it floats on the surface of fuels and creates a film (or blanket) that prevents the escape of vapors and thereby smothers the fire.

Permanently rigged AFFF stations are set up in high-risk and vital areas such as hangar bays on aircraft carriers. Usually called "HICAP" stations because of their high-capacity output, these systems do not need to be rigged before activating; they are ready for immediate use when needed. Injection pumps and balance pressure proportioners are used on high-capacity AFFF systems. Individual HICAP stations are able to serve many different firefighting systems. When the station is activated, the pump injects AFFF concentrate into the piping downstream of the firemain control valve after it opens.

The agitation of the water in the piping mixes the AFFF solution. The HICAP system can be activated from numerous local and remote stations, but it must be secured at the HICAP station itself. It is essential that the station be manned by qualified personnel once it is activated.

Portable AFFF systems require some rigging and servicing by the firefighting party. The male end of the hose line feeding seawater to the eductor (see below) is threaded into the female end of the portable eductor. A pickup tube (with a special ball-check valve that ensures one-way flow) must be inserted into a canister of AFFF. Seawater passing through the eductor causes a suction in the pickup tube that draws AFFF concentrate from the five-gallon container. The eductor mixes the AFFF concentrate and seawater and delivers them to a 95-gallon-per-minute (gpm) variable-pattern AFFF nozzle which is used to direct and distribute the solution.

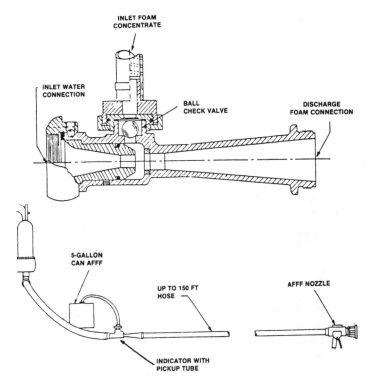

Figure 18.6. An in-line eductor is used to mix AFFF concentrate and seawater.

To maintain the correct AFFF concentrate-to-water ratio, firemain pressure should be maintained. A pressure decrease due to friction in the hose could reduce pressure sufficiently to cause an improper AFFF concentrate and water mixture. Limiting the lengths of fire hose to three (for a total of 150 feet) and a rise of no more than one deck between the eductor discharge and the AFFF nozzle will maintain the needed pressure. Continuous use requires approximately five gallons per minute of AFFF concentrate. Fresh five-gallon canisters of the concentrate must be provided as necessary to maintain the flow of AFFF.

Portable Extinguishers

There are two types of portable extinguishers used in the Navy: *carbon dioxide* (commonly called CO_2) and *dry chemical* (usually called PKP).

CO_2 extinguishers are used mainly for electrical (Class C) fires, but they are also effective on small Class A and B fires, such as an office trashcan or small amounts of oil, gasoline, and paint. Because CO_2 is heavier than air, it forms a smothering blanket over the fire. The extinguisher's effective range is four to six feet from the end of the horn.

To use the extinguisher, remove the locking pin from the valve, grasp the insulated handle of the horn with one hand, and squeeze the grip with the other. If you are in the open, approach the fire from the

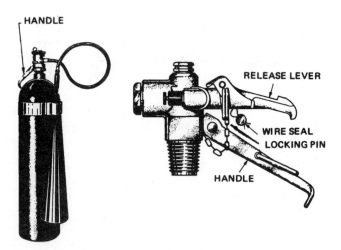

Figure 18.7. The portable CO_2 extinguisher with detail of the handle, release lever, and locking pin.

windward side (wind at your back). This extinguisher is quick to use, leaves no residue, and is not poisonous. But remember that CO_2 is capable not only of smothering fires but human beings as well. Use it sparingly in confined spaces. Also be aware that when released from the cylinder it expands rapidly to 450 times its stored volume, which causes the gas temperature to drop to minus 110° Fahrenheit. Contact with the skin can cause painful blisters.

Dry-chemical extinguishers are primarily used against Class B fires. The chemical used is purple potassium bicarbonate (similar to baking soda), also called "purple K powder" or "PKP."

PKP is nontoxic and four times as powerful as CO_2. It is also effective on Class C fires, but should not be used if CO_2 is available because it leaves a residue that may be harmful to the electronic components. PKP should not be used on internal fires in gas turbines or jet engines except in dire emergency for the same reason.

The dry-chemical extinguisher is available in two sizes. The K-20 contains 18 pounds of PKP, the K-30 contains 27 pounds of PKP, and both use CO_2 (from a cartridge) as a propellant. The extinguisher shell is not pressurized until it is to be used. Handling the extinguisher is simple. Pull the locking pin from the seal-cutter assembly, tilting the bottle away from you and others for safety, and strike the puncture lever to cut the gas-cartridge seal. The extinguisher is then charged and ready for use. Discharge the chemical in short bursts by squeezing the grip on the nozzle and sweeping the fire from side to side. Advance on the fire only if safe (a range of 19 to 21 feet is ideal). When you are finished, invert the cylinder, squeeze the discharge lever, and tap the nozzle on the deck. This releases all pressure and clears the hose and nozzle of powder.

Dry chemical is an excellent firefighting agent, but its effects are temporary. It has no cooling effect and provides no protection against reflash. Therefore it should be backed up by AFFF. In confined spaces, PKP should be used sparingly. Prolonged discharge of the chemical reduces visibility and makes breathing difficult.

There are often two types of fixed fire-extinguisher installations in areas such as machinery spaces and hangar decks. Fixed CO_2 extinguishers are a dependable, ready means of flooding spaces that are more-than-ordinary fire hazards. Cylinders have a 50-pound capacity and are mounted either singly or in banks of two or more. An installed CO_2 extinguisher is used as a flooding system for spaces not continually occupied by personnel, such as paint lockers.

An AFFF/PKP combination is an extremely effective means of controlling a Class B fire. The dry chemical is used to knock down the fire, and the AFFF blanket prevents a reflash. Aircraft carriers have a portable AFFF/PKP system known as a twin-agent unit (TAU) mounted either on its own carriage or on the back of an aircraft tractor.

Pumps

The P-100 is a portable diesel engine-powered pump designed to pump 100 gallons per minute (gpm). It can be used to fight fires or to dewater spaces, depending upon how it is rigged. It has a 3-inch inlet, attached to one or more lengths of hard-rubber suction hose, on the end of which is a foot valve and strainer assembly. The discharge is a 2½-inch gate valve with hose threads that can be attached to either a standard wye-gate (two 1½-inch hose connections), a special tri-gate (one 2½-inch and two 1½-inch hose connections), or a 2½-inch hose, depending on whether the pump is being used for firefighting or dewatering.

Like any other internal combustion engine, the P-100 produces carbon monoxide. When it is used below decks, the exhaust must be led outside the ship. Lengths of 2-inch hard-rubber hose are available for this purpose. This pump should never be run in a space containing explosive vapors.

In firefighting, a vast amount of water is often discharged into the ship. For instance, a 2½-inch hose with a pressure of 100 pounds per square inch (psi) pumps nearly a ton of water per minute. Obviously, this water must be removed or the ship's stability will be greatly impaired.

The P-100 pump can be used for dewatering by itself or with other equipment to increase the pumping rate dramatically. A pumping rate of 100 gpm is not always sufficient to dewater spaces. The dewatering rate of a single pump can be doubled with a jet pump called an eductor. The P-100 draws a suction from the space being dewatered and discharges it to an eductor in the same space. Since the eductor is virtually 100 percent efficient, the discharge from the eductor will be double the gpm of the P-100. Eductors are also used when the liquid to be pumped (gasoline or other flammables) cannot be handled by the pump itself. This practice eliminates the chance of damaging the pump or igniting the liquid. Eductors are also often employed alone, using the ship's firemain as a source of water pressure.

The electric submersible pump is the most versatile and easiest to rig of all dewatering pumps. It is powered by 440 volts of electricity and its pumping capacity depends upon the maximum height of the discharge hose. With the discharge hose at a height of 50 feet, the pump discharges 200 gpm, but when it is at 70 feet, it is capable of only 140 gpm.

When a large height is unavoidable, it is possible to rig two pumps in tandem with a length of $2^1/2$-inch hose between them. The lower pump is activated first and primes the upper pump, which is then activated. Since the water being pumped is also cooling the pumps, the upper one must be carefully monitored to prevent overheating. Overheating of the pump causes its internal seals to deteriorate and leak, resulting in an electrical short circuit that severely damages the pump.

Protective Clothing and Equipment

Any clothing that covers your skin will protect it from flash burns and other short-duration flames. In situations where there is a likelihood of fire or explosion, keep covered as much as possible, and protect your eyes with antiflash goggles.

If your clothes catch fire, don't run. This fans the flames. Lie down and roll up in a blanket, coat, or anything that will smother the flames. If nothing is available, roll over slowly, beating out the flames with your hands. If another person's clothes catch fire, throw the person down and cover him or her (except for the head) with a blanket or coat.

397

Aluminum-coated proximity suits are designed to protect the wearer from the radiant heat of fire. The suits offer only short-term protection. When worn by pilot-rescue personnel, the suits are continuously sprayed down to prevent overheating and should never make contact with actual flames. Proximity suits are used for open-air fires only and should never be used to combat fires inside the ship.

One piece of support equipment used by firefighting parties that is often invaluable is the *oxygen-breathing apparatus,* more often called simply an OBA. The replenishable canisters used with the OBA provide a supply of oxygen that gives the wearer the ability to go into compartments that have been robbed of adequate oxygen by a fire or that contain harmful gases, smoke, vapors, or dust. The oxygen is supplied by chemicals that purify exhaled air. The wearer's breath is circulated through the canister of chemicals, which react with CO_2 and the moisture in the wearer's breath to produce oxygen. The process continues until the oxygen-producing capacity of the chemicals is used up. When the face-piece of an OBA needs cleaning, use only soap and water, never alcohol. Never use grease or oil on any part of the OBA.

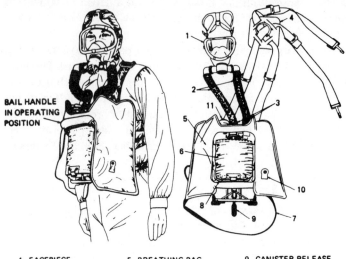

BAIL HANDLE
IN OPERATING
POSITION

1. FACEPIECE	5. BREATHING BAG	9. CANISTER RELEASE STRAP
2. BREATHING TUBES	6. BREASTPLATE	10. PRESSURE RELIEF VALVE AND PULL TAB
3. BREATHING TUBE COUPLINGS	7. WAIST STRAP	11. TIMER
4. BODY HARNESS AND PAD	8. BAIL ASSEMBLY HANDLE (STANDBY POSITION)	

Figure 18.8. The OBA allows you to enter a compartment that has been robbed of adequate oxygen by a fire.

Never enter a danger area until you are sure the apparatus is working correctly. OBAs are equipped with a timer that will tell you how much time has elapsed since you started your canister. Start the timer every time you start a new canister; when the timer goes off, or when it becomes difficult to exhale, return to fresh air.

For all their value, OBAs can be dangerous if mishandled. A used canister is very hot. Wear fire-resistant gloves or equivalent protection for your hands whenever you must handle a recently expended canister. Also be aware that the chemical in canisters is very caustic to the skin. If the chemical is accidentally spilled on deck, clean it up immediately using a nonflammable metal implement for a scoop. Oil, gasoline, or similar substances that come in contact with the chemicals can cause an explosion. Be sure you drop the used canister on a dry deck. Also be sure there is no chance for it to drop through or off a grating and into the bilges.

Expended canisters are normally discarded as hazardous waste. Never throw a canister overboard without getting permission from the OOD, and never throw a canister overboard if there is an oil slick on the water, or if the ship is in port. Also, do not hold your face or any part of your body over a canister opening.

Another important piece of support equipment is the *Scott Air-Pak 4.5*. Similar to the OBA, it also is a self-contained system, providing oxygen to the wearer by means of a self-contained air source. The face piece comes in three colors—green for small, black for large, and red for extra large. The face-piece contains a voice amplifier powered by a 9-volt battery.

Another alternative to the OBA, which may be used for entering smoke-filled compartments to rescue crewmembers, is the *air-line mask*. Since it produces no oxygen of its own, it should never be used when actually fighting a fire. The mask is a demand-flow air-line respirator with a speaking diaphragm, monocular lens with adjustable head harness, breathing tube, and belt-mounted demand regulator with quick-disconnect fittings. The mask comes with a 25-foot hose and quick-disconnect fittings. It is normally used with compressed air cylinders, but when these are not available, low-pressure ship's-service air may be used as an alternative, provided it is reduced to the proper operating pressure. Never use an oxygen cylinder with this

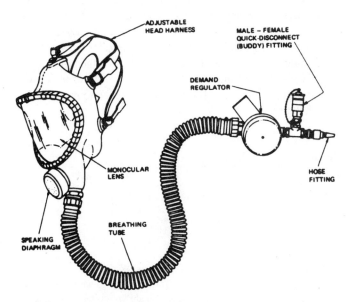

Figure 18.9. The air-line mask is normally connected to compressed air cylinders but may be connected to the ship's low-pressure ships'-service air system.

equipment. Oil, grease, or oily water in the apparatus might combine with the oxygen and explode. Before entering a space filled with toxic gases or smoke, check the mask to be sure it is working properly, then take a breath to determine whether there is sufficient airflow.

Tending lines are 50-foot lengths of nylon-covered steel wire used with the OBA or the air-line mask, with snap hooks at each end of the line. Tending lines are used as a precautionary measure in rescuing a fire investigator or firefighter. Rescuers equipped with OBAs follow the lines to the victim; they do not drag the person out by the lines except in cases when no other method of rescue is possible. Never attach a tending line to your waist. If, in emergency, you must be pulled from a space, a line attached at your waist might interfere with your breathing or cause internal injuries. OBAs are equipped with a D ring on the back of the harness assembly so that the tending line can be easily fastened.

The tending line serves another useful function in that it can be used to communicate. In order to accomplish this, a standard set of signals is used throughout the Navy (see Table 18.2). One way to remember the line signal is to think of the acronym OATH. *O* (okay), *A* (advance), *T* (take up slack), *H* (help).

The *emergency-escape breathing device* (EEBD), a fire-escape mask, consists of a head covering with a transparent face screen that can be donned quickly. Each EEBD carries a canister, which functions the same way as an OBA canister and provides the wearer with about 15 minutes' breathing time (depending upon the physical exertion involved). This should enable the wearer to escape from any space to the ship's topside. It is especially designed to protect against smoke inhalation.

Table 18.2. Tending Line Signals

	Pulls	Meaning
Tender to wearer	1	Are you OK?
	2	Do you want to advance?
	3	Should I take up slack?
	4	Do you need help?
Wearer to tender	1	I am OK.
	2	I am going to advance.
	3	I want you to take up slack.
	4	I need help.

Personnel working in engineering spaces wear *Supplemental Emergency Egress Devices (SEED)* on their belts for easy access. Unlike the EEBD, the SEED does not provide protection for the eyes and nose, and it has a short operational time. It is meant only as a supplementary device, used temporarily to allow a watchstander to get to an EEBD.

All closed or poorly ventilated compartments (particularly those in which a fire has just occurred) are dangerous because the air in them may lack oxygen or contain toxic gases. Three steps should be taken as a matter of routine to test for combustible or toxic gases in confined spaces. The first step should be to test for oxygen content; the second for combustible vapors or gases; and the third for toxic substances. There are several types of atmosphere-testing indicators available for use by firefighting personnel.

Combustible-gas indicators (explosimeters) are used to detect the level of explosivity of various flammable gases and vapors. Several different types of indicators are available, but all operate on the same principles. Operating instructions are attached to the inside of the case cover. This type of indicator can quickly, safely, and accurately detect all combustible gases or vapors associated with fuel oil, gasoline, alcohol, acetone vapors, illuminating gas, fuel gas, hydrogen, and acetylene in mixtures with air or oxygen. The indicator is sensitive to even small quantities of these substances. Although it does not actually identify specific combustibles, it indicates what their explosive level is. These instruments are equipped with flame arresters to prevent flashbacks.

Intended solely for the detection of oxygen deficiency in the atmosphere of a space, the oxygen indicator is designed to give a continuous reading of oxygen concentration from 0 to 25 percent. The oxygen indicator must be calibrated before each use.

The sensing head of the indicator should be introduced into every part of the compartment, from top to bottom. If a deficiency of less than 20 percent oxygen exists, the compartment should be fully ventilated and retested. Before using the oxygen indicator, you should become very familiar with the instructions for its operation.

The *Draeger toxic-gas detector* is a hand-operated, bellows-type aspirator pump into which the appropriate detector tube is inserted. The three gases commonly tested for are carbon monoxide, carbon dioxide (CO_2), and hydrogen sulfide.

After a fire has been extinguished, it is usually necessary to desmoke the affected compartment(s). This is done with natural or forced ventilation. In clearing the smoke out, several cautions should be noted:

Be sure the fire is really out.

Investigate the ventilation systems in the affected areas to make sure they are free of burning or smoldering materials.

Have fire parties and equipment standing by the blower and controller of the ventilation systems.

Obtain permission from DCC (or the engineer) to open ventilation-system closures and start the blowers.

Portable ventilating—blowers, electric or hydraulic (water operated) or pneumatic (air operated)—can be employed for de-smoking, although they are not as efficient or convenient as permanent ventilating systems. When explosive vapors or fumes are present, it may be dangerous to use the ship's permanently installed ventilation systems. Under these circumstances, use only portable blowers.

Firefighting Parties

Every shipboard firefighting party consists of two hose teams known as the attack party. The no. 1 hose team is the attacking unit, and the no. 2 team is the backup.

The *scene leader* is in charge of the firefighting party. The scene leader's first duty is to get to the fire quickly, investigate the situation, determine the nature of the fire, decide what type of equipment should be used, and inform DCC. Later developments may require different or additional equipment, but the scene leader must decide what equipment is to be used first.

The *team leader* for each hose team directs the action of the nozzlemen and the other members of her or his team.

Nozzlemen man the nozzles of the hoses wearing complete battle dress plus gloves, flash hoods, an OBA, and a miner's headlamp. Besides controlling the "business end" of the hose, nozzlemen help the scene leader investigate the fire when OBAs are needed to enter a compartment.

Hosemen lead out the hose from the fireplug, remove kinks and sharp bends, and tend it while it is being used. When fighting the fire, they too wear OBAs.

Investigators make continuous tours of inspection of those spaces adjoining the fire, looking for further damage, taking soundings (checking fluid levels in lower spaces), and leading personnel trapped in smoke-filled compartments to safety. In order to accomplish the latter, these team members also wear OBAs.

To ensure that those personnel wearing OBAs have a safety backup, they are assisted by team members called *OBA tenders*. They guard tending lines (when used) and keep spare OBA canisters available.

Plugmen stand by to operate fireplug valves when ordered. They also rig and stand by jumper hoses (used to bypass damage) when necessary.

Accessmen clear routes to gain access to the fire by opening doors, hatches, scuttles, and other closures. They carry equipment to open jammed fittings and locked doors.

AFFF supplymen prepare foam-generating equipment and keep the system supplied with AFFF.

CO_2 supplymen carry CO_2 and PKP extinguishers.

The *closure detail* secures all doors, hatches, and openings around the area to isolate the fire. All ventilation closures and fans in the smoke and heat area are secured by this detail, which also establishes secondary fire boundaries by cooling down nearby areas.

The *electrician* de-energizes and re-energizes electrical circuits in the fire area and rigs power cables for portable lights, tools, and blowers.

The *hospital corpsman* provides on-scene first aid and is responsible for supervising the movement of seriously injured persons to sick bay for treatment.

The *phone talker* plugs into the nearest JZ circuit to establish and maintain communication with DCC, either directly or through the local repair party.

The *messenger* delivers messages between the scene leader and the repair party leader.

Other personnel and equipment assigned to a firefighting party may include *foam-equipment operators,* additional hosemen, *proximity suitmen* (who wear special protective clothing that will allow them to get much closer to a fire than can someone with only normal protective clothing), a *portable (oxyacetylene) cutting outfit* (PCO) operator, the *de-watering/de-smoking equipment team,* and an *atmospheric test equipment operator* (who uses explosimeters, oxygen indicators, toxic-gas detectors, and other pieces of equipment to determine what dangers exist at the scene of the fire).

19 Seamanship

As a Sailor, whether you eventually strike for boatswain's mate or personnelman, there are certain basic skills of seamanship you will need to know or at least be familiar with. Few Sailors can say they've never handled a line or needed to tie a knot. All ships, whether they are patrol craft or aircraft carriers, use mooring lines to secure themselves to piers, anchors to hold them in place where there are no piers, special rigs to transfer supplies during an UNREP, and many other forms of equipment and skills that are unique but essential ships and boats.

Marlinespike Seamanship

The art of working with line or rope is called "marlinespike seamanship" or, sometimes, "marlinespiking." The name comes from a special tool used in working with rope which is called a "marlinespike."

It is important to learn the special terminology associated with marlinespike seamanship, primarily because you want to avoid confusion. But there is a good secondary reason as well. There are certain measures of professionalism in the Navy that have no official status and have nothing to do with getting you promoted, but are used to size you up as a true Sailor rather than a landlubber. If you want to be recognized as a true Navy professional—to earn the respect of those more experienced than you—you should make an effort to think, act, and speak like a Sailor. This means you should use 24-hour time, call a deck a deck (and not a floor), and know the difference between rope and line.

In the Navy, the term *rope* refers to both fiber and wire. Fiber rope includes those made of such natural materials as manila and hemp and those made of synthetic materials such as nylon. Here is the tricky part. Fiber rope is called "rope" only as long as it is still in its original coil. Once a piece has been cut to be used for some purpose (such as mooring or heaving), it is then called a "line." If you want to be considered a novice, call a line a rope. Rope made of wire (or a

combination of wire and fiber) is usually called "wire rope" or simply "wire" (even if it has been cut from its original coil and is being
used for some specific purpose). To make this just a little bit more
confusing, there are some exceptions. The life*lines* on ships are
nearly always made of wire, for example. You are probably pretty
safe if you just forget about the word "rope" and use the words "line"
and "wire."

What you would probably call a "loop" in a line is called a *bight*
in the Navy. "Looping" a line around an object is called *taking a turn*
or *taking a round turn*. Lines do not "break" in the Navy, they *part*.
The free end of a length of line is called the *bitter end*.

The simplest construction of a fiber line is to start with small
fibers, which are twisted until they form larger pieces called "yarns."
Then the yarns are twisted in the opposite direction to form "strands,"
after which they are twisted in the original direction to become a line.
The direction of this final twisting determines the "lay" of the line.
Line can be either three- or four-strand, though three-strand is most
common in the Navy. Nearly all three-strand line used in Navy ships
is what we call "right-laid," meaning that the strands are twisted to
the right. It is important to know this because you should always try
to coil a line in the direction of its lay. For example, right-laid line
should always be coiled in right-hand (clockwise) turns. This will
prevent kinking and extend the life of the line.

Lines can also be formed by a different process called "braiding."
Braided lines have certain advantages over twisted ones. They will
not kink and will not flex open to admit dirt or abrasives. The construction of some, however, makes it impossible to inspect the inner
yarns for damage. The more common braided lines are hollow
braided, stuffer braided, solid braided, and double braided.

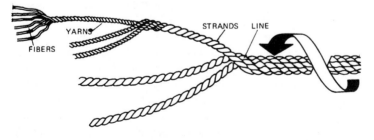

Figure 19.1. The components of a line.

Fiber Lines

Synthetic- and natural-fiber lines have certain advantages and disadvantages over one another. The common synthetic fibers—nylon, polyester (Dacron), polypropylene, and polyethylene (in descending order of strength)—ranging in size from $^5/_8$ inch to 12 inches in circumference, are generally stronger than natural fibers and not subject to rot. Nylon is over twice as strong as manila (the most common natural fiber), lasts five times as long, and will stand seven times the shock load. Dacron gets stronger when wet, and polypropylene is so light it floats, both of which are obvious advantages in a marine environment. The biggest disadvantages of synthetic line when compared to natural-fiber line is that synthetics stretch under heavy loads and it is more difficult to tell when they are going to part. Another disadvantage of synthetic line is that it does not hold knots as well as natural fibers. Some knots that are good for securing natural fibers, such as the square knot, are not adequate for synthetic. The bowline is one knot known to offer reasonable security when bending together or securing synthetic line.

Fiber lines are identified by their circumference and type; for example, "two-inch manila" or "three-inch nylon." Lines larger in circumference than five inches are called *hawsers*. Line that is less than one inch in circumference is usually called *small stuff*.

Synthetic Lines

Before you use new three-strand synthetic, it should be faked down on deck and allowed to relax for 24 hours. The period can be shortened to about two hours by hosing down the line with fresh water.

When it is wet, synthetic line shrinks slightly but does not swell or stiffen. When tension is applied to the line, water squeezes out; under working loads, it appears as vapor.

Oil and grease do not cause synthetics to deteriorate, but they make them slippery. When this happens, the line should be scrubbed down. Spots may be removed by cleaning the line with light oils such as kerosene or diesel oil.

Sailors who work with natural-fiber line soon learn how to judge tension by the sound the line makes. Unfortunately, although synthetic line under heavy strain thins down considerably, it gives no audible indication of stress—even when it is about to part. For this reason, a *tattletale* line should be attached to synthetic line when it is subjected to loads that may exceed its safe working load. A tattletale line is a piece of smaller line that is attached to a synthetic line at two carefully measured points so that it droops down. As the synthetic line stretches, the droop in the tattletale will get less and less. When the tattletale has become taut and is lying parallel to the synthetic line, you will know that the line is in danger of parting.

Natural-fiber Lines

Because of its tendency to retain water and to rot, special care and handling are required when using natural-fiber lines.

Coils of line should always be stowed on shelves or platforms clear of the deck. They should never be covered in such a way that may prevent the evaporation of moisture.

Whenever possible, a wet line should be dried before stowing. If line must be stowed wet, it should be laid up on gratings in long fakes or suspended in some other way so that it will dry as quickly as possible. It should never be covered until dry.

To prevent cutting or breaking of the outer fibers, keep lines from rubbing against other objects whenever possible, particularly sharp or jagged ones. Avoid dragging line over ground where it can pick up dirt and other particles; these can work their way into the line and weaken the line by cutting the inner strands.

Under normal working conditions, the strength of line exposed to the elements deteriorates about 30 percent in two years. Lines should be inspected frequently for deterioration. Open the lay by twisting in the opposite direction and inspect the fibers. A white powdery residue indicates internal wear. After particularly heavy use, inspect the inside threads to see if all or a portion of the fibers are broken.

Wire Rope

The construction of wire rope is similar to that of fiber lines. Wire rope consists of individual wires made of steel or other metal, in various sizes, laid together to form strands. The number of wires in a strand varies according to the purpose for which the rope is intended. A number of strands are laid together to form the wire rope itself. Wire rope is designated by the number of strands per rope and the number of wires per strand. Thus, a 6 by 19 rope has 6 strands with a total of 19 wires per strand.

Wire rope made up of a large number of small wires is flexible, but small wires break so easily that the rope is not resistant to external abrasion. Wire rope made up of a smaller number of larger wires is more resistant to abrasion, but less flexible.

Never pull a kink out of a wire rope by putting strain on either end. As soon as you notice a kink, uncross the ends by pushing them apart; this reverses the process that started the kink. Then turn the bent portion over, place it on your knee or some firm object, and push down until the kink starts to straighten out somewhat. Then lay it on a flat surface and pound it smooth with a wooden mallet.

Damage to a wire rope is indicated by the presence of what are called "fishhooks." These occur when individual wires break and bend back. If several occur near each other or along the rope's length, it is an indication that the wire rope is less reliable and may require replacement. Because of these "fishhooks," always wear gloves when handling wire.

You should inspect wire rope frequently, checking for fishhooks, kinks, and worn spots. Worn spots show up as shiny flattened surfaces.

Wire rope should never be stored in places where acid is or has been kept. Prior to storage, wire rope should be cleaned and lubricated.

Working with Line

Certain skills and practices, some of them simple and others more complicated, must be learned in order to work with line. The experts at working with line are the boatswain's mates, but every Sailor should be familiar with a number of these skills.

Stowing Line for Ready Use

Once a line has been removed from the coil, it may be prepared for storage or ready use, either by winding on a reel or in one of the following ways.

Coiling down. Lay the line down in circles, roughly one on top of the other. Right-laid line is always coiled down right-handed, or clockwise. When a line has been coiled down, the end that went down last on top is ready to run off. If you try to walk away with the bottom end, the line will foul up. If for some reason the bottom end must go out first, turn the entire coil upside down to free it for running.

Faking down. The line is laid down as in coiling down, except that it is laid out in long, flat bights, one alongside of the other, instead of in a round coil. A faked down line runs more easily than a coiled line.

Flemishing down. Coil the line down first, then wind it tight from the bottom end, counterclockwise, so that it forms a close mat. This method of stowing a line not only keeps it ready for use, it looks good.

Securing Ends

Never leave the end of a line without what is called a *whipping*. This can be a piece of small stuff tied to the end of the line or a piece of tape wrapped around it to prevent the end of the line from unravel-

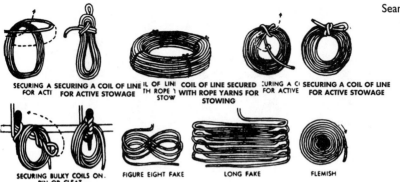

SECURING A SECURING A COIL OF LINE IL OF LINE COIL OF LINE SECURED CURING A CI SECURING A COIL OF LINE
FOR ACTI FOR ACTIVE STOWAGE TH ROPE) WITH ROPE YARNS FOR FOR ACTIVE FOR ACTIVE STOWAGE
STOW STOWING

SECURING BULKY COILS ON.   FIGURE EIGHT FAKE   LONG FAKE   FLEMISH
PIN OR CLEAT

Figure 19.2. Different ways of stowing line.

ing. A good method to use for nylon line is to wrap a piece of tape around the end, leaving the tufted end of the strands exposed. You should then singe the exposed strands, causing them to melt together.

Joining Lines Together

The most obvious method of joining lines together is to tie them with a knot. Other methods are also used for specific purposes because of the advantages they provide.

Knots, bends, and hitches. When you tie two lines together, you have formed a *bend.* When you tie a piece of line to some other object, it is called a *hitch.* To a seaman, a *knot* in a line usually means the line is tied to itself. In many cases, these functions may overlap, so these terms are not absolute. One guiding principle is that knots are usually meant to be permanent and are therefore more difficult to untie than are bends and hitches.

There are big, thick books describing the many varieties of knots, bends, and hitches, but if you are comfortable with just a few, you will be able to take care of virtually any common situation. If you learn no others, be sure that you can at least tie a *square knot* (also called a *reef knot*), a *bowline,* a bowline-on-a-bight, and a clove hitch. Others will prove useful in special situations, such as the *figure eight* (used to put a temporary end to a line), *catspaw* (secures a cargo sling to a hook), *timber hitch* (good for lifting or securing logs, planks, and other long, rough-surfaced objects), and *carrick bend* (used to bend two hawsers together). The more knots, bends, and hitches you know, the better you will be able to use line to your advantage in a wide variety of situations.

409

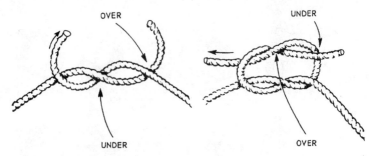

OVER

UNDER

UNDER

OVER

Figure 19.3. Tying the square knot.

Ornamental knots are used to give your ship a smart nautical appearance and to promote safety and habitability. Just as with practical knots, bends, and hitches, there are virtual encyclopedias of ornamental work. *Turk's heads, fox and geese,* and *sennits* are just a few of the many forms of ornamental knots you will more than likely encounter during your time in the Navy.

Seizings. Sometimes it is useful to secure two lines together side by side. This is accomplished by using a variety of what are called *seizings.*

Splices. When lines are to be joined end to end, they are *spliced.* A line can also be bent on itself and spliced to form a permanent loop on the end of the line. If properly done, splicing does not weaken the line. A splice between two lines will run over a sheave or other object much more easily than a knot.

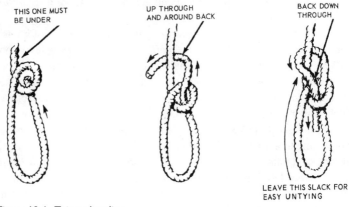

THIS ONE MUST
BE UNDER

UP THROUGH
AND AROUND BACK

BACK DOWN
THROUGH

LEAVE THIS SLACK FOR
EASY UNTYING

Figure 19.4. Tying a bowline.

Working with Wire Rope

The greater strength of wire rope as compared to fiber line is offset somewhat by its lesser flexibility and its tendency to rust if conditions are not right. Wire rope that is frequently exposed to weather or hard use requires some extra measures of protection to prolong its service life.

Worming. The lay of the rope is followed between the strands with tarred small stuff. This keeps moisture from penetrating the interior of the rope and fills out the rope, giving it a smooth surface ready for parceling and serving.

Parceling. This is accomplished by wrapping the rope spirally with long narrow strips of canvas, following the lay of the rope and overlapping turns to shed moisture.

Serving. The final step in preserving wire rope is accomplished by wrapping small stuff snugly over the parceling, pulling each turn as taut as possible so that the whole forms a stiff protecting cover for the rope. A tool called a *serving mallet* is used for passing the turns in serving, and each turn is pulled taut by the leverage of the handle. Remember this poetic rule:

> Worm and parcel with the lay,
> Turn and serve the other way.

Mooring

One very common and important use of lines in the Navy is mooring. Mooring is defined as securing a ship to a pier or to a mooring buoy, or by anchoring. In order to maximize pier space, Navy ships are also frequently moored to other ships, creating a *nest* of ships alongside a pier. In order to properly moor a ship to a pier, certain standardized procedures make the operation efficient and a knowledge of the appropriate terminology is essential. Standard commands, the deck fittings, and the lines themselves all are referred to in ways that must be understood by Sailors in order to take part in the operation or to stand watches properly once a ship is moored.

Mooring Equipment

In order to moor a ship properly, you will need to be able to identify certain items of equipment that are unique to ships. To begin with, a mooring line will do no good without the necessary fittings on the ship and on the pier to which the mooring lines are secured. A *cleat* consists of a pair of projecting horns for *belaying* (securing) a line. Bitts are cylindrical shapes of cast iron or steel arranged in pairs on the ship's deck and/or on the pier which are also used to belay lines. A *bollard* is a heavy cylindrical object with a bulbous top and a horn that is found on piers but not on ships. The eye or bight of a mooring line can be passed over it and, because of its design, the line will not slip off. A *chock* is different from the other fittings so far mentioned because lines are not secured to it but instead are passed through. Chocks come in three varieties—open, closed, and roller—and are used to feed lines in the direction you want, thereby increasing efficiency. A typical mooring configuration would have lines running from bitts aboard ship, through chocks, to a bollard (or a cleat or another set of bitts) on the pier.

To protect the sides of your ship from rubbing or banging against the pier, *fenders* and *camels* are used. Fenders are shock absorbers of various types (such as rubber shapes or clusters of line) suspended from the ship or pier to serve as a cushion between them. Camels serve the same purpose, but instead of being suspended from the deck, they float in the water. Besides protecting the ship and pier from contacting each other, camels are used to keep aircraft carriers further away from the pier because of their overhanging elevators. If you moored an aircraft carrier to a pier without camels to hold it off, the elevators would, in many instances, lower right onto the pier or

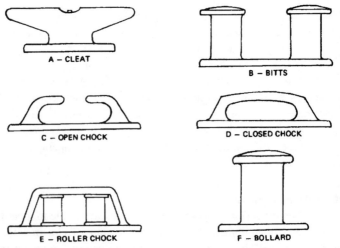

Figure 19.5. Cleats, bitts, and chocks are used on ships to secure lines. Bollards are found on piers or wharves.

dangerously close to it. To prevent rats from coming aboard your ship, using your mooring lines as convenient pathways, circular metal discs called (appropriately enough) *rat guards* are lashed to the mooring lines.

During the mooring process, a light line called a *messenger* is first sent over. Then, with the mooring line itself attached, it is hauled in. To help get the messenger across from the ship to the pier, a heaving line, bolo, or line-throwing gun is used, depending upon the distance of the ship from the pier. A heaving line is a light line with a weight, called a *monkey fist,* on one end; a bolo line is a nylon line with a padded lead weight or a monkey fist on it that is designed for throwing a greater distance by first twirling it in a circle to build up momentum before letting it go. A line-throwing gun is a modified shotgun that can fire a special projectile with a line attached. It will reach farther than a heaving line or bolo but, for obvious reasons, is dangerous to use, particularly when many people are standing on the pier.

Mooring Lines

Mooring lines are referred to by both numbers and by names. They are numbered starting with the forward-most one (number 1) and continuing aft in sequence. Mooring lines are named by a combination of their location, their use, and the direction in which they tend as they leave the ship.

Once a ship is moored to a pier or to another ship, it is important to prevent the ship from moving along (laterally) and to keep it from moving up and down (parallel to) the pier. Mooring lines are designed to prevent these two things. Lines that prevent ships from drifting away from the pier—in other words, that control lateral movement—are rigged perpendicular, or nearly so, to the pier and are called *breast lines*. Lines that prevent or minimize forward and aft movement—in other words, motion parallel to the pier—are rigged nearly parallel to the pier and are called *spring lines.*

The mooring configuration will differ depending upon the size of the vessel being moored and the surrounding conditions (tides, currents, weather), but a standard six-line moor will illustrate most of what you need to know about mooring a ship to a pier. The first line (farthest forward) is called the *bow line* and runs through the *bull-nose* (chock on the very front of the ship) and then to the pier. The next line aft is numbered "2" and is called the *after bow spring*. This name is derived from the fact that it *tends* (goes) aft, is located in the forward half of the ship (hence the word "bow"), and is a spring line (in this case it prevents the forward motion of the ship). Moving aft along the ship's main deck, the next line you would encounter would be the number three line, and it is called the *forward bow spring*. This, too, is a spring line because it keeps the ship from moving backward along the pier. The other parts of its name tell you it is located on the forward part of the ship (bow) and that it tends forward. The next two lines aft would be numbers four and five and they would be called the *after quarter spring* and the *forward quarter spring,* respectively. These lines are also spring lines and function the same as their counterparts on the bow. Because they are located on the after half of the ship, they are identified by the word "quarter" instead of "bow." The final line in a standard six-line configuration is called the *stern line.* Like the bow line, this line is usually rigged as a breast line, meaning that it runs perpendicular (or nearly so) to the pier and is used to prevent lateral (in and out) movement of the ship in relation to the pier. Larger ships will, of course, rig more lines to secure the ship more effectively to the pier or another ship. Those rigged in the middle (amidships) of the ship are called *waist* lines. So an extra line rigged amidships to keep the ship snug to the pier, for example, would be called a *waist breast* line. If more lines are rigged, they still follow the rule of numbering from forward, so that the last line aft on a ship moored with eleven lines would be called "number 11."

Once the ship is settled into her berth and all mooring lines have been rigged, they are usually *doubled up*. This is a somewhat misleading term because the way doubling up is actually accomplished results in *three* lines (actually *parts*) going from the ship to the pier instead of just one at each location.

Line-Handling Commands
During the process of mooring a vessel, it is vital that the conning officer be able to communicate efficiently with the line handlers. To

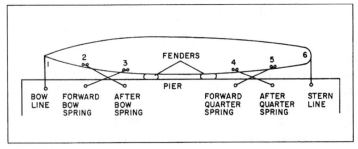

Figure 19.6. A six-line moor. Note the fenders used to keep the ship from rubbing against the pier.

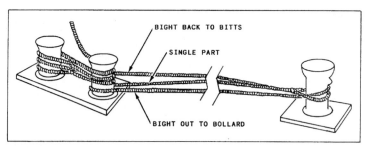

Figure 19.7. Correct method of doubling up.

make sure there is no confusion, commands that are commonly used in mooring operations have been standardized. This system can only be efficient if *both* the conning officer and the line handlers know what the various commands are and what they mean. (See Table 19.1.)

Mooring to a Buoy

There are, in some locations in the world, special buoys that are securely attached to the bottom and are equipped for mooring a ship. Rather than use lines in this type of moor, the ship detaches its anchor chain from its anchor and then reattaches the chain to the buoy. This method has the advantage of allowing a ship to be securely moored in a specific location without having to use its own anchor or its mooring lines. The disadvantage is that, like anchoring, this method of mooring leaves the ship out in the middle of the water, necessitating the use of boats to get personnel and supplies on and off the ship. This method of mooring is not as common as it once was but is still used in some ports.

Anchoring

Mooring to a pier is nearly always the preferred method for a ship to spend its time when not underway. When alongside a pier, personnel can come and go without much difficulty and supplies are easily brought aboard. Because there are not always piers available, and because there are occasions when it is preferable not to be alongside a pier (such as when political unrest in a region makes defending the ship from terrorist attack a priority), ships have the ability to use anchors as an alternative to mooring alongside a pier.

When anchored, boats must be used for transporting personnel and supplies to and from the ship. A careful watch on the sea and weather

415

Table 19.1. Line-Handling Commands

Command	Meaning
Stand by your lines	Man the lines; be ready to cast off or take in.
Pass number one.	Pass the number-one line to the pier and place the eye over the appropriate bollard or other fitting, but take no strain.
Take a strain on number two.	Put number two line under tension.
Slack number four.	Let all tension off the number four line.
Ease the bow line.	Let most of the tension off the bow line.
Hold number six.	Do not let the number six line pay out at all. (Best accomplished by taking turns around a cleat or set of bitts so that the line can't slip.)
Check the stern line.	Do not pay out the stern line but let it slip rather than part the line.
Heave around on number one.	Pull in the number one line using the capstan (mechanical device that can be used to efficiently pull in a line.)
Avast heaving.	Stop the capstan.
Take in number three.	Retrieve the number three line. (Bring your line back aboard your ship.)
Cast off number five.	Take the number five off the bollard or the fitting and let it go. (This command is used to tell line handlers on the pier or on an adjacent ship to return the number five line to the ship it belongs to.)

conditions must be kept and care must exercised to ensure that the ship does begin to move out of its anchorage by dragging its anchor.

The equipment associated with anchoring is called *ground tackle*. This includes the anchors themselves, the chains used to attach them to the ship, the windlasses used to lift the anchor back on board, and a variety of other components, such as shackles, chain stoppers, anchor bars, and detachable links.

Anchors

An anchor is a type of hook that embeds itself into the sea bottom to hold a ship in place. While the anchor itself is an important component of the process, the chain is also vital. The amount of chain used is very important because too much chain will allow the ship to move around too much within its anchorage, and too little may allow the ship to move out of its anchorage by dragging its anchor.

The *shank* is the body of the anchor and the *flukes* are the "teeth" (or hook part) that actually bite into the bottom. Some anchors have a *stock*, which is a kind of crossbar that prevents the anchor from flipping over once it is lying on the bottom.

Anchors are stored in a special tube called a *hawsepipe*. This tube also serves as a passage for the anchor chain that leads from the forecastle deck to the outer surface of the ship's hull closer to the water. The anchor chain is stowed in a large compartment called the *chain locker*.

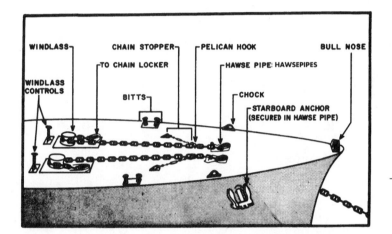

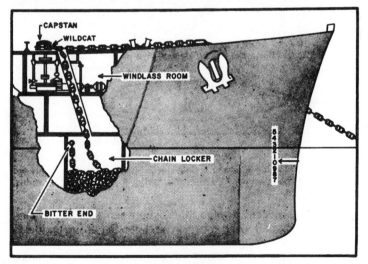

Figure 19.8. A typical ground-tackle arrangement.

There are various types of anchors and different methods of anchoring. The most common method of anchoring is to drop one or two anchors in relatively shallow water and pay out enough chain to ensure that the ship will stay in place. In a *Mediterranean moor,* a ship usually has the stern moored to a pier and an anchor out on each bow. An anchor carried aft by amphibious ships (that deliberately run aground in order to offload troops and supplies) to pull themselves

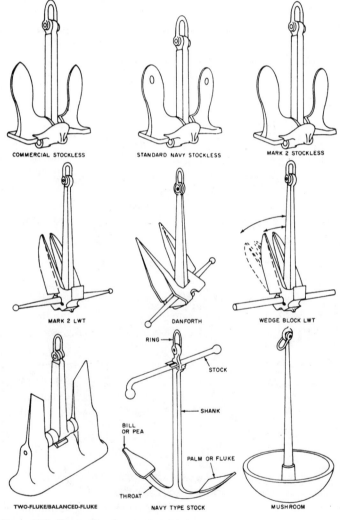

Figure 19.9. Types of anchors.

off the beach (retract) is called a *stern anchor.* A *stream anchor,* now seldom used, is a small anchor dropped off the stern or quarter of a ship to prevent her from swinging to a current.

Stockless anchors, because they do not have the crossbar to get in the way, are easy to stow and were adopted by the Navy for this reason, despite the fact that they do not have the holding power of old-fashioned anchors. Three types of stockless anchors are in use on naval ships: commercial, Mark 2, and standard Navy stockless. Of the three, the Mark 2, with its long flukes, has the greatest holding power. It is made only in the 60,000-pound size for use aboard aircraft carriers.

Mushroom anchors, once used in older submarines, are not used much anymore. They are very useful for placing buoys because, once planted (particularly in groups of three), they are not easily dislodged and are therefore very reliable.

There are three types of *lightweight* (LWT) anchors used on Navy ships. The Mark 2 LWT and the wedge-block LWT are the most common but the commercially made Danforth anchor is also used aboard some Navy craft and small boats. LWT-type anchors have a great deal of holding power for their weights, relying on their ability to dig in rather than their dead weight (as is the case for the stockless types). For example, in a sand bottom, 10,000-pound LWT anchors are designed to have a holding power approximately equal to the 22,500-pound standard Navy stockless. Sizes below 150 pounds are used as boat anchors.

Two-fluke/balanced-fluke anchors are used by surface ships and the newest submarines. They are normally housed in the bottom of the ship rather than in a hawsepipe on the forecastle. In surface ships, they are used in place of bow anchors, which could strike the large, bulbous sonar dome that bulges out beneath the water.

Although no longer used for practical purposes, *old-fashioned anchors* are the traditional anchors you see represented on officers' and chief petty officers' caps and on the rating badges of boatswain's mates. Also known as Navy type Stock anchors, they are commonly used as decorative items in front of Navy buildings and in various other locations.

Ground Tackle

Besides the anchors, there are other important components used in the anchoring process. Chains are the most obvious but there are a number of other components with which you should be familiar if you are going to understand the anchoring process.

Chains

Made of steel, Navy anchor chains vary in size according to the size of the ship and her anchors. Chain comes in 15-fathom lengths called *shots*. To understand this, you need to know that a fathom equals six feet. This means that a shot of anchor chain is 90 feet long. How many shots of chain a ship will carry depends upon the type of ship. Shots are connected to one another by *detachable links*.

A special color-coding system is used to identify the various shots so that when the ship is anchored, you can tell, just by looking at visible chain on deck, how much chain has been payed out and is underwater. Each of the detachable links that marks the beginning of another shot of chain is painted either red, white, or blue. The links on either side are painted white (the number of links corresponding to the number of shots) and pieces of wire are also twisted onto the last white link to further aid in identification (the latter is useful in the dark when you cannot see the links clearly but can feel the turns of wire). Every link in the last shot of chain is painted red and every link in the next-to-last shot is painted yellow. This will give you warning that you are almost out of chain. (See Table 19.2.)

Shackles

In ground tackle, these U-shaped or oval rings are used to attach chains to other objects. For example, the *bending shackle* attaches the anchor chain to the anchor.

Outboard Swivel Shots

On most ships, standard outboard swivel shots, also called *bending shots,* attach the anchor chain to the anchor. They make it possible to stop off (secure) the anchor and break (unfasten) the chain between

Table 19.2. Color-coding System for Shots of Chain

Shot Number	Color of Detachable Link	Number of Adjacent Links Painted White	Turns of Wire on Last White Links
1 (15 fathoms)	Red	1	1
2 (30 fathoms)	White	2	2
3 (45 fathoms)	Blue	3	3
4 (60 fathoms)	Red	4	4
5 (75 fathoms)	White	5	5
6 (90 fathoms)	Blue	6	6

the windlass and the anchor so that the chain can then be attached to a mooring buoy. Outboard swivel shots consist of detachable links, regular chain links, a swivel, an end link, and a bending shackle (which actually attaches the anchor to the chain). Outboard swivel shots vary in length depending upon the size and type of ship but will not normally exceed 15 fathoms.

Chain Stoppers

To hold the anchor securely in place when you are not actually in the process of letting it go or heaving it in, chain stoppers are attached to it. These consist of a *shackle* at one end (attaches the stopper to the deck of the ship) and a *pelican hook* (special hook that fits over a chain and can be securely closed—clamped on—or opened as needed) at the other. Several links of chain are included to give the stopper the desired length and a *turn-buckle* is included that is used to adjust the stopper so that there is no slack in the chain once the stopper is attached (in other words, it makes the stopper taut). The stopper located closest to the hawsepipe is called the *housing stopper.* Other stoppers are called *riding stoppers.*

Stoppers are used for holding the anchor taut in the hawsepipe when not in use, for keeping the chain secure when the ship is riding to an anchor, and for holding an anchor in place when it is disconnected from the chain.

Anchor Windlass

This machine is used to hoist the bow anchor. Those ships with stern anchors have a similar device on the ship's fantail called the *stern-anchor winch.*

On combatant ships, the anchor windlass is a vertical type with controls, including a friction-brake handwheel that can be used to slow down and actually stop the anchor from running out any further once it has been let go (dropped). Below deck is the drive motor with

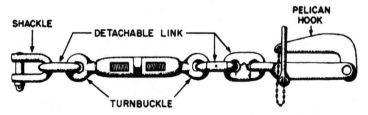

Figure 19.10. A chain stopper.

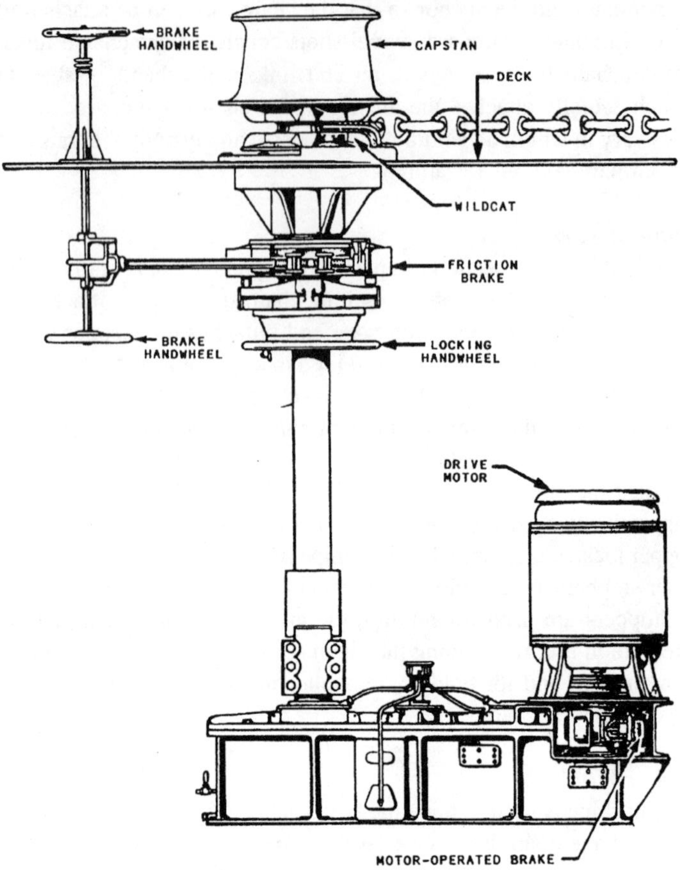

Figure 19.11. Vertical shaft anchor windlass.

its electric and hydraulic components. Above deck is a smooth cylinder called a *capstan* which can use the motor power to heave around on mooring lines. Beneath the capstan is a *wildcat* which is fitted with ridges called *whelps,* which engage the links of the chain and prevent it from slipping while heaving it in. The wildcat may be disengaged from the shaft so that it turns freely when the anchor is dropped; as mentioned before, it is fitted with a brake to stop the chain at the desired length (called *scope*).

On auxiliary ships, the anchor windlass is often a horizontal type above deck, with two wildcats, one for each anchor.

As mentioned earlier, if mooring buoys are available the anchor chain
may be detached from its anchor (leaving the anchor secured in its
hawsepipe by the stoppers) and then attached to a mooring buoy.
Mooring shackles are used to make the attachment. Forged-steel
mooring swivels with two links of regular chain at each end are
inserted into the chain outboard of the hawsepipe to keep the chain
from twisting as the ship swings.

The Anchor Detail

The anchor detail is normally headed by the first lieutenant, who is
assisted by one or more experienced boatswain's mates and a team of
Sailors who can perform the various tasks associated with anchoring.

Whenever a ship is entering or leaving port, the anchor detail is
set. This is true even if the ship has no intention of anchoring,
because the ship's anchors can be used in an emergency situation to
keep the ship from getting into serious danger—they serve as a kind
of emergency brake. For example, a ship coming into or leaving a
port often must travel through fairly restricted waters (such as a narrow channel or into a small mooring basin). If the ship should suddenly lose its propulsion power, it might coast or drift into danger
(such as running aground or colliding with other ships moored or
anchored nearby). If the anchors are ready for letting go, they can be
dropped and used to hold the ship in place temporarily until the problem can be fixed and propulsion restored.

Dropping the Anchor

With the anchor detail manned, the ship is carefully navigated into
position by the OOD and his or her special sea (navigational) detail.
When the ship is nearing the anchorage the bridge tells the forecastle
to stand by. Personnel on the forecastle will release all but one of the
chain stoppers and the windlass brake so that the weight of the anchor
is on the chain, which will then be held by the one remaining stopper.
When the ship is precisely in position, the bridge will tell the forecastle to let go the anchor. With everyone standing clear of the chain,
a Sailor will knock the pelican hook on the stopper loose and, with a
great roar, the anchor will plunge into the water and fall to the bottom. Allowing an anchor or its chain to run out using its own weight
is called *veering*.

The Sailor controlling the windlass will set the brake soon after
the anchor strikes bottom to prevent the chain from piling up. The
OOD will normally back the ship down to set the anchor (cause the

flukes to dig into the bottom). Then the OOD will order the brake released on the windlass and will back the ship down some more to veer more chain until it is at the desired scope (length). Stoppers will then be set and the ship is anchored.

Weighing Anchor

When the ship is ready to get underway from its anchorage, the sea and anchor details are set and the forecastle detail will set the brake on the windlass and remove the stoppers. Upon command from the bridge, the windlass operator will begin heaving around to bring in the chain. Normally, she or he will heave around to *short stay* (all the chain is retrieved leading up to the anchor, but heaving is stopped just short of pulling the anchor out of the ground) and wait for orders to proceed.

When so ordered, heaving is continued, and the bridge is informed when the anchor is *up and down* (pulled out of the ground, but still resting on the bottom). Once the anchor is clear of the bottom (the weight of the anchor is on the chain), the report "Anchor's aweigh" is sent to the bridge. At this point the ship is officially underway.

A hose team will spray the chain as it emerges from the water to remove the mud and debris accumulated from the bottom. Once the anchor can be seen, the forecastle will report its condition to the bridge. If it is ready to be housed (brought back into the hawsepipe), it will be heaved in and stoppers will be set to hold it in place.

Standard Commands

Just as it is vital for clear, concise communications during line-handling operations, so is it important to have the same during anchoring operations. (See Table 19.3.)

Scope of Chain

The ship is held in place not only by the anchor itself but by the chain as well. *Scope* is the amount of chain the ship puts out to hold the ship in place. This amount varies with the depth of the water. The scope is normally five to seven times the depth of the water. For example, if your ship is anchoring in 10 fathoms (60 feet) of water, the OOD will use between 50 fathoms (300 feet) and 70 fathoms (420 feet) of chain to hold the ship in place.

Towing

Most routine towing jobs in the Navy are handled by special vessels that are specially equipped to handle these operations, such as harbor

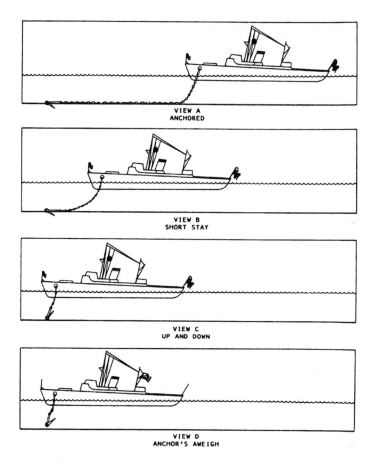

VIEW A
ANCHORED

VIEW B
SHORT STAY

VIEW C
UP AND DOWN

VIEW D
ANCHOR'S AWEIGH

Figure 19.12. From anchored to underway.

tugs, fleet tugs, salvage vessels, and submarine-rescue vessels. But
other Navy ships must, in emergencies, be able to tow other vessels
or be towed themselves.

The towing rig used varies among classes and types of ships, but
includes certain common items in one form or another. On the stern,
most ships have a *towing-pad eye* which is used to attach the *towing
assembly,* made up of a large pelican hook made fast to a towing
hawser. The hawser itself is usually a wire rope varying in length
from 100 fathoms for a destroyer to 150 fathoms for a larger ship. It
is normally attached to one of the towed ship's anchor chains, which
has been disconnected from the anchor, run through the bull-nose,
and veered to 20 to 45 fathoms.

Table 19.3. Anchoring Commands

Command	Meaning
Stand by.	Brake is released on the windlass so that the weight of the anchor is on the chain stopper
Let go.	The pin is removed from the pelican hook and a Sailor with a maul knocks the bail loose on the pelican hook so that it will release the stopper and the chain can run freely.
Pass the stoppers.	With the brake set, the stoppers are fastened around the chain to hold it in place, then the brake is released.
Heave around to.	The windlass brings the chain in until the short stay anchor is just about to break ground.
Anchor's up and down.	The anchor has broken ground but is still resting on the bottom.
Anchor's aweigh.	The anchor is clear of the bottom and the ship is under way.
Anchor is in sight.	The anchor detail on the forecastle can see the anchor well enough to report its condition.
Anchor is clear.	There is little or no debris from the bottom clinging to the anchor.
Anchor is shod.	The anchor is caked with mud and/or other debris from the bottom.
Anchor is fouled.	The anchor has hooked onto a cable or some other underwater obstruction that will prevent it from being brought into the hawsepipe.

The length of the towline—hawser and chain—is adjusted to hang in a deep underwater curve called a *catenary,* which helps to relieve surges on the line caused by movements of the two ships. Whether towing is done with two motor launches or two cruisers, the towline should be of such a scope (or length) that the two craft are *in step,* which means that they should both reach the crest of a wave at the same time. Otherwise, the towline will be whipped out of the water and may cause serious damage.

Once the towing hawser is rigged, the towing vessel gets under way very slowly. If the towing vessel moves too quickly, it may cause the line to part. Course changes must also be made slowly.

If you are involved in a towing operation, be aware that the towing line could part at any time and that, if it does, the potential for serious injury is very great. Never get any closer to a towing line than you have to.

Deck Seamanship

Despite all of their sophisticated electronics and modern engineering components, Navy ships must still rely on basic deck seamanship techniques to be able to move heavy loads about and to receive fuel, ammunition, and supplies on board. The principles—and, in fact, some of the actual equipment—used to accomplish these things are the same that Sailors have used for centuries. Mechanical winches may have replaced pure manpower in some cases, but the techniques and the rigs used are the same ones that Sailors used in the days of sail to get their work done. Because of this strong link to the past, many of the terms used in deck seamanship come down to us from centuries ago and will, therefore, take some getting used to.

Cargo Handling

Service and amphibious ships in the Navy, by the nature of their business, must be able to handle large amounts of cargo. But even combatants must be able to handle at least limited amounts. Therefore all ships have at least some cargo-handling equipment.

Basic Terminology

The most basic form of a cargo-handling rig is a boom attached to a kingpost that is operated by a combination of lines rigged for the purpose. A *kingpost* is a short, sturdy mast capable of supporting a large amount of weight. A *boom* is a sturdy pole that is attached to the king post by a swivel-type device called a *gooseneck*. The boom is lifted up and down by a *topping lift* and it is moved from side to side by *guys* (sometimes called *vangs*).

Rigging is a general term for wires, ropes, and chains used to support kingposts or other masts, or to operate cargo-handling equipment. *Standing rigging* describes lines that support but do not move. Examples of standing rigging are *stays,* which are rigged fore and aft to support masts, and *shrouds,* which are rigged athwartships to provide support. *Running rigging* includes movable lines such as topping lifts and guys.

Mechanical Advantage

One of the basic principles you must know if you are going to be able to work efficiently in handling cargo is that a device you probably would have called a pulley before becoming a Sailor is called a *block* and can be rigged to give you a significant mechanical advantage and thereby save you a great deal of work and energy.

When blocks and lines are combined either to change the direction of an applied force or to gain a mechanical advantage, the combination is called a *tackle*. The simplest tackle is called a *single whip* and is made by running one line through one block that has been attached to something (such as the end of a boom). This tackle give you no mechanical advantage and is used solely to cause a change of direction in the force applied; for example, it allows you to lift a load straight up while you are pulling downward.

Figure 19.13. Rigging detail for a single swinging boom. The basic elements are the kingpost, boom, gooseneck, topping lift, and vangs (guys).

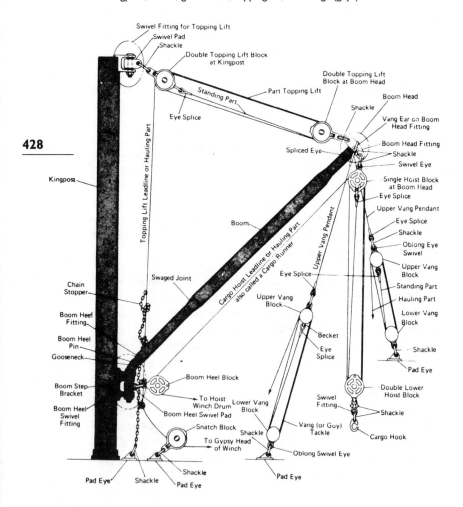

For obvious reasons, most tackles are rigged to achieve a mechanical advantage. The simplest tackle that provides this advantage is called a *runner*. Like the single whip, it uses only one line and one block, but by attaching the load to the block itself and allowing the block to move instead of attaching it to something, you gain a 2:1 mechanical advantage. (*Note:* In all cases described here, there is a certain amount of work lost because of friction, but the mechanical advantages gained are close enough for us to approximate them for simplicity.) That means that you will be able to lift a 120-pound load by using only 60 pounds of actual force—your load will seem only half as heavy as it actually is.

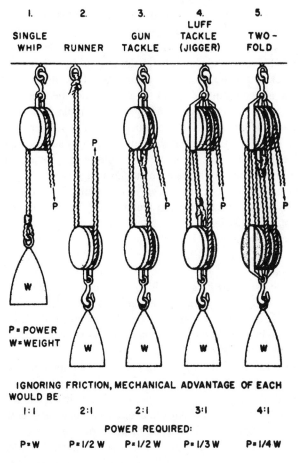

Figure 19.14. Blocks and tackles.

If you think about it, you can see that a runner would not be a very easy tackle to use (difficult to control), so a more common way to gain the same 2:1 advantage is to use *two* blocks (one moving and the other fixed) in a rig we call a *gun tackle.*

You have probably noticed that some blocks have more than one *sheave* (the "wheels" inside the block). Using a block with one sheave, combined with a block that has only two, we came up with a new rig called a *luff tackle.* This rig gives you a 3:1 mechanical advantage, which means your 120-pound load can now be lifted with only 40 pounds of force (it seems to weigh only one-third as much now).

Taking it another step, two blocks with two sheaves each can be rigged into a tackle we call a *twofold.* As you might have guessed, this rig provides an advantage of 4:1, meaning that you need only apply 30 pounds of force to lift your 120-pound load.

You may have noticed a pattern here that will help you to determine the theoretical mechanical advantage of a rig without having to come back to this book to look it up. If you look at the number of lines that are going in and out of the *moving* (not the fixed) block, it will tell you the mechanical advantage. For example, look at both the runner and the gun tackle. The number of lines running in and out of the moving block is two. This means the mechanical advantage is 2:1. The number of lines running in and out of the moving block on the twofold is four, so the mechanical advantage is 4:1.

Still more sheaves can be used in a two-block rig to gain even more advantage, but the friction factor begins to become sizable as you add more sheaves and lines so that the mechanical advantage is significantly degraded.

Basic Rigs

Perhaps the simplest cargo-handling rig is called a *single swinging boom.* If you have ever watched a crane at a construction site, this is comparable to a single swinging boom. The mechanical advantage of this rig can be increased by using one of the block-and-tackle combinations described above.

Booms can be used singly or in pairs. One common use of a pair of booms is the *yard-and-stay* rig. One boom, called the *hatch boom,* is positioned over the ship's deck or over a cargo hatch and the other, called the *yard boom,* is swung out over the side to hang over the pier. The cargo hook is attached to a pair of whips run from the end of each boom. The one attached to the hatch boom is called the *hatch whip* and the one attached to the yard boom is called a *yard whip.* By alternately easing out and heaving around on the two whips, the cargo hook (with its cargo attached) can be moved from the pier to the ship or vice versa.

Underway Replenishment (UNREP)

Before the techniques of underway replenishment (UNREP) were developed, a ship that ran low on fuel, supplies, or ammunition had to return to port, or she had to stop and lie to while she was replenished by small boats. This was a serious handicap that severely limited the effectiveness of ships at sea. With modern techniques of

Figure 19.15. A yard-and-stay rig.

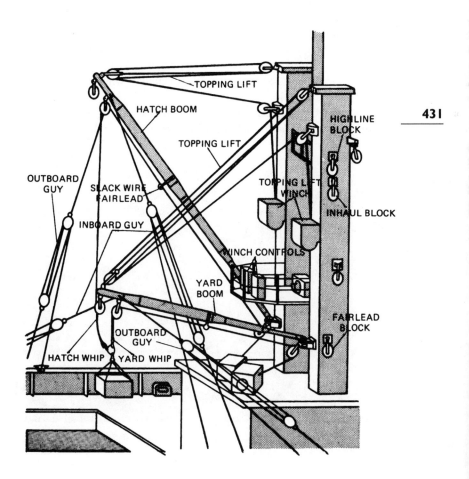

UNREP, an entire fleet can be resupplied, rearmed, and refueled within hours, while it is proceeding on its mission.

Some ships—such as replenishment tankers (AOR), oilers (AO), fast combat support ships (AOE), combat store ships (AFS), and ammunition ships (AE)—spend a great deal of their time conducting UNREPs. Other ships conduct UNREPs as necessary to keep themselves ready and on station. An aircraft carrier, for example, must UNREP with an ammunition ship to receive ordnance if it has been conducting strike operations and might conduct periodic UNREPs with its accompanying destroyers to replenish their expended fuel.

Different types of rigs are used for different purposes. In the discussion that follows, some of the more typical rigs will be described. For more detailed information, consult the naval warfare publication entitled *Replenishment at Sea* (NWP-14).

Cargo Rigs

Various combinations of winches, blocks, and booms have been found to be effective in passing cargo (such as ammunition, groceries, or spare parts) from one ship to another while they are both underway.

432

Burton rig. Cargo is moved from the delivering ship to the receiving ship by two burton whips, which correspond to the hatch whip

Figure 19.16. Underway replenishment (UNREP) keeps ships on station for long periods of time.

U.S. Naval Institute

and cargo whip in a *yard and stay rig* used alongside a pier. Winches on each ship handle the two whips involved. The delivering ship hoists the load clear, then the receiving ship takes in her burton whip as the delivering ship slacks hers off. When the load is spotted over the deck of the receiving ship, her whip is slacked and the load is eased to the deck. The entire operation requires skillful coordination between the two winchmen. They must keep constant tension on both whips at all times, whether they are running in or out, and they must keep the load just clear of the water. If the load is too high, the strain on all rigging is greatly increased. If the load is allowed to drop too low, it may be swept away by the passing sea. The maximum load that can be handled by this rig is 3500 pounds.

Housefall rig. In this method, both cargo whips are handled by the delivering ship. The whip that moves cargo to the receiving ship is called the outboard transfer whip (same as yard whip), and the whip that hauls the cargo hook back to the delivering ship is called the inboard transfer whip (same as cargo whip). Both winchmen are on the delivering ship. The maximum load is 2500 pounds.

Double housefall rig. This rig is used to speed transfers to ships that cannot handle more than one housefall rig. It is slower than housefalling to two separate receiving stations, but faster than house-falling to one station. In this method, the delivering ship uses two

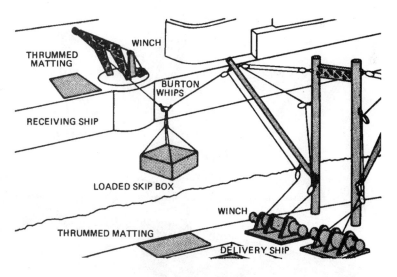

Figure 19.17. The Burton rig is similar to the yard-and-stay rig used alongside a pier.

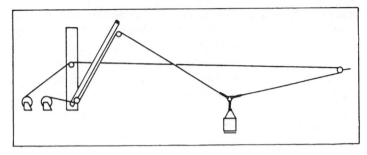

Figure 19.18. A basic housefall rig.

adjacent housefall rigs attached to a single point on the receiving ship. In handling cargo with this method, the delivering ship sends over a loaded net with one rig at the same time the other brings back an empty net from the receiving ship. The two nets pass each other in opposite directions each time a load is transferred.

Wire highline rig. This method involves a trolley moving on a highline that is attached to the receiving ship and kept taut by a winch on the delivering ship. An outhaul line (same as a yard whip) is heaved in by the receiving ship to move the load over. An in-haul line (same as a hatch whip) on the delivering ship returns the trolley for another load. The wire high-line is the standard procedure in trans-

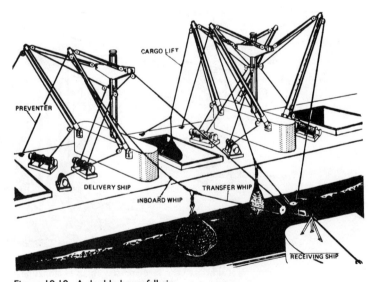

Figure 19.19. A double housefall rig.

ferring cargo to destroyers and other small ships, and at times is the best means of transfer to large ships. In order to use this method, the receiving ship must have a place in her superstructure high enough and strong enough to attach the highline.

Synthetic highline rig. This is the same as the wire highline rig, except that a synthetic (double-braided polyester) line is used instead of wire. Only light cargo can be handled. The receiving ship needs only a snatch block (block that can be opened up so that a line can be run through without using the bitter end of the line) attached to a pad-eye. The highline is kept taut during transfer either by 25 line handlers or by a capstan. The capstan cannot be used if personnel are being transferred. The trolley that rides the highline is moved by in-haul and out-haul lines, each handled by a minimum of ten personnel on deck. This rig is easily and quickly set up and is the safest method of transferring personnel from ship to ship.

STREAM rig. STREAM is an acronym for Standard Tensioned Replenishment Alongside Method. A wire highline is kept taut by a specially designed ram-tensioner assembly that automatically adjusts the tension as the two ships surge in and out (getting closer and farther away from each other), which inevitably happens as the ships steer into varying sea and wind conditions. With this stable line kept high and taut by the ram-tensioner, trolleys can be efficiently run

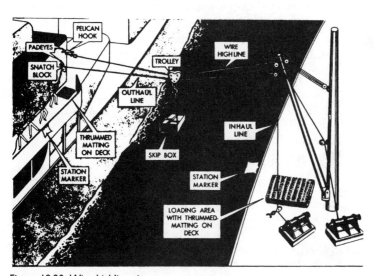

Figure 19.20. Wire highline rig.

back and forth on the wire. A device called a *traveling SURF* (standard UNREP receiving fixture) is sent over to the receiving ship and attached. This SURF combines in one device the wire tensioned highline and a combined in-haul/out-haul system that is used to run the trolley back and forth. This method has the advantage of simplicity for the receiving ship; she need only attach the traveling SURF to a secure point and everything that is needed is provided and controlled by the delivering ship. It also allows the ships to steam alongside at a safe distance (as much as 300 feet apart). This method can be adapted for transferring cargo or fuel.

Fueling at Sea

The method of fueling at sea depends upon the ships involved, the kind of fuel being transferred, and the weather and sea conditions. The various rigs differ mainly in the method by which the delivering ship sends the hose over to the receiving ship.

In the *conventional span-wire rig* the fuel hose is supported on a heavy wire that is attached to the receiving ship. This method allows the ships to refuel while maintaining an alongside distance of between 140 and 180 feet, which is a relatively safe distance that does not require any extraordinary shiphandling skills.

436

When the receiving ship is not equipped to handle a span-wire rig, the *close-in rig* is used. In this method, the hose is supported by whips leading from the hose-carrying saddles to booms, king posts, or other points high enough on the delivery ship to provide adequate support to keep the hose up and out of the water. This method (as you may have figured from its name) requires the ship to come in much closer than when using the span-wire rig—a 60- to 80-foot distance is required to effectively employ this method.

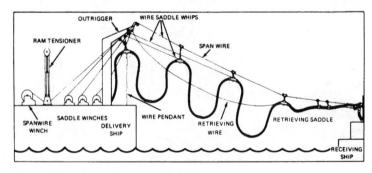

Figure 19.21. A typical refueling STREAM rig.

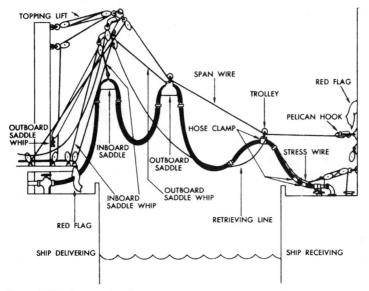

Figure 19.22. A span-wire rig.

437

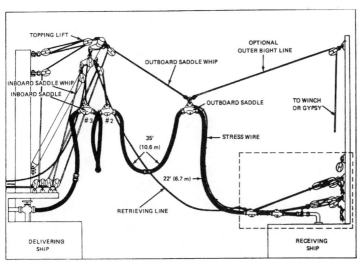

Figure 19.23. A close-in refueling rig.

The *fuel STREAM* rig is the same method used for transferring cargo (see above), having the advantages of simplicity for the receiving ship and a safer working distance.

Vertical Replenishment

Helicopters are often used to replenish stores and ammunition while ships are underway. Called *vertical replenishment* (VERTREP), this method can be used instead of, or at the same time as, alongside replenishment. By combining the two methods, a great deal of material can be transferred in less time. A particularly efficient method is to refuel alongside while receiving ammunition and/or stores via VERTREP. The two ships need not be alongside if VERTREP is the

Figure 19.24. A CH-46 Sea Knight helicopter lowers cargo to the flight deck of an aircraft carrier during a VERTREP.

only method of replenishment being used. The distance is limited only by the range of the helicopter(s) being used.

Cargo can be carried internally, but the preferred method is to sling it from a hook on the bottom of the helicopter. The load capacity of a Navy helicopter with an external load is as much as 7000 pounds.

Almost any ship can be replenished by helo if she has even a small open area for landing cargo, a larger unobstructed area overhead in which the helo can hover, and unobstructed access to the hover area so that personnel can clear out the delivered cargo.

20 Boats

The term "boat" refers to small craft limited in their use by size and usually not capable of making independent voyages of any length on the high seas. Do not make the mistake of calling a *ship* a "boat." It will mark you as a real landlubber.

The Navy uses thousands of boats, ranging from 9-foot dinghies to 135-foot landing craft. They are powered by either diesels, outboard gasoline motors, or waterjets. Most boats are built of aluminum, fiberglass, or steel. Newer Navy boats are designed and built using the International System of units (also known as SI or metric), but older craft were designed using the English units system (feet, inches, and so on).

Standard Boats

A standard boat is a small craft carried aboard a ship to perform various tasks and evolutions.

Landing Craft

These boats, carried by various amphibious ships, are designed to carry troops, vehicles, or cargo from ship to shore under combat conditions, to unload, to retract from the beach, and to return to the ship. They are especially rugged, with powerful engines, and they are armed. Landing craft are usually referred to by their designations (such as LCM or LCU) rather than by full names.

The principal types are the LCPL (meaning landing craft, personnel, large), LCM (landing craft, mechanized), and LCU (landing craft, utility). The most common in today's fleet are the LCMs.

There are two types of LCMs. Both types have a power-operated bow ramp, a cargo well, twin engines, and after structures that house enginerooms, pilot houses, and stowage compartments. The larger version, designated LCM-8 and often called "Mike 8," is 74 feet long, has a 21-foot beam, and is capable of carrying a heavy tank or

Figure 20.1. Landing craft, mechanized (LCM-6).

60 tons of cargo. The LCM-6 ("Mike 6"), is 56 feet long, has a 14-foot beam and a cargo capacity of 34 tons.

A much more sophisticated landing craft used in today's fleet is the LCAC (landing craft, air cushion). As you can tell by the name, this unusual craft floats on a cushion of air that allows travel over water and right up onto land to deliver troops, equipment, and supplies. They can clear an obstacle up to four feet high. They are 81 feet

441

Figure 20.2. An LCAC in the well deck of an LSD.

long and can carry a variety of vehicles or a load of more than 70 tons. Powered by four gas turbine engines, they are capable of speeds as high as 50 knots.

Workboats (WB)

There are two types of WBs, the 30-foot and the 15-meter (or 50-foot). The 35-foot WB is a twin screw craft with a forward cargo well and a bow ramp. The 35-foot WB is normally carried on board salvage ships and is used to assist ships in salvage operations, although it has been used for diving operations, underwater exploration, coastal survey, repair of other craft, and cargo transport between ships and shore. A portable "A-frame" is used to assist with cargo handling.

The 15-meter (50-foot) WB is a twin screw craft with steel hull construction and is a shallow draft cargo carrier. The 15-meter (50-foot) WB is intended for general-purpose missions and transportation of cargo. The craft has a pilot house aft and a forward cargo well deck.

Rigid Hull Inflatable Boats (RHIB)

These are versatile boats designed for service as a standard ship's boat. The seven-meter (24-foot) RHIB is a turbocharged, diesel-powered craft with a glass-reinforced plastic (GRP) hull. The hull form is

Naval Surface Warfare Center Detachment Norfolk, Carderock Division

Figure 20.3. A 15-meter workboat.

Naval Surface Warfare Center Detachment Norfolk, Carderock Division

Figure 20.4. Rigid hull inflatable boats (RHIB) have a glass-reinforced plastic hull.

a combination of a rigid planing hull with an inflatable tube. The craft are manned by a three-man crew and are provided with a canvas canopy forward.

443

Personnel Boats (PE or PERS)

These are fast, V-bottomed, diesel-powered boats with enclosed spaces specifically designed to transport officers, although smaller types are used for shore-party boats, lifeboats, and mail boats. They

Naval Surface Warfare Center Detachment Norfolk, Carderock Division

Figure 20.5. Personnel boats may become "gigs" when assigned to commanding officers, or "barges" when assigned to flag officers.

come in 8-, 10-, and 12-meter (26-, 33-, and 40-foot) lengths. The 8-meter (26-foot) boats have one enclosed cabin. The 10- and 12-meter (33- and 40-foot) boats have enclosed cabins forward and aft, and open cockpits amidships where coxswains steer by wheel. Those designed for officers are painted haze gray with white cabins. Those assigned for use by commanding officers, chief of staff, and squadron, patrol, or division commanders are called gigs and have a red stripe added just above the waterline. Personnel boats assigned to flag officers (admirals) are called barges. They have black hulls and a white stripe just above the waterline.

Utility Boats (UB)

These boats, varying in length from 18 feet to 15 meters (50 feet), are mainly cargo and personnel carriers or heavy-duty work boats. Many have been modified for survey work, tending divers, and minesweeping operations. In ideal weather, a 15-meter (50-foot) UB will carry 146 people, plus crew. Utility boats are open boats, though many of the larger ones are provided with canvas canopies. The smaller utility boats are powered by outboard engines. The larger boats have diesel engines.

Punts

These are open square-enders, 14 feet long. They are either rowed or sculled, and are generally used in port by side cleaners.

Special Boats

These boats, used by shore stations and for special missions, are not normally carried aboard ships as are the standard boats discussed

Naval Surface Warfare Center Detachment Norfolk, Carderock Division

Figure 20.6. This 15-meter (50-foot) utility boat can carry 146 people.

above. They include line-handling boats, buoy boats, aircraft rescue boats, torpedo retrievers, explosive ordnance disposal craft, utility boats, dive boats, targets, and various patrol boats. Many standard boats have been modified for special service.

Mark V Special Operations Craft (SOC)

This craft is also used for insertion and extraction of special warfare personnel. The craft is 82 feet long, and has twin diesel engines driving waterjets. The craft is capable of speeds in excess of 50 knots and is air deployable.

Patrol Boat, River (PBR)

This is a 31-foot, 25-knot, twin-diesel boat with a fiberglass hull and waterjet-pump propulsion that permits it to operate in 15 inches of water. The PBR is highly maneuverable and can reverse course in its own length. It carries radar, communications equipment, and machine guns.

Boat Crews

Most boats have permanently assigned crews. Crew size varies depending on the type of boat, but typically consists of the coxswain, engineer, and bowhook and sometimes a sternhook and boat officer. All must be qualified swimmers.

The boat crews represent their vessel and should for that reason take pride in their appearance and that of their boat. The efficiency and smartness of a ship's boats and boat crews reflect the standards of the ship. Clean white uniforms can be hard to maintain on some ships, but custom dictates that every day the ship's laundry wash and press a uniform for each member of the duty boat's crew. Ship regulations frequently require crewmembers to wear sneakers. This is a safety factor, but it also keeps the boats themselves looking good.

Coxswain

The coxswain is in charge of all personnel and equipment in the boat. Subject to the orders of the OOD and the senior line officer embarked, a coxswain otherwise has full authority and is responsible for the boat's appearance, safety, and efficient operation. The crew and passengers (including embarked troops) are required to cooperate fully with the coxswain. In fulfilling his or her responsibilities, the coxswain must be familiar with all details relating to the boat's care and handling. Equally important, the coxswain must be able to instruct the crew in all aspects of the general service and drills. The coxswain is also responsible for the appearance and behavior of the crew.

Engineer

The engineer must see that the engine is in good condition and ready to run. Only the engineer should work on the engine. The engineer may also perform the duties of the sternhook.

Bowhook

The bowhook handles lines forward when the boat is coming alongside a pier or ship. The bowhook also tends fenders and forward weather cloths (canvases spread for protection against the wind). In an open boat, the bowhook usually sits on the forward thwart (crossseat) on the starboard side, outboard. In bad weather, she or he may move to the lee side. The bowhook faces the bow and serves as a lookout. If the boat is decked over, the bowhook stands on the starboard after deck facing forward.

When the boat approaches the landing, the bowhook should be ready to spring ashore with the painter (a length of line secured to the bow of the boat for towing or making fast) and take a turn on the nearest cleat. When the boat approaches a ship's side, the bowhook should be in the bow with the boathook, ready to snag the boat line and make it fast. The bowhook should always have a fender ready to drop over the side if a bump is unavoidable.

Sternhook

The sternhook, likewise, should be ready at once to jump ashore with the stern line. In an open boat, the sternhook normally sits on the starboard side, outboard on the after thwart, facing aft. On decked-over craft, the sternhook usually stands on the port side of the after deck, facing forward.

Boat Officer

During heavy weather, and other times as deemed necessary, an officer (sometimes a chief petty officer) is assigned to each duty boat. A boat officer naturally has authority over the coxswain. The boat officer does not assume the coxswain's responsibilities, or relieve the coxswain of his or her normal duties, but is there to oversee the boat operations to ensure that safety is maintained at all times. The situation is somewhat like the relationship between the OOD and the commanding officer on the bridge. The coxswain and boat officer are responsible for the boat and for the safety and welfare of the crew and passengers.

Care of Boats

Maintenance greatly increases a boat's service life and assures its operational readiness. The boat crew takes great care to prevent corrosion of metal-hulled boats by maintaining the paint and specified preservation coatings in good condition and ensuring that the proper number of zincs are used to prevent electrolytic corrosion.

Maintenance and repair of fiberglass hulls involve the same materials and techniques used on sports cars. Do not use laminates, resin, or hardeners without fully reading the enclosed instructions.

Repair minor damage, tighten loose bolts, and fix or replace leaking gaskets as soon as possible to prevent more repairs later. Secure all loose gear to avoid damage when the water gets rough. Keep the boat and its equipment free of dirt, corrosion, and accumulated grease.

Proper preventive maintenance is essential. Engine oil changes, battery servicing, and other maintenance should be performed in accordance with the planned maintenance system (PMS) for the boat. Gear housings, steering mechanisms, and other moving parts must be well lubricated. Fenders should be placed between boats when they are tied up. All rubber exhaust couplings should be checked for tightness and condition. When a boat is hoisted out of the water, the struts, propeller, sea suctions, and shaft bearings should be checked. Dog-eared propellers or worn shaft bearings cause heavy vibration, which may result in severe damage to the hull and/or engine.

Oil-soaked bilges are a fire hazard. When draining or filling fuel tanks or engine crankcases, avoid spilling diesel fuel or engine oil.

Boat Customs

Just as Navy ships adhere to certain customs and traditions, so do Navy boats.

Etiquette

Whenever Navy personnel board a boat, junior personnel embark first and seniors last. When the craft arrives at its destination, seniors will disembark first and juniors last. While embarked, seniors sit aft and juniors forward.

Salutes

When underway, it is customary for boats to exchange salutes just as personnel and ships do. The coxswain (or boat officer, if embarked) will attend to all salutes, and the coxswain of the junior boat will initiate the salute and idle the boat's engine during the exchange. The rest of the boat crew will stand at attention. Passengers will remain seated but come to seated attention (sit erect, looking straight ahead and not talking).

Flags and Pennants

The national ensign is displayed from Navy boats when:

> they are under way during daylight in a foreign port;
> ships are dressed or full dressed;
> they are alongside a foreign vessel;
> an officer or official is embarked on an official occasion;
> a uniformed flag or general officer, unit commander, commanding officer, or chief of staff is embarked in a boat of his or her command or in one assigned for his or her personal use; or
> when prescribed by the senior officer present.

Since small boats are a part of a vessel, they follow the motions of the parent ship regarding the half-masting of colors.

When an officer in command is embarked in a Navy boat, the boat displays from the bow the officer's personal flag or command pennant—or, if not entitled to either, a commission pennant.

In a boat assigned to the personal use of a flag or general officer, unit commander, chief of staff, or commanding officer, or when a civil official is embarked, the following flagstaff insignia are fitted at the peak:

Spread eagle. For an official whose authorized salute is 19 or more guns (secretaries of the Navy, Army, Air Force, Chief of Naval Operations, Commandant of the Marine Corps, and so on).

Halberd. For a flag or general officer whose official salute is fewer than 19 guns and for a civil official whose salute is 11 or more, but fewer than 19 guns (assistant secretaries of defense down to and including consul generals).

Ball. For an officer of the grade or relative grade of captain in the Navy and for a career minister, counselor, or first secretary of an embassy, legation, or consul.

Star. For an officer of the grade or relative grade of commander in the Navy.

Flat Truck. For an officer below the grade or relative grade of commander in the Navy, and for a civil official on an official visit for whom honors are not prescribed.

The head of the spread eagle and the cutting edges of the halberd must face forward. The points of the star must face fore and aft.

Boat Markings

Admirals' barges are marked with chrome stars on the bow, arranged as on the admiral's flag. The official abbreviated title of the flag officer's command appears on the stern in gold letters—CINCPACFLT (for Commander-in-Chief Pacific Fleet), for example.

On gigs assigned for the personal use of unit commanders not of flag rank, the insignia is a broad or burgee replica of the command pennant with squadron or division numbers superimposed. The official abbreviated title of the command, such as DESRON NINE, appears on the stern in gold letters.

The gig for a chief of staff not of flag rank is marked with the official abbreviated title of the command in chrome letters, with an arrow running through the letters. Other boats assigned for staff use have brass letters but no arrows.

449

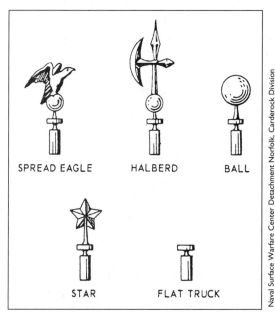

SPREAD EAGLE   HALBERD   BALL

STAR   FLAT TRUCK

Naval Surface Warfare Center Detachment Norfolk, Carderock Division

Figure 20.7. Flagstaff insignia.

Boats assigned to commanding officers of ships (gigs) are marked on the bow with the ship type or name, and with the ship's hull number in chrome letters and numerals. There is a chrome arrow running fore and aft through the markings. On boats for officers who are not in command or serving as chiefs of staff, the arrow is omitted and letters are brass. The ship's full name, abbreviated name, or initials may be used instead of the ship's type designation. An assigned boat number is sometimes used instead of the ship's hull number.

Other ship's boats are marked on the bow either with the ship's type and name or with her initials, followed by a dash and the boat number—for example, ENTERPRISE-1. These markings also appear on the stern of most boats. Letters and numbers are painted black. Numerals are painted as identifiers on miscellaneous small boats such as line-handling boats, punts, and wherries.

Boat Equipment

Every Navy boat in active service must have a complete outfit of equipment for meeting any ordinary situation. It is necessary to requisition part of the outfit. The coordinated shipboard allowance list (COSAL) lists items allowed for each boat. When a boat is turned in, its outfit also must be turned in, unless the boat is to be replaced by another of the same type. In that event, the outfit is retained. If a boat is to be replaced by one of a different type, the only items retained are those allowed for the new boat.

Hoisting and Launching Boats

The process of hoisting and lowering boats with a crane or davits is potentially dangerous and should be approached with the utmost attention to safety.

Launching

Before swinging out a boat to be lowered, first make sure that the hull drain plugs are in. Each person in the boat wears a life jacket, hard hat, and has a lifeline (monkey line) in hand. Run your sea painter outboard of everything on the ship, to the ship side of the bow, and belay with a toggle, so you can let it go without difficulty.

The boat's engine is started while the boat is in the air, but the clutch is never engaged until the falls are unhooked and hauled clear. In releasing the boat, the after fall is always unhooked first. Before starting ahead, take care that there are no trailing lines astern that

Figure 20.8. Hoisting and launching boats is an important seamanship skill.

might foul the screw. When the boat runs ahead and the painter slackens, the painter is thrown off by pulling out the toggle. The sea painter is hauled back to the ship by the light line attached to it.

Hoisting

When a boat comes alongside an underway ship to be hoisted in, it first secures the end of the sea painter. The shipboard end of the line is bent securely to a cleat or a set of bits. The boat end of the painter is lowered by a light line and made fast to a forward inboard cleat. The sea painter is never bent to the boat's stern or to the side of the bow away from the ship. If it is, the boat, when riding to the painter, will dive against the ship's side and perhaps capsize. It is also important that the boat be driven ahead and allowed to drop back on the sea painter to position itself exactly under the crane before lifting. Otherwise, it may broach to (turn crossways to the flow of water) and capsize as it starts to leave the water.

Once the boat rides to the painter, its engine is secured and the slings are attached. Steadying lines are secured to the cleats on the outboard side of the boat and brought back on deck to hold it steady as it rises. The bowhooks and sternhooks must fend if off the side.

Davits

Davits are devices specially designed to hoist and stow boats aboard ship. Hoisting boats with double-arm davits is somewhat more complicated than lifting them with a crane. The boat is attached to the sea painter in the same manner as with a crane—particularly if the ship has headway and must therefore take the same precautions against broaching to when the boat is lifted.

There are a number of different kinds of davits in use in the Navy.

Gravity davits are found on newer ships. Power is not required to lower boats. The boat lowers by gravity as it is suspended from the falls, and the descent speed is controlled with the boat's davit-winch manual brake. Several types of gravity davits are used. Depending on the design, a pair of modified davits may handle one to four boats; they are designated as single-, double-, or quadruple-davits. These are used mainly with amphibious craft.

An *overhead suspended davit* is a special gravity davit used beneath a sponson or other overhang found on aircraft carriers and helicopter landing ships.

A *slewing arm davit (SLAD)* is a mechanical davit with a single arm. The davit arm is mounted on a pedestal and rotates about a vertical axis when moving the boat outboard and inboard in a slewing type motion.

A *trackway davit* is a gravity davit consisting of an arm or arms mounted on rollers that run on an inclined trackway or trackways that are mounted on the deck. The incline on the trackway(s) is sufficient for gravity to cause the boat and arm(s) to move down the trackway(s) from the inboard position to the outboard position so that the boat may be lowered into the water.

Ready Lifeboat

Regulations require that a ship at sea have at least one boat rigged and ready to be lowered for use as a lifeboat. The ship's boat bill states the exact specifications a lifeboat must meet and the equipment it must have.

At the start of each watch, the lifeboat coxswain musters the crew, checks the boat and gear, has the engine tested, and reports to the OOD. Depending upon current operations, the crew may be required to remain near the boat.

The ready lifeboat, usually a RHIB, is secured for sea in the davits, ready for lowering. The lifeboat has its sea painter already rigged, and the lifelines are cleared for running. The boat should have a full tank of fuel, and the lubricating oil reservoir should be full. Keep an extra can of oil on board. The bilge should be clean and dry and the boat plug in place. Life-jackets are to be ready nearby or in the boat so the crew may don them quickly before lowering away.

21 Navigation

Every Sailor—even if she or he is an engineer, storekeeper, or airman—must have an understanding of basic navigational techniques. Living and working in the Navy you will serve in ships or at least have some contact with them. You may be tasked with standing a lookout watch or expected to help during a shipboard evolution that will require some knowledge of the skills discussed in this chapter.

Figure 21.1. Every Sailor must have an understanding of basic navigational techniques.

Knowing what a ship is doing and why it is doing it will greatly enhance your experiences at sea, even if you are not directly involved in the actual operations. Ships rely on boats for a variety of routine and emergency purposes and you may find yourself in a boat needing some basic navigational skills.

Elements of Navigation

Navigation is all about finding your position on the earth and then successfully moving to another position. The skills needed are based to a large degree on your ability to measure distance, speed, direction, and time. You may already have a good working knowledge of some of the skills and techniques described in this chapter. Others will probably be new to you.

Position

What you would call your "location" in civilian life is called *position* in nautical navigation. Using such things as visual bearings and radar ranges and then plotting them on nautical charts, navigators can determine their position.

455

Latitude and Longitude

To be able to pinpoint our position anywhere on the earth, ancient geographers came up with a grid system that covers the earth with imaginary lines called *latitude* and *longitude*.

Knowing that the earth spins on what is called its *axis* (notice that this word is similar to "axle," which is what a wheel turns about), these geographers chose the two points where the axis passes through the earth as their initial points of reference, calling them the *North* and *South Poles*.

Because these early geographers were Englishmen and England was, to them, of prime importance, they drew a line from one pole to the other that passed through the town in England where the Royal Naval Observatory was located—Greenwich—and called this line the *prime meridian* (sometimes called the *Greenwich meridian*). The rest was easy after that. They next extended the line up the other side of the world, so that it divided the earth into two halves. This other line—opposite the prime meridian—is called the *international date line*.

Another line was drawn at right angles to this prime meridian/international date line, exactly halfway between the poles, and was named the *equator*.

More lines were then constructed to gird the entire earth in a grid system. Lines drawn parallel to the equator are called parallels of latitude and lines drawn like the prime meridian (through the poles) are called lines of longitude.

The location of any place on Earth can be described by its latitude (the distance north or south of the equator) and longitude (the distance east or west of the prime meridian). Latitude is measured in degrees north or south of the equator, with 0 degrees at the equator and 90 degrees at each pole. Longitude is measured in degrees from the prime meridian, either east or west, and 180 degrees each way (until they meet at the international date line) so that they total 360 degrees. When a position is described using latitude and longitude together, it is often referred to as the position's *coordinates*.

For more precise measurements, degrees can be subdivided into *minutes* and they can be further subdivided into *seconds*. There are 60 minutes in a degree of latitude or longitude and 60 seconds in a minute.

456

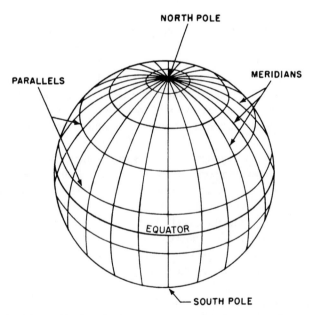

Figure 21.2. Parallels of latitude and meridians of longitude enable us to pinpoint a position anywhere on the earth.

Degrees are normally written using a small circle, minutes are written using a small symbol that looks like an apostrophe, and seconds are written using something that looks like quotation marks. So, "seventy-seven degrees, eighteen minutes, and eleven seconds" would be more simply written as 77°18′11″.

Using this standardized system of longitude and latitude, you can describe any point on Earth with great precision and consistency. For example, if you are standing in downtown Cleveland, Ohio, your position would be at coordinates 41°30′07″N and 81°45′17″W (read "forty-one degrees, thirty minutes, seven seconds north" and "eighty-one degrees, forty-five minutes, 17 seconds east"). Anyone with a map of Ohio could find your position with great precision using these coordinates.

Charts

On land, these positions would be plotted on maps that have latitude and longitude grids superimposed on them. But for plotting positions in the oceans, along shorelines, or on the waterways of the world, we use what are called *charts.* These, too, are marked with latitude and longitude lines and can be used to pinpoint positions, even in the middle of the world's largest oceans.

457

Distance

To find how far you are from land or how far you have to go to reach a rendezvous point, you will need some means of measuring distance. At sea, distance is measured in *nautical miles.* It is important for you to realize that a nautical mile and a land (or statute) mile are not the same. A nautical mile is about 6076 feet, or roughly 2000 yards. A land mile is 5280 feet. While this difference is not much (796 feet) when we are talking about one mile, it can become very significant when hundreds (or even thousands) of miles are involved.

A very useful aspect of the nautical mile is that it is equal to approximately one minute of arc measured along any meridian. On a map using land miles, you must refer to a mileage scale in order to measure distance, but because a nautical chart will always have longitude marked on it, you will have a handy reference for measuring distance simply by comparing it to the number of minutes of latitude along a nearby meridian.

Speed

In nautical navigation, speed is measured in *knots,* a seaman's term that means nautical miles per hour. Do not show yourself to be a landlubber by appending the words "per hour" to a ship's speed in knots. For example, a ship makes 27 knots, never 27 knots per hour.

Remember that a nautical mile is longer than a land mile. This means that a ship making 25 knots is traveling faster than a car on land that is clocked at 25 miles per hour. (In one hour, the ship will have traveled 151,900 feet [25 × 6076] while the car will have only gone 132,000 feet [25 × 5280].)

Direction

This is determined by a compass. You are probably already familiar with the four cardinal directions of north, east, south, and west. In the days of sail, when ships could not be steered with a great deal of accuracy, compasses with 32 divisions called *points* were the standard. These points had names such as "northwest-by-north" and "east-southeast."

Modern vessels can be steered much more accurately, so modern compasses have *360* divisions called *degrees*. Directions are always expressed in three digits and are measured clockwise from north, so east is 090 degrees, south is 180 degrees, west is 270 degrees, and

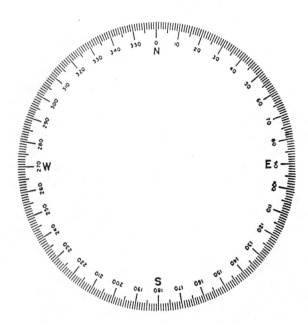

Figure 21.3. Modern compasses have 360 divisions, called degrees.

north is either 360 or 000 degrees, whichever designation is most convenient.

Nautical charts have what is called a *compass rose* printed on them (often there is more than one on a chart) which is used to determine accurate directions on the chart. Using a compass rose and the appropriate instruments, you can plot and measure lines in specific directions on a chart.

When ships steer in a specific direction, it is called a *course*. When you sight an object that is in a given direction from your ship, it is called a *bearing*.

Time

As already discussed in chapter 1, the Navy always uses 24-hour time, not civilian time with its confusing "A.M." and "P.M." designations. Some other things about time in the Navy are important not only for navigation but for clear communications and consistency of operations. Because, as a Sailor in the U.S. Navy, you are (either potentially or actually) a world traveler, you need to have an understanding of some of the fundamentals of world time.

You probably are aware that people living on the West Coast of the United States are in a different time zone from those living on the East Coast and that when it is 0800 in California, it is 1100 in New York. For convenience and to allow for the daily passage of the sun as the earth rotates on its axis, the entire world is divided into time zones.

Because there are 24 hours in the day and we know there are 360 degrees of longitude, it makes sense that each time zone would be 15 degrees of longitude wide ($360 \div 24 = 15$). And since the convention is to use the prime or Greenwich meridian as the beginning of longitude, it also makes sense that the first or reference time zone should be the one that includes Greenwich, England. This is called *Greenwich Mean Time* or *GMT*. The first time zone east of the one at Greenwich is one hour later (because the sun has already been there and passed on), and the first time zone west of Greenwich is one hour earlier.

In the Navy, because our ships and aircraft are mobile and often change time zones, and because it is important to military commanders to be able to refer to a common time when sending out messages to units scattered all over the earth, it is essential that we have a common reference time. For example, if the Chief of Naval Operations wanted to send out a message to all Navy submarines to report their positions at exactly the same time, he could not say simply "report at noon" because noon at San Diego is very different from noon in the Mediterranean Sea. He could say, "noon Washington, D.C., time,"

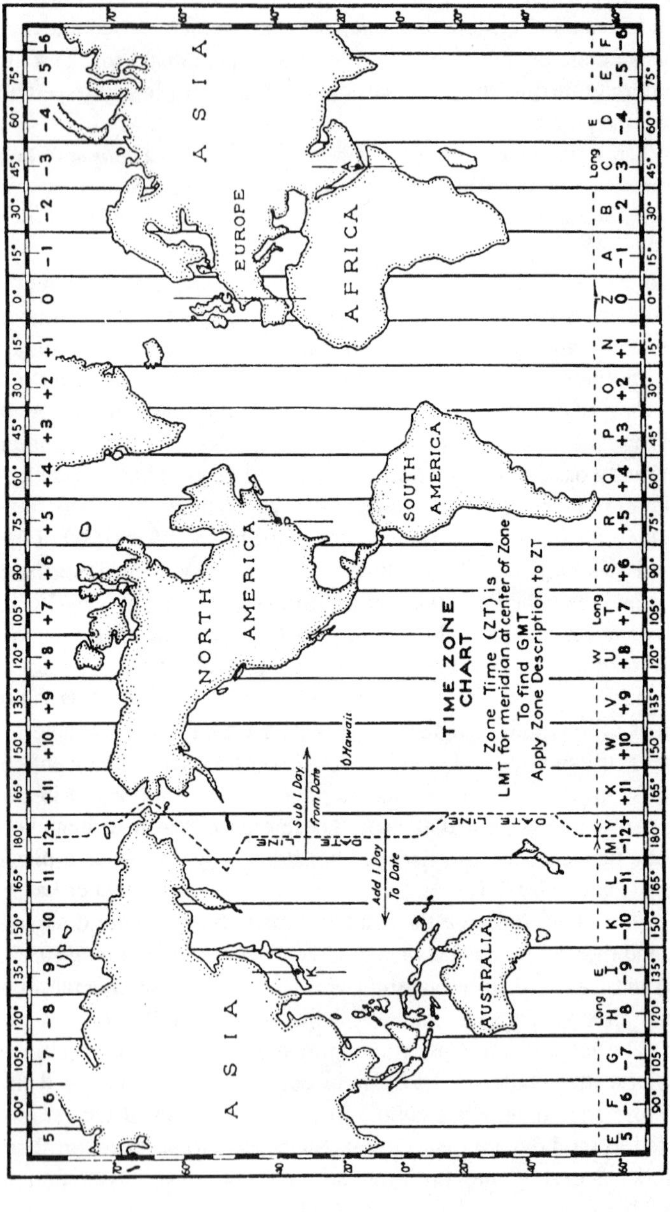

Figure 21.4. Time zone chart of the world.

but that would require every submarine to convert their local time to that of Washington. To simplify matters, the entire Navy, while keeping local time for convenience, also keeps GMT for common reference. You will often see clocks on ships (and at all naval installations for that matter) that are always kept set on GMT, no matter where in the world the ship might be. You will recognize these clocks as having been set to the reference time because they will be clearly marked either "GMT" or (more often) with a Z or "Zulu." This is because each time zone in the world is assigned a letter to identify it easily, and GMT is identified by the letter Z. You will often hear Sailors say something like "the last aircraft will take off at 0756 Zulu." This tells you that the time being used is the worldwide reference time rather than the local time.

If you look at a time-zone chart, you can see that each time zone is not only marked with a letter (Washington, D.C., is in time zone *R* or "Romeo" and Italy is in *A* or "Alfa"), but each one has a number preceded by a plus or minus sign. These numbers tell you what you need to do to convert your local time to GMT (or Zulu time). For example, Washington's Romeo time zone has the number "+5" marked on it. This means that you need to add five hours to your local time in order to know Zulu time. If it is 1322 on your wristwatch in Washington, you know the correct GMT is 1822.

Soundings

When navigating, you must obviously always be aware of the depth of the water in order to prevent your ship or boat from running aground. The depth of the water can also be a useful tool for determining your position. If you have a chart that shows the depths of the water, called *soundings,* you can use that information to help you decide where you are. For example, if your chart indicates a place where the bottom suddenly drops off into much deeper water (at an underwater cliff, for example), by watching your *fathometer* (an electronic instrument that reads the depth of the water by bouncing sound waves off the bottom) you will be able to tell when you have reached that point.

Soundings on a chart are sometimes given in feet and sometimes in fathoms. Be sure you know which your chart is using because there is a big difference (remember from a previous chapter that a fathom equals six feet). Steaming a ship with a 20-foot draft into waters that have been sounded at 11 fathoms (66 feet) is obviously a much better idea than taking that ship into 11 *feet* of water.

The Art and Science of Navigation

Mariners must rely upon a wide variety of methods, instruments, and sources of information in order to navigate effectively. Some of the techniques and practices described here you will never use, others you may use often. In any case, the professional Sailor will have a good working knowledge of the principles of navigation, and those who must navigate on a regular basis—such as quartermasters, OODs, and boat coxswains—come to appreciate why navigation is described as both an art and a science.

Methods of Navigation

Humans have been navigating the waters of the earth for thousands of years. In all that time, many means of navigation have been developed. All of them have in common the simple goal of determining one's position at sea (or in waterways), but how this is achieved can be as simple as taking visual sightings of objects on nearby land or as sophisticated as interpreting signals from a satellite orbiting the earth.

Piloting

Our earliest ancestors stayed within sight of land and used familiar landmarks to determine where they were and where they were going. This form of navigation—still used today—where the navigator relies on landmarks or on manmade navigational aids (such as buoys and lighthouses) is called *piloting*. This is the primary means of navigating when entering or leaving port or when traveling in coastal waters.

Dead Reckoning

With the invention of navigational instruments (such as the compass), navigators were able to venture onto the open sea by practicing an unreliable but better-than-nothing form of navigation called *dead reckoning*. This is simply the practice of starting from a known location and, with your compass, steering a specific heading. By calculating the elapsed time and your speed, you can come up with an estimate of where you think you are. This method can be refined by factoring in known current and wind conditions and is far better than merely blindly traveling about, but it is the least reliable means of navigation. In modern times, it is used only when no other forms of navigation are available.

From earliest times, man has been fascinated with the night sky; this
fascination eventually led to a more reliable method of navigating on
the open sea, called *celestial navigation*. By using the fixed stars and
the predictable planets, sun, and moon as guideposts, mariners developed ways of sighting these heavenly bodies (using a sextant). By
then performing mathematical calculations they were able to figure
out their own position on the earth. These methods were particularly
useful on the open sea where there are no other references available.
Assuming the navigator is able to get accurate sightings and performs
the calculations with precision, this method is a reasonably accurate
means of determining your position at sea.

Electronic Navigation

The advent of electricity ushered in a whole new realm called *electronic navigation*. Using radio beacons, radar equipment, satellites,
and other sophisticated developments, mariners can now navigate
with accuracy and relative ease so long as the needed electrical power
is available and the sophisticated equipment is functioning properly.

Combining Methods

463

The true mariner never relies on just one method of navigation. Fog
can obscure landmarks and buoys, making piloting difficult if not
impossible. Erratic currents and compass errors can reduce the reliability of dead reckoning. Clouds can obscure the heavenly bodies,
making celestial navigation impossible. And power failures or excessive moisture in an important electronic component can render the
most sophisticated electronic systems totally useless. The smart navigator uses all means available to check and double-check his or her
work.

Lines of Position and Fixes

The key to correlating where you are on the earth and where you are
on a chart is what navigators call a *line of position* (LOP). There are
many ways to obtain these LOPs and good navigators will use them
all whenever they can. Two or more (the more the better) LOPs will
give you a *fix*, which is your exact location on a chart.

Bearings

If you look at an object using a sighting device that is linked to a
compass so that you can accurately measure its direction, you have
taken what is called a *visual bearing*. For example, if you can see a

lighthouse from your ship and you sight it through an *alidade* (see "Navigational Instruments and Equipment") and see that it is exactly due north, you can then locate that lighthouse on your chart and draw a line from it that extends in a due-south direction. This is a line of position; you now have an important clue as to your whereabouts on the chart. You may be sure that your position is somewhere along that line.

For simplicity, let us say that you can also see a watertower, and its visual bearing turns out to be due east. When you find the tower on your chart and draw a line due west from it, you have created another LOP, and again you know that you are located somewhere along that line. Where these two LOPS cross (intersect) on your chart is your exact location, and it is called a *fix*.

If you think about it for a moment, you will probably see why we draw the LOP on the chart in the direction opposite to the visual bearing we sighted. In doing so, you have used what is called a *reciprocal bearing*. You know that south is opposite north and that west is opposite east, so in our example it was easy to figure the reciprocals. But it will rarely work out that your bearings will be exactly due north or east. More often they will be something like 047° or 239°, so their reciprocal bearings are not so obvious. However, the solution is fairly simple. To get a reciprocal bearing, you must add or subtract 180°. Due north is 000°, so adding 180 gives you the reciprocal bearing of 180° (due south). East is 090°, so adding 180 gives us 270°, which is due west. Adding 180 to 047° gives us 227° and subtracting 180 from 239° yields a reciprocal bearing of 059°. In deciding whether to add or subtract the 180, remember that your answer has to be within the compass limits of 360° in order to keep it usable on your chart, so *add* if the visual bearing is less than 180° and *subtract* if the visual bearing is more than 180°.

Bearings can also be determined using radar, but they are less accurate than visual bearings and should be used with caution.

Ranges

The more LOPs you obtain, the more accurate your fix will be. You may acquire LOPs using a variety of methods. Besides the visual bearings discussed in the example above, you may obtain an LOP by taking a *range* (measuring the distance) to an object. To accomplish this, you will most likely use a radar but stadimeters and sextants (see "Navigational Instruments and Equipment") can also be used in some circumstances. When you obtain a range, you must plot it on your chart as an *arc* rather than a straight line as you did with visual bearings. This curved line is another form of LOP—once again, you know your position is somewhere along that line. By combining this range LOP with one or more other LOPs (either other range arcs or visual bearings) you will have established a fix and know your position.

Celestial LOPs

When using celestial navigation techniques, you take visual sightings of a heavenly body using a sextant and, with the aid of mathematical calculations (that you can do with the help of a computer or special tables designed just for that purpose), you can plot the result on your chart. Each sighting of a heavenly body produces an LOP and, combined with more celestial sightings or other information (such as an accurate sounding), can lead to the establishment of a fix.

Electronic LOPs

Electronic navigation techniques—whether using highly sophisticated systems such as the NAVSTAR GPS (Navigation System using Timing and Ranging Global Positioning System—usually referred to as simply "GPS") or the older Long-Range Navigation (LORAN) system—also gather information that leads to the establishment of one or more LOPs. The more sophisticated systems today seem to be producing instantaneous fixes, but in truth they are computing the received inputs and working with them in a manner similar to plotting LOPs in order to produce fixes.

Time, Speed, and Distance

Besides determining where you are at any given moment, the art of navigation is about getting where you want to go. The key elements you will need to work with to accomplish this are time, speed, and distance.

These elements are related by simple formulas that can be used to do the calculations necessary for navigation.

$$\text{Distance} = \text{Speed} \times \text{Time} \ (D = ST)$$

$$\text{Speed} = \text{Distance} \div \text{Time} \ (S = D/T)$$

$$\text{Time} = \text{Distance} \div \text{Speed} \ (T = D/S)$$

In the above formulas, it is assumed that the values used are as follows:

Distance is in nautical miles.
Speed is in knots.
Time is in hours.

For example, if you know that your ship has traveled at a speed of 10 knots for 3 hours, you will have traveled 30 nautical miles ($D = ST$).

Tables and instruments available to the navigator can be used to perform these calculations, but it is useful to be able to do them manually because you might not always have these aids available and because it helps you become a better navigator if you understand these relationships.

Navigational Instruments and Equipment

Just as the chemist has her test tubes and centrifuge, and the artist has his paintbrushes and palette, the navigator has certain equipment that is used in gathering the necessary information and specialized instruments that are used in plotting that information on charts.

Compasses

One of the earliest inventions to have a major impact on the science of navigation was the compass. In its initial form—before the days of electricity—a compass relied on the magnetic properties of the earth. Later, another version that made use of the miracle of electricity was created, called a *gyrocompass*. Each has its advantages and limitations. The magnetic compass is less accurate and subject to disturbances in the magnetic field, but it will continue to function through a power failure. The gyrocompass is much easier to use and more accurate, but it must have electrical power in order to function. For these reasons, ships will have both.

Magnetic Compass

The typical magnetic compass used aboard ship consists of a floating card with magnetic needles attached which naturally align themselves with the earth's magnetic field. The floating card is supported in a bowl on a pivot in such a way that allows the card to stay in place (aligned with the earth's magnetic field) while the ship moves about beneath it. The stand in which the whole compass is kept is called a *binnacle*.

The floating card is marked with the cardinal points—North, East, South, and West—and the subdivisions in between. A line called the *lubber's line* is marked on the compass bowl and is aligned with the ship's fore and aft line. As the ship turns, the lubber's line will move with the ship and line up on the floating compass card, showing the direction the ship is headed—known in navigational terms as the ship's *heading*.

Figure 21.5. A typical Navy magnetic compass. Note the lubber's line just to the right of due East, indicating the ship's heading is between 100 and 110 degrees.

Compass Errors. The magnetic compass always points toward magnetic north. This is a near-perfect system for finding a ship's heading, but a problem arises because the magnetic north pole is not in the exact same place as the true north pole (the one that is located at the axis of the earth's rotation and is used as the starting reference for our coordinate system of latitude and longitude). Because of this difference we must always apply a correction to the magnetic heading on the compass in order to tell where true north is. This is not as difficult as it sounds because the information you need to make this correction is marked right on your chart as part of the compass rose. This difference between magnetic north and true north is called *variation*.

To further complicate things, your ship itself causes a disturbance in the natural magnetic field that the compass relies upon. This dif-

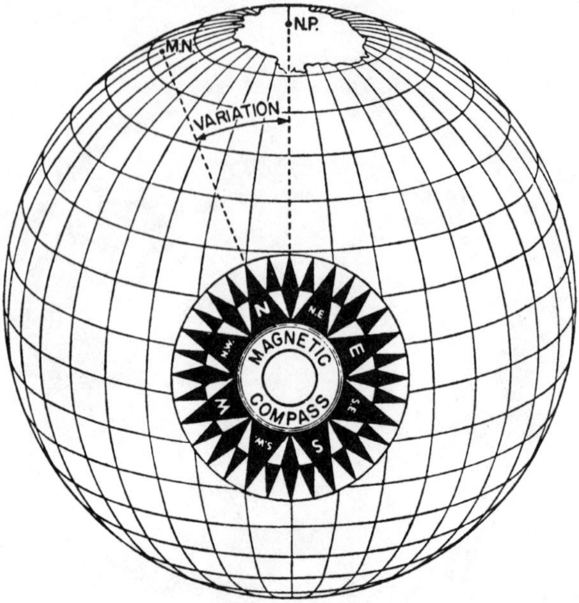

Figure 21.6. The magnetic compass aligns itself with the magnetic north pole (MN) instead of the geographic north pole (NP). The difference between the two is called variation.

ference is called *deviation* and requires another correction. The information you need to make this correction is also not far away. Each ship will have, either mounted to the binnacle or somewhere close by, a deviation table that tells you how much correction is necessary in order to convert the magnetic heading to true. A deviation table would look something like Table 21.1.

Periodically, the navigator and quartermaster perform an operation called *swinging ship* to update the deviation table for the vessel. To accomplish this, the ship steams in a complete circle from 0 to 360 degrees, and the amount of her compass deviation is noted at every 15-degree point. The results are compiled and new deviation tables made up and used from that point until the next swing ship is performed.

All compass errors (and their corrections) are described as easterly or westerly, never northerly or southerly.

Conversions. Because navigational charts can only be effectively used with *true* bearings and headings, it is important to know how to convert them from magnetic (what the compass is telling you) to true.

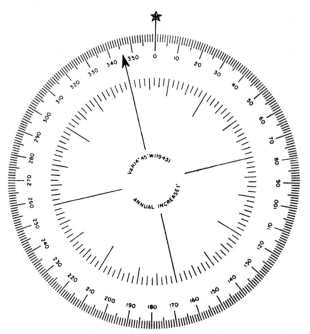

Figure 21.7. The compass roses that appear on nautical charts help the navigator to measure directions on the chart and to determine what the variation is in that part of the world. The star indicates true (geographic) north and the arrowhead is pointing toward magnetic north.

This is accomplished by applying the corrections for variation and deviation and is easier for most people to remember by the use of a nonsensical but effective memory aid. We begin by using certain letters to represent the parts of our calculation as follows:

C = Compass (the actual reading we get off the compass itself)
M = Magnetic (the actual magnetic heading after it has been corrected for deviation)
T = True (the true heading or bearing after all corrections have been applied)
V = Variation (from the compass rose of your chart)
D = Deviation (from the deviation table on your ship)

With these letters in mind, we can use the following memory aid to convert your compass readings to true: *C*an *D*ead *M*en *V*ote *T*wice *A*t *E*lections.

Table 21.1. Deviation table

Ship's Heading (magnetic)	Deviation	Ship's Heading (magnetic)	Deviation
000° (360°)	14°W	180°	13°E
015°	10°W	195°	14°E
030°	5°W	210°	12°E
045°	1°E	225°	9°E
060°	2°E	240°	4°E
075°	5°E	255°	1°W
090°	7°E	270°	7°W
105°	9°E	285°	12°W
120°	15°E	300°	15°W
135°	16°E	315°	19°W
150°	12°E	330°	19°W
165°	12°E	345°	17°W

Even though this phrase makes little sense, it has helped mariners remember how to convert their compass headings and bearings to true for centuries. What it tells us is to start with the reading on your *c*ompass (*C*an). Apply the correction for *d*eviation (*D*ead) to get the *m*agnetic (*M*en) heading. Then apply *v*ariation (*V*ote) to get your *t*rue (*T*wice) heading. The last part, *At E*lections, tells you that you should *a*dd *e*ast, which means that all easterly corrections should be added (and, conversely, all westerly corrections should be subtracted).

For example, if your compass is telling you that your ship is heading due east (090°) and you know from your deviation table that your correction should be 7°E, you would *add* 7 to 090 and find your magnetic heading to be 097°. If the compass rose on your chart told you that the magnetic variation for the part of the world covered by your chart is 4°W, you would then subtract 4 from 097 to get your true heading of 093°.

Sometimes, you will want to reverse the process, converting true headings or bearings to those you would expect to see on your magnetic compass. Some Sailors prefer to just use the "Can Dead Men Vote Twice At Elections" memory aid in reverse. But this can get a little confusing as to when to add or subtract, so others use "*T*imely *V*essels *M*ake *D*istance *C*ount *At W*ar" to remember this process. Still others make up their own memory aids.

This compass does not rely on the magnetic properties of the earth. Instead, it uses a heavy flywheel driven at high speed by an electric motor mounted on gimbals that free it to move in all directions. This mechanism allows the flywheel to remain more or less suspended in space, oriented with the axis of the spinning earth and, therefore, pointing toward true north.

The gyrocompass (often called simply "gyro") itself is usually located in a well-protected place below deck, but one of the advantages of this compass is that other compass cards that are electrically connected to the main gyro, called *repeaters,* can be placed on the bridge and in other parts of the ship, wherever they are needed. These repeaters show the same readings as the master gyrocompass and allow you to have many compasses from just one.

Gyro Error. The gyrocompass is not affected by variation or deviation. The motion of the earth causes the rotor to move so that its axis lies in a north-south direction. However, for mechanical reasons and because of the ship's vibrations, even the best gyrocompass will sometimes vary from true north. This gyro error is rarely more than a few degrees—often it is a half-degree or less—and normally it is constant over a long period of time and is not dependent on the heading of the ship.

Gyro error is determined at sea by shooting an azimuth (roughly equivalent to taking a bearing) to a celestial body where the exact bearing can be determined. In port or within sight of land, the error may be determined by sighting on two objects that are in line and their true bearing can be determined from a chart. This error is applied every time the compass is used, and the rule for these corrections is easy to remember if you use the word "GET" as a memory aid. Making a simple equation out of the word ($G + E = T$) will tell you that to go from *g*yro to *t*rue, you must add your *e*asterly error. For example, suppose you use your gyro to sight a church steeple and a watertower that are in a line, and the bearing you read is 277°, but a line drawn between the two on a chart indicates that the true bearing is actually 278°. You know that $277 + 1 = 278$, so you have a gyro error of 1°E. This means that all bearings taken by gyrocompass should have one degree added to them to get their actual true bearing for plotting on your chart.

Electronic Navigational Equipment

A variety of electronic systems are used by mariners to help them navigate. Some, such as LORAN and GPS, are specially designed as navigational systems that have transmitting stations on the earth or in orbit as satellites. Others, such as radar and sonar, are self-contained within the ship and do not have to rely on external stations.

Radar, originally developed as a means for detecting and approaching targets in warfare, has since evolved into a valuable electronic navigational aid. As a self-contained system it does not require external transmitting stations to be effective as a navigational tool. It is best suited for taking ranges, although it can be used (with caution) as a means of obtaining a bearing as well.

Sonar may also be used on a limited basis as a navigational tool. Designed primarily as a kind of underwater radar, using sound waves instead of radio waves to detect targets underwater, sonar can be used in conjunction with underwater topographical charts to determine one's position.

A device specifically designed for navigational purposes that is a kind of simplified sonar set is the *fathometer*. By sending a sound wave straight down beneath the keel of the ship and measuring the time required for it to return, you can determine the depth of the water.

Chronometers

The accurate measurement of time is critical to the success of the navigator. A simple clock is not normally accurate enough for navigational purposes, so navigators rely on a special device called a *chronometer*. Mounted in a brass case, which is in turn supported in gimbals in a wooden case to counteract the ship's motion, chronometers are kept in a cabinet in the chart room, usually on the ship's centerline, where they are protected against shock and temperature changes. A good chronometer never deviates more than a hundredth of a second from its average daily rate.

Chronometers are set to show Greenwich Mean Time and are wound every day at exactly the same time. Once a chronometer is started, it is never allowed to stop, and it is not reset while aboard ship. Chronometers are checked against radio time signals, or GPS readings, fast or slow.

Visual Equipment

A lot of navigating is done with the eye. Visual bearings are a key part of piloting, and observations of the heavenly bodies are an essential part of celestial navigation. A number of devices have been created to enhance the power of the eye and aid in its precision.

Bearing Circle

This ring is placed over a compass and is equipped with sighting vanes (similar to the gunsight on a rifle) which, when lined up on an object, permits you to read that object's bearing from you. When you are told to "shoot a bearing" or "take a bearing" to an object, this simple device will aid you in doing so.

Azimuth Circle

Similar to a bearing circle, this is also a ring that is placed over a compass, but it has some extra attachments that will help you make a visual sighting on a celestial body. Determining the direction to a star, a planet, the sun, or the moon is an important part of celestial navigation and is useful for other things such as determining your gyrocompass error. When determining the direction of an object on the earth, you obtain a *bearing;* when determining the direction of a celestial body, you obtain an *azimuth.*

Telescopic Alidade

This device—often called simply an alidade—is similar to a bearing circle, but has a telescopic device permanently mounted to it so that you can see the objects you are "shooting" more clearly. A cross-hair on the lens improves your accuracy and a mirror device in the telescope allows you to read the bearing off the compass while looking through the scope.

473

Sextant

The sextant is a precision instrument that can measure angles in degrees, minutes, and seconds. In its most common use, the sextant takes the image of a star (or other celestial body) and, through a mirror system, makes the star look like it has been moved from up in the sky down to rest on the horizon. Having done this, the precision scales on the sextant allow the navigator to read the exact angle between the actual star and the horizon. This angle, called the altitude, is the basic measurement in celestial navigation that will (after a series of calculations) yield an LOP.

The sextant can also be used to measure the angle between two objects on the shore which can be used to help determine your position.

Stadimeter

If you know the height of an object, such as a lighthouse, a water-tower, or the mast of another Navy ship, the stadimeter can be used to measure its distance from you. It is effective for heights between

50 and 200 feet, and at distances of 200 to 10,000 yards. Like a sextant, the stadimeter measures angles, but it accomplishes this a little differently. By setting the height of an object on an adjustable scale, you then look through the stadimeter to make a reflected image of your "target" coincide with the actual direct image. The distance is then read from another scale.

Lookouts

One of the most useful elements of navigation and of safe shiphandling is the lookout. Radars and sonars may fail to detect such things as smoke, small navigational markers, objects close to the ship, flares, or people in the water. These must be reported by the lookouts—the eyes of the ship. Upon their alertness rests much of the safety of the ship and her crew.

You may very well stand lookout watches at some time during your stay in the Navy. As a lookout, you must do much more than keep your eyes open. You must know how to search in a way that will cover every inch of the sector you are assigned, and you must be able to report the location of an object to the OOD in a way that will give her or him the information she or he needs. You must watch for ships, planes, land, rocks, shoals, periscopes, discolored water, buoys, beacons, lighthouses, distress signals, floating objects of all kinds, and anything else unusual. You must not only be the eyes but the *ears* of the ship as well, and report sounds, such as fog horns, ships' bells, whistle buoys, airplanes, surf, and anything unusual. The golden rule of being a good lookout is "If in doubt, report it." It is better to give the OOD too much information than to miss the one critical piece of information that can put the ship in jeopardy.

How many lookouts a ship will have at any given time depends upon the size and type of the ship and the conditions in which she is operating. Small ships will usually have only three lookouts: two in the vicinity of the bridge (port and starboard) and one after lookout somewhere astern. Larger ships may have more lookouts assigned to provide additional coverage. Each is stationed where he or she can best cover the surface and sky within his or her assigned zone. If lookouts are stationed any distance away from the OOD, they will wear sound-powered phones so that they may expeditiously send reports. It is good practice for a lookout to only use one of the earphones on the sound-powered set so that the free ear can be used to listen for relevant sounds as described above.

Low-visibility lookouts. In fog or bad weather, additional lookouts are stationed immediately in the eyes of the ship (as far forward as practical) and on the bridge wings. Sound carries much farther in fog than on clear days, so a lookout must listen closely—especially if he or she is located in the bow—for whistles, bells, buoys, and even the wash of water against the ship's stem. For this reason, fog lookouts do not wear sound-powered phones. Another Sailor is assigned to man the phones at each fog lookout station to make reports to the OOD.

Night vision. If you were to go on night watch directly from a lighted compartment, you would be almost blind for a while. As your eyes become accustomed to the weak light, your vision gradually improves. After 10 minutes you can see fairly well, and after 30 minutes you have your best night vision. This improvement is called dark adaptation.

Obviously, it is unsatisfactory to have someone standing a lookout watch who does not have 100 percent vision. To prevent this lost time while your eyes are adjusting to the dark, you must be sure that your eyes are not exposed to any white light (such as everyday light bulbs and fluorescent tubes) before going on watch. Fortunately, the human eye's ability to see in the dark is not affected by red light. That is why you will see only red lights on after dark in berthing compartments and at the various watchstations. Even with these precautions, there are places in the ship where you might encounter white light, such as on the mess decks where you might want to go get a sandwich or a cup of coffee before going on watch. To protect your eyes from any unwanted exposure to white light, you must put on specially designed red goggles before going on night lookout duty at least a half-hour before you must report for your watch. Be sure to leave them on for the full 30 minutes. These goggles prepare your eyes for darkness without affecting your ability to go about normal prewatch activities such as writing letters, watching television, or getting dressed and ready for your watch. Even with this precaution, you should still give yourself an additional five minutes of adjusting to the outside conditions before actually assuming the watch. As you know, it will probably take longer than that to get a full report from the person you are preparing to relieve.

Once you have assumed the lookout watch at night, you must learn to use your "night eyes" effectively. Because of the way your eyes are made—the light receptors for white (daytime) light are in the center of your eye, while your night-vision receptors are located around the daylight ones, off center—you normally look directly at an object to see it best in the daylight, but in the dark you should look to one side of an object to see it best. This will take some practice, but once you get used to it, you will be amazed at how well it works.

At night, it is easier to locate a moving object than a stationary one. But most objects in or on the water move relatively slowly. To counter this, move your eyes instead. This technique will significantly enhance your ability to pick up targets in the night. Slowly scan the area in broad sweeps instead of stopping to search a section at a time. If you think you see something while scanning, avoid the natural tendency to look right at it. Use the off-center technique to confirm the sighting and then report it.

Binoculars. Contrary to widespread belief, it is not always better to search with binoculars. Several factors govern when and how they should be used. In fog, for instance, they should not be used at all. At night, however, they will enhance your vision and should be used often.

Keep in mind that while they significantly magnify, binoculars' field of view is only about 7 degrees, which is pretty narrow. This means you can see objects at considerably greater distances than with the naked eye, but you are able to view only a very small portion of your assigned sector while looking through them. To counter this limitation, you should use the *scanning technique* when using binoculars to search for targets. This is a step-by-step method of looking. To understand this technique, try moving your eyes around a room or across the horizon rapidly and note that as long as your eyes are in motion, you see almost nothing. (You may have noticed this if you ever saw a video shot by someone who was moving the camera too rapidly—everything is a blur.) Now allow your eyes to move in short steps from object to object. You will be able to see what is there. When searching a seemingly empty stretch of sea, make yourself search your sector in short steps (approximately 5 degrees at a time), pausing between steps for approximately five seconds to scan the field of view. At the end of your sector, lower the glasses and rest

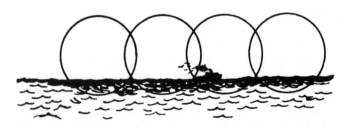

Figure 21.8. Step-by-step scanning.

your eyes for a few seconds, then search the sector in the reverse direction with the naked eye.

A sky lookout searches from the horizon to the zenith (overhead), using binoculars only to identify a contact. Move your eyes in quick steps—also about 5 degrees—across your sector just above the horizon, shift your gaze up about 10 degrees, and search back to the starting point. Repeat this process until the zenith is reached (you are looking straight up), then rest your eyes for a few seconds before starting over.

Reports. Every object sighted should be immediately reported to the OOD, no matter how insignificant it may seem to you. The report consists of two basic parts: what you see, and its bearing (direction) from the ship. Aircraft sighting reports also include altitude (called position angle).

Because they do not always have access to a compass at their watchstation, lookouts report objects in degrees of *relative bearing.* You will remember that navigational directions are described by true bearings where 000° represents true north, 090° is east, and so on. Relative bearings are similar to true bearings except that they are ori-

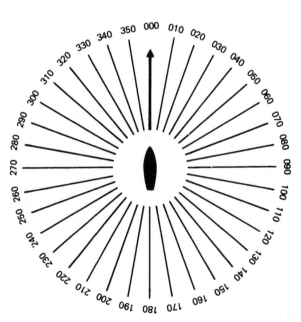

Figure 21.9. Relative bearings are measured clockwise from the ship's head and locate an object in relation to the ship. They have nothing to do with geographical directions.

ented on the ship's bow instead of true north. Therefore, 000° represents the ship's bow when using relative bearings. Just as true bearings progress in a clockwise direction, so do relative bearings. If you want to report a periscope that is broad on the ship's starboard side, its relative bearing is 090°. A fishing boat dead astern would be reported as 180°R, and a buoy approximately halfway between would be 135°R.

Bearings are always reported in three digits and spoken digit by digit. For example, you would report a merchant ship broad on your port side as "two-seven-zero degrees relative."

An object in the sky is located by its relative bearing and position angle. The position angle of an aircraft is its height in degrees above the horizon, as seen from the ship. The horizon is considered to be zero degrees and directly overhead is 90 degrees. Position angles can never be more than 90 degrees, and they are given in one or two digits and spoken as a whole number, not digit by digit. The words "position angle" are always spoken before the numerals. Thus, if you spot an aircraft flying just a little above the horizon halfway between the bow and the starboard side of your ship, you would report it as

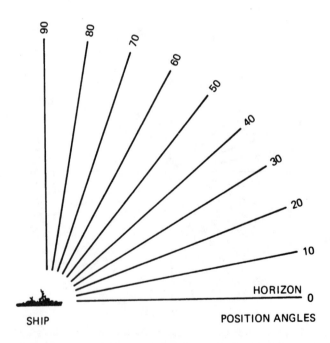

Figure 21.10. Position angles locate an object in the sky.

"zero-four-five degrees relative, position angle ten." A helicopter Navigation
hovering dead astern of your ship, about two-thirds of the way
between the horizon and straight up, would be reported as "one-eight-
zero degrees relative, position angle sixty."

Plotting Instruments

Once information, such as bearings or ranges, has been obtained
using the navigational equipment described above, it must be plotted
on a chart to be of use to the navigator. A number of instruments have
been developed—some of them centuries old—to aid the navigator in
this process.

Compasses and Dividers

Somewhat confusing is the fact that one of the instruments used by
the navigator has the same name as one of the major pieces of equipment also used in navigation—the compass. You probably are familiar with *this* compass from your math classes in school. It is a pencil
point and a sharp metal point joined in such a way as to facilitate the
drawing of circles and arcs. This instrument is particularly useful for
plotting ranges on charts.

A pair of dividers is much like a compass except that both points
are sharp metal ones. This instrument is primarily used to measure
distances on charts.

479

Parallel Rulers

The name of this instrument describes it well. Two straight-edged
rulers are joined by hinged arms that allow a direction to be moved
across a chart by "walking" the rulers, such as when the navigator
wants to move a bearing line across the chart to measure its direction
on the compass rose.

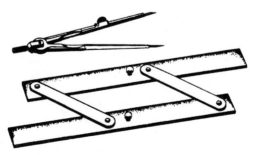

Figure 21.11. Dividers and parallel rulers.

Parallel Motion Protractor

Also called a universal drafting machine, this instrument is clamped to a chart table and aligned with the chart so that both distance and direction may be plotted at once. It is a fast and efficient means of plotting. The parallel motion protractor (often simply called a PMP) provides a very reliable method for plotting direction because, once aligned and set, there is little chance for it to slip as can happen with parallel rulers. This device, in essence, provides a movable compass rose that can be moved all over the chart with ease.

Nautical Slide Rule

This circular device simplifies time, distance, and speed calculations. By entering two known variables (such as distance and speed) on the appropriate scales, you can read the third (such as time) as needed.

Navigational Publications

Many publications are available which provide the information a navigator can use to better navigate his or her vessel. Nautical charts are printed and updated by the National Ocean Service (NOS) and the National Imagery and Mapping Agency (NIMA).

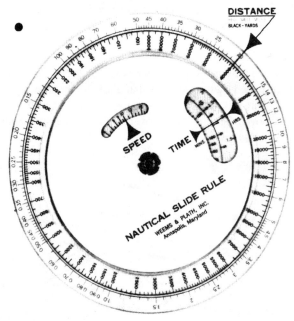

Figure 21.12. A nautical slide rule.

Additional valuable information about the various navigational aids found on these charts and supplementary information about what you can expect to find in the various waterways of the world is found in several important publications. For American waters, valuable supplementary information is contained in two publications: *Light Lists,* published by the U.S. Coast Guard, and *Coast Pilots,* published by NOS. For the other waters of the world, you must use the NIMA's *List of Lights* and *Sailing Directions* to obtain similar help.

NIMA also publishes useful information for U.S. Navy vessels in publications called *Fleet Guides.* These not only contain useful navigational information, but administrative and logistical data as well.

Tide Tables, which predict the height of the tide at given times, and *Tidal Current Tables,* which predict the direction and velocity of the currents associated with tidal variation at given times, are essential to the navigator.

Prepared jointly by the U.S. Naval Observatory in Washington, D.C., and the Royal Greenwich Observatory in England but published in the United States by the Government Printing Office, *The Nautical Almanac* (published once a year) and *The Air Almanac* (published twice a year) provide a wealth of data about the precise times and positions of celestial bodies as they rise, travel across the sky, and set.

Another set of publications used for celestial navigation is the *Sight Reduction Tables for Marine Navigation,* published by NIMA.

Various other publications are useful to the navigator, such as *Tables of Distances between Ports* (NIMA), *Tables of Distances between United States Ports* (NOS), *Handbook of Magnetic Compass Adjustment* (NIMA), and the *Radar Navigation Manual* (NIMA).

For those who want to become skilled navigators, much more detailed information about the art and science of navigation can be found in the NIMA publication, *American Practical Navigator* (also called "Bowditch" after its original author), and the following books, published by the Naval Institute Press: *Dutton's Navigation* and *Marine Navigation* by Richard R. Hobbs. Many other commercially produced publications can be useful to the serious student of navigation.

Tides, Currents, and Winds

Despite all of the advances of modern technology, ships are still very much subject to the natural forces at sea and in coastal waters. Anyone who ventures onto the great waters of the world must do so with an understanding that tides, currents, and winds will have an effect on what they do. Whether you are piloting a small boat on a narrow water-way or are part of the team that turns an aircraft carrier into the wind to launch aircraft, the more you understand about how these forces work and what their effects will be, the better mariner you will be.

Tides

Tides are very important in naval operations. Amphibious landings are normally scheduled for high tide so that troops and equipment can land well up on a beach. In some harbors, deep-draft ships may be able to enter only at high tide. Large ships are usually launched or dry-docked at high tide. Ships going alongside piers in channels subject to strong tides and currents normally wait for slack water, when the tide is neither ebbing nor flooding. Every Sailor whose responsibility is the handling of a vessel must understand the meaning and cause of various tidal conditions.

The term *tide* describes the regular rise and fall of the water level along a coast or in a port. The gravitational attraction of the moon is the primary cause of tides; it pulls water away from the earth. The earth's spinning motion also causes a bulge of water on the side of the earth opposite to the moon. Since the moon orbits the earth every 24 hours and 50 minutes, the result of these forces causes two low and two high tides at any given place during that period. The low and high tides are each 12 hours and 25 minutes apart. The sun also affects the tide, but it is so much farther away than the moon that its pull is not nearly as great. It does, however, have an effect such that the rise and fall of tides are more complicated than they would otherwise be. Despite these variables, tides can be predicted with relative certainty and the successful mariner will take advantage of this predictability whenever possible.

A tide rising or moving from low to high water is said to be *flooding*. When the tide is falling, after high tide, it is said to be *ebbing*. The difference in depth between a high tide and the next low tide is considerable in many harbors; areas that are safe for a powerboat at high tide may be completely dry at low water. In some areas of the world, you might board a vessel from a pier in the morning by stepping directly across, using a level brow, and that same afternoon, you would have to use a ladder to climb up to the main deck.

Currents

In most harbors and inlets, tides are the chief causes of currents; however, if the port is situated on a large river, its flow may also have a marked effect on tidal currents. The flow of a large river will prolong the duration of an ebbing current, and the velocity of that current will be considerably greater than that of the floodtide caused by effects of the moon and sun.

Where currents are chiefly caused by the rise and fall of the tide, their direction and speed are largely governed by the shape of the shoreline and the contour of the ocean bottom. In a straight section of confined waterway, the current tends to flow most rapidly in the center and much more slowly in the shallower water near either shore. If a boat goes with the current, the coxswain generally wants to stay near the center of the waterway. If a boat goes against the current, the coxswain stays as close to shore as the prevailing water depth will allow.

In many wide inlets, near the time of slack water the current may actually reverse itself in part of the inlet; while the ebb is still moving out of the main channel, a gentle flood may start near one shore. This condition, where it exists and is understood, can be helpful to a small-boat operator.

Where there is a bend in the channel, the current flows most strongly on the outside of the bend. This effect is very marked, particularly with a strong current. In some areas, a strong current can create rough water called tide rips. These are usually shown on charts and should be avoided. Every vessel, regardless of size, must make some allowance for the current's *set* and *drift* (direction and speed), which affects the course to be steered.

One more thing to bear in mind about currents: only on the coast does the turn of the current occur at the time of high water. In many ports, owing to the effect of the land's shape on water flow, there may be a very considerable difference between the time of high (or low) water and the time that the current starts to ebb (or flood).

Winds

Modern naval vessels are not dependent on the wind for power, as sailing ships were, but at times the wind's effect on a ship can be considerable. Although sails are no longer used on naval vessels, the area of the ship's hull and superstructure exposed to the wind is still called *sail area*. The more sail area a ship has, the more effect wind has on it. For example, an aircraft carrier, with all of its massive sail area, will have a more difficult time moving into a pier that has an offsetting wind blowing than will a submarine, which is low to the water and has much less area exposed to the effects of the wind.

The natural wind that is blowing at any given time (the breeze you feel on your face, for example, when you are standing on a beach looking out to sea) is called *true wind*. You know that on a perfectly still day, when there is no wind blowing, you can easily have your cap blown off while riding in a convertible with the top down. This air flow, caused by the vehicle moving through the air, is called *relative wind* (its velocity is directly *relative* to the speed you are traveling). When the effect of these two are combined, it is called *apparent wind*. For example, there will seem to be a lot more wind blowing if you drive down a road at high speed *into* the wind.

To illustrate these various winds, think about traveling in a small boat at a speed of 20 knots. If, when you start out, there is no (true) wind blowing, the relative wind (caused by your motion) will be 20 knots. An hour later, the wind has begun blowing out of the north at a speed of 10 knots. If you head north, the apparent wind will be 30 knots (20 relative + 10 true). If you head south, the apparent wind will be 10 knots (20 true – 10 relative). If you head in any other direction the apparent wind will be something in between 10 and 20 knots depending upon the course chosen.

The effect of wind on ship operations can be beneficial or detrimental. During flight operations, an aircraft carrier most often steams into the wind, because the increased speed of the apparent wind helps aircraft take off and land by providing them more lift. A strong wind can make mooring a ship more difficult by keeping it off the pier or causing it to blow down on the pier too quickly.

At sea, the direction of the true wind is indicated by streaks of foam down the back sides of waves, while the direction of the apparent wind is shown by the way the ship's flags are blowing. True winds are described by the direction *from* which they are blowing. A north wind is blowing from the north toward the south, for example.

The side of the ship toward the wind is the *windward* side, and the side away from the wind is the *leeward* side. When the wind changes direction to the right, or clockwise, it *veers;* when it changes in the other direction (counterclockwise), it *backs*.

The Beaufort Scale

Devised to help mariners describe wind and sea conditions, the Beaufort scale provides a guide that helps you equate what you are seeing with a range of wind speed. Study the scale below and you will be able to make assessments of the weather without the aid of instruments.

Table 21.2. The Beaufort Scale

Beaufort Number	Wind speed (knots)	Seaman's Term	Appearance of Sea
0	Below 1	Calm	Surface like a mirror
1	1–3	Light air	Ripples that look like fish scales, but without foam crests
2	4–6	Light breeze	Small wavelets, still short but more pronounced; crests look glassy and do not break
3	7–10	Gentle breeze	Large wavelets; crests begin to break; glassy-looking foam; perhaps scattered whitecaps
4	11–16	Moderate breeze	Small waves; becoming longer; fairly frequent whitecaps
5	17–21	Fresh breeze	Moderate waves, taking a more pronounced long form; many whitecaps are formed; chance of some spray
6	22–27	Strong breeze	Large waves begin to form; white foam crests are more extensive everywhere; probably some spray
7	28–33	Moderate gale (high wind)	Sea heaps up and white foam from breaking waves begins to move in streaks in the direction of the wind
8	34–40	Fresh gale	Moderately high waves of greater length; edges of crests break into spindrift; foam is blown in well-marked streaks in the direction of wind
9	41–47	Strong gale	High waves; dense streaks of foam in the direction of wind; sea begins to roll; spray may affect visibility
10	48–55	Whole gale	Very high waves with long overhanging crests; resulting foam is blown in great patches of dense white streaks in the direction of wind; whole surface of the sea looks white; rolling of the sea becomes heavy and shocklike; visibility is affected

11	56–63	Storm	Exceptionally high waves; small and medium-sized ships might be lost to view behind the waves; sea is completely covered with long white patches of foam lying in the direction of wind; everywhere the edges of wave crests are blown into froth; visibility is seriously affected
12	64–71	Hurricane	Air is filled with foam and spray; sea completely white with driving spray; visibility very seriously affected

Communications

Communications is a vital part of the Navy. Ships must be able to communicate with each other when operating together, aircraft must be able to talk to one another and to the ships they are operating with, and fleet commanders must be able to report to and receive instructions from Washington, D.C. These are all forms of *external* communications and are extremely important. But just as important, the various stations within a ship must be able to communicate with one another—called *internal communications.* For example, the ship's damage-control parties must be able to communicate with DCC and the bridge during an emergency, the bow lookouts must be able to report to the OOD what they see and hear, and Primary Flight Control on an aircraft carrier must be able to communicate with Sailors moving aircraft about on the flight deck.

Internal Communications

Probably the oldest form of internal communications—the messenger—is still among the most reliable. Modern ships have other means available which are much faster than sending a runner. Simple buzzer and light signals are used to attract attention when needed and to provide basic information about the current status of a system or component. Such things as rudder-angle indicators and engine-order telegraphs are more elaborate means of communicating equipment status. Computer links are used for sophisticated systems information, and synchro- and servo-systems are used with weapons systems to convey important information. Larger ships have telephone systems similar to the ones you have used all your life. The ship's bell is also used to convey information to the crew, and even the "aboard/ashore board" used on the quarterdecks of many ships to indicate who is aboard at any given time is a means of internal communications.

The two most widely used forms of internal communications are the *MC* and *J* systems. MC systems include one-way loudspeaker systems and special box systems that allow various stations to talk back and forth to each other. J systems are the Navy's sound-powered phone systems that have the advantage of not requiring electrical power to function.

MC Systems

The chief advantage of these systems is that they electrically amplify the human voice so that it can be heard by many people at one time and in noisy conditions. Their major disadvantages are that they cannot be depended upon if electrical power is lost and they add noise to an already noisy environment. Some of the MC systems are what you might call public-address systems. The Navy calls them central-amplifier systems. They use a system of speakers (located where needed) to broadcast information, but the receiving stations cannot answer back. Other MC systems are made up of two-way boxes in different locations around the ship which are wired to each other in such a way that the stations can talk to each other, either all at the same time or only one or a few at a time. These boxes are equipped with buttons that can be pressed so that only certain stations will hear what is being said. If you want to talk to all the stations on the circuit at the same time, push all of the buttons, but if only three of the stations on the circuit need the information you want to pass, you can press just the three buttons to those stations and not bother the others.

The 1MC System

In the old Navy, before the days of loudspeaker systems, the boatswain's mate passed any orders for the crew by word of mouth. The boatswain's mate of the watch (BMOW) sounded "Call mates" on his pipe to get the other boatswain's mates together, and they converged on the quarterdeck while answering repeatedly with the same call on their pipes. Upon hearing the word, they dispersed throughout the ship to sing it out at every hatch.

While this procedure was colorful, it took a lot of time. Today a single boatswain's mate can quickly pass the word over the MC circuit to reach all or part of the ship at one time.

The ship's general announcing system, over which the word can be passed to every space in the ship, is designated the 1MC system. Transmitters are located on the bridge and quarterdeck so that the word can be passed by the OOD at sea and in port.

On some ships an announcement is preceded by a boatswain's call or pipe to get the attention of the crew. A special call, called "All hands," is piped before any particularly important word, and a shorter call, called "Attention," is used before more routine announcements.

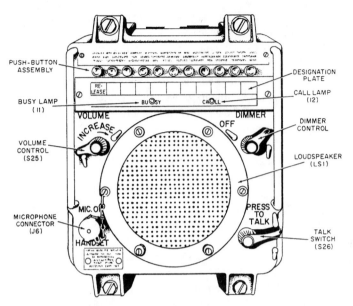

Figure 22.1. A two-way MC unit.

489

You will hear many different kinds of announcements over the 1MC. For most, the meanings will be obvious, but others will take some getting used to. Listed below are some of the more common announcements heard over the 1MC, followed by a brief explanation. The words used here are typical but may differ somewhat from ship to ship.

"Air bedding." Mattresses and pillows are to be removed from your rack and taken topside where they should be draped over the ship's rail for a few hours to air out.

"Haul over all hatch hoods and gun covers." A rain squall is approaching. All open hatches must be closed and protective tarps must be rigged.

"Mail call." Incoming mail is available for pickup.

"Mess Gear. Clear the mess decks." All personnel not assigned as mess cooks or attendants should leave the mess decks area so that preparations can be made for the next meal.

"The OOD is shifting his [her] watch from the bridge to the quarterdeck." This announcement alerts the crew that the OOD can now be found on the quarterdeck instead of the bridge. This occurs when the ship enters port. When the ship gets underway the opposite

announcement would be made (*"The OOD is shifting her [his] watch from the quarterdeck to the bridge."*)

"Reveille, reveille. All hands heave out and trice up." It's time to wake up and get out of your rack (bunk).

"Taps, lights out. All hands turn in to your bunks and keep silence about the decks." It is time to go to bed. If you are not going to bed at this time, you must be as quiet as possible when in the vicinity of berthing compartments.

"Turn to. Commence ship's work." Passed in the morning to announce the beginning of the work day. After the noon meal, a slightly modified version (*"Turn to. Continue ship's work."*) is passed.

"Up all late bunks." All personnel who have been sleeping in (beyond reveille) because they had the mid-watch the night before must now wake up.

The OOD is in charge of the 1MC. No call can be passed over it unless it is authorized by the OOD, the executive officer, or the captain.

Normally, the 1MC is equipped with switches that make it possible for certain spaces to be cut off from announcements of no concern to them. The captain, for instance, does not need to hear the call for late bunks, so his or her cabin can be cut out of the announcement.

Other MC Systems

Many MC systems are available for shipboard use, but not all of them will be found on every ship. They are listed below. (*Note:* Those systems with an asterisk are central amplifier [one-way] systems; the others are all two-way networks.)

*1MC	General
*2MC	Propulsion plant
*3MC	Aviators
4MC	Damage control
*5MC	Flight deck
*6MC	Intership
7MC	Submarine control
8MC	Troop administration and control
*9MC	Underwater troop communication
18MC	Bridge
19MC	Aviation control
21MC	Captain's command
22MC	Electronic control
23MC	Electrical control

24MC	Flag command
26MC	Machinery control
27MC	Sonar and radar control
*29MC	Sonar control and information
30MC	Special weapons
31MC	Escape trunk
32MC	Weapons control
35MC	Launcher captains
39MC	Cargo handling
40MC	Flag administrative
42MC	CIC coordinating
44MC	Instrumentation space
45MC	Research operations
*46MC	Aviation ordnance and missile handling
47MC	Torpedo control
50MC	Integrated operational intelligence center
51MC	Aircraft maintenance and handling control
53MC	Ship administrative
54MC	Repair officer's control
55MC	Sonar service
58MC	Hangar-deck damage control
59MC	SAMID alert

Sound-Powered Telephones

In battle conditions or during other emergencies, a ship may lose some or all of its electrical power. Battery-powered communication systems are good only as long the batteries hold out, and radio systems (such as walkie-talkies) are not always effective through steel bulkheads and decks (and they put radio signals into the air that can be detected by enemy forces in the vicinity). Because of these potential problems, ships must have some means of communicating internally that does not require an outside source of electrical power to function. For many decades, the Navy has relied upon a relatively simple but very reliable invention called the sound-powered telephone, which relies upon the energy generated by the user's voice to create enough current to power the circuit.

You will probably stand some sort of watch aboard ship that will require you to use a sound-powered telephone system. A ship at sea requires many talkers, even during a peacetime cruising watch. In addition to the lookouts, there are talkers on the bridge, in CIC, and in enginerooms, to mention only a few. These phones are used on all ships, and some ships have hundreds of them. To do your job properly, you must have a basic understanding of the ship's sound-powered system and you must learn proper telephone-talking procedures.

Ship's Sound-Powered System

For many years, sound-powered circuits were a primary source of interior communications. In ships with the newer IVCS system [see below], sound powered systems are now secondary.

Sound-powered systems are recognizable as such by the letter *J* in their circuit designation. Different circuits connect different parts of the ship for different purposes. An additional letter after the *J* represents the general purpose. For example, the letter *S* after the *J* in a circuit identifies that circuit as one used to gather sensor information (such as radar or sonar), the letter *L* would be used by lookouts to pass information to the bridge, CIC, and other stations that may need it, and so on.

As a further means of identification, numbers may precede the *J* to differentiate different circuits of the same general type. For example, on a ship that has only one primary weapons system, the circuit connecting key weapons stations would be simply designated the JC circuit. But on a ship with two major weapons systems, there would be two separate circuits, designated 1JC and 2JC. On most ships, the surface-search radar circuit is designated the 21JS while the air-search radar circuit is designated the 22JS.

Vital circuits are duplicated by what are called *auxiliary circuits.* Even though these circuits connect the same stations as the primary circuit, the wires connecting them are deliberately run through different parts of the ship so that damage to one is less likely to result in simultaneous damage to the other.

There are also some additional special circuits called *supplementary circuits,* which are short, direct lines used to connect key stations that need a source of quick, reliable communications, such as between the captain's sea cabin and the bridge. Because supplementary circuits are not manned, most of these circuits contain a buzzer system so that one station can alert another that communications between the two are desired.

The letter *X* precedes both auxiliary circuits and supplementary circuits, but you can tell the difference because the latter do not have an additional letter after the *J*. For example, the XJL and X22JS circuits are alternates of the JL and 22JS primary circuits, while the X1J and X8J would be supplementary circuits.

One last thing you should know about the numbers and letters assigned to sound-powered circuits is that individual stations on a circuit are distinguished from each other by the addition of yet another number at the end of the sequence. For example, 22JS7 identifies outlet number 7 on the 22JS circuit. Other outlets on the same circuit would be assigned individual numbers like 22JS6 and 22JS8, and so on.

Some of the more common sound-powered circuits you may encounter aboard ship are listed below.

JA	Captain's battle circuit
JC	Weapons control
JL	Lookouts
JW	Navigation
JX	Communications
1JV	Maneuvering and docking
21JS	Surface search and radar
22JS	Air-search radar
61JS	Sonar information
2JZ	Damage control

These circuits, and others like them, are manned when necessary but will remain unused at other times. For example, the JL circuit will be manned at all times while at sea but is unused when the ship is moored to a pier.

It is a good idea to familiarize yourself with the available jackboxes (outlets) in your work or watchstation area. That way, if something happens to a circuit you are assigned to talk on, you will know what alternatives are available. For example, if you are assigned as a talker on the JA circuit during GQ and that circuit sustains battle damage, you will save valuable time if you know where any nearby XJA outlets are. Knowing other circuits in your area may prove useful as well.

Some sound-powered circuits, particularly the supplementary ones, have a handset similar to a normal telephone handset that is always attached. These handsets will have a button that must be held down while talking, and they are often accompanied by a buzzer system that will alert you that someone wants to talk to you on that circuit.

Far more common, however, is the sound-powered telephone talker headset that is plugged into a sound-powered circuit outlet and worn by an individual who is specifically assigned as a talker on that circuit when needed.

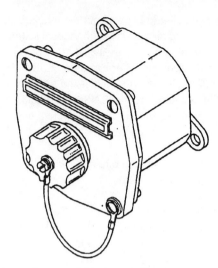

Figure 22.2. A sound-powered telephone jackbox.

Use of the Sound-Powered Headset

The typical headset used with the sound-powered phone consists of a headband that holds the receivers over the ears, a breastplate supported by a cloth neck strap, and a yoke that holds the mouthpiece transmitter in front of the mouth. The phone has a wire lead, which may be up to 50 feet long, with a jack on the end. The jack plugs into a box connected to the circuit.

Figure 22.3. Sound-powered handset.

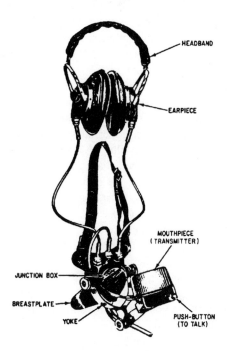

Figure 22.4. Sound-powered headset.

To put the gear on, first unhook the right side of the neck strap from the breastplate, pass the strap around your neck and rehook it. Next, put on the earphones and adjust the headband so that the center of one or both earpieces are directly over your ear(s). In most cases, you will want to keep one ear uncovered so that you can hear what is going on around you. Keep the unused earpiece flat against the side of your head to keep unwanted noises from being picked up. Adjust the mouthpiece so that it is about an inch in front of your mouth. In making this adjustment, remember that the fine wire that goes to the transmitter can be broken if mistreated. Be sure that there are no sharp bends in it, and do not allow it to get caught between the transmitter and the yoke that supports it. Last, insert the plug into the jack box and screw the collar on firmly.

When you are wearing the headset, always keep some slack in the lead cord, and be sure it is flat on deck. If you have the cord stretched taut, someone may trip over it and damage the wires, injure him- or herself, or injure you. Do not allow objects to roll over or rest on the cord.

After plugging in the phones, test them with someone on the circuit. If they are not in working order, report that to the person in charge of your station and don a spare set; don't attempt to repair the set yourself.

Never secure the phones until you have permission to do so. When permission is given, do not just remove the phones and leave them. Unless someone is relieving you and takes the phones from you, always make up the phones for proper stowage. Remove the plug from the jack box by holding the plug in one hand and unscrewing the collar with the other. When the collar is detached, grasp the plug and pull it out, lay it carefully on the deck. Immediately screw the cover on the jack box; dust and dirt can cause a short circuit in a box that has been left uncovered. (If you see an uncovered jack box cover it, even though you are not responsible for the carelessness.) Remove the headpiece and hang it over the transmitter yoke. Coil the lead cord, starting from the end at the phone. Coil the lead in a clockwise direction, holding the loops in one hand. The loops should be eight to ten inches across, depending on the size of the space where the phones are stowed. When you are coiling the lead, be careful not to bang the plug against anything.

When the lead is coiled, remove the headpiece from the transmitter yoke and put the headband in the same hand with the coil. Use this same hand to hold the transmitter while you unhook one end of the neck strap from the breastplate. Fold the transmitter yoke flat, being careful not to put a sharp bend in the transmitter cord. Wrap the neck strap around both the coil of wire you created and the headband two or three times and snap the end back on the breastplate, then fold the mouthpiece back up against the junction box. You then have a neat, compact package to be stowed. Put the phones into their box, or hang them on the hook provided. Be careful not to crowd or jam the leads.

One of the advantages of a sound-powered phone set is that in an emergency the earpieces and mouthpieces are interchangeable—you can talk into an earpiece and listen using the mouthpiece if you need to. This advantage is also a disadvantage, because an uncovered earpiece allows unwanted sound into the circuit that can make it difficult for others on the circuit to hear. Headset phones should, therefore, always be unplugged when not in use. If they are left plugged in, the earpieces will pick up noise and carry it into the circuit.

Never place the phones on the deck. Not only may someone step on them, but decks are good conductors of noise, which the phones can pick up.

Sound-Powered Telephone Talking Technique
The way you ordinarily talk is not the way you should talk on a sound-powered telephone. The person on the other end of the line cannot see you, may not know you, and may be unfamiliar with the things you are talking about. When you are functioning as a shipboard sound-powered telephone talker, you must speak clearly, be specific, and act businesslike. Use a strong (not loud), calm voice, and speak slowly, pronouncing each word carefully. Don't mumble, run things together, or talk with gum or other objects in your mouth. Always use standard terms and phraseology, avoiding slang.

Because sound-powered circuits are open to all stations simultaneously, circuit discipline is essential to prevent too much noise and confusion. Send only official messages. Do not engage in idle chitchat. Each phone talker is a key link in the ship's interior communications chain. Unauthorized talking means that the chain is weakened. Don't engage in it, and don't permit others to, either.

Keep the button in the off position except when you are actually talking. Avoid allowing anger, impatience, or excitement to be noticeable in your voice. Be professional. Few things can be as helpful or as reassuring as a calm voice in the middle of a crisis.

Standard Terms and Phraseology. When talking on a sound-powered telephone (or on a radio circuit and even a standard telephone), your voice does not have the same clarity that it does when speaking face to face with someone. That is one of the reasons why the Navy insists upon standardized terminology when communicating. You have already learned that course headings and bearings are always given as three digit numbers (zero-four-five) while position angles are spoken as "forty" or "seventy," for example. Numbers are often spoken individually rather than in the more conventional (but confusing) manner you were used to in civilian life. Because the numbers 5 and 9 sound very much alike on a sound-powered circuit or on a radio, the number "nine" is always pronounced "niner" in the Navy. This will seem strange to you at first, but after a while it will become second nature. Standardization of speech helps the listener to know what is being said by giving additional clues that will help overcome the reduced sound quality in these communication instruments.

One of the most valuable tools in maintaining clarity and avoiding confusion in communications is the use of the phonetic alphabet. *C, D, E, P, V, T,* and *Z* all sound very much alike on a sound-powered phone, for example. By using their phonetic equivalents (Charlie, Delta, Echo, Papa, Victor, Tango, and Zulu) there is no chance of

497

3

someone misunderstanding what letter you mean. If you say, "We need part number six alfa" instead of "six a," there is no chance that someone will confuse that with part 6k (which would be "six kilo"). The phonetic alphabet can also be used to spell out words that someone is having difficulty understanding.

The phonetic alphabet has been around for a long time, but has not always been the same. Back in the days of World War II, the phonetic alphabet began with the letters "Able, Baker, Charlie," K was "King," and S was "Sugar." After the war, when the NATO alliance was formed, the phonetic alphabet was changed to make it easier for the people who speak the different languages found in the alliance. That version has remained the same, and today the phonetic alphabet begins with "Alfa, Bravo, Charlie," K is now "Kilo," and S is "Sierra."

As you look over the phonetic alphabet, you will notice certain idiosyncrasies that you must accept. For example, the letter "Alfa" is spelled with an f instead of ph. This is because some of our allies do not have a ph in their language. Also note that "Whiskey" ends in "key," not "ky," and "Juliett" ends in two ts.

Pay close attention to the pronunciation of each letter. Note that in the table provided, each word is accented on the syllable in capital letters. This is no time for individuality—it is essential that everyone say these words as much the same as is possible to avoid any confusion, which is the whole purpose. The letter p should be pronounced "pah-PAH," not "POP-ah" as most Americans are more likely to say. L is "LEE-mah," not "LYE-mah," and q is "kay-BECK," not "quee-BECK."

a	alfa	AL-fah
b	bravo	BRAH-vo
c	charlie	CHAR-lee
d	delta	DELL-tah
e	echo	ECK-oh
f	foxtrot	FOKS-traht
g	golf	GOLF
h	hotel	hoh-TELL
i	india	IN-dee-ah
j	juliett	JEW-lee-ett
k	kilo	KEY-loh
l	lima	LEE-mah
m	mike	MIKE
n	november	no-VEM-ber

o	oscar	OSS-ker
p	papa	pah-PAH
q	quebec	kay-BECK
r	romeo	ROW-me-oh
s	sierra	see-AIR-rah
t	tango	TANG-go
u	uniform	YOU-nee-form
v	victor	VIK-ter
w	whiskey	WISS-key
x	xray	ECKS-ray
y	yankee	YANG-key
z	zulu	ZOO-loo

It is absolutely mandatory that you memorize the phonetic alphabet. You will be lost in the Navy without it.

Message Form. Most messages have three parts: the name of the station called, the name of the station calling, and the information to be sent. This format must always be followed. Call the station the message is for, identify your station, then transmit the message. It may seem strange to keep repeating these things, but keep in mind that there will probably be a number of people plugged into the circuit at the same time and they cannot see each other, so it is important to identify who you are and who you are talking to. Remember the order: who to, who from, what about. If you are on the anchor detail stationed on the forecastle and want to call the bridge, you would say:

"Bridge [who to], Forecastle [who from]; anchor secured [what about]."

When receiving a message, first identify your station, then acknowledge for the message with the words "aye, aye" or, simply, "aye." This means that you heard the message and understood it. It does *not* mean "yes." For example, if your station is the forecastle and the bridge has just ordered the anchor to be let go: "Forecastle, Bridge; let go the anchor."

Acknowledge that you understood what was said by answering with: "Forecastle, aye, aye" (or, "Forecastle, aye").

This does not mean that you (or anyone else) will let the anchor go. It means simply that you understood what was being said. When you pass this word on to the chief in charge of the anchor detail, she or he may tell you to tell the bridge that the anchor cannot yet be let go because the stopper is jammed. By saying "Aye, aye" you merely were saying "I heard and understood what you said."

You should note that in the above answer the forecastle did not say "Bridge, Forecastle, aye," but merely said "Forecastle, aye." This is because it is obvious who is being answered and to say "Bridge" would be unnecessary and unwanted talk to the circuit. It is acceptable (in fact, preferable) to abbreviate your conversation in this manner as long as it does not add to the confusion.

If you did not understand what was said, you should not answer "Aye, aye," but should say, "Bridge, Forecastle; repeat."

The following is a typical conversation you might have on the 1JV sound-powered circuit if you are on the forecastle as part of the anchor detail. For clarity, *your* words will appear in *italics*.

"Forecastle, Bridge; is the starboard anchor ready to let go?"
"Bridge, Forecastle; we are having trouble with the stopper."
"Forecastle, Bridge; report when the anchor is ready."
"Forecastle, aye."
[A minute goes by while the boatswain's mates are trying to free the stopper.]
"Bridge, Forecastle; the First Lieutenant says the bale is bent."

"Forecastle, Bridge; repeat."
"Bridge, Forecastle; the First Lieutenant says the bale is bent."
"Forecastle, Bridge; the 'what' is bent?"
"Bridge, Forecastle; 'bale.' Bravo, alfa, lima, echo."
"Bridge aye."
"Forecastle, Bridge; the Captain says he will back the ship down to keep us in our intended anchorage while you work on the stopper."
"Forecastle, aye."
"Bridge, Fantail; we have a small fishing boat astern of us."
"Bridge, aye."

In the last exchange, you can see that the talker at the fantail station, who is also on the circuit, warns the bridge that there is a fishing boat astern. This illustrates the importance of stations identifying themselves on the circuit when they speak. All of the prefacing with "Bridge, Forecastle" and "Forecastle, Bridge" in the above conversation seems unnecessary and awkward until you realize that there are other stations on the circuit, and it is important to know who is talking to whom in order to avoid confusion.

Circuit Testing. To find out if all of the stations on the circuit are manned and ready, the control-station talker would run a check of the circuit. For example, if the damage-control circuit is manning up and the control station (DCC) wanted to verify that all stations were on the line, the DCC talker would initiate the check by saying, "All Stations, Central; testing."

Each talker on the circuit then would acknowledge in the assigned order.

"Repair One; aye, aye."
"Repair Two; aye, aye."
"Repair Three; aye."
"Repair Four; aye, aye."

Normally each station answers in order, but does not wait more than a few seconds if the station ahead of it fails to acknowledge. If Repair Two fails to answer, Repair Three should, after giving Repair Two a few seconds to answer, go ahead and acknowledge for his or her station. If you were the talker in Repair Two and just came on the line while the check was going on, you should report in at the end, after all the other stations have made their reports in sequence. Do not try to jump in out of sequence—it may cause unnecessary confusion.

501

Integrated Voice Communications System (IVCS)

IVCS (spoken as "I-Vicks") combines the features of sound-powered phones, dial telephones, and intercom units into one sophisticated system with many advanced operating features. IVCS is capable of interfacing with other shipboard communications systems and consists of terminals (user access devices), computer-controlled interior communications switching centers (ICSCs), and a number of special accessories. In the event of a loss of electrical power, a battery back-up system keeps IVCS operating. Using "NETS" vice circuits, some of the more common ones are:

NET 15—-Command Net; used for Combat Information Center (CIC) coordination.
NET 25—Combat Systems Equipment Control
NET 27—Electronic Control
NET 29—Underwater Systems Control
NET 66—AEGIS/Air Weapons Control
NET 74—Surface Weapons Systems Control
NET 80—Damage Control
NET 85—Electrical Service/Engineering Systems Control

Voice Tubes

A voice tube is exactly what it sounds like—a metal tube that allows stations to communicate with one another simply by talking into it. Large cones are fitted onto the ends of the tube to amplify the sound of your voice. Voice tubes require no electrical power, but their effectiveness decreases in direct proportion to the length of the tube, so they are used for short-distance communication only. A typical voice-tube installation would connect the bridge wings to the helm, enabling the conning officer to pass orders to the helmsman without having to come into the pilot house from the bridge wing.

External Communications

External communication involves two or more ships, stations, or commands. A ship communicates externally by a wide variety of methods, including messenger delivery, mail, flaghoist, semaphore, flashing light, radio, facsimile (FAX), teletype, whistle signals, and foghorns. The most significant forms of communicating are visual and electronic.

Visual Signaling

Despite this age of high technology when satellites and radios transmit communications at incredible speed, the oldest form of communication continues to play a vital role in the Navy. Visual communication has a distinct advantage over other forms. For all its advances, science has yet to produce a silent form of communication, one that cannot be detected by advanced technological equipment. Visual communication fills the need for a reliable, silent, and relatively secure means of communication at ranges up to 15 miles.

The three main types of visual signals are flashing light, semaphore, and flaghoist.

Flashing Light

Letters and numbers are broken down into short and long flashes of light known as Morse code. A transmitting signalman sends messages one letter at a time with a slight pause between each letter. The receiving signalman flashes a light for each word received until the message is complete.

Flashing-light signaling is accomplished by two methods, directional and nondirectional. With the directional method, the sender aims his light directly at the receiving ship or installation. The ship's standard signal-searchlight is most often used but the *blinker tube* (or blinker gun) and the *multipurpose lamp* may also be used. The signal-searchlight is mounted to the ship's rail or to a special stand and is worked with levers attached to a blinking screen which allow the light to be quickly shown and blocked (to form the short and long flashes required for Morse code). The other two are portable, battery-operated lights with trigger switches to control flashes.

The nondirectional method is also called all-around signaling. Most of it is done by yardarm blinkers, lights mounted near the ends of the port and starboard yardarms on the mainmast and controlled by a signal key, similar to an old-fashioned telegraph, located on the signal bridge. This method is best for sending messages to several ships at once.

Lights used at night can be seen by an enemy, so an alternate system called "Nancy" uses invisible infrared light. Messages sent by this system can be seen only by those who have a special Nancy receiver, which gathers infrared rays and converts them to visible light. Nancy, with a range of from 10,000 to 15,000 yards, can be used only at night and is a more secure method of communication.

Semaphore

Semaphore requires little in the way of equipment and is relatively simple once the user becomes accustomed to it. Words are transmitted by holding the arms in a specific position to represent individual letters. When sender and receiver are close, as when their ships are alongside one another for UNREP, no special equipment is necessary. The semaphore characters are made simply by moving the hands to the proper positions. At greater distances, flags attached to short staffs held by the sender will make the signals much more visible. Standard semaphore flags are usually 15 to 18 square inches, and each staff is just long enough to grasp firmly. Most semaphore flags issued to the fleet today are fluorescent and made of sharkskin. For night semaphore, flashlights with special light-diffusing cones attached are held in the same manner as semaphore flags.

A good signalman can send or receive about 25 five-letter groups a minute. Only 30 positions need to be learned to be able to communicate by this method.

Semaphore is much faster than flashing light for short-distance transmissions. It may be used to send messages to several ships at once if they are in suitable positions but works best when used one on one. Because of its speed, semaphore is better adapted than the other visual methods for long messages.

PHC William H. Powers

Figure 22.5. Semaphore is a means of communicating that has stood the test of time.

Although semaphore's usefulness is limited somewhat by its short range, it is more secure than flashing light or radio because there is less chance of interception by an enemy or unauthorized persons. Speed and security, therefore, are the two factors favoring the use of semaphore.

Flaghoist
This is the most rapid system of visual signaling, but it can be used only in daytime. It is mostly used for transmitting tactical orders but

has some administrative uses as well. The meanings of each signal must be looked up in a signal book. There is a signal flag for each letter of the alphabet, a set of flags for each numeral 0 through 9, a set of pennants for each numeral 0 through 9, and other flags and pennants with special meanings. A compete set of signal flags will have sixty-eight flags and pennants. (See the appendices for a chart of all flags and pennants.)

Most ships carry only two or three complete sets of flags, but special substitute pennants may be employed to repeat flags that are already flying. The first substitute repeats the first flag or pennant in the same hoist, the second substitute repeats the second flag or pennant, and so on. With this system, there is virtually no limit to the combinations of flags and pennants that may be displayed (except for halyard space) and thousands of different signals can be sent.

Some signal flags have special meanings when used alone.

Bravo	Ship is handling explosives or fuel oil.
Five	Ship is broken down; cannot maneuver on its own.
Oscar	Man overboard.
Papa	Personnel recall. All hands return to ship.
Quebec	Boat recall. All boats return to ship.

Electronic Communications

Electronic communications used in the Navy take many forms. In the earliest days of radio, signals were sent by something called continuous wave which relied on Morse code as the means for transmitting signals. Later, voice radio came into being and revolutionized naval tactical communications. Other advances followed, including teletype, satellite communications, and facsimile (FAX).

Voice Radio

While you will certainly reap the benefits of modern electronic communications in the Navy, you will not be involved in using most forms unless you strike for radioman. One form, however, you will probably use on a frequent basis while standing watches or taking part in various operations. Voice radio or radiotelephone communications (RT) is often used as a fast, convenient, and efficient means of communicating. Ship to ship, ship to aircraft, aircraft to aircraft, ship to boat, and so on, voice radio is essential for many operations. Because of this, every Sailor should be able to communicate effectively using radio telephones, and because radios operate somewhat differently from the telephones you are used to, you

AND
ANSWERING
SIGN

Figure 22.6. The semaphore signaling system is fast and reliable but useful only at short ranges.

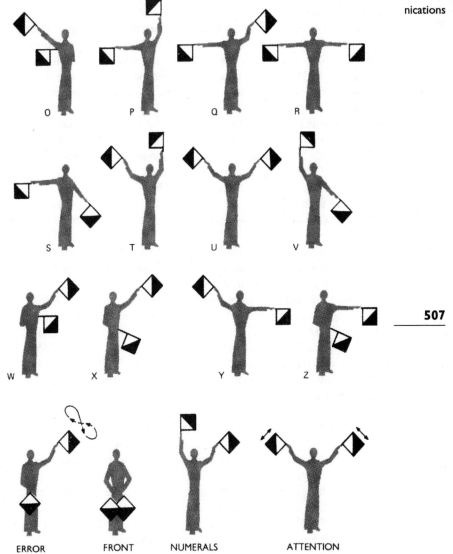

O   P   Q   R

S   T   U   V

W   X   Y   Z

ERROR   FRONT   NUMERALS   ATTENTION

will need to learn a few new things in order to be an effective radio communicator.

For example, if you have watched movies and television as most people have, you must begin by *un*learning a particularly bad habit that has, for some reason, made its way into 90 percent of all such productions. The oft-used expression "over and out" makes no sense whatsoever, yet you will hear it used time and again on the big and little screens. In radiotelephony, "over" is a shorthand way of saying "I am finished talking and now it is your turn." "Out" means "I am finished talking and we have nothing more to talk about, so I am signing off." In short, "out" is roughly equivalent to "goodbye" on a telephone. So when actors say "over and out," they are, in essence, saying, "I am finished talking and now it is your turn. Goodbye." Needless to say, this makes no sense. Never, never, *never,* say "over and out" on a Navy radio circuit unless you enjoy being the butt of jokes.

Other words and phrases, called "prowords," have special meanings when used in voice radio communications. You should familiarize yourself with the partial list in Table 22.1.

Voice radio transmissions take the following form: the station called followed by the words "this is" and the identification of the station doing the calling. For example, if the call sign of your station is "Tango Charlie" and you are trying to call station "Delta Whiskey," you would say, "Delta Whiskey, this is Tango Charlie." The following example illustrates a radio conversation between these two stations.

"Delta Whiskey, this is Tango Charlie, over."

"Tango Charlie, this is Delta Whiskey, roger over."

"Delta Whiskey, this is Tango Charlie. When will your last boat be departing? Over."

"Tango Charlie, this is Delta Whiskey. The last boat will depart one hour before sunset. Over."

"Delta Whiskey, this is Tango Charlie. The Chief of Staff wants you to wait until General Scarloni arrives. Over."

"Tango Charlie, this is Delta Whiskey. Spell last name of general. Over."

"Delta Whiskey, this is Tango Charlie. I spell SIERRA, CHARLIE, ALFA, ROMEO, LIMA, OSCAR, NOVEMBER, INDIA. Over."

"Tango Charlie, this is Delta Whiskey. Say again all after LIMA. Over."

Table 22.1. Prowords and Their Meanings

Proword	Explanation
Authenticate	The station called is to reply to challenge that follows.
Authentication is . . .	The transmission authentication of this message is _____.
Break	I hereby indicate the separation of the text from other portions of the message.
Call sign	The group that follows is a call sign (identification of a station—similar to a "handle" in CB radio).
Correction	An error has been made in this transmission. Transmission will continue with the last word correctly transmitted.
Figures	Numerals or numbers follow.
I say again	I am repeating my transmission (or the portion indicated).
I spell	I will spell the next word phonetically.
Out	This is the end of my transmission to you and no answer is required or expected.
Over	This is the end of my transmission to you and a response is necessary. Go ahead; transmit.
Relay (to)	Transmit this message to all addressees immediately following.
Roger	I have received your last transmission satisfactorily.
Say again	Repeat your last transmission.
Silence	[Repeated three or more times.] Cease transmissions on this net immediately. Silence will be maintained until lifted.
Silence lifted	The silence that was imposed on this net is now lifted.
Speak slower	Your transmission is too fast. Reduce speed.
This is	This transmission is from the station whose designator immediately follows.
Unknown station	The identity of the station with which I am attempting to establish communications is unknown.
Wait	I must pause for a few seconds.
Wait, out	I must pause for longer than a few seconds.
Wilco	I have received your signal, understand it, and will comply. [Since the meaning of "Roger" is included in that of "Wilco," the two prowords are never used together.]

"Delta Whiskey, this is Tango Charlie. I say again all after
LIMA: OSCAR, NOVEMBER, INDIA. Over."
"Tango Charlie, this is Delta Whiskey. Wilco. Out."

Transmitting Techniques

Because RT is used so widely in ships, aircraft, and motor vehicles,
everyone should understand the basics of circuit discipline. Under
most circumstances, the following practices are specifically forbidden:

Violation of radio silence
Unofficial conversation between operators
Transmitting in a directed net without permission
Excessive tuning and testing
Unauthorized use of plain language (no encryption)
Use of profane, indecent, or obscene language

Listen before transmitting—break-ins cause confusion. Speak clearly
and distinctly; slurred syllables and clipped speech are difficult to
understand. Speak slowly, so that the recorder has a chance to understand the entire message the first time. This way, you'll save time and
avoid repetitions. Use standard pronunciation, not regional accents.

Keep the correct distance (about two inches) between your lips
and the microphone. Speak in a moderately strong voice to override
background noise. While transmitting, keep your head and body
between sources of noise and the microphone.

Keep the volume of the headset earphone or speaker low. Pause
momentarily, when possible, during your transmission by releasing
the transmit button; pausing allows any other station with higher-
precedence traffic to break in. Transact your business and get off the
air. Preliminary calls are unnecessary when communications are
good and the message is short. Do not hold the transmit button in the
push-to-talk position until you're ready to transmit. Apply firm pressure to the transmit button to prevent an unintentional release.

Secure Voice Communications

If a transmission is in plain language, anyone can intercept and read
it. Important messages may be encrypted and sent in a code or cipher
known only to the sender and receiver. *Codes* are word-for-word substitutions, and both sender and receiver must use the same code book.
Ciphers are letter-for-letter substitutions, which may require a
machine for encoding and decoding. A coded message may be copied

by anyone, but without the code book it is difficult or impossible to read.

Modern communications equipment may include automatic encryption devices that "scramble" voice radio transmissions so that they are unreadable by unwanted parties and "unscrambled" by the intended receiver who has matching encryption/decryption devices.

23 Health, Fitness, and First Aid

In the days of "iron men and wooden ships," disease killed more men than did cannonballs. Sailors lived for months aboard damp and cold ships, ate salted or rancid meat and moldy or wormy bread, drank foul-smelling water, and bathed—if at all—in cold salt water.

Sailors in the Navy today live better and are safer and healthier than most people in the world. Even the smallest ship has facilities to provide nourishing meals, well-ventilated and heated berthing spaces, medical and dental attention, laundry services, hot and cold fresh water, and sanitary living conditions.

The Navy will train you to perform your military and professional duties, but your ability to perform them quickly and efficiently will depend to a large degree on your physical and mental condition.

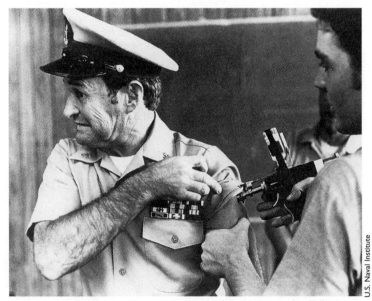

Figure 23.1. Regular medical attention is one of the benefits of Navy life.

U.S. Naval Institute

Health and Fitness

Earlier in this book, you learned that in dealing with equipment you must practice preventive maintenance (such as cleaning and lubrication) to keep the equipment functioning at its peak performance and to minimize the chances of it breaking down. You also learned that effective and expeditious damage control can minimize the harm done to a ship and its equipment. The same principles apply to the human body. You can do a great deal of "preventive maintenance" to keep your body operating in top condition, and you can minimize damage in an emergency by knowing the basics of body damage control, known as first aid.

Personal Hygiene

Keeping yourself clean is one of the important basics of the "preventive maintenance" required to keep your mind and body in top shape. Harmful bacteria have great difficulty surviving in a clean environment, and the close living environment often found aboard ship requires that all hands must stay clean not only for their own health and well-being but for that of their shipmates as well.

Bathing

Your skin is actually a large organ that covers your body. It protects the more sensitive internal organs, helps regulate body temperature, assists with the body's fluid and chemical balance, and contains nerve endings that serve as sensors to pain, temperature, touch, and pressure. Keeping this important organ clean and healthy is vital to letting it perform its many jobs efficiently.

Bathing is the most effective way of keeping your skin healthy. Whether you accomplish it in a tub or shower, bathing removes disease-carrying organisms, stimulates the circulation of blood, soothes sore muscles, improves your self-image, and relaxes you.

Hand Washing

Hand washing is the single most important thing you can do to prevent infections and stay healthy. Done often and well, it breaks the chain of infection by removing organisms from your hands and preventing the spread of infection to yourself or others.

There are five important steps to avoid the spread of infection with your hands. Do them as often as you are able and you and others around you will be healthier:

Wash hands as often as practical.

Always wash hands after going to the head and before meals.
Use soap; clean between fingers and around nails.
Dry with a clean towel.
Avoid touching your face, especially your nose, eyes, and mouth.

Scabies

Scabies is a parasitic disease of the skin. Microscopic scabies "bugs" burrow into the skin and lay their eggs, leaving small red bumps or clear blisters. The mode of transmission is usually direct skin-to-skin contact, and often from sexual contact. Scabies may also be picked up by bedclothes and using undergarments owned by someone else.
Suspect scabies if you:

experience intense itching (especially at night and at belt line);
see small raised red bumps in a line with blisters; or
have a rash on your fingers, genitals, waistline, or in the elbow
  crease.

Report to sick bay if you suspect you have scabies. Medical personnel will give you medications to combat the problem and will instruct you to launder your clothing and bed sheets.

Lice

Lice are very small and may require a magnifying glass to be seen. However, it is usually easier to find the "nits," which are clusters of louse eggs. Nits appear as tiny white lumps on the shaft of hairs.
Over-the-counter (OTC) RID shampoo works very well. Be sure to launder any clothing and bed sheets used 48 hours prior to treatment. If treatment is unsuccessful contact your medical provider.

Care of Teeth

The three most common dental diseases are tooth decay (caries), inflammation of the gums (gingivitis), and an affliction of the gums and bone that surround the teeth (pyorrhea). Any of these problems can lead to the loss of teeth.
There is no way to completely prevent tooth decay, but it can be cut down by brushing your teeth correctly and by avoiding sweets. Flossing, the only way to remove harmful deposits from between your teeth, should be done at least once a day.
Normal healthy gums are pale pink and firm in texture. If they are swollen or puffy, hang loosely about the teeth, and bleed easily, then you have gingivitis. If gingivitis goes untreated, you may notice

pockets or crevices between the tooth and gum, an indication of pyor-rhea. More teeth are lost from these two diseases than from tooth decay. It is required that all Navy personnel have their teeth checked at least once every year.

Tobacco, Alcohol, and Other Drug Abuse

One of the most effective ways to counter health and fitness is to introduce harmful substances into your body, particularly in large quantity. There are, unfortunately, parts of our society that encourage or even pressure us to practice such harmful behaviors. Before you consider using tobacco, alcohol, or any other drugs, and before you are tempted to write off some of the campaigns against these sub-stances as overzealous or misdirected, simply consider the implica-tions to your health. If you think these substances can be used with no consequences to your one and only body, you probably would also be willing to buy swampland as a real-estate development investment.

Tobacco

Once started, tobacco use is difficult to stop because the nicotine in tobacco is one of the most addictive substances known. Despite claims to the contrary by cigarette manufacturers, tobacco is as addic-tive as cocaine or heroin.

Tobacco use has many health hazards that the average smoker or dipper might not be aware of. Cigarette smoke contains 4000 chemi-cals, including the following highly toxic substances: carbon mon-oxide, a major component of automobile exhaust; formaldehyde, an ingredient of embalming fluid; and arsenic, a lethal poison. Smokeless tobacco is "doped" with higher concentrations of nicotine, sweeteners, and flavorings to make the product more addicting.

Tobacco use is the leading preventable cause of death in the United States; 500,000 Americans die of smoking-related illness each year, eight times as many as died in the Vietnam War. Everyone knows that smoking causes lung cancer. Some other cancers caused by tobacco include oral, bladder, kidney, prostate, uterine, ovarian, and cervical. People who use smokeless tobacco, or smoke cigars or pipes, think they are safe from the hazards of smoking, but the risks are potentially higher for mouth, tooth, and throat diseases and cancers.

Keep in mind that you are not only risking your own health by using tobacco, you risk the health of others around you as well. Pregnant women put their developing babies at serious risk of birth defects and other complications by using tobacco. One nonsmoker dies of passive smoke for every eight smokers.

The Navy is aggressively working toward becoming a tobacco-free organization in the near future. If you use tobacco products and would like to quit, there are several methods to help you. Ask the medical staff how you can get help quitting. If you do not use tobacco products, don't start. Your body, your mind, and your wallet will all be better off.

Alcohol

The abuse of alcohol by Navy members can seriously damage physical and mental health, may jeopardize safety, and can lead to criminal prosecution and discharge under other than honorable conditions. Alcohol is a drug and should be treated with caution. Although millions of people use this drug regularly, it is a dangerous substance that requires a great deal of common sense and caution to be used rather than abused.

Alcohol abuse leads to intoxication; this is often when people get into trouble. Violence, sexual assault, loss of coordination that causes an accident, and arrests for drunkenness are just a few examples of alcohol abuse.

Alcohol abuse can progress into alcoholism, as well as serious health problems, including damage to vital organs (such as your brain and liver) and extremely harmful psychological problems.

Pregnant women face special risks when drinking by risking fetal alcohol syndrome, which can cause serious problems for a developing child, including physical defects, mental retardation, and even death.

The Navy recognizes alcoholism as a disease and, as such, is committed to providing treatment. Every Sailor suffering from an alcohol problem has the opportunity to be treated. See your command drug and alcohol program advisor (DAPA) if you think you need help.

Illegal Drugs

Other drugs, such as marijuana and crack cocaine, are not only extremely dangerous to your health, they are illegal as well. The Navy has a "zero tolerance" policy for drug abuse. Therefore, mandatory separation and other consequences (such as prosecution and loss of benefits) follow any illegal drug-related incident.

To enforce this policy, the Navy uses periodic urinalysis testing and other methods to discourage and identify drug abuse.

Male Health

Men have special health needs which are important considerations when dealing with the prevention and early detection of disease. Good health is no accident but is achieved through careful attention to personal hygiene and seeking medical care when appropriate.

Testicular Exam

Early detection and early treatment are among the best tools available in the fight against testicular cancer. If cancer is detected early, it is most curable. Every male is at risk for testicular cancer and should do a monthly testicular self-exam to detect any swelling or lumps.

Cancer of the testes is one of the most common cancers in men 15 to 34 years of age. If discovered in the early stages, it can be treated promptly and effectively.

Problems other than cancer involving the genitals can arise. Report to the nearest naval medical facility if you experience any unusual genital conditions, such as painful urination, penile discharge, or pain. "Testicular torsion," which is caused when one of the testes twists on its cord, will result in the surgical removal of a testicle if not treated within the first six hours of occurrence.

Contraception and Disease Control

The most effective means of contraception and disease control is, of course, to avoid sexual relations. The use of condoms during sexual intercourse is a reasonably effective method of both birth and disease control. While it is not 100 percent effective in either case, it is vastly more effective than having unprotected sex. A condom is a disposable, thin sheath of latex rubber that is rolled over the erect penis just before intercourse. The condom usually has a place at the tip to hold ejaculated semen, stopping the sperm from entering the vagina and preventing pregnancy. The effectiveness of the condom as a birth-control measure is increased by the use of a spermicide as well. To be effective, a new condom must be worn with every sex act.

If birth control is the only consideration, a surgical procedure called a vasectomy is an option, but it should be considered only when the desired effects are meant to be permanent.

Female Health

Like men, women have special health needs. Practicing good health habits can allow for early detection of diseases and allow a healthy and more active lifestyle.

Breast Self-Exam

A breast self-examination is a regular exam you do to check yourself for lumps, thickening, and dimples in the breast, or an unusual discharge from the nipple. Most cases of breast cancer are discovered by women themselves, through self-exams.

The best time to examine your breasts is once a month, one week after your period starts when your breasts usually are not tender or swollen. If you do not have regular menstrual periods, check your breasts on the first day of the month.

If you do not know how to do a self-examination effectively, visit your nearest naval medical facility for instructions and assistance.

Pap Smear

The Pap smear is a simple, relatively painless procedure that when properly performed by trained medical personnel is highly effective in detecting abnormal cervical cells before they become cancerous. Pap-smear screening should begin when a woman becomes sexually active or no later than the age of 18. It should continue annually, unless otherwise directed by a health-care provider.

Prevention of Pregnancy

Unplanned pregnancies can be a devastating consequence of indiscriminate sexual activity. Abstaining from intercourse is the safest behavior, but if a woman is sexually active, she should consider the following alternatives.

Condoms. Latex condoms are up to 85 percent effective at preventing pregnancy. The use of condoms is especially important because they are the *only* method of birth control which may also prevent transmission of sexually transmitted diseases. (See "Male Health" for description of condom use.)

Spermicides. Foams, gels, and suppositories are very effective as birth control when used alone. When used with a condom, effectiveness approaches 95 percent.

Prescription barrier methods. Barrier devices, such as the diaphragm or cervical cap, require initial fitting by a health-care provider. When used with a spermicidal gel, effectiveness at preventing pregnancy approaches 95 percent.

Prescription hormonal methods. Hormonal methods (pills, shots, and implants) are highly effective at preventing pregnancy, approaching 99 percent.

Natural family planning. The so-called rhythm method requires special instruction or training on the timing of intercourse.

Effectiveness is variable and this method is not recommended when pregnancy must be avoided.

Tubal ligation. Tubal ligation is an extremely effective form of birth control but should be considered an irreversible option that is only suitable for those who want permanent pregnancy prevention.

Perineal Hygiene

It is important to keep your genital area clean and dry to help prevent irritation and yeast and bacterial infection. Always wipe from front to back to prevent the spread of bacteria and feces from the rectum into the vaginal area. Wear clean cotton underwear or underwear with cotton panels daily and avoid nonabsorbent, heat-retaining clothing such as nylon pantyhose and tights. Change tampons or pads frequently and avoid deodorant varieties. Douching is not necessary for effective hygiene.

Premenstrual Syndrome

Known also as PMS, this term is used to define the physical and emotional symptoms that some women have during the week or two before menstruation, such as bloated stomach, weight gain, fluid retention, enlarged and tender breasts, and tension. Treatment depends upon the symptoms manifested and their severity. Some changes in lifestyle may help, such as eating less salty food or chocolate and not drinking alcoholic or caffeinated beverages. Exercise may help both physical and emotional symptoms.

Menstrual Cramps

Menstrual cramps are lower abdominal pain or discomfort during or just before a menstrual period. Menstrual cramps are sometimes associated with specific diseases or an underlying disorder, so it is important to seek professional medical help if you experience cramps that are severe, unscheduled, do not seem normal, or last more than two or three days.

Mild menstrual cramps are relieved by pain relievers such as *acetaminophen* or *ibuprofen*. If you choose or are prescribed ibuprofen, it is important to take it at the earliest onset of symptoms (bleeding or cramping). You may want to carry your medication with you to avoid a delay when your symptoms begin. A heating pad or hotwater bottle can also be used on your lower back or abdomen, or soak in a warm tub to help decrease discomfort. Exercising regularly, such as walking, swimming, or bicycling, may improve blood flow and ease menstrual pain. Eat a diet rich in whole grains and green leafy vegetables. Drink plenty of fluids. Avoid smoking and excessive use of alcohol.

Nutrition

What we eat has a great deal to do with how we look and feel and plays a vital role in our ability to stay healthy. A good balanced diet will usually be available to you in most situations you will encounter in the Navy. Whether you reap the benefits of this opportunity is, of course, up to you.

Foods are grouped according to their benefits. A balanced diet uses an appropriate number of servings from each food group to provide enough calories and nutrients each day. Too much of any one food group is not good for you, nor is it healthy to completely avoid any one group completely.

If you have, or think you have, a weight problem, seek advice from professionals (trained medical personnel or certified nutritional experts) before embarking on a diet. Many diets do more harm than good.

Exercise

A regular exercise program has many benefits, including improving efficiency of the heart, increasing capacity of the lungs, decreasing body fat, and reducing the risk of coronary artery disease. Maintaining a regular fitness program can also allow you to pass the Physical Readiness Test (PRT) required on a periodic basis for all Navy personnel (see chapter 7).

When exercising, it is important to wear appropriate equipment. If you are running you should wear a good running shoe that is not old and worn out. If you run at least three times per week, you should get new shoes every six months. Playing court sports such as tennis or basketball require special court shoes. These shoes are designed to provide the proper support and prevent ankle injuries. If you are playing a sport where eye injury is a possibility (such as racquetball) it is important to wear the appropriate eye protection. Protective helmets, pads, and athletic supporters are vital when playing contact sports. If you exercise more than three or four times per week, it is important to mix activities like biking and running or stair-stepping and swimming. This is called cross-training and will be more effective overall as well as allowing your muscles, bones, and connective tissues to recover from the stresses of physical activity.

Treatment of Illness and Injury

Despite proper preventive health and fitness measures, illness and injuries will still occur for most people. This section is a basic guide to help you handle common illness and injury. It will give you information on the signs and symptoms, common causes, transmission, prevention, and treatment of these problems. It will also help you to decide when to seek medical attention. It is by no means meant to replace medical treatment. If you are in doubt it is always better to seek advice and treatment from trained medical personnel than to take unnecessary risks with your health.

Use this information as a tool to keep yourself healthy and safe, thereby maintaining your optimal physical and mental condition.

Foot Care

Few jobs or responsibilities in the Navy do not require you to use your feet in one way or another. Whether you must stand a quarterdeck watch or run to your battle station, your feet are a vital part of your ability to do your job. Some foot problems are relatively common and can be fixed with minor treatment. Others can be more serious and require medical assistance.

Blisters

Blisters are a buildup of fluid beneath the skin in response to friction. They are commonly caused by new or improperly fitting shoes, or a sudden increase in activity that results in harmful friction. If not treated properly, a "simple" blister can become infected and require hospitalization. Since the skin covering a blister provides protection from infection, it should be left intact when possible. If the lesion is in an area susceptible to continued irritation, then the fluid can be expressed by puncturing the base of the blister with a sterile needle. The blister should be padded with moleskin, gauze, or a bandage. Antiseptics such as betadine or antibiotic cream can also be applied.

Athlete's Foot

"Athlete's foot" is the common name given to a fungus skin infection of the feet that is characterized by dry white scaling skin on the sole of the foot. It can exhibit varying degrees of itching. Between the toes it can cause peeling and fissuring (cracking) of the skin. Sometimes it causes small blisters filled with clear liquid. It is usually located on the sole or instep of the foot. Contributing factors include occlusive excessive foot perspiration, humid weather, and walking barefoot in community shower facilities. Preventive measures include daily foot washes, sock changes twice per day, shower shoes, and antifungal medications. Treatment consists of seeking medical attention and proper foot care and hygiene.

Ingrown Toenail

An ingrown nail occurs when the side of the nail penetrates the skin. This can be caused by trimming the nail too short, tightly fitting shoes, or trauma. Once the nail has penetrated the skin, pain and infection result. The toe becomes red, swollen, and has a pus drainage. If left untreated, this can result in serious infection of skin and bone. Removal of the offending nail border by a medical provider is the best treatment. To prevent this problem, you should trim your toenails straight across and do not round the edges.

Stasis Cellulitis

Prolonged standing can lead to an accumulation of blood and fluid in the feet and legs, causing them to become red and swollen. If not properly treated, infection can occur. Seek medical attention immediately.

Eye Injuries

Even with the best of precautions, eye injuries are sometimes unavoidable. To help decrease the chances of permanent damage to the eyes, proper steps can be taken following an injury. The following information is provided to give you a basic understanding of which conditions can be self-treated and which ones need immediate medical attention.

Black Eye

A black eye can occur from a blow to the ocular region and is actually a bruise. Standard treatment is as follows:

A cold compress should be placed on the injured area right away.

Over-the-counter medicine such as acetaminophen can be taken to decrease the pain.

Warm compresses can be used afterwards to help the healing process.

If there is double vision, decreased vision, severe eye pain, or the above procedures do not help, seek medical attention.

Foreign Bodies in the Eye

Small objects such as paint chips, metal flecks, or sawdust can sometimes get into the eye. Treatment is as follows:

Wash your hands. Use a cotton swab, corner of a handkerchief, or twisted piece of tissue moistened with clean water (not saliva) to touch and lift away the particle from the eye gently. Never remove a foreign body from the eye using your fingers, tweezers, or sharp objects.

If the foreign body is embedded and not easily removed you should seek medical attention. Refrain from rubbing your eyes. If a foreign body is actually stuck into the eye or the eyeball itself is cut, *no pressure* should be placed on the eye. Cover the affected eye with a paper cup taped into place or other clean object that does not touch the eye. Cover the opposite eye with a sterile cloth bandage to reduce movement of both eyes. Seek immediate medical attention as soon as possible.

Abrasions to the Eye

The cornea (clear covering over the pupil) is very sensitive to pain; an abrasion to the cornea will cause the patient to be sensitive to light, experience sharp pain, and have red eyes and possible vision decrease. Seeking immediate medical attention is appropriate.

Burns to the Eye

After a chemical burn to the eyes, it is extremely important to immediately rinse the eye out with clean water or sterile saline solution for a minimum of 30 minutes. The proper procedure is:

Hold the affected eye open with your thumb and forefinger.

Pour large amounts of warm (not hot) water from a clean container over the entire eye. Direct the water from the inside corner of the eye (by the nose) and let the water run down toward the outside corner of the eye to keep the chemical from spreading to the other eye.

If both eyes are affected, quickly alternate the above rinsing procedure to both eyes.

If you are by yourself or you cannot keep the victim's eye open, you can fill up a sink or container with warm water, stick the victim's face in the water, and have them blink repeatedly.

After rinsing the eye out, loosely bandage the eye or eyes with a sterile cloth and seek immediate medical attention.

As with all injuries, it is far better to *prevent* a chemical burn to the eye than to treat it. Certain safety precautions are paramount when working with chemicals that can damage your eyes:

Always wear safety glasses.
Do not rub your eyes after using chemicals.
Always wear gloves.
Turn your head away from chemical vapors to prevent eye
    injury.
Wash your hands when finished.

Conjunctivitis (Pink Eye)

Conjunctivitis can be extremely contagious. You should see an eye doctor when your eyes burn, become red, watery, itchy, and/or present with mucous-like discharge. Precautions you should take are as follows:

Towels and linens should not be shared and should be washed
    frequently to decrease the spread of infection.
Never share eye makeup.
Avoid contact lens use when pink eye is suspected.
Avoid touching your eyes to decrease the chances of spreading
    the infection to the unaffected eye or to another person.
Wash your hands frequently.

Orbital Fractures

The most common cause of orbital fracture (skull fracture around the eye) is blunt trauma to the face. Seek medical attention immediately if a fracture is suspected. Bruising and swelling of the eyelids, difficulty with eye movements, and double vision are all possible indications of orbital fracture.

Retinal Detachment

The sudden appearance of flashes of light off to the side of your vision, numerous floating particles, or the feeling that a dark curtain is obstructing part of your vision are all symptoms of this serious problem. Immediate medical attention is needed to prevent permanent vision loss.

Ten Ways to Keep Your Eyes Healthy

1. Get a complete eye exam every year.
2. Wear your correct contact lens or glasses prescription as indicated by your eye doctor.
3. Do not sleep with your contact lenses in place unless your eye doctor specifically fit you with a special pair designed to be

worn overnight. Even then, you must never sleep in your contact lenses for more than six nights in a row before taking them out to clean and disinfect them. Failure to do so may result in permanent eye damage.

4. Contact lenses should be removed immediately if your eyes become red, painful, or if you notice a decrease in your vision. Carefully inspect the contact lens and do not wear again if you notice any chips or tears. You should see an eye-care provider before wearing your lenses again or if these symptoms persist.

5. Always wear suitable eye protection (shields, goggles, or safety glasses) when working with harmful chemicals and dangerous machinery. Safety glasses should also be worn during jobs that expose your eyes to materials such as sawdust, paint chips, or metal flecks.

6. Keep your eyelids healthy by cleaning the outside skin of the lids on a daily basis. This will reduce the formation of sties (painful lumps in the eyelid) and also decrease eye infections.

7. Do not share makeup as infections are easily spread this way.

8. Do not stare directly at the sun, bright lights, fires, or welding arcs.

9. Wear ultraviolet eye protection when in the sun or in tanning beds.

10. Eye injuries should be taken seriously. When in doubt, seek medical attention.

Diarrhea

Diarrhea is the passing of unusually loose and frequent bowel movements. It may cause discomfort and is often accompanied or preceded by cramping pains in the lower abdomen. Diarrheal illness can be very dangerous when dehydration develops. In this country, most attacks of diarrhea are the result of viral infection and last no more than 48 hours. No special treatment is usually warranted other than ensuring that you drink enough fluids. However, if diarrhea persists or recurs, seek medical assistance.

Diarrhea caused by bacteria is more serious. A visit to a country where sanitation standards are low may expose you to bacteria found in inadequately purified water or in contaminated milk and food. This is known as *traveler's diarrhea*. Therefore, eat only well-cooked food and drink only water and milk that have been boiled or sterilized. Again, if you have diarrhea lasting greater than 48 hours, seek medical attention.

Dysentery is a serious digestive-tract infection that is more common in hot countries but one that also occurs in the United States. It causes violent blood-stained diarrhea with fever, vomiting, and abdominal pain. If you have these symptoms, seek medical help immediately.

Sexually Transmitted Diseases

Sexually transmitted diseases (STDs) are infections that are usually spread by sexual contact. They used to be referred to as venereal disease or just "VD"; you may still hear that term or the slang term "clap" used when people are referring to STDs. The most effective means of avoiding STDs is, of course, to avoid sexual contact, but other effective means of reducing the risk are having only one sexual partner and the use of condoms.

It is a strange characteristic of our society that STDs are often the subject of jokes or are viewed by some as a badge of conquest. But make no mistake, there is nothing funny or admirable in contracting one of these diseases. STDs can permanently damage your reproductive organs, causing infertility. They can also cause heart disease, blindness, deafness, arthritis, and death. If a woman is infected during pregnancy she could have a miscarriage or pass the infection to her unborn baby.

If you suspect you have a STD or have been told by your partner that he or she was treated for a STD, refrain from further sexual encounters and seek medical treatment as soon as possible.

If you have any of the following symptoms, you should seek medical attention:

genital sores or warts
painful urination
genital pain during sex
unusual genital discharge
rashes in the genital area
swollen lymph nodes
unexplained weight loss
sudden loss of hair

Some of the common STDs can be treated or cured, others cannot. AIDS (acquired immune deficiency syndrome) is caused by HIV (human immunodeficiency virus). This virus infects a person's blood and attacks the cells that normally protect people from infection and cancer. An infected person may have no symptoms initially, but over the years the immune system weakens, causing the victim to lose the ability to fight off other diseases and disorders. The average time from HIV infection to the onset of AIDS is approximately 10 years. While advances have been made in medicine and treatment, there is no cure for HIV/AIDS.

First Aid

When an injury occurs, the first choice is obviously to have someone with the appropriate medical training take care of the problem. But it is also obvious that there will be many occasions when a person has been injured and there is no medically trained person around. Waiting for medical attention is not an option if the person is going to have any chance of survival in cases where breathing has stopped or there is severe bleeding. In these instances, what is popularly known as first aid can make the difference between life and death or between serious and minor injury.

CPR

Cardiopulmonary resuscitation (CPR) is used only for sudden cardiac or respiratory arrest. CPR is a temporary action performed by someone *trained* in performing CPR. This brief description of the emergency procedures for the adult cannot substitute for approved CPR training.

Important: Call for help as soon as the victim is discovered unresponsive. Then check ABCs (airway, breathing, circulation).

One-person Adult CPR

1. Gently position the person on his back and open the airway by pushing the head back and lifting the jaw.
2. Look, listen, and feel for breathing.
3. If the person is not breathing, seal your mouth around his and give two slow breaths, each lasting 1 to 1.5 seconds.
4. Feel for a pulse. If there is a pulse, breathe for the adult with one breath every 5 seconds. If no pulse, start chest compressions.
5. Chest compressions begin with the heel of one hand two-thirds of the way down the breastbone and your other hand on the top. Compress chest 1 to 2 inches. Continue compressing three times every 2 seconds (80 to 100 per minute). After 15 chest compression, give two breaths. Repeat until a pulse returns or medical help arrives.

Choking

The universal sign for choking is grasping the neck with both hands. If severe breathing difficulties occur and the victim is unable to cough up the object, such as a piece of food, use the following procedure (called the *Heimlich Maneuver*) to dislodge it:

Stand behind the victim and wrap your arms around the victim's waist (see figure below). Press one fist against the abdomen and below the rib cage. Then grasp your fist with the other and perform quick upward thrusts into the abdomen.

Unconscious victims should be rolled onto their back. Kneel astride the victim's thighs and use quick upward abdominal thrusts using the heel of your hand. Repeat 6–10 times, then check for the obstruction by sweeping the victim's mouth with your finger.

If you are the one who is choking, bend over the back of a chair thrusting your abdomen sharply. Repeat until object is dislodged.

Bleeding

It is important to note that the body only contains five quarts of blood. Prolonged bleeding from any type of wound can be life-threatening. Quick action in the rendering of first aid is required to minimize the loss of blood by controlling the bleeding.

Types of Bleeding

There are three types of bleeding:

Capillary bleeding is commonly characterized by a superficial wound with oozing blood easily controllable with direct pressure.

Venous bleeding is denoted by its dark color of red or maroon.

Arterial bleeding, which is easily recognizable by the bright red color and the typical pulsating bleeding at the wound site or, in the case of a deep wound, has a continuous bright red flow.

If you are confronted with multiple wounds on the same victim, you should treat them in the following order: arterial first, venous second, and capillary third.

Treatment of Bleeding

Treatment of the bleeding wound will depend upon the type and location of the wound. There are different methods that may be used to stop bleeding.

Direct pressure. Most external bleeding can be controlled by applying pressure directly over the wound. Use what is available (such as a clean cloth or a part of clothing). The cleaner the material the better in preventing infection. Application of the bare hand may be necessary in stemming a major loss of blood until more effective cloth material can be brought to use. After the bleeding has been controlled, apply layers of cloth to form a good-sized covering, and then bandage firmly. Do not remove the dressing. If blood saturates the dressing simply apply more cloth or dressing material to the site. Removal of the dressing may pull away the blood clot and bleeding may resume.

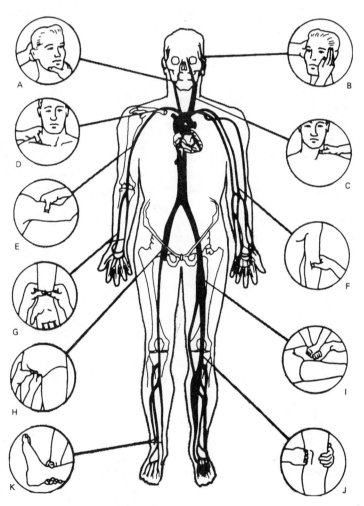

Figure 23.2. Pressure applied to the appropriate point on the body is an effective method of reducing or stopping blood flow.

Pressure points. For especially quick action, you can use your fingers or the heel of your hand to compress the supplying vessel against the underlying bone. Merely feel for the pulse directly above the wound (closer to the heart) and press against the bone in that particular area until the blood flow is diminished or stopped. Note that arteries run along the inner sides of the long bones in the body, and along the inner sides of the jaw. *Never* apply the pressure point method to injuries of the neck.

Tourniquet. This is the least desirable method of controlling bleeding because it is difficult to do correctly. It is and should always be the *last resort* when all other methods have failed. It is also important to note that any site at or below where the tourniquet is applied will have no nutrients or oxygen supply. The tissues will soon die, necessitating the ultimate loss of the limb.

When applying the tourniquet, place the dressing over the wound, wrap the bandage around the limb as close to the wound as possible and tear or cut the bandage into two tails at the exposed end. Tie an overhand knot around a stick, screw driver, pencil, or any material along those lines. Twist the bandage material until bleeding is stopped. Secure the stick or whatever the material you have used with a square knot to keep the bandage from unraveling and losing pressure over the wound. Once a tourniquet is applied it must never be removed except by a trained medical professional. If, for some reason (such as moving on to help other victims) you must leave the victim, mark her or his forehead with a *T*. Try to use something other than blood because it might be accidentally wiped away or might dry and flake off. On one side of the *T* write the location of the tourniquet (right leg, left arm, or whatever). On the other side of the *T* write the date and time it was applied.

Shock

Shock is a life-threatening condition that may occur with severe injury or illness. Shock may begin immediately, or it may be delayed for several hours. A shock victim has inadequate flow of blood to vital organs and tissues.

Signs and Symptoms of Shock

A person in shock may insist that they feel fine, and then pass out. The following indications will help you to identify when a victim is in shock:

Weak and rapid pulse
Breathing may be shallow, rapid, or irregular

Pale, cool, and moist skin
Dilated pupils
Drowsy, restless, or anxious

Treatment of Shock

Call for emergency medical help immediately. Do not give food or fluids. Lay the victim down on his or her back, raise both legs, loosen all tight clothing, and keep him or her warm.

Burns

Burns may be caused by dry heat (fire), moist heat (steam or hot liquids), electricity, or corrosive chemicals. To treat any burn, *first remove the cause.*

Superficial burns may not be serious but they are very painful, so first aid is performed mainly by cooling the area with cold running water for 10 minutes. If blisters form, do not break them. If the burn is on a part of the skin that can be rubbed by clothing, cover the area with a padded dressing. Do not apply any cream, grease, ointment, or butter. The exception is mild sunburn, which can often be soothed with over the counter anesthetic lotions or spray.

Serious burns cause extreme pain. Treat for shock immediately before trying to treat the burns. Keep the victim's head slightly lower than the feet and keep them warm. Cover all burns with dry, sterile dressings. A seriously burned person badly needs fluids. If the victim is conscious, able to swallow, and has no internal injuries, give her or him water, fruit juice, or sugar water.

Chemical burns can cause extensive destruction of body tissue. This kind of injury can be caused by acids such as nitric, sulfuric, and hydrochloric acid or by caustic alkalis such as potassium hydroxide (lye), sodium hydroxide, and calcium hydroxide. The best treatment of chemical burns is to wash the chemical off immediately with large amounts of clean, fresh, cool water. If possible, immerse the affected areas. Do not break any blisters. Cover the burns with dry sterile dressings and transport to nearest medical facility.

531

Fractures

There are two principle types of fractures, *simple* and *compound*. A simple fracture is a broken bone that does not break the skin. A compound fracture is characterized by the jagged edge of bone causing a break in the skin. The latter is more serious because of the high potential for infection and the potential loss of blood.

Since a fracture is an injury beneath the skin surface it cannot be seen except in rare cases. Always question the individual, "Do you think you may have fractured it?" Look at the person; do they appear in shock? Is there point tenderness over the injury site, localized discoloration of the skin, numbness, throbbing pain, or obvious deformity? All are signs and symptoms of a fracture. When in doubt, treat as if it is a fracture. You should be aware that an individual may be able to move the body or body part with a fracture so this is not a conclusive test, and may produce further internal injury. If you suspect the person may be in or going into shock, treat for shock first. With a compound fracture, control the bleeding first and when the blood loss is under control secure the fracture.

Treatment of Fractures

Effective splinting and immobilization of the fracture site is key to prevent further injury. Keep in mind that any joint above and below the site of fracture must also be immobilized. Virtually anything that immobilizes the fracture is appropriate, be it rolled newspaper, sticks, magazines, cardboard, or a metal pipe. Whatever you use for splinting, it should be padded for the victim's comfort and secured with strips of cloth. The rule of thumb in treating fractures is, *"Splint it as it lays."* Never attempt to straighten a fracture, this should only be attempted by trained medical professionals. Splinting supplies are provided on every naval vessel and installation.

Poisoning

Prompt action is paramount in poisoning cases. The objective is to dilute the poison as fast as possible or to induce vomiting, depending upon the kind of poison. This must be followed by swift medical evaluation at the nearest medical treatment facility. Great care must be given to assure the patient does not inhale any vomitus into the

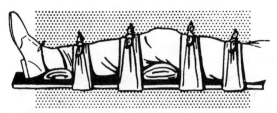

Figure 23.3. Effective splinting can prevent further injury once a fracture has occurred. Make sure splints are tied securely to immobilize the limb, but do not cut off blood circulation.

lungs. If this happens, immediate life saving professional medical intervention will be needed. All naval commands are required to have and maintain an antidote locker. In the locker you can find the "Handbook of Poison Antidotes," an antacid such as Maalox or Mylanta, vinegar, syrup of ipecac to induce vomiting, the phone number to the local Poison Control Center, activated charcoal to bind with the poison and prevent absorption in the intestine, a bottle of magnesium citrate to stimulate the bowel to allow for quick expulsion of the poison, medicine cups, ammonia capsules to arouse the unconscious patient, and your local emergency response phone numbers.

Caustic and corrosive poisons, such as ingested lye and strong acids, injure the lining of the food passages. The injury may be minimized when fluids are used to dilute the poison. First aid must be instantaneous as every second of delay will cause further injury. Water is usually the most readily available suitable substance. Four glasses of water will normally dilute the ingested caustic or corrosive enough to slow or subdue further damage to the lining of the food passage and stomach. For strong acids, glasses of water with several teaspoons of baking soda can be used. Mylanta or Maalox coats the lining of the food passages and stomach, preventing further injury.

Petroleum distillates such as gasoline, kerosene, paint thinner, and the like present a particular danger if vomiting is induced. *Do not induce vomiting!* The victim may breathe the poison into the lungs which may cause severe lung damage and death. Victims with this type of poisoning may exhibit violent behavior and should be closely guarded until help can arrive. These victims require immediate professional medical attention.

Narcotics and barbiturates depress the central nervous system and can depress the breathing center in the body, causing the victim to lapse into a coma and die. Close observation of pulse and respirations is very important. Call for help immediately. Provide CPR if indicated. The victim's pupils may be constricted and you may see little or no reaction to light. Watch for any signs of vomiting. Position the patient on his or her side if vomiting occurs. Protect the victim against physical harm if convulsions occur and always protect the airway until help arrives. Never give anything by mouth to an unconscious patient. If help is not readily available and the patient is awake and alert, syrup of ipecac may be given for ingested narcotics.

Heat Injuries

Exposure to extreme heat conditions can cause problems ranging in severity and can ultimately lead to death.

533

Dehydration

Dehydration can be very harmful but is easily preventable. The speed at which dehydration develops depends on body weight, activity, and loss of body fluids. In heat conditions, you can monitor your own hydration status by observing the color of your urine. The clearer the urine the better. Dark yellow urine means your urine is very concentrated and you are more prone to dehydration symptoms, heat exhaustion, and heat stroke. Other signs of dehydration are dry mouth and thirst and an increased heart rate.

The main objective when treating dehydration is to take in as much fluid as possible without causing increased nausea and subsequent vomiting.

To prevent dehydration, drink more water during heavy work or warm weather. If you should develop symptoms of dehydration, first begin by taking sips of water. Slowly increase your intake as tolerated. Avoid all juices and dairy products while trying to hydrate yourself.

Heat Exhaustion

Heat exhaustion occurs after sustained dehydration and heat stress. Heat exhaustion may progress to heat stroke which can lead to death. Signs and symptoms of heat exhaustion are fatigue, muscular weakness, profuse sweating, increased heart rate, dizziness, nausea, vomiting, and cool moist skin.

Treatment consists of rapid cooling of the body and rehydration. Call for medical attention immediately.

Heat Stroke

Caused by an imbalance between heat production and heat dissipation, heat stroke occurs when core body temperature increases. The body normally dissipates heat from the skin by radiation, conduction, convection, and evaporation. When the surrounding temperature rises the body loses its ability to effectively control heat release. This is especially true in a hot, humid environment. Heat stroke kills about 4000 people a year in the United States.

The most telling symptom of heat stroke is confusion and dizziness. Other symptoms include an absence of sweating; hot, dry skin; and collapse with loss of consciousness.

For the most part, heat stroke is preventable by adhering to a graduated schedule of increasing performance requirements in hot conditions and ensuring unrestricted access to drinking water. Salt replacement tablets, once thought to be effective in preventing heat stroke, are no longer recommended.

First aid treatment of a heat stroke victim is immediate rapid cooling. The most efficient method to reduce core body temperature is to remove all clothing, induce evaporative heat loss by spraying the victim with cool water, and fanning with warm air. Keep the victim's head above the level of the heart and transport the victim to a medical treatment facility immediately. Heat stroke is a very serious medical emergency.

Cold Injuries

Hypothermia, or abnormally low core body temperature, can result from exposure to cold weather or from total immersion in cold water. Signs and symptoms of severe hypothermia include unconsciousness, pale skin color, slow and shallow breathing, faint or undetectable pulse, and semirigid extremities. The victim may appear to be dead in these circumstances.

First aid consists mainly of bringing the body temperature back to normal. Wrap the patient in warm blankets in a warm room. Do not give the victim hot drinks or other stimulants until consciousness has been regained. Transport to a medical treatment facility immediately. Hypothermia is a very serious medical emergency.

Exposure to dry cold may cause frostbite, especially in the cheeks, nose, chin, ears, forehead, wrists, hands, feet, and genitalia. The skin turns white or gray, then bright pink.

Frostbite may also be caused by contact with certain chemicals that cause rapid freezing, such as liquid oxygen, carbon dioxide, Freon, and other industrial gases. Such injuries are often called chemical burns, but the body tissue is actually frozen.

When the frostbitten area is warmed up, it immediately becomes red and swollen. Large blisters develop. Severe frostbite causes gangrene, which destroys soft tissues and sometimes even bone. If deep tissue is destroyed, the injured part may have to be amputated. Do not thaw a frozen extremity until you can transport the patient to a medical treatment facility. *Do not rub or massage frostbitten tissues.*

Transporting Injured Personnel

The condition of the victim and the immediacy of danger will dictate the appropriate method of transportation. If the victim does not need to be immediately transported, wait for proper medical assistance. *Remember to give all necessary first aid before moving the victim.* Relieve the victim's pain and make him or her as comfortable as possible. Use standard stretchers when available. Make sure that the victim is securely fastened to the stretcher so that he or she will not slip, slide, or fall off. Use blankets, garments, or other available materials to pad the stretcher and to protect the victim from exposure.

Victims should usually lie on their backs while being moved, but a victim who is having difficulty breathing because of a chest wound may be more comfortable if the head and shoulders are slightly raised, or if he or she is placed on the side of injury. A victim with a severe injury to the back of the head should be kept on their side. A patient should always be carried *feet first* unless there is some special reason for carrying her or him head first, such as going up a ladder.

Stretchers

The most common method of transporting injured personnel is by using a stretcher. Because of the unique environments found in the Navy, there are several different types in use.

Stokes stretcher. This is a wire-basket type of stretcher that is adaptable to a variety of uses and is the most commonly used stretcher in the Navy. It will hold a person securely in place even when tipped or turned. The Stokes stretcher is generally used for transferring the injured to and from boats or ships. It can be used to rescue personnel from the water. Fifteen-foot handling lines are attached to each end.

These lines should be secured to stanchions or other solid objects when transporting victims from deck to deck. The stretcher should be padded with two blankets placed lengthwise so that one will be under each of the victim's legs, and a third blanket folded in half and placed in the upper part of the stretcher to protect the victim's head and shoulders. The victim should be lowered gently into the stretcher and made as comfortable as possible. The victim must be fastened to the stretcher by straps over the chest, hips, knees, and feet to prevent sliding up and down. The straps go over the blanket or over the covering.

Neill-Robertson stretcher. This stretcher is specifically designed for vertically removing an injured person from enginerooms, holds, and other compartments where access hatches are too small to permit the use of regular stretchers. It is all wood and canvas construction, and completely encloses the victim. When firmly wrapped around the victim, it gives the needed support for vertical lifting. A guideline is tied to the bottom ring to keep the victim from swaying against bulkheads and hatches while being lifted.

Army litter. This consists of two wooden poles, approximately seven feet long, with canvas stretched across the poles. It is used for evacuation of the injured at land-based facilities. It is hard to secure a casualty onto the Army litter, and for this reason its use is limited aboard ship. Check it for deterioration before using it.

Rescuer-Victim Carries

Some situations will require immediate transportation of an injured person. During these situations one of the following techniques may be used.

Three-man lift. One rescuer takes the head and shoulders of the victim, another takes the back and buttocks, and the third takes the legs and feet. The one with the victim's head says, "Ready, lift," and all lift together and keep the body straight.

Fireman's lift. Turn the patient face down. Kneel over the victim's head, facing the shoulders. Pass both your hands under the armpits and lift the victim to his knees. Then slide your hands down lower and clasp them around the victim's back. Raise the victim to a standing position, stick your right leg between the victim's legs, take the victim's right wrist in your left hand, and swing his or her arm around the back of your neck, holding the injured person close to you. Put your right arm between the victim's thighs, stoop quickly, pull his or her trunk across your shoulders, and straighten up.

To lower the patient, kneel on your left knee. Grasp the victim's left knee with your right hand. Slide the victim around in front of you

537

Figure 23.4. One person can transport an injury victim by using the fireman's lift.

and down your right thigh into a sitting position. Shift your hands to the victim's head and place the victim gently on his or her back.

Tied-hands crawl. Use this method when you must remain close to the deck or when you must have both hands free for climbing a ladder. Lay the victim on her or his back. Cross the wrists and tie them together. Kneel over the victim's stomach and lift the arms over your head so that the wrists are at the back of your neck. When crawling forward raise your shoulders high enough so that the victim's head will not bump against the deck.

Figure 23.5. A variation of the tied-hands crawl.

Navy Organization

A

The Navy, along with the Army and Air Force, is part of the Defense Department (DOD). Until 1947, the Navy and the Army were separate departments of the government and there was no such thing as DOD. The National Security Act of 1947 created the National Military Establishment (NME), which in 1949 became DOD. The Secretary of Defense (SECDEF) heads DOD and is an appointed civilian cabinet officer.

The original Department of the Navy (DON) was created in 1798 when Benjamin Stoddert was appointed the first Secretary of the Navy (SECNAV). In 1815, a three-man board of naval commissioners was created to manage the Navy. In 1842, this was changed to a bureau system, which lasted with minor changes until 1966. The position and title of Chief of Naval Operations (CNO) was created in 1915.

539

Department of Defense

DOD is the largest government agency in the United States. It is composed of the Office of the Secretary of Defense (OSD), defense agencies, the Joint Chiefs of Staff (JCS), unified combatant commands, and the Departments of the Army, Navy, and Air Force. It provides for military security and supports national policies and interests.

Secretary of Defense

The SECDEF is the principal defense policy adviser to the President of the United States and is responsible for the formulation of general defense policy and the execution of approved policy. Under the direction of the President, the SECDEF exercises direction, authority, and control over the department.

The Deputy SECDEF supervises and coordinates the activities of the department and takes the place of the SECDEF when necessary.

The Joint Chiefs of Staff

The JCS consists of a Chairman, the Chiefs of Staff of the Army and Air Force, the Chief of Naval Operations (CNO), and the Commandant of the Marine Corps (CMC). The JCS also has a Vice-chairman as a nonvoting member. The Vice-chairman acts as Chairman in the latter's absence.

The Chairman of the JCS, assisted by other JCS members and supported by the Joint Staff, is responsible for strategic direction of the armed forces; strategic planning; contingency planning and preparedness; advice on department and combatant command requirements, programs, and budgets; doctrine, training, and education for the joint employment of the armed forces; United Nations representational duties; and other duties prescribed by law, the President, or the SECDEF.

Unified Combatant Commands

Responsibility for military planning and operations in different parts of the world and for certain specialized aspects of the military establishment has been assigned to a number of unified commanders. A unified command, composed of elements of two or more services, has a broad continuing mission and a single commander. The current unified commands are Joint Forces Command, Central Command, European Command, Pacific Command, Southern Command, Space Command, Special Operations Command, Strategic Command, and Transportation Command. These commanders are responsible to the President and the SECDEF for accomplishing their assigned military missions and for exercising command authority over assigned forces. The operational chain of command runs from the President to the SECDEF to the unified combatant commanders through the Chairman JCS, who transmits orders to the commanders.

The Department of the Navy (DON)

Since its formal beginning as a military department in 1798, DON has consisted of three distinctly separate bodies: the Navy Department, the shore establishment, and the operating forces.

Navy Department

The Navy Department (as opposed to the Department of the Navy) refers to the central executive offices of DON located at the seat of government. Organizationally, the Navy Department comprises the Office of the Secretary of the Navy; the Office of the Chief of Naval

Operations; Headquarters, United States Marine Corps; and, under the command of the CNO, the Bureau of Naval Personnel. Headquarters, United States Coast Guard, normally is part of the Department of Transportation but can be a part of the Navy in time of war or national emergency.

The Navy Department establishes policy, provides direction, and exerts control over the operations of the other two components of DON, the shore establishment and the operating forces of the Navy.

Secretary of the Navy. The head of the Department of the Navy is a civilian and is called the Secretary of the Navy, abbreviated "SEC-NAV." Like all service secretaries, under secretaries, and assistant secretaries, she or he is appointed by the President and confirmed by the Senate. Under the direction, authority, and control of SECDEF, SECNAV is responsible for the policies and control of DON, including its organization, administration, operation, and efficiency.

The Office of the Secretary of the Navy is composed of the Undersecretary of the Navy, Assistant Secretaries of the Navy, General Counsel of DON, Judge Advocate General (JAG) of the Navy, Naval Inspector General (IG), Chief of Naval Research, and other offices and officials established by law or by the Secretary. The Office of the Secretary of the Navy is responsible for the following functions within the DON: acquisition, auditing and financial management, legal and legislative affairs, and the dissemination of information to the government and the public.

Undersecretary of the Navy. The Undersecretary of the Navy is the deputy and principal assistant to SECNAV. She or he is responsible for internal auditing (through the Office of the Auditor General), counterintelligence, security, law enforcement, and related investigative activities.

Assistant Secretary of the Navy (Manpower and Reserve Affairs). This assistant secretary supervises manpower and reserve component affairs of DON, including policy and the administration of affairs related to military (active and inactive) and civilian personnel.

Assistant Secretary of the Navy (Installations and Environment). This assistant secretary is responsible to SECNAV for the formulation of policies and procedures related to the construction, management, maintenance, and repair of facilities.

Assistant Secretary of the Navy (Research, Development, and Acquisition). He or she serves as the Navy's acquisition and procurement executive, establishing policies and procedures related to research and development.

Assistant Secretary of the Navy (Financial Management). This is the comptroller of the Navy, responsible for all matters related to the financial management of DON, including budgeting, accounting, disbursing, financing, internal review, progress and statistical reporting, and automatic data-processing systems and equipment (except for ADPE integral to a weapons system). He or she also serves as an advisor and assistant to the CNO and CMC with respect to financial and budgetary matters.

General Counsel. Reporting directly to SECNAV, the General Counsel provides legal advice and supervises matters relating to general legal issues, litigation, business and commercial law, real and personal property, civilian personnel law, patent law, the fiscal budget, accounting, and so on.

Chief of Information. Provides services to the public such as answering inquiries, assuring a prompt and accurate flow of information to the news media, and coordinating Navy participation in community events.

Judge Advocate General. Providing all legal services pertaining to functions of DON, except those areas of business and commercial law assigned to the general counsel of the Navy, the Judge Advocate General (JAG) supervises the administration of military justice (UCMJ) throughout DON and advises on matters involving admiralty law.

Chief of Legislative Affairs. Arranges and coordinates the presentation of statements, testimony, briefings, and reports to members and committees of Congress by military and civilian personnel of DON; monitors and evaluates congressional actions affecting DON; and arranges for congressional travel (an official responsibility of DON).

Director of Program Appraisal. Reporting directly to SECNAV, this office gives independent appraisals of existing and proposed Navy and Marine Corps programs. The office also analyzes DON objectives, and the validity, adequacy, feasibility, and balances of proposed programs to meet them, to help SECNAV assess the overall direction of DON's efforts.

Auditor General. Working under the direct supervision of the Under Secretary of the Navy, the auditor general is responsible for internal DON audits and commands the Naval Audit Service Headquarters and field regions.

Naval Inspector General. Serving as the principal advisor on all matters relating to inspection and investigation of importance to DON, with particular emphasis on readiness; identifies areas of inefficiency in DON and recommends improvement; and receives and investigates, or refers for investigation, allegations of inefficiency, misconduct, impropriety, mismanagement, or violations of law.

Director, Naval Criminal Investigative Service. Functioning as a kind of FBI for the Navy, this service commands an organization of people in more than 160 locations worldwide providing criminal investigative, counterintelligence, law enforcement, and physical and personnel security support to the Navy and Marine Corps, on land and sea.

Office of the Comptroller. This office, under the assistant secretary for financial management, is responsible for the Navy's budgeting, accounting, progress and statistical reporting, administrative organization, and related managerial tasks. The deputy comptroller advises both the CNO and the CMC.

Office of the Chief of Naval Research. Working for the assistant secretary for research, development, and acquisition, this office coordinates research programs for DON as well as administering activities within or on behalf of the Navy relating to patents, inventions, royalty payments, and other matters relating to the patent and copyright function.

Chief of Naval Operations. The CNO is appointed by the President of the United States and confirmed by the Senate to take precedence over all other officers of the naval service. As Navy representative of the JCS, the CNO keeps SECNAV informed on JCS activities and is responsible to the President and the Secretary of Defense for duties external to DON as prescribed by law. The CNO directs OPNAV (derived from "operations of the Navy" but is better thought of as simply the Office of the Chief of Naval Operations) and other major Navy headquarters and shore commands and activities, the operating forces of the Navy, and shore activities as assigned by SECNAV.

Vice Chief of Naval Operations. The VCNO is also appointed by the President, by and with the advice and consent of the Senate. Orders issued by the VCNO have the same effect as those issued by the CNO, who has delegated to the VCNO complete authority to act for him in all matters not specifically reserved by law to the CNO alone. The principal duty of the VCNO is to act as executive for the CNO.

Office of the Chief of Naval Operations. OPNAV is the headquarters of the CNO and is responsible for assisting in the execution of CNO duties. OPNAV also assists SECNAV, the Undersecretary, and the assistant secretaries of the Navy. Organizationally, OPNAV consists of the CNO, the Vice Chief of Naval Operations (VCNO), and

OPNAV principal officials (OPOs) as listed below. OPOs are responsible for the performance of assigned missions and functions within their respective areas of responsibility.

OPNAV Principal Officials. The CNO is assisted by a staff of principal officials, some of whom have the title of Deputy Chief of Naval Operations (DCNO) while others are directors or special assistants. The list that follows shows their codes and titles. It is by no means a complete listing and is subject to change, but it will give you an idea of how this is set up.

N1	DCNO Manpower and Personnel
N2	Director of Naval Intelligence
N3/N5	DCNO Plans, Policy, and Operations
N4	DCNO Fleet Readiness and Logistics
N6	Director of Space Information Warfare, Command and Control
N7	DCNO Warfare Requirements and Programs
N70	Warfare Integration
N74	Antisubmarine Warfare
N75	Expeditionary Warfare
N76	Surface Warfare
N77	Submarine Warfare
N78	Air Warfare
N79	Naval Training & Education
N8	DCNO Resources, Requirements, and Assessments
N09	Vice Chief of Naval Operations
N093	Surgeon General
N095	Director of Naval Reserve
N096	Oceanographer of the Navy (also Navigator of the Navy)
N097	Chief of Chaplains

Chief of Naval Personnel. Also known by the acronym CHNAVPERS, this officer directs the Bureau of Naval Personnel (BUPERS) which directs the recruiting, assignment, training, and career development of Navy personnel. Other personnel-related activities, such as the Navy Recruiting Command (CRUITCOM) and Navy Civilian Personnel Center (NCPC), report to CHNAVPERS as well.

Bureau of Medicine and Surgery. BUMED directs health care services for Navy and Marine Corps personnel and other authorized persons.

Commandant of the Marine Corps. Marine Corps equivalent to the CNO, the CMC is responsible, under SECNAV, for the administration, discipline, internal organization, training, efficiency, and readiness of the Marine Corps. As the Marine Corps representative on the JCS, the CMC keeps SECNAV informed on JCS activities and is responsible to the president and the secretary of defense for external duties as prescribed by law. The CMC's command includes Marine Corps headquarters, operating forces, support establishment, and reserve. The CMC is not a part of the command structure of the CNO; there is, however, close cooperation between the two.

The Navy Shore Establishment

The Navy shore establishment consists of major shore commands and shore activities that have been established by the SECNAV. A major shore command is generally charged with a Navy-wide or an area-wide mission and includes subordinate shore facilities to carry out its mission. For example, the Naval Computer and Telecommunications Command, a major shore command with headquarters in Washington, is responsible for the naval telecommunications system. Shore activities known as communications stations, located throughout the world, are included in this command.

Naval shore activities are formally organized installations with a prescribed mission for a specified local area. Naval shore activities include air stations, hospitals, submarine bases, amphibious bases, and shipyards. There are also many specified one-of-a-kind activities such as the Naval Academy and the Naval Observatory.

Chief Of Naval Education and Training. Also known as "CNET" (pronounced "seanet"), this officer is in charge of the Navy's education and training programs. CNET manages the funds that pay for education, the facilities that house classrooms, and the curricula used in naval training. Technical training at shore stations, at air stations, and at sea comes under CNET's jurisdiction. Under CNET are the Chief of Naval Air Training (CNATRA) and the Chief of Naval Technical Training.

Commander, Naval Computer and Telecommunications Command. COMNAVCOMTELCOM, under CNO, plans, operates, and maintains all Navy ashore communication resources and all non-tactical information resources for command, control, and administration of the Navy and those elements of the Defense Communication System assigned to the Navy.

Office of Naval Intelligence. The Director of Naval Intelligence, under the CNO, directs and manages ONI to fulfill intelligence requirements of the DON.

Commander, Naval Space Command. COMNAVSPACECOM, under the CNO, is responsible for all activities related to outer space that are conducted in conjunction with the accomplishment of the naval mission.

Commander, Naval Security Group. COMNAVSECGRU, under the CNO, is responsible for the Navy's cryptologic activities.

Commander, Naval Oceanography Command. COMNAV-OCEANCOM manages oceanographic activities (oceanography, meteorology, mapping, charting, geodesy, astronomy, and chronometry) under the Naval Oceanographic Program.

Commander, Naval Legal Service Command. COMNAVLEG-SVCCOM, under the CNO, administers the Navy's legal services program and provides command direction for all legal-service activities and resources.

Commander, Naval Sea Systems Command. COMNAVSEA-SYSCOM provides material support to the Navy and Marine Corps for ships, submersibles, other sea platforms, shipboard combat systems and components, other surface and undersea warfare and weapons systems, and ordnance expendables not specifically assigned to other systems commands.

Commander, Naval Air Systems Command. COMNAVAIR-SYSCOM is responsible for providing for material support to the operating forces of the Navy in the areas of aeronautical weapon systems, their associated subsystems, and related systems and equipment. COMNAVAIRSYSCOM provides similar material support to the Marine Corps, DON, DOD, Coast Guard, and other organizations as assigned. COMNAVAIRSYSCOM also operates shore facilities and ranges for the support of these needs.

Commander, Space and Naval Warfare Systems Command. COMSPAWARSYSCOM is responsible for providing material and technical support to the Navy and Marine Corps for space systems, command, control, communications, intelligence, electronic warfare, and undersea surveillance.

Commander, Naval Supply Systems Command. COMNAVSUP-SYSCOM is responsible for providing materials, supplies, and support services to the operating forces of the Navy and Marine Corps.

Commander, Naval Facilities Engineering Command. COM-NAVFACENGCOM is responsible for providing material and technical support to the Navy and Marine Corps in the following areas: shore facilities, real property, utilities, fixed ocean systems and structures, transportation equipment, and energy. This officer also controls the Naval Construction Forces.

Operating Forces

The operating forces of the Navy consist of fleets, seagoing forces, fleet marine forces, the Military Sealift Command, and other forces and activities assigned by the president or SECNAV.

Two chains of command apply to the operating forces. The *operational* chain of command runs from the president through the secretary of defense, to a commander of a unified or specified command, and then to those operational forces assigned to that commander. The *administrative* chain runs from SECNAV and the CNO to the operating forces.

It must be understood that the operating forces are permanently organized in the administrative chain of command, while the operational chain of command is task-oriented and can be structured as necessary to meet operational requirements.

The CNO commands the operating forces of the Navy and is responsible to SECNAV for their administration and use, including training and readiness.

Administratively, the Pacific and Atlantic fleets include ships and craft classified and organized into commands by type (for example, Surface Forces, Atlantic Fleet or Naval Air Forces, Pacific Fleet). Also included are the training commands and fleet marine forces. The operational chain of command can be a bit more complex.

547

To better understand these chains of command, let us look at a typical situation from the bottom up. Suppose you are assigned to the USS *Neversink,* which is homeported in Norfolk, Virginia. Administratively, your ship would be assigned to the Commander of Naval Surface Forces, Atlantic (COMNAVSURFLANT). While you are operating out of Norfolk—doing training exercises and getting important repairs completed—you would be operationally assigned to the Commander of the Second Fleet (COMSECONDFLT) as well. But when your ship deploys to the Mediterranean, you are no longer a member of the Second Fleet, but are transferred (operationally) to the Commander of the Sixth Fleet, who is the operational commander in the Mediterranean. He or she answers to CINCUSNAVEUR (Commander-in-Chief of Naval Forces in Europe), who would be an admiral in charge of all naval forces in and around the European continent. That admiral would also have a boss—who might be another admiral or a general from one of the armed forces—whose title is CINCEUR (Commander-in-Chief, Europe), who is in charge of all American armed forces in Europe (this includes Army and Air Force as well as Navy and Marine Corps). This commander would in turn answer to the Joint Chiefs of Staff, who are working directly for the

Secretary of Defense and the President of the United States (who is Commander-in-Chief of the Armed Forces of the United States).

A similar situation would exist if you had been assigned to the USS *Sailwell,* homeported in San Diego. Your ship would be administratively assigned to COMNAVSURFPAC and operationally to COMTHIRDFLT while operating in and out of San Diego. Once you deployed to the Western Pacific, however, you would change your operational chain of command to COMSEVENTHFLT (who is responsible for the Western Pacific) and the chain would extend upward through CINCPACFLT to CINCPAC to JCS to SECDEF to the President.

Task Force Organization. An entire fleet is too large to be used for specific operations and yet a particular task may require more than one ship. To better organize ships into useful groups, the Navy developed a system that has been in use since World War II.

Using this system, a *fleet* can be divided into *task forces* and they can be further subdivided into *task groups.* If these task groups still need to be further divided, *task units* can be created and they can be further subdivided into *task elements.*

A numbering system is used to make it clear what each of these divisions is. The Seventh Fleet, for example, might be divided into two task forces and they would be numbered TF 71 and TF 72. If Task Force 72 needed to be divided into three separate divisions, they would be task groups and would be numbered TG 72.1, TG 72.2, and TG 72.3. If TG 72.3 needed to be subdivided, it could be broken into task units numbered TU 72.3.1 and TU 72.3.2. Further divisions of TU 72.3.1 would be elements and would be numbered TE 72.3.1.1 and TE 72.3.1.2.

Regular Navy

The term "Regular Navy" refers to those people who serve in the Navy as a full-time job. The Navy also has a reserve component made up of men and women who serve in the Navy on a part-time basis, ready to serve full-time if war or other national emergency requires their help.

The regular Navy consists of officers, either in the line or in a staff corps, and enlisted men and women. The professional structure of enlisted Sailors has been covered extensively in other chapters, but some explanation of the officer part of the Navy is covered here.

Line and Staff Corps. All naval officers serve either in the regular line or in a special staff corps, according to their specialties. Depending on the uniform worn, officers wear the device of their specialty on the sleeve above the stripes, or on the shoulder boards, or on the collar. A line officer wears rank devices on both collar points, but a staff corps officer wears a rank device on only the right collar point and wears a special corps device on the left. Line officers exercise military command; only line officers command at sea and, in general, only line officers exercise command on shore. Members of certain staff corps, such as the Medical, Supply, and Civil Engineer Corps, command shore activities and units and come under the control of their respective bureaus.

Medical Corps (MC). Doctors in the Navy are commissioned staff corps officers. They provide medical services and administer hospitals, dispensaries, sick bays, and other medical units in the Navy. These doctors also serve the needs of the Marine Corps.

Dental Corps (DC). Dentists in the Navy are also commissioned officers. They provide dental services and run dispensaries on board larger ships. The Dental Corps, like the Medical Corps, Nurse Corps, and Medical Service Corps, comes under the Bureau of Medicine and Surgery, and serves the needs of both the Navy and Marine Corps.

Medical Service Corps (MSC). This corps has specialists in optometry, pharmacy, bacteriology, biochemistry, psychology, sanitation engineering, and medical statistics.

549

Nurse Corps (NC). Navy nurses are commissioned officers in the grades of ensign through admiral. They serve in a variety of settings, ranging from teaching hospitals to the relatively basic fleet hospitals and clinics.

Supply Corps (SC). This is the business branch of the Navy; it receives and disburses funds for supply and pay, subsistence, and transportation and handles the acquisition and distribution of spare parts and consumables.

Chaplain Corps (CHC). Officers of the Chaplain Corps are ordained ministers of various religions and denominations; they conduct religious services and promote the spiritual and moral welfare of the Navy and Marine Corps.

Civil Engineer Corps (CEC). This corps is composed of graduate civil engineers, who supervise the buildings, grounds, and plants as well as all construction of shore stations. This corps includes the Construction Battalions (popularly called "Seabees") who can build advance bases in new areas in relatively short periods of time when the need arises.

Judge Advocate General's Corps (JAG). Established in 1967, this staff corps is composed of lawyers certified to practice in the Navy.

Naval Reserve

As already mentioned, the Navy has an important reserve component. The mission of the Naval Reserve, like that of the other reserve components of the armed services, is to provide trained units and qualified individuals for active duty in time of war or national emergency and at other times required for national security.

Since its creation in 1915, the Naval Reserve has been a trained manpower source capable of rapidly augmenting active Navy forces to fill the gap between peacetime capability and wartime requirements. As part of the Navy's total force, the Naval Reserve—in addition to its wartime mobilization mission—is shouldering a greater share of day-to-day peacetime responsibilities. The integration of active and reserve forces ensures that Navy assets are fully utilized.

The Naval Reserve has many ships and air squadrons permanently assigned. The Commander, Naval Reserve Force (COMNAVRES-FOR), headquartered in New Orleans, is responsible for the administration and management of Naval Reserve programs in accordance with policies prescribed by the CNO, for the management of assigned reserves, and for supervising Naval Reserve activities.

There are three subordinate commands in New Orleans to help carry out this mission: Commander, Naval Surface Reserve Force (COMNAVSURFRESFOR), Commander, Naval Air Reserve Force (COMNAVAIRESFOR), and Commander, Naval Reserve Recruiting Command (COMNAVRESCRUITCOM). The senior of these officers also serves as deputy commander of the naval reserve force.

The Naval Reserve has several personnel components that provide different services and degrees of readiness to the Navy.

Selected Reserve. Selected reservists are the core of the Naval Reserve program. They are subject to involuntary recall for war or national emergency, or by the President for up to 90 days to support operational requirements without the declaration of a national emergency. Most selected reservists are Navy veterans who continue their affiliation with the service while at the same time pursuing civilian careers. These men and women usually meet one weekend a month and serve for two weeks each year on active duty designed to enhance their readiness. They are paid for their weekend drills and for their two weeks active duty.

Individual Ready Reserve. This component is also subject to involuntary recall for war or national emergency, but members are not required to train. Many do train without pay in volunteer training units established at most surface and air reserve activities. This voluntary training not only allows them to serve their nation in an important way, it makes them eligible for certain retirement benefits.

Training and Administration of Reserves (TARs). TARs are reserve training specialists who serve on full-time active duty in support of the Naval Reserve. TARs receive full active-duty pay and allowances and the same benefits as regular Navy personnel. TARs enlist in the TAR program or convert from Regular Navy or Selected Reserve status.

United States Marine Corps

The Marine Corps is a separate service under the Department of the Navy and consists of two fleet marine forces, one in the Atlantic, the other in the Pacific. The Marine Corps' primary mission is to provide the U.S. Navy with landing forces for amphibious operations. The United States is a maritime nation with worldwide interests; the Corps supports its global national strategy. During peacetime, Marines serve as essential elements of U.S. deterrence and project U.S. influence abroad.

The ability to project sea power ashore is an essential element of a maritime strategy, and the ability to execute an amphibious assault is an integral part of power projection. The Marine Corps is charged expressly with these tasks.

An organization unique to the Corps is the Marine Security Guard Battalion. Small, select, specially trained groups of Marines guard posts at American embassies and consulates around the world. These Marines are responsible for safeguarding classified material as well as protecting embassy personnel and property. Their duties are defensive, the overall protection of diplomatic missions being the responsibility of the host government.

The Marine Corps Reserve maintains the same high standards of performance and readiness as the Regular Marine Corps. The reserve augments and reinforces the active forces with well-trained units and highly qualified individuals.

Naval personnel also serve in Marine units, most especially as hospital corpsman. These Sailors must train with Marines, wear some of their uniforms, and become familiar with Marine Corps methods and equipment.

United States Coast Guard

The Coast Guard is the smallest of the nation's five military services. It operates under the jurisdiction of the Department of Transportation; upon declaration of war or when the President directs, the

Coast Guard operates within DON. Even though they are not normally part of the Department of Defense, Coast Guard personnel receive the same pay and benefits as DOD personnel and are subject to the Uniform Code of Military Justice.

The Coast Guard mission encompasses a variety of responsibilities. Primary among them is search and rescue, the saving of lives and property at sea. The Coast Guard operates search-and-rescue stations along America's coasts and inland waters, and stands ready 24 hours a day to dispatch rescue vessels to answer distress calls. Its numerous air stations assist in searches when rescue by vessel is impossible or speed is essential. A network of communication centers handles the vital communications necessary to integrate the work of these units.

The Coast Guard coordinates Automated Mutual-Assistance Vessel Rescue (AMVER), an international program of volunteer merchant vessels that provides the location of participating vessels to any vessel needing help at sea.

The Coast Guard also participates in the International Ice Patrol, begun in 1913. Each year, with other nations, it patrols a 45,000-square-mile area in the North Atlantic tracking icebergs.

As the nation's seagoing police force, the Coast Guard is the principal federal agency responsible for ensuring marine safety and enforcing maritime laws covering customs and immigration, drug interdiction, commercial fishing, international treaties, the marine environment, and even the protection of endangered marine mammals. To do this job, the Coast Guard uses a fleet of vessels ranging from small utility boats to highly sophisticated cutters, as well as helicopters and fixed-wing aircraft. When there is an oil or chemical spill, the Coast Guard deploys highly mobile "strike teams" of experts.

The Coast Guard is also responsible for recreational boating safety. It carries out a program that includes research in and development of safer boating practices and equipment, coordination and enforcement of industrial and water safety standards, cooperation with state boating authorities, and education of the boating public.

The Coast Guard maintains a volunteer auxiliary some 37,000 strong. Participants are trained in boat handling, sailing, rules of the road, marlinespike seamanship, weather, radiotelephone, search and rescue, navigation, meteorology, marine engines, and aids to navigation.

Keeping the nation's 40,000 miles of waterways safe for navigation is another Coast Guard responsibility. It maintains thousands of aids to navigation, from small buoys to large, sophisticated navigational buoys, offshore towers, lighthouses, and many other lesser lights. It also maintains and operates electronic navigation stations around the world.

The Coast Guard is also tasked with the safety of the nation's merchant marine fleet and ports. From design and construction to eventual scrapping, U.S. flag merchant vessels are under Coast Guard regulation. The Coast Guard approves new vessel designs and examines shipbuilders, prescribes a wide variety of safety and lifesaving equipment, licenses those who sail merchant ships, and investigates serious ship accidents.

Since its beginning in 1790 as the Revenue Marine, the Coast Guard has played a part in every national conflict. It participates in many DOD activities and in Navy fleet and interservice exercises. The Coast Guard is also involved in NASA launches and the Navy's maritime defense zone planning and operations in defense of coastal waters, ports, and harbors.

553

Navy History

What follows is a chronological listing of some of the significant moments in the Navy's history. This listing is meant as a reference only. To better understand your heritage, you should read one of the excellent histories of the United States Navy at your earliest convenience.

As you read American naval history, you will find some low moments—some times when the people who were serving in the Navy were unable or unwilling to meet the challenges at hand—but you will also soon realize that this is overall a history in which you may take a great deal of pride. The U.S. Navy has been built on the skill, determination, and valor of a great many Americans just like you, who have risen to the occasion when times and circumstances were difficult, who have learned from the mistakes and built on the achievements of the past, and who found the courage to do what was needed in the face of great adversity. Keep in mind that by serving as a member of the U.S. Navy, you are following in the footsteps of a great tradition, and you are helping to write the American history of tomorrow.

The Earliest Years

America was born of the sea. The people who made this nation came from over the sea, and they were sustained by goods exchanged by the shipload. Trade went on for 150 years before the desire to be master of their own destiny led the colonists to strike for independence. The first efforts at sea power were often feeble and fruitless, and yet they had their impact on the course of events. And at the critical juncture, it was the timely actions of the French Navy that resulted in the isolation of British General Cornwallis and his subsequent surrender.

12 Jun 1775 First engagement at sea during the Revolution. Citizens of Machias, Maine, under the command of Jeremiah O'Brien, seized a cargo sloop

and with her captured the cutter HMS *Margaretta.* [TB 30 and DDs 51, 415, and 725 were named *O'Brien.*]

6 Sep 1775   The schooner *Hannah* sailed as the first unit of a number of armed fishing vessels sent to sea by the Continental Army to intercept British supply ships during the siege of Boston.

13 Oct 1775   The Continental Congress authorized the outfitting of a ten-gun warship "for intercepting such transports as may be laden with stores for the enemy." This marked the beginning of the Continental Navy (forerunner to the U.S. Navy).

3 Dec 1775   The first man-of-war of the Continental Navy, the *Alfred,* was commissioned at Philadelphia. Her "first lieutenant" (XO) was LT John Paul Jones.

3–4 Mar 1776   A Continental squadron under the command of Commodore Esek Hopkins, composed of the *Alfred, Columbus, Andrea Doria, Cabot, Providence, Hornet, Wasp,* and *Fly,* successfully attacked the British at Nassau in the Bahamas. Captured were seventy-one cannon and fifteen mortars. This was also the first amphibious assault by American Marines, under the command of CAPT Samuel Nicholas. [DDs 311 and 449 were named for him.]

4 Apr 1776   The brig *Lexington,* under John Barry, defeated HMS *Edward* in lower Delaware Bay. This was the earliest of Barry's successes. [DDs 2, 248, and 933 were named for him.]

7 Sep 1776   Sgt. Ezra Lee of the Continental Army made the first "submarine" attack on a warship, an unsuccessful attempt to attach a powder charge to the hull of an anchored British ship from the submersible *Turtle,* designed by David Bushnell. [Submarine tenders AS 2 and AS 15 were named for Bushnell. The deep-submergence craft DSV 3 is also named *Turtle.*]

11 Oct 1776   A Continental Army squadron of gunboats under Col. Benedict Arnold fought a British force on Lake Champlain in the Battle of Valcour Island. This caused the British to delay the

invasion of the Hudson River Valley for a year, by which time the Continental Army was able to prepare and achieve a vital victory.

15 Nov 1776 Continental Congress set pay rates for officers and men. Petty officer rates were prescribed, though these were not divided into classes until 1885.

16 Nov 1776 The U.S. flag was saluted for the first time by the Dutch governor of St. Eustatius Island in the West Indies.

24 Apr 1778 John Paul Jones, in command of the sloop *Ranger,* defeated the sloop HMS *Drake* off Belfast, Ireland. The *Drake* became the first major British warship to be taken by the new Navy.

4 May 1780 An insignia, adopted by the Board of Admiralty (which had been set up by the Continental Congress to direct naval operations), became the Navy's first official seal.

23 Sep 1780 John Paul Jones, now commanding the converted merchantman *Bonhomme Richard,* defeated the frigate HMS *Serapis* in a night fight off Flamborough Head, England. His ship badly battered (she would sink after the fight), Jones rejected the British surrender question with his defiant, "I have not yet begun to fight!" [DDs 10 and 230 and DDG 32 were named in honor of Jones, and DDs 4, 290, and 353, and CG 19 in honor of his gallant first lieutenant, Richard Dale.]

5 Sep 1781 The French fleet, under ADM Comte de Grasse, blockaded Hampton Roads to keep reinforcements from Gen. Charles Cornwallis's British Army at Yorktown, Virginia, under siege by Gen. George Washington's Continental troops and by French forces under Gen. Jean-Baptiste Rochambeau. The *Comte de Grasse* (DD 974) honors this ally.

17 Oct 1781 General Cornwallis surrendered at Yorktown, thus ending the Revolutionary War.

19 Apr 1783 George Washington proclaimed the Revolution officially ended.

The frigate *Alliance,* last survivor of the Continental Navy, was sold out of service.

Rebirth and the Second War of Independence

The newly formed United States did without a navy for nine years. It
had been hoped that the world would leave the new country alone.
But that was not to be. Barbary pirate states on Africa's north coast
captured defenseless American ships, demanding ransom. When the
United States finally began reacting to that problem, war broke out
between France and Great Britain and U.S. neutral shipping (the
United States had one of the largest merchant fleets in the world then)
became a target for both sides.

America's tiny new Navy, whose first units were launched in
1797, first settled the French problem, then that of the Barbary
pirates, and finally fought the British. By the time the last of these
wars was over, the United States had become a significant sea power.

6 Jan 1791	A Senate committee reported that U.S. trade in the Mediterranean was impossible to protect without a naval force.
27 Mar 1794	President Washington signed into law "an act to provide a naval armament," which provided for the building of six frigates: the *Constitution, United States, Constellation, Congress, Chesapeake,* and *President.* The captains were to be paid 75 dollars a month, ordinary seamen 10 dollars. Rations were valued at 28 cents a day.
May–Oct 1797	The frigates *United States, Constellation,* and *Constitution* were launched.
30 Apr 1798	The Navy Department was established. Up to then, the secretary of war, a distant predecessor of today's secretary of defense, had directed both the Army and Navy.
May 1798	The converted merchantman *Ganges,* first warship to fit out and go to sea under the new federal constitution, put to sea to protect shipping off the U.S. East Coast.
18 Jun 1798	Benjamin Stoddert, first secretary of the Navy, took office. His salary was $3000 a year. The first actions in the undeclared quasi-war with

	France occurred in June. [DD 302 and DDG 22 were named *Stoddert.*]
9 Feb 1799	The *Constellation,* under Thomas Truxtun, defeated the French frigate *Insurgente* in 30 minutes. The Frenchmen had one hundred casualties, the Americans four.
1 Feb 1800	The *Constellation,* still under Truxtun, battered the French ship *Vengeance* for five hours, but nightfall and damage to the American vessel allowed the French to get away. Midshipman James C. Jarvis was lost when the *Constellation*'s mainmast gave way. [DDs 14 and 229 and CGN 35 were named for Truxton, DDs 38, 393, and 799 for Jarvis.]
7 Feb 1800	The thirty-two-gun frigate *Essex* became the first U.S. man-of-war to cross the equator.
31 Oct 1803	The frigate *Philadelphia,* under CAPT William Bainbridge, ran aground on a reef off Tripoli (Libya) while pursuing Barbary pirate craft; his ship and crew were captured. The American crew spent 20 months in a Tripolitan prison before being freed.
16 Feb 1804	LT Stephen Decatur, with eighty-three volunteers from the frigate *Constitution* and the schooner *Enterprise,* entered Tripoli harbor at night in the ketch *Intrepid* and destroyed the *Philadelphia* without a single loss. English admiral Lord Nelson termed it "the most daring act of the age." [DDs 5 and 341 and DDGs 31 and 73 have been named for Decatur.]
3 Aug 1804	Commodore Edward Preble in the *Constitution* led the U.S. Mediterranean Squadron in the first of a series of attacks against Tripoli that ultimately ended the Barbary wars and freed Bainbridge and the other Americans. The peace treaty was signed 5 June 1805. [DDs 12 and 345 and DDG 46 were named *Preble.*]
16 May 1811	In the mistaken belief he was attacking the frigate HMS *Guerriere,* which had been conducting some high-handed operations off the American East Coast, CAPT John Rodgers in the *President* blasted the sloop HMS *Little Belt*

in a night encounter begun by the smaller ship. [TB 4 and DDs 254 and 574 remembered him.]

18 Jun 1812 — Pres. James Madison declared war on Great Britain over "free trade and sailors' rights." The U.S. Navy then had but 17 warships, the British over 600.

16–28 Jun 1812 — The *Constitution,* under CAPT Issac Hull, escaped a five-ship British squadron in a classic 69-hour chase.

3 Aug 1812 — The *Essex,* under David Porter, captured HMS *Albert* after one broadside.

19 Aug 1812 — Isaac Hull and the *Constitution* defeated the frigate HMS *Guerriere* in a 35-minute slugfest that left the British vessel a hulk. This was the first time an American frigate had defeated a British frigate, and it greatly cheered the nation. As a result of the battle, the *Constitution* received her famous nickname Old Ironsides. [Hull has been remembered by DDs 7, 330, 350, and 945.]

18 Oct 1812 — Jacob Jones, commanding the sloop *Wasp,* smashed the brig HMS *Frolic* off the Chesapeake Capes. [Jacob Jones was honored by DDs 61 and 130 and DE 130.]

25 Oct 1812 — The frigate *United States,* sister ship of the *Constitution,* with Stephen Decatur in command, defeated the frigate HMS *Macedonian* in a two-hour combat that left more than 100 British casualties to twelve American. Taken into the U.S. Navy, the USS *Macedonian* served until 1828.

29 Dec 1812 — The *Constitution,* now commanded by William Bainbridge, left HMS *Java* a shambles in a hard two and a half-hour fight off Brazil. With this third loss in three frigate-to-frigate actions in five months, the Royal Navy received orders not to take on such American 44s as the *Constitution* and the *United States* with less than squadron strength. [DDs 1 and 246 and CGN 25 have been named after Bainbridge.]

14 Feb 1813 — The *Essex* became the first U.S. man-of-war to round Cape Horn and enter the Pacific Ocean.

559

24 Feb 1813   The sloop *Hornet,* under James Lawrence, defeated the brig HMS *Peacock* in two broadsides off Guyana.

1 Jun 1813   Rashly responding to a British captain's challenge, newly promoted Captain Lawrence, now commanding the frigate *Chesapeake* and a green crew, was defeated and killed off Boston in a fight with HMS *Shannon,* a frigate. Lawrence's dying words, "Don't give up the ship!" have lived on as one of the slogans of the U.S. Navy. [Lawrence was memorialized in TB 8, DD 250, and DDG 4.]

13 Aug 1813   The American brig *Argus,* under William Allen, was captured by the brig HMS *Pelican* in the Irish Sea after her raiding operations had taken twenty British merchantmen. [DD 66 was later named the *Allen.*]

5 Sep 1813   In a bloody engagement, William Burrows's brig the *Enterprise* (14) overcame HMS *Boxer,* a brig, off the coast of Maine. Both captains were killed, and they were buried side by side in Portland, Maine. [DD 29 and DE 105 honored Burrows.]

10 Sep 1813   The Battle of Lake Erie. Oliver Hazard Perry, commanding an American squadron of nine ships, defeated a British six-ship squadron to ensure U.S. control of the Great Lakes and the Northwest Territory. Perry carried Lawrence's dying command, "Don't give up the ship," on his battle flag, and the opening phrase of his victory report is still remembered today: "We have met the enemy, and they are ours. . . ." [Perry's name has been carried by DDSs 11, 340, and 844, and FFG 7.]

28 Mar 1814   After cruising Pacific waters in a highly successful operation against British whalers, the *Essex,* under David Porter, was trapped and defeated at Valparaiso, Chile, by the frigate HMS *Phoebe* and the sloop HMS *Cherub.* [David Porter has been remembered by TB 6 and DDs 59, 356, and 800.]

29 Apr 1814   The new American sloop *Peacock,* named after the British unit defeated by the *Hornet* the pre-

vious year, defeated the brig HMS *Epervier* off the Florida coast. The British ship was found to be carrying $25,000 in gold bullion! [Lewis Warrington, the *Peacock*'s captain, was memorialized in DDs 30, 383, and 843.]

22 Jun 1814   The *Independence,* first ship of the line in the U.S. Navy, was launched. She served in one capacity or another until 1912.

28 Jun 1814   The second *Wasp* of the War of 1812, a twenty-two-gun sloop commanded by Johnston R. Y. Blakeley, bested the brig HMS *Reindeer* in just 19 minutes in the English Channel. [TB 27, DD 150, and DE 140 have been named for Blakeley.]

24 Aug 1814   British invaders burned Washington, D.C. Sailors and Marines under CAPT Joshua Barney formed part of the American force that fought a delaying action at Bladensburg, Maryland, just outside Washington. [TB 25 and DD 149 bore his name.]

11 Sep 1814   Battle of Lake Champlain. A bloody engagement between Commodore Thomas MacDonough's sixteen-ship squadron and a British one of like number ended in defeat for the invaders (this is reminiscent of the Battle of Valcour Island during the Revolution, 11 Oct 1776). [MacDonough has been honored by DDs 9, 331, and 351, and DDG 39.]

16 Sep 1814   A Navy force, with Marines and Army troops, destroys Jean Lafitte's pirate base at Barataria, near New Orleans.

23 Oct 1814   A "floating steam battery" designed by Robert Fulton was launched for the Navy, which referred to her as the *Fulton* or *Fulton*'s Steam Battery. Carrying her paddlewheel between twin catamaran hulls, she had twenty guns and made five knots. Never actively used, the *Fulton* was demolished by explosion and fire in 1829.

24 Dec 1814   The Treaty of Ghent formally ended the War of 1812. Communications were poor in that day, and all the following engagements occurred

	because one or both sides failed to receive information.
8 Jan 1815	The Battle of New Orleans. Gen. Andrew Jackson and an army made up largely of militia defeated a British regular-army invasion force. Jackson's defenses had time to organize because a Navy gunboat force under Commodore Daniel T. Patterson and LT Thomas C. Jones had fought a successful delaying action at Lake Borgne. [Patterson's name has been carried by DDs 36 and 392 and FF 1061.]
15 Jan 1815	The frigate *President* was run down and captured by a four-ship British squadron.
7 Feb 1815	The Board of Naval Commissioners was established to oversee the maintenance and operation of the Navy under the direction of the secretary.
20 Feb 1815	Charles Stewart, in the *Constitution,* defeated the frigate HMS *Cyane* and the corvette *Levant* off Madeira Island. The *Levant* was later recaptured by the British, but the *Cyane* served actively in the U.S. Navy until 1827. [DDs 13 and 224 and DE 238 have borne the name of *Stewart.*]
23 Mar 1815	James Biddle, in the *Hornet,* took the brig HMS *Penguin* in 22 minutes. [Biddle has been honored by TB 26, DD 151, DDG 5, and CG 34.]
30 Jun 1815	In the final naval action of the War of 1812, the sloop *Peacock* captured the brig HMS *Nautilus* (14) off Java, while under the command of Lewis Warrington.

Until the Civil War

In the 45 years before the Civil War, the Navy fought in a small war with Mexico that gave it experience in amphibious and riverine operations. This was also a time of significant technological advances. Steam propulsion, iron hulls, exploding shells, and rifled guns all appeared in this period. U.S. men-of-war appeared in all corners of the world, showing the flag and protecting the rights of Americans overseas.

22 Mar 1820	CAPT James Barron killed the popular commodore Stephen Decatur in a duel at Bladensburg, Maryland. The resulting public outrage spelled the beginning of the end for duels.
23 Apr 1821	In an experiment typical of this time, the *Constitution* was propelled at three knots in Boston Harbor by hand-cranked paddlewheels. The experiment, which sought a way to power sailing ships in close quarters, was not repeated.
16 May 1821	The frigate Congress became the first U.S. warship to visit China.
2 Apr 1827	Construction of the first naval hospital was begun in Portsmouth, Virginia.
8 Jun 1830	The sloop *Vincennes,* under CAPT W. B. Finch, completed an around-the-world voyage—the first U.S. Navy warship to do so.
6 Dec 1830	The U.S. Naval Observatory—the first in the United States—was established.
17 Jun 1833	The ship of the line *Delaware* dry-docked in Gosport (now Portsmouth) Navy Yard. She was the first warship to be drydocked in the United States.
1838–42	CDR Charles Wilkes took a six-ship naval expedition around the world, exploring Antarctica and many places in the Pacific. [TB 35 and DDs 67 and 441 have borne the name *Wilkes.*]
Feb 1841	The first regulations providing details for enlisted uniforms, including the first specifics on rating insignia, were issued.
1 Sep 1842	The Board of Naval Commissioners was superseded by five technical bureaus. With variations in number and titles, they continue in existence today as the naval systems commands.
10 Dec 1843	The *Princeton,* the Navy's first screw-propelled steam frigate, was launched.
29 Mar 1844	Uriah Levy, the Navy's first Jewish officer, was promoted to captain. [DE 162 honored his service.]
1845	A captain's annual pay was a maximum of $4,500. The highest enlisted monthly pay was $40 (for a yeoman) and a ship's boy received $6 to $8 monthly. The rum ration was valued at 20 cents a day.

563

10 Oct 1845	The U.S. Naval Academy was established in Annapolis, Maryland.
18 Feb 1846	"Larboard" and "starboard" became "port" and "starboard" by general order.
11 May 1846	War was declared on Mexico.
20 Jul 1846	The *Columbus* became the first U.S. man-of-war to visit Japan.
1847	"The Kedge-Anchor," by Sailing Master William Brady, USN, was first published. This book was a forerunner of *The Bluejacket's Manual*.
9 May 1847	Twelve thousand Army troops under Gen. Winfield Scott made amphibious landings at Vera Cruz, Mexico, with the aid of the Navy. The city surrendered twenty days later, after a siege by Army and Navy forces.
14 Jun 1847	A squadron under Commodore Matthew C. Perry captured the Mexican city of Tabasco after fighting its way 70 miles upriver.
2 Feb 1848	The Treaty of Guadalupe Hidalgo ended the Mexican War, with the United States gaining most of its present southwestern territory.
28 Sep 1850	The punishment of flogging—whipping with a cat-o'-nine tails—was terminated in the Navy by Act of Congress.
31 Mar 1854	Commodore Matthew C. Perry signed a treaty with the Japanese at Yokohama, opening that country to western trade.
16 Jan 1857	An act of Congress established the rank of flag officer, the first actual rank higher than captain ever established in the U.S. Navy. Before this, commanders of forces and squadrons had held the operational title of commodore but the actual rank of captain.
2 Mar 1859	The first Navy ship to be built on the West Coast, the paddlewheel gunboat *Saginaw*, was launched at Mare Island, California.

The Civil War

The Navy's principal roles in this struggle were to blockade the South's coastline to prevent the export of cotton and the entry of munitions, and to cooperate with the Army in amphibious operations. On western rivers, the Navy developed specialized craft to dominate the Mississippi and its tributaries, and thus cut the Confederacy off from other supply sources via Texas. In this war, revolving turrets, ironclads, steam power, observation balloons, submersibles, and mines were tried, often for the first time in battle.

9 Jan 1861	The steamer *Star of the West* was fired on by South Carolinians while attempting to resupply Fort Sumter in Charleston Harbor. This was one of the events leading to the American Civil War.
27 Aug 1861	In North Carolina, a squadron under Flag Officer Silas Stringham bombarded Forts Hatteras and Clark into submission. [*Stringham* was the name of TB 19 and DD 83.]
7 Nov 1861	Flag Officer Samuel DuPont led his squadron to victory over Port Royal, South Carolina. [TB 7 and DDs 152 and 941 were named *DuPont*.]
21 Dec 1861	The Medal of Honor was authorized by Congress.
6 Feb 1862	A squadron under Flag Officer Andrew H. Foote helped take Fort Henry on the Tennessee River.
7 Feb 1862	A squadron under Flag Officer Louis M. Goldsborough captured Roanoke Island, N.C. [TB 20, DD 188, and DDG 20 all honored Goldsborough.]
14–26 Feb 1862	Foote's squadron again participated in the assault on a Confederate fort, this time helping to take Fort Donelson on the Cumberland River. [TB 3 and DDs 169 and 511 were named for Foote.]
9 Mar 1862	The *Monitor* (CAPT John L. Worden), first warship with a revolving gun turret, met the Confederate *Virginia* (ex-*Merrimack*) in the world's first battle of ironclads. The battle ended in a draw, but the *Virginia* never fought again. [DDs 16, 288, and 352 and CG 18 have been named *Worden*.]
14 Mar 1862	Flag Officer Goldsborough's squadron captured New Berne, N.C.
24 Apr 1862	Flag Officer David Glascow Farragut led his

565

squadron past Forts St. Phillip and Jackson up the Mississippi River to a commanding position above New Orleans, which surrendered the next day. [TB 11, DDs 300 and 348, and DDG 37 honor Farragut.]

10 Jun 1862
The *Red Rover,* the Navy's first hospital ship, went into operation on the Mississippi River.

16 Jul 1862
Congress established the ranks of rear admiral, commodore, lieutenant commander, master, and ensign. David Glasgow Farragut was appointed as one of the Navy's first four rear admirals. When the ranks of vice admiral (21 Dec 1864) and admiral (25 Jul 1866) were created, Farragut became the first officer appointed to them.

21 Aug 1862
The *New Ironsides,* the Navy's first *seagoing* armored ship, was completed. (The *Monitor,* mentioned above, was a shallow-draft ship designed for coastal operations.)

31 Aug 1862
The issuance of grog to ship's companies was ended, a year after being terminated for officers and warrant officers. Ship's wardrooms continued to operate "wine messes" until 1914.

17 Feb 1864
The Confederate submarine *H. L. Hunley,* commanded by Infantry LT G. E. Dixon, sank the Union steam sloop *Housatonic* with a spar torpedo, the first sinking of a warship by a submarine. The *H. L. Hunley* was also lost in the blast. [AS 31 recalls the builder of this craft, H. L. Hunley.]

19 Jun 1864
The Union steam sloop *Kearsarge* (CAPT John A. Winslow) sank the famed Confederate raider *Alabama* (CAPT Raphael Semmes) off Cherbourg, France. [Winslow has been honored by TB 5 and DDs 53 and 359 and Semmes by DD 189 and DDG 18.]

5 Aug 1864
A Union squadron under Vice Admiral Farragut assaulted Confederate forces in Mobile Bay and won a decisive victory. It was here, when mines (then called torpedoes) endangered his forces, that Farragut ordered, "Captain Drayton, go ahead! Damn the torpedoes! Go on!"

| 27 Oct 1864 | A steam launch, commanded by LT William B. Cushing, sank the large Confederate ironclad *Albemarle* with a spar torpedo. [Cushing was remembered by TB 1 and DDs 55, 376, and 797.] |
| 15 Jan 1865 | A squadron under Rear Admiral David D. Porter cooperated with an Army force under Maj. Gen. A. H. Terry in capturing Fort Fisher, N.C. [LSD 40 recalls the event.] |

Decline and Rebirth

After the Civil War, a combination of war weariness and westward expansion resulted in the Navy's decline. For nearly 20 years the Navy languished. Finally, in the mid-1880s, as nationalism gripped the country, the Navy once again received attention. On this wave of enthusiasm, the nation was swept into the Spanish-American War, the Great White Fleet was built, and the Panama Canal was constructed.

17 Apr 1866	Congress appropriated $5,000 to test the use of "petroleum oil" as fuel for ships' boilers.
1869	New regulations prescribed an enlisted working uniform for the first time. (Before, old dress uniforms were used.)
28 Jun 1869	William M. Wood was appointed first surgeon general of the Navy. [DD 715 was named for him.]
10 Jun 1871	A Navy-Marine Corps assault force made a landing in Korea in a punitive operation against a Korean fort that had fired on a peaceful American ship. LT Hugh W. McKee was killed in the attack and honored by TB 18 and DDs 87 and 575.
11 Sep 1872	James Henry Conyers became the first black to enter the Naval Academy.
9 Oct 1873	A meeting held by a group of naval officers resulted in the formation of the U.S. Naval Institute, publisher of *The Bluejacket's Manual.*
28 Jun 1874	The *Jeanette,* a supply ship, received the first Navy shipboard electrical system. While proceeding on a mission to the Arctic, she was crushed in an ice pack on 13 Jun 1881.

31 Jul 1874	The *Intrepid,* first experimental Navy torpedo boat to carry self-propelled torpedoes, was commissioned.
3 Mar 1883	The Navy appropriation act for Fiscal Year 1884 authorized construction of the cruisers *Atlanta, Boston,* and *Chicago,* and the "dispatch vessel" *Dolphin.* These were the first steel ships built for the U.S. Navy, and thus they mark the beginning of the transition from wood and sail to steel and steam. In these ships, the rank of master was changed to that of lieutenant (junior grade).
6 Oct 1884	The Naval War College was established.
8 Jan 1885	Petty officers were divided into first, second, and third class. For more than a hundred years there had been only the single grade of petty officer.
14 Feb 1885	Congress approved a military retirement act, the first formal retirement program for U.S. armed forces, but an oversight omitted the Navy, and it wasn't until 1899 that Sailors were included.
8 Dec 1885	The gunboat *Dolphin,* first steel warship for the U.S. Navy, was commissioned.
24 Sep 1894	The rate of chief petty officer was established by General Order No. 431.
15 Feb 1898	The battleship *Maine* was sunk by internal explosion (due to spontaneous combustion) in Havana Harbor. Belief that she had been attacked by Spaniards, encouraged by the press of the day, inflamed American public opinion and resulted in a declaration of war on 25 Apr 1898.
1 May 1898	Commodore George Dewey's Asiatic Squadron defeated the Spanish in Manila Bay. The battle had been begun by Dewey's order to his flagship captain, "You may fire when ready, Gridley." [DD 349 and DDG 45 were named for Dewey, and DDs 92 and 380 and CG 21 for Gridley.]
3 Jul 1898	Rear Admiral William T. Sampson's squadron defeated a Spanish force attempting to break out of Santiago, Cuba. Every Spanish ship was sunk

or run ashore. [Sampson has been honored by DDs 63 and 394 and DDG 10.]

13 Aug 1898   Spain asked for peace.

2 Mar 1899   George Dewey was promoted to Admiral of the Navy, a rank held by him alone. The act creating this rank also abolished the rank of commodore.

The Twentieth Century

In the last 95 years, the United States has been involved in two world wars, two Asiatic wars, and a variety of lesser incidents. At the end of World War II, the U.S. Navy was the mightiest the world had ever seen. Since then, other calls to duty have been met in a variety of ways, including a naval quarantine that took the United States to the brink of nuclear war, combat on the rivers and canals in Southeast Asia, and an assault on a desert nation, to name but a few. During this century, the Navy was a leader in technological development and contributed significantly to the exploration and utilization of the frontiers of both inner and outer space.

12 Oct 1900   The *Holland* (SS 1), the Navy's first submarine, was commissioned.

19 May 1902   The *Decatur* (DD 5), the Navy's first active destroyer, was commissioned. She was 250 feet long and carried two 3-inch guns and two 18-inch torpedo tubes.

4 Oct 1902   The first edition of *The Bluejacket's Manual* was published by the U.S. Naval Institute.

7 May 1903   The secretary of the Navy established thirteen Naval Districts, area shore commands intended to expedite defense, intelligence, and communications.

8 Jan 1907   By executive order, Pres. Theodore Roosevelt directed that all U.S.-commissioned ships be called United States Ship (USS). No standard existed before this, and usage varied widely.

16 Dec 1907   The four battleship divisions of the Atlantic Fleet, called the Great White Fleet by the press from the white peacetime color scheme then in use, began a round-the-world voyage, which ended in 1909.

6 Apr 1909	CDR Robert E. Peary became the first man to reach the North Pole. [DE 132 and FF 1073 have honored him.]
4 Jan 1910	The *Michigan* (BB 27), the first American "all-big-gun" or "dreadnought" battleship to enter service, was commissioned.
17 Sep 1910	The *Roe* (DD 24), the first destroyer of the *Paulding* (DD 22) class to enter active service, was commissioned. The ten *Pauldings,* completed in 1910-11, were the first American warships to use oil rather than coal for fuel.
14 Nov 1910	Eugene Ely, a civilian contract pilot, flew a plane off a temporary 57-foot wooden deck built over the bow of the cruiser *Birmingham*—the first aircraft launch from a ship.
18 Jan 1911	Ely landed on a platform built over the stern of the armored cruiser *Pennsylvania* in San Francisco Bay—the first shipboard landing.
Oct 1911	The Navy received its first aircraft. One was built by the Wright Brothers, and two others were built by Glen Curtiss.
5 Mar 1912	The Atlantic Submarine Flotilla, commanded by LT Chester W. Nimitz (see 31 Dec 1941), was established.
26 Jul 1912	The letter "D" in Morse code was sent by a plane to the destroyer *Stringham* a mile away—the first radio message received from an aircraft.
1 Jul 1914	Liquor was prohibited on all ships and stations.
6 May 1916	The first ship-to-shore radiotelephone conversation took place between the *New Hampshire* (BB 25) and Washington, D.C.
6 Apr 1917	The United States entered World War I.
4 May 1917	The first U.S. destroyer squadron arrived in Queenstown, Ireland, to help the British escort convoys. Asked by the English admiral when his ships would be prepared for duty, CDR Joseph K. Taussig replied, in a manner characteristic of "tin-can" Sailors, "We will be ready when fueled, sir."
17 Nov 1917	Germany's U-58 became the first submarine sunk by the U.S. Navy. She was done in by the

570

	destroyers *Fanning* (DD 37) and *Nicholson* (DD 52).
11 Nov 1918	An armistice ended World War I. Celebrated for years as Armistice Day, 11 Nov is now observed as Veterans' Day.
28 Feb 1919	The *Osmond Ingram* (DD 255), the first Navy ship named for an enlisted man, was launched. Ingram was the first enlisted man killed in action in World War I, lost when the destroyer *Cassin* (DD 43) was torpedoed in October 1917.
17 Jul 1920	General Order No. 541 established a system of letter-type symbols for ship designations (CV, DD, BB, AO, etc.). Continually modified to suit changes in the Navy's ship types, the system is still in use.
21 Aug 1920	The first radio message heard around the world was broadcast from a Navy radio station near Bordeaux, France.
20 Mar 1922	The *Jupiter,* a former collier (coal-carrier), was converted to be the Navy's first aircraft carrier, USS *Langley* (CV 1).
Feb 1923	Fleet Problem I was carried out in the Panama area. Through 1940 the annual fleet problem, an elaborate fleet-wide war game, was an important element of the Navy's strategic and tactical preparation for war.
17 Aug 1923	The Washington Treaty went into effect. This naval limitation pact placed limits on the size of naval forces of the United States, Britain, Japan, France, and Italy. The later London Treaty, in force 31 December 1930, placed additional restrictions. These treaties were attempts to prevent a naval arms race of the sort that preceded World War I.
8 Sep 1923	Seven destroyers and 23 men of Destroyer Squadron 11 were lost when the squadron ran aground at Devil's Jaw on the Southern California coast.
8 Aug 1925	The first night carrier landing took place aboard the *Langley.*
27 Feb 1928	CDR T. G. Ellyson, the Navy's aviator no. 1, was killed in an air crash.

571

28 Nov 1929	LCDR Richard E. Byrd flew over the South Pole. He had previously flown over the North Pole in 1926.
17 Sep 1936	Squadron 40-T was organized to protect American lives during the Spanish Civil War.
Apr 1937	The first sea trials of an experimental radar were conducted in the destroyer *Leary*.
1 Sep 1939	World War II began as German and Soviet troops invaded Poland. The president proclaimed neutrality but ordered the Navy to form a "neutrality patrol" to track and report belligerent ships near the United States or West Indies.
20 Jun 1940	The Bureau of Construction and Repair (ship design and construction) was merged with the Bureau of Engineering to form the Bureau of Ships, ancestor of today's Naval Sea Systems Command.
19 Jul 1940	Pres. Franklin D. Roosevelt signed the Two-Ocean Navy Act, authorizing 1,425,000 tons of new ships and 15,000 naval aircraft, an unprecedented increase in the size of the peacetime Navy.
3 Sep 1940	The "destroyers-for-bases" agreement was signed. The United States transferred fifty older DDs to Britain in exchange for base rights in British territories in the Western Hemisphere.
7 Dec 1941	In a surprise attack on Pearl Harbor, the Japanese inflicted severe damage on units of the U.S. Pacific Fleet and killed 2008 Navy men.
13 Dec 1941	Guam was captured by the Japanese.
23 Dec 1941	The Marines on Wake Island finally surrendered, after fierce resistance, to vastly superior Japanese forces.
31 Dec 1941	ADM Chester W. Nimitz took command of the Pacific Fleet. Nimitz commanded in the Pacific through V-J day and later became chief of naval operations.
26 Jan 1942	The Japanese submarine I-173 was sunk by the *Gudgeon* (SS 211), the first enemy naval vessel destroyed by a U.S. submarine.
27 Feb 1942	A combined American-British-Dutch-Australian

naval force was defeated by a Japanese force in the Battle of the Java Sea.

1 Mar 1942　　U.S. forces at Bataan in the Philippines surrendered to the Japanese.

4–8 May 1942　　The Battle of the Coral Sea was fought, resulting in the end of Japanese advances in the southwest Pacific. The USS *Lexington* (CV 2) was lost, as was the Japanese light carrier *Shoho*. This was the first battle fought solely by air groups—the ships of the opposing fleets never saw each other.

6 May 1942　　Corregidor surrendered.

4–6 Jun 1942　　At the Battle of Midway, four Japanese carriers were sunk and only one American (the *Yorktown*) was lost, ending the period of Japanese initiative in the Pacific War.

3 Aug 1942　　Mildred McAfee was commissioned as the first woman naval (line) officer.

7 Aug 1942　　U.S. Marines landed on Guadalcanal in the first American offensive action in the Pacific.

9 Aug 1942　　A Japanese cruiser force smashed a similar U.S.-Australian force in the Battle of Savo Island, sinking four cruisers in a half-hour night action.

11–22 Oct 1942　　The Americans won a night action in the Battle of Cape Esperance, sinking two Japanese warships and damaging two more, while sustaining one loss.

8 Nov 1942　　The U.S. Navy and Army participated in simultaneous amphibious landings in North Africa—at Algiers and Oran, Algeria, and Fedala, Morocco.

12–25 Nov 1942　　In two furious night actions, U.S. naval forces slugged it out with the Japanese in the Battle of Guadalcanal. The Japanese lost two battleships and three destroyers, the Americans two cruisers and seven destroyers—but the U.S. Navy had begun receiving new units at an increasing rate and so had more muscle left than the Japanese. [Five Sullivan brothers, who died in one of the lost cruisers, were honored by *The Sullivans* (DD 537), the first destroyer named for more than one person. It is now a memorial at Buffalo, New York. A second USS *The Sullivans* (DDG 68) was commissioned in 1997.]

30 Nov 1942 The Battle of Tassafaronga was the last Japanese try to save Guadalcanal. The *Northampton* was lost and so was a Japanese destroyer. The *Rogers* (DD 876) was named for three brothers lost with the cruiser.

9 Feb 1943 The last Japanese troops were evacuated from Guadalcanal, ending the six-month battle for that island.

9 Apr 1943 The rank of commodore was reestablished (but discontinued again after the war).

5 May 1943 The first antisubmarine hunter-killer group was formed, consisting of the escort aircraft carrier *Bogue* (CVE 9) and destroyers *Belknap* (DD 251) and *George E. Badger* (DD 196). During 1943, hunter-killer groups of jeep carriers, destroyers, and destroyer escorts went into widespread operation and effectively contributed to victory in the battle of the Atlantic. The *Bogue* and her consorts earned a Presidential Unit Citation for their antisubmarine work during 1943–44.

10 Jul 1943 The U.S. Navy participated in the invasion of Sicily.

13 Jul 1943 The Battle of Kolombangara resulted in the sinking of a Japanese light cruiser and the loss of the *Gwin* (DD 433).

25 Jul 1943 The *Harmon* (DE 678) was launched, the first ship to be named for an African-American.

6 Aug 1943 The Japanese lost three destroyers in the Battle of Vella Gulf. There were no U.S. Navy losses.

9 Sep 1943 U.S. naval forces landed the Allied Fifth Army at Salerno, Italy.

2 Nov 1943 At Empress Augusta Bay, U.S. Navy forces defeated a Japanese attack, sinking a cruiser and a destroyer.

25 Nov 1943 Five U.S. destroyers under CAPT Arleigh Burke, commander, Destroyer Squadron 23, defeated five Japanese destroyers off Cape St.

	George, New Ireland Island, sinking three and damaging another.
21 Jan 1944	The assault at Anzio was the last amphibious attack on Italy.
2 Feb 1944	Amphibious assaults were conducted against Kwajalein, Roi, and Namur Islands in the Marshalls. The islands were conquered quickly despite fierce resistance.
18 Feb 1944	Amphibious landings secured Eniwetok and Engebi Islands.
29 Feb 1944	The Navy landed Army forces in the Admiralty islands.
22 Apr 1944	U.S. landings at Hollandia, New Guinea, met little opposition.
May–Jun 1944	The *England* (DE 635) sank a record six Japanese submarines during this period. Three were killed in the first four days, and five of the six were downed without assistance! [CG 22 was later given the name *England*.]
4 Jun 1944	The U-505 was captured by a hunter-killer group of destroyer escorts led by the *Guadalcanal* (CVE 60).
6 Jun 1944	The Allies invaded Normandy. Nearly 2500 U.S. Navy ships and craft were involved in the largest amphibious assault ever. At one beach alone, 21,328 troops, 1742 vehicles, and 1695 tons of supplies were landed in 12 hours.
15 Jun 1944	The Second and Fourth Marine Divisions landed on Saipan and completed operations three weeks later.
19–20 Jun 1944	In the Battle of the Philippine Sea, also called the Marianas Turkey Shoot, naval aviators downed 426 Japanese aircraft while themselves losing only 95 planes.
21 Jul 1944	Marines and Army troops landed on Guam and took complete control of the island by 10 Aug 1944.
24 Jul 1944	The Marines landed on Tinian Island against light resistance.
15 Aug 1944	The Navy participated in amphibious landings in southern France, the last ones conducted in Europe.

15 Sep 1944	The Navy-Marine team assaulted Peleliu Island in the western Carolines.
20 Oct 1944	U.S. forces returned to the Philippines in an amphibious assault on Leyte Island.
23–26 Oct 1944	In three connected sea-air battles, known collectively as the Battle of Leyte Gulf, the Imperial Japanese Navy was virtually destroyed. The Japanese lost three battleships, one attack carrier, three light carriers, six heavy cruisers, four light cruisers, eight destroyers, and a submarine. U.S. Navy losses were one light carrier, two escort carriers, two destroyers, one destroyer escort, a submarine, and a torpedo boat.
14 Dec 1944	The five-star rank of fleet admiral was created. Fleet Admirals William Leahy, Ernest King, Chester Nimitz, and William Halsey have held this lifetime rank.
15 Dec 1944	The U.S. Army landed on Mindoro Island in the Philippines.
9 Jan 1945	Army forces landed at Lingayen Gulf, Luzon.
19 Feb 1945	The Marines landed on Iwo Jima. It took twenty-six days of bloody fighting to secure the island.
1 Apr 1945	In the final major amphibious assault of World War II, Army units landed on Okinawa on this Easter Sunday. In the heaviest use of Japanese kamikaze attacks in the war, thirty-four ships were lost, 288 others were damaged. The Japanese lost 1228 planes and pilots in this suicidal effort. Resistance finally ended on 21 June.
7 May 1945	Germany surrendered. Submarine losses by the Germans in the Battle of the Atlantic totaled more than 800.
6 Aug 1945	The first atomic bomb was detonated over Hiroshima, Japan. The weaponeer on the bomber *Enola Gay* was Navy CAPT W. S. Parsons. [DDG 33 was named after him.]
9 Aug 1945	A second atomic bomb was dropped on Nagasaki, Japan.
14 Aug 1945	V-J (Victory over Japan) Day. Hostilities ceased in the Pacific, putting an end to World War II.

2 Sep 1945	Japan formally surrendered on board the *Missouri* (BB 63).
2 Jul 1946	A jet aircraft operated from an aircraft carrier for the first time.
17 Sep 1947	James Forrestal became the first secretary of defense. The next day the National Military Establishment (NME) came into being. The NME coordinated service policies; in 1949 it became the Department of Defense (DOD), with the various services as its components.
3 Jun 1949	John Wesley Brown became the first African-American to graduate from the Naval Academy.
1 Oct 1949	The Military Sea Transportation Service (MSTS) was established, under Navy operation, as the consolidated sealift service for the Department of Defense. It absorbed the sea transportation services previously operated by the Army and Navy.
26 Jun 1950	U.S. forces ordered to support South Korea against invading North Korean troops.
3 Jul 1950	Panther fighter-bombers from the *Valley Forge* (CV 45) attacked Pyongyang, the North Korean capital, in the first strike by carrier-launched jet aircraft.
15 Sep 1950	Marines landed at Inchon, near Seoul, Korea, in a surprise thrust deep behind the front lines. This attack compelled the Communist invaders to fall back northward.
9 Nov 1950	The first dogfight involving a Navy jet and an enemy jet was fought. LCDR W. T. Amen, in a Panther, shot down a MiG-15, a Soviet-built fighter.
28 Aug 1952	First use of carrier-launched guided missiles. Pilotless, radio-controlled (via a TV guidance system) Hellcat fighters with high explosives were used against land targets from the *Boxer* (CV 21).
3 Nov 1952	Marine Maj. W. Stratton, in a Skyknight, scored the first kill by an airborne intercept radar-equipped fighter, shooting down a Soviet-built YAK-15.
27 Jul 1953	The Korean Armistice went into effect.

3 Dec 1954	The *Gyatt* (DD 712) was recommissioned as DDG 1, the first combatant Navy ship with anti-aircraft missiles.
17 Jan 1955	The *Nautilus* (SSN 571), the world's first nuclear-powered submarine, began operations.
7 Mar 1958	*Grayback* (SSG 574), built to carry Regulus II missiles, was commissioned as the Navy's first strategic missile submarine.
17 Mar 1958	The Navy's Vanguard I satellite was placed in orbit, where it should remain for 2000 years. It is the oldest manmade object in orbit today.
3 Aug 1958	*The Nautilus* became the first ship in history to reach the North Pole.
20 Dec 1959	*George Washington* (SSBN 598), the first Polaris missile submarine, was commissioned.
1960	The *Triton* (SSN 586) became the first submarine to circumnavigate the world submerged. The voyage covered 41,500 miles in 83 days at an average speed of 18 knots.
20 Jul 1960	The *George Washington* made the first submerged launching of Polaris ballistic missiles off Cape Canaveral.
15 Nov 1960	The first deterrent Polaris patrol was begun by the *George Washington*. It lasted 66 days, 10 hours.
5 May 1961	CDR Alan B. Shepard became the first American in space, riding Mercury capsule *Freedom 7* on a 15-minute suborbital flight.
9 Sep 1961	The *Long Beach* (CGN 9), the world's first nuclear-powered surface warship, was commissioned.
20 Feb 1962	Marine Maj. John Glenn became the first American to orbit the earth in *Friendship 7*.
Oct 1962	Pres. John Kennedy quarantined Cuba with naval forces to keep the Soviets from sending in strategic nuclear missiles. After a period of tension, in which nuclear war appeared very possible, the issue was resolved.
10 Apr 1963	The *Thresher* (SSN 593) was lost with all hands east of Portsmouth, N.H., because of material failure during a test dive. She was the first nuclear submarine to be lost.

May 1964	Seventh Fleet carriers deployed off northern coast of South Vietnam (Republic of Vietnam) in an area to be called Yankee Station.	Navy History
19 May 1964	The *Kitty Hawk* (CVA 63) began her first period of service off North Vietnam. She was the first U.S. carrier on station in the Tonkin Gulf during the Vietnam conflict.	
Aug 1964	The destroyer *Maddox* was attacked by North Vietnamese torpedo boats in the Tonkin Gulf on 2 Aug. Two nights later, the *Maddox* was joined by the destroyer *Turner Joy* and, in a confused melee in the dark of night, both ships believed they were attacked a second time by North Vietnamese patrol craft. Carrier planes from the *Ticonderoga* and *Constellation* later struck military targets in North Vietnam. On 7 Aug, Congress passed the Tonkin Gulf Resolution, the legal basis for U.S. armed support for South Vietnam.	
Mar 1965	Combined U.S.-Vietnamese patrol established to counter North Vietnamese coastal infiltration, soon named Market Time. This patrol also provided fire support to land forces, transported troops, and evacuated civilians from combat areas.	**579**
8 Mar 1965	Ninth Marine Expeditionary Brigade landed at Da Nang, the first battalion-sized ground combat unit to RVN.	
15 Apr 1965	Carriers struck Viet Cong forces in RVN from operating area southeast of Cam Ranh Bay, soon called Dixie Station.	
May 1965	Seventh Fleet ships began strike and fire-support missions in RVN.	
18 Dec 1965	River Patrol Force (TF 116) established to carry out Operation Market Time on South Vietnamese rivers.	
Oct 1966	Operation Sea Dragon began. Cruisers and destroyers, aided by carrier spotter planes, struck North Vietnamese military targets; the battleship *New Jersey* joined them for a short while in 1968. The operation ended in October 1968.	

13 Jan 1967	GMCM Delbert D. Black was sworn in as senior enlisted adviser of the Navy. This billet became master chief petty officer of the Navy (MCPON) on 28 Apr 1967.
28 May 1967	The *Long Beach* (CGN 9) fired a Talos missile at North Vietnamese MiG-21 in Tonkin Gulf, making it the first Navy ship to fire a surface-to-air missile at hostile aircraft.
30 Jan 1968	The Tet Offensive began as Communist forces threatened most population centers and captured the city of Hue, retaken by RVN troops and U.S. Marines in heavy fighting. North Vietnamese besieged the Marine base at Khe Sanh; massive Navy/Air Force air strikes helped defeat the attackers. The Communists suffered heavy losses. Large main-force units were pushed toward border areas. RVN control was extended.
6 Apr 1968	The battleship *New Jersey* (BB 62) was recommissioned for Vietnam service.
30 Sep 1968	The *New Jersey* fired her first mission off Vietnam, the first battleship combat firing since the Korean War.
Oct 1968	Beginning of Operation SEALORDS, a concerted U.S.-Vietnamese land/sea/air effort to cut supply lines from Cambodia and disrupt base areas in Mekong Delta.
20 Jul 1969	The lunar module *Eagle* landed on the moon's Sea of Tranquillity after detaching from Apollo 11. The commander of the mission and the first man to set foot on the moon was Neil Armstrong, who had been a Navy fighter pilot in the Korean War.
1 Aug 1970	The Military Sea Transportation Service was retitled the Military Sealift Command (MSC).
30 Mar 1972	North Vietnamese Easter offensive began. RVN forces prevailed with the help of U.S. naval forces providing naval gunfire, logistic support, and air/surface strikes on North Vietnam.
18–29 Dec 1972	Operation Linebacker II: Navy/Air Force planes conducted major strikes on North Vietnamese military targets in the Hanoi/Haiphong area after peace negotiations stalled and the North

Vietnamese strengthened defenses and built up supply lines and stockpiles.

Mar 1973 — Last U.S. forces withdrawn from RVN after extended transfer of resources and missions to RV Navy.

22 Jun 1973 — The Skylab I team, operating the world's first orbiting space laboratory, completed a 30-day operation. Its members were all naval aviators.

1 Jul 1973 — The traditional Sailor's white hat, broad collar, and bell-bottomed trousers were superseded by a more conventional, suit-like, CPO-type uniform.

18 Jul 1973 — Operation End Sweep, a clearance of mines from North Vietnamese waters, was completed by minesweepers and helicopters. Seventh Fleet ships departed Vietnamese waters.

Mar–Apr 1975 — Naval ships/aircraft evacuated U.S. allied personnel from Cambodia as that country was overrun by the Khmer Rouge (Operation Eagle Pull). As RVN fell to a full-scale North Vietnamese invasion, Operation Frequent Wind evacuated Americans, Vietnamese, and others from South Vietnam.

12 May 1975 — American containership *Mayaguez* was seized in the Gulf of Siam by Khmer Rouge gunboats and taken to Koh Tang Island. Marines boarded *Mayaguez* from USS *Harold E. Holt* (FF 1074) on 16 May as helicopter-landed Marines held a beachhead on Koh Tang against heavy opposition. *Mayaguez*'s crew was rescued.

1 Jan 1978 — The Navy returned to the traditional bell-bottom jumper uniform for Sailors in grades E-1 through E-4. On 1 May 1980, the Navy began issuing these uniforms to all male recruits, and by 1 Oct 1983 all enlisted men, E-1 through E-6, had resumed wearing them.

30 Sep 1980 — Naval Districts, established in 1903, were disestablished except for Naval District Washington. Facilities within previous district areas were transferred to area naval bases.

22 Dec 1980 — The aircraft carrier *Eisenhower* completed 152 consecutive days at sea, setting a new record.

581

27 Jun 1981	The *James K. Polk* (SSBN 645) completed the two-thousandth ballistic-missile deterrent patrol.
15 Sep 1981	The one-star flag rank of commodore was reestablished by an act of Congress. "Commodore" was an operational command title from the earliest days until 1862, when it became an actual officer rank. Abolished on 3 Mar 1899, it was restored on 9 Apr 1943 for use during World War II but was allowed to lapse in 1949. (See Nov 1985.)
11 Nov 1981	The USS *Ohio* (SSBN 726), the first of the Trident-firing ballistic-missile submarines, was commissioned.
2 Apr 1982	Argentine Marines and special forces captured the Falkland (Malvinas) Islands and nearby South Georgia Island from British defenders. Britain formed a task force to retake the islands; the United States announced its support. The islands were recaptured after a land-sea-air campaign in which ships and aircraft were lost or damaged by missiles, and the Argentine cruiser *General Belgrano* was sunk by submarine torpedoes.
28 Dec 1982	The USS *New Jersey* (BB 62), newly armed with missiles in addition to her five- and sixteen-inch guns, was placed in commission for the third time by President Reagan. Her three sister ships—*Iowa, Missouri,* and *Wisconsin*—later followed her into service.
23 Oct 1983	A terrorist truck bomb crashed into the headquarters and barracks building of Marines assigned to the Multinational Peacekeeping Force at Beirut, Lebanon, killing 241 Marines.
23 Oct 1983	U.S. forces landed on the Caribbean island of Grenada, expelling Cuban forces and capturing a quantity of Soviet-supplied arms.
Nov 1985	By act of Congress, the title of the Navy's one-star flag rank was changed from commodore to rear admiral (lower half). (See 15 Sep 1981.)
24–25 Mar 1986	In response to terrorist attacks on civilians, a Sixth Fleet force organized around the carriers

Saratoga, Coral Sea, America, and the new Aegis missile cruisers *Ticonderoga* and *Yorktown,* engaged Libyan forces in the Gulf of Sidra. Several Libyan missile patrol craft were sunk or damaged, and a missile battery at Sidra was hit.

14 Apr 1986   In coordination with Air Force F-111s flying from England, Sixth Fleet carrier planes struck military targets in Libya.

7 Mar 1987   Responding to Kuwait's request, the U.S. agreed to escort Kuwaiti tankers in the Persian Gulf during the Iraq-Iran War.

17 May 1987   The USS *Stark* (FFG 31), on patrol in the Persian Gulf, was damaged by two missiles fired from an Iraqi aircraft; thirty-seven of her crew were killed.

22 Jul 1987   Kuwaiti tankers began transiting the Persian Gulf under U.S. flag and Navy escort. The tanker *Bridgeton* was damaged by an Iranian mine.

12 Sep 1987   The *Avenger* (MCM 1) was commissioned. A wood-hulled ship designed to locate and sweep contact and influence mines, she was the first new USN mine countermeasures ship since 1960.

21 Sep 1987   Armed helicopters from the *Jarrett* (FFG 33) and Navy SEALs capture the Iranian craft *Iran Ajr* laying mines in the gulf.

8 Oct 1987   Iranian patrol craft fired on U.S. helicopters. U.S. forces sank at least one of the attackers.

19 Oct 1987   In retaliation for an Iranian missile attack on a U.S. flag tanker, the destroyers *Hoel* (DDG 13), *Kidd* (DDG 993), *Leftwich* (DD 984), and *John Young* (DD 973) bombarded two offshore oil platforms housing military radar and communications gear used in attacks on shipping. Navy SEALs finished the job with explosives, then destroyed a third platform.

14 Apr 1988   The USS *Samuel B. Roberts* (FFG 58) struck a mine in the Persian Gulf; though severely damaged, she was saved by the aggressive efforts of her professional crew.

| 18 Apr 1988 | In response to the mining of USS *Samuel B. Roberts,* American ships shelled Iranian oil platforms. Iranian frigates fired missiles at U.S. aircraft. Patrol craft fired on the *Wainwright* (CG 28). Planes and the *Joseph Strauss* (DDG 16) engaged patrol craft and two Iranian frigates. The Iranian patrol craft *Joshan* was sunk. The frigates *Sahand* and *Sabalan* were also severely damaged. An A-6 from the *Enterprise* (CVN 65) sank one, possibly more, Iranian patrol craft attacking commercial shipping. |

| 3 Jul 1988 | The cruiser *Vincennes,* while engaged in a skirmish with Iranian gunboats, mistook an Iranian airliner for a fighter on an attack run and shot it down. |

| Sep 1988 | The Navy began to scale down its Persian Gulf presence after an Iraq-Iran ceasefire of 20 Aug ended fighting. Tanker escort operations were replaced by a general "zone defense." |

| 19 Apr 1989 | A powder explosion in Turret II of battleship *Iowa* (BB 61) killed forty-seven crewmembers. It was the first "cold-gun" turret explosion since the Navy began using large-caliber breech-loading bag guns in 1895. |

| 16 Jul 1990 | A new service dress white jumper-style uniform with slacks/skirt became available in Navy uniform centers and was authorized for wear by all female E-6 and below. |

| 2 Aug 1990 | Iraq invaded and occupied Kuwait. The UN Security Council condemned the Iraqi invasion. |

| 8 Aug 1990 | Iraq declared annexation of Kuwait. President Bush ordered the commencement of Operation Desert Shield, deploying major U.S. forces to Saudi Arabia to assist in defending that country against possible Iraqi incursion. U.S. land and air forces were ordered in, reserves were recalled to active duty, and additional naval forces were deployed to reinforce those already in the Middle East area. |

| 17 Aug 1990 | U.S. naval forces in the Persian Gulf were ordered to intercept commercial shipping to and from Iraq and Kuwait to enforce UN sanctions. |

25 Aug 1990	The United Nations authorized the use of armed force to enforce sanctions.	Navy History
29 Nov 1990	The UN Security Council authorized use of "all necessary means" if Iraq refused to withdraw from Kuwait and release foreign hostages. This was the second UN resolution calling for forcible resistance to aggression; the first came when North Korea invaded South Korea in 1950.	
27 Dec 1990	Navy blue pullover sweater was authorized as part of service dress blue uniform for all hands.	
Jan 1991	The secretary of defense recommended a comprehensive scheme to acquire sealift ships to support overseas deployment of American troops.	
12 Jan 1991	Congress authorized President Bush to use military force if Iraq refused to withdraw from Kuwait. Deadline set for unconditional withdrawal by United Nations and Congress as 15 Jan.	
16 Jan 1991	Operation Desert Storm began with allied aircraft striking targets in Iraq and Kuwait. The *Wisconsin* and *Missouri,* followed by other ships, began first combat use of Tomahawk cruise missiles. Throughout Desert Storm, Navy surface and air forces supported air and land operations with strike missions using both cruise missiles and aircraft, fighter cover, search and rescue, mine countermeasures, and intercepts of Gulf shipping.	**585**
19 Jan 1991	U.S. carrier planes fired first SLAM ground attack missile in combat. The *Louisville* (SSN 724), operating in the Red Sea, fired first submerged Tomahawk combat strike.	
3 Feb 1991	The *Missouri* fired her first combat rounds since the Korean War, destroying prefabricated concrete command-and-control bunkers being moved into Kuwait. The *Nicholas* used sonar to guide the *Missouri* through hazards into the northern Gulf for the most advantageous firing.	
8 Feb 1991	The *Wisconsin* supported Marine reconnaissance into Kuwait by attacking Iraqi artillery	

sites, spotting fall of shots by television images transmitted by her remotely controlled aircraft. The *Wisconsin* fired in combat for the first time since Korea on 6 Feb, destroying an artillery battery.

18 Feb 1991   The *Princeton* (CG 59) and *Tripoli* (LPH 10) were damaged by mines in the northern Gulf. The *Tripoli* continued as flagship of mine-clearance operations. The *Princeton* proceeded to port.

21 Feb 1991   Marine AV-8B Harriers flew bombing strikes from the *Nassau* (LHA 4)—the first Marine combat air strikes from a helicopter landing ship.

24 Feb 1991   Ground war began after Iraq failed to respond to a 1200 EST 23 Feb deadline to comply with all UN resolutions and make large-scale withdrawal from Kuwait.

25–26 Feb 1991   Allied forces quickly defeated Iraqi troops in an unprecedented ground war.

27 Feb 1991   President Bush announced ceasefire effective 0800 28 Feb (Iraqi time). Defeated and forced out of Kuwait, Iraq accepted.

4 Jul 1991   *Arleigh Burke* (DDG 51), lead ship of a new class of missile destroyers. designed for battle group operations well into the twenty-first century, was placed in commission. Aegis, advanced sonar, LAMPS III, ASW torpedoes, five-inch, fifty-four guns, and a varied battery of missiles give the new ships formidable ability to operate against air, surface, and submarine targets.

27 Sep 1991   Pres. George Bush announced that all tactical nuclear weapons would be removed from Navy ships.

Nov 1991   The cruiser *Yorktown* (CG 48) conducted exercises with Bulgarian ships in the Black Sea, the first American operations with a navy of the former Warsaw Pact.

9 Nov 1992   An amphibious ready group (ARG) led by the helicopter carrier *Tripoli* (LPH 10) arrived off Somalia, supported by the carrier *Ranger* (CV

61), and landed troops at Mogadishu to oversee famine relief operations.

13 Jan 1993	During a period of tension between Iraq and allied forces, carrier *Kitty Hawk* launched a strike at Iraqi missile sites that had been playing their radars on patrolling allied aircraft. On 17 Jan, three U.S. destroyers launched Tomahawk missiles at a suspected Iraqi nuclear plant.
15 Apr 1993	U.S. naval forces begin participation in Operation Sharp Guard, a blockade of shipping into the former Yugoslavia in support of UN sanctions. This operation will continue until 18 Jun 1996.
26 Jun 1993	Responding to information of an Iraqi attempt to assassinate President Bush during his 1992 visit to Kuwait, two U.S. ships launched Tomahawk missiles at Iraqi intelligence headquarters in Baghdad.
11 Sep 1993	The aircraft carrier *Forrestal* commissioned on 1 Oct 1955 as the first of the post-World War II-designed "supercarriers," was decommissioned at Philadelphia. She ended her service as a training aircraft carrier at Pensacola, designated AVT 59.
Oct 1993	Navy and Coast Guard ships, with those of other navies, began an international quarantine of Haiti.
Mar 1994	Marines boarded ships off Mogadishu, ending U.S. operations in Somalia.
Oct 1994	President Clinton sent *George Washington* (CVN 73) to the Red Sea to protect Kuwait from threat of Iraqi troop concentration. Iraq withdrew from the Kuwaiti border.
Oct 1994	*Dwight D. Eisenhower* (CVN 69) was the first carrier to deploy with women as part of its crew.
Jan–Dec 1995	Throughout the year, U.S. forces played vital peacekeeping and "show the flag" roles in several of the world's trouble spots, including the Balkans, North Korea, and the Middle East. Navy and Marine units also joined the Coast Guard and other governmental agencies in counterdrug operations.

Jun 1995	A joint/multinational task force involving Marine and Navy units rescued Air Force CAPT Scott O'Grady after his F-16 was shot down by a Serb surface-to-air missile.
1 Jul 1995	A Fifth Fleet was designated for operations in the Middle East and Indian Ocean region. (There had been a Fifth Fleet operating in the Pacific during World War II.)
Aug 1995	Navy and Marine aircraft attacked Bosnian Serb surface-to-air missile sites to assist a UN peacekeeping contingent caught in the middle of an artillery exchange.
Aug–Sep 1995	During Operation Deliberate Force, aircraft from the carriers *Theodore Roosevelt* and *America* launched intense air strikes on various positions in war-torn Bosnia.
10 Sep 1995	The cruiser *Normandy* launched thirteen Tomahawk land-attack cruise missiles against targets in Bosnia.
1 Jan 1996	ADM Arleigh Burke, one of the great heroes of World War II and later a long-term Chief of Naval Operations who helped shape the Navy for the dawning nuclear age, passed away. At his request, his tombstone was inscribed with the single word "Sailor." [DDG-51 was named for him.]
Jan–Feb 1996	In response to Chinese threats to close the Straits of Taiwan, the carriers *Independence, Nimitz,* and *George Washington* and their supporting battle groups moved into the area as a deterrent show of force.
8–28 Feb 1996	Navy divers used their advanced technology to recover the flight data and voice recorders of a Dominican airliner crash in extremely deep and hazardous waters.
5–24 Mar 1996	In a classic example of deterrence and forward presence, two battlegroups centered around the carriers *Nimitz* and *Independence* were sent to patrol Chinese waters in response to a Communist threat to close part of the Taiwan Strait.
Apr 1996	U.S. warships and Marines were rushed to Monrovia, Liberia in the aftermath of an assault on

the U.S. embassy there. Many U.S. citizens were evacuated to safety in an operation dubbed "Assured Response."

16 May 1996   Chief of Naval Operations Jeremy "Mike" Boorda, the first former enlisted man to rise to the Navy's highest position, amid much turmoil and difficult times for himself and the Navy he loved, took his own life.

21 May 1996   In "Operation Quick Response" the *Guam* Amphibious Ready Group evacuated several hundred people from the land-locked Central African Republic using Marine aircraft.

10 Jul 1996   Patricia Tracey was promoted to vice-admiral, the first woman in the U.S. armed forces to wear three stars.

Jul–Oct 1996   Navy salvage vessels and divers recover the debris and victims from the depths of the Atlantic after TWA Flight 800 crashed into the waters off Long Island.

3–4 Sep 1996   The cruiser *Shiloh,* destroyers *Laboon, Russell,* and *Hewitt,* and the submarine *Jefferson City* launched Tomahawk missiles into Iraq in response to treaty violations there.

March 1997   In Operation Silver Wake, Marines from the amphibious ships *Nassau* (LHA-4), *Nashville* (LPD-13), and *Pensacola* (LSD-38) evacuated 877 Americans and foreign nationals from war-torn Tirana, Albania. Marine helicopters received and returned hostile fire during the operation.

May 1997   RTC Great Lakes introduced "Battle Stations" as the culminating challenge of Boot Camp [see Chapter 1].

21 Jul 1997   The 44-gun frigate USS *Constitution* ("Old Ironsides"), the Navy's oldest commissioned warship celebrated her 200th anniversary by getting underway under her own power (sails). During the War of 1812, she was undefeated in 30 engagements.

6 Aug 1997   Navy Sea Knight helicopters were among the first to arrive on the crash scene of Korean Air Lines Flight 801 and rescued 30 survivors from

the Guam jungle. Sailors from Naval Mobile Construction Battalion 133 ("SeaBees") cut through the dense jungle to permit rescue, medical, and investigative personnel to reach the site.

Feb–Apr 1998   In Operation Noble Response, naval forces join the other armed services in providing more than 800 tons of food and supplies to the flood-ravaged African nation of Kenya.

20 Aug 1998   Navy surface ships and submarines in the Red Sea and Arabian Sea launched a barrage of Tomahawk missiles against a suspected chemical weapons facility in Khartoum, Sudan and terrorist training camps in eastern Afghanistan in response to terrorist bombings of the U.S. embassies in Kenya and Tanzania, which killed some 200 people, including 12 Americans.

9 Sep 1998   USS *Grapple* (ARS-53) and members of Mobile Diving and Salvage Unit 2 arrived off Nova Scotia to assist in recovery operations after the crash of Swissair Flight 111.

7 Nov 1998   SeaBees from Gulf Port, Mississippi deployed to Honduras to support an international relief effort in the wake of Hurricane Mitch.

Dec 1998–Jan 1999   The carrier *Enterprise* and seven other ships (one CG, two DDs, three DDGs, and one SSN) launched aircraft and Tomahawk missile strikes against Iraq as part of Operation Desert Fox. An FFG, LHA, LPD, LSD, and two MCMs also played vital support roles in the campaign.

17 Feb 1999   After supporting U.S. operations in Antarctica for nearly 44 years, the final flight of the Navy's VXE-6 squadron departed the icy continent, ending the Navy's official presence there.

24 Mar 1999   Operation Allied Force (air strikes against Yugoslav targets) began. Many Navy ships and aircraft played major roles in the 78-day campaign that ultimately ended the killing in Kosovo.

22 Jul 1999   USS *Briscoe* (DD-997) buried the cremated remains of John F. Kennedy, Jr. at sea after a massive at-sea search effort by the Navy, Coast

	Guard, and Air Force recovered the 35th president's son's remains from his downed aircraft off Martha's Vineyard.
Aug–Sep 1999	The *Kearsarge* amphibious ready group provided massive humanitarian support in the wake of a devastating earthquake in northwestern Turkey.
October 1999	Several Navy ships, including the amphibious assault ship USS *Belleau Wood* (LHA-3), took part in vital peacekeeping operations off East Timor.
Oct–Nov 1999	Several Navy and MSC ships, including *Grapple* (ARS-53), *Austin* (LPD-4), *Oriole* (MHC-55), and *Mohawk* (T-ATF-170), participate in recovery operations off the coast of Nantucket following the crash of EgyptAir Flight 900.
8 Aug 2000	The Confederate submarine *Hunley* was recovered from the bottom of Charleston harbor. [See 17 Feb 1864.]
12 Oct 2000	Seventeen sailors died and 42 others were injured when suicide-terrorists blew a huge hole in the side of the guided-missile destroyer *Cole* (DDG-67) while the ship was refueling in Aden, Yemen. Through proficiency, determination, and courage the crew managed to save the ship.
9 Feb 2001	In a tragic accident that cost the lives of nine Japanese crewmen, the attack submarine *Greeneville* surfaced directly under the 190-foot fishing trawler *Ehime Maru*. The trawler sank within minutes and 26 crewmen were rescued.
1 Apr 2001	A VQ-1 (Fleet Air Reconnaissance Squadron 1) EP-3E Orion aircraft equipped with the Aries II electronic surveillance system was struck by a harassing Chinese fighter and forced to make an emergency landing on Hainan Island. All 24 crewmembers survived and were returned to the United States after being held 11 days by the Chinese.
11 Sep 2001	United States homeland was attacked by terrorists. The World Trade Center towers in New York were destroyed, and the Pentagon was severely damaged with many casualties. Presi-

dent Bush promised that terrorists will be brought to justice, pledging "we will not tire, we will not falter, we will not fail."

7 Oct 2001   U.S. forces began attacking targets in Afghanistan as the first military operation in the War on Terrorism. Among the many forces involved, U.S. aircraft carriers commenced air strikes; submarines and surface ships launched Tomahawk missiles; and Navy SEALs moved into positions to seek terrorist strongholds.

4 Oct 2002   The 100th anniversary of *The Bluejacket's Manual*.

Note: Future entries in this list may depend upon *you*.

Ranks and Rates

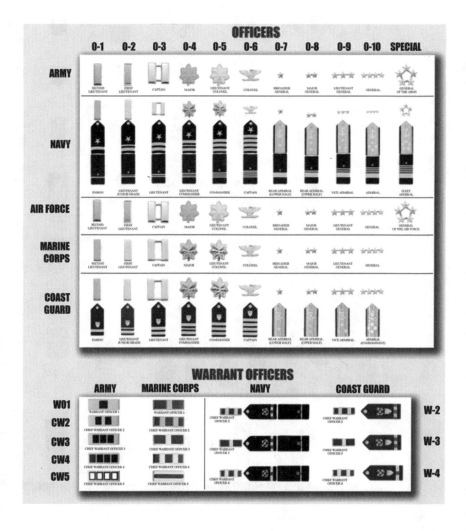

"Courtesy of *Military Times*"

Navigational Aids

Aids to navigation are lighthouses, lightships, minor lights, buoys, and day beacons. Aids are located so as to provide a nearly continuous and unbroken chain of charted marks for coast and channel piloting.

Buoys

Navigational buoys are floating markers, moored to the bottom, that guide ships in and out of channels, warn them of hidden dangers, lead them to anchorage areas, and the like. They are somewhat like road signs along a highway. Their location is usually shown by symbols on the area navigational chart. Buoys may be of various sizes, shapes, and colors. Color, markings, and to a lesser degree shape are the main means of identifying a buoy and correlating its location with that of the symbol on the chart. The following are the principal types of buoys used in U.S. waters:

Spar: A large floating pole, trimmed, shaped, and appropriately painted. It may be made of wood or metal. You will not see these very often in U.S. waters, but they are fairly common in other parts of the world.

Can and nun: Cylindrical and conical, respectively.

Spherical: Shaped like a ball. Used only as safe water marks (see below) and painted with red and white vertical stripes.

Bell: This buoy has a flat top surmounted by a framework supporting a bell. Older bell buoys are sounded by the motion of the sea. Newer types are operated automatically by gas or electricity.

Gong: Similar to the bell buoy except that it has a series of gongs, each with a different tone.

Whistle and horn: Usually cone-shaped with a whistle sounded by the sea's motion, or horns sounded at regular intervals by mechanical or electrical means.

Lighted: Surmounted by a framework supporting a light and powered by batteries or gas tanks.

Combination: Light and sound signals are combined in this type of buoy.

Large navigation buoys: Known as LNBs (and sometimes as LANBYs), these buoys were designed primarily to replace lightships and lighthouses. They are discs that may be as large as 40 feet in diameter and are equipped with lights, fog-signaling equipment, radio beacons, and meteorological sensors. They are normally placed relatively far from shore and therefore will not be encountered in navigational channels as are the other types discussed here.

In the United States, red buoys mark the right side of the channel and green buoys mark the left side when you are coming from seaward. Remember the saying, "Red-right-returning," to help you keep it straight. It means that if you are returning to port from sea, you should leave the red buoys on the right side of the ship to stay in the channel. If unlighted, red channel buoys are cone-shaped nun buoys, and green channel markers are cylindrical can buoys. If the buoys are lighted, it is their color that is most important.

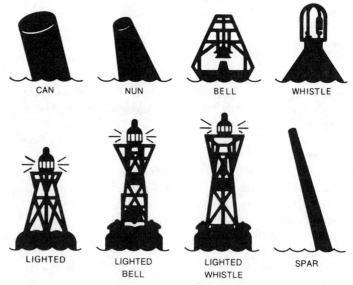

Figure D.1. Some of the buoys you may encounter.

Horizontal banded red and green buoys are used to mark obstructions or to indicate a fork in the channel and to show you which is the preferred way to go. If the top band is red, the preferred channel is to the left of the buoy coming from seaward; if the top band is green, the preferred channel is to the right. Buoys with red and white vertical stripes mark the middle of a channel and are called *safe water marks*. Black and red horizontally banded buoys are called *isolated danger marks* and are used to warn of such things as shipwrecks.

Buoys are valuable aids to navigation, but never depend on them exclusively. They may drag their moorings or go adrift. Lights on buoys are sometimes out of commission. Whistles, bells, and gongs that depend upon the sea's motion to sound may fail to function in smooth water. Anyone navigating by buoys must be alert to these possibilities.

Red buoys marking the right side of a channel bear *even* numbers, starting with the first buoy from seaward. Green channel buoys, to the left of the channel coming from seaward, have *odd* numbers. Banded or striped buoys are not numbered, but some have letters for identification.

Red lights are used only on red buoys or on ones that are horizontally banded in red and green, with the topmost band red. Green lights are only for green buoys, or for green and red horizontally banded buoys, with the topmost band green. Red and white vertically striped buoys that mark the middle of a channel or fairway have white lights.

The buoys discussed above are the ones you would expect to encounter in U.S. waters and some other parts of the world. In years past, mariners had to be familiar with many different buoyage systems in the world, but in the mid-1970s the International Association of Light Authorities reduced these many systems to two that have gained international acceptance. *IALA System A* is used in Europe, Africa, and much of Asia, including Australia and New Zealand. *IALA System B* is used in North, Central, and South America, Japan, South Korea, and the Philippines. Many of the conventions discussed above regarding U.S. waters (and therefore fall within IALA System B) are the exact opposite in IALA System A. *Green* buoys mark the *starboard* side of the channel when returning from sea in this system, for example. It is therefore essential for a mariner to know which system applies before attempting to navigate in the various waters of the world.

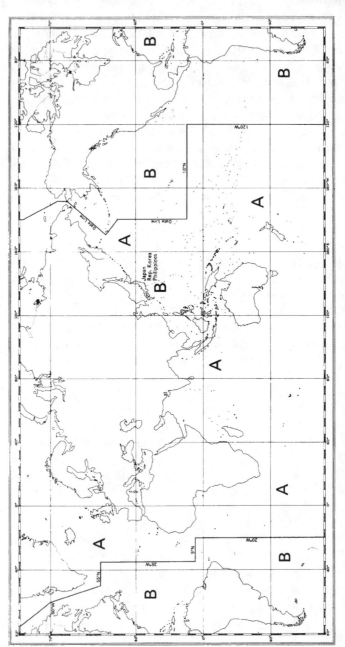

Figure D.2. IALA buoyage systems A and B. Note that U.S. waters are system B.

Day Beacons

In narrower waterways, structures that are fixed in place—either on shore or in shallow water—instead of floating and moored to the bottom like buoys are called day beacons. They usually consist of a piling with a colored and numbered or lettered geometric shape called a day mark near the top, triangular shapes to the right, and square shapes to the left (when you are returning from seaward). Their reflective colors and markings correspond to those a buoy would have at the same position. Often a night light is affixed to the top.

Two day beacons, located some distance apart on a specific true bearing, constitute a day-beacon range. When you can see two beacons positioned in line, your ship is "on the range," which means that you know you are somewhere along that bearing. Ranges are especially valuable for guiding ships through very narrow channels because it is a way of keeping exactly on track.

Storm-Warning Information

In the United States, information regarding weather and the approach of storms is furnished by the Weather Bureau. This information is disseminated by means of bulletins, reports furnished by newspapers, television and radio broadcasts, and, in certain ports, by flags during the day and lanterns at night.

If bad weather is approaching and it is expected that the winds will reach a speed up to 33 knots (approximately 38 miles per hour), one red pennant is displayed by day, and a red light over a white light is displayed at night to warn mariners. This is called a *small-craft warning*.

If the winds are expected to range somewhere between 34 and 47 knots (approximately 39 to 54 miles per hour) two red pennants are displayed by day and a white light above a red light at night. This is called a *gale warning*.

If the forecast calls for winds of 48–63 knots (55–73 miles an hour), a single, square red flag with a black center is displayed by day, and two red lights at night. This is called a *storm warning*.

Two square red flags with black centers displayed by day, and a white light between two red lights at night, forecast winds of 64 knots (74 miles per hour) or more and is called a *hurricane warning*.

E Morse Code

International Morse code is standard for all naval communications transmitted by flashing light. The code is a system in which letters, numerals, and punctuation marks are signified by various combinations of dots (.) and dashes (-). A skilled signalman sends code in evenly timed dots and dashes, in which a dot is one unit long, a dash three units long. There is a one-unit interval between dots and dashes in a letter, a three-unit interval between letters of a word, and a seven-unit interval between words.

A	Alfa	· —
B	Bravo	— · · ·
C	Charlie	— · — ·
D	Delta	— · ·
E	Echo	·
F	Foxtrot	· · — ·
G	Golf	— — ·
H	Hotel	· · · ·
I	India	· ·
J	Juliett	· — — —
K	Kilo	— · —
L	Lima	· — · ·
M	Mike	— —
N	November	— ·
O	Oscar	— — —
P	Papa	· — — ·
Q	Quebec	— — · —
R	Romeo	· — ·
S	Sierra	· · ·
T	Tango	—
U	Uniform	· · —
V	Victor	· · · —
W	Whiskey	· — —
X	X-ray	— · · —
Y	Yankee	— · — —
Z	Zulu	— — · ·

1	One	· — — — —
2	Two	· · — — —
3	Three	· · · — —
4	Four	· · · · —
5	Five	· · · · ·
6	Six	— · · · ·
7	Seven	— — · · ·
8	Eight	— — — · ·
9	Nine	— — — — ·
10	Ten	— — — — —
.	Period	· — · — · —
,	Comma	— — · · — —
?	Question Mark	· · — — · ·
;	Semicolon	— · — · — ·
:	Colon	— — — · · ·
-	Hyphen	— · · · · —
'	Apostrophe	· — — — — ·

Navy Flags and Pennants

Flag	Name – Written / Spoken	Flag	Name – Written / Spoken	Flag	Name – Written / Spoken
	A ALFA "AL-FA"		**M** MIKE "MIKE"		**Y** YANKEE "YANG-KEY"
	B BRAVO "BRAH-VOH"		**N** NOVEMBER "NO-VEM-BER"		**Z** ZULU "ZOO-LOO"
	C CHARLIE "CHAR-LEE"		**O** OSCAR "OSS-CAH"		**ONE - 1** "WUN"
	D DELTA "DEL-TAH"		**P** PAPA "PAH-PAH"		**TWO - 2** "TOO"
	E ECHO "ECK-OH"		**Q** QUEBEC "KAY-BECK"		**THREE - 3** "THUH-REE"
	F FOXTROT "FOKS-TROT"		**R** ROMEO "ROW-ME-OH"		**FOUR - 4** "FO-WER"
	G GOLF "GOLF"		**S** SIERRA "SEE-AIR-RAH"		**FIVE - 5** "FI-YIV"
	H HOTEL "HOH-TEL"		**T** TANGO "TANG-GO"		**SIX - 6** "SIX"
	I INDIA "IN-DEE-AH"		**U** UNIFORM "YOU-NEE-FORM"		**SEVEN - 7** "SEVEN"
	J JULIETT "JEW-LEE-ETT"		**V** VICTOR "VIK-TAH"		**EIGHT - 8** "ATE"
	K KILO "KEY-LOH"		**W** WHISKEY "WISS-KEY"		**NINE - 9** "NINER"
	L LIMA "LEE-MAH"		**X** XRAY "ECKS-RAY"		**ZERO - 0** "ZERO"

Pennant and Name	Written and Spoken	Pennant	Written and Spoken	Pennant	Written and Spoken
1	PENNANT ONE "WUN"		CODE or ANSWER CODE or ANS		PORT PORT
2	PENNANT TWO "TOO"		SCREEN SCREEN		SPEED SPEED
3	PENNANT THREE "THUH-REE"		CORPEN CORPEN		SQUAD SQUAD
4	PENNANT FOUR "FO-WER"		DESIG DESIG		STARBOARD STBD
5	PENNANT FIVE "FI-YIV"		DIV DIV		STATION STATION
6	PENNANT SIX "SIX"		EMERGENCY EMERG		SUBDIV SUBDIV
7	PENNANT SEVEN "SEVEN"		FLOT FLOT		TURN TURN
8	PENNANT EIGHT "ATE"		FORMATION FORM		FIRST SUB 1st.
9	PENNANT NINE "NINER"		INTERROGATIVE INT		SECOND SUB 2nd.
0	PENNANT ZERO "ZERO"		NEGAT NEGAT		THIRD SUB 3rd.
			PREP PREP		FOURTH SUB 4th.

Awards and Decorations

MEDAL OF HONOR

NAVY CROSS

DEFENSE
DISTINGUISHED
SERVICE MEDAL

LEGION OF MERIT

DISTINGUISHED FLYING
CROSS

NAVY AND MARINE
CORPS MEDAL

MERITORIOUS SERVICE
MEDAL

AIR MEDAL

JOINT SERVICE
COMMENDATION
MEDAL

COMBAT ACTION
RIBBON

PRESIDENTIAL UNIT
CITATION

JOINT MERITORIOUS
UNIT AWARD

POW MEDAL

GOOD CONDUCT
MEDAL

NAVAL RESERVE
MERITORIOUS SERVICE
MEDAL

NAVY OCCUPATION
SERVICE MEDAL

NATIONAL DEFENSE
SERVICE MEDAL

KOREAN SERVICE MEDAL

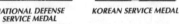

SOUTHWEST ASIA
SERVICE MEDAL

HUMANITARIAN
SERVICE MEDAL

MILITARY OUTSTANDING
VOLUNTEER SERVICE
MEDAL

NAVY AND MARINE
CORPS OVERSEAS
SERVICE RIBBON

NAVY RECRUITING SERVICE
RIBBON

ARMED FORCES RESERVE
MEDAL

REPUBLIC OF VIETNAM
PRESIDENTIAL UNIT
CITATION

REPUBLIC OF VIETNAM
GALLANTRY CROSS
UNIT CITATION

REPUBLIC OF VIETNAM
CIVIL ACTIONS UNIT
CITATION

INTER-AMERICAN
DEFENSE BOARD MEDAL

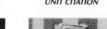

REPUBLIC OF VIETNAM
CAMPAIGN MEDAL

KUWAIT LIBERATION MEDAL
(Kingdom of Saudi Arabia)

DISTINGUISHED SERVICE MEDAL

SILVER STAR

DEFENSE SUPERIOR SERVICE MEDAL

BRONZE STAR

PURPLE HEART

DEFENSE MERITORIOUS SERVICE MEDAL

NAVY/MARINE CORPS COMMENDATION MEDAL

JOINT SERVICE ACHIEVEMENT MEDAL

NAVY/MARINE CORPS ACHIEVEMENT MEDAL

NAVY UNIT COMMENDATION

MERITORIOUS UNIT COMMENDATION

NAVY "E" RIBBON

FLEET MARINE FORCE RIBBON

NAVY EXPEDITIONARY MEDAL

CHINA SERVICE MEDAL

605

ANTARCTICA SERVICE MEDAL

ARMED FORCES EXPEDITIONARY MEDAL

VIETNAM SERVICE MEDAL

SEA SERVICE DEPLOYMENT RIBBON

NAVY ARCTIC SERVICE RIBBON

NAVAL RESERVE SEA SERVICE RIBBON

NAVAL RESERVE MEDAL

PHILIPPINE PRESIDENTIAL UNIT CITATION

REPUBLIC OF KOREA PRESIDENTIAL UNIT CITATION

UNITED NATIONS SERVICE MEDAL

UNITED NATIONS MEDAL

MULTINATIONAL FORCE AND OBSERVERS MEDAL

KUWAIT LIBERATION MEDAL (KUWAIT)

EXPERT RIFLEMAN MEDAL

EXPERT PISTOL SHOT MEDAL

The Navy's Service Song

The Master Chief Petty Officer of the Navy says, "Do more than learn the words; study them, understand them, and appreciate them. Stand crisply each time it is played."

Anchor's Aweigh

Stand, Navy, out to sea, fight, our battle cry;

We'll never change our course, so vicious foe steer shy.

Roll out the TNT, anchor's aweigh. Sail on to victory

And sink their bones to Davy Jones, Hooray!

Anchor's aweigh, my boys, anchor's aweigh.

Farewell to foreign shores, we sail at break of day, of day.

Through our last night on shore, drink to the foam,

Until we meet once more, here's wishing you a happy voyage home.

Blue of the mighty deep; gold of God's great sun,

Let these our colors be till all of time be done, be done.

On seven seas we learn Navy's stern call:

Faith, courage, service true, with honor over, honor over, all.

Internet Sources

The following is just a few of the many internet sites you can use to gather important information and stay on top of all you need to know to be a squared-away Sailor. This list is by no means complete but will get you started. Explore the many links that are available at these sites and you will be surprised how much information you can find. For example, at the Navy Directives website listed below you will be able to find the latest versions of Navy Regulations, the Ships Organization and Regulations Manual, Uniform Regulations, and many, many more.

Useful Internet Websites

All Hands Magazine	*www.mediacen.navy.mil/pubs/ allhands*
American Red Cross	*www.redcross.org*
Bureau of Naval Personnel	*www.bupers.mil*
Catalog of Naval Training Courses	*www.cnet.navy.mil/netpdtc/cantrac*
Chief of Naval Information	*www.chinfo.navy.mil*
Commissioning Programs	*www.neds.nebt.daps.mil/1420.htm*
Defense Financing and Accounting	*www.dfas.mil*
Defense News	*www.defenselink.mil*
Delta Dental	*www.ucci.com*
LifeLines Quality of Life	*www.lifelines4qol.org*
Naval Education and Training	*www.cnet.navy.mil*
Naval Historical Center	*www.history,navy.mil*
Naval Vessel Register	*www.nvr.navy.mil*
Navy College Program	*www.navycollege.navy.mil*
Navy Directives	*neds.nebt.daps.mil*
Navy Fact File	*www.chinfo.navy.mil/navpalib/ factfile/ffiletop.html*

Navy/Marine Corps Relief Society	*www.nmcrs.org*
Navy Mutual Aid Society	*www.nmaa.org*
NavyOnLine	*www.navy.mil*
Navy Personnel Locater	*www.chinfo.navy.mil/navpalib/faq/ .www/locate.html*
Navy Ships	*www.ncts.navy.mil/navpalib/ships/*
Task Force Excel	*www.excel.navy.mil*
Tricare	*www.tricare.osd.mil*
U.S. Naval Institute	*www.navalinstitute.org*
U.S. Navy Memorial Foundation	*www.lonesailor.org*
Veteran Affairs	*www.va.gov*

Official Publications and Directives

While the Constitution, various treaties, and Congress supply the fundamental laws governing the Navy, they are really only broad outlines. The Navy has various publications and official directives setting forth specific procedures for the daily operation of the Navy Department and for the administration of personnel.

Complete familiarity with these publications and directives is required for yeomen (YNs) and personnelmen (PNs), but to help you determine important policies and programs affecting your Navy career, regardless of your rating, you should have a working knowledge of many of them.

Important References

A very important publication that affects nearly everything you do—including application for various educational programs, transfers, discharges, and separations—is the *Naval Military Personnel Manual* (MILPERSMAN). Also of importance is *United States Navy Regulations* (NAVREGS), which outlines the organizational structure of the Department of the Navy and sets out the principles and policies by which the Navy is governed. The *Standard Organization and Regulations of the U.S. Navy* (SORM) (OPNAVINST 3120.32) sets forth regulations and guidance governing the conduct of all members of the U.S. Navy and sets the standards for the organization of naval units.

The *Manual for Courts-Martial, United States* (MCM) describes the types of courts-martial established by the Uniform Code of Military Justice (UCMJ), defines their jurisdiction, and prescribes their procedures. It also covers such matters as nonjudicial punishment (NJP) and reviews court-martial proceedings, new trials, and limitations on punishment.

The *Manual of the Judge Advocate General* (JAGMAN) (JAGINST 5800.7) covers legal and judicial matters that apply only to the naval service. Included among these are instructions regarding boards of investigation and examining boards—their composition, authority, and procedures.

U.S. Navy Uniform Regulations (NAVPERS 15665), or Uniform Regs for short, describes uniforms for personnel in all categories and contains lists of articles worn or used together. It tells you when various uniforms should be worn; how to wear medals, decorations, ribbons, rating badges, and special markings; and how to care for your uniforms.

Joint Federal Travel Regulations (JFTR) is issued in three volumes; only the first volume deals with actual travel. JFTR interprets the laws and regulations concerning the manner in which transportation is furnished, travel for family members, the transportation of household goods, reimbursement for travel expenses, and similar information.

U.S. Naval Travel Instructions (NAVSO P-1459) amplifies the rules laid down in volume 1 of the JFTR.

The *Department of Defense Military Pay and Allowance Entitlements Manual* (DODPM) covers statutory provisions for entitlements, deductions, and collections on military pay and allowances.

The *Navy Pay and Personnel Procedures Manual* (PAY-PERSMAN) (NAVSO P-3050) contains detailed information about the procedures of the military pay system for members of the Navy.

The *Enlisted Transfer Manual* (TRANSMAN) (NAVPERS 15909) is the official manual for the distribution and assignment of enlisted personnel; it supplements the MILPERSMAN.

The *Navy and Marine Corps Awards Manual* (SECNAVINST 1650.1), or simply Awards Manual, is issued by the secretary of the Navy for guidance in all matters pertaining to decorations, medals, and awards, including how they are worn.

The *Bibliography for Advancement Study* (NAVEDTRA 10052), published annually, is a list of training manuals and other publications used to prepare advancement examinations.

The *Manual of Advancement* (BUPERSINST 1430.16) addresses the administration of the advancement system. It explains the basic policies outlined in MILPERSMAN on eligibility requirements for advancement; the preparation of forms; the ordering, custody, and disposition of Navy-wide exams; the administration of examination for advancement; changes in rate of rating; and procedures for advancement.

The abbreviations used in identifying the originators of publications and directives can be confusing at times. A list of the common ones you will encounter is provided below.

Official
Publications
and
Directives

BUMED	Bureau of Medicine and Surgery
BUPERS	Bureau of Naval Personnel
CNET	Chief of Naval Education and Training
COMNAVAIRLANT	Commander, Naval Air Force, Atlantic Fleet
COMNAVAIRPAC	Commander, Naval Air Force, Pacific Fleet
COMNAVCRUITCOM	Commander, Navy Recruiting Command
DOD	Department of Defense
GPO	Government Printing Office
JAG	Judge Advocate General
NAVAIR	Naval Air Systems Command
NAVCOMP	Comptroller of the Navy
NAVEDTRA	Chief of Navy Education and Training (Command)
NAVMAT	Naval Material Command
NAVMILPERSCOM	Navy Military Personnel Command
NAVSO	Executive Offices of the Secretary of the Navy
NAVSUP	Naval Supply Systems Command
NAVTRA	Chief of Naval Training
OPNAV	Office of the Chief of Naval Operations
SECNAV	Secretary of the Navy
VA	Department of Veterans Affairs

Deciphering the Numbers

All of those confusing numbers you see attached to Navy publications and directives can be very confusing. You will note, for example, that many of the publications we have talked about and some that you will use to study for your advancement in rate are listed by the abbreviation "NAVEDTRA" followed by a series of numbers. These are publications issued by the Chief of Naval Education and Training (CNET) and are tracked by their own numbering system. Other commands sometimes use their own numbering systems as well.

Instructions and Notices

Most directives of an official nature within the Navy follow a consistent system that will help you to identify them and what they are about if you understand the system. These directives are either *instructions* or *notices*. The difference between the two is that instructions are more permanent (once put into effect they remain in effect until superseded or canceled), while notices are short-lived (they contain a self-cancellation date to indicate when they are no longer in effect). Both instructions and notices use the Navy's *Standard Subject Identification Code* (SSIC) system.

To understand this system and how it is used, you must begin with a publication identified as SECNAVINST 5210.11, which is a listing of the Navy's *Standard Subject Identification Codes* (SSIC). This publication (which is an instruction) lists four- or five-digit codes that are linked to particular subjects. The general divisions of these codes are as follows:

1000–1999	Military personnel
2000–2999	Telecommunications
3000–3999	Operations and readiness
4000–4999	Logistics
5000–5999	General administration and management
6000–6999	Medicine and dentistry
7000–7999	Financial management
8000–8999	Ordnance material
9000–9999	Ships' design and material
10000–10999	General material
11000–11999	Facilities and activities ashore
12000–12999	Civilian personnel
13000–13999	Aeronautical and astronautical material

You may have noticed that many of the publications listed above have the issuing authority followed by the abbreviation "INST," which tells you that this publication is an instruction. For example, the *Awards Manual* is identified by "SECNAVINST 1650.1," which tells us that this is an instruction issued by the secretary of the Navy.

Suppose that your ship wants to issue an official instruction establishing policies relating to tuberculosis testing of the crew. A closer look in the SSIC manual would show you that the 6000–999 (Medicine and Dentistry) codes are further broken down as follows:

6000–6099	General
6100–6199	Physical fitness

6200–6299	Preventive medicine
6300–6399	General medicine
6400–6599	Special fields
6600–6699	Dentistry
6700–6899	Equipment and supplies

This means that a directive addressing the subject of tuberculosis testing would best fall in the numbers assigned to "communicable diseases" and would therefore have a number somewhere between 6200 and 6299. In fact, the SSIC manual further breaks down the numbers as follows:

6200	General
6210	Quarantine
6220	Communicable diseases
6222	Venereal disease
6224	Tuberculosis
6230	Prophylaxis
6240	Hygiene and sanitation
(and so on)	

613

So you would know that a directive addressing communicable diseases would use a number in the 6220 series, and that if it was about tuberculosis, it would be assigned the number "6224." The ship's instruction addressing the subject of tuberculosis testing of the crew would therefore be numbered 6224. The number "6224.1" would further identify it as the first instruction on this subject issued by your ship. If the ship then issued another separate instruction that discussed the administering of tuberculosis tests to refugees brought aboard during evacuation operations, that directive would have the number "6224.2" to show that it is similar to, but different from, the first (6224.1). Any other instructions that might follow on the same subject would be given sequential numbers following the decimal point to tell them apart (6224.3, 6224.4, and so on).

If the ship later decided to make some changes to the original instruction (6224.1), the change would be identified by the letter *A*, making the new instruction 6224.1A instead of just 6224.1. Another change later would make the new instruction 6224.1B instead.

So, with the aid of the SSIC manual and an understanding of how these procedures work, you would be able to identify SECNAVINST 1650.1F as having been issued by the secretary of the Navy on the subject of "decorations, medals, and awards" and that this is the sixth change to the original instruction ("F" is the sixth letter of the alphabet).

If your ship wanted to put out a directive announcing when tuberculosis testing for the crew would take place, your ship would use a *notice* rather than an instruction. This notice would be numbered 6224 but would not have any decimals or change letters. This is because a notice is temporary. Included as part of the notice would be the date it would no longer be in effect (in other words, when it would be canceled). Any reference to it would include the date it was issued to identify it.

Glossary of Navy Terms and Acronyms

A person entering a new trade must learn the vocabulary of that trade. As you have probably already surmised, the Navy has a language all its own. In the list below, you will find many commonly used naval terms and acronyms. Words in italic appear elsewhere in the glossary.

Most of the terms you will have to learn pertain to shipboard life, but you should be aware that you will hear these terms used ashore in naval establishments as well. For example, Sailors will, more than likely, call a floor in a hallway at the Pentagon "a *deck* in the *passageway*."

Abaft—Farther aft, as in "abaft the beam."

Abeam—Abreast; on a relative bearing of 090 or 270 degrees.

Aboard—On or in a ship or naval station.

Accommodation ladder—A ladder resembling stairs that is suspended over the side of a ship to facilitate boarding from boats.

Adrift—Loose from moorings and out of control (applied to anything lost, out of hand, or left lying about).

AFFF—Aqueous film-forming foam.

Aft—Toward the *stern* (not as specific as *abaft*).

After—That which is farthest *aft*.

Afternoon watch—The 1200 to 1600 *watch*.

Aground—That part of a ship resting on the bottom (a ship "runs aground" or "goes aground").

Ahoy—A hail or call for attention, as in "Boat ahoy."

Alee—Downwind.

All hands—The entire ship's company.

Aloft—Generally speaking, any area above the highest deck.

Alongside—By the side of the ship or *pier*.

Amidships—An indefinite area midway between the *bow* and the *stern;* "rudder amidships" means that the rudder is in line with the ship's centerline.

Anchorage—An area designated to be used by ships for anchoring.

Anchor cable—The line, wire, or chain that attaches a vessel to her anchor.

Armament—The weapons of a ship.

Ashore—On the beach or shore.

Astern—Behind a ship.

Athwart—Across; at right angles to.

Auxiliary—Extra, or secondary, as in "auxiliary engine"; a vessel whose mission is to supply or support combatant forces.

Avast—Stop, as in "avast heaving."

Aweigh—An anchoring term used to describe the anchor clear of the bottom (the weight of the anchor is on the cable).

Aye, aye—Reply to a command or order, meaning "I understand and will obey."

Barge—A blunt-ended craft, usually nonself-propelled, used to haul supplies or garbage; a type of motorboat assigned for the personal use of a flag officer.

Barnacles—Small shellfish attached to a vessel's undersides, pilings, and other submerged structures, the accumulation of which can slow a vessel down.

616

Batten down—The closing of any watertight fixture.

Battle lantern—A battery-powered lantern for emergency use.

Beam—The extreme width (breadth) of a vessel, as in "a CV has a greater beam [is wider] than a destroyer."

Bear—To be located on a particular bearing, as in "the lighthouse bears 045 degrees."

Bear a hand—Provide assistance, as in "bear a hand with rigging the brow"; expedite.

Bearing—The direction of an object measured in degrees clockwise from a reference point (true bearings use true north as the reference, relative bearings use the ship's *bow* as the reference, and magnetic bearings use magnetic north).

Belay—To secure a line to a fixed point; to disregard a previous order or to stop an action, as in "belay the last order" or "belay the small talk."

Below—Beneath, or beyond something, as in "lay below" (go downstairs); or "below the flight deck."

Berth—Bunk; duty assignment; mooring space assigned to a ship.

Bight—A loop in a line.

Bilge—Lowest area of the ship where spills and leaks gather; to fail an examination.

Billet—Place or duty to which one is assigned.

Binnacle—A stand containing a magnetic compass.

Binnacle list—List of persons excused from duty because of illness.

Bitt—Cylindrical upright fixture (usually found in pairs) to which mooring or towing lines are secured aboard ship.

Bitter end—The free end of a line.

Block—Roughly equivalent to a pulley.

BMOW—Boatswain's mate of the watch.

Board—To go aboard a vessel; a group of persons meeting for a specific purpose, as in "investigation board."

Boat—A small craft capable of being carried aboard a ship.

Boat boom—A *spar* rigged out from the side of an anchored or moored ship to which boats are tied when not in use.

Boatswain's chair—A seat attached to a line for hoisting a person aloft or lowering over the side.

Boatswain's locker—A compartment, usually *forward,* where line and other equipment used by the deck force are stowed.

Bollard—A strong, cylindrical, upright fixture on a *pier* to which ships' mooring lines are secured.

Boom—A *spar,* usually movable, used for hoisting loads.

Boot topping—Black paint applied to a ship's sides along the waterline.

Bow—The forward end of a ship or boat.

Bow hook—Member of a boat's crew whose station is *forward.*

Break out—To bring out supplies or equipment from a stowage space.

Breast line—Mooring line that leads from ship to *pier* (or another ship, if moored alongside) at right angles to the ship and is used to keep the vessel from moving laterally away from the *pier* (another ship).

Bridge—Area in the superstructure from which a ship is operated.

Brig—Jail.

Brightwork—Bare (unpainted) metal that is kept polished.

Broach to—To get crosswise to the direction of the waves (puts the vessel in danger of being rolled over by the waves).

Broad—Wide, as in "broad in the beam."

Broad on the bow or quarter—Halfway between *dead ahead* and *abeam,* and halfway between abeam and *astern,* respectively.

Broadside—Simultaneously and to one side (when firing main battery guns); sidewise, as in "the current carried the ship broadside to the beach."

Brow—"Gangplank" used for crossing from one ship to another, and from a ship to a *pier.* (*Note:* "Gangplank" is not a naval term.)

Bulkhead—A vertical partition in a ship (never called a wall).

Buoy—An anchored float used as an aid to navigation or to mark the location of an object.

BUPERS—Bureau of Naval Personnel.

C M/C—Command master chief.

Cabin—Living compartment of a ship's commanding officer.

Camel—Floating buffer between a ship and a *pier* (or another ship) to prevent damage by rubbing or banging (similar to a *fender* except that a camel is in the water whereas a fender is suspended above the water).

Can buoy—A cylindrical navigational *buoy,* painted green and odd-numbered, which in U.S. waters marks the port side of a channel from seaward.

Carry away—To break loose, as in "the rough seas carried away the lifelines."

Carry on—An order to resume previous activity after an interruption.

Chafing gear—Material used to protect lines from excessive wear.

Chain locker—Space where anchor chain is stowed.

Chart—Nautical counterpart of a road map, showing land configuration, water depths, and aids to navigation.

Chart house—The navigator's work compartment.

Chip—To remove paint or rust from metallic surfaces with sharp-pointed hammers before applying paint.

Chock—Deck fitting through which mooring lines are led.

Chow—Food.

CO—Commanding officer.

Colors—The national ensign; the ceremony of raising and lowering the ensign.

Combatant ship—A ship whose primary mission is combat.

Commission pennant—A long, narrow, starred and striped pennant flown only on board a commissioned ship.

Companionway—Deck opening giving access to a ladder (includes the ladder).

Compartment—Interior space of a ship (similar to a "room" ashore).

Conn—The act of controlling a ship (similar to "driving" ashore); also the station, usually on the bridge, from which a ship is controlled.

Course—A ship's desired direction of travel, not to be confused with *heading.*

Cover—To protect; a shelter; headgear; to don headgear.

Coxswain—Enlisted person in charge of a boat.

CPO—Chief petty officer.

Crow's nest—*Lookout* station aloft.

Cumshaw—A gift; something procured without payment.

Darken ship—To turn off all external lights and close all openings through which lights can be seen from outside the ship.

Davits—Strong arms by means of which a boat is hoisted in or out.

Davy Jones' locker—The bottom of the sea.

DCC—Damage Control Central.

Dead ahead—Directly ahead; a relative bearing of 000 degrees.

Dead astern—180 degrees relative.

Deck—Horizontal planking or plating that divides a ship into layers (floors).

Deck seamanship—The upkeep and operation of all deck equipment.

Decontaminate—To free from harmful residue of nuclear or chemical attack.

Deep six—To throw something overboard (see also *Jettison*).

Dinghy—A small boat, sometimes equipped with a sail, but more commonly propelled by outboard motor or oars.

Dip—To lower a flag partway down the staff as a salute to, or in reply to a salute from, another ship.

Distance line—A line stretched between two ships engaged in replenishment or transfer operations under way (the line is marked at 20-foot intervals to aid the conning officer in maintaining the proper distance between ships).

Division—A main subdivision of a ship's crew (1st, E, G, etc.); an organization composed of two or more ships of the same type.

Dock—The water-space alongside a *pier*.

Dog—A lever, or bolt and thumb screws, used for securing a watertight door; to divide a four-hour *watch* into two two-hour watches.

Dog down—To set the dogs on a watertight door.

Dog watch—The 1600–1800 or 1800–2000 *watch*.

Double up—To double mooring lines for extra strength.

Draft—The vertical distance from the keel to the waterline.

Dress ship—To display flags in honor of a person or event.

Drift—The speed at which a ship is pushed off course by wind and current.

Drogue—Sea anchor.

Dry dock—A dock, either floating or built into the shore, from which water may be removed for the purpose of inspecting or working on a ship's bottom; to be put in dry dock.

EAOS—End of active obligated service.

Ebb—A falling tide.

Eight o'clock reports—Reports received by the *executive officer* from department heads shortly before 2000.

Ensign—The national flag; an O-1 paygrade officer.

Executive officer—Second officer in command (also called "XO").

Eyes—The forward most part of the *forecastle.*

F/MC—Fleet (or Force) master chief.

Fake—The act of making a line, wire, or chain ready for running by laying it out in long, flat *bights,* one alongside and partially overlapping the other.

Fantail—The *after* end of the main *deck.*

Fathom—Unit of length or depth equal to six feet.

Fender—A cushioning device hung over the side of a ship to prevent contact between the ship and a *pier* or another ship.

Field day—A day devoted to general cleaning, usually in preparation for an inspection.

Fire main—Shipboard piping system to which fire hydrants are connected.

First lieutenant—The officer responsible, in general, for a ship's upkeep and cleanliness (except machinery and ordnance gear), *boats, ground tackle,* and *deck seamanship.*

First watch—The 2000–2400 *watch* (also called evening watch).

Five-star admiral—*Fleet admiral;* a rank above admiral. No longer used.

Flag officer—Any officer of the rank of rear admiral (lower and upper half), vice admiral, or admiral.

Flagstaff—Vertical staff at the *stern* to which the *ensign* is hoisted when moored or at anchor.

Fleet—An organization of ships, aircraft, marine forces, and shore-based fleet activities, all under one commander, for conducting major operations.

Fleet admiral—A rank above admiral; no longer used. Also known as *five-star admiral.*

Flood—To fill a space with water; a rising tide.

Fore and aft—The entire length of a ship, as in "sweep down fore and aft."

Forecastle—Forward section of the main deck (pronounced "fohk-sul").

Foremast—First mast aft from the *bow.*

Forenoon watch—The 0800–1200 watch.

Forward—Toward the *bow.*

Foul—Entangled, as in "the lines are foul of each other"; stormy.

Gaff—A light *spar* set at an angle from the upper part of a mast (the national *ensign* is usually flown from the gaff under way).

Galley—Space where food is prepared (never called a kitchen).

Gangway—The opening in a bulwark or lifeline that provides access to a brow or accommodation ladder; an order meaning to clear the way.

General quarters—The condition of full readiness for battle.

Gig—Boat assigned for the commanding officer's personal use.

Ground tackle—Equipment used in anchoring or mooring with anchors.

Gunwale—Where the sides join the main deck of a ship.

Halyard—A light line used to hoist a flag or pennant.

Handsomely—Steadily and carefully, but not necessarily slowly.

Hard over—Condition of a rudder that has been turned to the maximum possible rudder angle.

Hashmark—A red, blue, or gold diagonal stripe across the left sleeve of an enlisted person's jumper, indicating four years' service.

Hatch—An opening in a deck used for access.

Haul—To pull in or heave on a line by hand.

Hawser—Any heavy wire or line used for towing or mooring.

Head—The upper end of a lower mast boom; compartment containing toilet facilities; ship's *bow*.

Heading—The direction toward which the ship's *bow* is pointing at any instant.

Heave—To throw, as in "heave a line to the pier."

Heave around—To haul in a line, usually by means of a capstan or winch.

Heaving line—A line with a weight at one end, heaved across an intervening space for passing over a heavier line.

Helm—Steering wheel of a ship.

Helmsman—Person who steers the ship by turning her helm (also called steersman).

Highline—The line stretched between ships under way on which a trolley block travels back and forth to transfer material and personnel.

Hitch—To bend a line to or around a ring or cylindrical object; an enlistment.

Holiday—Space on a surface that the painter neglected to paint.

Hull—The shell, or plating, of a ship from keel to *gunwale*.

Hull down—A lookout term meaning that a ship is so far over the horizon that only her superstructure or top hamper is visible.

Inboard—Toward the centerline.

Island—Superstructure of an aircraft carrier.

Jack—Starred blue flag (representing the union of the *ensign*) flown at the *jackstaff* of a commissioned ship not under way.

Jackstaff—Vertical *spar* at the stem to which the *jack* is hoisted.

Jacob's ladder—A portable rope or wire ladder.

Jettison—To throw overboard.

Jetty—A structure built out from shore to influence water currents or protect a harbor or *pier*.

Jump ship—To desert a ship.

Jury rig—Any makeshift device or apparatus; to fashion such a device.

Knock off—Quit, cease, or stop, as in "knock off ship's work."

Knot—Nautical mile per hour.

Ladder—A flight of steps aboard ship.

Landing craft—Vessel especially designed for landing troops and equipment directly on a beach.

Landing ship—A large seagoing ship designed for landing personnel and/or heavy equipment directly on a beach.

Lanyard—Any short line used as a handle or as a means for operating some piece of equipment; a line used to attach an article to the person, as a pistol lanyard.

Lash—To secure an object by turns of line, wire, or chain.

Launch—To float a vessel off the ways in a building yard; a type of powerboat, usually over 30 feet long.

Lay—Movement of a person, as in "lay aloft"; the direction of twist in the strands of a line or wire.

Lee—An area sheltered from the wind; downwind.

Leeward—Direction toward which the wind is blowing (pronounced "loo-ard").

LES—Leave and earnings statement.

Liberty—Sanctioned absence from a ship or station for a short time for pleasure rather than business.

Life-jacket—A buoyant jacket designed to support a person in the water.

Lifelines—In general, the lines erected around the edge of a weather deck to prevent personnel from falling or being washed overboard; more precisely (though not often used), the topmost line (from top to bottom, these lines are named lifeline, housing line, and foot-rope).

Line—Any rope that is not wire rope.

List—Transverse inclination of a vessel (when a ship leans to one side).

Log—A ship's speedometer; book or ledger in which data or events that occurred during a watch are recorded; to make a certain speed, as in "the ship logged 20 knots."

Look alive—Admonishment meaning to be alert or move faster.

Lookout—Person stationed topside on a formal watch who reports objects sighted and sounds heard to the officer of the deck.

LPO—Leading petty officer.

Lucky bag—Locker under the charge of the master-at-arms; used to collect and stow deserter's effects and gear found adrift.

Magazine—Compartment used for the stowage of ammunition.

Main deck—The uppermost complete *deck*. (An exception is the aircraft carrier, where the main deck is defined as the hangar bay rather than the flight deck which arguably fits the criteria of the definition.)

Mainmast—Second mast aft from the *bow* on a vessel with more than one mast. (On a ship with only one mast, it is usually referred to simply as "the mast.") The tallest mast on a vessel.

Main truck—The top of the tallest mast on a vessel.

Make fast—To secure.

Man—To assume a station, as in "to man a gun."

Man-o'-war—A ship designed for combat.

Marlinespike—Tapered steel tool used to open the strands of line or wire rope for splicing.

Marlinespike seamanship—The art of caring for and handling all types of line and wire.

Master-at-arms—A member of a ship's police force.

Mate—A shipmate; another Sailor.

MCPO—Master chief petty officer.

MCPON—Master Chief Petty Officer of the Navy.

Mess—Meal; place where meals are eaten; a group that takes meals together, as in officers' mess.

Messenger—A line used to haul a heavier line across an intervening space; one who delivers messages.

Midwatch—The *watch* that begins at 0000 and ends at 0400.

Moor—To *make fast* to a *pier,* another ship, or a *mooring buoy;* also, to anchor.

Mooring buoy—A large anchored float to which a ship may *moor.*

Morning watch—The 0400–0800 *watch.*

Motor whaleboat—A double-ended powerboat.

Muster—A roll call; to assemble for a roll call.

Nest—Two or more boats stowed one within the other; two or more ships moored alongside each other.

Nun buoy—A navigational *buoy,* conical in shape, painted red and even numbered, that marks the starboard side of a channel from seaward.

On the beach—Ashore; a seaman assigned to shore duty, unemployed, retired, or otherwise detached from sea duty.

623

OOD—Officer of the deck.

Outboard—Away from the centerline.

Overboard—Over the side.

Overhaul—To repair or recondition; to overtake another vessel.

Overhead—The underside of a deck that forms the overhead of the compartment next below (never called a ceiling).

Party—A group on temporary assignment or engaged in a common activity, as in "line-handling party," or a "liberty party."

Passageway—A corridor used for interior horizontal movement aboard ship (similar to a hallway ashore).

Pay out—To feed out or lengthen a line.

Pier—Structure extending from land into water to provide a mooring for vessels.

Pigstick—Small staff from which a commission pennant is flown.

Pilot house—Enclosure on the bridge housing the main steering controls.

Piloting—Branch of navigation in which positions are determined by visible objects on the surface, or by soundings.

Pipe—To sound a particular call on a *boatswain*'s pipe.

Pitch—Vertical rise and fall of a ship's *bow* and *stern* caused by head or following seas.

624

Plane guard—Destroyer or helicopter responsible for rescuing air crews during launch or recovery operations.

Plank owner—A person who was assigned to the ship's company when he or she was commissioned.

Plan of the Day (POD)—Schedule of a day's routine and events ordered by the *executive officer* and published daily aboard ship or at a shore activity.

POD—Plan of the day.

Pollywog—A person who has never crossed the equator (pejorative).

Port—To the left of the centerline when facing forward.

Quarterdeck—Deck area designated by the commanding officer as the place to carry out official functions; station of the officer of the deck in port.

Quartermaster—An enlisted assistant to the navigator.

Quarters—Stations for shipboard evolutions, as in "general quarters," "fire quarters"; living spaces.

Quay—A solid structure along a bank used for loading and offloading vessels (pronounced "key").

Radar—A device that uses reflected radio waves for the detection of objects. Derived from "radio direction and ranging."

Range—The distance of an object from an observer; an aid to navigation consisting of two objects in line; a water area designated for a particular purpose, as in "gunnery range."

Rat guard—A hinged metal disk secured to a mooring line to prevent rats from traveling over the line into the ship.

Reef—An underwater ledge rising abruptly from the ocean's floor.

Relief—A person assigned to take over the duties of another.

Replenishment—To resupply a ship or station.

Ride—To be at anchor, as in "the ship is riding to her anchor."

Riding lights—Navigational lights shown at night by a moored vessel.

Rig—To set up a device or equipment, as in "to rig a stage over the side."

Rigging—Line that has been set up to be used for some specific purpose (e.g., lines that support a ship's masts are called standing rigging, and lines that hoist or otherwise move equipment are called running rigging).

Rope—Fiber or wire *line* (fiber rope is usually referred to as line, while wire rope is called rope, wire rope, or wire).

Ropeyarn Sunday—A workday or part of a workday that has been granted as a holiday for taking care of personal business.

RT—Radiotelephone (voice radio).

Rudder—Device attached to the *stern* that controls a ship's direction of travel.

Running lights—Navigational lights shown at night by a vessel under way.

SCPO—Senior chief petty officer.

Scuttlebutt—A drinking fountain (originally, a ship's water barrel [called a butt] that was tapped [scuttled] by the insertion of a spigot from which the crew drew drinking water); rumor (the scuttlebutt was once a place for personnel to exchange news when the crew gathered to draw water).

Sea anchor—A device streamed from the *bow* of a vessel for holding it end-on to the sea.

Seamanship—The art of handling a vessel; skill in the use of deck equipment, in boat handling, and in the care and use of line and wire.

Sea state—Condition of waves and the height of their swells.

Seaworthy—A vessel capable of withstanding normal heavy weather.

Second deck—First complete deck below the main deck.

Secure—To make fast, as in "secure a line to a cleat"; to cease, as in "secure from fire drill."

625

Service force—Organization providing logistic support to combatant forces.

Shake down—The training of a new crew in operating a ship.

Shellback—A person who has crossed the equator.

Shift colors—To change the arrangement of *colors* upon getting under way or coming to moorings.

Ship—Any large seagoing vessel capable of extended independent operation; to take on water unintentionally.

Ship over—To reenlist in the Navy.

Ship's company—All hands permanently attached to a ship or station; the crew.

Shipshape—Neat, clean, taut.

Shoal—A structure similar to a reef, but more gradual in its rise from the floor of the ocean.

Shore—Land, usually that part adjacent to the water; a timber used in damage control to brace *bulkheads* and *decks*.

Sick bay—Shipboard space that serves as a hospital or medical clinic.

Side boy—One of a group of seamen who form two ranks at the gangway as part of the ceremonies conducted for visiting officials.

Side light—One of a series of running lights (the starboard side light is green and the port side light is red).

626

Sight—To see for the first time, as to sight a ship on the horizon; a celestial observation.

Skylark—To engage in irresponsible horseplay.

Slack—To allow a line to run out; undisciplined, as in a "slack ship."

Small craft—Any less-than-ship-size vessel.

Smart—Snappy, seamanlike, shipshape.

Sound—To determine the depth of water; to dive deep (of marine animals); a body of water between the mainland and a large coastal island.

Spar—The nautical equivalent of a pole.

Special sea detail—Crewmembers assigned special duties when leaving and entering port.

Splice—To join lines or wires together by intertwining strands; the joint so made.

Square away—To put in proper order; to make things shipshape.

Square knot—Simple knot used for bending two lines together or for bending a line to itself.

Stack—Shipboard chimney.

Stanchion—Vertical post for supporting decks; smaller, similar posts for supporting lifelines, awnings, and so on.

Starboard—Direction to the right of the centerline as one faces forward.

State room—A living compartment for an officer or officers.

Station—An individual's place of duty; position of a ship in formation; location of persons and equipment with a specific purpose, as in "gun-control station"; order to assume stations, as in "station the special sea and anchor detail."

Stay—Any piece of standing rigging providing support only.

Stem—Extreme forward line of *bow*.

Stern—The aftermost part of a vessel.

Stern light—White navigation light that can be seen only from *astern*.

Stow—To store or pack articles or cargo in a space.

Structural bulkhead—Transverse strength bulkhead that forms a watertight boundary.

Superstructure—The structure above a ship's main *deck*.

Swab—A mop; to mop.

Tarpaulin—Canvas used as a cover.

Taut—Under tension; highly disciplined and efficient, as in "a taut ship."

Tender—One who serves as a precautionary standby, as in "line tender for a diver"; a support vessel for other ships.

Topside—Weather *decks;* above (referring to the deck or decks above).

Trice up—To secure (older type) bunks by hauling them up and hanging them off (securing them) on their chains.

Truck—The uppermost tip of a mast.

Turn in—To retire to bed; to return articles to the issue room.

Turn out—To get out of bed; to order out a working party or other group, as in "turn out the guard."

Turn to—To start working.

UCMJ—Uniform Code of Military Justice.

UNREP—Underway replenishment.

Up all hammocks—Admonishment to personnel entitled to sleep after reveille to get up.

Void—An empty tank.

Waist—The amidships section of the main *deck*.

Wake—Trail left by a vessel or other object moving through the water.

Wardroom—Officers' messing compartment; collective term used to signify the officers assigned to a ship.

Watch—One of the periods, usually four hours, into which a day is divided; a particular duty, as in "life *buoy* watch."

Watertight integrity—The degree or quality of water tightness.

Weather deck—Any *deck* exposed to the elements.

Weigh anchor—To hoist the anchor clear of the bottom.

Wharf—Structure similar to a *quay* but constructed like a *pier*.

Whipping—Binding on the end of a line or wire to prevent unraveling.

Windward—In the direction of the wind.

XO—Executive officer; second in command.

Yardarm—The port or starboard half of a *spar* set athwartships across the upper mast.

Yaw—(Of a vessel) to have its heading thrown wide of its course as the result of a force, such as a heavy following sea.

Index

629

About the Author

Thomas J. Cutler enlisted in the Navy in early 1965 at the age of seventeen and has served the Navy in various capacities ever since. After a career that included service in patrol craft, destroyers, and aircraft carriers, as well as a combat tour in Vietnam, he retired in 1990 as a lieutenant commander. He is the founder and former director of the Walbrook Maritime Academy in Baltimore, Maryland, and spent nine years at the U.S. Naval Academy teaching seamanship, navigation, tactics, leadership, and history. He has been a professor of strategy and policy with the Naval War College since 1991. His published works include *Brown Water, Black Berets: Coastal and Riverine Warfare in Vietnam* and *The Battle of Leyte Gulf: 23–26 October 1944*. He was the recipient of the Navy League's prestigious Alfred Thayer Mahan Award and was named military teacher of the year at the Naval Academy in 1988–89. He currently serves as the senior acquisitions editor at the U.S. Naval Institute.